GERONTOLOGICAL PRACTICE

FOR THE TWENTY-FIRST CENTURY

END-OF-LIFE CARE

END-OF-LIFE CARE: A SERIES
Series Editor: Virginia E. Richardson

We all confront end-of-life issues. As people live longer and suffer from more chronic illnesses, all of us face difficult decisions about death, dying, and terminal care. This series aspires to articulate the issues surrounding end-of-life care in the twenty-first century. It will be a resource for practitioners and scholars who seek information about advance directives, hospice, palliative care, bereavement, and other death-related topics. The interdisciplinary approach makes the series invaluable for social workers, physicians, nurses, attorneys, and pastoral counselors.

The press seeks manuscripts that reflect the interdisiciplinary, biopsychosocial essence of end-of-life care. We welcome manuscripts that address specific topics on ethical dilemmas in end-of-life care, death and dying among marginalized groups, palliative care, spirituality, and end-of-life care in special medical areas, such as oncology, AIDS, diabetes, and transplantation. While writers should integrate theory and practice, the series is open to diverse methodologies and perspectives.

Joan Berzoff and Phyllis R. Silverman, *Living with Dying: A Handbook for End-of-Life Healthcare Practitioners*

GERONTOLOGICAL PRACTICE FOR THE TWENTY-FIRST CENTURY

A Social Work Perspective

VIRGINIA E. RICHARDSON & AMANDA S. BARUSCH

COLUMBIA UNIVERSITY PRESS   NEW YORK

COLUMBIA UNIVERSITY PRESS

Publishers Since 1893

NEW YORK, CHICHESTER, WEST SUSSEX

Library of Congress Cataloging-in-Publication Data
Richardson, Virginia E.
Gerontological practice for the twenty-first century : a social work
perspective / Virginia E. Richardson and Amanda S. Barusch.
p. cm. — (End-of-life care)
Includes bibliographical references and index.
ISBN 978-0-231-10748-8 (cloth : alk. paper) — ISBN 978-0-231-10749-5 (pbk. : alk. paper)
1. Social work with older people. 2. Gerontolgy. I. Barusch, Amanda Smith.
II. Title. III. Series.
HV1451.R53 2005
362.6—dc22   2005048437

For my mother,
Marjorie F. Richardson,
July 31, 1918–October 16, 2002

CONTENTS

PART 4   *Sociopolitical Issues*

PREFACE

THE DELIVERY OF SERVICES to older adults is a vital and expanding part of professional practice in the allied health professions. With the growth of this field has come recognition of the need for practice approaches that are empirically based and age-specific, that integrate "micro" and "macro" perspectives, and that are informed by contemporary themes in the fields of aging and social work.

This book is designed for students and professionals interested in serving older adults through direct practice. It reflects the needs that have emerged in the field, providing

- empirically based, age-specific interventions
- integrated "micro" (individual) and "macro" (policy-level) content
- a conceptual framework that recognizes contemporary themes in aging and social work

The book is organized in four parts: part 1 addresses theories and demographic realities; part 2 examines common psychological problems that arise in later life; part 3 considers the dynamics of family and work; and part 4 discusses sociopolitical realities that affect an aging population. Case examples are used throughout the text to integrate and illustrate specific interventions.

Part 1 includes chapters 1 through 4. In chapter 1 we review changing demographics, based on age, ethnicity, health, marital status, and living conditions. We review traditional and contemporary theories of aging in chapter 2 and introduce an integrated gerontological practice approach and the stages associated with this approach in chapters 3 and 4, respectively.

Part 2, which includes chapters 5 through 9, addresses psychological topics, including anxiety (chapter 5), depression (chapter 6), suicide (chapter 7), substance abuse (chapter 8), and dementia (chapter 9).

In part 3 we review social psychological issues, including social work practice with older families (chapter 10), end-of-life care (chapter 11), bereavement in the later years (chapter 12), and work and retirement (chapter 13).

Part 4, which addresses sociopolitical topics, includes economic policies (chapter 14), poverty in late life (chapter 15), health policies (chapter 16), and quality-of-life issues and important social services (chapter 17).

Many gerontology practitioners will struggle to apply these interventions effectively in demanding work settings that will require them to prioritize their work according to their clients' and agency's resources. Many age-specific interventions described here will require modification as the baby boomers and younger cohorts age. We encourage others to supplement and expand on what we present here. We focus on the most vulnerable older people, but we celebrate the many older people who age "successfully." Although we focus on social workers, other gerontological practitioners can modify the interventions described here in accordance with their clients' needs and their professional requirements.

ACKNOWLEDGMENTS

Virginia E. Richardson

Many people contributed to the development of this book. I am grateful to Rick Reamer, who approached me about writing the book and provided many excellent suggestions. Connie Corley read each chapter and offered specific feedback that enhanced the substance of the book. John Michel believed in and supported this project from the beginning, and this book was conceptualized, organized, and written under his direction and encouragement. I am especially grateful to Amanda Barusch, a gifted scholar, who collaborated with me on this project. Her integrity, enthusiasm, and commitment, more than anything else, resulted in the completion of this project. Dean Tony Tripodi of Ohio State University encouraged this project at every phase. Polly Kummel, an outstanding copy editor, substantially improved the book's clarity. Other colleagues who provided support include Shantha Balaswamy, Christine Price, Sandy Sullivan, and Gil Greene.

My family supported the writing at every stage. My older sister, Dr. Barbara Richardson, sent me daily e-mails to keep me on track during the most difficult periods. I can't thank her enough for her unconditional support. My younger sister, Janice Snowden, also provided unconditional support in numerous ways. I am forever indebted to them. I love and appreciate my daughter, Nikki Thomas, for boosting my spirits, making me smile, and teaching me about life while I worked on this. No one deserves more recognition than my husband, Michael Thomas, who read and edited every chapter and learned more about aging than he wanted. His love, generosity, and humor forced me to keep the book in perspective. I dedicate this book to my mother, Marjorie Richardson, to my mother-in-law and father-in-law, Joy and Gerald Thomas, and to all older people, who deserve as much quality of life as anyone.

AMANDA S. BARUSCH

It is a privilege to work with someone as dynamic, creative, and informed as Virginia Richardson, and I am grateful for her invitation to join in the development of this exciting book. I appreciate the counsel and support of Connie Corley, who not only read each chapter but encouraged us every step of the way. And the Columbia University Press team has been terrific. The University of Utah College of Social Work provides a work environment with the ideal mix of support and challenge—support from our dean and challenge from our students. For this I am always grateful. But most of all I am indebted to my family: Larry, Nathan, Ariana, Sunshine, and Maddie, who make life worth living; and Dr. Maurice Barusch, who is my favorite example of successful aging.

GERONTOLOGICAL PRACTICE
FOR THE TWENTY-FIRST CENTURY

PART 1

Overview and Theoretical Perspectives

CHAPTER 1

Social Work Practice in the Twenty-first Century

Tʜᴇ ᴀɢɪɴɢ ᴏꜰ ᴛʜᴇ Uɴɪᴛᴇᴅ Sᴛᴀᴛᴇs poses opportunities and challenges for social workers as the profession advances in this new millennium. The ethos of aging is changing as the population of older people becomes more ethnically diverse, lives and works longer, begins second and third careers, and struggles with chronic illnesses. The age considered to be "late life" has also changed. Middle age formerly began at 35, but today many view 45 and 67 as the beginnings of middle age and late life, respectively. In the new century midlife may commence around 50 and include the years between 50 and 69, with senescence not beginning until about 70.

How people will age in the future and how these changes will affect social work are important questions that we must answer. Other, related questions include what will become the most common problems of late life, and which elderly people will be most likely to encounter them? How will these transformations affect the psychology of aging? Will they alter how we age physically? Will age norms and roles change as demographics shift? How will communities respond to these transitions? Will society legislate social policies, laws, and regulations that adequately address elders' needs? What practice techniques will work best with which older people? These are only a few of the questions that social workers must consider.

The next four chapters describe an integrated practice model for social workers who work with older people. The model incorporates contemporary theories from gerontology and social work and reflects the changing demographics and paradigm shifts in the United States and around the world. The theoretical concepts illuminate the promises and limitations of prevailing treatment strategies and the importance of approaching clients' needs and concerns on multiple levels. Practitioners who understand the theoretical bases of the integrated practice model can be more effective in helping their older clients than those professionals who rely upon intuition and dated assumptions.

The complexity of the problems that older adults present to social workers requires a practice framework that incorporates micro and macro interventions as well as multidisciplinary practice. Well-developed therapies are more effective for older people when they are combined with social and environmental interventions. For example, a social worker may help a new widow cope with her feelings of loss and grief and recommend that she participate in a widow support group, thereby attending to the client's psychological and social needs. People who lose loved ones benefit from a holistic approach that encourages them to grieve and to accept support from others. Other people who are facing loss remind us of the universality of grief and loss, and people who share their suffering with others who are grieving feel empowered and less alone. By encouraging social workers to recognize multiple factors in their assessments and interventions—how a person's physical and mental well-being as well as his social needs and daily routines might be affected—, we will help older people from diverse backgrounds.

It is now axiomatic that not only do biological changes affect psychological functions but certain mental states affect physical status. Social events, such as caring for a sick relative or dealing with the loss of a spouse, can induce stress and other physiological changes. Stress lowers caregivers' immune system and increases their susceptibility to illness. Instead of working with clients' discrete problems, gerontological social workers must intervene on affective, cognitive, behavioral, and environmental levels simultaneously. Most gerontologists, regardless of discipline, agree that holistic treatment approaches help elderly people more than do strategies that treat cognitive, affective, or social functioning in a vacuum. The first chapter highlights demographic changes during the twentieth century that have important implications for gerontological practice.

Demographics of Aging

The number of Americans aged 65 and older increased tenfold during the twentieth century, from 3.1 million in 1900, when the median age was 22.9 and older people represented only 4% of the population, to 35 million in 2000, when the median age was 35.3 and older people comprised 12.4% of the United States population (see figure 1.1). The substantial increases also occurred in the group of people aged 85 and older (see figure 1.2). This group grew from 122,000 individuals in 1900 to 4.2 million in 2000. This graying of the population will continue as fertility rates decline and life expectancies, which are now at an all-time high at 77.2 years, continue to rise (National Center for Health Statistics [NCHS], 2003a).

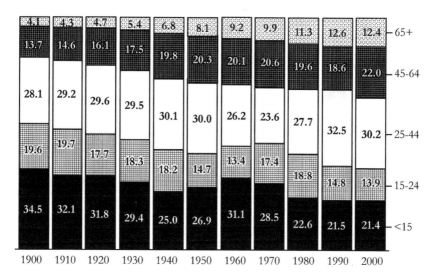

FIGURE 1.1 Distribution of the Total U.S. Population by Age: Percentages, 1900–2000
Source: Hobbs and Stoops, 2000, figure 2-4, p. 56.

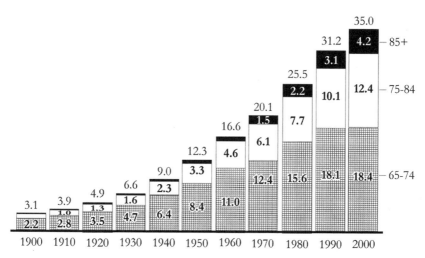

FIGURE 1.2 U.S. Population Aged Sixty-five and Older, 1900–2000 (Millions)
Source: Hobbs and Stoops, 2000, figure 2-6, p. 59.

Older women still vastly outnumber older men, especially in the oldest age groups (see figure 1.3). In 2002 the United States was home to 14.2 million men and 19.5 million women older than 65 and about 1 million men and 2.4 million women older than 85 (Spraggins, 2003). Gender differences in life expectancy (74.4 for males and 79.8 for females born in 2001) are expected to continue for at least the next fifty years.

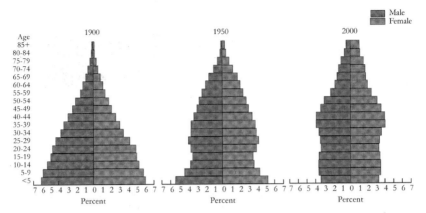

FIGURE 1.3 Age and Sex Distribution of the Total U.S. Population: 1900, 1950, and 2000
Source: Hobbs and Stoops, 2000, figure 2-1, p. 53.

Although most men older than 65 are married (approximately 75%), most women in this age category are single (almost 60%). Older women are four times more likely to be widowed than their male counterparts; there were 8.9 million widowed women (46%) compared to 2 million widowed men in 2002 (nearly 14%) (U.S. Census Bureau, 2003c) (see figure 1.4). Another 10% of older women were either divorced or separated, and about 4% never married. According to the Policy Institute of the National Gay and Lesbian Task Force, one to three million (3–8%) Americans older than 65 are gay, lesbian, bisexual, or transgender (Cahill, South, and Spade, 2000). Although we have minimal data from national samples, most experts estimate that the U.S. population in the twenty-first century will have a greater proportion of older lesbians than older gay men, especially among the oldest old (Barker, 2004).

Every census since 1970 has found more people living alone than the previous census recorded, and older women—73 to 77% of all female heads of household older than sixty-five during this period—were especially likely to live in one-person households (see figure 1.5).

The proportion of older men living alone remained substantially smaller than the proportion of older women who lived in single-person dwellings between 1960 and 2000. At the same time the percentage of male heads of household aged 65 and older who were living alone increased in every decade (see figure 1.5). The most common one-person households included older white adults; older blacks, Hispanics, and Asian and Pacific Islanders are less likely to live alone (U.S. Census Bureau, 2000).

The number of people who are members of ethnic minorities in the United States has increased dramatically since the mid-1970s. Figures 1.6 and 1.7 show the

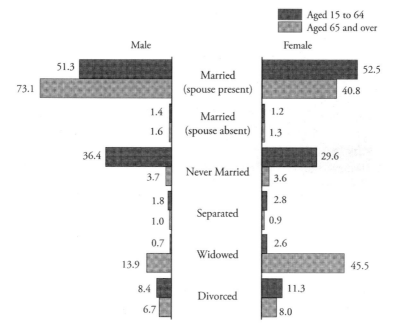

FIGURE 1.4 Marital Status by Sex and Age, 2002 (Percentages of Population Aged Fifteen and Older)

Source: Spraggins, 2003, figure 3, p. 2.

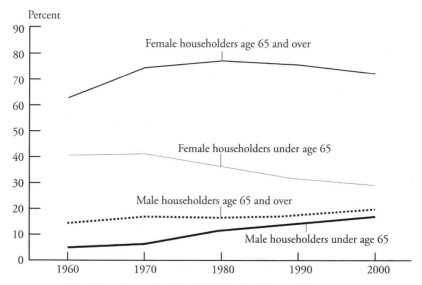

FIGURE 1.5 One-Person Households Within Age-Sex Groups: Percentages, 1960–2000

Source: Hobbs and Stoops, 2000, figure 5-7, p. 157.

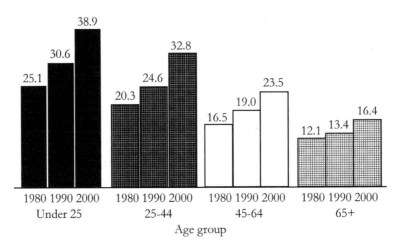

FIGURE 1.6 Percent Minority by Broad Age Group: 1980 to 2000
Source: Hobbs and Stoops, 2000, figure 3-21, p. 107.

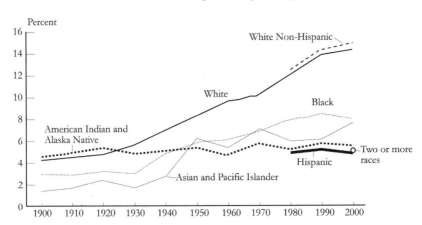

FIGURE 1.7 U.S. Population Aged Sixty-five and Older by Race and Hispanic Origin: Percentages, 1900 to 2000
Note: Complete data on Hispanic origin have been available only since 1980, and data on the population of two or more races are available only from the 2000 census.
Source: Hobbs and Stoops, 2000, figure 3-23, p. 109.

changes in the minority elderly population over time. Although minorities represent larger percentages of younger age groups, the minority population in every age group was larger in 1990 and 2000 than in 1980 (Hobbs and Stoops, 2002).

The older black population has grown steadily over time (see figure 1.7). In 1980 the U.S. population included 2.1 million blacks aged 65 and older, in contrast to 2.5 million in 1990 and 2.8 million in 2000, when older black men and older black women represented, respectively, 6.7% and 9% of the black population (figure 1.8).

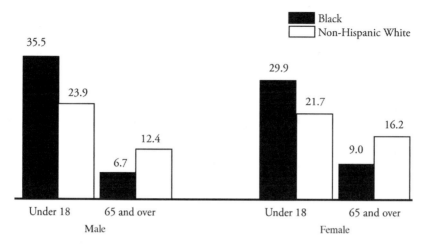

FIGURE 1.8 Population by Age, Sex, and Race, 2002 (Percentage of Population)
Source: McKinnon, 2003, figure 3, p. 2.

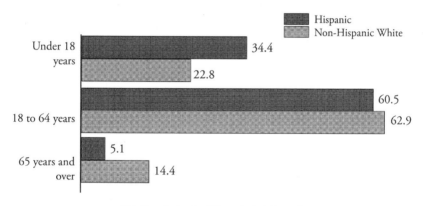

FIGURE 1.9 U.S. Population by Hispanic Origin and Age Group:
Percentages of Each Population, 2002
Source: Ramirez and de la Cruz, 2003, figure 3, p. 2.

Significant differences exist in the average life expectancies of blacks and whites. The average life expectancy for black males born in 2001 was 68.6, in contrast to 75 for white males. The average life expectancy for black females was 75.5, in contrast to 80.2 for white females (NCHS, 2003a).

The older Hispanic population has also increased. It rose from 0.7 million in 1980 to 1.1 million in 1990 to 2 million in 2002, when older Hispanics represented about 5.1% of the total Hispanic population (Administration on Aging [AOA], 2003b) (see figure 1.9). The number of these elderly people will continue to in-

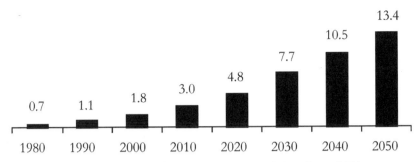

FIGURE 1.10 Population of Hispanic Origin Aged Sixty-five and Older:
1980– 2050 (Millions)
Source: Administration on Aging, 2003b, p. 1.

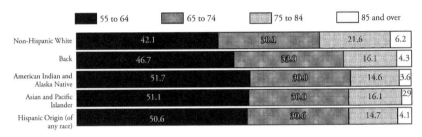

FIGURE 1.11 Percentage Distributions of People Aged Fifty-five and Older by Race,
Hispanic Origin, and Age, 2002
Source: D. Smith, 2003, figure 2, p. 2.

crease. Older Hispanics, who will soon become the largest minority group in the cohort of people aged 65 and older, are expected to account for 16% (13.4 million) of that group by 2050 (AOA, 2003b) (see figure 1.10).

Although the numbers of Asian and Pacific Islanders in this country have also risen since 1980, the percentage increase of those older than sixty-five has remained stable since 1980 at about 7% (Reeves and Bennett, 2003). Figure 1.11 illustrates the distribution of people aged fifty-five and older by race, Hispanic origin, and age.

Although poverty rates among older people have declined since 1990 (from 12.2% in 1990 to 10.4% in 2002), many older people remain poor (see figure 1.12). About 17% of people older than 65 and nearly 20% of people older than 75 were within 125% of the poverty level in 2002 (Proctor and Dalaker, 2003). The highest poverty rates continue among older blacks: 38.5% of black women were poor or near poor, compared to 18.6% of older white women and 10.8% of older white men in 2002. Among black women older than 75, almost half (41.5%) were poor or near poor (see figure 1.12). Hispanic men and women older than 65 also have high rates of poverty: 31.1% and 33.9%, respectively, were within 125% of the poverty

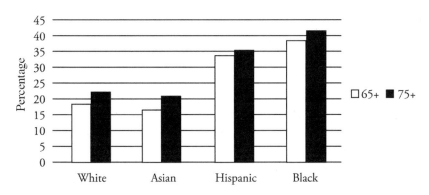

FIGURE 1.12 Poverty Among Older Women by Age and Ethnicity, 2002
Source: U.S. Census Bureau, 2003a, table 17.

level in 2002. The 31.6% of Hispanic men and 35.4% of Hispanic women older than 75 also were within 125% of the poverty level. Unlike other ethnic groups, Hispanics have seen poverty rates decline for those older than 65, but poverty rates have remained steady among all Hispanics. The Hispanic and black elderly continue to have higher rates of poverty than older white, non-Hispanic people and older Asian and Pacific Islanders, who have the lowest poverty rates (9.9%) of any ethnic group (Proctor and Dalaker, 2003).

Many older adults will remain productive and live in good health, free of substantial limitations on their activity. For people aged sixty-five, about 87% of white men, 83% of black men, 80% of white women, and slightly more than 72% of black women can expect to be able to remain independent (NCHS, 2003b). At the same time many older people, especially those in the oldest age categories, suffer from chronic illnesses, commonly heart diseases, hypertension, and diabetes. Chronic illnesses are especially prevalent among older women and older members of minority groups (NCHS, 2003a). While only 44.8% of sixty-five-year-old women can expect to live free of chronic arthritis for less than half of their remaining years, 58.1% of men of that age can expect to live without arthritis for the rest of their lives. Fifteen percent of women aged sixty-five and older are also more likely to require help with living independently than are men in the same age group (9%). Twenty-two percent of older non-Hispanic black women require more assistance in living independently than do older non-Hispanic white women (14%) or older Hispanic women (17%) (NCHS, 2003b). At each age and within each race, more men than women can expect to live a larger share of their lives free of any limitation (NCHS, 2003b). The difference between the white and black populations in the number of years that they are expected to live free of limitations is statistically significant (p < 0.05) at all ages, except for men aged eighty and older and for women aged eighty-five and older.

CONTEMPORARY AGING THEMES AND IMPLICATIONS FOR GERONTOLOGICAL SOCIAL WORK

These demographic changes have important implications for social workers generally and for gerontological social workers in particular. The data indicate the need for a practice model of aging that incorporates a multidisciplinary life course perspective and recognizes the importance of heterogeneity, diversity, and inequality. An integrative practice approach is especially important with older clients, who typically present complex issues involving interactive biological, psychological, and social factors. Although older adults today are healthier than any previous cohort of elderly people, many will need help managing chronic illness, coping with loss, and meeting financial exigencies. The integrative practice approach that we present in the chapters that follow reflect these changing demographics and embraces recent concepts that have emerged in gerontology and social work. Germain and Gitterman (1996) also incorporate these concepts in their model of social work practice (see also Germain and Bloom, 1999).

The Life Course Perspective

A life course approach assumes that the past and present are inextricably linked and that understanding one stage of life is necessary in order to understand the others. The approach views late life within the context of a person's previous choices and experiences. A central tenet of the life course perspective is to investigate and strengthen interactions between the individual and the environment, between the personal and the political, and between the micro (or clinical) and the macro (or policy) levels.

The life course perspective views the person within the context of historical, social, and individual time. Developmental and biological changes influence life experiences within the context of social and historical events as people age with others born at the same time, in other words, their age cohort. Even when they share similar historical and social experiences, however, older people will interpret events according to their subjective perceptions; personal characteristics, such as gender and ethnic background; and psychological orientations, including how they cope, feel, and react to life changes. Social time is based on age norms and expectations about how and when people should experience major life transitions. In late life the most common life transitions are widowhood and retirement. Historical events or social periods affect all people and age cohorts simultaneously. Examples of historical events that affected most older people include the depression and World War II.

Historical, social, and personal time affect all adults as they age and account for certain characteristics, including attitudes or beliefs, that simultaneously affect all members of a cohort. These three dimensions also explain the diversity of views and lifestyles among older adults and the differences in their responses to various treatment approaches, such as talking therapies and informal or behavioral interventions.

Elder and Johnson (2003) have identified five major principles that underlie a life course perspective. These are the beliefs that human development and aging are lifelong processes; that the life course of individuals is embedded in and shaped by the historical times and places that they experience during their lifetime; that the antecedents and consequences of life transitions and events vary according to their timing in a person's life; that people live their lives interdependently and this network of relationships expresses social-historical influences; and that individuals construct their own life course through the choices and actions that they take within the opportunities and constraints of history and social circumstances (see Elder and Johnson, 2003, for an in-depth discussion of these principles). Settersten (2003) proposes that the life course perspective is multidimensional (individual development occurs along biological, psychological, and social dimensions); multispheral (aging occurs in family, work, education, leisure, and other spheres); multidisciplinary (it requires contributions from biology, psychology, and sociology); and multidirectional (aging is characterized by varying levels and rates of change that affect many functions and cause both gains and losses). In short, developmental, social, and historical factors affect the life course. These multidimensional and multidirectional influences underscore the need for gerontology practitioners to intervene simultaneously on micro and macro levels, using basic and specialized approaches while taking into account normal and disordered aging. The multispheral and multidisciplinary forces presume a biopsychosocial perspective on gerontological practice that assesses the multiple dimensions—individual, social, and environmental—that simultaneously affect how people age.

Heterogeneity

People become increasingly differentiated as they grow older. Heterogeneity within a given birth cohort tends to increase during the lifetime because gender, race, religion, sexual preference, ethnic background, and individual characteristics all influence adult development. Carl Jung suggested it first: as people age they become increasingly individuated—more different from others in personality, income, education, health, and cognitive functioning. In her book *At Seventy: The Journal of May Sarton* (1987) the author May Sarton explained why she enjoyed growing older: "Because I am more myself than I have ever been. There is less conflict. I am happier, more balanced, and … more powerful" (p. 10).

Characteristics that distinguish a person earlier in life often become exaggerated with age. Cohorts also become increasingly variegated over time. Intracohort variability is as complex and multifaceted as intercohort differences (Dannefer and Uhlenberg, 1999; Dannefer, 2003). Practice models that are based on heterogeneity and individual differences enhance our understanding of aging and improve the efficacy of our interventions.

The marked individual variations inherent in older cohorts caution gerontological practitioners about inappropriately applying theories or interventions based on selected subgroups. On one hand, we must use best practices in social work. At the same time if social workers fail to tailor interventions in accordance with individual clients' circumstances and unique characteristics, social workers will be ineffective in treating many older adults. This is particularly important when gerontological practitioners use standardized assessments, especially those developed from research on younger or homogeneous populations. Social workers can take into account the heterogeneity among older people by using more subjective assessment techniques to supplement the objective assessments. Standardized instruments help social workers diagnose specific conditions, such as dementia or depression, while subjective assessments, such as narrative approaches, often yield valuable information from clients that might otherwise remain concealed. These more subjective approaches also work well when the goal is to help an older client find meaning or benefits in his life. Gerontological social workers should balance subjective and objective methods and tailor them to a client's circumstances.

Diversity

Calasanti (1996) distinguishes heterogeneity and diversity in her discussion of aging. She contends that the former focuses on individual variation and the latter applies to groups relative to their structure in society: "Incorporating diversity, then, ultimately means broadening our knowledge of *all* groups; uncovering and exploring the power relations constitutive of social reality stems from examining the similar and different experiences of a variety of groups. This comparative process is rendered even more complex by the dynamism and simultaneity of various power relations. That is, individuals experience their race/ethnicity, gender, class, and sexual orientation at the same time" (p. 149).

Calasanti argues that gerontologists must conceptualize diversity in terms of five factors: context, agency, dialectical processes, oppression and liberation, and historical influences. Context involves an examination of the circumstances surrounding a person's situation and automatically requires taking into account biological, psychological, social, and political factors. An older person seeking help with a problem does so within the context of diverse influences. These often include a person's physical and mental health, living arrangements, social supports, social class, and ethnic background. When social workers encounter an elderly person who is seeking help for depression, for example, the initial assessment should occur on multiple levels. Social workers must arrange for the person to have a complete medical evaluation because many illnesses result in depression, and depression can compromise a person's immune system and increase her susceptibility to disease. In addition, the person's living arrangements and social supports provide social workers with information on at least two fronts, helping them to determine which resources might be useful in intervention at a later time, as well as factors that may be contributing to the depression, such as social isolation and problems with transportation. The older person's social class and ethnic background expose some of the obstacles that she struggles against as well as norms and customs. Elderly people's sexual preferences are also important, although members of the current older cohort conceal their sexual identity more often than do their younger counterparts (Fullmer, Shenk, and Eastland, 1999).

The second factor affecting diversity is agency, which involves structural forces that are imposed upon individuals, often at an institutional level. These include economic systems, welfare institutions, and ideologies. Approaches that consider the effects of agency probe the ways that macro forces affect the lives of elders. Social Security regulations are examples of macro-level influences that affect many people and discriminate against those who worked intermittently for low wages. Advocates for elderly people can encourage older clients to lobby against such oppressive policies. Encouraging collective actions among older people increases others' awareness of ageism and sexism and, concomitantly, enhances older people's feelings of empowerment and emancipation. Other macro forces include the media's obsession with youth and youthful appearance (see Calasanti and Slevin, 2001, for more discussion of the social significance of the aging body).

The third concept underlying diversity, according to Calasanti (1996), is the dialectical nature of aging. By *dialectical* Calasanti means those processes that are dynamic as well as contradictory. An older person who struggles against ageism, for example, confronts both liberating and oppressive forces. On one hand, proponents of "productive aging" believe that most older people can work and remain in the labor force much longer than many people previously assumed. On the other hand, new policies, including changes in the age at which people will receive Social Security benefits, may increase poverty, especially among older women. The elimination of mandatory retirement laws is an important victory over ageist policies that forced people to terminate their employment prematurely. Yet in a society that offers limited opportunities to invest in pensions and other retirement benefits, some elderly people must work even though they are disabled or ill. The dialectic underlying diversity takes into account the complexities and ranges of motivations, desires, and feelings involved in growing older.

The fourth dimension recognizes the unequal power relations that the dominant population often displays toward minority groups. Theoretical assumptions that are based on majority populations and homogeneous samples can unfairly discriminate against older people who are homosexual, childless, or otherwise culturally different. Erik Erikson's model of psychosocial development (Erikson, 1963) exemplifies how practitioners can inappropriately apply concepts to older people who have not accomplished certain psychosocial tasks. According to Erikson (1963), adults who fail to master intimacy, generativity, or integrity face isolation, stagnation, or despair (see chapter 2 for a more in-depth discussion of Erikson's stages). Carol Gilligan and others now question the applicability of many established developmental theories, such as Erikson's, to women, various ethnic groups, and other minorities (Gilligan, 1982; Sands and Richardson, 1986). For example, Sands and Richardson (1986) found that many women wrestle with intimacy and identity and intimacy and generativity at the same stage instead of at different stages.

The fifth concept that Calasanti (1996) has identified as underlying diversity is historical context. This concerns the confluence of various power relations at a specific point in time and requires, "comparisons of similarities and differences in diverse aging experiences over time" (p. 154). Each person belongs to a birth cohort and is influenced by historical events. These cohort and historical events often become permanent markers that interact with aging. Current cohorts of older people who lived through the Depression view money and investments differently than members of subsequent cohorts; the "Depression babies" typically are more thrifty and economically cautious. At the same time, intracohort variations preclude practitioners from generalizing to all cohort members, each of whom idiosyncratically experiences the effects of age, cohort, and period.

Last, Calasanti (1996) emphasizes the fluidity of events and interactions: "Social reality neither consists of deterministic structures nor is it the result of random processes. Rather it is constituted by simultaneously dynamic and patterned processes that reconstitute and are shaped by permeable structures" (p. 155). She adds that "losing the rigidity that more static notions of social reality assume means that we cannot derive immutable 'truths' about the social aspects of aging" (p. 155).

The increasing diversity of the population requires practice approaches that consider the variability within and between groups that results from differences in gender, ethnicity, religion, social class, and sexual orientation. Gerontological social workers must know how older people from different ethnic groups differ from one another, but practitioners must also avoid inappropriate generalizations or stereotypes about individuals who have unique characteristics pertaining to culture, worldview, and level of acculturation. Gerontological social work must use a culturally competent practice model that integrates heterogeneity and diversity and individual and structural variations. Social work scholars, such as Geron and Little (2003) and Maramaldi and Guevara (2003), underscore the need for more culturally sensitive assessment instruments in gerontological social work to effectively evaluate older people from culturally diverse backgrounds.

Multidisciplinary Perspective

No single discipline can effectively meet the myriad of issues that emerge in later life. Practitioners need knowledge and skills from multiple disciplines to adequately care for older people. Biological and social processes interact as people age. Longevity, for example, is affected both by genes and by social factors, such as vigorous exercise, positive outlooks, diets low in animal fats, and moderate tobacco and alcohol use (Palmore, 1995; Leventhal et al., 2001). People with strong social supports typically live longer than socially isolated people. Social supports mitigate daily stresses by providing elderly people with confidantes with whom they can exchange information and share feelings (Chiriboga, 1995; Krause, 2001; Lubben and Gironda, 2003).

Most mental health experts now acknowledge the physiological contributions to many mental illnesses. Some medications, such as drugs for high blood pressure, can induce depression (Swartz and Margolis, 2004; Margolis and Swartz, 1999; Stevens, Merikangas, and Merikangas, 1995). Elderly people with auditory impairments sometimes become isolated or paranoid when extraneous noises prevent them from hearing well.

According to Light, Grigsby, and Bligh (1996), "Environments exert an effect on personality, and ... genes do also (how directly is at present largely unknown); but most important, genes also affect environments" (p. 167). Environmental factors, such as poverty and access to health care, can influence how genes are expressed. Conversely, genetic influences may be passive (when individuals are exposed to environments created by the behaviors of their relatives); reactive (when people create social environments by eliciting reactions from other people); or active (when individuals select appealing environments) (Light et al., 1996). Gold (1996) concludes that theories of aging "cannot capture the social or psychological parts of aging without incorporating—at some level—the biological as well" (p. 224).

In the final report of the 1995 White House Conference on Aging, the authors warn that "individual issues must not be looked at in a vacuum but must constantly be viewed as part of the whole, having an impact on each other in a variety of ways" (1996, p. 24). The delegates at the conference recognized the importance of personal and social roles and responsibilities and endorsed a biopsychosocial perspective: "A national aging policy must be sensitive to the interrelatedness of the myriad of issues that surround aging" (p. 24).

The authors of *A National Agenda for Geriatric Education: White Papers* advocate a similar position: the complexity of older adults' lives requires knowledge, skills, and delivery of services on multiple levels (S. Klein, 1996). The task force of the Association for Gerontology in Higher Education (which evaluates gerontology education) also emphasizes a comprehensive approach: "The study of aging occurring at both the macro- and micro-levels [is] built on an understanding that the underlying biological processes of aging unfold within an environment and are manifest as a result of the person-environment interaction. The outcomes of this interaction are affected by diverse dimensions, including, but not limited to, culture; demography; ethnicity; economy; geography; gender; history; political and social environments; and mental, physical and social status" (Wendt, Peterson, and Douglass, 1993, p. 11).

Multidisciplinary approaches have emerged in many areas. According to Birren and Schroots (1996), for example, "The psychology of aging may increasingly adopt an ecological point of view toward human aging that will embrace major modifications of our behavioral characteristics as we change our environments and styles of life" (p. 18). By "ecology of aging" they mean that " organisms not only express their genome but the expression is done in interaction with particular physical and social environments" (p. 18). Gold (1996) agrees: "In stark contrast to the narrowing fields of expertise in sociology, the study of aging relies upon a multidisciplinary approach. In fact, as we learn more about the processes of aging, it becomes even clearer that multiple disciplines and various methods are necessary for the study of aging. We cannot capture the social or psychological parts of aging without incorporating—at some level—the biological as well" (p. 224).

Gerontologists are increasingly involved in interdisciplinary teams that include nurses, physicians, dentists, allied health professionals, lawyers, psychologists, and social workers. Gerontological social workers understand, for example, that they often must work with physicians, who may prescribe antidepressants to supplement individual counseling, or with nurses and other allied health professionals to coordinate long-term care. Increasing numbers of social workers, especially those involved with health care, understand the need for multidisciplinary and interdisciplinary perspectives in gerontological practice (Berkman, Maramaldi, Breon, and Howe, 2002; Damron-Rodriguez and Corley, 2002). By focusing on multiple dimensions of an older adult from multiple viewpoints, gerontological social workers will more successfully address the myriad problems that most elderly clients present.

Power and Empowerment

Practice models of aging must also address unequal power relations in light of growing evidence that many older people lack access to adequate health care, live in poverty, and are socially isolated. Although older adults are better off on average than they were in the past, some experts, such as O'Rand (2001), have shown that inequality within and across age groups increased during the 1990s. Similarly, Gregoire, Kilty, and Richardson (2002) found that the economic status of older married white people improved during the 1990s, but the impoverishment of older single women, especially those who were members of racial minority groups, increased. Inequalities in health and life expectancies also continue despite advances in medical care (O'Rand, 2001). Hendricks (1996) argues: "Mythology notwithstanding, equality of opportunity is not inherent in the organization of life. Nor is it an intrinsic aspect of what it means to grow old. Not all of us resemble white, middle-class males. Not all of us grow old in families with loving spouses and attentive children. We do not come from optimal circumstances that ensure maximally successful aging. If they are to be useful, our conceptual models cannot afford to be myopic" (p. 142).

Hendricks also believes that "if we are to disentangle structural and ideological constituents of the way we age, we need to develop a better grasp of the real impact of power and prestige"(1996, p. 142). Similarly, Light and colleagues (1996) observe that "individuals whose social status characteristics afford them relatively high social rank (e.g., white, male, upper-class) will have more and better environments to choose from (or to choose them)" (p. 170). O'Rand (1996) explains that "patterns of inequality within and among cohorts emerge over time as products of the interplay between institutional arrangements and individual life trajectories.... In short, structural and temporal factors interact to produce inequality over time" (p. 230–31).

Traditional theories of aging have inadequately addressed diversity, power inequities during the life course, and oppression based on age, gender, ethnicity, religion, social class, and sexual preference. Practice perspectives that ignore these influences lead to ineffective interventions that benefit only the most privileged elderly people. According to Berkman and Harootyan (2003, p. 2), "The biopsychosocial frame is not sufficient without addressing economic, political, social, and environmental factors."

An integrated practice framework for aging embraces ideas that will empower older clients and free them from personal and social oppressions. It must synthesize practice dialectics, such as micro and macro practice, basic and advanced interventions, subjective and objective assessments, and normal and disordered aging in order to provide culturally competent solutions for the problems that elderly people will face in this new century.

Social work practice models that incorporate emancipatory agendas are important in working with older clients, many of whom have suffered the consequences of lifelong inequities. These models assume that social workers understand how social structural factors and social policies affect individual lives and that social workers advocate for more just social policies that will empower their clients. These models also emphasize clients' strengths and suggest ways to enhance their resilience and coping strategies. Social workers can empower older clients by working with others to change oppressive policies or by buttressing clients' skills and helping clients to use them. In social work these models are best exemplified in the empowerment-oriented models articulated by E. O. Cox and Parsons (1994) and J. Lee (2001), and in the strengths-based models described by Fast and Chapin (1997) and Chapin and Cox (2001).

Chapter 2 reviews theories of normal aging that were developed late in the twentieth century. Practice concepts based on the themes of the first two chapters are discussed within the context of an integrative aging practice model in chapter 3. In chapter 4 we apply these concepts to the listening, assessment, and intervention stages of practice. Parts 2 and 3 examine specialized direct practice interventions for specific aging problems, focusing on psychological issues, such as depression and dementia, and on social-psychological processes involving aging families, bereavement and end-of-life care, and work and retirement. These more specialized interventions supplement basic gerontological social work interventions. Although many advanced interventions are used to treat more serious problems in late life, social workers can also use them to address more typical aging problems. In part 4 we discuss economic policies, with particular attention to Social Security and poverty in late life; health policies, such as Medicare and Medicaid; and social services and aging, specifically, the Older Americans Act and the aging network. Gerontological social workers must understand how various health policies affect individual clients and advocate for more just policies that will empower aging people. As Estes (2001, pp. 39–40) articulately explains, "The state and economy (macrolevel) can be seen as influencing the experience and condition of aging, but individuals also actively construct their worlds through personal interactions (microlevel) and through organizational and institutional structures and processes (mesolevel) that constitute their social worlds and society."

Discussion Questions

1. How is the current cohort of older people different from younger cohorts?
2. What are some experiences of the current cohort of older people that influence their views on getting professional help?
3. How will the increase in the number of older people from diverse ethnic backgrounds influence gerontological social work?
4. How will demographic changes affect current aging policies?

CHAPTER 2

Theories of Aging

THEORIES OF NORMAL AGING address why people age; how they feel and experience aging; how roles, social relationships, and community affiliations vary
over time; and in what ways social structural factors and institutions affect aging.
This chapter examines four aspects of aging: biological aging, which is concerned
with the physical aspects of aging, specifically, why physiological capacities change
with age; psychological aging, which focuses on the individual and the intrinsic
processes that may change with age (including sensory capacities, perception and
cognitive abilities, and coping skills); social-psychological aging, which examines
the intersection of the individual with his environment and historically emphasizes social roles, family and social relationships, and adjustment to aging; and the
sociology of aging, which considers social constructions of aging and economic
and systemic influences that affect the organization of an aging society.

BIOLOGICAL THEORIES OF AGING

Biological aging refers to the physical changes that occur in vital organs, tissues,
and appearance over time. According to Cristofalo (1996), aging is not an event or
one thing that happens; rather it is "a period of the life history of organisms that
begins at maturity and lasts for the rest of the life span" (p. 737). Biological aging is
also characterized by an increasing vulnerability to environmental change, which
many refer to as senescence. Biological aging results from intrinsic and environmental sources and a combination of these (H. T. Blumenthal, 2003). Although
genetic factors may be especially influential during the prereproductive stages, the
accumulation of insults during the postmaturation years eventually takes its toll.

Most experts differentiate biological aging from age-related diseases (see, for
example, Olshansky, Hayflick, and Carnes, 2002). According to H. T. Blumenthal
(2003, p. 138), "Aging and disease are not synonymous. There are processes of ag-

ing and etiologies of disease. The relationship between the two is important, but not inevitable." Although manifested differently among people, biological aging is universal and results in death, whereas age-related diseases affect only certain people. Many changes evolve with age, such as the graying of hair, menopause, presbyopia, and other age decrements, but these age changes are not diseases; they are normal losses of function. These changes do not necessarily increase people's vulnerability to death, although decreased immune system functioning does increase susceptibility to disease that can lead to death.

Most contemporary theorists concur that biological aging and senescence occur as a result of the attenuation of natural selection forces, but they disagree about the nature and extent of these forces (Masoro, 2002; G. Martin, 2003). The theorists also distinguish biological changes caused by alterations in genetic structures from those caused by extrinsic sources, such as disease, accidents, and toxins. Although genetic processes may determine longevity indirectly, biological changes with age—the losses of physiological capacities that occur after the reproductive stage—are more often the result of random events that are not genetically determined (Hayflick, 1995; Olshansky et al., 2002). Thus most biological theories of aging are concerned with longevity determination, not age changes in biological functioning. This is an important distinction because it implies that losses in vision, hearing, and stamina do not necessarily affect longevity rates and that people can still live for many years despite the deterioration of these processes.

Recent research that focuses on aging cells instead of aging organisms may illuminate these complex issues (see, for example, Gil, Bernard, Martinez, and Beach, 2004). The role of telomeres, which are repeated nucleotide sequences at the ends of linear chromosomes, remains unclear. Telomere shortening in cells, more common in older people than in younger ones, occurs after a certain number of cell divisions and results in a permanent nonreplicating state called replicative senescence. Replicative senescence is not cell death; in fact, these cells may be more resistant to cell death than other cells that are not senescent (presenescent cells), but replicative senescence may contribute to some changes that occur with age. For example, the longer healing time for wounds or tissue injuries to elderly people is very likely due to replicative senescence (for a more detailed discussion of the ways in which senescent cells function differently, see Campisi, Dimri, and Hara, 1996). This process, perceived as normal and most typical of human cells, contrasts with what happens to telomeres in cancer cells, which can produce the enzyme telomerase. This results in the indefinite lengthening of telomeric sequences to the ends of chromosomes. Thus replicative senescence may act as a mechanism to suppress tumors, which result from the uncontrolled proliferation or dividing of cells.

Although senescence results from multiple factors, including errors, free radicals, and vulnerable immune system, and no or few genes may directly determine biological aging, genetic influences may indirectly affect aging. Evolutionary theorists argue that natural selection plays a less significant role than other factors later in life (see Kirkwood, 2002, for a more detailed discussion of aging and natural selection theories). For example, genes may ensure that people live long enough to reproduce, after which other processes, sometimes referred to as stochastic, or random, influences, predominate (H. T. Blumenthal, 2003; Olshansky et al., 2002). Genes that are advantageous early in life may harm people later (this is called the pleiotropic genes theory). According to Kirkwood (2002), biological aging is also influenced by how much investment is needed to maintain effective functioning in the early years (this is known as the disposable soma theory). Most biological theorists concur that the processes that influence biological aging differ from those that are significant during the reproductive years.

Finch and Seeman (1999) believe that environmental factors, such as stress, contribute more to aging losses than experts have previously acknowledged and that scientists have underestimated the influence of environmental factors on morbidity and mortality. The long-term effects of individual variations and reactions to physiological processes over time remain unresolved; however, the effects of psychosocial factors (social supports, attitudes, and perceptions of personal control) on endocrine responses and morbidity are intriguing and provide support for conceptual approaches to aging that acknowledge interactions between physical, psychological, and social factors. Finch and Seeman (1999), for example, explain how prolonged exposure to cortisol increases susceptibility to such age-related diseases as arteriosclerosis, hypertension, diabetes, and reduced immune function, as well as cognitive impairments. Finch and Seaman also believe that diet and lifestyle changes can modify these pathological endocrine patterns.

What biological changes typically occur with age? With the understanding that individual variations are enormous, not only in when people age but also in how (that is, in what capacities), experts have identified some general processes that occur as people grow older. Despite individual variations, most people experience age changes in vision, hearing, touch, taste, smell, reaction time, hair color, skin, physiological capacity, and sexuality.

Changes in the Senses

James Fozard and Sandra Gordon-Salant (2001) offer a comprehensive report on age changes in vision and hearing in the *Handbook of the Psychology of Aging*. They explain that declines in vision vary enormously, but the most significant changes in auditory and visual functions occur among those older than seventy-five. Most people eventually experience changes in the eye's ocular media, retina, visual cortex, ocular control, contrast sensitivity, visual accommodation, and sensitivity to light (Fozard and Gordon-Salant, 2001; Kline and Scialfa, 1996). The most common visual changes include the ability to adjust to the dark, color discrimination (with declines in the ability to differentiate blues and greens occurring earlier and to a lesser extent in discrimination of the reds and yellows), glare and glare recovery (increased susceptibility to glare), and perception of motion. Warren, Blackwell, and Morris (1989) found that declines in ability to perceive motion have a significant, although small, association with older people's increased risk of falling. Branch, Horowitz, and Carr (1989) found that self-reported vision loss among older people sometimes leads to unmet needs in daily activities, both physical and emotional.

Many older adults complain about hearing losses that often cause speech and communication difficulties. Although the ability to hear high-frequency tones typically declines first, most older people will also lose hearing sensitivity, as well as facilities in temporal processing and in discriminating frequencies and intensities of sound (Fozard and Gordon-Salant, 2001).

Many older people lose their ability to differentiate and notice many smells. The most common olfactory losses are the ability to detect the smells of coffee, peppermint, coal tar, and almonds (Schiffman, 1995a). Age declines in taste acuity are also common, although these changes may result mostly from declines in smell sensitivity (Aldwin and Gilmer, 2004; Schiffman, 1995b). Losses in older people's ability to identify sweet, sour, salty, and bitter compounds are especially acute, and preferences for stronger, more tart, and less sweet tastes may increase.

PSYCHOLOGICAL THEORIES OF AGING

Personality Changes

Carl Jung was one of the first psychologists to consider the psychological changes that occur in the latter part of the life cycle. Earlier theorists of psychological aging assumed that most of a person's personality, values, and beliefs were formed during childhood and that adulthood was primarily an experience of juggling various roles, such as marriage, work, and parenting. Psychoanalytic theories, such as those of Freud (1949), reinforced these ideas by emphasizing stages of development in children. These theorists assumed that the basic personality forms during the first five years of life and then serves as the underlying foundation from which later needs and desires in adulthood are expressed.

Carl Jung (1933, 1960) organized psychological development into two stages: the preforty stage and the postforty stage. In the first stage, according to Jung (1933), people are confronted with demands from the outer world, specifically, family and career responsibilities. Jung believed that people expand their social networks and turn outward as they struggle to find their niche in the occupational world and in their families.

The second stage, according to Jung, involves a reassessment of the first. This is an introspective stage, precipitated primarily by biological changes that occur with age. These biological changes confront people with their mortality and lead adults older than forty to become more reflective about meaning and purpose in their lives. Jung viewed this stage as a time of turning inward, or a period of contraction, when people reflect upon who they are and who they want to be. Often this leads individuals to recognize other aspects of themselves that they previously have not expressed. Jung believed that most people suppress these other aspects of their personality during the preforty stage, when they must conform to society's expectations for them as spouses, parents, and workers. The recognition of the finiteness of life, precipitated by many biological changes (in taste and smell, eyesight, hearing, touch, sexuality, and physiological capacity), causes people to redefine their priorities and their commitments. Neugarten (1973) called this period the "return of the repressed," when whatever a person suppressed during the first stage of life bursts forth. By recognizing previously concealed aspects of themselves, people become more accepting of themselves, that is (in Jungian terms), more "individuated," more aware, and more accepting of their idiosyncrasies. In this respect people become more integrated and more androgynous. Men who previously silenced the more feminine aspects of their personality become more nurturing and affiliative; women become more autonomous and assertive. David Gutmann (1964) and others, including Sheehy (1976) (who refers to this as the stage of sex role reversal), believe that these changes are inevitable and are linked to reproductive capacities. Others view the "return of the repressed" more broadly, in that whatever a person suppressed emerges later, although individual variations in the process prevail.

Whatever the reason for this period of reassessment, most people confront their mortality at some point during their adult years. This often leads not only to a greater acceptance of themselves but also to an increased tolerance of others. In the lexicon of Carl Jung (1969) people become "more individuated" with age. The numerous studies that document extended heterogeneity with age corroborate these ideas.

Like Jung's (1933) and Freud's (1949), Erikson's model of psychosocial development is a linear one. It shares concepts of expansion and contraction with the Jungian model (Erikson, 1963). Erikson, who built his conceptual framework for the life cycle on the foundation laid by Freud (1949), described eight life stages. A conflict between two polarities of a psychosocial issue characterizes each stage. According to this model, late life involves a crisis of "integrity versus despair." This is a time for final reflection and a review of one's life. A positive resolution of this conflict occurs when older people conclude, after careful contemplation, that they have contributed something worthwhile to society and that life has meaning. A negative resolution occurs when an older person regrets her past decisions, wishes she had taken other paths, and finds only despair after a thoughtful assessment. A person who successfully manages this stage resolves the conflict in favor of integrity but is aware of feelings of despair.

Herzog and Markus (1999) describe a dynamic system of the self that incorporates cognitive, affective, and somatic functions and that adapts and reacts to life changes that occur with age. This system assumes multiple selves, including future and past selves, that contribute to the maintenance of continuity and identity, adaptation to losses, and changes in self-esteem, which may occur when people become ill or chronically incapacitated. Herzog and Markus's conceptualization of the self is important for gerontological social workers, who must understand why some people cope well with difficult life changes, whereas others need support and assistance negotiating their self-perceptions under circumstances of trauma, stress, and loss.

Theories of cognitive processes throughout adulthood, which we discuss later in this chapter, explain how people adapt to age and social changes. These theories illuminate the ways that social workers can intervene and bolster older people's self-esteem, particularly during difficult times. Because older people incorporate more "past selves" than younger people do (Herzog and Markus, 1999), gerontological social workers may find reminiscence therapy especially effective with depressed or lonely people. When social workers implement narrative intervention strategies with older people, they help these clients revive and revise their life stories and self-perceptions (Rubinstein and de Medeiros, 2004). These narratives help others grasp the personal, environmental, and cultural contexts, in which elderly people reside and the meanings that they attach to these contexts. Smith and Freund (2002) were surprised that so many older people maintain their expectations and hopes about their future selves, even in the face of significant health declines. These scholars concluded that these findings contradict the conclusions of disengagement theorists, who believe that people withdraw later in life, and that the findings of Smith and Freund (2002) instead support the view that older people remain involved with life. Their research also found that older people who conceptualize many selves that occupy multiple domains—such as work and relationships—adapt better to late life challenges than older people with fewer selves. When people conceptualize multiple selves, they are less vulnerable to losses and to adverse life circumstances. Social workers should avoid stereotypes that reinforce the notion that older people focus only on their past selves. By listening to older clients explain themselves and by enhancing and/or broadening older people's self-perceptions, gerontological social workers will empower their older clients and help them revise their stories and their roles in these life scripts.

Cognitive Changes

Schaie has studied intellectual development in adulthood for more than forty years. He concludes that there are no "uniform patterns" of age changes in cognitive development during adulthood and that individual differences obscure overall age changes in intellectual decline (Schaie, 1995). Schaie (1995) argues for the importance of conceptualizing intelligence as multidimensional rather than as a unitary factor.

Schaie examined five dimensions of intelligence: verbal meaning, spatial orientation, inductive reasoning, number skills, and word fluency (see figure 2.1). He found that adult age changes occur at different rates along the different dimensions.

Although he found general average age declines for certain abilities, he emphasizes that marked intellectual decline does not occur for most people until late in life and that the greatest declines occur in the dimensions that people use infrequently. Many age differences also decline when researchers control for per-

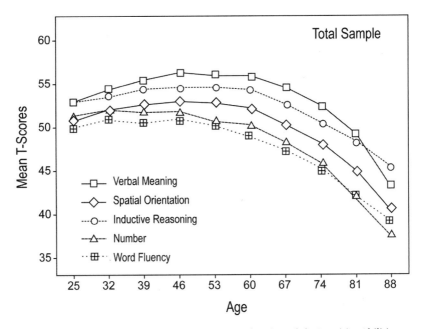

FIGURE 2.1 Schaie's Rate of Change over Time for Five Adult Cognitive Abilities
Source: Schaie, K. W. (1996). *Intellectual development in adulthood.* New York: Cambridge University Press, p. 112. Used by permission.

ceptual-motor speed (Madden, 2001; Zimprich and Martin, 2002). Most cognitive declines manifest themselves in a stair-step fashion: typically, an event will lead to a decline, followed by a period of stability until the next drop (Schaie, 1996). This description of gradual deterioration stands in contrast to ideas of linear declines with age. Schaie found that by the age of sixty, everyone has experienced a drop in at least one of the five dimensions. On the other hand, none of the respondents in his study declined in all five abilities, even at eighty-eight (Schaie, 1996).

Reliable age decrements, however, occur around the age of seventy-four. Perceptual speed and numeric abilities typically decrease first, usually in the midfifties. By their late sixties most people experience observable decrements in inductive reasoning and spatial orientation; verbal changes are rare for most people until their late seventies. Many investigators, for example, Salthouse and Ferrer-Caja (2003), have found age declines in physical and mental speed and memory, but the sources of these age changes remain unclear.

These changes are consistent with data that show that functions related to the frontal lobes of the brain are especially susceptible to age declines (Woodruff-Pak and Papka, 1999). These functions are most often considered the executive functions of the brain, specifically, planning, organizing, thinking divergently, inhibiting, and self-monitoring.

Schaie (1995) has found significant cohort differences in these age changes. He found tremendous individual differences and that generations vary in the dimensions that they perform best. Future cohorts of older people may demonstrate different patterns from those that are reported now. These cohort differences in intelligence are often underestimated. According to Staudinger and Bluck (2001) and Willis and Schaie (1999), when researchers compared adults born from 1889 to 1966, they found increases in some intellectual abilities, stability in others, and decreases in still others.

Many other factors, including health, marital status, educational achievement, and type of occupation, affect patterns of cognitive changes in adulthood as well (Schaie, 1996). For example, Schaie (1996) found that individuals from privileged backgrounds that included complex jobs or continued involvement in stimulating intellectual and social activities had fewer age changes in cognitive functioning than those who were more sedentary, withdrawn, and involved in family distress. He also observed that those who had flexible mind-sets and were less bothered by disruptions in familiar routines performed better on cognitive assessments. The plasticity of the aging mind is clearly greater than experts have previously assumed.

In his landmark Kleemeir lecture on the aging mind at the annual meeting of the Gerontological Society of America in 1992, Paul Baltes presented an overview of decades of work on cognitive processes and aging, specifically, memory and wisdom. He also proposed a model for successful and optimal aging that takes into account broader psychological concepts such as cognitive aspects of the self, self-development, and self-management (P. Baltes, 1993). The contributions from Paul Baltes's research have helped experts organize the complexities of studying the aging mind. All social workers should be familiar with his findings. We can identify abnormal cognitive changes only if we understand the normal processes that occur with age.

Like Schaie, Paul Baltes argues that cognitive functioning, including intelligence, involves multiple dimensions and that intelligence is not a single factor. He distinguishes fluid from crystallized intelligence. *Fluid intelligence* focuses on the speed and accuracy of processing sensory information, visual and motor memory, and processes of discrimination, comparison, and categorization. Paul Baltes considers fluid intelligence similar to cognitive mechanics, or the "hardware of the mind." He refers to *crystallized intelligence* as cognitive pragmatics, or the "culture-based software of the mind." Crystallized intelligence is knowledge that is typically acquired over time and includes reading and writing skills, language comprehension, educational qualifications, professional skills, and life skills. This distinction between fluid and crystallized intelligence is useful, according to Baltes, because the life trajectories of these two kinds of intelligence differ. Fluid intelligence, for example, peaks around the age of twenty-five and then begins to decline. Conversely, crystallized intelligence also peaks around age twenty-five but then stabilizes. In some instances crystallized intelligence improves until after age seventy, when biological factors can lead to declines in both fluid and crystallized intelligence (P. Baltes and Smith, 1999).

Schaie and Willis (1986) and Willis and Schaie (1994) report positive results from training programs in intellectual development. They found that about two-thirds of participants in these programs showed improvement in cognitive functioning, although there were differences in the maintenance or long-term benefits of these interventions. Paul Baltes and Smith (2003) studied the effects of training on fluid intelligence and found that cognitive training improved memory outcomes in their experiments, although they also found that none of the older people performed in the top of the distribution even after training. Not a single older person functioned above the mean of young adults; aging losses in cognitive functioning persisted. Over time, as the aging loss became more pronounced, speed and accuracy of performance suffered. The performance of older people was especially poor when the training involved relearning, revising, or updating memory. That is, substituting new information for previously learned material is especially difficult for older people; old information appears to interfere with memory processing. Although Paul Baltes infers that training does have some positive effects and that those who failed to respond to practice and cognitive exercises may have been exhibiting signs of "pathological aging" of the mind, others, for example, Salthouse, Berish, and Miles (2002), have found no beneficial effects from cognitive interventions. Declines in cognitive performance are most pronounced in advanced old age (seventy to one hundred or older) (P. Baltes and Smith, 1999). Kramer and Willis (2002) believe that practitioners will have more success if they tailor cognitive training to an individual's unique cognitive strengths and weaknesses. Until more studies on cognitive training are conducted, gerontological social workers can help older adult clients identify realistic ways to compensate for cognitive declines.

Selective Optimization with Compensation

Paul Baltes proposes a model of aging that he refers to as "selective optimization with compensation" (P. Baltes and Smith, 1999; M. Baltes and Carstensen, 1996). He suggests that people compensate for age declines and are more resilient than many gerontologists have previously recognized. Paul Baltes identified four important coping factors that enhance resiliency. The first is the use of *different possible selves.* This underscores the ability of people to modify themselves and respond as needed, depending on the context. The young often do not have this flexibility. Second, over time people acquire a *realistic perspective:* they transform their goals and aspirations to fit within their current context. Changes in goals coincide with the third dimension, *shift in priorities.* Goals that a person once considered crucial no longer seem as important ten or twenty years later, as the content and structure of life goals change. These reassessments play an important role in helping people achieve integrity and satisfaction with their lives. Fourth, *social comparison,* which many social psychologists have emphasized for years, also facilitates successful adaptation to late life. Individuals change their reference groups and modify them to better fit their needs and circumstances. Groups that people once perceived as critical sources of social comparison lose their centrality as individuals develop affinities with others to whom they feel most similar. These psychological processes are valuable and, in many instances, necessary changes that result in successful aging.

Wisdom

Wisdom is an attribute that enhances older adults' well-being; gerontological social workers can assess wisdom and encourage it in older clients. Although many experts have assumed that wisdom is a desirable attribute in late life and that wise people are more satisfied with their lives than unwise adults, until recently few researchers have evaluated wisdom empirically.

Most scholars have focused on the concept of wisdom. Paul Baltes defines wisdom as "an expert knowledge system in the fundamental pragmatics of life permitting excellent judgment and advice involving important and uncertain matters of life" (1993, p. 586). He states, "At the center of wisdom are questions concerning the conduct, interpretation, and meaning of life" (p. 586). Paul Baltes identified five properties of wisdom: wisdom involves struggles with the human condition and meaning of life; wisdom includes a knowledge, judgment, and advice; it involves breadth, depth, and moderation; wisdom combines mind and virtue, and exists for the benefit of oneself as well as humankind; and wisdom is difficult to attain but readily identified. Sternberg and Lubart (2001) define wisdom as the application of tacit knowledge to the achievement of a common good by balancing interpersonal, intrapersonal, and extrapersonal interests. Staudinger (1999) suggests that life experience and knowledge are more important than age in developing wisdom. In a phenomenological study of wisdom with selected older adults, Montgomery, Barber, and McKee (2002) concluded that wisdom is a multidimensional concept, comprised of several components, specifically, guidance, experience, moral principles, time, and compassionate relationships. Webster (2003) has identified multiple components that underlie wisdom, specifically, experience, emotions (i.e., regulation of emotions), reminiscence, openness, and humor. Ardelt (2003a) organizes the dimensions that comprise wisdom into cognitive, reflective, and affective factors. The cognitive dimension "refers to a person's ability to understand life, that is, to comprehend the significance and deeper meaning of phenomena and events, particularly with regard to intrapersonal and interpersonal matters" (Ardelt, 2003a, p. 278). The reflective dimension, which is a prerequisite of the cognitive dimension, describes people's abilities to transcend self-centeredness and better understand others' perspectives. Finally, the affective component includes the presence of positive emotions, especially compassion for others and an absence of negative emotions toward people.

Paul Baltes (1993) empirically tested the relationship of aging and wisdom by comparing younger and older adults from various backgrounds and occupations, and he found that older people compared favorably with younger age groups. Those who exhibited the highest scores in wisdom were people who had lives that favorably disposed them to the acquisition of wisdom (in Paul Baltes's experiments these were clinical psychologists and others previously identified for their wisdom). The most wise were in their late sixties; no individual younger than fifty scored at the top of the distribution on wisdom. In her attempt to create a three-dimensional wisdom scale, comprised of cognitive, reflective, and affective components, Ardelt (2003a) confirmed that those who scored highly on a wisdom scale also demonstrated greater well-being, higher purpose in life, and mastery, and they scored lower on depression and fear of death. Webster's wisdom scale correlates positively with generativity and ego integrity, Erikson's two concepts. Although more research on wisdom is needed, gerontological social workers may find that wisdom is a better representation of well-being in late life than traditional measures of life satisfaction or happiness.

Gerotranscendence

Tornstam (1992, 1994) suggests that people shift away from obsessions with material satisfaction as they age and move toward more spiritual or nonmaterialistic yearnings, in other words, they move toward "gerotranscendence." Tornstam (1992, 1994) introduced the components of gerotranscendence on three levels: cosmic, self, and social and individual relations. The *cosmic level* refers to changes in perception of time, space, and objects. People perceive their past and mortality differently, with greater acceptance of death and of the inexplicable, unexpected events that occur in life. These changes often lead a person to an appreciation of the nonmaterialistic, or spiritual, dimensions of life. This shift in perspective from tangible to intangible pursuits resembles the transformation, or "return of the repressed," androgyny, and individuation that Jung associates with the second half of life and that Erikson associates with the concept of integrity.

The second level of gerotranscendence, according to Tornstam, involves the *self*, which once again suggests an integration and acceptance of good and bad aspects of one's personality. This leads to a decline in self-centeredness and egoism toward self-transcendence and altruism.

Finally, Tornstam refers to *changes in social and individual relations*, which he claims become less superficial and more genuine as a person's tolerance for good and bad increases. People evaluate success less in terms of material gains and more in terms of spiritual accomplishments, such as fulfillment from giving to other people and to the next generation, as well as in terms of caring for others and living a life that has meaning and integrity. Gerontologists need to conduct more empirical studies of gerotranscendence in order to refine, understand, and corroborate these precepts.

The Fourth Age

Paul Baltes and Smith (Baltes and Smith, 1999, 2003) differentiate the third age, that is, the years between sixty and eighty, from a fourth age, which begins after eighty. They suggest that compensatory mechanisms and other resources from cultural and environmental factors may successfully compensate for aging losses during the third age but that their effectiveness declines as biological factors increase in importance during the fourth age. Paul Baltes and Smith (2003) define the fourth age in two ways. First, they provide a population-based definition, which is the chronological age at which 50% of the individual's birth cohort is no longer alive.

Second, a person-based definition begins at different ages for different people and depends on whether an individual's quality of life is predominately positive or negative. Paul Baltes and Smith identify several characteristics of the fourth age, which are mostly negative. These include significant losses in cognitive potential and ability to learn; an increase in chronic stress syndrome; significant prevalence of dementia (about 50% in ninety-year-olds); high levels of frailty, dysfunctionality, and multimorbidity. They also contrast these characteristics with those factors associated with the third age, or the young old, that are more positive, such as an increase in life expectancy (more older people live longer); substantial latent potential for better fitness (physical, mental) in old age; the gains in physical and mental fitness shown by successive cohorts (generations); evidence of the cognitive-emotional reserves of the aging mind; the increasing number of people who age successfully; high levels of emotional and personal well-being (self-plasticity); and effective strategies for mastering the gains and losses of late life. Most important, Paul Baltes and Smith (2003) argue that we must be cautious about extending life expectancies, given the negative characteristics associated with this fourth age. If we expect to maintain the quality of these people's lives, we will need more societal supports, applicable social policies, and effective genetic interventions to compensate for the many declines that occur among those who live longer. Paul Baltes and Smith (2003) conclude that we must also prepare people better for their longer lives so that they are better able to compensate and optimize life during the fourth age.

SOCIAL-PSYCHOLOGICAL THEORIES OF AGING

Role Theory

Role theory was commonly used in the late 1960s and early 1970s to explain adjustment to late life. It was often applied to widowhood and retirement to explain the behavioral changes that occur after these life events. According to role theorists, society is structured around various roles that prescribe norms and expectations regarding behavior and attitudes. Some argue that personality is comprised of the different roles that people occupy in their lives or that a specific set of roles is the culmination of an individual's existence (Blau, 1973; Cottrell, 1933). Although theorists have presented various definitions of *role,* Thomas and Biddle (1966) conclude that it commonly refers to a set of prescriptions defining the proper behavior for a position. A position is a collectively recognized category of people differentiated on the basis of a common attribute, common behavior, or the common reaction of others toward them. The category must be distinct in the minds of most people (Thomas and Biddle, 1966). Presumably, roles are socially defined, that is, role behaviors are learned (Strean, 1979). Examples of roles include worker, student, spouse, parent, and caregiver (Thomas and Biddle, 1966).

Streib and Schneider (1971) and Blau (1973) were among the first to apply concepts from role theory to late life, specifically, to retirement and widowhood, respectively. Streib and Schneider as well as Blau hypothesized that the work role is one of the most important that individuals (especially men) assume and is a strong source of a person's identity. For example, many men and women refer to their work or occupation when describing themselves to others. The work role provides standards and guidelines for behavior and values. Employers often dictate regulations governing performance, behavior, and even personal appearance; professions develop and enforce codes of ethics. Role theorists argue that people lose a major source of their identity when they retire. This loss of the work role presumably makes people discontent, anxious, and sometimes depressed.

Blau (1973) believes that retirement threatens people's self-esteem in several ways. It decreases their opportunities for daily social contact. It sometimes dismantles relationships with coworkers, customers, clients, and other occupational contacts, and it inevitably leads to a loss of professional group affiliation.

Blau (1973) uses the term *role exit* to describe how roles affect people in late life. Role exits are problematic when they require people to relinquish roles that they have already mastered and to learn new roles, which may be more complex, more demanding, and less rewarding. Blau argues that role exits in later life, such as widowhood and retirement, differ from role exits that people experience earlier in life. Widowhood and retirement involve a departure from two major societal roles, marriage and work. According to Blau (1973), no new roles are available to replace these. Consequently, these role exits produce stress and strain no matter how satisfied or dissatisfied a person might have felt with her previous role. Declines in morale often ensue.

Blau (1973) also distinguishes between voluntary and involuntary role exits. Voluntary role exits usually involve hope of a new life, including anticipation of greater satisfactions or rewards from some other role. Involuntary role exits are more destructive: people who are forced to leave a role often feel rejected, abandoned, betrayed, and unappreciated. Because voluntary and involuntary retirements have different effects on adjustment, practitioners must consider the circumstances of their clients' retirement and, specifically, whether they wanted to retire. Workers who have planned to retire for several years frequently know how they will spend their retirement years and often adjust well. Those whose retirement occurs unexpectedly, because of ill health or involuntary layoff, have typically made no plans for retirement; this group is most susceptible to adjustment problems.

The role exits that adults undergo during widowhood are equally distressing. In these instances people have lost a familiar companion with whom they have many associations. The extent of the disruption varies according to the circumstances of the death, such as the timing, whether it was anticipated or unanticipated, the nature of the relationship and how conflictual it was, and the resources available to the surviving partner (Richardson and Balaswamy, 2001). We will discuss these issues in greater depth in chapter 12.

Rosow (1974) believes that, regardless of the voluntary nature of the role exit, most people experience some anxiety when they exit major roles. The distress is greater, however, when people are not prepared for the changes and when they lose valuable resources as a result of the change in roles (Richardson and Kilty, 1991).

Many criticize role theory for failing to consider the unique mental processes of people and for devaluing subjective, intrapsychic functioning (Strean, 1979). Critics also censure role theory for underestimating the important effects of culture, social class, and power. Most researchers who have used role theory in their investigations also have used cross-sectional research designs that emphasize group differences. Longitudinal research designs, although more costly and cumbersome to conduct, more often demonstrate stability. Researchers have found minimal support for the kind of distress and anomie that many role theorists predicted after exit from a major role.

Disengagement Theory

In their outline of disengagement theory Cumming and Henry (1961) postulate that older people gradually and inevitably withdraw from the various roles that they occupied in middle age and reduce their level of activity or sense of involvement in life. Cumming and Henry theorize that elders turn inward and become increasingly preoccupied with themselves. Cumming and Henry also argue that this disengagement is demonstrated by a shift in preference from the more engaging, affective, obligatory, vertical ties of work and family to less demanding, less affective, voluntary, horizontal peer relations. Although Cumming and Henry believe that this shift is inevitable and intrinsic, they acknowledge that the smoothness of the transition depends upon other social events. According to Cumming and Henry, an older person's withdrawal benefits society. They used a systems framework to explain the relationship of the individual to the society, focusing on individual adjustment and life satisfaction. Many years of research failed to show that disengagement is either natural or inevitable. Those who do withdraw do so more often from a lack of opportunities and social or economic constraints than from choice.

Activity Theory

In response or reaction to disengagement theory activity, theorists like Havighurst (1957) argue that people adjust best to late life when they maintain high levels of activity and continue the levels of involvement that characterized their middle age (Friedman and Havighurst, 1954). Older people who lead active lives will have higher levels of self-esteem and will generally be more satisfied and/or happier with their lives than those whose lives are less dynamic. Many studies (e.g., Albrecht, 1951; Burgess, 1954; Havighurst, 1957) report strong associations between levels of activity and well-being. This theory, however, places impractical expectations on many older people who may be comfortable living their lives at a more relaxed pace than they did during their middle years.

Continuity Theory

Continuity theory dominated the gerontological literature for many years, especially during the 1980s. The shift from cross-sectional to longitudinal research designs emphasized stability in well-being and personality. Continuity theorists purport to explain why levels of life satisfaction, well-being, and happiness remained stable over time for most people.

Atchley (1989) organized continuity into internal and external continuity. He describes internal continuity as a person's fundamental structure of ideas, based on memory that persists over time. External continuity focuses on the person's social and interpersonal surroundings. Atchley asserts that people seek continuity in both external and internal events. Not only do people maintain stability in temperament, identity, and attitudes as they age, but they prefer familiar surroundings and the advantages that come from maintaining lifelong friendships. Thus the maintenance of continuity is advantageous. People desire and pursue continuity.

Research that used longitudinal designs supported many ideas from continuity theory. For example, George and Maddox (1977), as well as Wan and Odell (1983), suggest that most people maintain continuity in well-being and in their social engagements regardless of the changes that they experience as they age, such as retirement.

Other research, for example, Richardson & Kilty (1997), suggests that the key to maintaining continuity lies with a person's ability to maintain his resources. That is, if people can keep their resources at the same level that they were during midlife, continuity will prevail. But if a person's resources decrease, as occurs for many older women after retirement, discontinuity will result. In an analysis of older people's expectations and resources before and after retirement, Richardson and Kilty (1997) found many gender differences in maintenance of financial assets after retirement.

Older women, more so than older men, expected to have more lucrative resources during retirement. But many older women found that their resources dissipated unexpectedly when they stopped working upon retirement. They were not prepared for the declines in their standard of living and new restricted lifestyle. Ethnicity also affects how easily a person sustains continuity; for example, income levels among blacks decline with age. As we discussed in chapter 1, substantial numbers of black elderly are poor. Inequalities that existed earlier in life worsen over time.

Socio-emotional Selectivity

Five studies—Carstensen (1993, 1995), Carstensen, Gross, and Fung (1997), Carstensen, Isaacowitz, and Charles (1999), and Lang and Carstensen (2002)—applied P. Baltes's theory of selective optimization with compensation in an attempt to understand older people's relationships. Carstensen and colleagues (1999) proposed a theory of socio-emotional selectivity to understand why many older adults prefer to interact with those who help them regulate their emotions. Older people discard associations that disrupt their emotional equilibrium, according to Carstensen. Carstensen and others, for example, Lang and Carstensen (1994, 2002) and Lang, Staudinger, and Carstensen (1998), empirically demonstrated how selectivity in social relationships enhances well-being in later life. They explained why many elderly people withdraw from interpersonal associations that demand energy, commitment, or time, especially if these associations are not rewarding. Older people prefer meaningful interactions, in part because they perceive their time as more limited than younger people's. Such selectivity is adaptive (Carstensen et al., 1999).

M. Baltes and Carstensen (1999) expounded upon these ideas when they described collective optimization with compensation. They suggest that couples, families, and groups, as well as individuals, select events and experiences that sustain their well-being. Future analyses will illuminate how these ideas apply to groups and organizations as well as individuals. These speculations buttress contemporary views in social work and gerontology that endorse multilevel interpretations within a person-environment paradigm.

Sociological Theories of Aging

Social Phenomenological Theories of Aging

Social phenomenological theorists (e.g., Gubrium and Holstein, 1999) challenge dominant ideologies in gerontology research that deify positivist approaches. Gubrium and Buckholdt (1977), as well as Reker and Wong (1988), argue that objective measurements of aging are overvalued and that many gerontologists have ignored subjective perceptions of aging. The meaning attached to growing older remains unclear. The ways that people subjectively experience aging and attach meaning to their lives are fundamental to understanding aging, according to Gubrium and Holstein (1999). The meaning of an event for each individual enlightens practitioners as to what it feels like to age. This view assumes that people differ in their perceptions and interpretations of their experiences. These ideas are especially important for social workers interested in clients' subjective perceptions and objective conditions.

Gubrium and Holstein (1999) argue that gerontologists must attend to the existential concerns of older people. According to Gubrium and Holstein, practitioners who help older people interpret and make meaning from their experiences broaden our knowledge of aging and, concomitantly, assist those elderly persons who are reflecting and searching for some purpose to their experiences. Sands (1986) argues that the search for meaning during a crisis or transition is a natural process that facilitates the moving on to new experiences. People late in life face mortality more directly, and finding meaning becomes even more important. A life interpreted as meaningful has integrity and is purposeful. As Erikson (1963) noted, when upon reflection one finds emptiness, despair sets in. Whether it involves contemplation about the past or thoughts about the present, establishing meaning for one's experiences is helpful to many people in late life. Social phenomenologists have contributed enormously to theories of aging by raising gerontologists' awareness of the subjective nature of experiences and of how differently people interpret their lives.

Age Stratification Theory

When Riley (1971) introduced age stratification theory, she argued that age groups share important characteristics, specifically, demographics (e.g., size, racial composition, and sex ratio), history, and unique intergenerational relations. She argues that gerontologists can better understand aging people by considering the age cohort into which they were born. Historical and social influences on their lives should be taken into account because these forces explain why many individuals within a particular age group perceive sex roles, race relations, and economics in the ways that they do. For example, the current cohort of adult older people experienced economic collapse in the 1930s. This historical event affected many of the attitudes, decisions, and beliefs of this age cohort. It clarifies, for example, why many older people who experienced the Great Depression later distrusted the stock market, spent money cautiously, and saved carefully. Another common cultural belief among the current older cohort is that anyone who undergoes therapy or counseling for mental health problems must be "crazy." Many elders of this generation eschew mental health centers. In contrast, many members of the baby boom generation have sought help from social workers at mental health centers, and the stigma once attached to mental health counseling has lessened. Practitioners must understand these cohort influences.

Aging and Society Paradigm

Riley (1996), as well as Riley, Foner, and Riley (1999), suggest that gerontologists replace the term *age stratification* with *aging and society—A&S paradigm*. The distinctive features of individuals on the one hand and social structure on the other are still important, but the interplay between these two features, or "dynamisms" (sets of processes), is crucial, according to Riley (1996): "The dialectical interplay between lives and structures is two-directional. A change in one direction tended to produce changes in the other direction" (p. 257). This paradigm moved away from perceiving the individual and society as static. Instead it recognized that both features constantly change. Riley, Foner, and Riley (1999, p. 327) suggest that, "against the backdrop of history, changes in people's lives influence and are influenced by changes in social structures and institutions. These reciprocal changes are linked to the meanings of age, which vary over time." The dynamic nature of the individual and of society is crucial to an understanding of aging and society, according to Riley, and these are interdependent; each influences the other. Hence the aging-and-society perspective emphasizes the dialectical interplay of changes in individuals and changes in social structure.

Subcultures of Aged

Rose (1965) suggests that older Americans are a subculture of society and are often discriminated against because they are perceived as having less status than younger people. A subculture of older people emerges when age peers interact mostly with each other and are isolated from those of dissimilar ages. The increase in segregated housing for older people is likely to promote such interactions. For example, the proliferation of retirement villages, elder hostels, and other forms of segregated lifestyles means that elderly people will spend more time with each other, develop friendships with same-age peers, and interact less with those who are younger, regardless of how much time they spend with relatives of different ages. Some agencies assume that it is easier to deliver services to similar age groups that share a common lifestyle, food preferences, and health needs. These assumptions are probably inaccurate and are based on group averages instead of individual characteristics. The long-term consequences of such social assumptions include undermining cooperative and potentially amiable intergenerational relationships.

Social Exchange Theories

Kuypers and Bengston (1973) argue that interactions in late life are best under-stood as complex processes of exchange between society and older people. An unfavorable balance of power between older people and the larger society arises when fewer older people participate in paid work. When people retire, the power differential shifts as society provides more material resources, in the form of Social Security, Medicare, and other forms of assistance than the elders give back. The unbalanced exchange leads to disempowerment and loss of status for many older people. Zusmand (1966) conceived of a multistage cycle of social breakdown that starts when society labels older people as deficient and powerless. Older people internalize such negative messages and become increasingly vulnerable to future losses. Kuypers and Bengston called this the social breakdown syndrome and de-veloped the social reconstruction syndrome, a model used to teach practitioners to interject reconstructive suggestions depending upon which part of the cycle an older person is struggling with most (see figure 2.2).

This was one of the first intervention models that incorporated micro and macro levels of treatment. For example, intervention on a societal level can be directed at mitigating elderly people's overall vulnerability and susceptibility to attacks on their self-esteem. A society that was not so attuned to the work ethic and productivity and was more open to defining people in broader ways would in-corporate those who are not engaged in paid work and would value them as much as those who are working. A change in society's values regarding the work ethic would require major reconstruction of an economic philosophy that is intrinsic to the traditional American character.

Geriatric social workers can buttress the individual's strength by helping her to increase her coping capacities and feelings of control. Those who feel greater internal locus of control are presumably less affected by society's admonishments or external labeling. Such interventions can occur with individuals or groups. Community services, such as improved housing, more accessible transportation, nutrition programs, and other social services, can also promote self-reliance, in-dependence, and thus self-control.

The importance of the social breakdown and social reconstruction model lies in the attention that it focuses on perceiving both individual and social structural forces that influence elderly people.

Political Economy of Aging

According to Quadagno and Reid (1999), the political economy of aging perspec-tive focuses on the interplay of private and public, state and market. Old age is

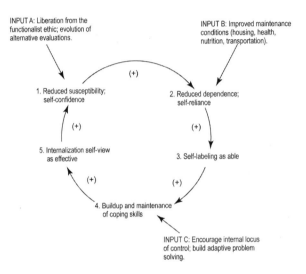

FIGURE 2.2 Social Reconstruction Syndrome
Source: Bengston, V. L. (1973). *The social psychology of aging.* Upper Saddle River, N.J.: Prentice Hall,, pp. 47–48. Used by permission.

socially constructed, "a product of struggles that result in the unequal distribution of societal resources" (Quadagno and Reid, 1999, p. 344). Similarly, Estes (2001) argues that aging cannot be understood unless one considers important sociostructural factors that substantially affect older people. Estes' description of the political economy of aging (2001) is especially relevant here because of her emphasis on the linkages between the micro, meso, and macro levels of aging (Estes, 2001). Estes states (2001, p. 2) "The power struggles between these institutional forces occur within the context of the 'interlocking systems of oppression' (Collins, 2000) of gender, social class, and racial and ethnic status across the life course (Dressel et al., 1999; Street and Quadagno, 1993)." She explains that the political economy of aging is based on several premises: (1) Society shapes how older individuals are perceived and how they perceive themselves, affecting their sense of worth and power; (2) attributional labels applied to the elderly shape not only the experience of old age but also societal decisions concerning public policy for the elderly; (3) social policy and the politics of aging mirror the inequalities in society and the outcomes of power struggles around those structured arrangements. Policy is not neutral. Rather, it reflects the advantages and disadvantages of capital and labor, whites and nonwhites, men and women in society. The fourth premise is that social policy reflects the dominant ideologies and belief systems that enforce, bolster, and extend the structure of inequalities, advantages, and disadvantages in the larger economic, political, and social order. The political economy of aging focuses on the sociostructural conditions of society. Studies that examine the influence of the state, class, gender, and racial and ethnic divisions in society are especially relevant. The political economy of aging also draws from multiple theories and levels of analysis (Estes, 2001).

Minkler and Estes (1991) define the state as being "comprised of the major social, political, and economic institutions including the legislative, executive, and judicial branches of government; the military and criminal justice systems; and public, educational, health, and welfare institutions" (p. 22). According to Estes (2001), many scholars concur that the state, which is a patriarchal institution, is a major force behind the subjugation of women. The concern is with how patriarchy (i.e., the dominant culture of white men) oppresses women and people of color. Many ethnic groups share a common culture or set of physical attributes that is different from and devalued by the dominant culture; they typically have less power and control over their lives than dominant groups.

Personal problems, including mental health, unemployment, and illness, become public concerns. Political economy theorists emphasize how the dominant culture, institutions, and social classes shape both subjective and objective conditions of older people.

Estes (1993) proposes an approach to intervention that incorporates an *empowerment imperative* and involves "a commitment to the design and evaluation of social interventions that enhance the capacity of the older and chronically ill for self-esteem, personal control, individual and social involvement, and social action" (p. 294). The empowerment imperative "is committed to the development and implementation of interventions that modify the structural conditions (e.g., inadequacies in health or housing policy) that contribute to or generate dependency problems in old age" (p. 294). Estes (1993) argues for three levels of intervention: the first focuses on the concerns of everyday life. These interventions should be created to increase personal control by older people in daily life. Level 2 interventions, emanating from institutions and professionals in the community, must also focus on improving individual personal control. Improving access to community services for all older people, regardless of gender, social class, or race and ethnicity is crucial. The third level involves interventions that challenge ingrained social structures, discriminate against older people, and promote inequities by age as well as by gender and ethnicity.

Critical Gerontology

Critical gerontology is concerned with relations of domination and exploitation of older people as they age, and with the ways that hierarchy, inequality, and oppression underpin social patterns and relations in late life (Richardson and Kilty, 1997). Critical theorists, including Habermas (1976), as well as those from the Frankfurt school (e.g., Horkheimer and Adorno, 1972), concur that a preeminent goal is helping older people to achieve an emancipatory ideal, that is, to identify and overcome the oppressive forces that are dominating them and/or preventing them from achieving autonomy, wisdom, and transcendence (Held, 1980; Moody, 1988). Ovrebo and Minkler (1993) assert that "critical gerontology embraces a broad framework of political economy of aging and considers how political, socioeconomic, and related factors interact to shape and determine the experience of growing old" (p. 289). It is "deeply concerned with the intersection of gender and aging and views gender, race, and class as pivotal variables influencing the trajectory of growing old by predetermining an individual's location in the social order" (Ovrebo and Minkler, 1993, pp. 289–90). This perspective seeks emancipation from all forms of domination, including prevailing ideologies and hidden interests (Moody, 1993). People become freer when they analyze the dominant viewpoints and ideas and expose the covert oppressive influences.

Although most critical theorists find great fault with positivism and have more natural affinities with qualitative methods, they do not endorse a single method and reject no particular approach (Morrow, 1994). Habermas (1976), in particular, argued for the use of a range of approaches and suggested that we should not replace all methods of causal analysis with interpretive approaches or vice versa. Instead, he argued that the goal should be to transcend dualities and reach a higher synthesis in which both perspectives have their place (Best and Kellner, 1991; Fraser and Nicholson, 1988; Hollinger, 1994; McCarthy, 1982). Best and Kellner (1991) assert that the best products of critical theory are multidimensional and use multiple perspectives and methods. Adorno (1973), as well as Hollinger (1994), argued for an integrated social theory that takes into account macro *and* micro influences as well as consensus *and* dissensus.

Atchley (1993) proposes, for example, a critical perspective on retirement that he believes will help us achieve a more integrated view of the experience by taking into account social structural and economic influences along with individual and human development viewpoints. An in-depth analysis of retirement as a so-cial institution, according to Atchley (1993), would attempt to "expose further the deeper motives behind the institution and to expose the patterns of domination contained within them" (p. 7). The prevailing hegemony of retirement does not incorporate many of the existing inequities in pension coverage, Social Security, and other retirement resources. In contrast to some eminent postmodern theo-rists, such as Lyotard (1984), most critical theorists believe that it is important and necessary to retain certain categorical distinctions such as gender, race, and class (Best and Kellner, 1991). A critical gerontological perspective on retirement planning would therefore focus on access to pensions and jobs and equal distribu-tion of income by race, class, and gender. Gender inequities in the distribution of pensions and in retirement planning in general are a major concern for critical theorists in gerontology (Richardson and Kilty, 1997).

Feminist Gerontology

Feminist scholarship has largely ignored older women, and gerontologists have overlooked feminism. Colette Browne, Dianne Garner, and Nancy Hooyman, all social workers, wrote the first important works in feminist gerontology: *Women, Feminism, and Aging* (Browne, 1998), *Fundamentals of Feminist Gerontology* (Gar-ner, 1999), and *Feminist Perspectives on Family Care: Policies for Gender Justice* (Hooyman and Gonyea, 1995). Feminist gerontologists focus on the intersection of aging and gender from a life course perspective (see Hooyman, Browne, Ray, and Richardson, 2002). The approach resembles critical gerontology in its concern with emancipation and liberating older people from political and structural fac-tors that oppress them. Feminist gerontology incorporates gender, as well as race, social class, and sexual preference, by examining how these influences accumulate during the life course and contribute to poverty and social inequality in late life. Feminist gerontologists argue that gender oppression is inextricably connected to oppression by race, class, age, and sexual preference and advocate for social changes that will promote social and economic justice and empower older people. Feminist gerontologists identify nine elements underlying this perspective. These include the need to document inequality and oppression by gender, race, and class across the life course and the added oppression by age; identify the sociocultural, historical, and political forces that shape aging among diverse groups; analyze the interactions of production and reproduction within a Western capitalistic mar-ketplace; critique the ideologies of separate spheres and of familism; advocate for gender justice by seeking political and structural change; reconceptualize power and empowerment; adopt a holistic ecological perspective; seek opportunities for solidarity within and across genders; and search for new and alternate methods for gerontological practice, policy, research, and education. Feminist gerontologists pay particular attention to gender inequities in caregiving, work, and retirement that must be challenged if older women expect to achieve parity with older men. Feminist gerontology fits with an integrated gerontological practice that concomitantly implements micro and macro interventions and individual and environmental conceptualizations of problems and concerns in late life. In addition to endorsing holistic views of people's lives, these theorists emphasize people's strengths and embrace their diversity and individual differences. Empowerment and advocacy are also fundamental to feminist gerontology (Garner, 1999). According to Garner (1999, p. 10), advocacy involves "pressuring organizations or governments to respond to the needs of older women and working to eliminate stereotypes, change societal attitudes, and broaden the range of roles available to aging women." As the gap between rich and poor widens, gerontological social workers will need to apply ideas and intervention strategies endorsed by critical and feminist gerontology theorists if they expect to help older adults and to eradicate current health and economic inequities that accumulate over the lifespan.

CRITIQUE

Social workers must know classic as well as contemporary theories of aging to understand normal age changes and disordered processes. Social workers who understand how theorists conceptualize aging will recognize developmental processes that commonly occur in late life and better differentiate the disordered processes that affect many older adults. Social workers must remain aware of new studies that challenge traditional views and discover new approaches and understandings.

The theories reviewed in this chapter emerge from psychology, social psychology, and sociology and are based on research that generally used samples of older people from the dominant white male culture. Gerontologists now realize that many theoretical conclusions drawn from these investigations are inapplicable to older adults from diverse ethnic backgrounds. For example, recent research on retirement demonstrates the need for conceptualizations or theories that reflect many women's intermittent, irregular career trajectories or the blurred distinctions between work and retirement for many older African Americans. Although adult cohorts grow more heterogeneous over time, theories of aging have yet to incorporate this diversity.

Social workers strive to emancipate older people from oppression, but traditional theories of aging neglect this issue. They understate or ignore the many inequalities in income, access to health care, and quality of life that extant studies of older people from various ethnic backgrounds reveal. Social workers must better understand how to incorporate salient values basic to the profession of social work with theories of aging.

Discussion Questions

1. Which theory of aging makes most sense to you and why?
2. How do older and new theories of aging differ in their assumptions about growing older?
3. What implications do the theories of aging have for social work practice with older adults?
4. Take a theory that this chapter describes and apply it to one of your older clients.

CHAPTER 3

Integrated Gerontological Practice

THE GERONTOLOGICAL PRACTICE MODEL that we are proposing synthesizes aging and social work practice theories by taking into account relevant themes from both. These include the applicability of a life course perspective; the use of the concepts of heterogeneity and diversity, which are especially relevant to the twenty-first century; the need for a multidisciplinary framework; and attention to power and inequality. These themes translate into practice approaches that are especially relevant to gerontological social work. First, a life course perspective integrates individual and social forces, that is, micro and macro influences, and thus incorporates both micro and macro practice approaches. A life course perspective also implies that the social worker will pay attention to normal and disordered aging by using basic and specialized skills. In addition, the greater heterogeneity of the older cohort demands practice strategies that are subjective and tailored to individuals. Yet another factor especially relevant to gerontological social work is the diversity of subgroups in American society, which requires a perspective that recognizes the importance of culturally competent practice. Also, a multidisciplinary framework, which is a central premise in gerontology, complements social workers' commitment to biopsychosocial practice. Finally, power and inequity, which are salient themes in many contemporary aging theories, are also fundamental aspects of social work and are represented in emancipatory enterprises and empowerment practice. The aging themes that are outlined in chapter 2 are associated with the practice approaches identified here. See table 3.1.

COMBINING MICRO AND MACRO PRACTICE FOR A LIFE COURSE PERSPECTIVE

A life course perspective underscores interactions between individuals and their environment and between individual, social, and historical time. This approach

TABLE 3.1 Components of Integrated Gerontological Practice

Aging Themes	Practice Approaches	Implementation Stage	Practice Strategy
Life course perspective	Micro and macro practice Normal and disordered aging Basic and specialized interventions	Intervention stage	Prevention Individual treatments Family therapy Group interventions Community interventions Advocacy
Heterogeneity	Sensitivity to individual differences Subjective/interpretive/ meaning	Listening stage	Empathic listening Cultural empathy Narration Life review Subjective assessments
Diversity	Cultural sensitivity	Assessment and intervention stages	Culturally valid assessments and interventions
Multidisciplinary perspective	Biopsychosocial practice	Assessment and intervention stages	ABCDEF guide Standardized assessments Interdisciplinary teams Holistic practice
Power and inequality	Emancipatory practice mutuality	Intervention	Empowerment Advocacy Social change

is multidimensional, multispheral, multidisciplinary, and multidirectional. One way to ensure that individual and social forces, and individual and social time, are taken into account simultaneously is to use an integrated practice approach with gerontological practice strategies. Although many social work programs divide clinical practice and policy, gerontological social workers must integrate micro and macro practice when treating older clients. These interactions between individual and social events, which are central to a life course perspective, demand an integrative approach. For example, when the social worker who had worked with one client, Ms. Jones, for many years visited her, the social worker noticed that Ms. Jones was losing weight; she recently had suffered a fall, breaking her ankle, and could not walk. Ms. Jones was transferred to a skilled nursing facility after three days in the hospital because she was unable to care for herself at home. This transfer plummeted her into a serious depression. After comprehensively evaluating Ms. Jones's circumstances, the social worker learned that Ms. Jones was worried about how she could pay for the nursing home because Medicare discontinues payments after one hundred days. The assessment revealed how depressed Ms. Jones was about her fall, her need for care, and her failing health. The social worker referred Ms. Jones to a physician to determine whether antidepressant medication was appropriate, and she helped Ms. Jones assess her financial situation in light of the limitations of Medicare.

The multifaceted nature of most problems in later life requires interventions on multiple levels, and social workers must coordinate services at practice, program, and policy levels. This means that gerontological social workers should be proficient in policy analysis and advocacy, clinical practice, and case management. Although social workers might select one intervention strategy or combine several in ways that work best for a particular client, they must work in several modes simultaneously and become adept at a wide range of skills. Germain and Gitterman (1996) maintain that the most important criteria that social workers must take into account when selecting a practice modality are client choice and comfort. Germain and Gitterman have identified circumstances in which a social worker would use various modalities. A summary of these follows, but social workers seeking more detailed knowledge should consult Germain and Gitterman's book, *The Life Model of Social Work Practice* (1996).

Individual Modalities

Individual modalities are used for people who are

- Under intensive stress, requiring frequent and immediate contact
- In need of specific concrete entitlement resources
- In need of privacy
- In a state of extreme anxiety and shyness
- In need of a long-term, trusting relationship
- In a situation for which the family modality is inappropriate

Family Modalities

- Family modalities are recommended
- When life stressors are located in family relationships and communication patterns

or

- When life stressors are located in family developmental transitions, traumatic life events, and other critical life issues

Group Modalities

Group modalities work best for people who

- Share a common set of threatening life events
- Share a common set of life tasks and issues
- Suffer from isolation or stigmatized status
- Need to act and gain greater control and mastery over their environment

Community Modalities

Community modalities are necessary for people who need to work to improve community or neighborhood conditions.

Generic and Specialized Interventions

Gerontological social workers need to know the theories of biological, psychological, and sociological aging that we discussed in the previous chapter in order to understand and differentiate normal and disordered aging. For example, although most people's vision deteriorates with age, the elderly are more likely to suffer eye diseases, such as glaucoma and macular degeneration. Many older people also struggle to hear high-frequency sounds, and increasing numbers of people need hearing aids as they age. The oldest old have more sensory deficits than other adults, but people react differently to these changes. People sometimes become depressed when they confront multiple sensory deficits along with chronic illnesses that interfere with their daily routines and, in some instances, with their independence. Gerontological social workers who understand normal age changes will avoid pathologizing older clients and will know when and how to intervene to help them.

Although most people adapt well to age changes, more specialized intervention strategies are necessary when an elderly person's coping skills are ineffectual, when multiple conditions interact, or when a medication used to treat one condition exacerbates another, such as when a drug for hypertension induces depression. More advanced techniques to treat specific late life problems have emerged since the 1990s, and gerontological social workers must keep abreast of newly developed treatments. For example, many interventions effectively manage wandering and other inappropriate behaviors associated with dementia, and experts now differentiate between substance abuse in early and late life and recommend different treatments depending on the age at which someone develops problems. Such innovative interventions, which we discuss in later chapters, appear constantly.

SUBJECTIVE PRACTICE FOR HETEROGENEOUS OLDER COHORTS

Gerontological social workers must respect the various ways in which older clients differ from one another. As they age, people become increasingly differentiated with respect to health status, intellectual abilities, psychological functioning, income, and lifestyle (Dannefer, 1988). One way to account for this heterogeneity is to use subjective practice approaches, which are less structured than objective methods. These approaches seek clients' understanding of their circumstances, so gerontological social workers hear their clients' perspectives from their viewpoint without interrupting them or hastily attributing causes to problems. Life review and other approaches that encourage older people to tell their stories are examples of subjective techniques that gerontological social workers can effectively apply during assessment and intervention stages. Narrative approaches, described in chapter 4, are especially relevant.

A practice approach that focuses on subjective and interpretive dimensions of older clients ensures that social workers will respect individual differences among older people and avoid inappropriate interventions. Subjective approaches help social workers to individualize their interventions with older people and to treat them more effectively in accordance with clients' unique circumstances. Older clients also feel freer to express their feelings and tell their story in a style that befits their gender, age, and culture. They often ascribe meaning to their experiences after sharing their life experiences with practitioners who use open-ended techniques. When subjective practice strategies are combined with objective approaches, such as standardized assessments, gerontological social workers obtain a more valid picture of a client's functioning.

CULTURALLY COMPETENT PRACTICE FOR DIVERSE ELDERS

Culturally competent practice will become especially important as the number of older members of minority groups increases in the twenty-first century. Although the demographic trends at the end of the twentieth century confirmed the need for a more gerontological focus in social work, they also underscored the need for more culturally competent practices. Germain and Gitterman (1996) use the term *diversity-sensitive* when they describe culturally competent practice in the life model of social work practice. The term encompasses sensitivity in several areas: sensitivity to difference, sensitivity to race and ethnicity, sensitivity to gender, sensitivity to differing developmental issues, sensitivity to chronic conditions, and sensitivity to sexual orientation. Sensitivity to difference means that social workers must accept and respect each client's race, ethnicity, socioeconomic status, religion, sexual orientation, gender, age, and physical state. Social workers must maintain a high level of self-awareness to accomplish diversity-sensitive practice. They must also acquire specialized knowledge about specific populations or people that they serve. Germain and Gitterman assert that "The combination of self-awareness and specialized knowledge helps to assure a practice that is sensitive to difference and is responsive to the needs and aspirations of vulnerable and oppressed populations and to the consequences of discrimination. Sensitivity to difference also requires respect and understanding of people whose characteristics and values may differ from those of the group around them or of the worker" (1996, p. 29).

Germain and Gitterman (1996) maintain that social workers cannot act sensitively about race, ethnicity, and recent immigrants unless they understand revolution, traumatic expulsions, mass murders, and atrocities; regional and class differences within a group; characteristics of family structure, gendered role expectations, the status of women, and generational relationships; values, attitudes, and beliefs, and the significance of religion; health and illness patterns, the meaning attributed to physical and mental symptoms, and natural helping traditions; worldview and the social construction of reality; a group's acculturation experience in North America; and the ways in which a particular individual or family differs from cultural patterns usually found in a group. Social workers must also recognize gender issues that include awareness of male dominance and the oppressiveness of patriarchy in the culture. Many experts have formulated culturally competent practice models in the twenty-first century; the most well developed are described by Sue and Sue (2003) and Pedersen, Draguns, Lonner, and Trimble (2002).

Finally, Germain and Gitterman (1996) emphasize that social workers must maintain sensitivity to sexual orientation and understand the way that gay and lesbian people have been oppressed, as well as alternative lifestyles, gay and lesbian family life, and gay and lesbian rights. Gerontological social workers must become familiar with the needs and concerns of older people who are gay or lesbian. In a recent survey of gay and lesbian elders, McFarland and Sanders (2003) learned that a majority of gay and lesbian elders worry about social workers' knowledge of gay lifestyles. McFarland and Sanders also identified several factors that prevent gay and lesbian elders from using community services and recommended that social workers increase their understanding of these minority people and advocate for more "gay-friendly" agency environments.

Biopsychosocial Practice for a Multidisciplinary Perspective

A multidisciplinary perspective advances social work's commitment to biopsychosocial practice with a focus on individuals and their environments and on the interactions that inevitably occur between these two areas. Biopsychosocial assessments are essential in gerontological practice for several reasons. They ensure that social workers will examine an elderly client multidimensionally, in multiple spheres, looking, for example, at the individual, family, and community, and from a multidisciplinary perspective. These assessments facilitate micro and macro practice by taking individual characteristics and strengths into account while evaluating the effect of current policies on a client's options. Social workers will help older people from diverse backgrounds and will identify potentially oppressive social forces, such as racism and sexism, that require social change on a systemic level by considering multiple factors in social work assessments and interventions. Berkman and colleagues (2002, p. 5) state, "Our biopsychosocial approach gives social workers a carefully balanced perspective that takes into account the entire person in his or her environment, and helps in the assessment of the needs of an individual from a multidimensional point of view." The interactions that occur among the multiple systems of an elderly person's life are especially important to consider.

This approach is best suited to gerontological practice in which clients present complex problems involving multiple dimensions (Berkman et al., 2002; see also Greene and Galambos, 2002, and Mellor and Ivry, 2002, for in-depth discussions of education strategies for gerontological social work). For example, there are often multiple contributors to depression in late life, and many of these sources interact with and exacerbate other problems. Depression is more common among older people who have the worst health and substantial functional limitations. The loss of independence is especially demoralizing to older people. Social workers must consider the biological and social causes of depression and use treatment strategies from biological, psychological, and sociological perspectives. Interactions between physical and mental health functioning are more common in late life than in early adulthood and illustrate the importance of a biopsychosocial practice model in gerontological social work practice.

Social workers have used biopsychosocial practice in various ways. Germain and Gitterman (1996) advise practitioners to consider a person-environment fit when assessing and intervening with a client. Others refer to the individual-environmental nexus. In chapter 4 we articulate a framework that ensures the implementation of a multidisciplinary perspective by taking into account biological, psychological, and sociological dimensions.

Emancipatory Practice to Address Late Life Inequalities

Power and inequality are central concepts in contemporary theories of aging and social work practice. O'Rand (1996) explains that growing inequality is "a central principle of the life course perspective" (p. 230). Similarly, Hendricks (1996) asserts, "If we are to disentangle structural and ideological constituents of the way we age, we need to develop a better grasp of the real impact of power and prestige" (p. 142). Unequal power relations in late life are manifested in various ways but most conspicuously in older people's inadequate access to health care, retirement benefits, housing, occupational opportunities, and education. Economic inequities, for example, accumulate over time. Many older women, especially minority and unmarried women, live in poverty later in life because of lifelong inequities in the workforce, in aging policies, and in caregiving demands. Several studies have found cumulative advantages and disadvantages as a result of income inequality within cohorts in the United States (Dannefer, 2003). Prevailing hegemonies about the best way to grow older are also oppressive, especially when they dictate a "right way to age" or focus on "successful" and "productive" aging from economic or competitive views. Moody (1988) maintains that perspectives that do not incorporate these ideas create a risk that the knowledge that they generate will be used for purposes that would lead not to freedom but to a new domination by professionals, policy makers, and practitioners.

The Code of Ethics of the National Association of Social Workers (NASW) clearly articulates social workers' obligation to promote social justice (see Reamer, 1998, for more discussion of this standard). Reamer (1998, p. 254) explains that "social work ... must maintain its fundamental commitment to serving those who are most at risk." This includes learning about oppression, injustice, and exploitation and, states Reamer, "to this end, ideally social workers should devote at least a portion of their professional time and expertise to efforts to challenge oppression and injustice" (1998, p. 255). In their discussions of ecological practice Germain and Gitterman (1996) consider the concepts of power, powerlessness, and disempowerment. They distinguish coercive power, which they define as "withholding of power by dominant groups from other groups on the basis of personal or cultural features," from exploitative power, which they describe as "abuse of power by dominant groups that creates technological pollution around the world, endangering the health and well-being of all people and communities and, most especially, poor people and their communities" (p. 23). Germain and Gitterman explain that oppression results when dominant groups withhold power from vulnerable groups because of their color, ethnicity, gender, age, sexual orientation, religion, socioeconomic status, or physical or mental conditions.

Germain and Gitterman (1996) acknowledge Bertha Reynolds's prescient belief that clients have the right to decide when they need help, what help is useful,
and when they no longer need help (B. Reynolds, 1934). Thus social workers must
respect clients' strengths and desire to maintain self-control. Social workers empower their clients by working with them to develop mutually agreed-upon goals,
instead of unilaterally deciding what is best.

Barbara Solomon was one of the first to address empowerment in social work
practice in her observations about African Americans and women (1976). She defines empowerment as a set of activities in which the "aim is to reduce the powerlessness that has been created by negative valuations based on membership in a
stigmatized group" (1976, p. 19). More recently, Simon (1994) and J. Lee (2001) have
contributed invaluable suggestions for enhancing clients' sense of mastery, control,
and empowerment. Simon (1994) underscores clients' strengths and the need to
help them acquire the resources to which they are entitled, such as health insurance,
long-term care, and Social Security and other disability and retirement benefits.

An empowerment perspective incorporates an integrative practice approach,
according to Lee (2001), and addresses personal, interpersonal, and political factors, especially resource problems. Lee explains, "It is therefore a clinical and com-
munity-oriented approach encompassing holistic work with individuals, families,
small groups, communities, and political systems" (2001, p. 31). The personal (or
micro) level affects self-concept and well-being; the interpersonal (or meso) level
is "the ability to influence others to attain desired resources and goals" (Lee, 1994,
p. 24). The political (or macro) level involves providing knowledge about oppression and the processes that might bring about collective action and social change.
E. O. Cox and Parsons (1996, p. 130) describe it as "a process through which individuals and groups become strong enough to participate within, share in the
control of, and influence events and institutions affecting their lives." According
to Chadiha and Adams (2003), social workers must seek to empower their black
female clients through multilevel practice approaches and sociopolitical change in
order to enhance their physical and economic well-being.

Empowerment practice can emancipate older clients by raising their awareness
of oppressive social policies and by encouraging them to advocate for fair policies. Social justice is a central principle in empowerment-oriented practice (E. O.
Cox, 1999). When social workers incorporate an emancipatory goal in their practice, they help older clients understand how discrimination and socioeconomic
forces contribute to current deprivations. Social workers can discuss the effects of
economic recessions and political ideologies on, for example, Social Security and
Medicare with older clients as they learn how these conditions exacerbate ongoing inequities. This strategy helps clients uncover environmental constraints that
prevent them from seeking and getting help and from achieving autonomy and

fulfillment. It includes accepting clients' definitions of their life issues; identifying and building on clients' strengths; engaging in a power analysis of their situation; mobilizing resources and advocating with them and on their behalf; teaching specific skills such as problem solving, community and organizational change, parenting, job seeking, assertiveness, competence, and self-advocacy. When helping clients to develop these skills, the social worker consults, facilitates, or guides but does not instruct. This avoids replicating the power relationships that clients are attempting to overcome (Germain and Gitterman, 1996, p. 32).

ETHICS IN GERONTOLOGICAL PRACTICE

Ethical dilemmas are ubiquitous in social work practice with the elderly, and they are becoming increasingly complex as advances in medical treatment expand, as the number of older clients increases, and as debates about assisted suicide intensify. Gerontological social workers must address many ethical issues and know how to help families resolve ethical dilemmas, which are highly charged and complicated. Practitioners must consult the profession's code of ethics and other relevant ethics statements when they are confronted with ethical dilemmas. NASW's Code of Ethics will help gerontological social workers address many common ethical issues that arise in their practice.

NASW adopted a new code of ethics that took effect on January 1, 1997. It was the first major revision of the Code of Ethics since 1979. All members of NASW are required to uphold these new standards. All gerontological social workers must know, understand, and adhere to the 1997 NASW Code of Ethics.

The code includes four sections: the "Preamble," which addresses the mission of social work and the core values of the profession; the "Purpose of the NASW Code of Ethics," which offers a general guide for approaching ethical issues or dilemmas in social work practice; "Ethical Principles," which outlines the profession's broad ethical issues; and "Ethical Standards," which offers specific ethical standards for social workers who face moral dilemmas or legal questions in their practice.

The preamble states that "the primary mission of social work is to enhance human well-being and help meet the basic human needs of all people, with particular attention to the needs and empowerment of people who are vulnerable, oppressed, and living in poverty" (NASW, 1997, p. 1). This mission concurs with the guidelines of the Council on Social Work Education, which unequivocally identify social work as a profession that focuses on disenfranchised populations.

Social work is a value-based profession. It underscores environmental obstacles that interfere with people's optimal functioning and sometimes create egregious inequities, especially in income, education, and social status. It also takes into account biologically based factors. For example, most social workers now recognize the role that heredity and physiology play in the onset of bipolar disorder. Attention to social structural forces does not preclude biological or medical interventions, such as psychopharmacological treatment or even electroconvulsive (shock) treatments in certain situations. Biological factors are especially important considerations when social workers help older people. Many age-related health problems affect how people feel and interact with others. Gerontological social workers should understand the chronic illnesses that occur in late life and know how they can affect older people's psychological and social lives.

The NASW Code of Ethics is unequivocal about social workers' dual focus in practice and emphasizes empowerment and self-determination. It also recognizes cultural diversity as an important ingredient in social work practice. The code reminds social workers of the importance of identifying and advocating against oppressive social practices that prevent clients from achieving freedom, equality, and justice. Social workers must increase clients' awareness of and access to information, services, and resources while working toward social justice by confronting or fighting policies that foster poverty, discrimination, and prejudice.

Subsequent chapters identify common ethical dilemmas that social workers encounter in their work with older people. The most difficult ethical issues facing gerontological social workers today include assisted suicide and the right to die; health reform; guardianship; work and retirement; nursing homes; and managed care. When social workers are confronted with an ethical dilemma, they should consult NASW's Code of Ethics and ascertain whether it offers a resolution to the problem. The code provides guidelines for social workers, but it is not a cookbook that resolves all ethical dilemmas. E. P. Congress (1999) proposes that social workers who must make a fast decision in the face of an ethical dilemma use the ETHIC model:

Examine relevant personal, societal, agency, client, and professional values.
Think about which ethical standard of the NASW Code of Ethics applies to the situation, as well as about relevant laws and case decisions.
Hypothesize about the consequences of different decisions
Identify who will benefit and who will be harmed in view of social work's commitment to the most vulnerable.
Consult with supervisors and colleagues about the most ethical choice.

The two cases that follow illustrate the importance of an integrative practice model when social workers assist older people. These cases illuminate the value of interventions that address these inevitably complex problems from a life course and multidisciplinary perspective that takes into account biological, psychological, and social influences.

Ms. D'Amico is forty-five, married, and has two children, aged seven and ten. During the last year Ms. D'Amico's widowed mother, who is seventy-eight, has gradually evidenced cognitive impairment. The mother, who has always taken impeccable care of herself, has stopped bathing regularly, washing her hair, and brushing her teeth. On two occasions she forgot to turn off the stove after cooking, and Ms. D'Amico worries that her mother will harm herself. Ms. D'Amico is the only daughter in her family; she has two brothers, who are also married with children.

Ms. D'Amico feels most responsible for her mother's care, and she has experienced conflict when trying to meet the needs of her mother and the demands of her own immediate family. Ms. D'Amico frequently drives her children to events and various activities, and she feels pressure from their teachers to drive on field trips, assist with school parties, and volunteer in the classroom. When she avoids these requests, she believes she is a "bad mother."

Meanwhile, Ms. D'Amico works full time as an administrative assistant at a company that is threatening layoffs. Her husband also works long hours. Ms. D'Amico has felt enormously stressed and exhausted from the many demands placed upon her. She is uncertain how to engage her brothers in their mother's care, and she did not know where she might find help. She called a local senior information and referral service, which connected her with a social worker.

The social worker recognized that Ms. D'Amico's problems incorporate biological, psychological, and social influences that have to be considered simultaneously. The social worker is aware that Ms. D'Amico's situation is becoming increasingly common: middle-aged women who work while raising children and caring for older parents. As in most families, Ms. D'Amico feels more responsible for her mother's care than her brothers do. The social worker understood that she needed to educate others about the social and psychological effects of caregiving on family members, the workforce, and society. Caregiving usually involves personal and political issues. Ms D'Amico's problems are personal and political.

During the first stage of intervention the social worker listens reflectively and emphatically as Ms. D'Amico shares her feelings about how stressed and frightened she is. The social worker and client concur that her mother needs a proper and comprehensive assessment of her cognitive functioning to rule out potentially reversible causes of cognitive impairment, such as malnourishment, drug interactions, and sleep problems.

The social worker also considers Ms. D'Amico's biological health, cognitive and other psychological functioning, background characteristics (specifically gender, marital, and parental status), financial resources, and environmental supports. In addition to conducting a comprehensive assessment, the social worker respects Ms. D'Amico's attitudes toward respite care that could offer her support and flexibility at work, reducing the strains from caregiving. Ms. D'Amico might also benefit from participation in a support group for family caregivers. The social worker discusses the cultural and familial factors that contributed to the caregiving decisions that she has already made. By respecting the individual circumstances surrounding Ms. D'Amico's problems, the social worker tailors her intervention in accordance with Ms. D'Amico's unique difficulties. At the same time the social worker understands the broader ramifications of Ms. D'Amico's plight. Many caregivers struggle with inordinate burdens, stress, burnout, and conflicting demands between work and family.

Caregiving is one of the most demanding issues confronting families today. In addition to helping families through counseling and support groups, gerontological social workers must advocate for universally accessible programs for caregivers; social policies that encourage gender parity in caregiving; and services that are affordable, culturally sensitive, and comprehensive. As more and more families undertake caregiving responsibilities, often at the most inopportune times, Americans will need more services that assist caregivers with the stresses and hardships that they will inevitably endure.

Three thousand representatives came to Washington, D.C., in 1995 to participate in the fourth White House Conference on Aging (WHCOA). Of the sixty preliminary resolutions that delegates proposed, forty-one were approved (Saltz and Rosen, 1997). The delegates identified caregiving as one of the highest priorities for the country to address. According to resolution #28, entitled "Support for Caregivers," the average American woman will spend sixteen years caring for children and seventeen years caring for an older relative. The 1995 WHCOA report also noted that Alzheimer's disease already afflicts more than four million Americans, and the number of Americans affected will rise by 50%—to six million—by 2012. It will exceed fourteen million by the middle of the twenty-first century and is expected to consume more of our national wealth than any other illness except cancer and heart disease.

Caregivers gained more services with the inclusion of the National Family Caregiver Support Program (NFCSP) in the reauthorization of the Older Americans Act in 2000; these included information, caregiver training and counseling, and respite care. Many caregivers have used services in their communities that this program supports. Most states report a need for more funding, especially to provide additional respite and supplemental service support (Administration on Aging, 2002). The Lifespan Respite Care Act of 2003 is another much-needed program that will provide grants for community-based respite services for caregivers, which are among the services most frequently requested.

Instead of relocating older relatives, increasing numbers of families are respecting their elders' wishes to remain at home. Many elderly people prefer to avoid the loss and stress involved in moving into a child's home, especially if the residence is out of state. These families also seek assistance from community resources. The next case illustrates the importance of transportation in keeping older people in their homes.

CASE 3.2

Mr. Paul, an eight-six-year-old African American, lives alone about eight miles from the city. He has led an active life despite worsening problems with his senses. Until recently, he attended a nearby senior center that offers social contact and recreation, and he rarely missed church, where he has many close friends. His only son lives in another state with his wife and three children. Because Mr. Paul's vision and hearing are gradually deteriorating, he does not drive. At his last doctor's visit he learned that he has glaucoma, which went untreated for many years. His hearing loss, originally confined to one ear, now affects both ears. When his physician told him that he should stop driving, Mr. Paul was devastated. Driving always represented freedom and independence to him. He wants to stay in the community where he has many close friends and where his church and senior center are located. Mr. Paul's doctor has referred him to a social worker to help him evaluate his options.

The social worker evaluates Mr. Paul's situation on several levels. Mr. Paul is alert, gregarious, and, except for his visual and hearing problems (assessment of biological and health factors), healthy and independent (assessment of cognitive and behavioral functioning). He is happy, has many friends, cooks for himself, and takes good care of himself. He needs only transportation. Although the social worker finds transportation to get Mr. Paul to his medical appointments, she is unable to locate someone to drive him to the grocery store, church, or senior center. Many older people cite transportation as one of their most important problems (Richardson, 1992). Transportation problems underscore why social workers need to intervene on micro and macro levels.

But the social worker persists, contacting the local Area Agency on Aging; she obtains the telephone number for the senior information and referral service. The social worker and Mr. Paul call this service. After asking Mr. Paul many questions, an intake worker concludes that he is eligible for taxi vouchers for getting to the grocery store or visiting his friends. He uses the vouchers selectively because they provide for a limited number of taxi trips per month. The social worker also consults with Mr. Paul about transportation to his church and the senior center. He realizes that he has friends who might pick him up on their way to church and that the senior center sometimes provides people with transportation. The social worker encourages Mr. Paul to ask his friends for a ride and to inquire about transportation assistance at the senior center. By encouraging Mr. Paul to ask for help from friends and from the directors of the senior center, the social worker empowers Mr. Paul and supports his independence.

The social worker is disappointed that the area lacks a central source for transportation services, and although she helped Mr. Paul solve his transportation problems, she realizes that she needs to advocate for better and more centralized transportation assistance for the community's senior population, given that the number of older nondrivers is expected to grow substantially as the baby-boom generation ages.

Although many adult day care and some senior citizen centers offer participants transportation, many do not, and the existing resources inadequately address the transportation needs of many older people who can no longer drive. Resolution 30 from the White House Conference on Aging (1995) calls for maximizing transportation choices and implementing policies that promote elderly people's access to transportation. The resolution arose from complaints about transportation by many older people. More than half of all older people live in areas where access to social, economic, health, and recreational services is difficult, according to the Conference on Aging report (1996). The lack of transportation threatens the independence of many elderly people. The reauthorization of the Transportation Equity Act for the Twenty-first Century will allow states to develop and improve more transportation programs that will target elderly people. Although the U.S. Department of Transportation (2004) identified $90.7 million, from the Consolidated Appropriations Act of 2004, that it could use to support transportation for elderly people and people with disabilities, the agency also found that amount is insufficient to support the growing needs of older nondrivers. Medicare would save millions of dollars in long-term medical costs if the program covered transportation costs for nonemergency services, such as trips for preventative medical treatments (Burkhardt, 2002). Lack of access to medical services is especially significant among older people from rural areas and from low-income groups (Burkhardt, 2002). Although more and more communities are providing innovative transportation programs that will improve older people's access to medical services, many elderly people would need less costly care if these services were more comprehensive. Social workers who advocate for such transportation services can improve the quality of life for many older clients.

These examples demonstrate the need for an integrative practice approach that takes into account micro and macro issues. Although the social workers can help by linking Ms. D'Amico to a caregiver support group and by finding transportation for Mr. Paul, important changes in policy are needed to help them and other older people in similar situations. By helping these elderly people recognize the multiple layers of issues that contribute to their circumstances, social workers will empower them and they will feel less stigmatized by their problems.

In chapter 4 we discuss the three stages of intervention—listening, assessment, and intervention—that gerontological social workers typically use. Within the context of basic interventions on behalf of elderly clients, we also discuss the major practice concepts behind an integrated gerontological practice, including combining micro and macro practice and implementing a biopsychosocial framework, culturally competent counseling, and emancipatory and empowerment practice, which we reviewed in this chapter.

DISCUSSION QUESTIONS

1. Identify a case in your practice that required that you implement micro and macro interventions.
2. What is an example of a situation in which you would need to use generic and specialized interventions with an older client?
3. How does culturally competent practice change how you will intervene with older clients?
4. Identify some ways that older people are oppressed or treated unfairly in society.

CHAPTER 4

Stages in Gerontological Practice

SOCIAL WORKERS TYPICALLY use three stages in counseling. While some so-cial workers, for example, Germain and Gitterman (1996), refer to these as the initial, ongoing, and ending phases, others, such as Gilliland and James (1988), describe them as the listening, assessment, and intervention stages. However prac-titioners refer to these practice stages, most gerontological social workers focus on establishing rapport, building trust, and showing support when they first meet a client. They achieve these goals by listening intently, carefully, and skillfully to older people's stories and by offering them the space and time to share their sub-jective perceptions of events. We refer to these activities as the listening stage. Social workers gain important information during this stage that will assist them with the next stage—the assessment stage. The assessment stage should incorporate the ABCDEF practice guide (discussed shortly), which is based on biopsychosocial and multidisciplinary perspectives. Specific objective assessments will ensure the inclusion of these perspectives, although subjective approaches should be used as a supplement. In addition, selected comprehensive assessments are sometimes useful in gerontological practice. Finally, the intervention phase that follows from the assessment should incorporate micro and macro factors along with basic and specialized interventions. We discuss the intervention phase within the context of how directive social workers need to be during that phase, and we give special at-tention to the practice strategies that underpin culturally competent practice.

THE LISTENING STAGE IN GERONTOLOGICAL PRACTICE

Older clients typically want a safe and secure setting where they can talk freely about their problems. Because many older people distrust mental health profes-sionals and believe that they treat only "crazy" people, gerontological social work-ers must expend extra effort to establish rapport with these clients. The listening stage is usually the first tool that social workers use when they meet older clients. The most important goals of this stage are establishing rapport and trust; helping clients manage, accept, and control their feelings; and assisting clients in finding meaning and identifying stressors in their lives.

Goals of the Listening Stage with Older People

Establishing Rapport and Trust with Older Clients

Gerontological social workers must establish rapport and trust with the older client through verbal and nonverbal exchanges during the listening stage. The social worker must avoid dominating the relationship or acting "overprofession-ally." Social workers should begin by allowing the older client to tell his own story, although practitioners may share similar experiences in response and, in some instances, may physically demonstrate their regard. Social workers must attend to nonverbal as well as verbal cues from their elderly client to determine the most appropriate responses for the individual. The distance, objectivity, and neutrality emphasized in traditional methods of counseling are often unnecessary and sometimes countertherapeutic in social work practice with older people.

Managing, Accepting, and Controlling Feelings

Social workers who establish rapport and trust with older clients usually elicit greater verbalization of their feelings. These clients benefit from the opportunity to share without interruption and within a genuinely caring environment. Many older clients learn to manage, accept, and gain control of their feelings by talking about them. They learn that some of their most painful feelings are normal reactions to life events that become less frightening and more manageable when they share their experiences with others.

Searching for Meaning

The listening stage also helps clients find meaning in their lives, which is especially important in later life. Existential challenges frequently surface as people grow older and become increasingly susceptible to chronic illnesses. Many people contemplate death for the first time. Carstensen and colleagues (see Lang and Carstensen, 2002; Carstensen, Isaacowitz, and Charles, 1999) have demonstrated empirically that when older adults perceive time as limited, they socialize more selectively, that is, with people who provide them with intimate and meaningful interactions. Those older people who find meaning often feel comforted and have something to hold on to during hard times. They also cope with aging better than those who feel empty inside. When confronted with major losses involving a spouse, friends, or physical deterioration, many older adults find strength through the meaning in their lives. In her book *The Wheel of Life: A Memoir of Living and Dying*, Kübler-Ross explains, "At those [difficult] moments you can either hold on to negativity and look for blame, or you can choose to heal and keep on living. Since I believe our only purpose for existing is to grow, I had no problem making a choice.... When you learn your lessons, the pain goes away" (1997, p.18).

Older adults often derive meaning through contemplation, reflection, and self-evaluation. According to Reker and Wong (1988), "Meaning embraces the connotations and denotations of what is conveyed when individuals speak of their lives and the significance they attach to their existence. ... It includes the value that individuals place upon the events and flow of life" (p. 217). Rowles and Reinharz (1988) say that many older clients construct meaning while sharing their thoughts and feelings during unstructured conversations. Reker and Wong (1988) emphasize that, as individuals construct and reconstruct "reality" over time, these internal representations may or may not resemble objective reality.

Erikson (1963) believed that the last psychosocial task people confront in later life is the attainment of integrity, which refers to a feeling of wholeness or unity of personality and includes a sense that life has purpose and meaning. Jung (1933) also believed that people focus on meaning during the second half of life. He claimed that people younger than forty are primarily concerned with meeting the obligations of work and family but that this changes later in life when the demands of family and work subside. Paul Baltes (1993) emphasizes the development of wisdom in the later years; he demonstrates that many older people acquire wisdom as they pursue their questions about conduct, interpretation, virtue, and meaning.

Social workers facilitate the development of meaning, integrity, and wisdom by encouraging older clients to review their feelings and thoughts and to share their experiences in their own words. Narrative approaches to therapy that emphasize meaning and encourage clients to tell their story from their own viewpoint are especially efficacious at this stage (see Abels and Abels, 2001, for more detail about implementing this approach).

Identifying Stressors in Older People's Lives

Finally, social workers must help older people identify the sources of stress in their lives. Germain and Gitterman (1996) describe "life stressors" that include difficult life transitions, traumatic life events, harsh social and physical environments, and dysfunctional interpersonal processes. These stressors are usually externally generated and manifest as harm, loss, or a threat of future harm or loss. Social workers identify older clients' life stressors by evaluating their social context and examining their interactions with family members, friends, groups, and institutions.

Several specific techniques encourage older clients to share and reflect upon their feelings.

Specific Strategies During the Listening Stage

Empathetic Listening with Older People

The gerontological social worker demonstrates that she is listening to a client through her posture, facial expressions, voice tone and pitch, nodding, and eye contact. These behaviors help establish trust with older clients by communicating involvement, concern, and compassion. In addition to expressing appropriate nonverbal behaviors, the gerontological social worker must speak empathetically to the client. The social worker must have an ample vocabulary that conveys a wide variety of feelings and must be adept at identifying, translating, understanding, and verbally responding to the older client's feelings.

Social workers communicate empathetic understanding to clients by addressing their affective and cognitive messages, that is, by focusing not only on their clients' feelings but also on their thoughts and ideas. For example, practitioners must recognize inconsistencies between what clients say and do. Older people may deny feeling anxious but exhibit symptoms of anxiety, such as shortness of breath, tenseness, excessive worrying, or somatic disturbances. Social workers also communicate empathy through silence, which can provide clients with time for reflection and is often therapeutic.

Expressing Cultural Sensitivity and Cultural Empathy with Older People

Sue and Sue (2003) identify three characteristics of culturally sensitive counselors. First, culturally skilled counselors are aware of their own values and biases. The culturally skilled social worker has "moved from being culturally unaware to being aware and sensitive to his or her own cultural heritage and to valuing and respecting differences" (p. 19). Second, he recognizes the assumptions that he makes about human behaviors and the preconceived notions that he may have about a client. The counselor who remains unaware of his biases unwittingly imposes those prejudices and stereotypes on his clients. Third, the culturally aware counselor is "sensitive to circumstances (personal biases, race, gender, and sexual orientation identity, sociopolitical influences, etc.) that may dictate referral of the minority client to a member of his or her own sociodemographic group or to another therapist in general" (Sue and Sue, 2003, p. 19). Social workers must be aware of their own racist, sexist, heterosexist, or other attitudes, beliefs, and feelings.

Culturally competent practitioners also appreciate the worldviews of their clients and seek to understand their perspectives in a nonjudgmental manner. They view clients' worldviews within the context of sociopolitical systems that often promote domination of some groups over others. Culturally aware counselors do not assume that one cultural view transcends another merely because it is dominant. Culturally skilled gerontological counselors acquire specific knowledge about the social groups that they work with and recognize the sociopolitical forces that affect the lives of group members. For example, counselors must recognize how institutional barriers can prevent older members of minority groups from receiving social services, and practitioners must advocate for their older clients' rights to these services and strengthen their indigenous support systems.

Finally, culturally competent counselors use interventions that are appropriate for their clients and consistent with their life experiences and cultural values. This means that the social workers must know how and when to use different interventions. Traditional approaches that emphasize talking or require clients to come to the social worker's office are often inappropriate with older adults. In contrast to other groups that use services, older people are more likely to require in-home assistance (Emlet, Crabtree, Condon, and Treml, 1996). Culturally skilled counselors will also recognize the importance of nonverbal communication and engage in outreach and community interventions when appropriate. Social workers must also understand that many older clients resist formal help and distrust social workers. (See Pedersen et al., 2002 for a more in-depth discussion of culturally competent counseling.)

Gerontological social workers must also convey cultural empathy, which is the learned ability to accurately understand the experiences of a client from another culture by demonstrating culturally empathetic responsiveness and understanding. According to Ridley and Udipi, culturally empathetic responsiveness is "the process through which counselors communicate their understanding of the self-experience of culturally different clients" (2002, p. 320). This involves such skills as conveying naïvêté, verbally reflecting the client's descriptions, and expressing interest in the client's background and culture.

Culturally empathetic understanding is "the process through which counselors perceive the meaning of the self-experience of culturally different clients" (Ridley and Udipi, 2002, p. 319). Social workers convey accurate understanding in several ways. One approach involves summarizing what the client has said in words that she understands and that convey empathy. Another strategy involves identifying and prioritizing issues by offering explanations that give meaning to the client's experiences. This often brings closure to a session and is especially valuable after an emotionally intense discussion of difficult events or painful feelings. Social workers who are culturally empathetic come to appreciate that clients are a product of their culture, which shapes and instills values, feelings, attitudes, thoughts, values, motivations, coping patterns, and behaviors.

Cultural empathy is comprised of cognitive and affective dimensions. The cognitive component involves knowing how an older client perceives a situation. Although no one ever completely grasps another's feelings or fully understands what someone else is going through, social workers who attend to relevant cultural signals will better empathize with their older clients than will those who ignore these signals. For example, a social worker who meets with a Korean American family for the first time should begin by asking family members to describe the problem and allowing them to present the problem from their perspective. The social worker might focus on the actions of family members and ask them to interpret what happened. A social worker who asks Korean American clients to describe their feelings toward a family member may find that the relatives retreat from the question and are reluctant to talk and share. The social worker may infer that this particular Korean American family responds more comfortably to discussions about actions and behaviors than to questions about personal feelings, especially about family members. Social workers must respect their clients' cultural boundaries and remain sensitive to cues that certain questions are offensive. Narrative practice approaches help to ensure that social workers take into account clients' perspectives and stories.

The cognitive dimension also involves the processes of cultural self-other differentiation and perspective taking. Cultural self-other differentiation counteracts a counselor's unwitting tendency to impose on clients his cultural background or style of responding. Substantial cultural differences between social workers and their older clients can give rise to complex ethical dilemmas. For example, a social worker working with an older male client who has the dominant role in the family faces different issues if the client's cultural context condones this. If a social worker's beliefs interfere with her ability to conduct treatment, she should refer the client to someone who is less conflicted about the cultural differences. Social workers must separate their own values and biases from those of their clients. Pedersen and colleagues (2002) recommend that the best way for counselors to achieve this differentiation is to examine themselves as cultural beings. Social workers who adopt reflexive attitudes toward themselves and their practice will respond more sensitively and respectfully to cultural differences.

Another cognitive process, perspective taking, requires the social worker to learn about older clients from an external frame of reference —to understand cultural variations among older people (Pedersen et al., 2002). Although gerontological social workers must recognize the limits of their cultural understanding, they must also strive to learn as much as possible about other cultures and ethnic groups.

The affective processes involved in cultural empathy are vicarious affect and expressive concern (Pedersen et al., 2002). Vicarious affect occurs when a social worker tries to experience the same emotions in the same way as his client. Social workers can empathize with a client's experiences by remembering similar feelings that different events evoked in their life. Because empathetic listening occurs only within the boundaries of vicarious experience, it has inherent limitations.

Developing this skill is especially important for counseling clients from unfamiliar backgrounds.

Expressive concern is another affective process involved in cultural empathy. Social workers must genuinely care about their clients and never feign concern. The NASW Code of Ethics unequivocally states that a social worker who is indifferent toward a particular client's oppression should transfer that client to a social worker who does empathize. Genuineness is a critical component of the listening phase and involves being role-free, that is, true to oneself and real, regardless of one's role; being spontaneous and freely expressing oneself; being nondefensive and understanding of hostile or critical comments; being consistent in one's values, regardless of the situation; and being self-disclosing (Egan, 1986).

Social workers who successfully communicate empathy, genuineness, and acceptance achieve better rapport and trust with their older clients, who benefit in turn from the increased understanding of their concerns and feelings. When social workers need to probe for clarification or information, they may quickly establish rapport during a shortened listening stage and then focus on assessment.

These are some approaches that culturally competent practitioners use, but gerontological social workers must seek in-depth training in culturally sensitive practice to effectively prepare themselves for the diverse older clients whom they will meet. After the listening stage, the gerontological social worker should conduct comprehensive assessment of the older client. The assessment stage, which we discuss next, varies according to the types of problems that clients present and the amount of time that social workers have to work with them.

The Assessment Stage in Gerontological Practice

Social workers continue to listen during the assessment stage but ask more questions. The ABCDEF practice guide helps social workers apply a multidisciplinary and biopsychosocial practice approach with older clients, who typically present problems involving physical and mental health, subjective and social states, and social policies and inequalities.

The ABCDEF guide serves as an assessment and intervention tool that considers the client's

Actions or behaviors
Biological and health factors
Cognitive functioning, including mental health and coping styles
Demographic effects, such as age, gender, and marital status

Environmental forces, including cultural and ethnic influences and community resources

Feelings, that is, affective states and worldviews

See figure 4.1 and the discussion that follows.

The assessment of action and behaviors (A) involves systematic evaluations of older clients' behaviors, that is, how they have reacted to the problems that they have presented. With depressed clients, for example, social workers determine how the clients spend their time, how much they participate in gratifying activities, whether they are lethargic, and whether they eat and sleep well. When social workers assess actions, they examine older people's behaviors as symptoms or as contributors to problems. They evaluate clients' activities of daily living (ADL) as well as their instrumental activities of daily living (IADL). An ADL assessment typically evaluates skills in basic self-care, such as eating, mobility, using the toilet and bladder functioning, dressing, and bathing. An IADL evaluation considers more complex activities, such as cooking, cleaning, doing laundry, paying bills and managing finances, driving, doing housework, and attending to home maintenance. Older adults interested in living independently should be able to perform all these skills.

Assessment of biological and physical functioning (B) includes learning about an older client's health and biological predispositions. This often requires contact with the client's primary care physician to obtain reports about health conditions and current medications. Evaluations of physical functioning typically include di-

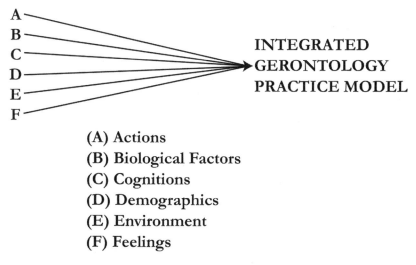

(A) Actions
(B) Biological Factors
(C) Cognitions
(D) Demographics
(E) Environment
(F) Feelings

FIGURE 4.1 ABCDEF Practice Framework

agnosis, symptoms, reported health, days in bed during a specified period, use of hospitals or physicians during a specified period, and expressions of pain and discomfort. Social workers should always inquire about older people's use of over-the-counter medications. Psychiatric and medical histories will reveal any familial patterns of depression, substance abuse, heart disease, or other physical conditions.

Cognitive assessments (C) usually include questions about short- and long-term memory and orientations to time, place, and person. The social worker might conduct a mini mental status examination to evaluate a client's cognitive skills. In many instances social workers refer clients to specialists who are trained to evaluate cognitive functioning and to diagnose dementias in older people. The social worker should consider the older person's coping patterns, for example, how he approaches problems, what he says to himself, whether he is typically hopeful or pessimistic. These cognitive evaluations can help the social worker differentiate whether an older client is struggling with a dementia or depression. They also provide insights into the client's personal strengths and resources.

The demographic profile (D) reveals important information about the older client, including economic resources, work status, and marital situation. The demographic profile of an older client is important for several reasons. An older person's income identifies for the social worker the parameters for intervention, that is, whether and how much an older client must work, what resources she has for long-term care, and what types of services she might use. It divulges background information, such as age, race, and gender, which correlates statistically to such behaviors as attempted suicide. Older men, for example, attempt suicide more often than older women, especially if the men are unmarried and suffer from a medical illness or are depressed. An older person's marital status and health are also important predictors of the lethality of a suicide attempt. Social workers who deem an older client a high risk for suicide will use more direct interventions, for example, recommending hospitalization, than they will for older people who have lower suicide potential. When assessing the risk of self-harm, these demographic indicators are critical clues.

Assessments of older clients' environmental resources (E) reveal information about their support networks, including their relationships with family, friends, and neighbors. The assessment of environmental influences must take into account not only the quantity but also the quality of the older person's social supports, including what resources and services are available to him. It includes the evaluation of the client's housing arrangements, finances, and use of and access to services. Environmental assessments include identifying and understanding cultural norms and behaviors that will increase the social worker's understanding of the context and unique circumstances comprising the older client's lifestyle, worldview, and values.

Finally, older adults' feelings (F) reveal the extent of their psychological pain. Their feelings also shed light on how they express themselves. For example, many older people from the current cohort are reluctant to share their feelings and try to avoid "complaining," although this varies by ethnic and cultural background. Some older people are highly demonstrative.

The ABCDEF model encourages gerontological social workers to consider the multiple sources of older people's problems. It is holistic and synergistic and guards against fragmented practice strategies by requiring social workers to carry out comprehensive assessments that consider many dimensions. It also encourages social workers to view older people within the context of their environment and to look for transactions that occur on multiple levels and in many areas.

For example, when a family seeks alternative living arrangements for an aging parent who is being released from the hospital after treatment for a stroke, social workers typically will encounter several problems. Social workers who apply the ABCDEF practice guide will first examine the older person's actions and behaviors (A) to assess how much mobility the older person lost from the stroke. Social workers should examine how well the person can manage the activities of daily living and instrumental activities of daily living in order to determine how much help she needs. This assessment will offer insight into how to maintain the older person's independence, what care the family might be able to provide, and what services are offered in the community that would lend additional support.

Second, the social worker should understand the biological changes (B) that strokes cause. Strokes vary from mild to severe and may result in complete paralysis or affect only one side of the body. The social worker should arrange for the evaluation of any dementia following a stroke because it can substantially affect the progression of the older person's health and care. In this case the social worker can evaluate the stroke victim's cognitive functioning (C) by choosing among various assessment tools for dementia described in chapter 9.

The family's demographic profile (D) will help the social worker determine the extent of economic resources available to help the stroke victim. Depending upon the seriousness of the stroke and subsequent rehabilitation requirements, the family may need to find a suitable nursing home for their elderly relative. The family's economic situation will influence the type of nursing home it will consider, for example, a private or nonprofit nursing home, and whether Medicaid will provide funds. See chapter 16 for a discussion of public and private insurance policies to cover the cost of a nursing home. The demographic assessment will also reveal the client's marital status, parental status, religion, and living arrangements, all of which will help the social worker assess her potential resources.

Environmental influences (E) are especially important in stroke cases. For example, older people who are recovering from a stroke might adjust well to living at home with sufficient formal and informal supports and suitable housing. Ecological factors, such as the location of family members, will influence nursing home placement if the older person prefers to live near kin. An older client's desire to remain in her neighborhood may depend on the accessibility of services. Many older people who have had strokes feel depressed, and social workers must carefully evaluate their feelings (F) and overall affective state. In addition to arranging physical care for the older person, the social worker should evaluate how she is coping with the illness and how she feels about it. Supportive counseling may help the family and elderly person to adjust, especially during crucial transition periods.

The example of a stroke victim illustrates how a social worker could implement the ABCDEF practice guide. It also reveals why gerontological social workers should use an integrated practice approach and apply multiple interventions. Here, the social worker had to understand how strokes affect families, know how to assess impairment, be adept in family and individual counseling, understand health insurance and resources, and effectively advocate for the best interests of the client. This comprehensive practice approach decreases the chance that the family will receive fragmented, redundant, contradictory, or discordant services.

Gerontological social workers should also evaluate the older client's worldview, level of acculturation, when appropriate, and their familiarity with psychological terminology.

Assessment of Worldview

Older clients' worldviews are based on cultural and individual influences that determine how they perceive, interpret, and understand their lives and experiences. Assessments of older people's worldviews usually involve exploring their individual, group, and cultural identities, their values, beliefs, and language, and their perceptions of the helping process (Grieger and Ponterotto, 1995). Social workers can best learn about older clients' worldviews by listening as they tell their stories and by attending to how they present their problems, although social workers may also inquire about attitudes, religion, language, and rituals. The Scale to Assess World View (SAWV) is a useful instrument that many gerontological social workers use with clients (see Ibrahim and Owen, 1994, for more information about this scale). Assessment of clients' worldviews is the most significant part of cross-cultural assessment and counseling (Ibrahim, Roysircar-Sodowsky, and Ohnishi, 2001).

Assessment of Acculturation Among Older People

Acculturation refers to how a person adapts from one culture to another. Landrine and Klonoff (1996) describe acculturation as "the extent to which ethnic-cultural minorities participate in the cultural traditions, values, beliefs, and practices of their own culture versus those of the dominant 'White' society" (p. 1). Paniagua (1998) defines *acculturation* as "the degree of integration of new cultural patterns into the original cultural patterns" (p. 8). The level of acculturation often varies within families from diverse ethnic backgrounds. These differences sometimes create intergenerational tensions and conflicts and become exacerbated when caregiving is involved. Gerontological social workers should evaluate how different degrees of acculturation contribute to family strife.

Information from assessments of acculturation also guides the practitioner's interventions. Although instruments now exist for specific ethnic groups, gerontological social workers may prefer to assess acculturation with more generic tools, such as the Brief Acculturation Scale, which assesses three areas: generation (whether the person is from the first, second, third generation and so on); the family's preferred language; and social activity, ranging from a desire to interact only with others from the same ethnic group to a desire to interact only with people from a different ethnic group (Paniagua, 1998). This scale provides information about clients' perceptions of and attitudes toward formal services and helps social workers determine how best to intervene. Assessment of the older client's level of acculturation encourages the gerontological social worker to individualize the treatment plan and avoid applying to his clients generalizations about large groups. Contrary to previous assumptions, substantial variations exist among elderly members of a given cultural group. Landrine and Klonoff (1996), for example, found differences within African American culture in coping styles and beliefs about work, family, and childrearing. Their research revealed that African Americans who exhibited the highest levels of acculturation blamed themselves more for their problems than did those with the lowest levels of acculturation. Conversely, those who were more immersed in their ethnic culture more commonly used distraction and distancing methods of coping. These findings underscore the need for gerontological social workers to accurately assess the older client's level of acculturation by using assessment tools that are reliable and valid (see Berry, Trimble, and Olmedo, 1986, and Berry and Sam, 1997, for a detailed discussion on the assessment of acculturation).

Assessment of Feelings and Familiarity with Psychological Terminology

Assessments of older clients' feelings offer social workers insights into how older clients subjectively experience their problems, into the intensity and complexity of clients' psychological pain, and into how particular older clients express themselves. Clients who demonstrate minimal affect, for example, may need help showing and sharing feelings, while those who feel overwhelmed often need help managing their emotions. Assessments of older clients' feelings usually include psychological evaluations to detect any depression, anxiety, loneliness, substance abuse, or other psychiatric conditions.

Older people's views of mental illness, psychological distress, and counseling often differ from those of younger people and can affect an older person's receptiveness to psychological explanations and psychology-related material. Many older people resist and lack confidence in mental health services. For example, Waxman, Carner, and Klein (1984) found that older people believe that physicians are more effective than mental health professionals in treating psychiatric symptoms. Lawton (1979) and Germane, Shapiro, and Skinner (1985) found that older adults are generally unwilling to interpret their problems as psychological, preferring instead to attribute them to physical conditions. Given many older people's skepticism about mental health services, gerontological social workers must establish rapport with older clients and guard against paternalizing by using discussion and a mutual setting of goals. Spar (1988) suggests using "symbolic giving" (offering a cup of coffee) and physical expressions of affection (touching on the arm) to make contact with older people.

It is important to assess the extent to which people understand, interpret, label, and explain their experiences in psychological terms and principles. For example, older people who talk about stages of grief may interpret their feelings of loss as denial, shock, sadness, or depression, whereas others may have more idiosyncratic or culturally based interpretations. Social workers need to evaluate the older client's familiarity with psychological terminology to determine the most appropriate assessment and intervention strategies. This information also offers social workers guidance in how to incorporate psychological language and psychological references during treatment. Older people's knowledge of psychology usually corresponds to their knowledge of human behavior and practice theories. Social workers must sometimes teach clients this information, for example, when using cognitive therapy for anxious elderly clients, who must learn such concepts as catastrophizing and distorted thinking. Social workers who take time to explain assessment and intervention strategies give clients more control of their lives by providing valuable therapeutic information that they can use outside treatment. This is one way that gerontological social workers can empower older clients.

Examples of Comprehensive Assessment Instruments for Older People

Gerontologists and social workers often use three major multidimensional assessment instruments to assess older people: Duke University's Older Americans Resources and Services questionnaire (OARS); the Comprehensive Assessment and Referral Evaluation (CARE); and the Minimum Data Set (MDS+) for assessment and care screening of nursing home residents. Social workers must receive adequate training and supervision before they attempt to use these instruments.

OARS

OARS is one of the most commonly used comprehensive assessment instruments for older people. It was developed from Duke's Older Americans Resources and Services Program in 1975 (Fillenbaum, 1995). OARS evaluates older people's physical, psychological, ADL, social, and economic functioning and includes questions about the client's involvement with approximately twenty-four different services, such as transportation or homemaker services. It also yields demographic and administrative information. Social workers can use the OARS Multidimensional Functional Assessment Questionnaire (MFAQ) during face-to-face interviews, although it can be administered by mail or telephone under certain circumstances. It typically takes forty-five minutes for older people to complete the questionnaire, which is available in English, Spanish, Italian, and Portuguese

Social workers should investigate the psychometric properties of assessment instruments before using them with older clients. An instrument's reliability and validity reveal important information about its rigor. Only instruments that consistently and accurately measure phenomena should be used. The instrument should have high external and internal reliability and strong validity with older people, including those from diverse ethnic backgrounds. This psychometric information helps social workers decide whether an instrument is appropriate for a particular client.

OARS has excellent test-retest reliability (about 96%). The interrater reliability is between 0.66 and 0.87. The validity of OARS has been measured with criteria obtained from clinical interviews and other sources. More information is available from OARS, Center for the Study of Aging and Human Development, Duke University Medical Center, Durham, NC 27710.

CARE

The Comprehensive Assessment and Referral Evaluation (CARE), which was originally developed for a cross-national study of older people living in New York and London, provides an in-depth evaluation of older people's psychiatric status (Gurland et al., 1977–78). It was designed to evaluate the effectiveness of therapy by monitoring the older client's symptoms over time (R. A. Kane and Kane, 1981). In addition to the psychiatric assessment, which differentiates a wide range of symptoms and syndromes, this instrument includes a geriatric mental status schedule. CARE is especially beneficial for multidisciplinary teams interested in triangulating information. Researchers, for example, Gurland and colleagues

(1977–78), have expended enormous efforts to make CARE appropriate, under-standable, interesting, and minimally stressful for older people. A SHORT-CARE version, which focuses on dementia and depression as well as disabilities, has also been created (Gurland, Golden, Teresi, and Challop, 1984).

The interrater reliability correlations of CARE are especially high for the psy-chiatric dimensions (e.g., 0.88 for memory disorientation and 0.92 for the depres-sion-anxiety items). Reliabilities for the medical and social dimensions are more moderate (ranging from 0.48 to 0.79) (Gurland et al., 1977–78). Data from inter-views were used to analyze CARE's face, concurrent, and predictive validities.

The Minimum Data Set

All nursing homes require that new residents be assessed with the Minimum Data Set (MDS). When Congress passed the Omnibus Budget Reconciliation Act of 1987 (OBRA), it mandated the establishment and use of a national resident assess-ment system with a uniform set of items and definitions for assessing older people living in nursing homes. The Health Care Financing Administration (HCFA) con-tracted with the Research Triangle Institute, the Hebrew Rehabilitation Center for the Aged, Brown University, and the University of Michigan to create the MDS in 1988. It has been extensively tested for validity and reliability. The MDS covers a range of topics and includes questions about personal care and the amount of supervision that an older person requires to conduct specific personal care activi-ties. The section concerned with psychological status assesses the resident's moods and behaviors. Social functioning covers self-initiated activities and the extent of the resident's involvement with roommates, friends, and family members. It also considers service use, including participation in behavior management programs, occupational therapy, psychological therapy, and recreation therapy. Questions about advance directives and guardianship, attitudes about role changes, com-munication, and hearing patterns are also included. Administering the MDS re-quires approximately ninety minutes. Changes are monitored over time as well as by place and context, although the instrument is most reliable when several people from various disciplines contribute to the assessment (Mor and Morris et al., 1995). Some experts (for example, see R. L. Kane, 2000) have raised questions about how well this tool assesses mental health, social relationships, and quality of life, although Ruckdeschel, Thompson, Datto, Streim, and Katz (2004) found that the MDS 2.0 was as reliable and valid as the Geriatric Depression Scale in identifying depression. R. L. Kane (2000) also recommends different applications of the MDS for cognitively intact and cognitively impaired older people. The over-reliance on observations lessens the validity of this instrument's data on highly functioning elderly people.

Comprehensive multidimensional assessments, although consistent with an integrative perspective, are often cumbersome and difficult to implement. In some settings social workers act as care managers who not only gather relevant information about a client but also monitor residents' functioning over time. For example, they record when older clients see their physicians, when medications change, or when social circumstances change, such as when a spouse dies, or when the client changes rooms. Intake specialists at nursing homes also use comprehensive assessments, but interdisciplinary teams also increasingly use them.

Interdisciplinary Teams

During a routine physical examination Ms. Marly's doctor discovered that her blood pressure was elevated and prescribed medication to treat the hypertension. Ms. Marly also complained of insomnia, weight loss, and boredom, but the physician overlooked her depression because she did not specifically mention it. After Ms. Marly took her blood pressure medication for a few weeks, her depression worsened and she became suicidal. Her physician had failed to consider the effect of the prescribed drug on Ms. Marly's psychological functioning.

Several commonly prescribed medications for hypertension list depression as a possible side-effect. Specifically, the chronic use of beta-blockers or reserpine derivatives can cause depression (Swartz and Margolis, 2004). An interdisciplinary team that included a gerontological social worker would have recognized Ms. Marly's depression and recommended that she be evaluated for an alternative medication. Ms. Marly's experience exemplifies the need for interdisciplinary teamwork and underscores how social workers might contribute to these teams.

Interdisciplinary teamwork with older people has many benefits. It increases the likelihood that older people's needs are treated holistically and that a biopsychosocial approach to assessment and intervention is used (Mellor and Lindeman, 1998; Damron-Rodriguez and Corley, 2002). Interdisciplinary programs save clients from having to visit numerous specialists and from receiving fragmented and redundant services. Older people who obtain treatment from interdisciplinary teams experience fewer problems from interaction effects of different interventions.

Interdisciplinary teams include professionals who work collaboratively from multiple disciplines and share information about clients at regularly scheduled meetings. They jointly agree on treatment plans after each participant contributes. Leadership is shared—the interdisciplinary team, instead of one person, takes responsibility for implementing and monitoring treatments. Social workers contribute to these teams by focusing on role changes in late life, socioeconomic issues, and family and social supports (Damron-Rodriguez and Corley, 2002).

Most interdisciplinary teams have nonhierarchical group arrangements, and they function best when all participants have received training in interdisciplinary practice and are committed to the team approach. This avoids protracted discussions about terminology and the types of turf battles that can otherwise arise when professionals from different disciplines work together.

Gerontological social workers should receive training in interdisciplinary practice and should be able to conceptualize assessments and interventions from an interdisciplinary perspective. This requires awareness of the terminology, theoretical approaches, and typical intervention strategies used by different professions as well as skills in communication, group dynamics, and conflict resolution.

Social workers can occupy several roles on an interdisciplinary team, including assessor of the client's biopsychosocial functioning; care manager; monitoring and linking the client and family to appropriate agencies; provider of psychosocial counseling; group facilitator, which is especially important when working with families or groups; liaison to the professional community; advocate to obtain services and ensure that a client's rights are not abridged; and community resource expert who knows what services are available (Mellor and Lindeman, 1998).

The Limits of Assessment

Gerontological social workers are sometimes unable to conduct comprehensive assessments, which can be time consuming, costly to administer and interpret, or not feasible for many older clients. A detailed assessment is countertherapeutic in some situations. Social workers who encounter older people in crisis may, for example, shorten the assessment phase and use alternative methods of assessment. Telephone interviews may substitute for face-to-face assessments, especially when families and clients need immediate attention. Shorter screening devices can provide preliminary information about whether more comprehensive assessment methods are necessary, although they typically are less reliable and less valid than the longer versions. The SHORT-CARE takes about thirty minutes to complete, in contrast to the ninety minutes involved in the comprehensive version. The Medical Outcomes Study (MOS) Short Form (SF-36) has thirty-six items, and a MOS six-item general health form, which assesses chronic conditions in older people, also is available (Stewart and Ware, 1992; Ware and Sherbourne, 1992). Short instruments to measure depression and cognitive functioning are also available. The widely used Center for Epidemiological Studies Depression Scale (CES-D), has two short forms (see Kohout, Berkman, Evans, and Cornoni-Huntley, 1993). Zarit (1997) recommends use of the Mini-Mental State Examination (MMSE) for brief screenings of cognitive functioning but cautions that short versions of the MMSE are often inaccurate.

Cultural biases reduce the validity of many standardized instruments, especially if researchers excluded diverse groups in their initial analyses. According to Geron (1997), a good assessment instrument considers differences in cultural, linguistic, and other modes of expression. It also takes into account the ways that an assessor's values and beliefs can inhibit elders, especially if they are from atypical backgrounds, from responding comfortably and answering truthfully. Clients often have expectations about which responses are appropriate, expected, or desired, and they often misinterpret questions (see Luborsky, 1997). According to Yee (1997, p. 26), "Culture affects how individuals understand illness and disability, how they seek help and perceive assessment and service acquisition mechanisms, and how they attach meaning to interactions with representatives of a service system."

Gerontological social workers who adopt a biopsychosocial perspective recognize the limitations of standard instruments and the ways that their biases, imperfect reliabilities, and implementation problems can affect clients' responses. Many gerontological practitioners supplement standardized instruments with other methods of assessment, such as clinical interviews, that allow them to evaluate nonverbal as well as verbal responses, communication styles, and clients' perceptions and interpretations of questions.

The Intervention Stage with Older People

As with the listening and assessment stages, gerontological social workers intervene on multiple levels and use various strategies for intervention. Social workers can use the ABCDEF practice guide to organize their interventions and to ensure an integrative approach. Based on the assessment, they can apply specific micro and macro intervention techniques that will lead to changes in older clients' actions or behaviors (A), biological functioning (B), cognitions (C), demographic resources (D), environmental supports (E), and feelings (F). For example, an ABCDEF assessment of Ms. Reed reveals that her actions are restricted (A); she is homebound because she fears going out to public places. She recently fell at a local mall (B) and believes that everyone was making fun of her (C). She is a seventy-five-year-old widow who lives alone and lacks environmental supports (D, E), and she often feels lonely, frightened, and anxious (F). The social worker concludes that Ms. Reed suffers from agoraphobia and that a combination of influences, including her recent fall and increasing social isolation, has contributed to her irrational thoughts and negative feelings.

An integrative practice approach that incorporates a multilevel intervention strategy is the most effective way to address the multiple influences that are simultaneously and interactively causing Ms. Reed's fears. The social worker contracts with Ms. Reed to intervene on both individual and environmental levels. Specifically, the social worker recommends that Ms. Reed undergo exposure techniques to gradually address her fears (F) about leaving home. See chapter 5 for a more in-depth review of interventions for anxiety. In addition, after Ms. Reed and the social worker realize that Ms. Reed stopped socializing with friends and neighbors after her husband died, they identify multiple strategies for increasing her involvement with others (E). For example, Ms. Reed agrees to participate in a widow support group offered by a nearby agency (D, E). The social worker also links Ms. Reed to a telephone reassurance and companionship program funded under the Older American Acts (see chapter 17) that will increase her social involvements (E) and arranges a life line so that someone will immediately come to her assistance if something happens to her (B, E). These individual and social interventions are intended to modify Ms. Reed's restricted actions (A) by enhancing her social contacts. The social worker understands and empathizes with Ms. Reed's feelings (F) and irrational thoughts (C) but helps her experience fewer anxiety attacks by becoming more confident about going out.

The social worker uses a collaborative intervention approach with Ms. Reed, who feels empowered by contributing to her treatment plan. Together, they agree upon how to proceed.

Level of Directiveness

The assessments of older clients' situations—the severity and nature of their problems, their personal and social resources, the cultural context, and the efficacy of particular interventions—affect whether gerontological social workers will use a client-centered, collaborative, or practitioner-directed approach during the intervention stage. Although social workers will rarely use confrontational approaches with an elderly client, they must protect the client by using directive interventions in some cases. For example, when an elderly client is in a serious crisis that could cause harm to others, social workers must use directive approaches to safely resolve this situation. See James and Gilliland (2001) and Gilliland and James (1988) for more information about directive approaches during crises.

Simon (1994) recommends that social workers implement collaborative instead of hierarchical worker-client relationships and emphasize mutuality in their practice to decrease unnecessary inequities between themselves and clients. This will also enhance the older client's feelings of mastery and self-control. Rowles and Reinharz (1988) refer to this practice as *cooperative dialogue,* which is achieved when practitioners avoid unnecessary authoritarian or dominating relationships with clients. Germain and Gitterman (1996) advocate the establishment of humanistic partnerships between workers and clients that minimize power inequities. They note that "the relationship between client and worker shifts from subordinate recipient and superior expert to a relationship characterized by mutuality and reciprocity" (Germain and Gitterman, 1996, p. 39). They explain that while social workers bring professional knowledge and skill to the helping relationship, clients bring their unique experiences and life stories. A collaborative, nonhierarchical intervention approach is consistent with an empowerment orientation that strives to support the client's participation in the helping process. When older clients have stable resources, social workers can buttress their support systems and their problem-solving skills. This bolsters clients' feelings of self-efficacy and self-determination.

The Client-Directed Approach

The client-directed approach is generally recommended when older clients have many personal strengths and community supports and their problems are less serious. The receptiveness of clients to this approach is also important. As discussed earlier, older clients vary in the extent to which they feel comfortable about self-disclosing. Some older clients prefer a highly directive social worker, but others want the responsibility of making their own decisions and initiating treatment plans while their social worker offers support and encouragement. Social workers facilitate listening by asking many open-ended questions that help older clients work through difficult feelings and thoughts and decide upon a course of action. During a client-directed treatment approach, gerontological social workers might ask an older client the following questions: How do you view your situation, and what do you think is the best thing to do? Have you given much thought to how you might resolve the problem? These questions work best with older clients after they have shared their stories during the listening stage and their social worker has conducted a comprehensive assessment. Social workers who use a client-directed approach provide reflective and empathetic listening and ask questions that encourage clients to share feelings and identify solutions. Questions also help older clients identify their personal strengths and resources, coping strategies that have worked in the past, and realistic and appropriate intervention strategies. Client-directed interventions are often empowering, and they frequently incorporate psychoeducational counseling approaches. Many older clients feel less alone and more comfortable when they realize that their responses are normal. Self-help groups, such as caregiver and bereavement support groups, are usually client directed and often include psychoeducational counseling; they help participants by providing them with a context in which they can observe how others cope with similar circumstances.

The Collaborative Approach

A collaborative strategy typically requires more mutual work with older clients to identify problems, evaluate potential solutions, and implement changes. Gilliland and James (1988) believe that practitioners who use a collaborative approach function as a catalyst to clients searching for solutions to their problems. Instead of doing all the problem solving, social workers work with clients to evaluate options together. The social worker might say, for example: "There seem to be several issues going on for you right now. Perhaps we should prioritize them and identify which ones you want to work on first." Or the social worker might rephrase it this way: "Let's consider several alternative solutions and examine each of their strengths and weaknesses." Social workers can support older clients, help them understand their feelings and circumstances, and sometimes offer solutions in a collaborative approach, but they generally avoid managing clients' problems for them.

The Practitioner-Directed Approach

Social workers must intervene quickly when older clients have severe problems and feel out of control or incapable of solving problems. Gilliland and James (1988) believe social workers need to use a directive approach with clients who (1) need immediate hospitalization because of chemical use or organic dysfunction; (2) are suffering from such severe depression that they cannot function; (3) are experiencing a severe psychotic episode: (4) are suffering a severe shock, bereavement, or loss; (5) have an anxiety level that is temporarily so high that they cannot function; (6) are out of touch with reality; or (7) are a danger to themselves or others. When a client is suicidal or severely anxious and demands immediate attention, social workers must quickly manage any feelings of immobilization that the client may have, identify solutions, determine intervention strategies, and intervene immediately. Clients are usually relieved that a trusted professional has taken control.

CASE 4.1

Ms. Revor, a sixty-five-year-old African American, was referred to counseling by her sister, who worked for a local agency. Ms. Revor met with the social worker and reported that she has been feeling "stressed out" about caring for her father; he was diagnosed with Alzheimer's disease a few years earlier. The social worker applied the ABCDEF practice guide to assess Ms. Revor's individual and social circumstances and to create a treatment plan using an integrated practice model.

During the listening stage the social worker heard Ms. Revor talk about how difficult it has become to care for her father as his condition worsens. The social worker was aware that she and Ms. Revor have different ethnic backgrounds and demonstrated cultural empathy to Ms. Revor from the outset of treatment. Ms. Revor had lived most of her life in an African American community in the South, whereas the social worker had lived in a suburban community on the East Coast. The social worker recognized that she and Ms. Revor have different perspectives on caregiving and that she must refrain from imposing her beliefs on Ms. Revor, that is, the social worker understood cultural self-other differentiation. The social worker probed for insight, a strategy to enhance the communicative processes involved in cultural empathy, by listening to how Ms. Revor presented her caregiving experiences and described her struggles in her own words and from her own perspective. The social worker focused on the four major goals of the listening stage: establishing rapport and trust, encouraging the expression of feelings, searching for meaning, and identifying life stressors.

The social worker began treatment by asking Ms. Revor an open-ended question about why she sought help at this time. Such questions facilitate sharing and convey openness and interest to the client. Before revealing her feelings, Ms. Revor talked about her discomfort with formal services and her reluctance to seek help. She explained that she finally came to this agency to appease her sister. She also felt desperate and knew that she needed help. The social worker engaged in empathetic listening by using nonverbal and verbal responses to reflect Ms. Revor's feelings and convey understanding.

The social worker focused on Ms. Revor's feelings while encouraging her to share more about her background. This helped the social worker learn more about Ms. Revor's attitudes about caregiving. The social worker discovered, for example, that Ms. Revor felt strongly about avoiding nursing home placement for her father because her family does not believe in using nursing homes to care for relatives. Ms. Revor clearly articulated her worldview while talking about her feelings. As the social worker listened empathetically and conveyed cultural understanding, Ms. Revor began to recognize her feelings of loss about her father's condition. The social worker started to establish rapport and trust with Ms. Revor by recognizing how painful it is to watch one's father deteriorate. During this stage the social worker enabled Ms. Revor by encouraging her to express her feelings; explored or probed for insight into important background information and into sources of stress; and validated Ms. Revor's feelings and educated her about the stresses of caregiving and the need for social supports.

The social worker then conducted a more comprehensive assessment of Ms. Revor, using the ABCDEF model as guide to her evaluation. She also visited Ms. Revor at her home. This helped Ms. Revor, who had problems with transportation, and it helped the social worker obtain a better understanding of her family's environmental context. The assessment stage revealed important information about Ms. Revor's worldview, level of acculturation, actions and behaviors (A), biological or health status (B), cognitive functioning (C), demographic background (including her marital and work status) (D), environmental resources (including family supports and friends) (E), and feelings and psychiatric state (F). The social worker concluded that Ms. Revor has a solid belief system that emphasizes caring for elderly members in the home but that she has become increasingly isolated as the demands of caregiving have increased. These demands have exacerbated Ms. Revor's hypertension and left her feeling exhausted and depressed. Although Ms. Revor was once actively engaged in the community, she has retreated from these gratifying activities to take care of her father.

The social worker sought more precise information about Ms. Revor's father's diagnosis and prognosis from their physician. The background information that Ms. Revor provided about her family also helped the social worker assess this family's interpersonal dynamics.

The social worker used the ABCDEF guide and concluded that Ms. Revor lacks adequate personal *and* environmental resources. Based on a comprehensive assessment, the social worker decided to use a collaborative intervention approach with Ms. Revor. Together they considered various options, ranging from individual treatment to community intervention. Although reluctant to use formal services, Ms. Revor was receptive to adult day care that primarily serves the African American community and offers familiar foods, activities, and social norms. The social worker also connected Ms. Revor to respite services and a caregiver support group funded by the National Caregiver and Family Support Program (E). In addition to helping Ms. Revor access these community services, the social worker recommended that Ms. Revor obtain individual treatment for her depression (A, B, C, E, F). During the intervention stage the social worker used a wide range of skills: empowering Ms. Revor by providing her with relevant information about coping and community supports (E); facilitating change by helping Ms. Revor break through her resistance to counseling and receiving services (D); coordinating community resources and putting Ms. Revor in contact with them; and supporting her while using cognitive behavioral interventions to treat Ms. Revor for depression (A, B, C).

Case 4.1 illustrates how a social worker can apply multiple modes and methods of intervention and embrace a biopsychosocial practice model that considers multiple sources of stress. A gerontological social worker who focused only on the individual level and relied solely upon psychotherapy to treat Ms. Revor's depression and stress would ignore community interventions that empowered Ms. Revor. Conversely, a social worker who arranged for services for Ms. Revor without helping her to cope better with caregiving could damage Ms. Revor's physical and psychological functioning. The social worker integrated several levels of intervention while respecting and supporting Ms. Revor's worldviews about family and caregiving and arranging for family, group, and community supports.

This discussion of the need for an integrated gerontological practice approach as well as the basic elements of that approach concludes the first part of the book. Part 2 presents innovative assessments and advanced intervention techniques that are used to treat particular problems.

Discussion Questions

1. In what ways does social work practice with older clients differ from that used with younger clients?
2. What are the advantages and disadvantages of using subjective and objective methods of assessment?
3. What are some examples of situations in which you would need to implement a practitioner-directed intervention approach with an older person?
4. Take an older client from your practice and assess the client by using the ABCDEF practice guide. Then implement an intervention based on the assessment derived from this practice guide.

PART 2

Psychological Problems and Interventions

CHAPTER 5

Anxiety Reactions Among Older People

A NXIETY IS A COMMON AND NORMAL response to many life events. When it interferes with daily functioning or is excessive, anxiety becomes dysfunctional. In contrast to depression, anxiety among older adults has received scant attention. The dearth of information on anxiety in later life continues despite data that show that anxiety reactions are the most common types of psychiatric distress among elderly people (Wetherell, Gatz, and Craske, 2003; Gatz, Kasl-Godley, and Karel, 1996). Anxiety disorders are more than twice as prevalent as mood disorders and four to eight times more common than major depressive episodes in people aged sixty-five and older (Reiger, 1998). The reason for the lack of attention to anxiety among older people by health professionals, including social workers, is unclear.

Given the prevalence of anxiety and recent findings that indicate an association between chronic anxiety and hypertension, heart attacks, and mortality, especially in older men (Lavretsky et al., 2003; J. G. Beck and Averill, 2004), gerontological social workers who work with elderly people must learn more about the incidence of anxiety and anxiety disorders among elderly people; the circumstances of its occurrence, for example, variations in rates of anxiety in nursing homes and community dwellings; differences in its expression in younger and older adults; sources of anxiety; and interventions recommended for anxiety in older people. The purpose of this chapter is to increase social workers' awareness of the prevalence of anxiety among older adults and of contemporary treatment approaches to reduce older people's anxieties.

DEFINITION OF ANXIETY

Anxiety is a cognitive-affective state characterized by a negative feedback cycle, varying degrees of high negative affect, and feelings that are future oriented but out of control. It involves a sense that both internal and external events are proceeding in an unpredictable and uncontrollable fashion. Maladaptive shifts in attention (usually from external orientation to an emphasis on internal processes) typically occur (Barlow, 1988). In contrast to depression, anxiety is a more diffuse emotion and difficult to define and measure. Because anxiety and depression often occur together, especially in late life, differentiation between the two is often difficult.

Incidence of Anxiety Among Elderly People

Experts have underestimated the extent of anxiety and anxiety disorders among older adults for many of the same reasons that the experts believe that most symptoms of mental health distress are underrated in older people. The current cohort of older adults more often presents psychological problems in somatic terms and was raised when many psychological terms, such as anxiety, were hardly mentioned. Many elderly people mention their "nerves" or "worries" when describing their anxieties. Although future cohorts of older people will, presumably, feel more comfortable talking about psychological issues, many older people today express negative feelings reluctantly. For these reasons social workers must cautiously interpret epidemiological data on anxiety from the current cohort of older people and understand that incidence rates for this age group are probably underrated.

The incidence varies according to the sample that was used, how anxiety was measured, and how the information was reported. Most reports used data obtained from the National Institute of Mental Health Epidemiological Catchment Area Project at Duke University Medical Center (Blazer, George, and Hughes, 1991).

Knight, Teri, Wohlford, and Santos (1995) estimate that as many as 22% of individuals older than sixty-five present symptoms of anxiety, and almost 6% of older adults meet the criteria for an anxiety disorder (Rabins, 1992). Mehta and colleagues (2003) examined anxiety rates among 3,041 well-functioning older adults and found that anxiety symptoms occurred in 15% of older people without depression and 43% of those with depression. In general, anxiety rates decrease with age, and older women report higher rates of anxiety than do older men (Fisher and Noll, 1996; J. G. Beck and Averill, 2004). Mehta and colleagues (2003) also found that white women had the highest anxiety rates of any race/gender group.

Phobias, which are the most common type of anxiety in late life, are provoked by exposure to a specific feared object or situation. Common phobias among older people include fears of airplanes, heights, falling, storms, and certain illnesses. Flint (1994) found that among those older than sixty-five, about 6% of the women and 3% of the men evidenced a phobic disorder in a reanalysis of the Epidemiological Catchment data.

The *Diagnostic and Statistical Manual of Mental Disorders* says that a diagnosis of agoraphobia—fear of public places—is appropriate when the primary features involve "anxiety about being in places or situations from which escape might be difficult (or embarrassing) or in which help may not be available in the event of having a panic attack or panic-like symptoms" (*DSM-IV*, 1994, p. 396). In contrast to generalized anxiety disorders, most cases of agoraphobia in older people are of recent onset. The lifetime rates reported by people older than sixty-five are about 8.4%, whereas the rates that they report for the last six months are about 5.2% (Blazer, et al., 1991; Margolis and Rabins, 1997). Various cultures continue to perceive agoraphobia in different ways. In some settings, for example, women who spend all their time in the home and who do not go out in public are perceived as virtuous, not abnormal (Friedman, 1997). Most experts, such as White and Barlow (2002), identify panic as the central experience of agoraphobia.

Generalized anxiety disorders are characterized by excessive anxiety and worry (apprehensive expectation) that occur more days than not for at least six months, in regard to several events or activities; difficulty controlling worries; irritability, restlessness, or feeling keyed up; difficulty concentrating or mind going blank; muscle tension; and sleep disturbance. These disorders are often preceded by a negative life event that causes adverse reactions, including negative affect, arousal, stress-related neurobiological reactions, and, most important, the feeling that life is progressing in an unpredictable and uncontrollable manner (Barlow, 1988). The individual's level of arousal increases as she shifts her focus of attention from her regular activities to the topic of concern. This leads to more vigilance and self-evaluation that, in turn, raises her anxiety. She becomes anxious not only about the immediate issue but also about her agitated response. People are sometimes so alarmed that they become immobilized and unable to perform. They feel out of control, fear that things will worsen or that something terrible will happen, and, most important, worry that the future is unpredictable. When individuals repeatedly confront situations that they cannot influence, they often feel helpless and anxious and rehearse various reactions to potential unpleasant experiences in an attempt to gain control and prepare for the next adversity.

The salient feature of generalized anxiety disorders is that the individual has an apprehensive expectation about the future. The person is usually constantly anxious or worried; the sudden attacks of anxiety that characterize panic attacks are less frequent. The most common worries in later life center around health and illness, money, transportation, and family.

About 4.6% of elderly people have suffered from a generalized anxiety disorder at some time in their lives, and 1.9% were diagnosed with this during the previous six months (see J. G. Beck and Averill, 2004, for a discussion of anxiety rates). Although many older people who are diagnosed as experiencing a generalized anxiety disorder experienced symptoms of anxiety earlier in their lives, sometimes the symptoms reappear in later life when new stressors arise.

Older women typically report more symptoms of anxiety than older men, in part because men and women face different sources of anxiety. Older women, for example, worry more about taking care of an ill spouse, losing friends and other family members, and paying bills. They also worry about basic material resources such as food, transportation, home repairs, heating, and telephone bills (Kastenbaum, 1994). Ethnic differences in coping styles also affect rates of anxiety. For example, Neighbors and Jackson (1996) explain that although African Americans have confronted more environmental stressors, they exhibit lower rates of psychological distress than do whites. Neighbors and Jackson attribute this difference to the successful problem-solving skills that many African Americans have learned and their use of more "active behavioral strategies," such as seeking outside help for their problems.

Obsessive-compulsive disorders typically appear in childhood or early adulthood. Epidemiological data on the incidence of obsessive-compulsive disorders reveal a prevalence rate of 1.3% in those aged sixty-five to seventy-five and 0.6% in those older than seventy-five (Kohn, Westlake, Rasmussen, Marsland, and Norman, 1997). A disproportionate number of highly educated older women experience obsessive-compulsive disorders. Older people who exhibit symptoms of an obsessive-compulsive disorder have probably lived with these problems intermittently throughout their adult lives. Kohn and colleagues (1997) caution, however, that few researchers have examined obsessive-compulsive disorders among older people. Kohn and colleagues found that although fewer older adults were diagnosed with obsessive-compulsive disorders, the course of the disorder in later life is usually more severe and more chronic than it is among younger people. We need more research on how obsessive-compulsive disorders manifest in later life because it is likely to increase as older people live longer.

People can experience a posttraumatic stress disorder (PTSD) at any age. The *DSM-IV* defines PTSD as "the reexperiencing of an extremely traumatic event accompanied by symptoms of increased arousal and avoidance of stimuli associated with the trauma" (1994, p. 393). Although individuals vary in how they reexperience a traumatic event, people suffering from PTSD usually exhibit recurrent and distressing recollections of the event, such as images, thoughts, or perceptions, and recurrent distressing dreams. They experience intense psychological distress at exposure to internal or external cues that symbolize or resemble any aspect of the traumatic event. Difficulties falling or staying asleep, irritability or outbursts of anger, difficulty concentrating, hypervigilance, and exaggerated startle responses are common. Older people who have recently emigrated from countries where there has been a lot of violence and disorder may have elevated rates of posttraumatic stress disorder. These individuals may fear expressing their feelings and experiences and avoid discussing previous experiences of torture and trauma.

Panic disorders or panic attacks are the least common type of anxiety found among elderly people (Blazer et al., 1991; Gatz et al., 1996). Although the onset of panic disorders at age forty-five is unusual, this can appear in certain circumstances.

The essential feature of a panic attack is "a discrete period of fear or discomfort that is accompanied by at least four of thirteen somatic or cognitive symptoms" (see *DSM-IV,* 1994, p. 395, for a list of these symptoms). The anxiety involved in panic disorders is usually acute, sudden, and short lived. When left untreated, panic disorders sometimes develop into agoraphobia (Margolis and Swartz, 1999). Panic disorders are also associated with higher levels of major depression, alcohol and drug dependency, and suicide (Margolis and Swartz, 1999).

When older people exhibit symptoms of panic disorder, gerontological social workers should first consider certain medical conditions that sometimes evoke acute anxiety. Older people at greatest risk for these disorders are those struggling with impairments in instrumental activities of daily living (IADLs), and there is evidence that this association persists across cultures and ethnic categories (Ormel et al., 1994).

Gerontological social workers should also rule out anxiety disorders caused by substance misuse or abuse when assessing sudden anxiety in older people. Panic attacks can arise from intoxication or withdrawal from certain substances, such as benzodiazepines, which many older people use.

CHARACTERISTICS OF ANXIETY IN LATER LIFE

Kastenbaum (1994) identifies four unique features of anxiety in later life. Realistic concerns, such as those about health, housing, money, and crime, often are behind the anxiety in older people. Loss of resources, which happens to many older people after retirement and widowhood, frequently evokes feelings of anxiety. Some older people worry about dying and illness and especially about becoming incapacitated. While younger people's concerns about death often focus on the loss of self, elderly people more often worry about the process of dying and becoming a burden to others (Kastenbaum, 1992). Finally, cultural differences in anxiety are common in all age groups but especially among older adults. Prevailing conceptualizations of anxiety exclude some cultural expressions of anxiety. In an analysis of the mental health of adults in Puerto Rico, S. Friedman (1997) learned that other cultures view as typical many symptoms that the *DSM-IV* (1994) considers to be abnormal. For example, the syndrome *Ataques de nervios*, which involves "screaming uncontrollably" and "attacks of crying" and is common in Puerto Rico, is omitted from the *DSM-IV* under anxiety and appears only in the somatization section. S. Friedman (1997) argues for an expanded set of symptoms to define anxiety and greater acknowledgment of overlaps that sometimes occur between affective, somatoform, and dissociative disorders. He also recommends that clinicians seek information from families and others, especially when treating people from different cultural backgrounds.

In addition to these characteristics, some experts, for example, Mehta and colleagues (2003), caution that the constructs underlying anxiety as well as depression differ from those that emerge among younger people. Because many older people learn better ways to experience and express their negative emotions over time, they often experience multiple feelings simultaneously, resulting in what some refer to as "more diffuse cognitive representations." The co-occurrence of anxiety and depression is more common later in life than among younger people (Mehta et al., 2003; Beekman et al., 2000). These differences may or may not be related to more overlap among affective states later in life. These differences in the manifestation of depression and anxiety later in life have led increasing numbers of experts to question the applicability of traditional diagnostic criteria for these disorders among older people (J. G. Beck and Averill, 2004).

Causes of Anxiety Among Elderly People

Biological Sources

When assessing an older person's anxiety, social workers should first rule out other psychiatric conditions, such as depression and delirium, which often coexist with anxiety and are frequently mistaken for it. Social workers should also consider side-effects from medication and situations in which anxiety might be secondary to a medical illness. Examples of medications that are known to contribute to anxiety in older people include bronchodilators, such as ephedrine or epinephrine; psychostimulants, such as methylphenidate (Ritalin); and thyroid hormones (Swartz and Margolis, 2004). Social workers should identify patterns from a client's medical history that might indicate the presence of a medical problem. Finally, social workers should recognize that anxiety reactions are often normal reactions to medical problems. Other health conditions associated with anxiety include hypertension, visual impairment, urinary incontinence, insomnia, and alcohol use (Mehta et al., 2003).

Some medical illnesses, such as cardiac conditions, seizure disorders, hyperthyroidism, hyperparathyroidism, pheochromocytoma (an adrenal gland tumor), and vestibular dysfunctions can evoke panic attacks (Swartz and Margolis, 2004). (See the *DSM-IV,* 1994, on p. 400 for a detailed discussion of differential diagnosis.) Certain metabolic conditions (e.g., hypoglycemia, anemia), respiratory conditions (e.g., asthma, chronic obstructive pulmonary disease, pneumonia), and overuse of caffeine can also incite anxiety reactions (Carstensen, Edelstein, and Dornbrand, 1996). Diabetes mellitus has been associated with higher rates of phobias, and Parkinson's disease is disproportionately associated with social phobias. High rates of generalized anxiety disorders (65%) have been noted in individuals with Graves' disease (Trzepacz, McCue, Klein, and Levey, 1988). Several studies suggest an association between dementia, especially in the early stages, and anxiety (see Cartensen et al., 1996, for more discussion of this topic). Generalized anxiety disorders also occur more often among people who have suffered a stroke (Margolis and Swartz, 1999).

Because older adults are more likely to suffer from health impairments than younger people, social workers should give substantial and careful consideration to illness as a source of an elderly person's anxiety. Medical illnesses and anxiety symptoms can also interact and exacerbate each other.

Psychological and Social Causes

Many psychological events can cause anxiety in late life. For some older adults, especially those who have always struggled with anxiety, theories that emphasize early childhood experiences are probably relevant. Many older people feel anxious after an accumulation of losses. When people are repeatedly confronted with situations that they cannot influence, they often feel helpless and anxious. Mehta and colleagues (2003) found that older people who had confronted negative life events, such as death of a spouse or partner or illness of a family member or friend, during the previous year had significantly more anxiety than those who experienced more stability in their lives. Catastrophic financial loss has also been associated with the emergence of anxiety problems later in life (J. G. Beck and Averill, 2004).

The types of life events that older people encounter differ from those that younger people experience. While the losses that people experience in their early years are usually related to growth and development, such as graduation, marriage, and parenthood, in the later years losses become less celebrated. In one way or another many older people confront losses related to youth, family, parents, work, spouse, health, and independence. Although each person resolves these differently and most people adjust well to these changes, some elderly people feel overwhelmed, especially if the losses are sudden and unexpected, close in time, or cause major disruptions in interpersonal or financial resources. An older person's anxieties are often realistic responses to extremely threatening situations.

According M. Baltes and Carstensen (1996), older people seek "optimal" settings during adulthood. When faced with age-related obstacles, such as declines in physical stamina, reaction time, or health, people find alternative ways to continue their engagement in activities that they enjoy. When an older person fails to find a way to compensate for losses, he can become anxious or depressed. These older people are more likely to report less than optimal mental health (Aldwin, 1994). Take the case of Ms. Levin, who prides herself on her self-sufficiency and independent lifestyle. She recently suffered a stroke and realizes that she must learn to compensate for her physical deficits if she is to continue living independently. If Ms. Levin fails to learn how to compensate, she may worry about how long she can continue on her own, whether she can live by herself, what she will do if she has another stroke, whether she will have to relocate to a nursing home, and, if so, whether she will have to leave the neighborhood. If she ruminates too much about these issues, her anxiety may develop into panic attacks, phobias, and or even agoraphobia.

Social workers should use an integrated framework to determine the most appropriate solution for a particular client, regardless of the sources of the anxiety, and the interventions should emerge from the ABCDEF practice guide that we discussed in chapter 4. Comprehensive assessment of an older client's anxieties provides the gerontological social worker with the essential information he needs to individualize the interventions, based on the patterns of the client's responses. Specific assessment tools for measuring anxiety in older people offer in-depth information about the frequency, intensity, and severity of a particular client's anxieties, which the social worker can compare with normal and clinical populations. Next we describe a select group of instruments for assessing anxiety in older people.

Assessment of Anxiety in Older People

Few instruments are available to assess anxiety specifically among older people, and those that exist ignore the growing heterogeneity and cultural variation inherent in the older adult population. Despite these limitations, some instruments help gerontological social workers understand the severity and types of anxieties that older clients have. When these instruments are used in conjunction with a comprehensive evaluation, they will enrich the assessment.

The Anxiety Disorders Interview Schedule for DSM-IV (ADIS-IV) (R. A. Brown, DiNardo, and Barlow, 1994) and the Structured Clinical Interview for

DSM (SCID) (Spitzer, Williams, Givvon, and First, 1992) are rigorous and well-established diagnostic inventories for diagnosing anxiety. These are the only two interview schedules that demonstrate good potential for use with older people (J. G. Beck and Stanley, 1997; Stanley, Beck, and Glassco, 1996). Data on the reliability look promising for both instruments (Wetherell et al., 2003; see J. G. Beck, Stanley, and Zebb, 1995 and Stanley et al., 1996, for more detail on the ADIS-IV, and Segal, Hersen, Van Hasselt, Kabacoff, and Roth, 1993, for information on the SCID). These instruments require extensive clinical experience and familiarity with the *DSM-IV* (1994), and both take more than an hour to administer (Carmin, Pollard, and Gillock, 1999). The Clinician Administered PTSD Scale (CAPS) is another well-established instrument that evaluates posttraumatic stress disorder in older people (Blake et al., 1990).

In contrast to the ADIS-IV and the SCID, which clinicians use for diagnostic purposes, several scales have emerged that evaluate symptoms of anxiety. The Hamilton Anxiety Rating Scale (HARS), which is a clinician-rating scale designed to assess the severity and intensity of thirteen symptoms of anxiety, works well with elderly people (J. G. Beck et al., 1999; J. G. Beck and Stanley, 1997). Sinoff, Ore, Zlotogorosky, and Tamir (1999) developed the Short Anxiety Screening Test (SAST) specifically for assessing older people who might also have depression. This instrument takes only about fifteen minutes to administer. The Anxiety Status Inventory (ASI), which is an observer-rated instrument, is also useful for evaluating anxiety in older people (Zung, 1971). The Self-Rating Anxiety Scale (SAS) resembles the ASI, but older people rate themselves (Sheikh, 1991; Zung, 1971). Both instruments are excellent for assessing older clients' anxieties and take only five minutes to administer. The Beck Anxiety Inventory (BAI) (A. T. Beck, Epstein, Brown, and Steer, 1988) is another self-report questionnaire; it measures twenty-one common somatic and cognitive symptoms of anxiety and demonstrates good psychometric properties with older people (Wetherell et al., 2003; Carmin et al., 1999).

Some social workers will find that older people are more comfortable talking about their "worries" than their "anxieties." The Penn State Worry Questionnaire (PSWQ) is a self-report inventory that was designed specifically for older people (Meyer, Miller, Metzger, and Borkovec, 1990). This is a sixteen-item questionnaire that measures trait worry, defined as "the generality of worry over time and situations, the intensity/excessiveness of the experience, and the uncontrollability of the process" (Carmin et al., 1999, p. 77). J. G. Beck and colleagues (1995), who examined the psychometric aspects of the PSWQ on a sample of older people, found that the instrument's reliability and validity were excellent. A shorter version of the PSWQ, comprised of just eight instead of sixteen items, appears to work especially well with older people (Hopko et al., 2003). The Worry Scale (WS), which is a thirty-five-item scale that measures severity of worry about financial, health, and social concerns, was also developed for older adults (Wisocki, Handen, and Morse, 1986) and now includes questions about the amount of time spent worrying, the age at which worrying began and was most common, and significant life events associated with worry (Wisocki, 1994). These worry scales, which are highly associated with generalized anxiety disorders (Carmin et al., 1999), are excellent alternatives to the more traditional anxiety inventories for measuring anxiety because of their references to "worries" instead of "anxieties."

Future attempts to create anxiety scales for elderly people need to consider several factors (Salzman and Lebowitz, 1991). Self-rating scales should be short: no more than thirty items or ten minutes. Yes/no formats work best. The scale must be readable for elderly people with vision impairments, and the instructions and questions must be clear and appropriate for elderly people from various ethnic backgrounds, educational levels, and income groups. Observer-rated scales should also tap multiple aspects of anxiety, specifically, cognitive, affective, behavioral, and physiological. These scales should discriminate between anxiety and depression and allow for their coexistence. Panic attacks and overall anxiety must be clearly differentiated. Anxiety symptoms caused by medical illnesses should be taken into account. Open-ended questions should also be included to provide flexibility, and geriatric norms must be established. Finally, the instruments should be sensitive to therapeutic interventions.

SPECIFIC INTERVENTIONS FOR ANXIETY AMONG OLDER PEOPLE

Anxiety often is the most salient problem that an older person presents, and it requires immediate attention if the person is in great distress. Unless the older person is in crisis, social workers should apply the integrated practice model, described in earlier chapters, to ensure that comprehensive assessments and interventions will occur on multiple levels. Advanced techniques for particular problems, such as anxiety, have burgeoned since the 1990s and should enhance generic practice. Next we review the most effective techniques for treating anxiety in older people. These include exposure techniques, cognitive restructuring, coping strategies, supportive psychotherapy, and psychopharmacological treatment.

Exposure Techniques

Exposure techniques, which are one of the most helpful interventions for treating older people with phobias, require that older clients confront the situation that they fear, which can be real or imagined, while they are relaxed (Barlow, 1988). Because social workers can modify the administration of exposure techniques, including the intensity of the exposure and the directiveness of the clinician, and incorporate supplemental coping strategies (see White and Barlow, 2002, for an in-depth discussion of implementation of exposure techniques), social workers should carefully assess the older client so that they may tailor this treatment strategy to their client's unique circumstances. The approach generally involves the following procedures. The social worker presents each anxiety-provoking situation for a long or short period of time with mild or intense arousal and teaches the client how to control her breathing, think constructively, and relax using progressive relaxation techniques. The intent is to weaken the association between the feared object and anxiety. With repeated exposure and without negative consequences, the feared reaction, for example, the phobia, is eventually extinguished. If the client does not escape or avoid the treatment, she learns new responses to the feared situation. The procedures are organized in a graduated format, that is, from least to most anxiety provoking. Repeated exposure begins with lower anxiety conditions, and the older client practices encountering each situation until the most anxiety that she experiences is mild (Craske, 1996). The social worker instructs the client to use breathing strategies to help her relax and to use appropriate cognitive strategies. The client learns the difference between breathing that leads to hyperventilation and high anxiety and breathing that originates from the diaphragm, which promotes relaxation. The client also counts during inhalation and says or thinks the word *relax* as she exhales.

Progressive relaxation techniques teach a client how to systematically relax her muscles. The method involves first tightening dominant muscles, for example, the right arm, for a period of time and then relaxing it. The client usually does this twice before she begins to tighten and relax other muscles. Once the client is relaxed, the social worker exposes her to the feared situation. With proper breathing and appropriate thought processes, clients presumably unlearn their fears and replace the anxiety response to the specific situation with a calm one. Progressive relaxation is easy to learn, and most clients become relaxed after following the procedures. Social workers often use audiotapes that provide the client with detailed instructions. The techniques are usually modified with older people who are arthritic or have other physical limitations. Barlow and Craske (2000) have developed in-depth manuals that articulate the procedures involved in administering exposure techniques.

Many experts, such as Barlow (1988) and White and Barlow (2002), have demonstrated the efficacy of these procedures in eliminating panic attacks and agoraphobia. When used to treat agoraphobia, the procedures are usually carried out in situ, that is, in the natural setting under the condition that the client fears. The involvement of significant others, such as family members and friends, improves the success rate of exposure to eliminate agoraphobia. Cognitive restructuring is an excellent supplement to these techniques (Craske, 1996).

Social workers should cautiously implement exposure techniques with older people who might experience cognitive impairments if aroused too much, and some elderly people have trouble with progressive relaxation techniques. Social workers should use exposure techniques only after they have conducted a thorough assessment of an older client's physical, emotional, and cognitive functioning to avoid any adverse effects.

Cognitive Restructuring

Some clients respond to exposure techniques only when the intervention includes cognitive restructuring. Clark (1997) observed that people who catastrophize events, that is, exaggerate negative events, usually need additional cognitive interventions. These individuals often misinterpret bodily sensations and become frightened by them. Then they become hypervigilant, and if they manage to avoid the precipitating situation, their catastrophizing increases. Unless these clients learn how to "reframe" and more accurately interpret these sensations, exposure techniques will fail with them. When clients reframe events, they identify and label irrational thoughts and then substitute more constructive cognitions. When clinicians incorporate education and information, Socratic questioning, role playing, and video and audio feedback, cognitive restructuring is especially efficacious with older people.

Cognitive restructuring methods also work well with older clients suffering from generalized anxiety disorders, although recent studies, such as that by Wetherell and colleagues (2003), who used more rigorous research designs, indicate that cognitive restructuring methods are about as effective as supportive counseling. These methods focus on challenging negative beliefs that maintain and promote meta-worrying, that is, the worry about worrying that people often develop when they use worrying as a coping strategy (A. Wells, 1995, 2004; A. Wells and Butler, 1997). Strategies such as asking the client to engage in worry postponement often help because they help clients feel more in control of their worries. Another major component of this treatment is the concomitant emphasis on helping the client "generate alternative positive endings to worry scenarios" (A. Wells and Butler, 1997, p. 170). The social worker encourages the client to use coping strategies that include more positive content. This shifts the client's attention away from worrying about worrying. Homework assignments that the client can practice outside the treatment session are also an integral aspect of cognitive therapy. Because many elderly clients are unfamiliar with this approach, social workers must explain the assumptions behind this treatment, seek questions to clarify any misunderstandings the client may have, and encourage collaboration between the social worker and client. If the social worker provides the client with feedback about his progress in treatment, both client and worker will feel responsible for achieving the desired outcome. The feedback also helps the social worker more credibly assess the effectiveness of treatment.

Cognitive behavioral approaches fit well with an integrated practice model and are especially effective with older people whose problems result from physiological as well as psychological and environmental sources. In addition, cognitive behavioral therapy can incorporate various modalities. Although many assume that the primary modality is individual, cognitive behavioral therapy works with families and groups (Zeiss and Steffen, 1996). Many excellent training manuals on cognitive behavioral therapy are also available.

Laidlaw, Thompson, Dick-Siskin, and Gallagher-Thompson (2003), as well as Gallagher-Thompson and Thompson (1996), suggest that practitioners modify their cognitive interventions when using them with older people. These researchers recommend that clinicians be more active during treatment sessions, reduce the pace, and convey information in sensory, visual, and verbal modalities. Barrowclough and colleagues (2001) also recommend that practitioners use short treatment sessions when implementing cognitive approaches with older people.

Older clients who fail to respond to cognitive approaches may also require medication and alternative treatment approaches, such as supportive psychotherapy and interventions that focus on coping.

Coping with Anxiety in Late Life

Some older people feel more comfortable and benefit from nondirective treatment approaches when social workers listen more and emphasize the client's strengths. Coping frameworks work with various clients and are not restricted to people with psychiatric disorders. By emphasizing people's strengths and successful aging, and assuming that coping styles are learned, coping approaches "destigmatize" the client's emotional and psychological problems. The facilitation of optimal aging is another advantage of the coping perspective. Because negative life events can increase anxiety in late life, social workers will enhance clients' resilience and feelings of mastery by helping them to use functional coping strategies. After evaluating several studies, Aldwin and Gilmer (2004) concluded that although adverse experiences often lead to psychological distress, those who evidence the most distress are usually older people who perceive an event as uncontrollable.

Coping involves "the use of strategies for dealing with actual or anticipated problems and their attendant negative emotions" (Aldwin, 1994, p.107). Coping strategies help people adapt to their culture and social background of origin. Clients also learn to use different coping strategies for each context or situation that they encounter. Because coping is a function of personal and environmental factors (Aldwin, 1994), the styles of coping that people acquire are based on multiple influences, including personality and cultural factors. People may maintain self-destructive patterns because they adopted inappropriate coping skills, and with appropriate treatment they can learn more effective coping strategies. Social workers first need to evaluate the effectiveness of the client's coping strategies, that is, how well she mitigates distress and optimizes her environment.

After client and social worker determine how well the coping strategies alleviate the client's anxieties, the client can decide whether and how he will modify these techniques. For example, after examining the effectiveness of using alcohol to reduce anxiety, clients presumably will conclude that the deleterious long-term consequences of drinking are too great. Other clients, perhaps those facing an uncertain medical diagnosis, may find that distraction is far more effective than monitoring as a coping method when events are unalterable. The use of coping models in practice with anxious older adults has enormous potential for treating the older person's suffering from anxiety and will become an increasingly important approach in the future.

Supportive Psychotherapy

Supportive psychotherapy, which emphasizes the expression of feelings, symptoms, and experiences, has successfully reduced symptoms of anxiety with many older people (J. E. Fisher and Noll, 1996; Crits-Christoph, Gibbons, and Crits-Christoph, 2004). Although cognitive behavioral approaches effectively reduce many older people's fears to specific events, supportive psychotherapy is more appropriate when elderly people's anxieties focus on existential issues that concern death, meaning, and loneliness. Stanley and colleagues (1996) found that nearly twice as many anxious older people responded to supportive therapy as responded to cognitive behavioral approaches, and Wetherell and colleagues (2003) found similar results when they compared cognitive behavioral techniques with a discussion group. Because supportive approaches encourage older people to share their thoughts and feelings with an empathetic listener, people feel less alone and less afraid. When these techniques are used in groups, older clients benefit from the knowledge that others are struggling with similar issues. These opportunities for reflection are especially efficacious for older people seeking help with existential issues. Gerontological social workers may combine interventions, for example, supportive therapy, with coping or cognitive behavioral as well as exposure or medication, when clients present multiple concerns and as problems change during treatment. Older clients usually have many issues that make them anxious. Some are concrete and specific, like phobias, whereas others are more free floating and abstract. A single method of treatment is often insufficient, especially with older people. Thus gerontological social workers must be adept at a wide range of skills if they plan to use an integrated treatment model to treat older people's anxieties.

Specific Worry Techniques

Thought-stopping approaches, which confront clients when they start worrying and teach them to yell "Stop!" to themselves when they start ruminating, is commonly used to interfere with uncontrolled worrying. Many clients worry because they become superstitious and believe that because they worried about an event that they feared and it didn't occur, the worrying prevented the feared experience from happening. Social workers can evaluate these "fears about *not* worrying" by encouraging clients to think about similar experiences in the past and to examine how well worrying helped them (see Laidlaw et al., 2003, for a more in-depth discussion of these issues). The Worry Half-Hour, when clients are told to schedule specific times to worry, has also lessened clients' overall anxiety. Because worry is a central component of generalized anxiety, a common anxiety problem in late life, these techniques could help many older people cope better with their anxieties.

Psychopharmacological Treatment for Anxiety in Late Life

Some older people fail to respond to cognitive behavioral and supportive therapy approaches and need medication, especially if their anxiety is long standing, intractable, and nonspecific. Many older people today will seek help first from a physician, who is likely to prescribe drug treatment. In addition, because the stigma attached to mental illness among the current cohort of older people predisposes them to interpret their anxiety in somatic terms instead of in psychological terms, they will see a doctor before they will contact a social worker.

When doctors treat older people's anxieties, they often prescribe tranquilizers. Twenty-seven percent of tranquilizer prescriptions are written for older people, and about 20% of these older adults use tranquilizers daily (Blow, 1998). Benzodiazepines are the medications prescribed most frequently for older people complaining of anxiety (Salzman and Lebowitz, 1991), and 95% of benzodiazepine prescriptions for older adults in this country are ordered for treatment of anxiety and insomnia; only 5% are used with general anesthesia, as a muscle relaxant, or as an anticonvulsant (Blow, 1998).

Older adults who use benzodiazepines claim that they help, and the majority uses them as prescribed, that is, for short periods of time. A few, usually older women who experience multiple chronic physical illnesses and are under great distress, use them on a long-term basis. More nursing home residents use benzodiazepines than older people in the community, although this has changed since 1987 when the Nursing Home Reform Act was passed (Franson, Chesley, and Kennedy, 2003). Physicians sometimes prescribe benzodiazepines to manage older clients who are agitated, restless, or disruptive (Greenblatt and Shader, 1991).

The greater frequency of prescribing antianxiety medications for older people has many implications, especially given that older adults respond differently to psychopharmacological treatment than younger people do. The same dose of an antianxiety medication in an older person will yield different results in a younger person. It takes older people longer to completely metabolize the medication, and longer effects mean that these drugs are more likely to adversely affect more facets of the older person's life, such as driving during the day, walking and exercising, and activities involving intense cognitive concentration.

Because people's abilities to absorb and metabolize drugs decrease with age, toxicity from medications can easily occur in older people; this is especially common if the dose is too high. Elderly people, especially those who have used benzodiazepines for a year or more, are more susceptible to impairments in cognitive functioning, such as increased forgetfulness, decreased attention, worsened short-term recall, greater confusion, and decreased reaction time (Salzman and Lebowitz, 1991). Many antianxiety drugs also cause drowsiness, which increases accidents, interferes with social functioning, and disrupts sleep cycles.

Older people are also more likely to have physical illnesses that can influence the absorption of drugs, and older people use more over-the-counter medications than younger people. Many of these interact with the antianxiety medications and result in drug toxicity. Drug toxicity also can occur if the older client is already taking a prescribed medication, and the physician or pharmacist is unaware of the other medication(s) that the older person is taking. Unless physicians carefully monitor the effects of these medications on older clients, these interactions will be overlooked until a crisis occurs.

Salzman and Lebowitz (1991) offer guidelines that clinicians should consider when recommending benzodiazepines or working with older clients who are taking benzodiazepines. First, he recommends that clinicians cut the dosage (perhaps by 50 to 75%) for the older client to minimize side-effects. Second, he suggests that benzodiazepines not be used for long periods of time, perhaps no longer than four weeks. This reduces dependency, cognitive impairments, and other side-effects. Third, if older people who are taking benzodiazepines have certain physical illnesses, such as those that affect balance and could lead to falls, physicians should monitor them carefully for adverse reactions. Fourth, the physician should conduct a complete assessment of other medications that the client is taking, including over-the-counter drugs.

Buspirone, another antianxiety medication, is not habit forming and can work well for the treatment of older people's anxieties. Buspirone has demonstrated effectiveness, especially for generalized anxiety disorders and for agitation (Swartz and Margolis, 2004; J. E. Fisher and Noll, 1996). One advantage of using buspirone instead of benzodiazepines is that it creates less dependency. The side-effects are less serious. The most commonly reported side-effects of buspirone include dizziness, headache, nervousness, and nausea (Swartz and Margolis, 2004). The disadvantages of this medication are that some older people experience nausea when they first use it, and it takes as long as four to six weeks for most clients to notice any therapeutic benefit (Laidlaw et al., 2003). Sometimes buspirone can precipitate manic effects. Older people who have decreased renal or hepatic functioning should be given reduced dosages (Blow, 1998).

Physicians frequently prescribe antidepressant medications to treat anxiety. Specifically, the tricyclics and selective serotonin reuptake inhibitors (SSRIs) are now viewed as the most desired form of psychopharmacological treatment for anxiety (Swartz and Margolis, 2004). In 1996 Zoloft, Prozac, and Buspar were among the top ten drugs prescribed for nursing home residents (Blow, 1998). Tricyclic antidepressants are recommended for panic disorders, although they take six to twelve weeks to become effective. Alprazolam (Xanax) has also been used to treat panic attacks, although it can be habit forming. Paroxetine (Paxil) and (Zoloft) are also used to treat panic attacks (Swartz and Margolis, 2004).

Other types of medication that physicians sometimes prescribe for older clients complaining of anxiety are beta-blockers. These are more effective for generalized anxiety than for panic attacks. Beta-blockers also effectively reduce extreme agitation in older people; however, because beta-blockers are known to cause tardive dyskinesia as well as other kinds of toxicity among elderly people, they are used less frequently.

Gerontological social workers should recommend psychopharmacological treatment for older people only after conducting a comprehensive assessment. Social workers must carefully assess older clients' health and medication use and investigate any past history of substance misuse or abuse. Even if a physician prescribes medication for anxiety, social workers must address the psychological and environmental influences that contribute to the older client's anxiety. For example, an older woman experiencing anxiety because of inadequate finances will continue to feel distressed regardless of medication if no one helps her to address her economic concerns. Or an older person diagnosed with agoraphobia may feel enough relief from medication to seek help but will most likely need additional exposure interventions to recover completely. Medication and psychosocial interventions are usually complementary.

CASE 5.1

Ms. Friedman, seventy-five, has sought help from a local senior information and referral hotline. Her rabbi contacted her after she failed to attend several Friday night services at the temple. He visited her at home and learned that she has become increasingly isolated and fearful about going out. Ms. Friedman has agreed to see a social worker who also will visit Ms. Friedman in her home. During a listening stage the social worker listens empathetically as Ms. Friedman describes her fears about leaving home. She no longer can get groceries, visit her doctor, or obtain prescriptions at the pharmacy without experiencing severe anxiety. Ms. Friedman explains that she feels nervous about leaving home because "something bad" might happen to her.

The social worker uses the ABCDEF practice guide to structure the assessment and intervention. Ms. Friedman's actions are severely restricted (actions). Her anxiety about going out began after she fell and broke her ankle recently. Except for feeling unsteady on her feet, Ms. Friedman is in good health (biological condition). She suffers from mild cognitive impairment and exhibits symptoms of an obsessive-compulsive disorder (cognitions). She frequently struggles with unhappy, anxiety-provoking thoughts that she feels unable to control. The social worker also considers Ms. Friedman's demographic profile (demographic profile) and learns that she regularly attended Friday night services until she became afraid of going outside. The social worker's examination of environmental influences (environmental factors) in Ms. Friedman's life is revealing. The social worker realizes that some of Ms. Friedman's fears about leaving home are based on realistic concerns. Neighborhood crime has recently increased, and several elderly people's homes have been burgled. Ms. Friedman also is aware of neighbors who have been assaulted while grocery shopping. The social worker considers Ms. Friedman's anxiety (feelings) to be severe and administers the Anxiety Status Inventory (ASI) to acquire more in-depth information about the intensity, duration, and frequency of Ms. Friedman's anxiety.

The social worker concludes that Ms. Friedman's actions and fears about leaving her home may be the result of agoraphobia. She is anxious about being in places or situations from which escape might be difficult (or embarrassing), and she avoids several kinds of transportation; she avoids or endures being away from home with marked distress; and no other mental disorder accounts for the anxiety or phobic avoidance.

Based on the ABCDEF practice guide and a collaborative intervention approach, the social worker and Ms. Friedman agree to modify her actions (A) and feelings (F) by using exposure techniques. In addition, they conclude that environmental interventions (E) are necessary. Ms. Friedman has learned that several other older women in the neighborhood also worry about leaving home because they fear for their safety. The temple has agreed to provide Ms. Friedman and other elderly people with transportation and to organize a meeting of residents in the area. They plan to discuss how they might reduce neighborhood crime and improve safety. Ms. Friedman is relieved to know that other women share her fears and is empowered by working with other members of the temple to improve their neighborhood.

This case demonstrates why gerontological social workers should incorporate individual and environmental interventions in their treatment plan. An integrated practice approach, delineated by the ABCDEF practice guide, involves the comprehensive assessment of the older person's situation and a holistic treatment strategy. A treatment approach that used only exposure techniques to modify Ms. Friedman's behaviors and feelings would have been inadequate. Ms. Friedman's problems were beyond her individual issues. Empowerment focuses on emancipating clients from oppressive situations and enhancing their well-being and sense of mastery. By increasing Ms. Friedman's awareness of environmental obstacles and by encouraging her participation in the temple's intervention, the social worker helped Ms. Friedman to feel empowered, in more control, and less anxious about leaving her home.

Discussion Questions

1. Why do you think that older people experience less anxiety than younger people?
2. What are some causes of anxiety in late life?
3. Which treatment approaches to anxiety do you prefer and why?
4. Which approaches work best with what types of older people or problems?
5. What are the advantages and disadvantages of using medication to treat anxiety among older adults?

CHAPTER 6

Depression Among Older People

DEPRESSION CAN AFFECT AN OLDER PERSON'S LIFE in many ways. It is a major cause of cognitive impairment, disease, and disability in later life, and depressed elderly people recover more slowly from hip fractures, strokes, and chronic arthritis than older people who are not depressed (Montano, 1999). Older people fall and have perceptions of poor balance more often than younger people do, and they are more likely to experience early nursing home placement (Koenig and Blazer, 1996). Elderly people who are depressed have twice as many hospitals stays for medical reasons as those who are not depressed, and they have higher morbidity rates and slower recovery after surgery (Montano, 1999).

In a study of 6,247 elderly people who had been free of disability six years earlier, Penninx, Leveille, Ferrucci, Van Eijk, and Guralnik (1999) found that those who were depressed at the baseline measure were significantly more likely than nondepressed elderly people to develop disabilities in activities of daily living (ADL) and loss of mobility. The differences between the two groups were apparent within one year. The depressed group also had more first-time heart attacks and hip fractures than the nondepressed group. The authors speculate that lower levels of physical activity and more limited social contacts by the depressed older people accounted for the increase in ADL disability and loss of mobility six years later. They also suggest that other biological processes, such as poor immune response, may have intensified the susceptibility of depressed elderly people to diseases and declines in physical health. Ormel and colleagues (1999), whose results corroborated those of Penninx and colleagues (1999), found that older depressed people also suffered social disabilities, that is, limitations in their performance of complex social and occupational activities, more often than nondepressed older adults. Premorbid depressed people, that is, those who are depressed before becoming ill, decompensate more socially and psychologically than do their nondepressed peers when they develop medical conditions (de Jong et al., 2004).

Researchers also have reported significant associations between depression and heart disease. People who have heart disease are more likely to be depressed, and people with depression appear more likely to develop heart disease; those who have depression and heart disease have poorer prognoses and higher mortality rates than people who do not (Fraser-Smith, Lesperance, and Talajic, 1995; Roose and Dalack, 1992; K. B. Wells, Rogers, Burnam, and Camp, 1993; Whooley and Browner, 1998). But few depressed heart patients seek help, and when they do, their depression is often overlooked or misdiagnosed.

The comorbidity of depression and medical illnesses is complex and often interactive. Unless depressed older adults receive adequate treatment, many will spend money on unnecessary health care. The total median annual health care costs of depressed primary care patients are twice as high as those of nondepressed patients (Katon, Lin, Russo, and Unutzer, 2003). As the number of older people with depression increases as we approach 2020, geriatric depression—especially in those older than seventy—will become one of the major contributors to global disease in the twenty-first century (Murray and Lopez, 1996; C. Reynolds et al., 1999).

In this chapter we first present epidemiological data on the incidence of depression among older adults. After a brief discussion of causes of depression in later life, we focus on assessments and interventions for depressed elderly people. The chapter concludes with a case example that illustrates how an intervention for a depressed older person might unfold.

INCIDENCE OF DEPRESSION AMONG ELDERLY PEOPLE

The reported incidence rates of depression in late life vary widely, depending upon how epidemiologists define depression, how they differentiate between younger and older people, what types of depression researchers include in their study, how they measure depression (e.g., through self-report, observation, or interview), and how they analyze the data. The incidence rates also depend upon characteristics of the sample, with clinical and community samples yielding different results. Finally, the rates also depend on whether the instrument used was designed to measure depression among elderly people and whether the researchers measured diagnostic indexes or symptoms of depression.

Most experts agree that while depression disorders decrease with age, depression symptoms increase. The relationship between age and depression symptoms is curvilinear: younger and older people have the highest numbers of depression symptoms, whereas middle-aged people have the lowest. These age differences continue even when researchers control for comorbid physical illnesses (Koenig, 1997; Fiske, Gatz, and Pedersen, 2003). Most researchers estimate that 1% to 6% of older people in the community are diagnosed with a depression disorder, and about 27% of older people display symptoms of depression (Blazer, Hughes, and George, 1987; Eaton et al., 1989; Koenig, 1997). Depression rates are especially high among patients in primary care settings (approximately 37%). The rates in hospitals are between 10% and 13%, and about 30% suffer from minor depressive disorders.

Rates of depression are highest among older people living in long-term care settings. Thirty to 50% of nursing home residents demonstrate depressive symptoms (Katz and Parmelee, 1997). Rovner (1993) found that even when controlling for other medical conditions, nursing home residents with depression were 59% more likely to die during their stay than were residents who were not depressed.

Older women are depressed more often than older men (J. J. Weissman et al., 1988). Lack of adequate economic resources is consistently associated with higher rates of depression among these women. Although bereavement is not an inevitable precursor to depression, many widows and widowers experience clinical depression during the early years of bereavement (Futterman, Thompson, Gallagher-Thompson, and Ferris, 1995).

Ethnicity is also a factor in rates of depression in late life. Richardson (1999a) found significant differences in depression among elderly white and African American widowers. White widowers exhibited more negative affect, depression, and feelings of powerlessness than their African American counterparts. Turnbull and Mui (1995) and Teresi and colleagues (2002) also observed that older white adults were more depressed than elderly African Americans. In a study of African American and white men and women aged fifty-eight to sixty-four, Fernandez, Mutran, Reitzes, and Sudha (1998) found that income had a significantly greater effect on depression among African American women than on African American men or white men and women, because African American women were more economically impoverished than members of those other groups. These income effects on depression remained even when the researchers removed their controls for social support and poor health. The relationship between depression and age among African Americans also is curvilinear: the young and the elderly evidence more depressive symptoms than those aged forty-five to sixty-four. According to Turnbull and Mui (1995), depression with anxiety is the most common psychological problem that older African Americans report.

Elderly Hispanic people typically demonstrate higher rates of depression than non-Hispanic older adults, but the rates vary according to population: Mexican Americans, Puerto Ricans, and Cuban Americans have different rates of depression (Bastida and Gonzalez, 1995). For example, elderly Mexican Americans and Puerto Ricans show the highest rates of depression among older Hispanic groups (Falcon and Tucker, 2000; Gonzalez, Haan, and Hinton, 2001).

Among Asian Americans, older people's worldviews and ethnic and socio-economic background influence the occurrence of depression in the later years (Kang and Kang, 1995). Many elderly Chinese have high rates of depression, but the incidence is highest among elderly Chinese immigrants (Casado and Leung, 2001). Mui (1998) found that perceived dissatisfaction with family, poor self-rated health, living alone, number of stressful life events, and higher levels of education predicted depression in a study of 147 elderly Chinese immigrants. She argues that practitioners need to acquire a greater understanding of intergenerational conflicts in Chinese families. Among elderly Indian immigrants high rates of depression are related to poor physical health, stress, and urban residence (Manson, 1995). A qualitative study of elderly Japanese Americans' conceptualizations of depression and anxiety found considerable overlap between these two disorders (Iwamasa, Hilliard, and Kost, 1998). Cultural differences in the meaning of depression among elderly Asian Americans and whites suggest that a clinician can be more helpful to many older Asian Americans if the clinician focuses on families and community associations and frames necessary individual changes within the client's cultural context (Wong, Heiby, Kameoka, and Dubanoski, 1999). In addition, social workers must carefully assess intergenerational differences among minority families. When Shibusawa and Mui (2001) examined depression among elderly Japanese Americans, they found that those with fears of dependency on family members exhibited higher rates of depression than their peers who did not have these fears. Harel and Biegel (1995) caution that ethnicity alone does not determine mental health status and that factors associated with ethnicity, such as the strength of an individual's community and culture, determine a minority older person's psychological state and susceptibility to depression. In addition, the accuracy of reported rates of depression among ethnic groups is questionable because many depression tools are inappropriate for many older adults from minority groups.

Cohort differences in perceptions of depression also exist. Older people are less inclined to use psychological terms, such as depression or feeling blue, or to express their feelings, and many experience depression and anxiety more somatically than younger people. Older people are often unaware that they are depressed and attribute their feelings to normal changes associated with aging. Even if they acknowledge their depression, many older people associate depression and other mental health disorders with "crazy" people and avoid seeking help. The National Alliance for the Mentally Ill (NAMI) reports that as many as 9 in 10 older people with depression do not receive treatment (NAMI, 1997).

Symptoms and Types of
Depression Among Elderly People

Major Depressive Disorders

According to the fourth edition of the *Diagnostic and Statistical Manual* (*DSM-IV*; 1994), the essential feature of a major depressive disorder is one or more major depressive episodes without a history of manic, mixed, or hypomanic episodes. Social workers should be familiar with the several criteria that constitute a major depressive episode in the *DSM-IV* and they should also recognize the unique features associated with depression in late life. Although there are more similarities than differences in the ways that older and younger people experience depression, older people often exhibit symptoms differently. Many older depressed people complain about physical distress, such as insomnia, weight loss or gain, low appetite, and loss of interest in sexual activities, but they are less likely to verbalize their unhappiness or sadness than younger depressed people (Swartz and Margolis, 2004). Gottfries (1998) observed that elderly people with depression also exhibit high rates of anxiety and concluded that in later life depression is part of a depression-anxiety syndrome in which either depressed mood or anxiety is the predominant symptom. Anhedonia and lack of interest in pleasurable activities are also common among elderly depressed people (M. D. Blumenthal, 1975). C. Murphy and Alexopoulos (2004) found that psychomotor retardation, reduced interest in activities, and executive dysfunction were especially characteristic of late life depression. In addition, Mueller and colleagues (2004) found that the course of depression differs in younger and older age groups and that early relapse and recurrence are more frequent among older depressed people. Cognitive impairments, such as difficulties in concentration and attention, lack of alertness, and memory complaints, also frequently accompany depression in late life. Signs of distress, including agitation, irritability, anxiety, and anger, are other significant indicators of depression in late life (Wolfe, Morrow, and Fredrickson, 1996).

When assessing older people for depression, social workers should distinguish major depression disorders from mood disorders that result from a general medical condition, substance-induced mood disorders, dysthymic disorders, and dementias. We describe these in the pages that follow.

Mood Disorders Resulting from a General Medical Condition

Several types of medical disorders are associated with depression. The most common are strokes, cardiovascular diseases, certain cancers, and thyroid diseases

(Blazer, 2002; Swartz and Margolis, 2004; U.S. Department of Health and Human Services [DHHS], 1999). Malec, Richardson, Sinaki, and O'Brien (1990) estimate that the rates of depression among those who have experienced a stroke might be as high as 30% (Gottfries, 1998). According to Margolis and Rabins (1997), approximately 25% of cancer patients, 40% to 65% of heart attack survivors, and 10% to 27% of stroke survivors experience some type of depression. Major depression is three times more likely among people with diabetes, and about half of those who suffer from chronic pain syndrome (fibromyalgia) experience an episode of depression. Other medical conditions associated with depression include hyperthyroidism, hypothyroidism, myocardial infarction, congestive heart failure, chronic obstructive pulmonary disease, Parkinson's disease, cancers of the pancreas and lung, and specific brain diseases or lesions (Koenig and Blazer, 1996; Margolis and Rabins, 1997).

The differential diagnosis of major depression disorders and dysthymia from depression caused by a medical condition is one of the most important assessment tasks of gerontological social workers, for several reasons (Wolfe et al., 1996). First, physical illness and disability are often risk factors for depression. Second, physiological changes often occur as a result of depression. Third, psychological moods and physical reactions typically interact, especially among older people. Finally, the diagnosis of depression among elderly people is further complicated by their frequent use of over-the-counter and prescription medications, which also interact with their physiological state and often lead to adverse side-effects.

Other Mood Disorders

Many prescription and over-the-counter drugs can cause substance-induced mood disorders and lead to depression. These include antihypertensives, drugs used to treat Parkinson's disease, minor and major tranquilizers, alcohol, drugs that target tumors, and steroids (Koenig and Blazer, 1996; Margolis and Rabins, 1997; Swartz and Margolis, 2004). Dysthymic disorders, which are more moderate types of depression, occur more frequently in later life than major depressive disorders. Social workers will identify more elderly people who will benefit from treatment for depression when clinicians view depression along a continuum from severe to moderate to mild. Although dysthymic disorders are relatively less severe, they cause suffering and can adversely affect an older person's autonomy, interaction with others, health status, and well-being. Adjustment disorder with depressed mood is one of the most commonly found subsyndrome depressions among older people. Social workers can typically connect the onset of an adjustment disorder with depressed mood to a difficult event in the life of an older person who has generally avoided major depressions in early and middle adulthood.

Depression Versus Dementia

Many depressed elderly people exhibit cognitive impairments, such as problems with concentration and memory, that resemble dementia. Upon formal testing, however, depressed people usually do well; they underestimate their cognitive abilities (Harwood, Barker, Ownby, Mullan, and Duaru, 1999). A cognitive decline associated with depression is typically more abrupt than a decline that results from dementia. Depressed elderly people typically have fewer problems than people with dementia in carrying out such daily tasks as finding their way home, following directions, and understanding how to complete activities (Wolfe et al., 1996). However, the depressed elderly are more inclined than elderly people with dementia to report symptoms of anxiety, loss of interest in sex, and sleep disturbances. People with dementia have more impairments in recognition and delayed memory than people who are depressed, and many people with dementia are unaware of their cognitive impairments (Laidlaw et al., 2003). Differential diagnosis of these two disorders is complicated because approximately 30% of elderly people with dementia may suffer from either a major depressive disorder or depressive symptoms (Laidlaw et al., 2003; Wolfe et al., 1996). Recent studies also show that depression can precipitate Alzheimer's disease even in people whose depression first appeared twenty-five years before the onset of Alzheimer's disease (Green et al., 2003). Van Reekum, Simard, Clarke, Binns, and Conn (1999) found that depressed elderly people were twice as likely as nondepressed older adults to develop dementia. However, the exact nature of this association—that is, whether depression is merely an early sign of dementia or a causative factor—remains unclear.

A depressed elderly person should have a thorough medical evaluation with particular attention to the onset of symptoms, course of illness, and response to treatment. Because depression is more treatable than dementia and, in most instances, reversible, social workers must carefully and systematically differentiate between these two conditions. (We discuss the assessment and treatment of dementia in chapter 9.)

CAUSES OF DEPRESSION AMONG ELDERLY PEOPLE

Many factors, both alone and through interactions with other factors, contribute to depression among older people. The greatest risk factors for depression in late life are physical illness, disability, pain, loss, and lack of social support. Genetic influences contribute to many types of depression, although some experts, for example, Blazer (2002), suggest that genetic causes are more significant during early adulthood. Psychological and social factors, especially worldview, cognitive and coping styles, and life circumstances (such as economic and widowhood status), are also important contributors to late life depression that presumably interact with biological influences. In the next section we briefly discuss these biological, psychological, and social contributions to depression in late life. Readers interested in more in-depth discussion of this material should consult the reference list at the end of the book.

Biological Factors

Blazer (1995) reports that depressed older people exhibit decreased blood flow to the hypothalamic region, which affects moods, and that depressed elderly people respond differently from those who are not depressed when given a synthetic corticosteriod, specifically, dexamethasone. Blazer (2002) also notes that some psychobiological changes that naturally occur with age could increase some older people's vulnerability to depression, but late life depression is more likely caused by an interaction between biological changes and psychological and social factors. Many older people become depressed when illness interferes with their activities of daily living (ADL) and self-care. Steffens, Jays, and Krishman (1999) found that older people who lost their ability to carry out instrumental activities of daily living (IADL) were substantially more depressed than those who experienced deficits in "self-maintenance skills." Researchers suspect that both organic and psychological factors play a role in the onset of depression after a stroke (see Mast, MacNeill, and Lichtenberg, 2004, for a more in-depth discussion of cardiovascular symptoms and depression). Depression can also contribute to greater mortality and morbidity. Penninx and colleagues (1999) found that chronic depression (lasting an average of about four years) raises the risk of cancer by 88% in elderly people.

About 10% to 15% of mood disorders are caused by medications, illegal drugs, or neurological or medication conditions (Swartz and Margolis, 2004). Some medications that are used to treat hypertension and other medical conditions contribute to the onset of depression among older adults. These medications include beta-blockers, other antihypertensives, reserpine, digoxin, L-dopa, steroids, benzodiazepines, and some cancer-fighting drugs (Gottfries, 1998; Swartz and Margolis, 2004).

Deficiencies in essential nutrients have been linked to depression among older people (Swartz and Margolis, 2004; Gottfries, 1998). Elderly people with low levels of vitamin B12 and low folate levels are more prone to depression. Folate deficiencies can cause insomnia, irritability, fatigue, and forgetfulness and can interfere with therapeutic responses to electroconvulsive therapy and certain antidepressants, such as fluoxetine and sertraline (Gottfries, 1998).

Chronic pain is another significant factor related to depression in late life. Ohayon and Schatzberg (2003) report that people with chronic pain are four times more likely to become depressed than those without chronic pain. These investigators also report that depressed people were five times more likely to report backaches, four times more likely to report headaches, three times more likely to have limb pain, and two times more likely to mention gastrointestinal and joint/ articular diseases than nondepressed people. The connection between pain and depression remains unclear; further studies are needed of the mechanisms underlying this association.

Psychological and Social Causes

Loss and Adverse Life Events

Although most elderly people cope well with bereavement, the loss of a spouse is an important risk factor for depression in late life (Wolfe et al., 1996). Van Grootheest, Beekman, Broese van Groenou, and Deeg (1999) found that elderly widowed men and women have significantly more symptoms of depression than elderly married men and women and that men are more likely to be depressed upon losing a spouse than are women. G. Lee, Willetts, and Seccombe (1998), who found similar gender differences in widowhood, discovered that time moderated the effects of widowhood on depression for women, but high rates of depression among men continued three years later. Among African Americans, however, widowed men are less symptomatic than their female counterparts (Brown, 1996).

Newly bereaved elderly people are especially at risk for depression that can last for several years (Turvey, Carney, Arndt, Wallace, and Herzog, 1999). The *DSM-IV* (1994) recommends a diagnosis of major depressive disorder only when symptoms last longer than two months after the loss; however, in a longitudinal cohort study of 5,449 older adults, Turvey and colleagues (1999) found that high rates of depression are common as long as two years after the loss of a spouse. Although most bereaved elderly people eventually adjust, depression may last longer than experts have previously assumed. Complicated grief reactions should be considered if a client feels excessive guilt, ruminates about death, morbidly dwells on feelings of worthlessness, or exhibits hallucinations, marked psychomotor retardation, or prolonged and marked functional impairment.

The accumulation of losses—for example, losing friends or spouses, relocating, developing illnesses—is especially common during late life and often leads to depression. The circumstances surrounding losses, as well as the coping strategies that older people use to manage multiple losses, often determine whether and how much they will become depressed.

Negative life events often precipitate late life depression (Fiske et al., 2003; Kraaij, Arensman, and Spinhoven, 2002). Fiske and colleagues (2003) also found that the association between depression and negative life events is reciprocal, that is, depressed older people are more likely than nondepressed older adults to experience negative events in the future. Fiske and colleagues surmise that poor social adjustment among these depressed people contributes to the occurrence of additional adverse experiences in their lives.

Lack of Social Supports

Several studies have found an association between lack of social support and depression in late life (Craft, Johnson, and Ortega, 1998; Blazer, 2002; George, 2004). Among low-income, frail elderly, Rogers (1999) found that those who were the most depressed had the least adequate and least satisfying social relationships. Similarly, Hays and colleagues (1998) investigated correlates of four dimensions of the Center for Epidemiological Studies—Depression (CES-D) Scale—among a large sample of community-dwelling elderly people and found only one variable—having a confidante—that influences all four dimensions. Forsell and Winblad (1999) also found a significantly greater incidence of long-term depression among older people who have insufficient social networks than among those who have adequate social support. Studies of depression among elderly people consistently show the importance of social supports in mitigating depression, although the type of support matters. Fukukawa and colleagues (2004) found that emotional support from family members more effectively buffers depression than instrumental support from these relatives.

Caregiving

Those who care for aging relatives frequently demonstrate high levels of depression, even when their previous experiences with depression and the prevalence of depression in their family are taken into account; this is especially true for those caring for someone in the later stages of dementia (Dura, Stukenberg, and Kiecolt-Glaser, 1990; Hannappel, Carslyn, and Allen, 1993; Tennstedt, Cafferata, and Sullivan, 1992). The social isolation that caregivers frequently experience is one of the most significant contributors to depression. Many caregivers have minimal opportunities for respite from caring and are unable to leave their ailing spouse or parent alone or with someone else. Insufficient pleasure is another reason that caregivers become depressed. Because caregiving is demanding and often requires complete attention, caregivers, who typically are women, may be unable to satisfy their own needs or take time to participate in activities that they enjoy. When caregivers consistently lack positive experiences and interactions, depression ensues.

Caregivers are often tired from sleep deprivation, which also exacerbates depression. Gerontological social workers can help caregivers with their depression by linking them to supportive services, such as caregiver support groups, that offer contact with others similarly situated, who understand what they are feeling and experiencing.

Socioeconomic or Income Factors

Studies consistently demonstrate a higher incidence of depression among lower socioeconomic groups (Carstensen et al., 1996). The strength of this association lessens, however, when controls for illness, social supports, and other social stresses are considered. In addition, Chodosh, Buckwalter, Blazer, and Seeman (2004) demonstrated that social class differences influence how people report and experience depression.

Stress and Coping

How older people cope with stressful events may be more important than the events themselves in determining the risk for depression. For example, not all elderly people who suffer from a chronic illness experience depression; many older people adapt by compensating for their health limitations in other ways. Individual appraisals of stressful events as positive, negative, or neutral affect how strongly the person reacts to threatening situations (Lazarus and Folkman, 1984). Coping mediates between a crisis and a response to a crisis. People who have adequate personal and social resources will persevere, change, or adapt to their circumstances. Those who appraise their situations as beyond their resources and capabilities will manage less well. In addition, elderly people with high levels of personal meaning, that is, a purpose in life and a strong personal identity and social conscience, are less likely to succumb to depression (Reker, 1997). Elderly people who feel they have a high degree of personal choice are also less likely to become depressed. According to Reker (1997), elderly people with a meaningful existential outlook cope with personal and social losses by transcending depression and finding meaning in their experiences. When Mazure, Maciejewski, Jacobs, and Bruce (2002) analyzed the effects of stressful life events on depression among elderly people, the researchers confirmed that people's coping strategies mediate their reactions to life events. Those with the most effective coping strategies avoid depression, whereas those with inadequate coping resources become depressed more frequently.

Several studies reveal an association between depression and emotion-focused coping, that is, venting and expressing feelings (Aldwin and Gilmer, 2004; Stanton, Danoff-Burg, Cameron, and Ellis, 1994; Zeidner and Endler, 1996). These findings suggest that elderly people who regulate their feelings by reframing events will cope better than those who feel overwhelmed by their emotions and dwell on their feelings. Zeidner and Endler (1996) and Nolen-Hoeksema (2000) have found that depression occurs more frequently among those who ruminate and are preoccupied with their affective state. Emotion-focused coping is especially maladaptive when it interferes with problem-solving coping, which works best when events are amenable to change. Problem-solving coping is directed at analyzing and solving a problem. Emotion-focused coping is more appropriate when stressful events are uncontrollable or intractable. In these situations active emotion-focused coping that includes positive reappraisal or self-control alleviates depression better than problem-focused coping. Seeking social support, finding meaning, and religious coping are also effective ways to cope with stress (Aldwin and Gilmer, 2004)

A biopsychosocial view of depression that focuses on the connections between biological, psychological, and social functioning will ensure that older people who are depressed are identified and treated appropriately. Interdisciplinary teams that include physicians, nurses, social workers, and other health professionals are especially important when treating elderly people because they typically struggle with medical, psychological, and environmental impediments. No one profession can address all the multifaceted problems that older people encounter. When health professionals work in teams and share different viewpoints, assess different areas, and apply holistic interventions, they can more successfully address these complicated problems.

ASSESSMENT OF DEPRESSION IN OLDER PEOPLE

The two instruments that are most widely used by clinicians to evaluate depression during interviews are the Schedule for Affective Disorders and Schizophrenia (SADS) and the Hamilton Rating Scale for Depression (HAM-D). The SADS requires that elderly people discuss the history, characteristics, and symptoms of their depression with clinicians, who then rate the intensity and duration of the symptoms on a seven-point scale. Social workers need extensive training to administer this instrument correctly, and the interviews are lengthy (about two hours), but the SADS is widely recommended because it accurately discriminates between depressed and nondepressed elderly (Gallagher, 1986).

The HAM-D has the advantages of taking less time to administer (usually about thirty minutes) than the SADS and of distinguishing different levels of depression. The HAM-D provides more information about the various ways that symptoms are organized and a more qualitative understanding of an elderly person's depression. The instrument covers seventeen areas related to depression that clinicians rate on either a five-point or three-point scale for severity. Although many use the

HAM-D, some question its validity and efficacy with older people and its overemphasis on somatic symptoms.

Social workers can obtain objective and subjective data on an older adult's depression by using self-report inventories along with interviews. The self-report inventories that are most often used with older adults are the Zung Self-Rating Depression Scale and the Beck Depression Inventory. Both scales measure depressive symptoms and are easy to administer; both are based on the assumption that depression can be measured along a single continuum from mild to moderate to severe. The Geriatric Depression Rating Scale, which was designed specifically for older people, measures the presence or absence and severity of various symptoms. This scale is also brief and simple to administer.

Futterman and colleagues (1995) recommend a three-stage procedure for assessing depression in older people. All older people who demonstrate physical or emotional distress should be screened for depression. The social worker should use an interview-based assessment, such as the SADs, to acquire a more in-depth evaluation. Finally, the clinician and client should identify treatment goals during the third stage that they can specify, monitor, and use to evaluate the treatment.

Because substantial cultural and class differences exist in how people express and experience depression, social workers should consider the potential cultural biases of depression assessment tools. In an in-depth analysis of two widely used depression instruments, Chodosh and colleagues (2004) found significant differences by race, income, and education in people's response styles. They found that although older people from low-income groups report more symptoms of depression, they bother the poor older people less than they bother older adults from higher socioeconomic backgrounds.

Some assessment instruments have been translated into other languages. For example, Gupta and Yick (2001) have successfully used the CES-D with Chinese immigrants, and Stokes, Thompson, Murphy, and Gallagher-Thompson (2001) have translated a version of the GDS into Chinese. A Japanese version of the GDS is widely used in Japan (Matsubayashi et al., 1994).

SPECIFIC INTERVENTIONS FOR DEPRESSION AMONG OLDER PEOPLE

Gerontological social workers must intervene on multiple levels to successfully treat late life depression. Clinicians should use interventions that address the environmental stressors contributing to an older person's depression, in conjunction with individual interventions that help the client reappraise and cope with problems. Social workers can easily incorporate treatment strategies designed specifically to treat depression in older people within an integrated practice framework. Next we discuss selected approaches that have been empirically validated or specifically recommended with depressed older people. These include psychotherapy (specifically, cognitive therapy, interpersonal therapy, and life review), psychopharmacological treatment, and electroconvulsive therapy (ECT). Although a physician usually supervises drug treatments and ECT, social workers often team up with other health professionals to work with depressed older adults.

Psychotherapy/Psychosocial Interventions

Psychotherapy almost always occurs during face-to-face meetings and emphasizes verbal and nonverbal communications between social worker and client. Psychotherapy helps clients manage difficult situations by focusing on how they feel, perceive, and react to stressful events experienced recently or in the past. The emphasis is on the client's affect, cognitions, behaviors, and communications, depending upon the treatment approach that the social worker uses. Many clinicians engaged in psychotherapy with older people who once were perceived as rigid and "too old to change." These views have changed, and many types of psychotherapy are effective with older people (Blazer, 2002). The most common types of psychotherapy used to treat depression in older people include dynamic psychotherapy, supportive therapy, brief therapy, interpersonal therapy, behavioral therapy, group therapy, and cognitive therapy (Blazer, 2002). Cognitive interventions, which focus on clients' thoughts, are especially efficacious for treating late life depression, although life review and interpersonal therapy are also recommended (Laidlaw et al., 2003). Psychopharmacological treatment is often used in conjunction with psychotherapy, whereas ECT is usually implemented when an older person's depression is unresponsive to other interventions.

The current cohort of older people rarely seeks care from social workers or other mental health specialists. Many older depressed people are treated with medication because they more often seek help from their family physician, who typically treats patients with antidepressants (J. Gallo, Rabins, and Illife, 1997). Alvidrez and Arean (2002–3) found that physicians infrequently refer their depressed older patients for psychotherapy or behavioral treatment. Many more depressed older people could benefit from psychosocial interventions than receive these services. These interventions are especially relevant in gerontological practice because of the potential adverse interaction effects of antidepressants and other medications that older people may be taking. One promising psychosocial intervention for older people is cognitive behavioral therapy.

Cognitive Behavioral Therapy with Older People

Several studies (e.g., Thompson, Gallagher, and Breckenridge, 1987; Laidlaw et al., 2003) have confirmed the efficacy of cognitive behavioral therapy (CBT) for depression in older adults. The best interventions for depressed older adults are those that combine cognitive interventions with medication (Gerson, Belin, Kaufman, Mintz, and Jarvik, 1999; Blazer, 2002). Cognitive therapy is based on the assumption that maladaptive perceptions and beliefs about the world and about one's experiences cause depression and anxiety. According to A. T. Beck, Rush, Shaw, and Emery (1979), distorted cognitive functioning occurs in three areas: the negative triad, underlying beliefs or schemas, and errors in logic. The negative triad represents one's perceptions of oneself, one's experiences, and the future; depressed people usually have negative self-concepts and experience themselves as inadequate and incompetent. They remember the past pessimistically, as if nothing worked out well, and they expect awful events to occur even when they are enjoying life. Their underlying beliefs are often negative and reflect a morbid outlook, and they view misfortunes out of context and more negatively than they really are; in short, they perceive and expect the worst. Their thinking often reflects errors in logic, and they are inclined to exaggerate, catastrophize, overgeneralize, and overemphasize the negative.

According to Gallagher and Thompson (1983), three kinds of cognitive distortions consistently appear in older people. One is a distorted belief that they are too old to change and that seeking help for problems is useless because they have been like this for most of their life and cannot change. Another common distorted belief is the view that everything would be fine if only one specific problem changed. This is a common fantasy among widows who ruminate about the return of a deceased spouse. The third cognitive misperception that often occurs in late life is expressed as "You're too young to help me" or "If I had only done it differently earlier in my life, I wouldn't be depressed now."

The goal of cognitive therapy is to help older people identify cognitive statements that are so irrational and self-destructive that they result in depression and to substitute positive and constructive statements for these negative cognitions. Clinicians first teach elderly people to recognize how they exaggerate, catastrophize, and overemphasize the negative. Then the clinicians encourage their elderly clients to substitute healthier, less dismal cognitions for the negative ones. Social workers must usually educate older clients about this approach, teach them how to implement it, and then monitor their progress. The "daily thought record" is an excellent monitoring device (Thompson and Gallagher-Thompson, 1997). It organizes the assessment into five areas: the situation or event that led to the negative feelings; unhelpful thoughts and what they mean and how strongly the client believes in them; feelings (sadness, anger, anxiety, etc.) and how strong these emotions are; confrontation of negative thoughts and their replacement with more helpful and adaptive thoughts; and extent of the client's belief in the original negative thoughts after they are replaced with more constructive ones.

Cognitive therapy helps depressed older adults for several reasons. Social workers work collaboratively with older clients when using cognitive therapy, and clients do not have to converse in sophisticated psychological and therapeutic language. Older clients can carry out simple homework assignments that they can use outside the therapeutic setting. Family members are easily included in the treatment process, and diagnosing clients into specific categories of mental illness is not necessary. Cognitive therapy also works well within an integrated practice framework and with interdisciplinary teams (Zeiss and Steffen, 1996).

Cognitive therapy works best with elderly people when social workers include multimodal training (visual aids, demonstrations of techniques), memory aids (tapes and written assignments), clear and careful presentation of material, and an emphasis on strengths as well as deficits (Zeiss and Steffen, 1996). Laidlaw and colleagues (2003) have outlined several procedural modifications to cognitive behavioral therapy when practitioners use it with older people. First, memory problems in older clients may require social workers to present information slowly and repetitively. Laidlaw and colleagues recommend taping meetings with practitioners to allow older clients to hear the meetings again and practice homework assignments between sessions. Second, interdisciplinary teams that shed light on physiological and health problems, along with environmental ones, are especially important. Third, social workers must instill hope by sharing with their older clients information about the efficacy of treatment for late life depression. These clients need to know that most people's depression improves over time and especially as a result of treatment. Finally, Laidlaw and colleagues (2003) recognize the benefits and limitations of storytelling when implementing cognitive behavioral therapy with older people, and these researchers suggest that practitioners carefully examine when narrative approaches are most helpful (see Laidlaw et al., 2003, for information about specific techniques for using cognitive behavioral therapy with older people).

In their constructive model for depressed older adults, Ronen and Dowd (1998) explain that writing about positive thoughts and positive actions empowers depressed older people and helps them to acquire a more positive outlook. The Daily Mood Rating Form as well as the Older Person's Pleasant Events Schedule promote positive feelings and experiences among depressed older adults (see Zeiss and Steffen, 1996, for more details about these assessment tools).

Interpersonal Therapy

Klerman, Weissman, Rounsaville, and Chevron (1984) developed interpersonal therapy after observing many interpersonal problems among depressed people (see M. Weissman, Marowitz, and Klerman, 2000, for additional information about interpersonal therapy). Klerman and colleagues assumed that if depressed people's social relationships improved, their depression would subside. Interpersonal therapy is especially useful for older adults because it is short term and goal oriented. Clinicians are active and focus on a problem area that the social worker and older client identify together. The emphasis is on current interpersonal conflicts rather than on underlying issues from previous relationships.

Interpersonal therapy focuses on loss and grief, interpersonal disputes, role transitions, and interpersonal deficits (Miller and Silberman, 1996). A psychoeducational component, which teaches older clients about typical responses to loss, role changes, and interpersonal disputes, is especially therapeutic (Hinrichsen, 1999). Discussing useful coping strategies is also important. Most researchers who have investigated the efficacy of interpersonal therapy have ignored geriatric populations. Miller and Silberman (1996) found promising results for interpersonal therapy when they compared it with treatment with antidepressant medication (nortriptyline), and a combination of both with depressed elderly people. In a review of psychosocial treatments for depression among older people, Niederehe (1996) reported that interpersonal therapy was just as effective as psychopharmacological intervention (specifically, nortriptyline in this study) in treating depression and resulted in fewer dropouts from treatment. Some, such as Swartz and Margolis (2004), suggest that interpersonal therapy is especially efficacious with older people when their depression stems from a life event, such as a death of a spouse.

Life Review

Life review is another useful technique that is widely used with depressed older people. According to Butler (1963), life review is a "naturally occurring, universal mental process characterized by the progressive return to consciousness of past experiences, and, particularly, the resurgence of unresolved conflicts" (p. 66). Life review is broader than reminiscence, which involves the process of recalling past events or experiences and is merely one component of life review. A. Pincus (1970) observed that depressed elderly people reminisce less than nondepressed older adults and that reminiscing sometimes alleviates their depression. Social workers who use life review to treat depression in older people typically encourage them to reevaluate their life by reflecting on past events and by integrating those events into their overall life schemata. People usually begin by reviewing their lives as children, then as adolescents and young adults, and eventually as middle-aged adults. Some clients emphasize significant life events. Whatever form it takes, the process helps people understand why they make certain decisions and put their lives in perspective. Life review usually helps older people find meaning in their lives as they review past events and reflect upon salient events. When they reminisce, people identify what was important to them, what memories were significant, and what events contributed to who they are now. They think about what made them sad and what seemed meaningful at the time but now seems unimportant.

Social workers can use various techniques to elicit memories and recall (Burnside, 1996). These include (1) flashbulb memories of specific past events that often evoke vivid recollections of what one was doing at a specific time, such as when John F. Kennedy was assassinated or when a particular airplane crash occurred; (2) genograms: people diagram their family tree and include family members in their life review; (3) props such as old newspapers, antiques, pictures, and music to stimulate long-term memories; (4) themes that are therapeutic and relevant for a particular older client or group; and (5) time lines, which people use to identify important life events along a continuum from birth to the present, helping them to understand how perspectives change over time.

Life review can be conducted in groups or in a one-to-one interaction between a social worker and an older client. Although group reminiscence is beneficial, individual meetings are especially efficacious because depressed older people often prefer the intimacy and confidentiality afforded by one-on-one encounters. Individual sessions are also more amenable to comprehensive assessment, and private sessions work particularly well with older clients who are prone to wander, experience agitation, or have severe cognitive impairments. When life review is used with a depressed older person who is in the early stages of a dementia, long-term memories may predominate over current or short-term cognitive states, but the intervention is just as effective.

Because some older people dislike reminiscing, social workers should use life review cautiously and should never assume that elderly people want to discuss the past merely because they are older. J. Wallace (1992) observed that some older people reminisce because they assume that others expect it of them. Gerontological social workers must carefully assess the appropriateness of life review for each client and use alternative treatment methods with older people who are reluctant to talk about the past.

Psychopharmacological Treatment of Depression

Social workers should refer older clients for medical evaluation when they believe that the older person will respond well to psychopharmacological treatment or when his depression is intractable to psychotherapy or other psychosocial treatment. Physicians must prescribe antidepressants cautiously because adverse side-effects can sometimes negatively affect an older person's health and create iatrogenic reactions. Nevertheless, many depressed elderly people respond well to antidepressant medications, especially when they are used in conjunction with psychosocial interventions.

Until recently, the antidepressants most widely used with older people were tricyclic antidepressants, specifically, nortriptyline, desipramine, and maprotiline. Although the side-effects from these medications, which are often called secondary amines, are less serious than some other tricyclic antidepressants (such as amytriptyline, imipramine, protriptyline, and doxepin, which are known as tertiary amines), side-effects such as confusion or delirium can result from interactions with other medications (Dick and Gallagher-Thompson, 1996; Meyers and Young, 2004).

Many depressed older people have improved after being treated with the monoamine oxidase inhibitors (MAOIs), but these can have serious side-effects, such as elevated blood pressure, dizziness or lightheadedness, and insomnia. The potential interaction effects between MAOIs and other drugs are especially dangerous in older people and can be toxic.

Excellent results have been achieved when older clients have been treated with selective serotonin reuptake inhibitors (SSRIs), specifically, Prozac, Paxil, and Zoloft. More recent medications, such as Lixapro and Effexor, which can cause an increase in blood pressure, need more testing on older people. Because older people metabolize drugs more slowly and take more medications than younger people, older people more often experience adverse side-effects and toxic reactions from drug interactions. Many antidepressants also take longer to work with older people. Older people should begin with a lower-than-recommended dosage of antidepressant medications, and the dosage should be increased gradually only after it is clear that potentially dangerous interactions or side-effects can be avoided.

Electroconvulsive Therapy

Older clients who are suicidal and fail to respond to medication and psychosocial treatments may be candidates for electroconvulsive therapy (ECT), which has immediate therapeutic effects. Depressed older people with psychosis might benefit more from ECT than depressed elderly people who are not psychotic (Blazer, 2002; Flint and Rifat, 1998; M. K. O'Connor et al., 2001). ECT is most advantageous when older people respond poorly to antidepressant medications or are severely depressed. The safety of ECT has improved since it was first introduced in the

1930s, but side-effects, such as memory problems, headaches, nausea, and muscle pain, are still common. It is usually administered about two or three times a week for a total of six to twelve sessions. Although the efficacy rates are high, the benefits are short term. Most patients (50% to 60%) relapse within a year (Swartz and Margolis, 2004). Blazer (2002) recommends placing patients on antidepressant medication for at least six months to avoid relapse, even if their initial response to psychopharmacological treatment was poor.

ECT should be avoided with older people who have cardiovascular problems, neurological diseases, and other degenerative diseases (Dick and Gallagher-Thompson, 1996). It is recommended cautiously for the treatment of depression in later life because of the number of older adults who have these health impairments and the frequency with which older adults report confusion after ECT treatment.

CASE 6.1

Mr. Antoine, a seventy-five-year-old retired salesman, has rheumatoid arthritis and often complains about pain. He has become increasingly discouraged about his future. He called the local elder-care hotline and was referred to a social worker.

Mr. Antoine met with the social worker and explained that his arthritis has become so bad that he has had to give up golf and walking. He feels unhappy, lethargic, and disinterested in everything. The social worker listens to Mr. Antoine describe the various experiences that led to his current situation. The social worker uses the ABCDEF model to assess Mr. Antoine and concludes that his actions and behavior (actions) are lethargic, torpid, and restricted, although he has no limitations in his ADLs or IADLs. She recognizes that Mr. Antoine's pain (biological state and health) contributes to his negative feelings and that he needs a thorough consultation with his doctor. Mr. Antoine has avoided discussing his pain with his doctor because Mr. Antoine feels that he should tolerate it. Mr. Antoine's thoughts and expectations for himself (cognitions) exacerbate his situation. He is otherwise alert and well aware of his surroundings.

Demographic indicators (demographics)—his age, race (he is white), and gender—suggest that Mr. Antoine is a high risk for suicide. The social worker asks Mr. Antoine whether he feels suicidal or has attempted suicide in the past, along with other questions about suicide (see chapter 7 for a discussion of the suicide lethality index and assessment of suicide potential). Mr. Antoine explains that he sometimes has suicidal thoughts but he has no plans to kill himself, has no means to carry it out, and would not do it even if he could. After evaluating Mr. Antoine's suicidal potential, the social worker concluded that Mr. Antoine was not a high suicide risk based on his past history, low suicide ideation, and lack of access. She asks him several questions about his present and past history, his symptoms (e.g., his negative feelings, inactivity, apathy, and somatic complaints), how often they appear, and over what period of time. The social worker suspects that Mr. Antoine meets the criteria for a major depressive disorder but still needs to rule out other possibilities. His social supports are limited (environmental factors); he lives in semi-independent quarters at a life care community center and rarely sees his children. The social worker listens attentively to Mr. Antoine explain how his unhappiness (feelings) has developed during the last several years, especially since his pain has worsened.

Based on the integrated model, the social worker concludes that Mr. Antoine lacks personal and environmental resources and has problems in several areas. Mr. Antoine's arthritis has created multiple losses for him. In addition, his expectations that he should remain "tough" prevent him from obtaining the pain relief that he needs. These perceptions and the persistent pain have increased his depression and social isolation.

After listening to Mr. Antoine discuss his feelings (F) and comprehensively assessing his circumstances, the social worker addresses the biological and health factors (B) behind Mr. Antoine's depression by referring him to a geropsychiatrist for a medication evaluation and by counseling Mr. Antoine to tell his doctor about his pain. She uses the Numeric Rating Scale, commonly used with older people, to determine the severity of Mr. Antoine's pain (see Chibnall and Tait, 2001, for more information about this scale). She addresses the cognitive issues (C) by explaining cognitive behavioral treatment to Mr. Antoine; she suggests that he monitor his thoughts for a few weeks by using the daily thought record, which is organized by situation (a brief description of the stressful event); beliefs (thoughts associated with the stressful event); and emotions, (emotions/feelings associated with the stressful event). (See Laidlaw et al., 2003, for more information about this tool.) The ultimate goal is to work with Mr. Antoine to substitute more positive thoughts for his automatic negative ones. The social worker also encourages Mr. Antoine to engage in more pleasurable activities (A), and during the next few meetings they identify activities that he enjoys. The social worker enhances his environmental supports (E) by referring Mr. Antoine to a support group for people with chronic illnesses.

The social worker also helps Mr. Antoine with his insurance; although his managed care company will pay for most of his counseling, his pain and depression treatments are reimbursed differently, and the required out-of-pocket payments are more than he can afford. The social worker contacts the

American Pain Society, which has a position statement on pain assessment and treatment in the managed care environment (see Fox et al., 2000, for more information) and obtains information that will help Mr. Antoine negotiate with his insurance company. These activities lift Mr. Antoine's spirits and help him feel more in control of his life by providing a stronger sense of mastery and self-sufficiency. The social worker has met her profession's ethical obligations to enhance her clients' well-being by advocating for better services and health coverage for older people suffering from pain.

The association between chronic pain and depression, which is interactive, is common in late life (Blazer, 2002). Older people in pain are more depressed than older people who are free from suffering, but depression also decreases people's tolerance for pain. This association underscores the inextricable connection between biological and psychosocial functioning and the need for an integrated practice model that addresses micro and macro dimensions. The social worker intervened on multiple levels with Mr. Antoine. She saw him for his counseling; consulted with his doctor; referred him to a support group; helped him with his insurance; and advocated for better health coverage of his pain treatments. (See chapter 11 for more information about pain assessment and chapter 16 for a more in-depth discussion of health policies.) Although the social worker's involvement with Mr. Antoine will continue for several months, she initially assessed and intervened on micro, meso, and macro levels.

DISCUSSION QUESTIONS

1. How do older people manifest depression differently from younger people?
2. What are the advantages and disadvantages of treating depressed older people with antidepressants?
3. What are some ways that social workers might educate older people and prevent depression in late life?
4. Discuss the strengths and limitations of the various psychosocial treatments available for depressed older adults.
5. How might social workers combine subjective and objective methods when assessing older people for depression?

CHAPTER 7

Suicide Among Older People

INCIDENCE OF SUICIDE IN LATE LIFE

Suicide rates increase with age, although these rates have declined since 1990. Such age-related changes in the suicide rate demonstrate why gerontological social workers must carefully assess older clients for suicide potential, especially if they are depressed or suffering with a medical illness. These changes also underscore why we must continue to enhance quality of life in the later years. A review of recent suicide rates by age, gender, and ethnic background reveals those who are at greatest risk for suicide, but let us first discuss ethical issues that often arise in these situations.

Recent debates about end-of-life decisions, death with dignity, and advance directives have changed people's attitudes toward death and life. The passage of the Patient Self-Determination Act of 1990, as well as Oregon's decision to regulate and legalize assisted suicide, have profound implications for social workers practicing with older people. Social workers will more frequently become involved with older people who have more end-of-life choices today than they did in the past. This chapter focuses on suicide among people who are not terminally ill. It also recommends interventions for suicidal elderly people. In chapter 11 we discuss death and dying, including physician-assisted suicide, in the context of end-of-life care. This includes a discussion of advance directives, living wills, health proxies, and assisted suicide. The discussion also incorporates the contributions of the hospice movement, which has challenged many traditional ideas about dying and quality of life among people with terminal illnesses. We discuss these issues again in the chapter on health policies, chapter 16.

Although a salient ethical value for social workers is self-determination, this assumes that all people have equal access to information and options for treatment, and act out of "free will"—minimal coercion from outside forces. Social workers value individual choice but only when they are satisfied that a particular client is well informed and has exhausted all treatments.

The National Association of Social Workers (NASW) has a policy statement regarding client self-determination in end-of-life decisions. All gerontological social workers should be familiar with it. NASW's position recognizes the diversity of viewpoints on end-of-life issues as well as the individual's right to determine level of care. NASW does not promote social workers' direct involvement in end-of-life decisions; in almost all states this would lead to criminal charges. Rather, "the appropriate role for social workers is to help patients express their thoughts and feelings, to facilitate exploration of alternatives, to provide information to make an informed choice, and to deal with grief and loss issues" (NASW Delegate Assembly, 1993). In *Assisted Suicide* (1997) Jamison writes that "aid in dying should be reserved for extraordinary cases. At a minimum, I believe that a patient's condition must be incurable and associated with unrelenting and intolerable suffering. I do not see assisted suicide as equivalent to other interventions, particularly when more than one option is available. I believe that the issue needs to be dealt with on a case-by-case basis and answered anew by each clinician, preferably working as part of a health care team or with input from colleagues whenever possible" (p. 179).

Jamison also argues that regardless of practitioners' initial ethical response, they are obligated to clearly assess the patient's motives and refer her to appropriate treatment. An in-depth assessment of a client's suicide risk is imperative, first to prevent an impulsive decision, one that has not been clearly thought through, and, second, because in most cases multiple treatment options are available to the suicidal elderly person that often effectively deter suicide and improve her quality of life. Improving the quality of the older client's life, whether the person is terminally or chronically ill, ought to be the clinician's first line of defense when confronted with an elderly person who wants to commit suicide. The rise in effective treatments for the depressed elderly, including those who are terminally ill, offers hope that did not exist in the past for these people. The remainder of this chapter provides a brief review of suicide prevalence based on sociodemographic factors, such as gender, income, ethnic background, and other important categories. Next, we present a suicide lethality index that gerontological social workers can use in practice. It will help them assess those who are at greatest risk. We conclude with suggested interventions for elderly people who are suicidal.

Sociodemographic Differences in Elderly Suicide

Despite the decrease in suicide rates since 1990, older adults, specifically, older men, complete suicide more often than younger men. The overall rate of suicide among people older than sixty-five was 15.2 per 100,000 in 2000, down from 20.5 per 100,000 in 1990. The rates have declined for both men and women among all older subgroups, those 65 to 74, 75 to 84, and 85 and older (National Center for Health Statistics, 2003a). Older men who attempt suicide succeed more often than younger men who try to kill themselves. The ratio between attempted and completed suicide among young men is 200:1 in contrast to 4:1 among older men (Conwell, Duberstein, Cox, et al., 1998; Conwell, Duberstein, Connor, et al., 2002).

In addition to associations between age and suicide, substantial gender differences in completed suicide persist. Older men were almost eight times more likely to commit suicide than were older women in 2000, and this ratio has increased somewhat despite suicide declines overall since 1990. In 2000 the suicide rate for older women was 4.0 per 100,000 in contrast to 31.1 for older men. The rates increase with age. For example, among older men aged 65 to 74, the rate was 22.7 per 100,000 in 2000, whereas it was 38.6 among those aged 75 to 84 and 57.5 among those older than 85. Contrast these rates with those for women in the same age groups, which are 4.0, 4.0, and 4.2 per 100,000, respectively. Men are also more likely to attempt suicide following the onset of depression in late life, whereas women are more likely to attempt suicide with onset of depression early in life. Various factors have been suggested for these gender differences. The most common differences are that women have stronger support systems, greater ease in expressing intimate feelings, and less commitment to work than men do. The gender differences in suicide rates may change as women use more lethal methods and as they become increasingly identified with work and occupational status. Thus we must keep in mind that current differences between older men and older women in suicide may be a result of factors associated with a particular cohort and are already changing in subsequent cohorts. Practitioners must cautiously infer how these incidence data do or do not transfer to baby boomers and younger cohorts. Clinicians must also be cautious in making inferences from these gender differences: although older men complete suicide more frequently, older women express more suicidal ideation (Ron, 2002). Women also have higher depression rates. Older women's suicide rates are low (about 4%), but older women may experience more psychological distress more often than older men. Ron (2002) found that single women, specifically, recently widowed women, were especially at risk for suicidal ideation. These findings confirm that gerontological social workers must also address older women's depression and suicidal feelings.

Ethnic differences in suicide rates are revealing. Older white men (65+) have the highest rates (33.3 per 100,000) followed by older Hispanic men (19.5) and older Asian men (15.4). Older African American men have the lowest suicide rates

(11.5 per 100,000). The highest suicide rates of any subgroup are found among white men older than 85 (61.6 per 100,000) and white men aged 75 to 84 (41.1). Substantial variations within ethnic groups exist. For example, in their study of elderly Hispanics in Florida from 1990 to 1993, Llorente, Eisdorfer, Loewenstein, and Zarate (1996) found that elderly Cuban men had a suicide rate per 100,000 that was 1.67 times higher than that of older Americans in general. Cuban men older than 65 had the highest rates (66 per 100,000), followed by the general population of U.S. men (39.6 per 100,000), Cuban women (9.0 per 100,000), and the general population of U.S. women (6.2 per 100,000). In general, older men in minority populations are less likely to commit suicide, presumably because of their family support network is stronger and more extensive than that enjoyed by the general population of older people in the United States (Llorente et al., 1996).

In addition to age, gender, and ethnic differences in suicide rates, marital status is significantly associated with completion of suicide. Those who are single, especially those recently divorced or widowed, have higher rates of suicide than their married counterparts. In their comparison of recently and remotely bereaved older people, Duberstein, Conwell, and Cox (1998) found several factors that increased the likelihood of suicide. For those who had been widowed for less than four years, these factors included whether they had received psychiatric treatment, experiences with early loss and separation, and slightly higher rates of lifetime substance abuse.

Older people who commit suicide are typically socially isolated. They are less involved with neighbors, friends, and family members who might be around to rescue them after a suicide attempt. Inadequate emotional support and social interaction are especially predictive of suicide in later life. Several studies, for example, Beautrais (2002), Bartels, Coakley, and colleagues (2002), and Turvey, Conwell, and colleagues (2002), document that suicide rates increase among older people, even if they have health problems, when they lack confidantes or other close relationships. An older person who lives alone is at especially high risk for suicide for many of the reasons just cited. In addition, older people with health problems are less likely to survive an attempt.

Health problems are related to suicidal ideation. If a person suffering from poor health is also depressed, the risk of suicide is even higher (Turvey, Conwell, et al., 2002; Waern, Rubenowitz, and Runeson, 2001). Some experts report that at least one-third of older people who committed suicide had a physical illness (Blazer and Koenig, 1996). Recent studies suggest a decline in suicide attempts by people with physical illnesses as new psychotherapies, such as cognitive therapies, effectively lessen depression and suicidal ideation among older people diagnosed with medical problems.

Other Factors Associated with Suicide in Late Life

Fifty to 80% of all older people who committed suicide had been diagnosed with a major depression (Szanto et al., 1996; Blazer and Koenig, 1996; Conwell, 1992). Turvey, Conwell, and colleagues (2002) found that depression was the strongest predictor of late life suicide. Those who have a mixed depression and anxiety are especially vulnerable to suicide (Bartels, Coakley, et al., 2002). Suicide rates are also high among older people who often abuse substances, including alcohol, as well as prescription and nonprescription drugs. Those who have access to medications are more likely to attempt suicide than those to whom such substances are less readily available. Older people who have recently experienced loss, especially an accumulation of losses, are more vulnerable to depression and suicide than those who are fortunate enough to maintain their resources. More rigorous studies, for example, Heisel, Flett, and Besser (2002), that used specific suicide assessment instruments and examined specific psychological constructs, confirm that depression, combined with feelings of hopelessness, especially interpersonal hopelessness and pessimism about the future, are the most significant risk factors for suicide. These findings corroborate Baumeister's "escape from self" theory that suggests that people at risk for suicide are seeking a way to stop intense negative affect, disappointment, and painful self-awareness (Baumeister, 1990; Heisel et al., 2002).

Szanto and colleagues (1996) compared active and passive suicidal ideation among elderly depressed people. Active suicidal ideators were defined as people who were seriously thinking, planning, or wishing to commit suicide. Passive suicidal ideators referred to those who responded that they would avoid steps to save or maintain their life or that they had thoughts of killing themselves but that they would not do it. First, Szanto and colleagues corroborated earlier research indicating the salience of feelings of hopelessness among those who want to kill themselves. Both the passive and active ideators scored significantly higher on hopelessness on the Beck Depression Inventory than nonsuicidal ideators. Second, the overall scores for active and passive ideators on the Beck Depression Inventory were also higher, and they had more often attempted suicide in the past. Finally, Szanto and colleagues found that active suicidal ideators expressed more feelings related to self-disgust and self-hatred than the passive suicidal ideators. In general, there were more similarities between these two groups than differences. The findings suggest the importance of social workers' taking seriously all older people who express suicidal ideation, especially those who are depressed and feel hopeless. Szanto and colleagues also observed that self-report measures and semistructured interviews were effective tools for detecting suicidal ideation among older people. These researchers found the Beck Depression Inventory to be especially useful.

Attitude differences apparently also are important. According to Butler, Lewis, and Sunderland, (1998), older people who express more "lenient" or liberal views about assisted suicide have more risk factors for suicide, such as depression, alcoholism, and recent losses, than older adults who have more objections to assisted suicide. Llorente and colleagues (1996) hypothesize that the greater the loss in social status and resources, the greater the likelihood of depression and suicide. They postulate that this explains higher rates of suicide among older white males and, specifically, among older Cuban men, who are more likely to encounter disruptions or discontinuity in social and occupational status, than among older women or older people from minority backgrounds who have struggled with disenfranchisement and oppression throughout their lives. Studies suggest that many older people from traditionally oppressed groups learn coping strategies that allow them to manage the typical assaults of late life more effectively than can those who confront these challenges and other obstacles for the first time (Richardson, 1999b).

Older people use more lethal methods to attempt suicide than do younger people. For example, Butler and colleagues (1998) and Conwell, Duberstein, Connor, and colleagues (2002) report that firearms and explosives were the most commonly used methods of suicide among older people who attempted suicide in the United States. Other methods included drugs, guns, hanging, and jumping off high places. Their suicides tend to be more premeditated, with fewer warnings than those of younger adults (Conwell, Duberstein, Cox, et al., 1998). In addition, suicide rates are higher when older people have guns, specifically, handguns, in their homes (Conwell, Duberstein, Connor, et al., 2002). Older people are also more inclined to engage in what is referred to as "chronic suicide," which involves a process of slow deterioration because their will to live decreases and they become increasingly neglectful of self-care (Butler et al., 1998). According to Blazer and Koenig (1996), chronic suicide, from such causes as failure to eat, sustained drug and alcohol abuse, refusal to use life-sustaining medications, and self-neglect, is the most common form of suicide among older adults.

Assessment of Suicide in Late Life

The first and most important step that social workers must take toward intervening in suicide among older people is similar to the initial step with younger people. The social worker must know the warning signs of suicide and know how to acquire information about how great a risk an elderly client is for suicide. There are standard or key questions that all social workers should ask older people who are depressed, have a history of psychiatric illness, abuse substances, or express symptoms of depression. First, and most important, social workers should ask the person directly whether he is suicidal. A question such as, "Do you feel like killing yourself?" typically gets an honest response. Most people who are suicidal will respond truthfully to this question. One of the biggest mistakes that practitioners make is not asking the client whether she feels like killing herself, lest asking this question puts the idea in her head. If anything, by asking questions about suicide and death directly, social workers reveal that they are comfortable talking about death and suicide. This often minimizes the anxiety that clients have in talking about dying and their wish to kill themselves.

Most clients who are suicidal will acknowledge their feelings upon being asked whether they feel like killing themselves. Older people carry out more premeditated suicides and may not willingly volunteer the information that they are planning to kill themselves. But, if asked, they will usually admit to suicidal thoughts and plans. This is why it is so important for social workers to ask this question.

If an older person responds affirmatively to the first question and reveals that he feels suicidal, the social worker next should ask whether he has decided how he will kill himself. Among those who have thought carefully about how and where they will kill themselves, the risk for suicide increases. Therefore inquiring about the specificity of the plan is useful. The more detailed and specific the plan, the greater the risk. For example, an older client who responds by saying, yes, I have thought about killing myself when a social worker asks, could be a high risk. If the social worker then asks whether he has a plan about how to do it, and he says, "I planned on using a gun," the risk increases again. Clients who have plans to kill themselves are more likely to follow through than clients who provide a vague answer to the question. For example, many older clients who express suicidal ideation indicate that although they are tired of living and want to die, they could not kill themselves because of their religion. The risk of suicide among these older people is lower than it is for someone who has a specific plan worked out, a method that is highly lethal, such as a gun, and lives alone, so the chance of rescue is minimal.

It is important to ascertain the method by which people plan to kill themselves because some methods are more lethal than others. If the client suggests that he will use a gun or hang himself, the social worker should perceive this as another warning sign. Taking an overdose of medication and slitting one's wrists typically are perceived as less lethal methods of suicide. Social workers must make cautious inferences from the responses because older people have greater access to medications than younger people and have more opportunity to either take multiple drugs that could create deathly toxic reactions or take so much of a drug that they so seriously damage their bodies that they cannot rebound.

A related question involves the person's access to lethal substances or devices. As we mentioned earlier, if an older client acknowledges having a plan to kill herself, and she has easy access to highly toxic substances, the social worker should be more concerned than if the client has no ready access to drugs. If an older male client says he plans to use a gun to kill himself and has such a weapon in his desk drawer at home, his risk of suicide is greater than if he has to go buy a gun to use. Accessibility of means and lethality of the method are two important indicators that help social workers assess how likely the client is to commit suicide.

Finally, another critical question involves the client's previous history. The social worker should always ask the client whether she has ever attempted suicide in the past. It is a myth that those who attempt suicide are only seeking attention and are not serious about killing themselves; those who have tried to kill themselves are the ones who are most likely to eventually succeed. Practice makes perfect.

A few assessment instruments exist that social workers might use as a supplement to face-to-face interviews. One is the Geriatric Suicide Ideation Scale (GSIS), one of the only multidimensional instruments available for assessing suicidal ideation. The validity of this scale for predicting suicidal thoughts is excellent. The other is the Scale for Suicide Ideation (SSI), which is a clinician-administered scale and has good reliability and validity (see Beck, Kovacs, and Weissman, 1979, and Heisel et al., 2002, for more information on these instruments). The GSIS scale appears to be a more valid predictor of suicidal ideation and suicide risk than the SSI (Heisel et al., 2002).

Based on the substantial associations between suicide and depression and hopelessness, gerontological social workers should probe carefully for these feelings. If they are unable to determine older clients' affect in these areas, clinicians should use the GSIS or the Beck Hopelessness Scale, another strong scale, to assess these issues (Beck, Weissman, and Lester, 1974).

Warning Signs and the Suicide Lethality Index

A suicide lethality index that takes into account warning signs, background factors, and subjective distress helps social workers working with older people to determine the degree of suicide risk that the client represents and how to intervene.

Upon questioning by the social worker, the client usually reveals the warning signs that we discussed earlier: expressions of suicidal ideation, a plan for suicide, specificity of the plan, lethality of the method, access to method, and previous history.

The social worker should consider the warning signs in the context of background factors. For example, an older client who lives alone is higher on the suicide lethality index than someone who lives with family members. The most critical background factors that the social worker should consider are age, gender, marital status, ethnicity, living arrangements, employment situation or occupational status, substance abuse, and health. The profile of a high suicide risk is an older white man in poor health who lives alone and recently was widowed. He is depressed and admits that he feels like killing himself to escape the psychological pain that he feels. He has a gun at home and plans to kill himself on his wedding anniversary.

No one fits the profile this perfectly. Some older people exhibit some warning signs and background characteristics, but others do not. For these reasons social workers should use the suicide lethality index cautiously and only as a supplement to a more in-depth assessment of the client's subjective distress.

Basing their work on Shneidman's many years of investigation into suicide (1985), Leenaars, Maltsberger, and Neimeyer (1994) suggest that clinicians consider three subjective states when evaluating a client's risk for suicide: level of perturbation, lethality, and cognitive constriction. This information should supplement the clinician's assessment of the client's background factors.

Perturbation refers to the extent to which the person is upset, disturbed, troubled, anguished, and experiencing subjective distress and psychological pain. Although this is often difficult for clinicians to assess, it is one of the most significant predictors of suicide risk. Perturbation is also one of the first subjective states that social workers should try to mitigate in an older person who is suicidal. Later in the chapter we discuss specific suggestions for how to intervene under these circumstances, but in general social workers should model calmness and demonstrate acceptance of the person's suffering. The social worker whose client is suicidal will try to move toward empathy and the gentle introduction of alternatives and tolerance for examining options. Elderly people who are determined to commit suicide and have developed a detailed plan may exhibit high levels of perturbation but not necessarily admit suicidal ideation. Social workers who work with the client to lessen her degree of upset are more likely to bring about a positive outcome, regardless of how forthright the client is about revealing her suicide intentions.

The second subjective state, lethality, refers to the extent to which the client perceives death as a viable solution to his suffering. Some clients may exhibit high levels of perturbation but exclude suicide as an option because their religion forbids it. Those who view suicide as a reasonable option for solving life's problems are at greater risk for suicide than those who do not. Someone who considers joining her loved one in the afterlife is at great risk for suicide. Many elderly people philosophically believe that they will reunite with their loved ones after death. The extent to which these elderly people view death as an option is an indicator of how likely they are to commit suicide.

Cognitive constriction, a third high-risk subjective state, occurs when the elderly person perceives suicide as the sole option for escaping his suffering. This person is more apt to kill himself than is an elderly person who conceptualizes various problem-solving strategies. These individuals are considering only one way out of their troubles. When questioned about considering other options, clients who have high lethality levels respond by saying, "Killing myself is the only way I can get away from these horrible feelings and the ultimate despair that I feel right now." These elderly people feel hopeless. They perceive the consideration of alternatives to suicide to be a waste of time. As we noted earlier, elderly men who are recent widowers are especially vulnerable. When the death of a loved one occurs unexpectedly, complicated grief reactions, including suicidal wishes, are more common than when the surviving spouse prepared for the loss while caring for and observing her loved one's gradual decline. The pain and loss that some elderly people experience is intolerable, and they are often unable to contemplate continuing their lives without their spouse. These people have high levels of cognitive constriction and need help escaping from their limited perceptions. They exhibit what many clinicians refer to as tunnel vision. In these instances the goal of the social worker is to help the elderly person consider alternatives to suicide. Together the social worker and client can examine all the choices and evaluate the consequences that are likely to ensue from each option. This may include raising the client's awareness of how committing suicide will affect his loved ones or how inadequately this option resolves the problems.

The social worker assesses the older person's level of perturbation, lethality, and cognitive constriction. When clinicians analyze these subjective states as well as the specific background factors that we described earlier, social workers will have more success identifying those who are at greatest risk for suicide. This process becomes increasingly complex when the elderly person shows some warning signs and not others. In general social workers should err on the side of caution and intervene by ensuring as much protection for a suicidal elderly person as possible.

Interventions Recommended for Elderly People with Suicidal Ideation

Social workers treating elderly people who express a suicide wish must first determine how likely the person is to carry out her suicidal thoughts. A careful assessment that incorporates an evaluation of the background factors, as well as the warning signs that we described earlier, is critical in treating suicidal elderly people. The results of this assessment will determine how the social worker will intervene. These situations typically call for a crisis intervention model. But social workers who are working with suicidal people move quickly from the initial stage of building rapport to assessing the suicide risk and immediate intervention. Although clinicians expedite the initial listening stages, which underpin most models of crisis intervention, when working with people who are suicidal, developing rapport, listening empathetically, and helping the client to find meaning remain relevant in these cases. Without adequate rapport the social worker will acquire limited information from the client and inadequately assess the older person's risk for suicide. The elderly person must feel comfortable about revealing her suffering and pain and her suicidal intentions. Establishing rapport and listening empathetically are important in suicidal situations. This stage differs from that in nonsuicidal cases because the social worker must conduct a more detailed assessment more quickly of the client's intentions when he reveals that he has suicidal ideation. In these circumstances social workers are literally dealing with life and death issues. They are obligated to determine how great a risk the client poses for attempting suicide. Social workers assess suicide risk by using the suicide lethality index, which involves gathering background information and assessing the subjective state, specifically, levels of perturbation, lethality, and cognitive constriction. Once social workers determine an older person's risk for suicide, they know better how to intervene.

Hospitalization is sometimes necessary when the client's high level of subjective distress continues and especially if the client remains hopeless, which is one of the most significant predictors of suicide. In this instance social workers should know the procedures that they must follow in their agency and in their state to have an older client admitted for in-patient treatment. The respite from daily difficulties that the hospital environment offers is often therapeutic to older people who feel overwhelmed, depressed, and suicidal. This more secure environment allows clients in distress a relief from day-to-day maintenance activities. It provides a setting where they can safely let go and accept that others are caring for them. This "time-out" is necessary and helpful to some clients who are suicidal. Social workers should work swiftly toward the hospitalization of any client who is at high risk. A psychiatric facility that has a geriatric unit is preferable to hospitals without geriatric experts. In these specialized units the physicians, nurses, and social workers have special training in treating older people who are depressed and suicidal. As we discussed in chapter 6, recent research has shown that older people today often present with complex issues that require careful medical attention and assessment of multiple physical, psychological, and social factors.

The goals during the intervention phase are to help the client identify alternatives to suicide for alleviating her distress; to delay suicide, because most suicidal feelings abate; to decrease perturbation, lethality, and cognitive constriction; and, ultimately, to increase the client's involvement with others. The most significant predictors of late life suicide, according to the empirical studies that we presented earlier, demonstrate that hopelessness, especially social hopelessness, and negative thoughts about the future increase older adults' suicide risk. Gerontological social workers must attend to the older clients' painful negative affects if the clinicians are to reduce their clients' suicidal ideations, and the clinicians must instill hope.

These tasks are accomplished by using multiple modes of intervention, including individual interventions and family therapy, if possible.

Social workers must also develop community programs and advocate for the prevention of suicide by the elderly. Social workers who have developed programs have found that they in fact reduce the number of suicide attempts by older people. For example, Morrow-Howell, Becker, and Judy (1998) evaluated Link-Plus, a social work program used by a community crisis agency. This program provided case management and supportive services by telephone to older adults who were depressed, socially isolated, and needed assistance. These efforts reached the most vulnerable older people in the community, and the social workers' accessibility by telephone was especially important for those who lacked transportation. The Center for Elderly Suicide Prevention and Grief-related Services, a program of the Goldman Institute on Aging in San Francisco, offered another telephone program that included counseling and home visits for at-risk older people. Finally, the Gatekeepers Program of Spokane, Washington, involved the community by training meter readers, postal workers, bank personnel, and the fire department's emergency medical response teams to identify potentially suicidal older people living in the community (Raschko, 1997). The most socially isolated older people need aggressive outreach to find them.

CASE 7.1

In chapter 6 Mr. Antoine, an older white man in pain and socially isolated, was deemed a low risk for suicide after the social worker conducted a thorough assessment. Based on the suicide lethality index, most social workers should conclude that Mr. Antoine is at high risk for suicide. He is a white male with health problems, unmarried, and lives alone. Another social worker evaluates Mr. Antoine, who now feels suicidal, and learns that in addition to the high-risk demographic characteristics, Mr. Antoine exhibits several warning signs for suicide and demonstrates a distressed subjective state. First, the social worker asks Mr. Antoine whether he feels suicidal. This time he responds affirmatively to this question. Next, the social worker asks him whether he has thought about how he would kill himself. After he responds that he plans to use a gun, which is a highly lethal method, and that he has a gun at home in a drawer next to his bed, the social worker concludes that Mr. Antoine is a high risk for suicide. The social worker learns that Mr. Antoine plans to kill himself on the anniversary of his wife's death and that he intends to pull the trigger late at night when no one is likely to hear the shot. The method, detailed plan, and minimal chance of rescue all increase Mr. Antoine's risk of suicide.

The social worker also evaluates Mr. Antoine's subjective state by evaluating his level of perturbation, lethality, and cognitive constriction. Mr. Antoine exhibits high anxiety and reports that he can no longer tolerate the pain that he feels when he is alone and because he misses his wife. He says that, given all his medical problems and physical pain, his life is not worth living. Mr. Antoine is perturbed and perceives death as an escape from his suffering. He is cognitively constricted because he considers suicide the *only* reasonable solution.

The social worker talks with Mr. Antoine about alternatives to suicide. They outline and list other solutions that he might consider. As Mr. Antoine and the social worker discuss each option, Mr. Antoine gradually recognizes other possibilities. This process of considering alternative solutions helps the elderly client recognize other avenues that he might pursue. The act of evaluating alternatives to suicide is one of the most important interventions that social workers will use with elderly suicidal clients. At the same time, by listening reflectively, showing empathy, and emphasizing hopeful alternatives, the social worker also helps lower the client's level of perturbation. When the client becomes less perturbed and less committed to suicide as the only alternative, the social worker could consider working with the client on an outpatient basis. Several precautions are imperative. In this case the social worker would first ask Mr. Antoine to turn over his gun. It is important that the access to suicide be blocked by removing all potential suicide methods. Second, the social worker would ask Mr. Antoine's permission to talk to his extended family, as well as neighbors, to alert them to Mr. Antoine's feelings and intentions. These informal support systems are often underused and are an excellent resource for assistance. Third, the social worker should work with Mr. Antoine and his support system to arrange for someone to be available to him at all times, at least during this crisis period. Fourth, many social workers use suicide contracts with clients. This typically involves working with the client on a written agreement that specifies that if the client feels suicidal, he will refrain from acting on this impulse and will contact either the social worker or another mutually agreed-upon person as a first step. Most clients who are suicidal respond well to such a contract and usually do call the social worker when they are feeling suicidal. This arrangement is surprisingly very effective. Finally, social workers who work with clients at risk for suicide must remain accessible. They may meet with the clients several days a week rather than the traditional schedule of an hourlong office visit once a week. The social worker must convey to the client that he is available at any time if the client feels suicidal. During this crisis period the social worker engages in frequent interactions as needed with this client. Over time the social worker can lessen the frequency of contact while the client, now less perturbed and cognitively restricted, and the social worker uses a cognitive behavioral therapy approach, interpersonal intervention, psychopharmacological treatment, and any other interventions that the social worker can administer in an outpatient basis. If the client improves and feels less depressed and suicidal, the social worker infers that the immediate crisis is over and institutes other treatments. However, a client such as Mr. Antoine always remains at high risk for suicide, given his past history and background.

After the crisis the social worker must work with Mr. Antoine on long-term goals, that is, those that empower him and, in particular, restore hope. The recommended approach would be a collaborative intervention in which the social worker and Mr. Antoine together explore the sources contributing to his hopelessness as well as new activities in which he might participate. The first effort might require interpersonal therapy, described in chapter 6, and it might require family therapy, involving those with whom he quarrels or those from whom he has disengaged. The second effort, involving community and other empowering interventions, would address Mr. Antoine's feelings of hopelessness. The social worker and Mr. Antoine must brainstorm and identify pleasant activities in which he might engage. Many older depressed people have withdrawn from others and from rewarding participations that might empower and revitalize them. Practitioners must address the immediate crisis but also address these more ongoing, albeit more intractable, problems if they expect to alleviate depression and feelings of despair in older suicidal clients.

DISCUSSION QUESTIONS

1. What are the most significant predictors of suicide in late life?
2. How might you intervene differently with older suicidal clients than you would younger suicidal people?
3. What aspects of a biopsychosocial assessment are most important when assessing an older person's risk of suicide?
4. How might interventions that the social worker might use with an older client during a suicide crisis differ from those that the clinician might use after the crisis has resolved?

CHAPTER 8

Substance Abuse Among Older People

SUBSTANCE ABUSE BY ELDERLY PEOPLE is a neglected area in gerontological practice. Social workers' training in substance abuse typically emphasizes alcohol and drug problems among young and middle-aged adults. Clinicians learn little about the substance abuse problems of older people. Most practitioners underestimate the seriousness of substance abuse and misuse among older adults. Social workers also erroneously assume that elderly people are unlikely to respond to treatment. Some practitioners question why they should treat anyone with a drinking problem at such a late stage. Other clinicians believe that the consequences of drinking too much are innocuous for older people and may even keep their cholesterol level down. Although older people who drink moderate amounts of alcohol derive some health benefits, especially in cardiovascular functioning, they face more problems from consuming alcohol too frequently or too excessively (Blow and Barry, 2003).

These ageist attitudes deter social workers from evaluating and identifying alcohol and drug problems among older people. Contrary to prevailing views, studies (e.g., Linn, 1978; Carstensen, Rychtarik, and Prue, 1985; Kashner, Rodell, Ogden, Guggenheim, and Karson, 1992; and Atkinson, 1995; Lemke and Moos, 2002, 2003) show that older people complete and benefit from addiction treatment more often than younger people do. The inattention to older people's substance abuse problems is particularly troublesome, given the strong statistical associations between substance abuse and suicide, morbidity, and chronic health problems.

Those who drink alcohol excessively are especially vulnerable to serious health conditions, including gastritis, pancreatitis, chronic obstructive pulmonary disease, peptic ulcer disease, and psoriasis (Liberto, Oslin, and Ruskin, 1996). Long-term drinkers are more likely than nondrinkers to have reduced capabilities to combat infection and cancer, impaired immune systems, cirrhosis and liver diseases, decreased bone density, gastrointestinal bleeding, malnutrition, and mental health problems. They are also at greater risk for dementia and impairments in activities of daily living (Blow and Barry, 2003).

Drinking in late life can also exacerbate existing medical conditions, such as hypertension, cardiac arrhythmia, myocardial infarction, and cardiomyopathy, as well as increase the risk of hemorrhagic stroke. Drinking even small amounts of alcohol can cause problems for older people with a variety of conditions, including hypertension and diabetes mellitus.

The Center for Substance Abuse Treatment (CSAT; Blow, 1998) and the National Institute on Alcohol Abuse and Alcoholism (NIAAA) recommend no more than one drink per day (NIAAA, 1995) for individuals older than sixty-five who are in good health and are not taking psychoactive medications. Because older people are more sensitive to the effects of alcohol and metabolize it more slowly than young adults, similar amounts of alcohol have a greater effect on elderly people (Blow, 1998). Elderly people can experience substantial adverse consequences from consuming relatively small amounts of alcohol.

In the first part of this chapter we review the incidence rates and risk factors for alcohol and drug problems in late life. They underscore the significance of substance abuse problems among older people and the need for gerontological social workers to carefully evaluate older clients for alcohol and drug problems. Too many older people who would benefit from intervention remain misdiagnosed, underdiagnosed, and untreated. The assessment and treatment section, which comprises the second part of the chapter, discusses age-specific interventions that are often more appropriate for older people than established interventions that were developed for younger people.

CHARACTERISTICS OF SUBSTANCE ABUSE IN LATE LIFE

Incidence of Alcohol Problems

The general decline in diagnoses of substance abuse problems in later life (which is more typical of elderly whites than elderly members of minority groups) is attributed in part to the higher mortality rates among alcohol and drug abusers. Some studies have found that the mortality risk among alcohol abusers is as much as five times that for nonabusers of the same age and gender (Allen and Landis, 1997). One study found that female alcoholics died fifteen years earlier than women in general (U.S. General Accounting Office, 1995). Higher mortality rates are also found among those who have abused drugs and medications. Despite age declines in drinking, alcohol and substance abuse is the third leading health problem among those aged fifty-five and older (King, Van Hasselt, and Segal, 1994). Because the threshold for at-risk alcohol use decreases with advancing age, smaller amounts of alcohol cause physiological and psychological impairments in later life than bring about the same effects in younger drinkers.

Depending on the populations sampled, response rates, terms used, and methodologies, various studies have found that 3% to 25% of all older adults engage in "heavy alcohol use" and from 2.2% to 9.6% have moved on to "alcohol abuse." Of course, alcohol use and abuse are notoriously difficult to measure accurately because of the stigma associated with alcoholism and because denial is a common coping strategy for many problem drinkers. Community surveys estimate that 1% to 15% of older people engage in problem drinking (Blow and Barry, 2003); some estimates are higher, between 4% and 23% (Atkinson, 2002). About 2% to 4% of older men and about 0.5% to 1% of older women are alcohol dependent (Atkinson, 2002). Among hospitalized individuals older than sixty, 21% were diagnosed with alcoholism (U.S. Congress, 1992). The rates are much higher in nursing homes, ranging from 2.8% to 49%, depending on the institution and methods used (Joseph, 1997).

Researchers have also found high rates of alcohol use in some retirement communities (Atkinson, Tolson, and Turner, 1990). Few researchers have examined alcohol problems in nursing homes or assisted living facilities. W. L. Adams and Cox (1997) found that 20% to 25% of residents in certain retirement communities drank heavily. When W. Klein and Jess (2002) examined alcohol policies in more than one hundred intermediate care facilities and homes for older adults, they found many ambiguous policies about alcohol use and inattention to these issues.

Types of Alcohol Problems Among Elderly People

At-Risk and Problem Drinkers

CSAT, a division of the Substance Abuse and Mental Health Service Administration, created a consensus panel comprised of clinical researchers, clinicians, program administrators, and patient advocates to identify the most up-to-date incidence rates, assessment instruments, and treatment options for substance abuse problems in late life. The panel's conclusions (Blow, 1998; Barry, 1999) provide important guidelines for gerontological social workers. One recommendation offered by the panel involves classifying older drinkers. It recommends distinguishing "at-risk drinkers" from "problem drinkers" and including "heavy drinkers" in the problem drinker category when conceptualizing types of alcohol problems among older people. An at-risk drinker is "one whose patterns of alcohol use, although not yet causing problems, may bring adverse consequences, either to the drinker or to others" (Blow, 1998, p. xvi). Older people who drink and drive are examples of at-risk drinkers. Although older at-risk drinkers are often difficult to detect because they are inconspicuous and rarely get into trouble as a result of their drinking, they can be regular heavy drinkers or engage in binge drinking (Atkinson, Turner, and Tolson, 1998). At-risk drinkers are usually older people who have more than one drink a day. Problem drinkers consume more alcohol than at-risk drinkers and are often referred to treatment because of a specific problem, such as a legal problem (e.g., driving while drinking), medical complication (e.g., cirrhosis of the liver), psychiatric difficulty (e.g., a mood disorder), or interpersonal conflicts (e.g., with a spouse or adult child) (Atkinson et al., 1998; Blow and Barry, 2003). They often appear at hospital emergency rooms because they have fallen or suffered some other sort of accident, liver disease, delirium, malnutrition, incontinence, or hypothermia (Atkinson et al., 1998). Problem drinkers sometimes appear at senior meal sites or at shelters for the homeless, and they often present with substantial social deficits. They are also found on medical wards and in nursing homes. The adverse event(s), rather than the drinking itself, typically impel treatment for older problem drinkers. Blow and Barry (2003) characterize alcohol abuse as continued drinking despite negative consequences and the inability to fulfill responsibilities. See the criteria for substance dependence outlined in the *DSM-IV* (1994).

Early Versus Late Onset Problem Drinkers

Late onset problem drinkers experience their first problems with alcohol after the age of forty or fifty. They tend to drink smaller amounts and less often than early onset problem drinkers (Brennan and Moos, 1991). Because their drinking problems are less severe, late onset problem drinkers encounter fewer alcohol-related problems, such as driving while drinking, and only occasional family conflicts compared to early onset problem drinkers.

About one-third of older adults with alcohol problems are late onset problem drinkers (Bucholz, Sheline, and Helzer, 1995), and about one-third of late onset problem drinkers are women. The percentage of women who are late onset problem drinkers increases with age. Bucholz and colleagues (1995) observed that among women aged 50 to 59, 16% reported first having a symptom of alcoholism after age 49. The percentage increased to 24% among women aged 60 to 69 and to 28% among those aged 70 to 79. Among men in these age groups, the percentages were smaller (3% of men aged 50 to 59, 15% of those aged 60 to 69, and 14% of those aged 70 to 79) (Bucholz et al., 1995).

Late onset problem drinkers are the most common type of problem drinkers among elderly people, and, like younger alcoholics, they often drink because they cannot cope with their problems. Although some speculate that late onset drinkers are more influenced than their nonalcoholic peers by financial problems and life events, such as widowhood and retirement (Liberto and Oslin, 1997), few studies support the notion that stress precipitates late life drinking problems. Earlier studies, with fewer controls, smaller samples, and biased samples, indicated that an association might exist between stress and problem drinking among older people, but recent studies show no relationship between stress and excessive alcohol use in the later years (Welte, 1998). Instead, recent data show that older adults who are under the most stress drink less than those without stress, that the most active and vigorous elderly people drink the most, and that alcohol may buffer the negative effects of stress and depression when used in moderate amounts (see Welte, 1998). The most critical factor associated with late life problem drinking is a history of alcohol problems during early adulthood, according to Welte (1998). These findings challenge previous assumptions about the causes of late life problem drinking and illustrate how commonly accepted assumptions about the elderly are sometimes extremely inaccurate.

Early onset problem drinkers often have had lifelong patterns of problem drinking. They have more psychiatric disorders than late onset problem drinkers, especially major depression and bipolar disorders, and they sometimes use alcohol to self-medicate these conditions (Liberto et al., 1996). Studies consistently show that early onset problem drinkers have a more extensive family history of alcoholism, more diagnoses of antisocial personality, and a poorer prognosis than late onset problem drinkers (Gomberg and Zucker, 1998). See table 8.1 for characteristics of early onset and late onset problem drinkers.

Because their drinking usually increases with age, early onset problem drinkers may experience such alcohol-related health impairments as diabetes mellitus, cirrhosis, and pancreatitis. In severe cases cognitive impairments can occur in visuospatial, memory, and perceptual-motor function. Many cognitive deficits improve when individuals cease drinking, but some functions never return fully (Liberto et al., 1996; Allen and Landis, 1997). Both early and late onset problem drinkers use alcohol almost daily in social and nonsocial settings, and both types drink to mitigate psychological pain and emotional distress (Blow, 1998).

Risk Factors for Alcohol Abuse in Later Life

Gender

Men at all ages are more likely than women to report problems with alcohol, and men are four times more likely than women to abuse alcohol and become dependent on it (Grant, Harford, Dawson, Chou, Dufour, and Pickering, 1994). According to findings from the Epidemiological Catchment Area study, alcohol abuse and dependence are the most common psychiatric disorders among men (J. K. Myers, Goldman, Hingson, Scotch, and Mangione, 1984). Although men abuse

TABLE 8.1 Clinical Characteristics of Early and Late Onset Problem Drinkers

Variable	Early Onset	Late Onset
Age at onset	Various, e.g., < 25, 40, 45	Various, e.g., > 55, 60, 65
Gender	Higher proportion of men than women	Higher proportion of women than men
Socioeconomic status	Tends to be lower	Tends to be higher
Drinking in response to stressors	Common	Common
Family history of alcoholism	More prevalent	Less prevalent
Extent and severity of alcohol problems	More psychosocial, legal problems, greater severity	Fewer psychosocial, legal problems, lesser severity
Alcohol-related chronic illness (e.g., cirrhosis, pancreatitis, cancers)	More common	Less common
Psychiatric comorbidities	Cognitive loss more severe, less reversible	Cognitive loss less severe, more reversible
Age-associated medical problems aggravated by alcohol (e.g., hypertension, diabetes mellitus, drug-alcohol interactions)	Common	Common
Treatment compliance and outcome	Possibly less compliant; Relapse rates do not vary by age of onset	Possibly more compliant; Relapse rates do not vary by age of onset

Source: Blow, 1998, p. 21.

alcohol more than women at all ages, late onset problem drinking is more common for women (W. L. Adams and Cox, 1997; Blow, 1998; Dupree and Schonfeld, 1999). Experts, for example, Blow and Barry (2003), are now reporting that the risks related to problem drinking are greater among older women than among older men because the women outlive their spouses, confront additional losses, tolerate alcohol poorly, and often mix alcohol with prescription medications, especially benzodiazepines.

Most studies probably underestimate the amount of alcohol use and abuse by older women. Definitions of alcohol problems that are based on the number of drinks that a person consumes are misleading when applied to older women. Few studies take into account women's lower tolerance for alcohol, and the health risks of alcohol are greater for older women than for older men who drink the same amount because men and women metabolize alcohol differently. At any age women are more sensitive than men to the effects of alcohol and consequently develop alcohol dependence faster. Many older women are surprised when they develop alcohol-related health problems after drinking less alcohol than men who do not develop those problems.

Many practitioners fail to detect alcohol problems in older women because they resist disclosing how much alcohol they use, drink alone, and often hide their drinking from others. Denial of alcohol problems may be especially common among the current cohort of older women, who often feel embarrassed about drinking and consider excessive drinking inappropriate for elderly women. In addition, those who mix alcohol with prescription drugs (a potentially fatal combination) may report use of the medication but not of the alcohol (Glied and Kofman, 1995). Many health professionals also misinterpret older women's symptoms of alcohol abuse as age-related problems or other physical symptoms, simply because clinicians do not expect an older woman to have a drinking problem. See table 8.2 for some signs and symptoms of alcohol problems among older women that could lead to a diagnosis of problem drinking. These signs suggest that social workers should probe carefully for and at least rule out drinking.

Ethnic Differences

The results from studies that have compared elderly members of minority groups and elderly whites remain contradictory, in part because ethnic differences in drinking typically vary by income and type of drinking. Gomberg and Zucker (1998), for example, found that among low-income groups, African Americans drink more and experience more alcohol-related problems than white men. Jackson, Williams, and Gomberg (1998) observed that middle-income African Americans drink more than African Americans from lower and higher income groups. In contrast to the pattern of age decline in drinking found among whites, problem drinking increases with age among African Americans. Similar age increases in drinking appear among Hispanics. Hispanic males have one of the highest rates of problem drinking among older adults (Zucker, 1998).

In a review of the literature Kail and DeLaRosa (1998) concluded that Latinos drink more than Latinas among all age groups and that alcohol consumption in-

TABLE 8.2 Signs and Symptoms of Alcohol Problems in Older Women

• Anxiety	• Increased tolerance to alcohol or medications
• Depression, mood swings	• Memory loss
• Disorientation	• New difficulties in decision making
• Poor hygiene	• Falls, bruises, burns
• Family problems	• Idiopathic seizures (i.e., seizures with an unknown origin or cause)
• Financial problems	• Sleep problems
• Headaches	• Social isolation
• Incontinence	• Poor nutrition

Source: Blow and Barry, 2003; Barry, Oslin, and Blow, 2001.

creases after the age of fifty among certain subgroups. Although more research on the use and abuse of alcohol among older people is needed, these reports suggest that marked cultural and intragroup variations permeate late life drinking.

Income

Many studies show that the frequency of drinking increases with income but that alcohol abuse and dependence occur more often among lower income groups, at least among men (Liberto et al., 1996). Among older women, the most affluent drink more than women in lower income groups. Older women who have annual incomes of more than $40,000 are three times more likely to drink heavily than older women who have annual incomes of less than $40,000 (National Center on Addiction and Substance Abuse [NCASA], 1998).

Marital Status

Some studies, for example, Glynn, Bouchard, LoCastro, and Laird (1985), suggest that unmarried older men drink more and have more alcohol problems than elderly married men, whereas others report no marital status differences (Sulsky, Jacques, Otradovec, Hartz, and Russell, 1990). Married women drink more than unmarried women, but elderly divorced women drink more heavily than older married women (Bucholz et al., 1995). Problem drinking occurs more frequently among never married, divorced, and separated elderly women than among elderly married women (Blow, 2003; see also Wilsnack, Vogeltanz, Diers, and Wilsnack, 1995, for more discussion of marital status and problem drinking).

Medical Problems

Although older people in good health are more likely to drink than elderly people in poor health, older adults with health problems abuse alcohol more frequently than those who are healthy. Several studies document that hospitalized older people have higher rates of alcoholism (almost 50%) than elders who receive treatment as outpatients (Buschsbaum, Buchanan, Lawton, and Schnoll, 1991; Liberto et al., 1996). The greatest number of older people in poor health with current or past problems with alcohol are living in nursing homes. More studies of alcohol use and abuse in nursing homes are needed.

Depression

Depression contributes substantially to alcohol abuse. Alcoholic women are twice as likely as nonalcoholic women to be depressed, and alcoholic women are four times more likely than men to be depressed (Brennan, Moos, and Kim, 1993). Many older women drink alone to lessen their depression and feelings of loneliness (Gomberg, 1990). When depressed older people experience health problems or transportation problems that increase their social isolation, their risks of alcohol abuse are even higher.

Psychosocial Factors

Liberto and Oslin (1997) proposed a "biopsychosocial hypothesis" to explain problem drinking in late life. They suggest that certain physiological characteristics, personality traits, psychopathological conditions, and social experiences interact to cause alcohol misuse—and sometimes alcohol abuse—in the later years. Atkinson (2000) suggests a biopsychosocial model of late life problem drinking that considers three factors: predisposing factors (family history of alcohol problems, previous substance abuse, previous pattern of substance consumption, and personality traits); factors that increase substance exposure and consumption level, such as gender (alcohol and illicit drugs for men and sedative-hypnotics and anxiolytics for women), chronic illness associated with pain, insomnia, anxiety, long-term prescriptions, caregiver overuse of as-needed medication, life stress, loss, social isolation, negative affects, family collusion, drinking partners, and discretionary time and money; and factors that increase the effects and abuse potential of substances, such as age-associated drug sensitivity, chronic medical illness, and use of other medications that may interact with each other and with alcohol.

Access to alcohol and opportunities to drink also contribute to late life alcohol abuse problems. A study that queried older people six months after their retirement and again at the end of their first year of retirement found that their drinking had increased (Richardson and Kilty, 1995). Older people who are accustomed to occasional social drinking may drink more after retirement, when they have more time and easy access to alcohol. In some retirement communities residents routinely drink with dinner meals and at weekend socials and sometimes unwittingly develop dependency on alcohol. Retirement communities that link socializing with drinking have more residents who begin to drink excessively after moving into the community (Alexander and Duff, 1988).

Research on the reasons why older people abuse alcohol in later life remain contradictory, which is not surprising, given the heterogeneity within this population. Older people drink for different reasons, depending on their gender, ethnic status, and medical condition. These variations underscore the need for comprehensive assessments of an older person's drinking and interventions tailored for each client's unique circumstances.

Incidence of Prescription and Over-the-Counter Drug Problems

Older people use prescription drugs approximately three times more often than the general population, and their use of over-the-counter medications is even higher (U.S. Department of Health and Human Services, 1999). Although older people account for only 13% of the population, they consume 25% to 33% of all prescription drugs (Finlayson, 1998; Ondus, Hujer, Mann, and Mion, 1999). About 83% of adults older than sixty-five take at least one prescription drug, and 30% of those older than sixty-five take eight or more prescription drugs daily (Blow, 1998; Oslin and Holden, 2002). In nursing homes half of all residents take at least one psychoactive drug (Sandburg, 1998), and about 82% of nursing home residents use over-the-counter medications. The combination of prescription and over-the-counter medications is especially troublesome for elderly people, who experience more than half of all adverse drug reactions that result in hospitalization (Chastain, 1992).

The most common over-the-counter drugs used by older people are analgesics, vitamins, and laxatives, whereas the most frequently prescribed drugs for this age group are diuretics, cardiovascular drugs, and sedative-hypnotics. The prevalence of benzodiazepine dependence is about 11% (Finlayson and Hofman, 2002). Twenty percent of all prescriptions for tranquilizers and 38% of prescriptions for hypnotics were written for older adults in 1991. In addition, older women are 37% more likely to receive a prescription for a tranquilizer than men during a visit to their physician (Simoni-Wastila, 1998). Many elderly people misuse medications, that is, they underuse, overuse, or erratically use medications, and some become dependent on drugs, which can lead to abuse (Gomberg and Zucker, 1998).

Types of Drug Problems

Patterns of use among older adults are often categorized as proper use, misuse, abuse, and dependence. Misuse is the most common type of medication problem among older people and typically results from misunderstanding or forgetting directions. It includes taking more or less than the recommended dose, skipped dosages, medicine taken for contraindicated purposes or used in conjunction with other medications with undesirable interactions, or consumption with alcohol. Physicians contribute to misuse by prescribing unnecessarily high dosages, neglecting to consider potential drug interactions with other medications, and failing to clearly explain how medications should be used.

Elderly people misuse medications for various reasons, including (1) lack of judgment or misconceptions about the prescribed drugs; (2) inability to manage the medication regimen, either because it is complex or because the older person has persistent memory problems and needs regular supervision; (3) insufficient resources for purchasing or storing medications; and (4) a desire for results other than those for which the medications were prescribed, such as using pain pills to sleep, relax, or cope with negative feelings.

Misuse can progress into abuse and dependence in some circumstances. Abuse occurs when problems related to the medication emerge at home or in risky situations, such as driving. Dependence occurs when tolerance for the medication arises, withdrawal symptoms appear, and the older person neglects his regular activities and is unable to go without the medication. Dependence includes situations in which the older person uses the medication for longer than recommended or needed, her inordinate efforts to obtain the drug interfere with her daily routines, or her use of the medication continues despite adverse physical or psychological effects. In all these circumstances an older person can develop problems without realizing it. For example, an elderly woman who is prescribed a tranquilizer for a specific traumatic incident may unwittingly continue to take the medication until she develops a tolerance for it. When she later stops taking the drug, she can experience withdrawal effects and may start taking the drug again to alleviate these symptoms.

Risk Factors for Drug Misuse and Abuse

Gender

Older women are at a much greater risk of abusing prescription medication, especially psychoactive drugs and benzodiazepines, than are older men (Finlayson and Davis, 1994; Finlayson, 1995). Older women take an average of five prescription drugs at the same time, and about 25% (6.4 million) use at least one psychoactive prescription medication (Baum, Kennedy, Knapp, Juergens, and Faich, 1988; H. A. Pincus et al., 1998). The correlates of psychoactive drug use among women include middle and late life divorce, widowhood, limited education, poor health and chronic somatic problems, high stress, lower income, depression, and anxiety (Closser and Blow, 1993; Gomberg, 1995). Because older women are more sensitive than men to many medications, especially psychoactive prescription drugs, and have a reduced tolerance, older women often develop substance abuse problems more quickly than older men and with greater consequences (NCASA, 1998).

Elderly women are especially vulnerable to the adverse effects of benzodiazepines, The sedative effects of tranquilizers can lead to falls, insomnia, car accidents, and unpleasant withdrawal effects, and they can also increase depression. Long-term use of these drugs can lead to confusion and memory loss. Although many doctors now prescribe the shorter-acting benodiazepines, such as Xanax and Ativan, and medications that are less addictive and sedating, including Buspar, Prozac, and Zoloft, the potential for unintentional misuse, through inadvertently mixing medications, misunderstanding directions, or developing a tolerance and physical dependence, remains high for older women.

Ethnicity and Income

Data on racial and ethnic patterns of drug use by older people are limited. White women use benzodiazepines more often than do minority women, with one exception: older Hispanic women report higher rates and longer periods of using Valium, Librium, and Tranxene than older non-Hispanic women (CSAT, 1994; Page, Rio, Sweeney, and McKay, 1985).

Older women with incomes of more than $75,000 are 44% more likely to report using psychiatric prescription drugs than older women with incomes that are less than $15,000 a year, but affluent women presumably have easier access to prescription medications (NCASA, 1998).

ASSESSMENT OF SUBSTANCE ABUSE IN OLDER PEOPLE

Assessing Alcohol Abuse

If social workers work within an integrated practice model, they can assess potential alcohol problems in older adults on several levels. At the least intensive level social workers can integrate questions about alcohol use when they attend to other tasks, such as discharge planning, case management, care planning, or counseling for other problems. The consensus panel of CSAT recommends asking the following questions (Blow, 1998, p. 50):

Do you ever drink alcohol?
How much do you drink when you do drink?
Do you ever drink more than four drinks on one occasion?
Do you ever drink when you're lonely or upset?
Does drinking help you feel better [or get to sleep more easily, etc.]? How do you feel the day after you drink?
Have you ever wondered whether your drinking interferes with your health or any other aspects of your life in any way?
Where and with whom do you typically drink? (Drinking alone at home alone signals at-risk or potentially abusive drinking.)
How do you typically feel just before your first drink on a drinking day?
What do you typically expect when you think about having a drink? (Positive expectations or consequences of alcohol use in the presence of negative affect and inadequate coping skills are associated with problem drinking.)

Social workers can usually ask these questions during conversations with an older person about his health, nutrition, social functioning, or use of services.

Screening instruments offer social workers useful tools for conducting preliminary but systematic assessments of an older person's drinking behaviors that easily supplement informal discussions about alcohol use.

The CAGE Questionnaire Screen

The CAGE is an easily administered screening instrument that takes only about one minute to complete (Ewing, 1984). It consists of four questions that are scored with a zero for no and one point for yes. (The acronym CAGE derives from key words—italicized here—in each question.) The questions are

1. Have you ever felt you should *cut down* on your drinking?
2. Have people *annoyed* you by criticizing your drinking?
3. Have you ever felt bad or *guilty* about your drinking?
4. Have you ever had a drink first thing in the morning to steady your nerves or to get rid of a hangover (*eye opener*)?

High scores indicate problems with alcohol, and a score of more than two points is clinically relevant. The CAGE will identify the most serious problem drinkers, including those with abuse and dependence, but will miss less serious problem drinkers as well as those in the early stages of alcohol abuse. In addition, the validity of the CAGE for older adults, and for older women in particular, is questionable (Blow and Barry, 2003; Moore, Seeman, Morgenstern, Beck, and Reuben, 2002). Moore and colleagues (2002) recommend using both the CAGE and MAST-G (discussed next) when screening older people because these instruments tend to measure different problems and the CAGE is less sensitive to many older people's issues.

The MAST-G

The Michigan Alcoholism Screening Test—Geriatric Version (MAST-G) was developed specifically for older people. It is also appropriate for screening older women (Blow and Barry, 2003). It is usually completed in writing and takes about twenty minutes (Blow, 1998). It contains twenty-four questions, including:

After drinking, have you ever noticed an increase in your heart rate or beating in your chest?

When talking with others, do you ever underestimate how much you actually drink?

Does alcohol make you so sleepy that you often fall asleep in a chair?

Does having a drink help you sleep?

Do you like to end an evening with a nightcap?

Have you ever increased your drinking after experiencing a loss in your life?

In general, would you prefer to have a few drinks at home rather than go out to social events?

Do you usually take a drink to relax or calm your nerves?

When you feel lonely, does having a drink help?

See Blow (1998) for more information about this instrument.

The MAST-G will effectively identify those with drinking problems, but it will also uncover drinkers who do not have clear alcohol problems. The MAST-G works well in various settings, including hospitals, nursing homes, counseling centers, senior citizen centers, and adult day care centers.

The Alcohol Use Disorders Identification Test (AUDIT)

The Alcohol Use Disorders Identification Test (AUDIT) is a ten-item screening instrument, developed by Babor, de la Fuenta, Saunders, and Grant (1992), that is based on the World Health Organization's evaluation of harmful and hazardous alcohol consumption. It is the only alcohol-screening instrument that practitioners can use with older people from nontraditional and diverse ethnic backgrounds, although the applicability of the instrument to older people needs further study (see Barbor et al., 1992, or Blow, 1998, for more detail about AUDIT).

Other Screening Instruments

The Alcohol-Related Problems Survey (ARPS) is an excellent and valid tool for assessing drinking problems among older people (Moore, Morton, and Beck, 1999). Another useful instrument is the Drinking Problem Index (DPI), a seventeen-item measure designed to detect alcohol problems among older people (Finney, Moos, and Brennan, 1991). This index focuses on negative consequences of drinking, excessive use, dependence, and drinking for escape. Two self-report instruments, ARPS and its shorter version, Short ARPS (SHARPS), improve upon other measures by identifying older people who will experience adverse medical consequences from excessive alcohol abuse or dangerous interactions from mixing alcohol and medications. These have high sensitivity and adequate psychometric properties (Moore, Beck, Babor, Hays, and Reuben, 2002).

Another screening measure that shows promise with older people is the U-Open Screen, which emerged from the Substance Use Disorders Diagnostic Schedule (SUDDS). The U-Open Screen examines factors that are especially relevant to older people, such as unplanned use of alcohol, objections, preoccupation with use, use in response to emotional distress, and neglect of responsibilities.

Clinical Assessments

Social workers who suspect that older clients have alcohol problems should clinically assess their drinking behavior. Many practitioners have successfully used the Substance Use Disorders Diagnostic Schedule—IV (SUDDS-IV) to assess potential substance abuse among older people. This tool includes sixty-four questions to help clinicians diagnose substance abuse problems according to the *DSM-IV* (1994) criteria (Hoffmann and Harrison, 1995). The SUDDS-IV is administered during interviews and requires about one hour to complete. Older people simply respond yes or no to questions about alcohol and drug use, stress, anxiety, and depression.

The Addiction Severity Index (ASI) is also an appropriate instrument to use with older people (Satre, Mertens, Arean, and Weisner, 2003). It evaluates medical, employment, drug, alcohol, legal, psychiatric, and family/social and legal problems in the client's lifetime and past thirty days. The CSAT consensus panel recommends that clinicians use age-appropriate criteria, which we discuss in the sections that follow, when applying *DSM-IV* criteria for substance dependence and substance abuse in older people.

Modifying DSM-IV Criteria for Use with Older People

When applying the *DSM-IV* (1994) criteria to older people, social workers should consider several issues. First, factors that involve failure to meet work, legal, and school obligations are irrelevant diagnostic criteria for older people who are retired and less likely to come in contact with legal authorities. Also, diagnoses based on self-report are limited by the reluctance of many older people to disclose alcohol problems; they are more likely than people in younger age cohorts to feel stigmatized by a diagnosis of alcohol abuse. In addition, some elderly people are unable to accurately report the amount and frequency of their drinking. Another factor to consider is that many older people are unaware of physical and psychological problems created by substances that their physicians prescribed and recommended. Physicians sometimes overlook substance abuse problems among older people and may prescribe psychoactive medications that worsen existing conditions (NCASA, 1998). Further, the use of tolerance as a criterion is problematic for elderly people because of their greater sensitivity to substances. Clinicians who disregard age differences in drug tolerance may fail to diagnose older people who would benefit from substance abuse treatment. An older person with low tolerance to alcohol, for example, could still have a drinking problem; conversely, an older person with high tolerance is not necessarily physiologically dependent. Also, the *DSM-IV* criteria ignore the many deleterious health effects (such as cognitive impairments, diabetes, and hypertension) that moderate alcohol consumption can have on older people. Finally, marked withdrawal effects can occur among older

TABLE 8.3 Applying *DSM-IV* Diagnostic Criteria to Older Adults with Alcohol Problems

Criteria	Special Considerations for Older Adults
1. Tolerance	May have problems even with low intake because of increased sensitivity to alcohol and higher blood alcohol levels.
2. Withdrawal	Many late onset alcoholics do not develop physiological dependence.
3. Taking larger amounts or over a longer period than was intended	Increased cognitive impairment can interfere with self-monitoring; drinking can exacerbate cognitive impairment and monitoring.
4. Unsuccessful efforts to cut down or control use	Same issues across lifespan.
5. Spending much time to obtain and use alcohol and to recover from effects	Negative effects can occur with relatively low use.
6. Giving up activities because of alcohol use	May have fewer activities, making detection of problems more difficult.
7. Continuing use despite physical or psychological problems caused by use	May not know or understand that problems are related to use, even after receiving medical advice.

Note: Diagnostic criteria for alcohol dependence are subsumed within the *DSM-IV*'s general criteria for substance dependence. Dependence is defined as a "maladaptive pattern of substance use, leading to clinically significant impairment or distress, as manifested by three (or more) of the following, occurring at any time in the same 12-month period" (*DSM-IV,* 1994, p. 181). Listed here are special factors to consider when applying *DSM-IV* criteria to older adults with suspected alcohol problems.
Source: Blow, 1998, p. 18.

problem drinkers after insubstantial alcohol consumption. Delirium tremors are more common among elderly people than among younger adults during withdrawal (Brower, 1998), and these often lead to more frequent and longer hospitalizations. See table 8.3 for suggestions about how to apply *DSM-IV* criteria to older people who may have problems with alcohol.

Assessing Prescription Drug Use

Although no effective screening tools for prescription drug misuse or abuse by older people currently exist, the CSAT consensus panel has identified several discriminating questions that practitioners can ask (Blow, 1998, p. 50). These include

1. Do you see more than one health care provider regularly? If so, why?
2. Have you switched doctors recently?
3. What prescription drugs are you taking? Are you having any problems with them?

4. Where do you get your prescriptions filled?
5. Do you use any nonprescription medications? If so, what, why, how much, how often, and how long?

A more in-depth assessment should be made of an older client who seems confused about her prescriptions, sees more than one doctor, uses more than one pharmacy, or seems reluctant to discuss her drug use (Sullivan and Fleming, 1997). Additional warning signs of medication problems include

- Excessive worrying about whether a prescription psychoactive drug is really working or complaints that the drug has lost its effectiveness, suggesting tolerance
- Displaying detailed knowledge about a specific psychoactive drug and attaching great significance to its efficacy and personal effectiveness
- Worrying about having enough pills or about whether it is time to take them, to the extent that other activities revolve around the dosage schedule
- Continuing to request and to use refills when the condition for which the drug was originally prescribed has or should have improved, or other signs of resistance to stopping or reducing use of the medication
- Complaining about doctors who refuse to write prescriptions for the drug
- Self-medicating, by increasing doses or by supplementing the prescribed drug with over-the-counter medications
- Excessive sleeping during the day

INTERVENTIONS FOR SUBSTANCE ABUSE PROBLEMS IN OLDER PEOPLE

Specific Interventions for Alcohol Problems

Many older people need treatment for alcohol problems, but few receive it. Social workers and other practitioners assume that drug and alcohol abuse are intractable problems in older people, even though studies demonstrate that older people respond just as well (and sometimes better) to alcohol treatment as younger people (Lemke and Moos, 2003; Reid and Anderson, 1997; Fitzgerald and Mulford, 1992; Dupree, Broskowski, and Schonfeld, 1984; Helzer, Carey, and Miller, 1984).

Although researchers have evaluated the effectiveness of a wide variety of alcohol treatment programs, few have focused on alcohol programs for older people. Treatment improvement protocols (TIPs), which are published periodically by CSAT, provide the most up-to-date information on treatments for older people.

Blow and Barry (2003) have examined several alcohol treatment programs for older people and for older women. Based on the recommendations of the CSAT consensus panel, they advise practitioners to proceed slowly with older people to allow for their hearing, visual, and cognitive problems. In addition, panel members noted that many older people resist talking about private concerns, especially to strangers, require home visits, and respond less well to traditional confrontational approaches (Blow, 1998). Alcoholics Anonymous meetings that are age specific, less confrontational, and more flexible about alcohol consumption, for example, generally work better with older drinkers than regular AA groups.

Detoxification

Social workers must first help older problem drinkers decide whether they need medical care for detoxification and, if so, whether inpatient or outpatient treatment is more appropriate. Elderly drinkers are more likely than younger ones to require inpatient treatment because they are typically at greater risk for medical complications. Dangerous abstinence reactions, such as seizures or delirium, can occur during alcohol withdrawal, especially if alcohol use was excessive for prolonged periods and then abruptly stopped. Older people who are suicidal, have serious mental health problems or medical conditions that are unstable or uncontrolled, or need twenty-four-hour care will require careful monitoring in inpatient settings. When multiple addictions, for example, to alcohol and certain prescription drugs, are involved, hospitalization is usually unavoidable. Inpatient detoxification is also recommended for socially isolated elderly people who live alone, have continued access to abused substances, or respond poorly to outpatient treatment.

Older people should take lower doses of benzodiazepines than younger people if those medications are prescribed during detoxification. Doctors should begin with one-third to one-half the usual adult dose for twenty-four to forty-eight hours and carefully monitor these patients' reactions (Blazer, 2004; Blow, 1998).

Age-Specific Approaches

Although older people benefit from mixed-age alcohol treatment programs as much as younger people, some experts maintain that age-specific substance abuse programs work better with older people for several reasons (Atkinson, 1995; Blow, 1998; Lemke and Moos, 2002, 2003). First, older people frequently drink for different reasons than younger people. For example, many older people drink to combat loneliness, depression, loss, and chronic pain (Schonfeld and Dupree, 1995). In addition, older clients usually respond better when treatment moves more slowly, repeats important issues, provides emotional support, and avoids confrontation. Group sessions that include reminiscence promote bonding and support among elderly people from the same generation. Older clients frequently require compensatory aids to assist them with their visual and hearing impairments and other physical disabilities. Daytime meetings and appointments are also more appropriate for elderly people, who may see poorly at night or fear going out in the evening. The most effective programs combine cognitive behavioral approaches that teach older people social skills to restore their social supports and management techniques to mitigate depression, grief, and loneliness (Blow, Walton, and Chermack, 2000; Schonfeld, Dupree, and Dickson-Fuhrmann, 2000).

Brief Intervention

Brief interventions without intensive care for detoxification are especially efficacious for older adults who are not alcohol dependent but need to reduce their alcohol consumption. Brief intervention is also recommended for older people who are resistant to specialized treatment but agree to explore their fears about treatment and alcohol abstinence or reduction. Many late onset problem drinkers with milder alcohol problems are excellent candidates for brief intervention, which can occur during home visits, at adult day care programs, or during the course of long-term interventions. These interventions are flexible, goal oriented, and, of course, expeditious, qualities that are particularly important for older clients (see Barry, Oslin, and Blow, 2001, for specific guidelines for implementing brief interventions).

Confrontation is generally not recommended for older problem drinkers (Blow, 1998). Studies increasingly show that confrontation only strengthens denial and resistance to treatment among older people (W. R. Miller, Benefield, and Tonigan, 1993). When a confrontation meeting is necessary with an older client who becomes confused easily, only one or two relatives or close friends should attend; grandchildren should not participate. References to highly charged terms, such as *addict* or *alcoholic*, should also be avoided.

Motivational Enhancement Therapy

The goal of motivational enhancement therapy (MET) is to motivate clients to stop or reduce their drinking based on individualized feedback about drinking patterns and the effects of drinking on the client's physical health. It involves four treatment sessions over twelve weeks after a comprehensive assessment of an older person's drinking behaviors and patterns (DiClemente, Bellino, and Neavins, 1999). Social workers usually provide clients with feedback about their drinking during the first session and review the frequency of the drinking, intensity (amount of drinking), level of intoxication, risk for negative consequences (specifically, liver function and neurological function), and risk factors for alcohol problems (such as family history of drinking, tolerance, and age-specific alcohol effects). The social worker then devises a treatment plan that delineates goals, how the client will achieve them, and the support that the client will need. MET is client centered and tailored to an older person's drinking profile. Clients set the pace in motivational counseling, but the social worker also holds them responsible for their drinking and for any changes that they make. MET often prepares clients for more intensive treatment, which is delivered only when the person is ready for it.

Cognitive Behavioral Therapy Approaches
Cognitive behavioral therapy works best with people who are mildly dependent on alcohol, and it typically follows earlier, more intensive treatment. It is based on the assumptions that maladaptive behavior, specifically, problem drinking, is learned and that teaching the client to modify his dysfunctional behavior—by eliminating incentives for drinking and by promoting activities that are incompatible with alcohol use—will help the problem drinker learn alternatives to drinking. Cognitive interventions are implemented alone or in combination with behavioral strategies. The goal is to help clients manage their negative thinking, use constructive cognitions, and replace inappropriate expectations about alcohol with more innocuous and more adaptive coping strategies (see chapters 5 and 6 for more detailed information about cognitive behavioral therapy). Schonfeld, Dupree, and Dickson-Fuhrmann (2002) have effectively integrated age-specific cognitive behavioral and self-management therapy approaches with relapse prevention to treat older people with drinking problems.

Drug Dependence Treatment

The CSAT consensus panel recommends that practitioners use psychosocial interventions to treat older people's drug misuse; any modification or discontinuation of an older person's medications should occur only under the supervision of qualified health care professionals. Social workers must first identify why an older client misuses or abuses medications. For example, some elderly people misuse medications because they forget how to take them properly. Others may intentionally overuse their drugs, particularly if they have become dependent. Whereas daily pill boxes might help the forgetful older client, those who deliberately use their medications for nonprescribed purposes require more involved interventions, including inpatient treatment.

Schonfeld and colleagues (2002) have adapted an age-specific cognitive behavioral and self-management therapy program, called GET SMART (Geriatric Evaluation Team: Substance Misuse/Abuse Recognition and Treatment), to assist the many older people who need help with multiple substances, especially prescription medications. These researchers have modified the approach to assess use and abuse of multiple substances, including alcohol, illicit drugs, and/or improper use of prescribed medications. The program teaches participants how to cope with social pressure; being at home alone; feelings of depression and loneliness, anxiety and tension, anger and frustration; cues for substance use; urges (self-statements); and slips or relapses.

These specific techniques for treating older adults with substance abuse problems should be used with the ABCDEF practice guide to determine the choice of treatment, the need for inpatient or outpatient care, whether brief intervention is appropriate, and whether motivational enhancement therapy should be implemented before trying more intensive treatment. Education and information about potentially addictive properties of the client's medications should accompany all treatment plans. Many state and local offices on aging, home health care agencies, and national alcohol and drug organizations distribute excellent brochures and other materials about the potential misuse of prescription and over-the-counter medications. Some programs engage in outreach and in-home services to assist those who need motivation to participate or who are unable to attend group programs (Atkinson and Misra, 2002). Social workers must also encourage clients to ask their doctors and pharmacists about the proper use of their medications.

Health care providers need more training about drug misuse and abuse among older people. Many health providers remain ignorant of the differences in the ways that older adults and younger people metabolize drugs and the need to adjust dosages accordingly; the potentially dangerous drug interactions for older people with multiple prescriptions; the warning signs of drug abuse and misuse in older people; the need for age-specific assessment and screening instruments for drug misuse and abuse; and the availability of specific treatments for older people with substance abuse problems. Workshops and programs that focus on substance abuse in late life should be offered to those who work closely with older people, including workers at local area agencies on aging, community mental health centers, adult day care facilities, senior citizen centers, hospitals, and nursing homes. The case example that follows demonstrates the many ways that social workers coordinate their work with physicians and coordinate care when they treat elderly people with substance abuse problems.

CASE 8.1

Ms. Jasper, seventy-five, has sought help for anxiety that began after her husband died a few years ago. She states that she is unable to sleep and that she worries about her safety and health. She constantly feels tired during the day and reports that she "doesn't think as well as I used to."

Her primary care physician previously prescribed two tablets of Valium at night before bedtime. She started taking three tablets when she felt that two were insufficient but then complained that these also "stopped working." Ms. Jasper has become increasingly anxious and depressed. A friend suggested that she contact a social worker at the local community mental health center.

After conducting a comprehensive assessment, the social worker realizes that Ms. Jasper has developed a tolerance to Valium and uses the ASI to evaluate the extent of Ms. Jasper's dependence. The social worker also learns that Ms. Jasper has continued to mourn the death of her husband and feels depressed about this loss (F). Her cognitive functioning is adequate (C). She is in excellent health and has just seen her physician for a complete physical examination (B). Background information (D) reveals that Ms. Jasper stayed home to care for her two children, who now live out of state. She lives alone in an apartment complex for senior citizens, but she rarely socializes with others (E). The social worker conducts a more in-depth assessment of Ms. Jasper's depression to determine its severity and whether she is suicidal (see chapters 6 and 7 for more detail about depression and suicide in late life).

With Ms. Jasper's written permission, the social worker contacts her physician to discuss whether Ms. Jasper could be dependent on Valium. The doctor becomes concerned and agrees to work with the social worker to reduce Ms. Jasper's dependence on Valium.

The social worker and physician work out a brief intervention strategy, which Ms. Jasper endorses, to taper off the Valium and to treat her anxiety and depression. The social worker uses the approach known by the mnemonic *FRAMES* to guide treatment in the brief intervention (see Blow, 1998). *F* refers to feedback about personal risk or impairment; it involves providing education and information about the client's drug behaviors, the reasons that the client should discontinue the drug, the effects of long-term drug use (e.g., tolerance and dependence, and potential adverse cognitive, physical, psychological, and social consequences). *R* represents personal responsibility for change and the notion that older people must actively contribute to decisions about their treatment. *A* refers to advice about change and the dissemination of accurate information about recommended changes in the use of medications. The social worker should offer a menu (*M*) of options to clients to provide them with choices and motivate them to use medications properly. *E* signifies empathetic and supportive counseling rather than confrontational treatment. *S* refers to the importance of enhancing clients' feelings of self-efficacy and strengthening their confidence about discontinuing medications.

The social worker, the physician, and Ms. Jasper agree to the following treatment goals: Ms Jasper will taper off Valium (A—actions, behavior) to improve her energy level (B), depression (F), and mental alertness (C). She will explore and work through her feelings about her husband's death and learn more appropriate coping strategies in counseling sessions with the social worker (F). This treatment will offer Ms. Jasper support and incorporate relevant cognitive behavioral therapy techniques, such as thought stopping, reframing, positive self-talk, and relaxation techniques, to help Ms. Jasper manage her emotional distress. In addition, the social worker agrees to set up environmental supports (E) from the local area agency on aging.

Ms. Jasper's situation demonstrates the complexities involved in helping older people who develop iatrogenic drug dependencies. Benzodiazepines are one of the most inappropriately prescribed medications for older women, who are more likely to be hospitalized for substance abuse–related problems than for heart attacks. According to a report published in 1998 by the National Center on Addiction and Substance Abuse at Columbia University, "By ignoring the substance abuse of mature women, we compromise the quality of these years or we condemn these women to early death or disability from a broken hip, emphysema, a heart attack or lung cancer, or an inadvertent overdose of sleeping pills taken after having a few drinks too many. We leave millions of grandchildren without grandmothers, and children without mothers. We saddle others with the avoidable burden of caring for an ailing parent" (1998, p. iii).

DISCUSSION QUESTIONS

1. Why have social workers and other professionals largely ignored the substance abuse problems of older people?
2. In what ways do older men and women differ in how they use and abuse substances?
3. How will cohort differences affect substance use and abuse among older people, and how will the baby boom generation differ from the current cohort of older adults?
4. What are the social policy implications of substance abuse problems in later life?

CHAPTER 9

Dementia

A S DEMENTIA (AND, SPECIFICALLY, ALZHEIMER'S DISEASE) affects more and more older people, social workers will need to know how to help elderly people and their families cope with this devastating disorder. Practitioners should understand the nature and progression of dementia, how to inform and instruct families about Alzheimer's disease (often referred to as AD) and related disorders, and be able to determine which interventions work best for elderly people and their families at different stages of dementia, in different contexts, and under different circumstances.

AD, the most common form of dementia, challenges the coping strengths of many families and often depletes their emotional, social, and family resources. Although many dementias are treatable, some, such as vascular dementia and Alzheimer's disease, are irreversible and require substantial care, especially during the later stages. For example, while non-Alzheimer's caregivers average about 11.8 hours per week in caregiving activities, those who are tending to people with Alzheimer's spend an average of 17.6 hours per week giving care (National Alliance for Caregiving, 1997). According to a national study conducted by the National Alliance for Caregiving and the AARP in 1996, many caregivers of people with Alzheimer's spend more than 40 hours a week assisting them, and older caregivers provide the most intensive care (National Alliance, 1997).

The financial costs of Alzheimer's disease are onerous. Annual direct and indirect national costs involved in caring for Alzheimer's patients are at least $100 billion (National Institute on Aging, 2004). American businesses spend as much as $61 billion a year on Alzheimer's disease, and of this amount $24.6 billion covers health care related to Alzheimer's, and $36.5 billion is related to caregivers' expenses (U.S. Department of Health and Human Services [DHHS], 2003a).

This chapter focuses on older people with dementia and begins with a discussion of the definition and incidence rates of dementia. (We discuss caregivers' concerns in chapter 10.) Next, we review selected assessment tools for screening dementia clients and evaluating their behaviors, moods, functional and psychiatric status, and overall quality of life. Then we present interventions that address these issues. The chapter ends with a case example that demonstrates how a social worker might intervene in a specific instance.

Dementia Defined

Dementia refers to the loss of cognitive functioning, memory, planning, language abilities, and abstract thinking. It involves a significant intellectual decline or impairment that persists over time in several cognitive areas (Rabins and Margolis, 2004). Memory impairment is an essential aspect of dementia, along with impairments in speech, motor functioning, and perception. It is typically manifested by language problems, an inability to learn new material, and problems remembering recently learned information. The client increasingly uses words such as *it* or *thing* to represent specific items for which she has lost the word, and the content of her talk lacks its usual structure and meaning. Impairments in motor functioning also lead to failures in self-care, including cooking, bathing, and dressing. Loss of perceptual and cognitive skills contributes to an inability to think abstractly, name familiar objects, and follow through with projects, plans, and activities. Because people with dementia often display poor judgment, they can overestimate their performance in certain areas. Some people engage in inappropriate "disinhibited behavior," including openly displaying sexual behaviors or exhibiting disruptive and potentially hurtful aggressive actions. People with severe dementia fail to recognize their surroundings, friends, and relatives and ultimately themselves.

Dementia differs from age-associated memory impairment (AAMI) and from mild cognitive impairment (MCI), which falls somewhere between AAMI and Alzheimer's disease (Rabins and Margolis, 2004). AAMI refers to normal declines in memory, including the occasional forgetfulness that is associated with age, such as difficulty remembering a name, a word, or the location of one's keys. When people are tired, sick, distracted, or under stress, they forget more easily. Unlike dementia, AAMI is neither progressive nor disabling. In addition, many people with dementia are unaware of their forgetfulness, but those with AAMI usually recognize and worry about their memory lapses.

Elderly people with mild cognitive impairment (MCI) forget more frequently than those with AAMI but not as much as those with Alzheimer's disease. In comparison with those who have Alzheimer's disease, people with MCI have fewer problems with language and are less disoriented and confused about daily tasks. Memory loss (especially visual memory loss) that is more severe than normal memory loss is one of the most salient characteristics of mild cognitive impairment (Petersen et al., 1999; Petersen, 2000). Those with MCI annoy family and friends by repeatedly asking the same question, but they otherwise function well and demonstrate no cognitive impairment in such areas as orientation, language, and attention (National Institute on Aging [NIA], 1999). Petersen and colleagues (1999) identify five criteria suggestive of MCI. These include memory complaints, abnormal memory for age, ability to carry out normal activities of daily living, normal general cognitive function, and the absence of dementia. Each year 12% to 15% of MCI cases (or 40% after three years) develop Alzheimer's disease (DHHS, 2003a).

INCIDENCE OF AND TYPES OF DEMENTIA

Alzheimer's disease accounts for 60% to 70% of all dementias in late life (Grossberg and Desai, 2003). About 4.5 million Americans have Alzheimer's disease, and their numbers will increase substantially by the middle of the twenty-first century; the number of people older than sixty-five who have Alzheimer's disease doubles every five years (NIA, 2004). Experts estimate that by 2050, the number of Americans with Alzheimer's could range from 11.3 million to 16 million (Alzheimer's Association, 2003; Katzman, 2000). In a study of almost fifteen thousand adults, von Strauss, Viitanen, DeRonchi, Winblad, and Fratiglioni (1999) found that the prevalence rates for dementia increases from 13% among those aged 77 to 84 to 48% for those aged 95 and older. Those aged 90 to 94 were about four times more likely to have dementia than those in the younger group; those older than 95 were six times more likely.

Vascular dementia develops after several small strokes. It is the most common cause of memory loss after Alzheimer's disease and accounts for about 10% to 20% of dementia cases (Rabins and Margolis, 2004). Other less common dementias include dementia with Lewy bodies, frontotemporal dementias, dementia from Huntington's disease, Creutzfeldt-Jakob disease, and amnestic syndrome. Dementia with Lewy bodies sometimes occurs along with Alzheimer's or Parkinson's disease and accounts for 5% to 10% of cases. It is probably the second most common type of dementia after Alzheimer's disease. Lewy bodies are abnormal structures in the brain. People with this type of dementia have more problems with spatial working memory than those diagnosed with Alzheimer's disease. They also experience more hallucinations, especially visual hallucinations (Rabins and Margolis, 2004; Conn, 2004). Frontotemporal dementia, which occurs in about 5% of dementia cases and is less common than Alzheimer's disease and dementia with Lewy bodies, involves substantial abnormalities in the frontal lobes. In addition, diseases such as Huntington's and Parkinson's can lead to dementia. Creutzfeldt-

Jakob disease, named after the German neurologists Hans Gerhard Creutzfeldt and Alfons Maria Jakob who first described the disease in the 1920s, is rare (affecting about 1 in 1 million people), has a rapid onset, and is fatal, usually within eighteen months of the appearance of symptoms. Amnestic syndrome refers to an inability to remember anything immediately after the onset of the illness, although on rare occasions people fail to recall events before the emergence of this disorder. Despite the severe memory loss, people with amnestic syndrome have normal intelligence. The amnesia results from damage to the temporal lobes, which can be caused by various factors, including an accident, severe alcoholism, prolonged low blood pressure, thiamine deficiencies, and brain inflammation.

Dementias are typically categorized as reversible and irreversible. Reversible dementias are those that result from causes that can be treated and controlled, such as depression, illness, and reactions to medication. Depressed people sometimes have trouble concentrating, remembering, and learning new things, but they recognize their cognitive problems, whereas people with dementia tend to overestimate their abilities. Moreover, depressed people's cognitive problems usually clear up once they feel better. The relationship between depression and dementia is complex, in part because depression and dementia often coexist, and depression often precedes dementia (Yaffe et al., 1999).

Medications can sometimes provoke dementia reactions. Prescription and nonprescription drugs are far more likely to cause elderly people to suffer adverse side-effects that mimic dementia (see chapter 8 for more in-depth discussion of substance abuse and misuse among older people). Medications that can cause memory impairment include some anti-inflammatory drugs, such as prednisone; heartburn medications, specifically, cimetidine (Tagamet), famotidine (Pepcid), and ranitidine (Zantac); certain heart medications; and antianxiety/sedative drugs, such as triazolam (Halcion), alprazolam (Xanax), and diazepam (Valium).

Certain medical conditions can also lead to dementia. For example, infections, specific vitamin deficiencies (e.g., vitamin B-12 and niacin), hormone imbalances from thyroid disorders, and such diseases as AIDS, neurosyphilis, chronic meningitis, and brain tumors (especially those of the cerebral cortex that cause memory and other cognitive problems) are also associated with dementia (Rabins and Margolis, 2004).

The most common type of irreversible dementia is Alzheimer's disease, a progressive disorder of the brain characterized by nerve cell damage and ultimately death, as amyloid plaques (dense pieces of dendrites from nearby nerve cells and related proteins) and neurofibrillary tangles (twisted and convoluted material found in nerve cell bodies) accumulate. As the amyloid plaques collect in the hippocampus, which controls memory, language, reasoning, and perception, and in the cerebral cortex, which regulates judgment, cognitive declines and changes in behavior and personality occur. Neurofibrillary tangles destroy the delicate nerve cell transmissions that are needed for normal cognitive performance. When neurotransmitters such as acetylcholine weaken, memory and learning abilities decline, and other changes in sleep patterns, moods, and personality emerge.

THE MANIFESTATION OF ALZHEIMER'S DISEASE

Alzheimer's disease typically progresses in three stages. During the first stage people forget names, appointments, recent conversations, recent events, or where they parked their car; they sometimes misplace their keys, purses, and books; they often repeat questions and become frustrated because they are unable to remember the answers; and they frequently struggle with directions, complicated instructions, and abstract discussions. As the disease progresses, people lose the ability to care for themselves, including dressing, bathing, brushing their teeth, and other grooming activities; they also become increasingly incapable of expressing themselves orally or in writing. They continue to decline until they stop recognizing themselves and lose the ability to walk or feed themselves. By this stage they are completely dependent on others, and they become increasingly vulnerable to infections, such as pneumonia, as their bodies weaken and deteriorate. Pneumonia is the most frequent cause of death among people with Alzheimer's disease.

Many behavioral symptoms appear as the disease progresses, including insomnia; incontinence; verbal, emotional, or physical outbursts; sexual disorders; weight loss; psychosis; depression; agitation; and wandering. According to some reports, 25% to 50% of people with Alzheimer's disease demonstrate symptoms of depression, 30% to 50% have delusions, and 10% to 25% have hallucinations (Bartels et al., 2003; S. Cook et al., 2003; Volicer and Hurley, 2003; Mega, Cummings, Fiorello, and Gornbein, 1996). Those with psychotic symptoms typically have more cognitive impairment and more rapid deterioration. They are also more inclined to wander, to undergo personality changes, and to express agitation, anger, depression, and personality changes than people without psychotic symptoms (Rockwell, Jackson, Vilke, and Jeste, 1994; Sultzer et al., 1995). When people with Alzheimer's disease become irritable, frustrated, and angry, they sometimes scream or yell, demand attention, refuse to cooperate, or hit, bite, or kick. Agitation usually worsens as Alzheimer's disease progresses.

Sudden illnesses (especially bladder infections, other infections, bronchitis, or pneumonia) as well as dehydration or poor nutrition can easily precipitate confusion and agitation for older adults with Alzheimer's disease. Strokes and flare-ups from diabetes or diseases of the heart, liver, or kidneys can also lead to agitation or delirium. Adverse side-effects from drug interactions and toxic reactions to medications are often responsible. Sleep problems, resulting from lack of sleep or frequent awakenings during the night, can induce agitation if the Alzheimer's patient becomes overtired.

Environmental stressors that can lead to agitation include disruptions in routine, excessive isolation, overstimulation, and physical discomfort resulting from noise, temperature, or other environmental stimuli. Hospitalization, including a temporary stay in a nursing home, can exacerbate symptoms and generate fear.

Certain psychiatric conditions (including anxiety, depression, psychosis, anger, and aggression) sometimes provoke behavioral disturbances, especially when people with Alzheimer's feel mistreated, misunderstood, or unable to complete a task that they could perform earlier in life. Refusing to cooperate, especially when caregivers try to help with basic care needs, is another way that many express their anger. Depressed adults with Alzheimer's disease may cry constantly, withdraw, and isolate themselves from others. Those who are already predisposed to anxiety often regress when their routines are disrupted, uncertainties arise, or pressures mount to be on time, complete certain tasks, or respond to requests or interactions that they fail to understand.

Cohen-Mansfield (2000) conceptualized disruptive behaviors as verbally aggressive and nonagressive, and physically nonaggressive and aggressive. The verbally aggressive people include more women than men, and these people experience more pain and discomfort than those in the other categories. Their agitation more frequently emerges at night, when they are alone or when they are using the toilet or bathing (Cohen-Mansfield, Werner, and Marx, 1990). Physically nonaggressive people typically have a more advanced dementia, even though they are healthy in other respects. These individuals often seek stimulation by wandering and pacing, especially when more appropriate activities are unavailable. They roam for self-stimulation rather than from discomfort. Finally, the most physically aggressive are often men with severe cognitive impairments who struggle to communicate or who feel threatened, such as when someone tries to bathe them (Bridges-Parlet, Knopman, and Thompson, 1994). See figure 9.1 for a depiction of this model. The most disruptive older people are often suffering from unrecognized and untreated pain (Volicer and Hurley, 2003; Cohen-Mansfield and Creedon, 2002).

Causes of Dementia

Researchers continue to search for the causes of Alzheimer's disease. The most common causes still under investigation include genetic factors, head injuries, immune system disorders, oxidative damage, and inflammation. Early onset Alzheimer's disease (occurring in people younger than sixty-five), which accounts

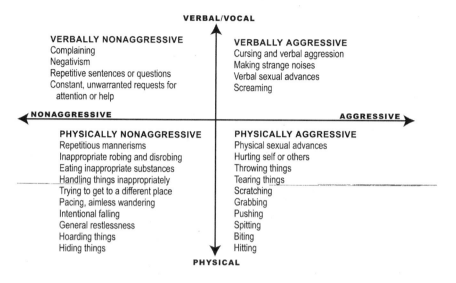

FIGURE 9.1 Cohen-Mansfield Agitation Inventory
Source: Cohen-Mansfield, J. (2000). Approaches to management of disruptive behaviors.
In Lawton & Rubinstein, *Interventions in dementia care*. New York: Springer. Used by permission.

for about 10% of all Alzheimer's cases, often runs in families. Apolipoprotein E (APOE), found on chromosome 19, is associated with the formation of amyloid plaques. It has received considerable attention as a suspect in the development of late onset Alzheimer's disease. The role of beta-amyloid remains unclear, although experts know that people with Alzheimer's disease have an accumulation of this protein. Most experts concur that Alzheimer's disease results from the buildup of these plaques (Rabins and Margolis, 2004).

Inflammation—another process that increases with age—may also contribute to the development of Alzheimer's disease. Studies demonstrate a lower incidence of Alzheimer's disease among people who frequently use anti-inflammatory agents, suggesting that inflammation (and particularly brain inflammation) causes cell damage that either exacerbates on-going Alzheimer's disease activities or eventually leads to substantial cognitive malfunction or dysfunction.

Researchers are also trying to determine whether a connection exists between brain infarction (stroke) and Alzheimer's disease. Preliminary research indicates that infarctions may interact with or exacerbate the progression or manifestation of Alzheimer's disease (Alzheimer's Disease Education and Referral Center [AD-EAR] and National Institute on Aging, 1999).

Vascular dementia, which results from several ministrokes, is the second most common type of irreversible dementia. When a stroke occurs and areas in the brain are deprived of oxygen, brain damage can result in the loss of such functions as thinking, movement, and speech. A single infarct is often inconsequential, but the damage caused by several of these tiny strokes can accumulate. This damage affects the client's memory, language, and other cognitive abilities.

Diagnostic Criteria for Dementia of the Alzheimer's Type

Clinicians typically use one of two sets of diagnostic criteria from the *DSM-IV* (1994) (and, more recently, the *DSM-IV-TR*, 2000) or from the National Institute of Neurological and Communicative Disorders and Stroke in collaboration with the Alzheimer's Disease and Related Disorders Association (NINCDS-ADRDA) (see McKhann et al., 1984).

According to the *DSM-IV*, five major criteria comprise the basis for making a diagnosis of dementia of the Alzheimer's type; all are based on how the client's cognitive deficits developed, their effect on the individual's social or occupational functioning, and the course of the disease (see *DSM-IV*, 1994, for more details).

Table 9.1 lists the criteria for a clinical diagnosis of Alzheimer's disease according to the NINCDS-ADRDA. These criteria generally are consistent with those identified in the *DSM-IV*; however, important differences exist. First, unlike the *DSM-IV*, the NINCDS-ADRDA criteria require formal neuropsychological and mental status testing to diagnose Alzheimer's disease, and memory deficits, although noted, are unnecessary for a diagnosis of Alzheimer's disease; thus those individuals who have more language deficits than memory problems could still be diagnosed with Alzheimer's disease. Second, the two sets of criteria also differ in their emphasis on how the client fares in occupational and social activities. Finally, in contrast to the *DSM-IV* criteria, the NINCDS-ADRDA criteria identify two levels: possible Alzheimer's disease (when symptoms are consistent with Alzheimer's disease but include atypical features) and probable Alzheimer's disease (when the indicators clearly suggest Alzheimer's disease, and other causes of dementia have been excluded or ruled out). Hogervorst and colleagues (2000) recommend combining the categories for possible and probable Alzheimer's disease in order to increase the sensitivity of these criteria; they also suggest including additional assessments to improve specificity, especially when minimal or mild dementias are involved (Morris and Fulling, 1988).

When physicians evaluate an older person for dementia, they conduct clinical interviews with the patient and with her caregivers. The doctor obtains a history of complaints, including cognitive, medical, neurological, and psychiatric symptoms, as well as of the date of onset, precipitating factors, and duration and

TABLE 9.1 Criteria for Clinical Diagnosis of Alzheimer's Disease*

Criteria for Diagnosis of Probable Alzheimer's Disease

- Dementia established by clinical examination and documented by a standardized test of cognitive function (e.g., the Mini-Mental Test, Blessed Dementia Test) and confirmed by neuropsychological tests

- Deficits in two or more areas of cognition (language, memory, perception)

- Progressive worsening of memory and other cognitive functions

- No disturbance of consciousness

- Onset from age 40 to 90, typically after 65

- Absence of other systemic disorder or brain disease

Factors Supporting Diagnosis of Probable Alzheimer's Disease

- Progressive deterioration of specific cognitive functions such as language (aphasia), motor skills (apraxia), and perceptions (agnosia)

- Impaired activities of daily living and altered patterns of behavior

- Family history of similar disorders, particularly if confirmed by neurological testing

- The following laboratory results:

  - Normal cerebrospinal fluid (lumbar puncture test)

  - Normal electroencephalogram (EEG) test of brain activity

  - Evidence of cerebral atrophy on computer tomography with progression documented by serial observation

Other Clinical Features Leading to Diagnosis of Probable Alzheimer's After Excluding Other Causes of Dementia

- Plateaus in the course of progression of the illness

- Associated symptoms, including depression, insomnia, incontinence, delusions, hallucinations, weight loss, sex problems, and significant verbal, emotional, and physical outbursts

- Other neurological abnormalities, especially in advanced disease, including increased muscle tone and a shuffling gait, seizures in advanced disease, and CT normal for age

Features That Make Diagnosis of Alzheimer's Uncertain or Unlikely

- Sudden onset

- Such early symptoms as seizures, gait problems, and loss of vision and coordination

*Criteria as established by the National Institute of Neurological and Communicative Disorders and Stroke in collaboration with the Alzheimer's Disease and Related Disorders Association.

Source: McKhann et al., 1984. Clinical diagnosis of Alzheimer's disease. Report of the NINCDS-ADRDA Work Group under the auspices of the Department of Health and Human Services Task Force on Alzheimer's disease. *Neurology,* vol. 34, pp. 939–44. Used by permission.

manifestation of symptoms. The physician takes into account complete medical, social, vocational, educational, and family histories, especially any family history of dementia. Reviewing the client's medication is especially important. The physician usually performs physical, neurological, and mental status examinations that include ratings of dementia severity. A comprehensive evaluation for dementia in an elderly person should also include functional assessments of activities of daily living (ADL) and instrumental activities of daily living (IADL) and of caregivers' support and stress levels. In addition, the physician typically orders appropriate laboratory tests, especially if a reversible dementia is suspected. Neuroimaging, based on a computed tomography (CT) or magnetic resonance imaging (MRI), is especially important when vascular dementia seems likely.

Interdisciplinary teams comprised of physicians, nurses, occupational therapists, and social workers are especially helpful during these diagnostic stages. Physicians can examine patients and review their medications, laboratory results, and other diagnostic tests, while occupational therapists evaluate their functional abilities. Gerontological social workers often uncover behavioral and psychiatric problems. The social workers also work as advocates for the client, refer him to appropriate community services, and help caregivers redesign their homes to facilitate care or arrange for nursing home placement.

The diagnosis of Alzheimer's disease is no longer a "diagnosis of exclusion," in which all other possible disorders must be ruled out before the diagnosis can be made. Clinicians now have access to more diagnostic tools created specifically to identify dementia. For example, advances in the use of MRI can reveal the existence and extent of any shrinkage that has occurred in the hippocampus, which is associated with Alzheimer's disease. Genetic testing for the APOE ε4 gene, which increases the risk of Alzheimer's disease, or the presenilin genes associated with early onset Alzheimer's is also available, although it is not routinely recommended at this time (NIA, 2004). Regardless of the setting, social workers need to know what screening instruments to use, as well as when and how to use them. Most dementia instruments focus on specific areas, such as cognitive functioning, psychiatric status, and behavior or functional capacities.

ASSESSMENT

Social workers encounter people with dementia in various settings. For example, hospital social workers often use crisis intervention techniques when older people injure themselves because of a suspected dementia. In these situations social workers must arrange for a qualified physician with special training in diagnosing dementia to conduct the assessment of cognitive functioning. Social workers must also work with the client's family to find safe living arrangements and appropriate resources to assist in the care of the relative with dementia.

Many elderly people who seek help for depression or anxiety or home maintenance are unaware that they have a dementia. Social workers often are the first to identify dementia, to refer these older people for evaluation, and to arrange community support. Nursing home social workers usually know about residents' dementia and are consulted when elderly people exhibit disruptive behavioral or psychiatric symptoms.

Cognitive Assessments

The most widely used screening instrument for dementia, the Mini-Mental State Examination (MMSE), was originally developed for use with psychiatric inpatients but is now used more often in community or outpatient settings (Folstein, Folstein, and McHugh, 1975). Although the MMSE has excellent reliability and validity, clinicians must use it cautiously with older people with advanced impairments and with those from diverse ethnic and socioeconomic backgrounds. The accuracy with which clinicians detect dementia improves substantially when they use the MMSE along with the clock drawing test (CDT), which is efficient and inexpensive to administer (Peters et al., 2000; K. S. Brown, 1999). The CDT and the Short Portable Mental Status Questionnaire (SPMSQ) work well with elderly people from a variety of ethnic backgrounds (Borson et al., 1999; Pfeiffer, 1975).

More and more clinicians are using telephone interview versions of the MMSE, especially with older adults who for various reasons are unable to visit the clinic for a face-to-face interview. However, some modifications are required. Although most geriatricians emphasize that a telephone assessment is not a substitute for a personal interview, telephone interviews are surprisingly effective for identifying overall cognitive impairment. For more information about telephone assessments see Monteiro, Boksay, Auer, and Torossian (1998).

People who are given the clock drawing test are first asked to draw a clock by drawing a circle, then adding numbers, and finally setting the clock to a specific time. Clinicians who are appropriately trained can easily administer the CDT in less than five minutes, and older adults feel comfortable with the instructions. This test works especially well with adults who are poorly educated and speak languages other than English. Borson and colleagues (1999) found that the CDT has greater specificity than the MMSE and is more effective as a first-level dementia screen for elderly people whose first language is not English. It can also be administered rapidly with minimal training.

The Mental Status Questionnaire (MSQ) was originally developed for institutionalized older people. It includes ten items that assess general orientation to current location, time, person, and current events, and it can be administered in five to ten minutes (Kahn, Goldfarb, Pollack, and Peck, 1960). Although the MSQ has excellent specificity and moderate sensitivity, it needs further testing in non-institutionalized settings and with elderly people from a variety of ethnic backgrounds.

The Short Portable Mental Status Questionnaire (SPMSQ), which includes items from the MSQ, evaluates orientation, location, personal information, current events, and counting backward by threes, beginning with twenty. Clinicians have used it with various populations of older adults in different settings, and it effectively distinguishes the presence or absence of dementia (Pfeiffer, 1975). Its sensitivity (34%), however, is low relative to most other dementia measures.

The 7-Minute Screen (7MS), developed by P. R. Solomon and colleagues (1998), differentiates Alzheimer's disease from age-related cognitive impairments by focusing on four cognitive activities: enhanced cued recall, verbal fluency, temporal orientation, and clock drawing. Although the 7MS demonstrates excellent potential for accurately identifying older adults with Alzheimer's disease, more information on its clinical utility in various settings is needed.

The Alzheimer's Disease Assessment Scale (ADAS) is a twenty-one-item scale requiring about thirty minutes to administer. It focuses on cognitive functioning and psychiatric symptoms that clinicians observe and uses information from caregivers (W. G. Rosen, Mohs, and Davis, 1984). The ADAS detects early Alzheimer's, offers information about which stage the client is in, measures the severity of the dementia, and effectively tracks changes over time. A different version, the ADAS—Late Version, was developed to measure advanced dementia (Kincaid et al., 1995). Many experts believe the ADAS is more discriminating than the MMSE (Inzitari et al., 1999). The ADAS is also less influenced by educational differences and is available in German, Spanish, Japanese, French, Greek, and Italian (see Inzitari et al., 1999, for more information about these foreign-language versions). Researchers who have studied Alzheimer's in different ethnic, cultural, or linguistic settings find that the clinical characteristics of the disease remain the same (Inzitari et al., 1999). Few assessment instruments have been subjected to such rigorous cross-cultural analyses.

Although the Clinical Dementia Rating (CDR) has been used more frequently in research than in practice, geriatricians recommend it when the clinician needs standardized information about the severity and stage of a client's dementia. The CDR, which was developed by Hughes, Berg, Danziger, Coben, and Martin (1982), assesses memory, orientation, judgment and problem solving, community affairs, hobbies, and personal care. It is based on direct assessment, observation, and information from informants and provides an overall rating of dementia severity (i.e., healthy, questionable dementia, mild dementia, moderate dementia, and severe dementia). Although administering the CDR is more time consuming than some other instruments, and it requires specific training, clinicians will appreciate the information that this instrument provides about the stages of dementia.

The Global Deterioration Scale (GDS) also provides stage information. Many clinicians use the GDS because it includes an evaluation of functional status and an assessment of dementia along a seven-point rating scale that reflects the progress of the disease (Reisberg, Ferris, de Leon, and Crook, 1982). Clinicians have also successfully administered the GDS over the telephone. Paveza and colleagues (1992), however, found that many ADL impairments appeared earlier than the GDS predicted, and this group questions the appropriateness of this scale (and others that provide single-score staging).

Psychiatric Assessments

Social workers should always evaluate Alzheimer's patients for depression because many people with dementia, especially those in the early stages of the disease, become depressed. The Cornell Scale for Depression in Dementia was developed specifically for this purpose (Alexopoulos, Abrams, Young, and Shamoian, 1988). Social workers can also use other standardized instruments, such as the Geriatric Depression Scale.

One of the first dementia instruments to include noncognitive items was the Behavioral Pathology in Alzheimer's Disease Rating Scale (BEHAVE-AD), which was developed from retrospective chart reviews of outpatients with Alzheimer's disease (Reisberg, Borenstein, et al., 1987). The BEHAVE-AD scale assesses paranoia/delusions, hallucinations, activity disturbance, aggression, sleep-wake cycle disturbance, affective disturbance, and anxiety/phobic symptoms. Two similar scales, the Columbia University Scale for Psychopathology in Alzheimer's Disease (CUSPAD) (Devanand et al., 1992) and the Behavioral Rating Scale for Dementia of the Consortium to Establish a Registry for Alzheimer's Disease (CERAD) (which is based on the BEHAVE-AD), also include psychiatric items.

Functional Status

Social workers should always evaluate the functional status of people with Alzheimer's disease, including their capabilities for managing ADL and IADL. Although many elderly people with mild or moderate dementia function well, some need help with cooking, cleaning, and basic care.

Nursing homes regularly use the Minimum Data Set-based Cognitive Performance Scale (CPS) to gather information on residents' functional skills. The Bedford Alzheimer Nursing Severity Scale, which also evaluates residents' functional performances, takes into account mobility, dressing, eating, sleeping, and cognitive abilities (Volicer, Hurley, Lathi, and Kowall, 1994).

Although the ADAS-L also includes a few items on ADL skills, some experts question the accuracy of these ratings (see Teresi and Evans, 1996). The GDS, described earlier, includes functional status measures that gauge the severity of a person's dementia. Reisberg, Ferris, de Leon, Schneck, and colleagues (1984) modified the GDS and created the Functional Assessment Staging Test by adding several major functional stages as well as eleven substages.

Behavioral Assessments (Including Agitation and Wandering)

The disruptive behaviors of people with dementia, especially agitation and wandering, distress many caregivers. When elderly people with dementia continually disrupt caregivers' sleep, emotional functioning, and basic routines, caregivers become increasingly stressed, unhappy about caregiving, and more inclined to institutionalize the person with dementia. Social workers can mitigate caregivers' stress by targeting and assessing the problem areas, by intervening with approaches that lessen disruptive behaviors, and by concomitantly improving the moods of people with dementia, ultimately improving the quality of living for everyone. Although many people with dementia act inappropriately when they feel frustrated or when some need of theirs is not met, various factors, including brain dysfunction, overstimulation, and understimulation, contribute to their agitated behavior (Cohen-Mansfield, 2003). When family members have the right resources and adequate supports, they can usually care for a person with dementia at home without undue stress and depression.

Cohen-Mansfield (2000) defines agitation or disruptive behavior as "inappropriate verbal, vocal, or motor activity that is not judged by an outside observer to result directly from the needs or confusion of the agitated individual" (p. 40). An older adult who screams because she needs help eating is not exhibiting a disruptive behavior, according to Cohen-Mansfield. People with dementia often need assistance for legitimate reasons. Cohen-Mansfield (2003) stresses that agitation includes a range of behaviors that are perceived as inappropriate by someone else; the older person often perceives his actions differently.

The definition of *agitation* varies among caregivers, depending on the context and their circumstances. The BEHAVE-AD, described earlier, includes a section on activity disturbances, and the CUSPAD addresses psychotic reactions, but both disregard many other agitation reactions. The CERAD Behavior Rating Scale for Dementia (BRSD) (Tariot et al., 1995), which was developed in a comprehensive, multidisciplinary effort from a review of existing scales, thoroughly assesses disruptive behaviors. It covers depressive features, psychotic features, defective self-regulation, irritability/aggression, vegetative features, apathy, and affective lability. With adequate training, interviewers can easily administer the BRSD.

Another instrument that is easy to use, comprehensive, and appropriate for the assessment of disruptive behaviors is the Neuropsychiatric Inventory (NPI), developed by Cummings, Gega, Gray, Rosenberg-Thompson, and Carusi (1994). The NPI measures delusions, hallucinations, agitation, depression, anxiety, euphoria, apathy, disinhibition, irritability, aberrant motor behavior, night-time behaviors, and appetite and eating changes according to four scores: frequency, severity, total (frequency multiplied by severity), and caregiver distress. It is also possible to produce detailed analyses of specific areas.

The Behavioral Symptoms Scale for Dementia was developed by Devenand and colleagues (1992). It contains thirty items that examine areas of disinhibition, catastrophic reaction, apathy/indifference, sundowning (when people become especially agitated and restless as evening approaches), and denial that are troublesome for caregivers. The Dementia Behavior Disturbance Scale also emphasizes behaviors that upset many caregivers, including repetitive questioning, purposeless activities, and changes in sleep, continence, and eating (Baumgarten, Becker, and Gauthier, 1990). Although experienced clinicians usually administer this scale to family members, caregivers can administer it.

An instrument that rapidly assesses disruptive behaviors in nursing homes is the Nursing Home Behavior Problem Scale, developed by Ray, Taylor, Lichtenstein, and Meador (1992). It includes six subscales: uncooperative/aggressive, irrational/restless, annoying, inappropriate, dangerous, and sleep disturbance.

The Revised Memory and Behavior Problems Checklist is another easily administered scale developed for caregivers that assesses their reactions as well as the frequency of the older person's behaviors during the previous week (Teri et al., 1992). Most caregivers complete the list in fifteen to twenty minutes. A version that was developed for nursing homes, the Memory and Behavioral Problem Checklist—Nursing Home, is also available (Wagner, Teri, and Orr-Rainey, 1995). Other scales designed specifically to measure agitation include the Cohen-Mansfield Agitation Inventory and a reduced version called the Brief Agitation Rating Scale (Cohen-Mansfield, 2000; Cohen-Mansfield, Marx, and Rosenthal, 1989; Finkel, Lyons, and Anderson, 1993); the Disruptive Behavior Rating Scales (Mungas, Weiler, Franzi, and Henry, 1989); the Discomfort Scale for Advanced Alzheimer Patients; the Pittsburgh Agitation Scale, which includes items concerned with resistance to care; and the Ryden Aggression Scale, one of the first scales to measure sexually aggressive behaviors.

Although the sources of agitation vary from medical conditions to environmental disruptions, social workers should first consider medical problems, especially if the disruptive behaviors appear suddenly. Infections, nutritional problems, strokes, complications from chronic illnesses, toxic reactions to drugs, and drug interactions can all evoke inappropriate behavior. Chronic sleep problems can disorient and confuse someone with dementia. Psychiatric problems, especially psychosis expressed as delusions or hallucinations, are another source of disruptive behavior, and people with severe cases of depression and anxiety sometimes become agitated. When environmental changes occur, people with dementia often react disruptively. Most respond best when their environments are stable, uncertainties are minimized, and schedules and routines are consistent.

Cohen-Mansfield (2000) identifies four models, which are often interactive, that are used to explain problem behaviors: direct effects of dementia, unmet needs, behavioral reinforcement, and environmental vulnerability. She also explains that different types of problem behaviors are related to different needs. For example, verbal behaviors are often related to distress and loneliness, whereas physically nonaggressive behaviors are unrelated to suffering and are often adaptive. Cohen-Mansfield argues that aggressive behaviors, which occur more frequently during severe cognitive impairment, are poorly explained by the unmet needs model and are, more likely, attempts to communicate discomfort. Practitioners must first consider the sources of agitated behavior and create intervention models based on these factors.

Mood Assessment

Lawton, Van Haitsma, and Perkinson (2000) argue that "dementia patients have the same right that all people have to maximize positive feelings and minimize negative feelings" (p. 99). Radford and Bucks (2000), who examined emotion processing among people with Alzheimer's, found that their emotional reactions, specifically, perceptions of nonverbal cues, were more resistant to damage from Alzheimer's disease than were their cognitive abilities and that deficits that do occur are typically in the expression of emotions. People with dementia continue to feel, but they struggle to talk about and describe their emotions (Bowlby Sifton, 2000; Shue, Beck, and Lawton, 1996).

Sinha and colleagues (1992) developed the Behavioral and Emotional Activities Manifested in Dementia Scale to assess the feelings of people with Alzheimer's disease. It is easy to administer to people with Alzheimer's or to their caregivers and measures the severity and intensity of emotions. C. Beck (1995) developed the Observable Displays of Affect Scale to examine facial expressions, vocalizations, and body movements as indications of affect among adults with dementia. Although this scale was developed for researchers, clinicians can also use it.

Lawton, Van Haitsma, and Perkinson (2000) have developed a comprehensive affect training program for clinicians for assessing the feelings of people who have Alzheimer's. The training begins with didactic instruction on how to observe emotions and uses the Apparent Affect Rating Scale, which was developed by Lawton, Van Haitsma, and Klapper (1996). Clinicians are taught to interpret the emotions of people with Alzheimer's by reading their faces, voices, bodies, eyes, and contacts or touch. For more information about this training, see Lawton and colleagues (2000).

Quality of Life

More and more clinicians seek to enhance the quality of life for people with dementia. We discuss three scales that assess quality of life—the Dementia Quality of Life Scale (D-QOL), Quality of Life—Alzheimer's Disease (QOL-AD), and Quality of Life Assessment Schedule (QOLAS). These measures assume (1) that quality of life is important to all humans; (2) that despite severe impairments, people with dementia have feelings and preferences; (3) that it is philosophically and morally important to understand the subjective perceptions of people with Alzheimer's disease; and (4) that individuals with Alzheimer's are as entitled to experience pleasure as people without cognitive limitations.

Lawton (1991) measured quality of life through "the multidimensional evaluation, by both interpersonal and social-normative criteria, of the person-environment system of the individual" (p. 6). Lawton and colleagues (2000) incorporate a biopsychosocial perspective, a holistic view of people with dementia that emphasizes their strengths and ongoing positive contributions rather than their deficits, disruptive behaviors, and their need for burdensome caregiving. Lawton's definition of quality of life takes into account both objective and subjective elements. The objective factors focus on sensitivity and individualization of care as well as environmental factors, including staff-patient ratios, in-service training programs, and residential ambience. Behaviors, functional capacities, social supports, and cultural influences all comprise the objective assessment of quality of life (Lawton et al., 2000). The subjective components include the views and emotions of people with dementia.

Brod, Stewart, Sands, and Walton (1999) and Brod, Stewart, and Sands (2000) developed the dementia-specific Dementia Quality of Life Scale (D-QOL) with five domains: positive affect, negative affect, sense of aesthetics, and feelings of belonging and self-esteem. The D-QOL differs from most objective assessments of quality of life in that it is "patient-administered," that is, administered to the person with dementia; caregivers usually serve as proxies and answer the questions for the person with dementia. The D-QOL was designed for people with MMSE scores greater than 12. Logsdon, Gibbons, McCurry, and Teri (2000) also created an instrument, the Quality of Life—Alzheimer's Disease (QOL-AD), to measure quality of life among people with dementia, specifically, those with Alzheimer's disease. It differs from the D-QOL in its inclusion of items that pertain to physical condition, energy level, finances, interpersonal relationships, and involvement in meaningful activities. Caregivers can complete the QOL-AD, and people with dementia can follow along if they are given clear instructions and a copy of the questions. Logsdon and colleagues (2000) found that the QOL-AD works best with people whose MMSE scores were between 10 and 28; those with scores below 10 failed to complete the instrument.

Two outcomes from the evaluation of this instrument by Logsdon and colleagues (2000) are worth noting. First, caregivers and people with dementia agree on most of the items, specifically, those that measure mood, energy, physical health, and self, but they disagree on items that focus on memory or ability to do chores. Second, based on their analysis of the responses from caregivers and people with dementia, Logsdon and colleagues (2000) found that depression and frequency of pleasant events were the most important predictors of quality of life.

The Quality of Life Assessment Schedule (QOLAS) was created to help clinicians individualize their assessments of people with Alzheimer's disease (Selai, Trimble, Rossor, and Harvey, 2000). Similar to the other quality-of-life scales, the QOLAS is effectively implemented with mildly and moderately impaired people with dementia, who usually understand the questions on the instrument and can complete the interview. For those who have a severe dementia, caregivers serve as proxies.

Intervention

Social workers are often the first to suspect a dementia in an older person. They must know how to screen for dementia and the steps involved in diagnosing it. Social workers' initial discussions with families of aging relatives usually involve helping them to manage their feelings of anxiety, fear, loss, and shame, which often emerge when the family initially suspects dementia. Social workers should encourage family members to express their concerns about an impending dementia diagnosis. By listening to their feelings, answering their questions, and describing how others have coped, social workers offer hope to family members and aging people during these difficult prediagnosis stages. In these early stages social workers can support the relatives, inform them about what to expect, and counsel elderly people who are in early stages of dementia and who often feel depressed.

Later, when families feel overwhelmed and need help managing disruptive behaviors, social workers can recommend interventions that improve the quality of life for caregivers and people with dementia and reduce the overall stress for everyone. Nursing home social workers also organize activity groups for people with dementia and support groups for their families.

In the next section we discuss interventions for people with dementia in four problem areas: mental status, moods, behaviors, and functional skills. For a complete review of dementia interventions, see Lawton and Rubinstein (2000), as well as Kumar and Eisdorfer (1998). See also Hay, Klein, Hay, Grossberg, and Kennedy (2003) for an in-depth discussion of assessments and interventions recommended for agitation, depression, and other behaviors associated with dementia.

Interventions for Cognitive Impairment

The first line of treatment for an older person with dementia, especially one who has recently been diagnosed, is pharmacological, that is, medication with cholinesterase inhibitors. In fact, the practice guidelines for treating Alzheimer's disease and other dementias that were established by the American Psychiatric Association in 1997 maintain that nonpharmacological therapies for improving cognitive function are ineffective. They do not stop or reverse the disease, although they may improve people's cognitive functioning for a few months and, in some instances, a few years (NIA, 2004). Some experts nevertheless believe that memory-enhancing treatments can help in certain circumstances, particularly in the early stages of dementia. Although social workers need to know about the medications available, the present discussion focuses on nonpharmacological interventions.

The Memory Enhance Program was developed for adults with early stage Alzheimer's disease or mild cognitive impairments who are living in assisted living facilities (Simard, 2000). It provides an example of a nonpharmacological cognitive enhancement intervention. People with dementia participate at least five days a week in memory classes, brain exercises, and other cognitive activities, as well as physical exercise, stress reduction, dining, and evening events. The intent is to mentally stimulate the residents by involving them in word games, puzzles, other games, and social activities. This memory program differs from many others by integrating mental challenges with social interaction. The broader goal is to improve quality of life for cognitively impaired people. Simard and colleagues are developing a similar memory enhancement program for people with more severe dementia.

Reality orientation, which was first described by Taulbee and Folsom in 1966, was one of the first cognitive training programs used with dementia patients in nursing homes. The intent of reality orientation is to bring the demented older person back to "reality." By correcting elderly people who are confused about dates, places, or people, caregivers and professionals presumably stimulate and enhance their cognitive capacities. Nursing home staff and family members often work together by constantly reminding the aging relative of the correct facts about people, events, or other information.

Group or classroom reality orientation is usually offered at specific times during the day. Several residents, selected because of their dementia, gather for group sessions that are typically led by a professional staff member. Session leaders introduce "reality" by asking each group member to read from a bulletin board that lists the date, time, weather, and current events and by encouraging group discussions about specific issues. Posting calendars and bulletin boards throughout the residence is usually referred to as "environmental reality orientation." In a comprehensive meta-analysis of the literature, Spector, Davies, Woods, and Orrell (2000) found that residents with dementia who participate in reality orientation are more alert, cognizant, and functional than residents with dementia who are not exposed to reality orientation. Spector and colleagues (2000) found no evidence of adverse effects from participation in reality orientation.

Many clinicians object to the confrontational style of reality orientation and worry about insulting and distressing clients. Some, for example, Woods (1999), argue that reality orientation's excessive emphasis on the cognitive status of people with dementia deprives them of dignity, respect, and, in some instances, their personhood; these critics believe that approaches such as reality orientation assume that "cognitive abilities underpin personhood and accordingly, that cognitive impairment must therefore pose a threat to full status as a person" (p. 17). Despite these objections, clinicians can effectively offer reality orientation in a nonconfrontational manner in some circumstances.

Interventions to Enhance Functional Capacities

Functional performance, specifically, engagement in meaningful activities (occupation), contributes substantially to the well-being of people with dementia. Data consistently show reductions in behavioral and psychiatric problems among those who remain active (Bowlby Sifton, 2000). People with dementia seek purposeful activity, that is, to engage in meaningful activities, as much as people who do not have dementia. Social workers should ensure the availability of appropriate activities in which people with dementia can participate. By helping these people to maintain their investments in rewarding activities, such as managing and picking up the mail, visiting with grandchildren, cooking and cleaning, gardening, watching television, or listening to music, social workers improve the quality of living for people with dementia and their families (see Bowlby Sifton, 2000, for an in-depth discussion of these activities).

Bowlby Sifton (2000) outlines specific guidelines for health care professionals to use in engaging people with dementia in meaningful functional activities. She advises that clinicians emphasize the semantic and procedural memories rather than episodic memories, which decline more rapidly. Episodic memory (memory of specific events) usually fails first, followed by semantic memory (memory of general knowledge), and, finally, procedural memory (memory of how to do things), which is the most basic. With prompting and appropriate assistance, especially nonverbal cueing, many people with dementia can continue to brush their teeth, wash dishes, and locate the kitchen or dining room.

Humor and the ability to laugh persist after other cognitive functions fail. Laughter relieves tension, builds rapport between the caretaker and the person with dementia, and preserves the dignity of people with dementia by helping them to save face. People with dementia remain emotionally aware and sensitive to others even during severe stages of dementia, although they often have trouble verbalizing their feelings. Bowlby Sifton recommends that caregivers and health professionals encourage the nonverbal expressions of feelings, such as through music or art. Because people with dementia often remember the emotional moods associated with events and activities, for example, whether the ambience of an event was sad or joyous, clinicians should capitalize on these remaining capacities to maximize the pleasures and delights for people with dementia.

Many people with dementia enjoy the company of others long after they have suffered substantial cognitive declines; most people's social skills remain automatic and overlearned. When caretakers ensure that people with dementia socialize adequately, their alertness and equanimity are enhanced.

Music, exercise, and sensory experiences, the other areas that people with dementia often retain a capacity to enjoy, also enhance well-being. The major sensory areas, including sound, smell, sight, taste, and movement, remain mostly intact as dementia progresses. According to Bowlby Sifton (2000), the human need for sensory stimulation, referred to as "sensoristasis," is essential until death. Structured sensory stimulation is a specific clinical intervention carefully designed to enhance the functional capacities of people with Alzheimer's disease. It encourages people with dementia to make a functional response (for example, arrange flowers or use fragrant soap to bathe) by using sensory-rich but familiar everyday objects while focusing on one sense at a time. Caregivers can easily integrate sensory stimulation while carrying out routine caregiving tasks. For a more detailed discussion of this intervention, see C. Bowlby (1993).

Interventions for Psychiatric Problems

Although many pharmacological and nonpharmacological interventions are effective for treating people with dementia who have psychiatric conditions, social workers must carefully assess the circumstances before they choose interventions. For example, when people with dementia suddenly hallucinate or become delusional, caretakers should consider infection, medication, or marked disruptions in environmental conditions, which can be resolved quickly. But when psychotic symptoms persist, psychopharmacological treatment may be needed. As we discussed earlier, depression commonly accompanies early stage Alzheimer's disease. Although psychopharmacological treatment (i.e., antidepressant medications) works well with many people with dementia, social workers should first implement psychosocial interventions. If the major source of the depression is environmental, and it is not modified, the depression will continue. In addition, people with dementia may be more susceptible than others to the adverse side-effects of antidepressants (Katz, 1998). Nonpharmacological interventions have become more widespread since the passage of the Nursing Home Reform Act (NHRA) in 1987, which provides that "residents have the right to be free from any physical or chemical restraint imposed for purposes of discipline or convenience and not required to treat the resident's medical symptoms."

Psychotherapy (including reminiscence, cognitive behavioral therapy, behavioral interventions) works well with older people with dementia when it is tailored to their needs and capacities. Teri and Gallagher-Thompson (1991), who developed a cognitive behavioral intervention approach for depressed people with dementia, maintain that the goals for depressed people are the same, whether they have dementia or not (i.e., to identify negative cognitions and substitute these with more positive ones; see chapter 6 for a more detailed discussion of cognitive behavioral therapy). Laidlaw and colleagues (2003) recommend modifications of cognitive behavioral therapy when using it to treat depression in older people with dementia. Laidlaw and colleagues suggest that practitioners become familiar with the older person's strengths and weaknesses, keep goals realistic and simple, and conduct more structured sessions with people who have Alzheimer's than they would with people who do not. Clinicians should also simplify homework assignments, offer shorter but more frequent sessions, and use more behavioral strategies, especially with the most severely impaired people. Behavioral approaches can also effectively treat depression in people with dementia. When Teri, Logsdon, Uomoto, and McCurry (1997) taught caregivers behavioral strategies for alleviating depression (including problem solving or increasing the frequency of pleasant events), the moods of both the caregivers and the people with dementia improved; this worked as well as most antidepressants.

Teri and Logsdon (1991) developed the Pleasant Events Schedule—Alzheimer's Disease (PES-AD) to enhance well-being among people with Alzheimer's disease; it is widely used and improves the treatment of depression for people with dementia. The PES-AD includes fifty-three items that identify a range of potentially rewarding activities for people with dementia. Dementia patients and their caregivers work together to rate the activities according to frequency, availability, and enjoyability. Caretakers often recall other activities that the patient enjoys that are not included on the list in PES-AD. Social workers and caregivers then develop interventions based on the responses. Caregivers can complete the form in less than thirty minutes, or they can work on it intermittently for several days. Most caregivers report that the PES-AD is simple to use and that it helps them plan gratifying experiences for their relatives who have dementia.

Validation fantasy, developed by Naomi Feil (1992, 1993), is another approach designed to enhance the emotional well-being of people with dementia. This approach encourages clinicians and caregivers to respond empathetically and to use verbal and nonverbal expressions to demonstrate their concern. They validate the feelings of the people with dementia by reflecting and accepting their feelings. Caregivers and clinicians avoid confrontations and corrections about reality. Validation therapy is usually applied in groups of six or seven elderly people with dementia and a leader who encourages participants to share their feelings. Although few investigators have systematically evaluated validation therapy, or compared it to appropriate controls and to other interventions, many social workers find this approach intuitively appealing.

Interventions for Behavioral Disturbances

After extensive study of agitation among people with dementia, Cohen-Mansfield (2000) created an innovative treatment known as TREA (treatment routes for exploring agitation). She proposed the following intervention guidelines (2000, p. 53):

- Treatment of disruptive behaviors should be individualized.
- The different syndromes of disruptive behaviors ... have different etiologies and different meanings; therefore, they require different approaches to treatment.
- Nonpharmacological approaches to treatment should precede pharmacological approaches.
- The first step in developing a specific treatment plan for a specific person is to attempt to understand the etiology of the agitated behavior or the need it signals.

- In developing a treatment plan, the remaining abilities, strengths, memories, and needs should be utilized, as well as recognition of disabilities, especially those in sensory perception and mobility. Unique characteristics of the individual—such as past work, hobbies, important relationships, and sense of identity—need to be explored to best match current activities to the person.
- Prevention, accommodation, and flexibility are essential elements of intervention.

Prevention includes arranging environmental design, structure, and ambience in the most appropriate manner to minimize disruptive behaviors by the person with dementia. For example, the environment must offer enough social stimulation to reduce isolation. Accommodation occurs when minor or innocuous environmental modifications satisfy the needs and thus reduce the agitation of a person with dementia. For example, nursing home residents who continually wander to the receptionist's desk might benefit from increased social opportunities. Caregivers must also remain flexible and adjust elements of older people's daily routines to meet the needs and wishes of people with dementia. For example, instead of insisting that elderly people eat three meals a day at specific times, caregivers may be able to provide snacks and meals when the person with dementia wants to eat.

Cohen-Mansfield (2000, 2003) recommends using different interventions depending on the type of disruptive behavior, that is, whether the behaviors are verbally disruptive, physically nonaggressive, or aggressive. Cohen-Mansfield and Werner (1998a) found that the most common causes of verbal aggression were pain, depression, and poor health. Social workers and caregivers can prevent hostile verbal actions by effectively treating the person's depression or discomfort. Social isolation and boredom can often be resolved by enrolling the person with dementia in adult day programs that offer structured activities and social opportunities. In nursing homes, day programs that include lunch and structured activities, such as gardening, singing, or crafts, stimulate and appeal to many people with dementia. Some like to relax while watching videotapes of relatives talking. Cohen-Mansfield (2000) found that both face-to-face and simulated interactions decreased verbally disruptive behaviors. Physically nonaggressive behaviors, such as pacing and wandering, also have multiple causes (Logsdon et al., 1998). D. Klein and colleagues (1999) found that wandering occurs most among people with Alzheimer's whose dementia is severe and whose depression is moderate to severe with delusions or hallucinatory thoughts.

Using a behavioral approach, Heard and Watson (1999) found that they could modify wandering among people with dementia by offering alternatives. In one instance, an elderly person wandered to experience sensory stimulation, but the wandering ceased when this stimulation—music, hugging, or touching—was offered directly.

Environmental interventions, such as monitoring devices, help caregivers keep track of aging relatives who wander. Cohen-Mansfield and Werner (1998b) decreased problem wandering behavior, such as exit seeking and inappropriate trespassing, among nursing home residents by enhancing certain corridors with visual, auditory, and olfactory stimuli. They found that people with dementia preferred the enhanced corridors to the halls that lacked such stimulation.

Social workers should first assess people with dementia to determine the optimal amount stimulation that they need and structure their environment in accordance with their circumstances. In a study of caregivers of people with dementia, Olsen, Hutchings, and Ehrenkrantz (1999) found that several design features were particularly helpful. Ranch-style homes or one-floor apartments work better than two-story dwellings with stairs. Adequate space provides people with dementia with room to wander; both caregivers and care recipients feel less confined in open settings. Simple and understandable floor layouts, with few curves and walls, prevent people with dementia from getting lost or confusing their surroundings. Signage throughout the residence, especially when used in familiar settings such as the dining room or bedrooms, can enhance their orientation. Familiar surroundings offer stability, continuity, and reassurance. Several studies demonstrate that homelike environments improve well-being, reduce behavioral disturbances, and enhance functional capacities among people with dementia (see Day, Carreon, and Stump, 2000). A layout that provides visibility between rooms helps caregivers to monitor the actions of a person with dementia and reassure the older person that a caregiver is accessible. Privacy is especially important for caregivers when they need to retreat and refuel. Bathrooms that are visible, safe, and spacious enough to bathe aging relatives are important. When kitchens or special sections within kitchens are arranged to accommodate people with dementia, they can maintain their independence and functional capacities for longer periods. Electric stoves are less hazardous than gas stoves for people with dementia, and some automatically turn off after a certain period of time. Day and colleagues (2000) also found that specific dining areas for people with dementia reduce inappropriate outbursts in other areas. Finally, outdoor access, where people with dementia can walk freely and safely in a yard or garden and experience fresh air, stimulates the senses and enhances their well-being.

Functional analyses of disruptive behaviors help caregivers determine the precipitants and consequences of problem behaviors. These analyses usually reveal specific patterns. For example, some people with dementia become anxious only at night when they are tired. Others clash with caregivers when forced to bathe or dress. Once caregivers identify the events that provoke problem behaviors, they can modify or avoid those situations.

Social workers, caregivers, and anyone interacting with people with dementia should intervene to minimize agitation on the basis of the following guidelines. The environment of the person with dementia should be safe, comfortable, at an appropriate temperature with good lighting (especially at night), and soothing (e.g., with pictures of relatives, bright colors). Overstimulation from noise or excessive activity should be avoided. Open spaces accommodate wandering better than confined areas, and living quarters for people with dementia must be physically safe. For example, caregivers should remove knives from the kitchen and use safety locks and monitoring devices. Regular routines and structured environments are very important, and disruptions in routine should be avoided as much as possible. Tasks, such as dressing, dining, and bathing, should be simplified. Social workers should ask questions that require recognition rather than recall to answer. Caretakers should talk slowly and distinctly, use familiar words and short sentences, and use nonverbal gestures and signs or prompts to facilitate understanding. When a topic elicits agitation, social workers should never persist or argue with the older person who has dementia. In a qualitative research study of care providers, Beach and Kramer (1999) learned that people with Alzheimer's become far more compliant when health professionals avoid using the word no, make connections to the client's history when trying to distract him, change caregivers to end obstinacy connected with one person, and confirm rather than deny residents' realities. In addition, when attempting to modify disruptive behaviors, social workers should consider whether the person with dementia perceives the behaviors as inappropriate and problematic or as necessary under the circumstances. For example, a social worker may discover that a person with dementia feels neglected and ignored. By encouraging caregivers to understand the sources of the agitation, social workers can often mitigate the tensions. To the extent possible, social workers should include many people—including family members, nurses, aides, and other staff members—when creating and implementing interventions. Finally, social workers should also identify strategies that families and others have used successfully in the past.

More and more programs offer special care units (SCUs) for people with dementia. The quality of care in SCUs depends on several factors, including staff ratios, staff training, environmental features, the programs offered, and the type of facility, for example, whether it is a nursing home or residential care facility. While some offer better care than others, SCUs have generally disappointed health care professionals (Ory, 2000). Studies increasingly demonstrate few differences between SCUs and non-SCUs. In a comprehensive evaluation of 510 residents with dementia at seventy-seven intermediate care facilities in Canada, Chappell and Reid (2002) found no differences between SCUs and non-SCUs in cognitive functioning, agitation, social skills, physical functioning, affect, or expressive language.

Social workers should integrate the specialized assessments and interventions for dementia, which we have discussed in this chapter, with the integrated practice model that we described earlier. This will ensure that the treatment is individualized. What follows is an example of how a social worker supplemented the integrated practice model with more specialized assessment and intervention techniques for dementia.

Case 9.1

Ms. Heinz, eighty-five, moved to a lifetime care community several years ago. Her husband died about ten years before she relocated, and her three children live in different states. Ms. Heinz is a gregarious person, generally optimistic with an even disposition. Although she felt lonely when she first moved into the facility, she gradually befriended several older women. Ms. Heinz functioned well until recently, when the staff social worker and several residents noticed that she seemed confused and unusually anxious. She began forgetting and misplacing things, repeating herself in conversations, and misidentifying friends. She was increasingly overwhelmed by trying to maintain her household, especially buying groceries, arranging home repairs, and paying bills. When Ms. Heinz started wandering around the facility and visiting the receptionist's desk several times a day, usually in a state of anxiety, the social worker consulted with Ms. Heinz and members of her family.

The social worker referred Ms. Heinz to a geriatric physician for a physical examination and complete neurological assessment. It revealed that although she is in good physical health, Ms. Heinz suffers from a mild dementia—probably early stage Alzheimer's disease, based on results from the MMSE and other tests. Although the physician prescribed Aricept for Ms. Heinz, she refuses to take it. Her wandering has increased.

The social worker comprehensively assesses Ms. Heinz' situation by using the ABCDEF practice guidelines. Her actions (A), specifically, her wandering, jeopardize her safety; in some instances, she has gotten lost in the corridors of the building. Her health and biological functioning (B) are excellent. After discussions with Ms. Heinz's physician, her children, and the aides who visit her regularly, the social worker rules out sudden changes in Ms. Heinz's health, nutrition, or sleep as reasons for the wandering. The social worker determines that Ms. Heinz's cognitive state (C) becomes more confused when she feels overwhelmed by the demands in her life. She is white, a widow, and a college graduate (D). Several environmental factors (E) seem to trigger her wandering (these are described shortly). Ms. Heinz is generally in good spirits but becomes anxious in certain situations (F). The social worker uses a modified version of the Hamilton Anxiety Rating Scale (HARS; see chapter 5), a brief interview-administered tool, to assess Ms. Heinz's anxiety.

The social worker also conducts a functional analysis of Ms. Heinz's wandering and identifies its antecedents (A), behavioral characteristics (specifically, its frequency, duration, and intensity) (B), and the consequences (C) or results of the activity. Ms. Heinz usually wandered on Sundays, holidays, and late afternoons (the antecedents) until she stumbled upon an area where many people congregate (the consequences). These were typically "downtimes" when the facility was quiet. The social worker uses Cohen-Mansfield's TREA model for intervention and follows its guidelines. For example, she individualizes the treatment and tailors it to Ms. Heinz's preferences. The social worker identifies the underlying motivations for Ms. Heinz's wandering, recognizes her interests and strengths, specifically, her gregariousness, and first tries a nonpharmacological intervention.

After a comprehensive assessment the social worker concludes that Ms. Heinz's wandering is related to disorientation, lack of structure, and the anxiety that seems to emerge on Sundays when daily routines are different, fewer staff members are around, and no formal activities are offered. Ms. Heinz's children call this the "Sunday syndrome" because she calls them several times on these days and acts upset and disoriented.

The social worker uses prevention, accommodation, and flexibility to design an intervention. The social worker designs a structured activities program from 10 A.M. until 3 P.M. The intent is to reduce the disruptive behaviors exhibited by Ms. Heinz as well as a few other residents by engaging them in rewarding and appropriate activities. The social worker hires more staff for weekends and arranges for a companion to help Ms. Heinz more successfully carry out her daily routines, keep her company, and encourage her involvement in enjoyable activities. The social worker uses the Pleasant Events Schedule—Alzheimer's Disease to identify the most rewarding events and activities for Ms. Heinz. Although family members initially resist this intervention because they doubt that their mother will accept a stranger, they are pleasantly surprised. Not only does Ms. Heinz welcome the idea but she feels more secure because she knows that someone is available to keep her company and help her with her chores. Ms. Heinz's wandering as well as her agitation and anxiety decrease substantially. This intervention addresses Ms. Heinz's quality of life as well as her wandering and considers objective and subjective aspects of her well-being. For example, by adding more staff on Sundays and implementing a structured day program, the social worker considered environmental factors. Ms. Heinz's strengths and interests, particularly her gregariousness, were taken into account by hiring a companion who could help her perform more activities of daily living and engage her in productive and enjoyable activities. By intervening on multiple levels, behaviorally and programmatically, and by taking into account Ms. Heinz's feelings and preferences, the social worker used a more holistic approach to treat her wandering, the problem that initially raised concerns.

Discussion Questions

1. In what settings are social workers likely to work with older people with dementia? How will these settings influence the assessment and intervention approaches that social workers will use with people who have dementia?
2. How can social workers prepare for the baby boom generation, which will include more people with Alzheimer's disease?
3. What types of problems do people with dementia typically experience, and which interventions work best with what problems?
4. What social policies should gerontological social workers know about when working with people with dementia and their families? How might these be modified to more effectively address the needs of older people with dementia and their families?

PART 3

Social Psychological Problems and Interventions

CHAPTER 10

Social Workers and Aging Families

S OCIAL WORKERS HAVE ALWAYS worked with families, but today these families include older relatives who need care as well as more multigenerational households comprised of grandparents who are raising grandchildren. Increases in life expectancy and societal changes in urbanization, geographic mobility, and gender roles have led to families that are smaller and more dispersed around the country. Although married couples still comprise the majority of U.S. households, they are older and make up a smaller proportion of households than in the past (Fields and Casper, 2001). In addition, more people live alone today, especially older women who have outlived their spouses, were divorced, or never married.

Family members are more involved with caregiving than at any other time in history despite the obstacles created by smaller families, geographic mobility, and working women. Intergenerational relationships have become more common as greater numbers of adult children and their aging parents coexist. By 2020 most middle-aged adults will have a surviving parent (Mabry, Bengston, and Rosenthal, 2001). Changes in life expectancy and the shift from acute to chronic illnesses have resulted in aging parents who live longer but also have lengthier illnesses. About one hundred million Americans suffer from a chronic illness or disability for which they need help, and at least 40% of people older than seventy need help with one or more daily activities (National Academy on an Aging Society, 1999).

Grandparents live longer and maintain more extended relationships with grandchildren and other family members than in the past. Early in the twentieth century only 20% of young adults had a living grandparent whereas 68% had a living grandparent in 1980 (Uhlenberg, 1996). Increasing numbers of these grandparents are raising grandchildren. According to the U.S. Census of 2000, more than six million children are living in households maintained by a grandparent or another relative, and more than 2.4 million grandparents have primary responsibility for their grandchildren's care (Generations United, 2002). Although all types of households led by grandparents have increased, the greatest growth has occurred among grandparent households in which neither parent is present; since 1990 the number of these households has increased by 53% (U.S. Census Bureau, 2004a).

Social workers are in a unique position to work with older families. The commitment of social workers to biopsychosocial practice has prepared them, more than any other professionals, to help aging families in various settings, for example, in the community and in hospitals, hospices, and nursing homes. In this chapter we focus on three critical areas—caregiving for older relatives, elder abuse, and grandparents who are raising grandchildren—in which social workers are most likely to work with aging families. We will highlight specific assessment and intervention techniques designed for these situations within the perspective of an integrated gerontological practice framework.

Caring for Elderly Parents

More than 23% of American households report that they are caring for a relative or friend who is at least fifty years old, and family members (especially women) provide most of the care for aging relatives (see figure 10.1). Among African Americans, 77% of caregivers are women (Older Women's League [OWL], 2001). Slightly more than half of all caregivers provide help to elderly family members every day, and an additional 21% report that they assist relatives at least several times a week (National Academy on an Aging Society, 2000). Adult daughters (42%) are the most common caregivers, followed by spouses (25%) (National Alliance for Caregiving, 1997; National Academy on an Aging Society, 2000). Daughters are three times more likely to assume the primary caregiving role than sons, although increasing numbers of men are becoming caregivers (Stephens and Franks, 1999). Women caregivers usually provide assistance to aging relatives for longer time periods than do male caregivers. Eighty percent of those who provide constant care—forty or more hours per week—are women, regardless of race or ethnic background (Calasanti and Slevin, 2001).

B. Kramer (2002) and E. Thompson (2002) argue that the number of male caregivers is underestimated, and experts predict that increasing numbers of men (especially husbands) will become more involved with caregiving in the future. Men frequently serve as secondary caregivers, and they are most often the caregivers of people with AIDS (E. Thompson, 2002).

Ethnic differences in caregiving also influence how care is provided. African Americans provide more informal care than the national average (OWL, 2001). Approximately 42% of African American adult children and 52% of Hispanic adult children care for aging relatives. Four percent of all adult grandchildren care for

Sex

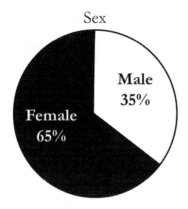

FIGURE 10.1 Gender Differences in Caregiving
Source: Alecxih, Zeruld, and Olearczyk, n.d., p. 5.

their grandparents, and the figures are even higher for adult grandchildren who are African American and Hispanic, 10% and 6%, respectively. African American caregivers more frequently care for a sibling, other relative, or friend and use a broader support network than white caregivers, who are more inclined to care for a spouse and involve mostly immediate family members (Gallagher-Thompson et al., 2003; Dilworth-Anderson, Williams, and Gibson, 2002).

Braun and Browne (1998) found significant variations in dementia caregiving within a group of Asian Americans and Pacific Islander Americans. Braun and Browne noted that the generations perceive dementia differently and that these differences are important, especially among the first four generations of Japanese Americans. For example, while more and more younger Japanese and Chinese Americans understand Alzheimer's disease as a medical condition, many older people in these families, especially those who recently immigrated to this country, view dementia as a mental illness requiring family problem solving rather than professional assistance. These variations underscore how differently people within groups conceptualize dementia.

The Stresses of Caregiving

Most people take pleasure in caregiving. They enjoy giving back to someone who cared for them and knowing that their aging relative is well protected. Caregiving offers people a chance to express love and affection for a family member. It can increase family cohesiveness as families unite to deliver care that a sick relative needs. The ability to find meaning in stressful situations is a valuable coping strategy that can improve caregivers' well-being, especially when the demands of care escalate (Noonan and Tennstedt, 1997).

Although many people benefit from helping their aging relatives, most caregivers eventually encounter difficulties, and they experience more distress than non-caregivers (Gallagher-Thompson, 2001; R. Schulz, O'Brien, Bookwala, and Fleissner, 1995). The most common emotional stresses for caregivers are depression, loneliness and social isolation, difficulty sleeping, role stress and role conflict, and disruptions in other family relationships. Behavioral problems among care recipients contribute most to caregivers' levels of stress, along with the number of hours of informal care and infrequency of breaks (Chappell and Reid, 2002). Caregivers who assist relatives with dementia or other serious memory impairments experience the greatest stress, particularly if care recipients exhibit disruptive behaviors. The more severe the care recipient's condition, the greater the stresses and disruptions for caregivers. Many people report that watching their loved ones deteriorate is the hardest part of caregiving (National Alliance for Caregiving, 1997).

Although minority caregivers often provide more care to more disabled elderly, they often report fewer burdens than do members of other groups surveyed (Noelker and Whitlach, 2001). Many African American caregivers interpret stressors and cope with caregiving differently from white caregivers. African American caregivers are more likely to cognitively reappraise their experiences, and they often experience less stress than those who use noncognitive coping approaches (Dilworth-Anderson et al., 2002). For example, many African American caregivers find meaning in helping elderly relatives. Coping styles significantly influence which caregivers become distressed and which adjust well to caregiving.

The context of caregiving is also important. For example, AIDS caregivers are likely to be gay male partners and friends, and they are more vulnerable to role overload, financial problems, and isolation than those tending to people who do not have AIDS (Wight, 2002). These caregivers often struggle with lack of acceptance, feelings of alienation, and, in many cases, their own poor health because they too are infected with HIV. Discrimination is especially problematic for gay and lesbian elders, such as when employers decline to extend health care benefits to the partners of employees. In addition, because caregivers for elderly gays and lesbians are often reluctant to disclose their sexual preferences to health care workers, they frequently feel even more alone and alienated.

Social isolation and loneliness are commonly associated with caregiving. Many caregivers say that caregiving has reduced the time that they spend with other family members or in leisure activities (see figure 10.2). Feelings of loneliness are especially prevalent among spouse caregivers who are losing the support and companionship of their ailing partner. Those who lack community support feel even more cut off from others (Tebb and Jivanjee, 2000).

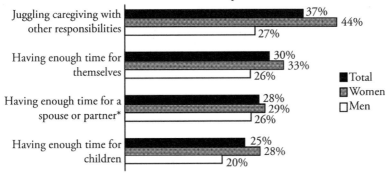

FIGURE 10.2 Concerns of Caregivers
Note: Differences by gender are not statistically significant at $p < .05$.
Source: National Survey on Health Care and Other Elder Issues (#1603). The Family Circle and the Henry J. Kaiser Family Foundation, September 2000. Used by permission.

Caregivers typically report worse health and more chronic illnesses than non-caregivers, and they have weaker immune systems (Adler, Patterson, and Grant, 2002; Glaser and Kiecolt-Glaser, 1997). They also use more psychotropic medications than noncaregivers (Gallagher-Thompson, 2001). Male caregivers are especially vulnerable to health problems and may be more physiologically reactive to psychosocial stressors than female caregivers (Adler et al., 2002).

Conflict with work is another concern for caregivers; many miss work (see figure 10.3) or quit their jobs because of caregiving demands. About 20% of caregivers stop working to care for loved ones, according to a survey conducted by the National Alliance for Caregiving (1997). This percentage is even higher among Hispanic and Asian caregivers. By relying on close friends and formal services, many African American caregivers continue to work and manage to provide satisfactory care for relatives (Bullock, Crawford, and Tennstedt, 2003). Caregivers who quit work or miss work for caregiving reasons experience more economic problems than those who are able to continue working (Richardson, 1999b).

Pinquart and Sorensen (2003) conducted a meta-analysis of 228 studies, focusing on factors that contribute to caregiver burden. They found that the most significant contributor to caregiver burden and depression was behavior problems among care recipients. Caregivers also were more burdened and more depressed when care recipients had more physical and cognitive impairments and required more caregiving and more hours of care per week. Caregivers of relatives with dementia experienced more depression and burden than caregivers for family members who did not have dementia. Also, the burden and depression increased with

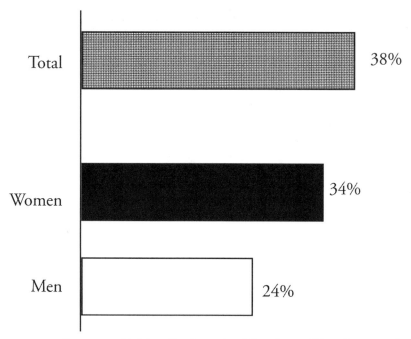

FIGURE 10.3 Percentage of Adults with a Parent Aged Sixty-five or Older Who Have Missed
Work to Care for Their Parent
Source: National Survey on Health Care and Other Elder Issues (#1603). The Family Circle and the
Henry J. Kaiser Family Foundation, September 2000. Used by permission.

the duration of caregiving. Finally, Pinquart and Sorensen (2003) observed that
coping processes (such as perceiving benefits and meaning), valuing the increased
closeness to the care recipient, and strong social supports mitigated these negative
consequences.

Assessment of Caregivers

How caregivers are affected by their responsibilities varies according to the type of
illness involved and the coping strategies used. Social workers must comprehensively assess these clients because multiple factors affect the manner in which they
manage their caregiving experiences. The ABCDEF practice guide, presented in
earlier chapters, ensures that the assessment takes into account multiple levels of
functioning and that social workers tailor their interventions to the unique needs
of caregivers and care recipients. Social workers should supplement this approach
with specific caregiving assessment tools to obtain more in-depth information
about specific problems.

The ABCDEF practice approach includes the assessment of clients' actions (A), biological/health functioning (B), cognitive status (C), demographic indicators (D), environmental influences (E), and feelings (F). The actions (A) assessment focuses on the behaviors and activities of care recipients and caregivers alike. In some cases a functional assessment, which focuses on the antecedents and consequences of an action, will help reveal the motives and circumstances behind care recipients' behavior problems. Assessing the biological status (B) or health of caregivers and care recipients is important. Care recipients with serious illnesses require more assistance than healthier people. The cognitive (C) assessment covers family members' coping approaches, and demographic (D) factors shed light on a family's cultural context. When evaluating the clients' environment (E), their living arrangements and the physical design of their residence are important considerations. In addition, the social worker should evaluate family interactions and other family systems as well as clients' informal and formal systems. The feelings (F) of the care recipient and his caregivers reveal a family's overall functioning and well-being.

Specific Caregiving Assessment Tools

As experts continue to create specific instruments to assess caregivers and their families, social workers must select instruments that demonstrate adequate reliability and validity and are easy to administer to older family members. Next we describe a few of the most common instruments for assessing caregivers; these primarily focus on the caregiver's burden and well-being.

The Caregiver Burden Interview (CBI) and the Revised Memory and Behavior Problems Checklist (RMBPC) devised by Teri and colleagues (discussed in chapter 9) are the two most widely used instruments (Teri et al., 1992; Zarit and Zarit, 1983; Zarit, Reever, and Bach-Peterson, 1980). Many experts view these as the "gold standards," especially for those caring for people with dementia (Gaugler, Kane, and Langlois, 2000). Social workers can easily administer the twenty-two items of the CBI in person, over the phone, or as part of a questionnaire. The RMBPC includes three subscales: depression, memory problems, and problem behaviors. It assesses the objective burden, specifically, the frequency of troubling behaviors, and subjective burden, that is, the extent of distress caused by these behaviors. These instruments (and their revised versions) have excellent reliability and validity, although social workers should use the RMBPC cautiously with minority families (Whitlatch, Zarit, and von Eye, 1991; Bedard et al., 2001; O'Rourke and Tuokko, 2003). Gottlieb, Thompson, and Bourgeois (2003) found that the RMBPC inadequately assesses the caregiving experiences of African American and Latino families. Social workers and other practitioners must develop more culturally sensitive caregiver assessment tools that are valid with all populations.

The Caregiver Reaction Assessment (CRA) asks caregivers about their schedules, health, finances, family support, and self-esteem. This instrument is also easy to administer and has excellent psychometric properties. In addition, it works equally well with care recipients who do and do not have dementia.

Pearlin, Mullan, Semple, and Skaff (1990) have developed several brief measures that assess caregiver stress by measuring primary stressors (e.g., role captivity, role overload, and loss of intimate exchange) and secondary stresses (e.g., family conflict, work strain, and financial strain). Zarit, Stephens, Townsend, and Greene (1998) added more items to the role overload scale. These measures also have excellent psychometric properties and evaluate important areas, such as financial and work strain, that social workers need to consider.

The Caregiver Appraisal Measure, which includes forty-seven items developed by Lawton, Kleban, Moss, Rovine, and Glicksman (1989), assesses subjective perceptions of caregiving and provides a more culturally unbiased view than other instruments of clients' caregiving experiences. Many social workers have used the Caregiver Well-Being Scale, designed by Tebb (1995), which examines caregivers' overall functioning and quality of life. This scale addresses caregivers' feelings, physical needs, self-security (i.e., feeling loved and secure about the future), family support, leisure experiences, and satisfaction with activities of daily living, including household tasks and repairs, and maintenance of functions outside the home, such as maintaining hobbies and visiting friends. Berg-Weger, Rubio, and Tebb (2000a) found that the scale had satisfactory reliability and validity. Unlike many scales, this instrument takes caregivers' strengths into account, and social workers have used it successfully with caregiver support groups. Social workers can also use this instrument to screen a caregiver before a crisis occurs and to identify the at-risk caregiver (Berg-Weger et al., 2000b).

Caregiving Interventions

Coon, Ory, and Schulz (2003) claim that the most effective caregiving interventions incorporate strategies that have several components. Sorensen, Pinquart, and Duberstein (2002) reached the same conclusion after reviewing several different treatment approaches. They found that multimethod interventions (specifically, respite and adult day services) are necessary to alleviate the burden on the caregiver and restore her well-being. When respite care was combined with skills training and support groups, Sorensen and colleagues (2002) found that practitioners were able to reduce the disruptive behaviors of care recipients. Skills training alone was ineffective in helping depressed caregivers, who more often needed individual counseling. Table 10.1 presents specific problems and selected interventions.

TABLE 10.1   Selected Caregiver Problems and Interventions

Type of Problem	Recommended Intervention
Behavior problems in care recipients	Skills training for caregivers in groups
Depression	Individual counseling (CBT)
Other emotional issues	Individual counseling
Social isolation/loneliness	Caregiver support groups
Caregiver burden and overload	Respite care Adult day programs Individual counseling
Caregiver well-being	Information about caregiving Links to services

Skills Training

Because problem behaviors appear as a result of certain conditions, such as inactivity, abrupt change, overstimulation, or frustrating tasks, social workers can empower caregivers by teaching them how to conduct a functional assessment of the person for whom they are caring, as discussed in chapter 9. Most caregivers can effectively reduce problem behaviors in care recipients when this assessment is combined with skills training. This will reduce the caregiver's level of stress and improve his sense of well-being (Levesque et al., 2002).

An example of a program designed to improve caregivers' problem-solving skills is the Environmental Skill-Building Program (Gitlin and Gwyther, 2003). Caregivers were taught how to modify troublesome behaviors by following a sequence of steps, beginning with naming and framing problem areas by evaluating and understanding them, and then identifying potential solutions or actions. Caregivers were shown how to use environmental and personal resources to intervene. For example, one caregiver modified her house to limit wandering to a particular room that was safe and secure. Another reduced his back strain by lifting a care recipient in a different way. Caregivers were also taught various distraction techniques and how to communicate better with care recipients by speaking calmly and avoiding complicated instructions. The caregivers learned to avoid arguments about reality and to validate care recipients' feelings or comments even when they were inaccurate. This program used standardized as well as individualized interventions. When skills training incorporates information about adaptive coping strategies and household maintenance, such as cooking and grocery shopping, social workers can empower caregivers. Many male caregivers in particular benefit from this information and from assistance with understanding and coping with feelings (Femiano and Coonerty-Femiano, 2002).

Individual and Family Counseling

Individual training programs work better than support groups when caregivers need help with emotional problems. However, many practitioners use groups because they help a larger number of people and are more cost effective (Toseland and Smith, 2003). Psychotherapy, specifically, cognitive behavioral therapy, is especially efficacious with caregivers who are depressed or feel overburdened (Sorensen et al., 2002). When the focus of the therapy is on the caregiver's well-being, individual interventions work better than group approaches, according to Sorensen and colleagues (2002), who conducted an extensive meta-analysis of caregiver interventions. The most common concerns among caregivers involve family conflict, emotional reactions to a care recipient's chronic illness, and problems resulting from a care recipient's cognitive or emotional impairment. Spouses who are caregivers often grieve the loss of the emotional and physical intimacy that they once shared with their loved one, and they find that individual counseling is a safe environment in which to discuss these concerns (Mittelman, Zeiss, Davies, and Guy, 2003). The caregiving spouses can explore various options for meeting their intimacy needs without concern about being judged by others. Individual counseling can also help caregivers reflect on and reframe their experiences into a more acceptable framework.

Sherrell, Buckwalter, and Morhardt (2001) suggest that adult children who view caring for their parents as a developmental transition will more easily find benefits from caregiving than those who remain unaware of these inevitable life changes. During individual counseling social workers can help caregivers better understand their parents' needs by encouraging the caregivers to reassess their previous interactions with their parents and to discover meaning from their caregiving role.

Family counseling is sometimes necessary to lessen dysfunctional interactions between family members and to improve their communication skills. Social workers also meet with subgroups, such as siblings, or with people who are external to the family, including other relatives or friends who are directly involved in the caregiving. Walsh (1999) and Greene (2000) underscore the importance of reducing families' levels of stress by providing family members with information about various topics, especially medical ones; helping them set concrete guidelines for sustaining care, problem solving, and optimal functioning; and linking them to community services. Home assessments with family members often shed light on how well they are caring for their loved one. Other useful family interventions include conducting a genogram of the family, facilitating life review, advocating to obtain services for families such as adult day care or respite care, and mediating between families and other institutions (Greene, 2000; Argüelles, Klausner, Argüelles, and Coon, 2003).

When caregivers seek alternative living arrangements for their aging relatives, social workers can guide family members through this difficult process. Some caregivers need individualized attention to cope with their feelings of loss and guilt, which often arise during these transitions. Although many family caregivers feel physically better after placing a relative in a long-term care setting, they often report high levels of depression, anger, and anxiety, lasting in many instances for several years (Zarit and Whitlatch, 1992).

Individual and family counseling vary according to caregivers' background characteristics, including gender, education, social class, and ethnicity. Gallagher-Thompson and colleagues (2003) outline several recommendations for practitioners who are working with African American caregivers. Gallagher-Thompson and colleagues advise that practitioners develop rapport with available members of the caregiver network and identify one or two key relatives who can mediate between the practitioner and other family members. Gallagher-Thompson's team also suggests that the practitioner working with African American families determine how much information the caregiver wants to have about an elderly relative's medical condition before providing details about an illness. In addition, Gallagher-Thompson and colleagues (2003) recommend that practitioners discuss an aging relative's medical condition several times if necessary and ensure that services, such as adult day programs or support groups, are located nearby. Ideally, these services should include professionals from the local community. Culturally sensitive practice is especially important when social workers help families with caregiving. Caregiving norms vary considerably between families, and within families generational alliances about filial responsibilities commonly occur.

Latinos often believe that it is their duty to care for aging relatives who need help, although substantial variations exist across Latino subgroups. Gallagher-Thompson and colleagues (2003) point out that many Latino families become more receptive to formal help if it will improve their loved one's care and well-being. Spanish-speaking caregivers also communicate more easily with social workers who are bilingual and bicultural.

Social workers involved with Japanese American caregivers need to be aware of the intergenerational and geographic differences that influence these families. According to Braun, Takamura, Forman, Sasaki, and Meininger (1995), these families are more likely to use social services if social workers provide culturally sensitive outreach materials written in the language of the targeted population; present materials in an appropriate context; disseminate information through minority-oriented media; use services that are accessible and acceptable to the target population; and collaborate with established community groups and leaders who provide high-quality, highly regarded services.

Caregiver Support Groups

Caregiver support groups, which can be facilitated by peers or professionals, are designed to provide emotional and informational support and to enhance caregivers' coping skills. Because many caregivers feel lonely and socially isolated, they appreciate the camaraderie that they often find in these groups. Most caregivers benefit from sharing their problems with others in the same situation and learning how others have managed similar problems. These support groups also ease the stresses and strains of caregiving and reduce distress by offering respite from the caregiving role and lessening the participants' feelings of isolation and loneliness. In addition, these groups offer families hope by educating them about what to expect with different illnesses (Toseland, 1995).

Hebert and colleagues (2003) designed a group intervention for caregivers that includes cognitive appraisal and other coping strategies, based on Lazarus and Folkman's transactional theory of stress and coping (Lazarus and Folkman, 1984; Folkman et al., 1991). Caregivers are taught to distinguish unalterable from modifiable stressors and to apply a coping approach, for example, a problem-solving strategy or an emotion-focused one (specifically, reframing), based on the type of stressor.

Social workers who develop caregiver support groups should first decide whether participants will be of the same gender, include spouses or adult children, or will be involved with caregivers of people who do or do not have dementia. Harris (2002) found that most male caregivers prefer to talk to other men and that spouses and adult children typically confront different problems. Adult children who are caregivers often struggle with the change in their role as son or daughter and with what their parent meant to them, both earlier in their lives and later as they both aged; adult children benefit most from respite care and adult day services. On the other hand, spouses who are caregivers more frequently appreciate help with intimacy issues and with IADLs and household tasks. When forming these groups, social workers should take into account caregivers' race, ethnicity, and socioeconomic status; whether the focus is on prevention or remediation; and special populations, such as grandparent caregivers (Toseland and Smith, 2003).

Respite Care/Adult Day Services Programs

Respite programs that provide temporary relief or breaks from caregiving range from adult day care to in-home or overnight respite (Zarit, 2001). Several researchers have found that caregivers' moods improve when they use respite services, although the benefits may be short term and success depends on the type and length of the respite (see Curran, 1995; Harper, Manasse, James, and Newton, 1993).

Adult day service programs usually follow a medical or social model. The medical approach is more rehabilitative and focuses more on participants' health conditions, whereas the social model typically emphasizes recreational, interpersonal, and environmental interventions. The funding for these programs also differs. In a study that compared outcomes of programs, Leitsch, Zarit, Towsend, and Greene (2001) found that both models successfully reduce caregivers' depression, anger, role overload, and worry, although the medical programs are more expensive for private pay clients than the social programs are. Gaugler and colleagues (2003) found similar benefits in a different evaluation of adult day services, that is, that caregivers' feelings of role overload are substantially reduced when they use these programs.

In addition to intervening directly with family members, social workers must advocate for more progressive policies that alleviate caregivers' burdens. More companies need to offer flexible schedules that allow employees to manage their family and work lives. Paid leaves are essential to keep workers from quitting their jobs for caregiving reasons. Employees also require better protection from the loss of pay and seniority, health, and pension benefits that often result from taking family leave.

The Family and Medical Leave Act, enacted in 1993, ensures that workers can take as long as twelve weeks of unpaid leave for caregiving if they are employed by an organization with at least fifty employees, work at least 1,250 hours a year, and have worked for at least twelve months. Unfortunately, few employees take advantage of these rights because the leaves are unpaid. In addition, these companies infrequently provide health care coverage for domestic partners or for grandparents raising grandchildren. Another program designed to assist caregivers is the National Family Caregiver Support Program (NFCSP), which was launched with the reauthorization of the Older Americans Act in 2000. The NFCSP provides informal caregivers with information, training, counseling, and respite services. These initiatives still barely cover the emotional, social, and financial needs that most caregivers have.

A major overhaul of national policy in regard to long-term care is needed in order to eradicate the many inequities that result from caregiving, especially among women and many minority groups. Hooyman and Gonyea (1999) claim that most interventions inadequately reduce caregivers' stress because the techniques focus too much on changing caregivers' attitudes and perceptions instead of on the fundamentally oppressive experience of caregiving. Hooyman and Gonyea argue that traditional approaches inadvertently exacerbate caregivers' frustrations because these techniques fail to acknowledge the involuntary nature of caregiving. Instead of validating caregivers' feelings associated with involuntary or obligatory caring, practitioners teach caregivers that they will feel better if they reinterpret the situation, that is, reframe their interpretation. Hooyman and Gonyea (1999) also state that the benefits from participating in caregiver support groups are typically short term because these groups inadequately address the underlying problems of gender inequities in caregiving and because the groups assume that care is women's "natural" life work—and they assume that this work is unpaid. Feminist gerontologists contend that such oppressive circumstances will continue until the United States makes fundamental structural changes in its social values and institutions.

Hooyman and Gonyea propose a model of caregiving based on gender justice that emphasizes information and advocacy; caregivers' rights to comprehensive and culturally competent services to facilitate caregiving; and empowerment, that is, choice, because many women would choose not to provide care. Educational programs would focus on prevention and planning to help caregivers anticipate service needs before a crisis occurs. The programs would be offered locally, perhaps in churches and neighborhood centers, to increase people's knowledge of and access to community services. Support groups would raise caregivers' awareness of structural factors that limit their rights, reinforce gender inequities, and abnegate society's involvement with families that provide elder care. Hooyman and Gonyea (1999) recognize that such a model of care requires major changes in economic support and in people's assumptions about caregiving, but these researchers maintain that many caregivers will continue to feel oppressed and burdened unless such changes are implemented.

ELDER ABUSE

Most families grow stronger as a result of caregiving, and few people abuse their older relatives. At the same time, as people live longer and need more care because of chronic illness, some family members will feel burdened and will mistreat their aging relatives.

The incidence of elder abuse is difficult to determine because many people are reluctant to report it. The National Center on Elder Abuse (NCEA) estimates that about 500,000 Americans older than sixty were abused by a family member in 1996 (NCEA, 2003c). Domestic elder abuse varies minimally across ethnic subgroups, and more similarities than differences exist among ethnic minority families (A. Moon, 2000; M. Hudson et al., 1999). Spousal abuse is the most common type of domestic elder abuse, followed by abuse by adult children, which is on the rise (Schiamberg and Gans, 2000).

Elder abuse refers to any knowing, intentional, or negligent act by a caregiver or other person that causes harm or a serious risk of harm to a vulnerable adult, although definitions vary from state to state (NCEA, 2003c). According to Carp (2000, p. 9), "Domestic elder abuse occurs in situations that include an elderly person and a family caregiver in which the needs of the older individual are in-adequately met, whether through ignorance, inability, neglect, frustration, or in-tent, by the caretaker or other relative." Carp explains that "domestic elder abuse is manifested in various forms including but not limited to physical attack, threaten-ing or intimidating physical or verbal behavior, unnecessary or demeaning con-finement or isolation from other people, failure to follow physicians' instructions regarding medication and other care, exploitation of the elder's financial assets or dependence, or any combination thereof" (2000, p. 10).

NCEA (2003c, p. 1) identifies six types of abuse:

- Physical abuse—inflicting, or threatening to inflict, physical pain or injury on a vulnerable elder, or depriving them of a basic need.
- Emotional abuse—inflicting mental pain, anguish, or distress on an elder person through verbal or nonverbal acts.
- Sexual abuse—non-consensual sexual contact of any kind.
- Exploitation—illegal taking, misuse, or concealment of funds, property, or assets of a vulnerable elder.
- Neglect—refusal or failure by those responsible to provide food, shelter, health care, or protection for a vulnerable elder.
- Abandonment—the desertion of a vulnerable elder by anyone who has as-sumed the responsibility for care or custody of that person.

The most common types of abuse are neglect and emotional abuse, followed by physical abuse (Schofield and Mishra, 2003). Carp (2000) also includes, as forms of abuse, failure to provide elders with proper assistance with their activities of daily living, and families' disrespect for a care recipient's right to autonomy and to make his own decisions.

Quinn and Tomita (1997) identify the following suspicious signs and symptoms: (1) someone other than the caregiver brings the client to a hospital emergency room, or someone finds the client alone in the home; (2) the interval between injury or illness and presentation for medical care is prolonged; (3) a suspicious history exists; or (4) the caregiver is failing to administer prescribed medications. The NCEA (2003c) has identified bruises, pressure marks, broken bones, abra-sions, and burns as indications that physical abuse, neglect, or mistreatment may be occurring; unexplained withdrawal from normal activities, a sudden change in alertness, and unusual depression are indicators of emotional abuse; bruises around the breasts or genital area can be signs of sexual abuse; sudden changes in the elder person's financial situation could be the result of exploitation; bedsores, unattended medical needs, poor hygiene, and unusual weight loss can be signs of neglect. Belittling behavior, threats, and other uses of power and control are indicators of verbal or emotional abuse, as are strained or tense relationships or frequent arguments between the caregiver and elderly person.

Family members, whether men or women or adult children or spouses, are the most frequent abusers (NCEA, 2003c). Abusers typically have more mental or physical health problems, alcohol or drug dependence, financial problems, resentment toward the elderly person, and social isolation than nonabusers (Wolf, 1996; Schofield and Mishra, 2003). Caregivers are more likely to mistreat aging relatives when caregivers view what they do as a burden and feel stressed from the demands of care, especially when they perceive that they are not receiving adequate help or support from others. These caregivers often provide care to children *and* elderly relatives at the same time.

Elderly people with dementia and those who are socially isolated are at greatest risk of abuse (Carp, 2000; NCEA, 2003c). Women are victims in 75% of psychological abuse and 92% of financial abuse cases (NCEA et al., 1998). Some care recipients, especially those who become aggressive, combative, or verbally abusive, or who exhibit disturbing behaviors such as sexual acting out or embarrassing public displays, are more likely to experience caregiver abuse than others. A history of alcoholism, financial problems, tension, conflict, and violence in the marital relationship, and mental illness, are other risk factors (Kosberg, 1988; Lachs and Pillemer, 1995; Wolf, 1996). The incidence increases when caregivers and care recipients live together, had a poor relationship before the onset of the illness or disabling condition, and, if married, experienced a conflictual relationship (Anetzberger, 2000; NCEA, 2003a). Some investigators, for example, Comijs, Dijkstra, Bouter, and Smit (1999), have suggested that abuse is more common when elderly people resolved problems more passively than nonvictims. Comijs and colleagues also found that financial mistreatment occurred more often when victims had low self-efficacy. Because of stereotypes, biases, and preconceived expectations about elder abuse, many practitioners fail to recognize abuse directed against elderly men, according to Kosberg (1998). Older men are particularly vulnerable to abuse in situations in which they resent and become angry about their growing dependency from an illness or as a result of alcohol abuse.

Assessment of Elder Abuse

Social workers should interview family members alone and, ideally, in the home setting if abuse is suspected. The social worker should speak calmly and allow sufficient time for the clients to feel comfortable (see Quinn and Tomita, 1997, for a detailed outline of assessment of elder abuse). Social workers should prepare for the interview by anticipating how they will intervene in certain situations. In addition, social workers must eschew stereotypes about abuse and remember that it occurs in all families, regardless of gender composition, ethnic background, or sexual orientation. Domestic elder abuse can happen in all types of families, including lesbian, gay, bisexual, and transgendered relationships. Practitioners need not identify the sexual orientation of a care recipient and caregiver, but clinicians should assess the relationship and potential for abuse in gay, lesbian, bisexual, and transgendered relationships, just as they would in any other suspected domestic abuse situation. Social workers must be aware that the lack of legal protections for gay and lesbian couples affects the manner in which social workers will intervene if they identify elder abuse (Cook-Daniels, 1997). Although few caregiver programs exist specifically for lesbian, gay, bisexual, and transgendered partners, caregiver support groups increasingly include people with diverse sexual orientations.

Screening Tools

Specific screening and assessment tools for evaluating elder abuse typically focus on caregivers, health professionals, or care recipients. An example of a screening instrument for caregivers is the Caregiver Abuse Screen (Reis and Nahmiash, 1995). The Texas Elder Abuse and Mistreatment (TEAM) battery, which focuses on the root causes of abuse, is easily incorporated in a comprehensive geriatric assessment (Dyer and Goins, 2000). One of its strengths is its multifaceted approach to elder abuse. In Ohio experts have published the *Screening Tools and Referral Protocol for Stopping Abuse Against Older Ohioans: A Guide for Service Providers* (STRP), which includes three screening tools: the Actual Abuse Screening Tool, the Suspected Screening Tool, and the Risk of Abuse Screening Tool. These may be used separately or in combination (Nagpaul, 2001).

Reis and Nahmiash (1998) developed the Indicators of Abuse Screen (IOA) for health professionals; it is brief, inexpensive, and easy to use. This instrument covers a range of abuse indicators, including marital and family conflicts, financial problems, and substance abuse. It provides three categories of abuse indicators: intrapersonal and interpersonal problems of caregivers; past abuse of the care receiver; and a lack of social support for the care receiver. Reis and Nahmiash argue that these categories provide helpful information about caregivers and their potential for abusing care recipients. The instrument has demonstrated high internal consistency as well as adequate construct, divergent, and concurrent validity. Practitioners can effectively individualize their interventions by isolating more specific problem areas. For example, if the assessment indicates a lack of social support, social workers can focus on enhancing these resources, either informally or by linking caregivers to community services. When the strains lie within the marriage, social workers may need to conduct marital counseling or help the caregiver and care receiver cope differently with conflict. Reis (1999) developed a shorter version, the Brief Abuse Screen for the Elderly and Caregiver Abuse Scale, which takes less than a minute to complete.

The Elder Assessment Instrument (EAI) is a forty-four-item Likert scale that includes seven sections for evaluating the signs, symptoms, and subjective complaints of elder abuse, neglect, exploitation, and abandonment (Fulmer, Street, and Carr, 1984; Fulmer, 2003). Clinicians complete this instrument, which has excellent psychometric properties even though it is also brief; it takes only about twelve to fifteen minutes to implement, and it is easy to use.

Shugarman, Fries, Wolf, and Morris (2003) have developed an index comprised of specific risk factors with more than 90% sensitivity (60% specificity) that social workers can use to screen for potential elder abuse. The index evaluates short-term memory problems, psychiatric diagnoses, alcohol abuse, interpersonal skills, conflicts with family or friends, loneliness, and social support. Unfortunately, this instrument concentrates on care recipients and pays little attention to caregivers.

Schofield and Mishra (2003) criticize current elder abuse screening tools on the ground that they inadequately consider family members' reluctance to report abuse and tendency to give socially desirable responses, especially during face-to-face interviews. Schofield and Mishra suggest that practitioners use more self-report instruments to reduce people's feelings of shame when reporting abuse and that clinicians focus on specific rather than general perceptions. The Hwalek-Sengstock Elder Abuse Screening Test (H-S/FAST) was one of the earliest self-report instruments to assess a person's risk of elder abuse (Hwalek and Sengstock, 1986). This instrument was eventually revised into a twelve-item scale, now called the Vulnerability to Abuse Screening Scale (VASS).

The VASS, which is also a self-report instrument, includes four factors: vulnerability, dependence, dejection, and coercion (Schofield and Mishra, 2003). The vulnerability factor validly measures physical and psychological abuse and is a good measure of violence committed by an intimate partner. The dependence factor focuses more on the environment, such as the amount of privacy at home, need for assistance (such as medication help), and trust of family members. Dejection evaluates loneliness and alienation from family members; it correlates strongly with depression, anxiety, and dementia. The coercion factor includes items such as family members' forcing elderly people to do things or inappropriately taking their belongings. This instrument is also easy to administer.

Comprehensive Assessment

Comprehensive assessments of domestic elder abuse are considered necessary because of the complex influences underlying elder abuse, but some experts, for example, Wasylkewycz (2002), criticize such approaches as cumbersome and unwieldy. Despite the difficulties involved with comprehensive assessments, most experts, for example, Anetzberger (2000), underscore the need for intervention models that take into account the context and complexities involved in elder abuse. Anetzberger proposes a practice framework that considers whether protection, empowerment, or advocacy intervention is most appropriate; the target(s) of intervention, that is, the victim, perpetrator, or family system; and the functions of the intervention, such as whether the response requires emergency, supportive, rehabilitative, or preventative services.

Carp (2000) similarly defines elder abuse as an outcome of transactions between people and their environment that produce adaptive/maladaptive behaviors and experiences. She explains that abuse stems from many factors, including interactions among family members and economic influences, as well as environmental, housing, and community influences. It involves personal factors (i.e., characteristics of the elderly person and characteristics of the caretaker or perpetrator), environmental influences (i.e., physical and personal components of the immediate situation plus influences from the broader society), and the transactions between these.

These approaches underscore the need for social workers to comprehensively assess caregiving families and to intervene on multiple levels. Social workers should first assess the care recipient, the caregiver, and the family. Then clinicians should consider whether they must implement emergency, supportive, rehabilitative, or preventative interventions. Finally, they should implement a protective, empowerment, or advocacy model, depending on the type of abuse, the characteristics of the family, and the individual circumstances involved.

Social workers can modify the ABCDEF practice guide in several ways to assess transactions between elderly people and their caregivers. Practitioners should assess the family members' actions (A), biological functioning/health (B), cognitive status (C), demographic indicators (D), environmental resources and constraints (E), and feelings (F), including their psychiatric history. Social workers should especially attend to care recipients' functional performance, for example, ADLs and IADLs, because these are indicators of the extent of the elderly person's dependence on others. Caregivers' knowledge and skills are also critical areas to consider. The environmental assessment should cover living arrangements, privacy, the home environment, and community resources. The practitioner also should take social influences into account, for example, ideological views on caregiving, ethnic differences about filial obligations, and governmental policies about caregiving, such as who should be eligible for paid leave for caregiving and how they will be compensated. Ideally, social workers should work in interdisciplinary teams comprised also of physicians who specialize in geriatrics and nurse-practitioners, to assess elder abuse. Multiple professions must work together to assess family members' health, nutrition, activities, and social factors (Dyer and Goins, 2000).

Intervention for Suspected Elder Abuse

Although social workers are often the first to recognize domestic elder abuse and to address issues with family members, they are often unprepared to handle these cases (Choi and Mayer, 2000). In most states social workers who suspect elder abuse or neglect must report the mistreatment to proper authorities and reveal the name and address of the abused older person, along with the nature of the abuse and the basis for the suspicion (Moskowitz, 1998). Failure to report elder mistreatment to public agencies is a criminal offense in most jurisdictions, although prosecutions of such cases have been rare.

Elder abuse cases are difficult for social workers for various reasons. Inconsistent definitions and inadequate legal definitions of elder abuse can prevent social workers from effectively identifying and assessing elder abuse. Also, the emphasis on detection and reporting of abuse has hampered social workers' efforts to devise appropriate interventions. Finally, many ethical dilemmas arise that can immobilize inexperienced social workers. On the one hand, social workers want to protect care recipients' rights to self-determination and their preferences regarding intervention. On the other hand, most social workers feel protective of aging clients. Unless an elderly person is mentally incompetent, he or she has the right to refuse help. Bergeron (1999) recommends that social workers collaborate with other professionals when evaluating elder abuse because the mutual decisions that arise from these collaborations usually result in more prudent judgments, especially when difficult ethical dilemmas are involved.

Community Services

Social workers will initially link family members to appropriate community services, such as homemaker services, home health aides, respite care, adult day care, and other support services. In addition, many care recipients benefit from increased contact with others and the productive and more structured activities of adult day care centers. These services also offer caregivers a respite from watching their relatives. The Alzheimer's associations offer educational materials and meetings, friendly visitor and volunteer programs, and support groups for caregivers, while some local agencies provide financial assistance. Homemaker services, home skilled nursing, chore services, and Meals-on-Wheels may be appropriate. Mental health and substance abuse interventions can supplement these services. In addition, social workers should strengthen families' support systems by encouraging family members to socialize with friends or to engage in religious activities. These involvements frequently help family members relax and get their minds off their problems. More often than not, such involvements also reveal different but more constructive ways of handling conflicts that reduce maltreatment and feelings of alienation.

Multicomponent Interventions

In an effort to educate caregivers about elder abuse, Anetzberger and colleagues (2000) developed an intervention program that successfully coordinates the efforts of an adult protective services agency and a local Alzheimer's association. Anetzberger and colleagues developed a caregiver handbook that includes three brief self-assessment instruments to help caregivers determine whether they are at risk of abusing the person they care for. One instrument identifies disruptive behaviors of care recipients that caregivers often find to be stressful. Another lists physical and emotional indicators of strain to help caregivers recognize stress and their reactions to it. The third instrument outlines behaviors that suggest elder abuse. Caregivers who recognized that they were potential abusers were provided with assistance and suggestions about how to modify their reactions in order to reduce potentially abusive interactions. This model demonstrates how agencies can collaborate to train caregivers of relatives with dementia to recognize abuse and to change their responses with or without professional assistance. Social workers can incorporate more direct interventions if necessary.

Nahmiash and Reis (2000) outline a five-step multidisciplinary intervention that is based on empowerment theory and focuses on strengthening care recipients' resources and strengths while advocating for their rights. Social workers help caregivers by educating them about community services, adaptive coping strategies, and resources to reduce their feelings of burden and social isolation and therefore their frustration and mistreatment of care recipients. This approach uses home care interventions led by various professionals, volunteers, and community experts. Empowerment support groups for care recipients and family support groups for caregivers are part of the strategy. Individual counseling alleviates family members' stress, anxieties, and depression. The model uses the Abuse Intervention Description Tool, which is unique in several respects. It takes into account abuse and nonabuse issues, prioritizes interventions, evaluates families' receptiveness to different strategies, and monitors whether the abuse is reduced or stopped. Unlike other approaches, this model includes well-designed interventions that target specific problems. The model also incorporates an evaluation component.

Individual and Family Interventions

As practitioners continue to focus on domestic elder abuse, they will create more individual, family, and group interventions to treat these problems. Reay and Browne (2002) found positive results from a psychological intervention that includes an educational program administered by a trained clinician on a one-to-one basis with caregivers. During ninety-minute semistructured interviews, clinicians talked with caregivers about their relatives' illnesses, services and other available resources, and the nature of caring for an elderly person, especially common feelings of isolation, loss of control, and stress. Four weeks later the caregivers entered an anger management program that taught them how to manage the stages of anger, deal with triggers by monitoring their reactions, manage their arousal through relaxation, and cope with care recipients' behavior by using time-out and assertion skills. The investigators found that although both components reduce caregiver strain, depression, and anxiety, the anger management intervention works especially well with physically abusive caregivers, and the education component produces the greatest change among neglectful caregivers.

Few family interventions that focus specifically on elder abuse have been developed or evaluated, but most experts recognize that domestic elder abuse involves dysfunctional or problematic family interactions that can be treated through family counseling. Family therapy is recommended with caregivers and aging relatives when families are receptive and when social workers have the time and appropriate resources to modify dysfunctional familial interactions. The goals are to assess the family's cultural milieu along with its communication patterns and to reduce its stress (Greene, 2000). Social workers should also offer family members concrete guidelines for sustaining appropriate care and link them to supplemental services.

Mediation

Mediation is another strategy that helps families reduce conflict and maladaptive interactions, and it often prevents problems from escalating or becoming uncontrollable. While counseling emphasizes personal growth, mediation involves helping clients find their own solutions to problems by using impartial and independent clinicians or older trained mediators (Craig, 1998). Face-to-face mediation is the preferred approach, but "shuttle mediation," which involves carrying messages back and forth between participants, is also possible. The approach emphasizes confidential communication (with no office records kept, if possible); voluntary participation; impartiality; self-determination; a lifespan perspective; affirmation that promotes improved self-worth; realism; problem solving instead of blaming; and shared communication.

Mediation is not effective when mental incompetence or long-standing dysfunctional interactions are involved. It works best when multiple perspectives require expression or when social workers must shift allegiances or fairly represent different viewpoints (Craig, 1998). Multiple strategies, ranging from family meetings to linking family members to community services, are usually needed, but the ultimate goals are to empower caregivers and care recipients and to improve their lives.

Ethical Issues

The ethical issues that arise in domestic elder abuse cases usually involve care recipients' rights to self-determination and to refuse treatment. Ethical dilemmas also occur when social workers try to differentiate psychological abuse from neglect or to identify disruptive behaviors on the part of care recipients. Caregiver support groups present other ethical problems. For example, social workers often struggle with how to encourage open discussion while maintaining group members' rights to confidentiality and self-determination. Caregivers who self-disclose may inadvertently mention domestic abuse, and the ensuing group discussion could deter future mistreatment. Many practitioners might not want to report abuse in these situations. At the same time social workers who fail to report abuse might violate the law and fail to protect a vulnerable older adult.

Bergeron and Gray (2003) offer several recommendations for social workers who are directing caregiver support groups that address these ethical dilemmas. Bergeron and Gray suggest, first, that social workers learn more about elder abuse by reading current literature on the topic. Bergeron and Gray emphasize that social workers should know and understand the laws pertaining to reporting elder abuse in their state. And, because many cases are unclear, social workers must develop relationships with practitioners who work in the elder abuse field to better understand how abuse laws work. Communities that have interdisciplinary teams will more effectively address elder abuse cases when they arise. Before starting a caregiver support group, social workers must discuss exceptions to confidentiality with every potential group member. The statement about confidentiality should be in writing, and each group member should sign it. The social workers should educate group members about state laws pertaining to abuse so that they clearly understand the circumstances under which the social worker must report abuse. Further, social workers should monitor group members' self-disclosures to prevent them from prematurely disclosing information. Social workers must also feel confident that they have the professional skills that they need to intervene in situations of suspected abuse and to effectively manage the situation. By meeting one on one with group members, social workers can often preserve caregivers' dignity and avoid public embarrassment. Social workers can communicate directly and empathetically during individual meetings with caregivers and discuss specific interventions or services that could improve their caregiving experiences.

Social workers must carefully evaluate caregivers and care recipients' perspectives without patronizing them. Immediate professional intervention is usually needed when care recipients' cognitive capacities are impaired or when elderly people willingly seek legal intervention as a result of abuse, but in most cases the elderly recipient of care is able to express her preferences for care (Harbison, 1999).

The emphasis on elderly people's rights to autonomy and self-determination has replaced earlier models of elder abuse that experts, for example, Nerenberg (2000), now call the protective service models. Many view these models as paternalistic and demeaning to older people, who are often treated like child abuse victims. Unlike children, most elderly people can make their own decisions. These criticisms are especially relevant, given recent data showing associations between the involvement of adult protective services agencies and premature nursing home placement (Lachs, Williams, O'Brien, and Pillemer, 2002).

Empowerment

Nerenberg (2000) argues for more collaborations between elder abuse and domestic violence advocates that focus on empowerment, self-help, and peer support. Support groups for older victims of domestic violence exemplify such a collaboration (Wolf, 2001). Wolf explains that such groups offer older women opportunities to form healthy relationships with others and that these groups build participants' self-confidence and self-esteem by validating their fears and strengthening their resolve. These groups, which are typically comprised of five or six members, meet continuously on a weekly basis for about two hours. Open discussions are mixed with exercises, educational sessions, and outside speakers, such as experts knowledgeable about legal, financial, or Social Security issues. Groups should include both a leader and a coleader, and at least one of these should have training and experience or previous participation in a group (Wolf, 2001). Experienced clients should also reach out to others (Vinton, 1999). Intake procedures should remain simple, and meeting sites should be accessible, provide parking, and preserve anonymity. The safety, well-being, and support of women clients are critical. Hospitals, shelters, and senior centers are prime places for meetings, but practitioners should meet with clients in their homes to boost rapport and enhance the women's comfort.

Prevention

Prevention is crucial. Social workers can often prevent elder abuse by recognizing risk factors. Sometimes a brief respite is all that caregivers need to reduce their stress. National efforts are underway to increase people's awareness. For example, the National Center on Elder Abuse organized a National Summit on Elder Abuse in 2001 to publicize the issue and to recommend policies to reduce and eliminate elder abuse. The summit focused on service gaps, public education about elder abuse, professional training, adult protective services, prosecution, maximizing resources, and policy barriers. Since the summit the NCEA has been promoting the proposed Elder Justice Act in the U.S. Senate (NCEA, 2003b). This measure would establish dual offices of elder justice in the U.S. Department of Health and Human Services' Administration on Aging and in the U.S. Department of Justice to coordinate elder abuse prevention efforts nationally. The law would also require that long-term care nursing aides undergo an FBI criminal background check before they are hired and that they receive better training in the detection of elder abuse. The bill also would create an office of adult protective services within the Department of Health and Human Services' Administration for Children and Families. A similar bill, the Elder Justice Act (HR 2490), has been introduced in the House of Representatives.

Grandparents Who Are Raising Grandchildren

More and more older families include grandparents and great-grandparents, and, as people live longer, the duration of grandparenthood has lengthened and grandparents have taken on more diverse roles. Social workers will encounter increasing numbers of multigenerational families that include grandparents who are actively involved with adult children and grandchildren. The average age at which people become grandparents is forty-eight, although this varies by ethnicity and socioeconomic status. About 80% of grandparents have telephone contact and more than half—64%—see their grandchildren at least every couple of weeks (Davies and Williams, 2002). Frequency of contact between grandparents and grandchildren depends on various factors, but proximity, access to transportation, and the health and employment status of the grandparents are the most significant.

Grandparents increasingly maintain separate residences from their adult children and grandchildren and take on grandparent roles associated more with companionship than the authority of the past (Gratton and Haber, 1996). Grandparents are more likely to act as babysitters when their grandchildren are young, but different interactions, such as sharing ideas and problems, become more salient as the grandchildren grow up.

Some families live together in multigenerational households. Grandparents who emigrate from Mexico and other Latin American countries, for example, often live, at least initially, with their adult children (Applewhite, 1988). Limited financial resources have led to coresidence in many families, especially among African Americans and subgroups comprised of young, unmarried mothers. These housing arrangements have profound significance for the role of grandparents. When multigenerational families share a residence, grandparents' roles often become more functional, that is, they begin caring for young children and assisting in other household responsibilities (Gratton and Haber, 1996). Grandparents serve as surrogate parents and provide financial assistance in many families (Silverstein and Marenco, 2001).

More and more grandparents are raising their grandchildren, especially among African American and Latino families (Silverstein and Marenco, 2001). About 5% of white grandparents and 14% of African American grandparents have grandchildren residing in their homes (Lugaila, 1998). About 6% of Hispanic children reside with their grandparents, but these families more often live in three-generation families in which grandparents and their adult children are coparents (Saluter, 1996; Bryson and Casper, 1999). The number of children raised solely by grandparents or other relatives increased by more than 50% between 1990 and 1998 (U.S. Census Bureau, 2001b; Casper and Bryson, 1998; Lugaila, 1998). In 2000 about 2.35 million grandparents were raising grandchildren in the United States (U.S. Census Bureau, 2001b). The increase in the number of families is the result of many factors but primarily is related to changes in child welfare reimbursement policies, policy shifts away from nonrelative foster parenting, and rising rates of divorce and single-parent households.

Some grandparent caregivers welcome the opportunity to parent a second time, nurture their grandchildren, and transmit their family's beliefs and values. At the same time grandparents raising grandchildren are older than they were when they parented their own children; the average age of custodial grandparent-caregivers is fifty-nine (Fuller-Thomson and Minkler, 2000). Most grandparents who raise grandchildren experience stress for various reasons. The most common problems revolve around poor health, economic hardships, inadequate government support, housing limitations, and difficulties in raising special needs grandchildren.

Health problems are the most significant difficulties that these grandparents face (Hayslip, Emick, Henderson, and Elias, 2002). Even when controls for age, social class, and ethnicity are considered, grandparents raising grandchildren experience worse health than noncaregiving grandparents (Solomon and Marx, 2000), and many grandparents attribute their worsened health to their caregiving (Minkler, Roe, and Price, 1992). They also struggle with more functional limitations than other grandparents. Fuller-Thomson and Minkler (2000) found that 56% of caregiving grandmothers report at least one limitation in activities of daily living (ADLs), such as caring for their personal needs, climbing a flight of stairs, or walking six blocks. African American grandparent-caregivers have twice as many ADL limitations as noncaregiving African American grandparents.

Caregiving grandparents often have more mental health problems than noncaregiving grandparents do. About one-third (32%) of caregiving grandmothers meet clinical criteria for depression, in contrast to 19% of noncaregiving grandmothers (Minkler and Roe, 1996; Burnette, 2000a; Fuller-Thomson and Minkler, 2000). Caregiving grandmothers are also more likely to experience a less satisfactory quality of life and more anxiety than noncaregiving grandmothers. The psychological distress that these caregivers experience results from changes in their routine, stresses associated with raising grandchildren, the untimeliness of this role, and the loss of what they perceive as "real" grandparenthood. Another frequently overlooked source of depression arises from the circumstances in which grandparents become caregivers for their grandchildren. The precipitating conditions sometimes include an unfortunate event in the life of their adult child, such as incarceration, incapacitation, or substance abuse. These grandparents feel a sense of loss and disappointment that their adult child is unable to parent.

Practitioners need to identify and address the sources of these grandparents' depression and to help them find constructive ways to cope with these losses. In addition, practitioners should focus on improving these caregivers' access to medical care that would improve their physical and mental health (Pruchno and McKenney, 2002).

Grandparent-caregivers are also more likely to live in poverty, and they often lack health insurance (Generations United, 2002). Their adult children rarely contribute enough to help these households rise out of poverty. In addition, many grandparents either quit work or reduce their work hours to care for their grandchildren, and welfare programs provide insufficient financial support. "Child only" grants from Temporary Assistance to Needy Families are one source of funding for which these households may be eligible, but this program offers only minimal assistance. Strict legal requirements detailing who can receive financial support also is a hindrance to helping these grandparents to supplement their household income, and grandparents who do not have legal custody of their grandchildren and try to obtain financial assistance are often unsuccessful.

Many states limit economic aid to direct child care expenses or to foster care payments for those who have formalized their caregiving arrangements, but obtaining legal custody when the parents are opposed can be costly and time consuming. Many grandparent-caregivers avoid legal action because they hope that their adult children will eventually resolve their problems and become full-time parents. Subsidized guardianships, offered by some states, allow grandparents to have legal guardianship without terminating the parents' rights. These provisions are generally designed for children who have been in state custody with a relative or nonrelative for at least six months, although some states require as long as two years.

Housing is another concern, because most grandparent caregivers are initially unprepared to raise grandchildren. Arrangements are often made precipitously and abruptly, and grandparents rarely have proper accommodations. Their homes are often too small to raise young children or lack childproofing. In some instances rental managers will evict grandparents when grandchildren arrive because of public housing limits on the number of residents. In their analysis of census data, Fuller-Thomson and Minkler (2003) found that grandparent-caregivers who rent spend inordinate amounts of their income on housing costs; although almost a quarter (23%) receive a housing subsidy from the government, many who live below the poverty line receive no help although they are eligible. Fuller-Thomson and Minkler (2003) also found that about 25% of these caregivers live in overcrowded conditions.

Social isolation and feelings of alienation from other parents commonly occur among grandparents raising grandchildren. The demands of caregiving often prevent them from attending meetings or socializing with others. Although cultural factors influence the amount of social support available to grandparent-caregivers, most grandparents raising grandchildren experience a decline in social contact (Burnette, 1999).

In contrast to grandparents in coparenting arrangements, grandparents with custody of grandchildren more often struggle with grandchildren's behavioral and mental health problems, including poor schoolwork, fights with other children, disobedient behaviors, sadness and low self-esteem, and hyperactivity (Kolomer, McCallion, and Janicki, 2002; Pruchno and McKenney, 2000; Burnette, 2000a, 2000b).

Assessing Grandparents Raising Grandchildren

Social workers should assess grandparents' and grandchildren's individual functioning, including their physical and mental health, along with environmental influences, such as housing, income, and social support. The complexities involved in grandparents' raising grandchildren demand a comprehensive assessment and interventions at individual, family, and environmental levels. The ABCDEF practice guide considers family members' actions (A), which include assessments of family interactions and dynamics, as well as evaluations of individuals' behaviors at home and outside the home. The biological functions (B), specifically, the health status of family members, are crucial because physical and mental health interact. The assessment of cognitive status (C), including coping strategies that grandparents and grandchildren use, offers insights into how well family members manage stress. The demographic (D) indicators shed light on the cultural context in which these grandparents are raising their grandchildren. Goodman and

Silverstein (2002) found substantial cultural differences in well-being and in the meaning of grandparent-caregiving in an analysis of minority grandparents who were raising their grandchildren. For example, Goodman and Silverstein found that African American grandparents function better when they are custodial grandparents, but Latino grandparents are happiest when they are coparenting in three-generation households (C. Cox, 2000a; Goodman and Silverstein, 2002). These differences underscore the variations within families and the importance of respecting grandparents' preferences. The environmental context (E) considers family income, housing arrangements, and social support, including the use of and access to community services for these families.

Interventions with Grandparents Who Are Raising Grandchildren

Information

The most widely used and efficacious interventions for grandparents who are raising grandchildren include the dissemination of information, especially the availability of support groups, respite services, financial assistance, and individual and family counseling. The Grandparent Information Center, created in 1993 by the AARP, is one of the most powerful resource centers in the country and handles referrals in English and Spanish. The center, which publishes a widely disseminated newsletter and links people to support groups and other services, has greatly enhanced the public's knowledge of policies and services related to grandparents who are raising grandchildren. Some states offer hotlines, coordinate volunteers, and train social workers. Generations United, another advocacy organization, provides up-to-date information about grandparents who are raising grandchildren and advocates for legislation involving legal and custody issues. The Grandparent Caregiver Law Center at the Brookdale Center on Aging at Hunter College in New York is an example of a legal resource center that helps grandparent-caregivers to modify custody options, obtain public benefits, or resolve other legal problems (G. Wallace, 2001). The Brookdale Foundation Group's Relatives as Second Parents Program in New York (not affiliated with the center at Hunter) has improved services for grandparent-caregivers by offering seed grants. Its efforts, and an annual national training conference, have educated numerous professionals on the best practices for grandparents who are raising grandchildren. This program also offers grandparent support groups throughout the state and a network for professionals and caregivers.

Support Groups

Support groups for grandparents are widely used and range from informal groups that meet in people's homes to formal ones provided by agencies. Most grandparent-caregivers will participate in these groups if they are constructive and provide the grandparents with valuable information, such as on legal options, health care, and day care. The most appealing groups structure meetings, focus on problem solving, and emphasize positive and tangible issues. When support groups turn into gripe sessions, many grandparents stop participating (Strom and Strom, 2000).

Strom and Strom (2000) identified three stages that grandparents experience when they participate in groups. Participants first want to share their stories and experiences with grandparent-caregiving and discuss their disappointments, anger, and hopelessness; this is the self-disclosure stage. During the constructive self-evaluation stage participants share and identify solutions to their problems and focus on modifying their lives and enhancing their well-being. By the third stage, healthy adjustment, most participants have eschewed any feelings of bitterness or regret and have adapted well to parenting. Most participants are stronger and more hopeful by the end of the program. Those who seem stuck receive individualized attention to help them move forward. Strom and Strom recommend that groups include participants from all three stages to encourage everyone's progress. Strom and Strom (1993) have also devised a Grandparent Strength and Needs Inventory for trained clinicians to use in assessing grandparents before they enter the groups.

Empowerment Training

C. Cox (2000a, 2002) has effectively reached many African American and Latino families with empowerment training, which emphasizes caregivers' strengths and deficits. This training enhances grandparents' personal power (C. Cox, 2000a). Social workers can improve grandparents' feelings of self-efficacy by implementing multiple techniques, including role playing, video feedback, lectures, and discussion. Although group leaders often facilitate the groups, social workers should view the participants as the experts. Social workers can maintain continuity between group meetings by assigning the grandparents to keep a journal, as well as homework assignments that involve grandparents' interactions with their grandchildren. Grandparents who have established trust and rapport with other group members more often reveal their worries and fears, which usually revolve around losing their grandchildren, their health, and who will care for their grandchildren if they die or become ill.

C. Cox (2000a) has also implemented empowerment training with Latina grandmothers who are raising their grandchildren; she notes several differences between these caregivers and African American grandparent-caregivers. In contrast to the African American grandmothers who were raising their grandchildren, fewer Latina grandmothers with similar responsibilities had legal custody of the grandchildren in their care. Contact between grandchildren and their parents was more frequent among the Latino families. However, language barriers, along with such cultural influences as the role of women and familism, sometimes prevent these families from using services.

Individual and Family Counseling

Individual counseling is recommended when grandparent-caregivers demonstrate depression, anxiety, or other symptoms of distress. Individual counseling that includes information about positive health behaviors, for example, nutrition, exercise, and weight management, will also improve these grandparents' physical and mental health (Whitley, Kelley, and Sipe, 2001). Sands and Goldberg-Glen (2000) recommend that practitioners learn more about family therapy with grandparents who are raising grandchildren and attend especially to the interactions between these grandparents and grandchildren. Sands and Goldberg-Glen found that the well-being and mental health of the grandparents is directly related to the grandchildren's behaviors and problems. When social workers increase the prevalence of positive interactions between family members, Sands and Goldberg-Glen (2000) found, family members connect better and become closer. Specific strategies that these families need include focusing on and buttressing family strengths, demonstrating parenting skills and behavior management, and helping family members access and use community resources.

Respite Services

Respite programs range from those at recreational facilities, camps, or day care centers to more formal programs offered by residential and mental health facilities. Before- and after-school programs give grandparent-caregivers time to visit doctors, complete household chores, and socialize with friends. In addition, libraries, churches, recreational facilities, and formal service organizations can offer intergenerational activities for these families. One survey found that more than three-fourths of grandparent-caregivers rank joint social and recreational activities with their grandchildren as the most valuable service they use (Landry-Meyer, 1999).

Policy Changes

In 2000 Congress authorized the Older Americans Act, which included the National Family Caregiver Support Program (NFCSP). It provides funds to support family members who care for older relatives with serious chronic illnesses or disabilities, and 10% of this money was set aside to assist grandparents who are raising grandchildren. Services are available in five categories: information for caregivers about services; assistance to caregivers in gaining access to services; individual counseling, organization of support groups, and training caregivers to make decisions and solve problems related to their caregiving roles; respite care; and supplemental services for caregivers.

A proposed measure known as the Legacy Act of 2003 was introduced in the Senate in 2003. It would increase the amount of housing available to households headed by a grandparent or other relative. The GrandFamilies House in Boston is the nation's first housing program specifically designed for grandparent-headed families. Support groups and other programs like Generations United KinNet, the only national network of support groups for relatives caring for kin in formal foster care programs, will reach more of these families.

C. Cox (2000b) offers several guidelines for developing policies on behalf of grandparents who are raising grandchildren, including involving grandparent-caregivers at every step when designing programs, engaging in aggressive outreach to the most vulnerable caregivers, offering basic assistance in various ways, supporting the collaboration of multiple networks, building more intergenerational programs, sustaining funding at all levels, and using grandparents as advocates. Policies that fail to incorporate these recommendations will inadequately address the multidimensional needs of these caregivers.

CASE 10.1

Ms. Anderson, a fifty-year-old married mother of three teenage boys, sought help and is attending a caregiver support group at an agency that focuses on helping older people and their families. During one group session Ms. Anderson shares her frustrations in caring for her mother, who is suffering from a dementia that has worsened during the last six months. She is concerned because her mother has become increasingly isolated, and she has stopped visiting friends, cooking, and shopping for groceries.

Ms. Anderson's father is his wife's primary caregiver, but he has withdrawn from friends and activities as he spends increasing amounts of time caring for her. Although Ms. Anderson works full time as a sales clerk, she delivers two meals to her parents every day. Ms. Anderson's husband can offer only minimal assistance because he travels a lot during the week, and her sons are busy with school and other activities. Ms. Anderson feels that she has been neglecting her own family and worries because her middle son has started fighting with other boys after school.

The social worker suggests that she and Ms. Anderson meet privately to discuss the problems in greater depth and to identify potential solutions. The social worker comprehensively assesses Ms. Anderson by using the ABCDEF assessment guide and meets with Ms. Anderson and her family at their home and at the home of Ms. Anderson's parents. The social worker evaluates family members' behaviors, health, cognitive functioning, and coping approaches and examines the physical layout of the grandparents' home. The social worker assesses family members' feelings as well as their interactions and social supports. The social worker gives Ms. Anderson and her father the CBI so that they may evaluate how overloaded they feel from caregiving. The social worker also uses the Revised Memory and Behavior Problems Checklist (RMBPC) to identify and assess any behavior problems of Ms. Anderson's mother in more depth. Both Ms. Anderson and her father show evidence of being greatly burdened by their caregiving duties, and the problem behaviors of Ms. Anderson's mother contribute significantly to their stress. The social worker also talks with Ms. Anderson's mother to assess her needs and uses the Pleasure Events Schedule—Alzheimer's Disease (PES-AD) scale with her to identify activities in which she might participate.

After several sessions with Ms. Anderson and her family, the social worker outlines several potential interventions, which they all discuss and evaluate. The social worker collaborates with family members to determine and implement the interventions. The family agrees to bring Ms. Anderson's mother in for a comprehensive assessment of her dementia (which eventually is diagnosed as Alzheimer's disease). Next, the social worker shows family members how to functionally assess the wandering of Ms. Anderson's mother. Because Ms. Anderson and her father were initially reluctant to accept help, the social worker introduces interventions by discussing them and gradually demonstrating their potential. For example, the social worker talks with family members about adult day care before bringing them to the program to observe, talk to participants, and consult with the professionals and volunteers who work there. After many conversations with the social worker, Ms. Anderson's father concludes that an adult day program would benefit his wife. His wife is also willing to attend. Mr. Anderson recognizes that his wife would receive better medical care at the adult day program than what he can offer at home and that most participants enjoy the structured activities that the program provides. His wife especially enjoys the crafts, a major activity at the center.

The social worker also evaluates the depression of Ms. Anderson's father and refers him to a geriatric psychiatrist for a medication evaluation. In addition, the social worker puts the family in contact with the Alzheimer's Association, which provides Ms. Anderson's father with more information about his wife's illness. After talking with volunteers, he begins to attend a support group for male caregivers, where he meets men in similar situations who suggest how he might cope better with his wife's illness. Although his wife's disease is progressing, he feels less depressed and less overwhelmed with caregiving. Ms. Anderson feels better because her mother is spending time in a safe place, where she enjoys the activities and socializing with the staff and other clients. Ms. Anderson also feels closer to her father and more understanding of his needs. She continues to participate in the caregiver support group but now feels able to spend more time with her sons.

This case demonstrates the value of respite care and, specifically, adult day care, for caregivers, and care recipients with Alzheimer's disease. It benefited Ms. Anderson and her father by relieving them of constant caring, and it helped Ms. Anderson's mother by engaging her in productive activities that enhanced her pleasure. The social worker used a collaborative approach to intervene and patiently developed rapport with family members before recommending interventions. By gradually introducing interventions and using several methods, the social worker increased the family's receptiveness to services. The social worker continued to have contact with Ms. Anderson and her parents and to prepare them for what they might expect and what services they might use during the later stages of Alzheimer's disease.

DISCUSSION QUESTIONS

1. How will women's increased participation in the labor force affect caregiving?
2. How can social workers lessen the stresses and strains of caregiving? For what changes might they advocate?
3. What can social workers do to decrease elder abuse in families?
4. In what ways do intergenerational family interventions differ from traditional approaches to family therapy?

CHAPTER 11

Social Work Practice and End-of-Life Care

MOST DEATHS IN THE UNITED STATES occur among people older than seventy-five. Three-quarters of deaths in 2000 involved people older than sixty-five, and 56% were attributed to those older than seventy-five (Miniño, Arias, Kochanek, Murphy, and Smith, 2002). Although AIDS has affected mortality rates and decreased life expectancies around the world, especially in sub-Saharan African countries, in the United States mortality has increasingly become associated with old age as people live longer and die from chronic illnesses.

Social workers are encountering increasing numbers of terminally ill older people in hospitals, hospices, private homes, nursing homes, and other alternative living situations. The psychosocial issues that social workers must address are crucial at the end of life. These issues affect dying people's views about how and where to die and generally influence the quality of the death experience. Most information available about the end of life focuses on medical care, but social workers are beginning to develop broader information about end-of-life care, including the psychosocial aspects of dying.

Elderly people are more likely than younger people to know that they are dying and to value the quality of their lives instead of trying to extend their years (Ross, Fisher, and MacLean, 2000). Multiple chronic illnesses, especially cancer, cardiovascular disease, respiratory illnesses, and dementia diseases, afflict elderly people more often than they do young adults. As a result older people's deaths often are more prolonged than those of younger people, which more often result from accidents or acute illnesses.

Physicians and other health professionals use more experimental and innovative interventions with young patients than with elderly patients. For example, some cardiologists consider certain treatments too risky for elderly patients, and oncologists often treat older people differently from younger adults who have the same disease (National Institute on Aging and National Cancer Institute, 2002). In a review of age differences in cancer care, Mor (2002) found that diagnostic intensity declined with the age of the patient, and physicians used less aggressive treatment and sometimes not even standard treatment with older people.

This chapter addresses contemporary issues about death and dying, specifically, the causes, definition, and attitudes toward death that are relevant to end-of-life care with older people in the twenty-first century. We also discuss end-of-life care for older people at different phases of the dying trajectory: (1) when death is still remote; (2) when a life-threatening illness is diagnosed; (3) during treatment, when most people cope with the realization that they are dying and with the pain and physical discomforts of their illness; and (4) at the deathbed or death setting in homes, hospitals, and nursing homes. We address didactic information, that is, knowledge that social workers need about death and dying, and practice approaches: interventions at different phases, in different settings, and for different issues. In chapter 12 we discuss bereavement associated with death.

DEATH IN THE TWENTY-FIRST CENTURY

Defining Death

The absence of a heartbeat and breathing, resulting in a drop in body temperature, discoloration of the body, rigidity of the muscles, and unresponsive reflexes in the eyes, were traditionally used to determine death. The concept of brain death emerged only after artificial means of maintaining breathing and a heartbeat developed.

Although definitions of death have fluctuated over time, most states use the definition endorsed by the President's Commission for the Study of Ethical Problems in Medicine and Biomedical and Behavioral Research, which states that "an individual who has sustained either (1) irreversible cessation of circulatory and respiratory functions, or (2) irreversible cessation of all functions of the entire brain, including the brain stem, is dead." This definition was codified as the Uniform Determination of Death Act and was endorsed by the American Bar Association and the American Medical Association in 1981 (President's Commission, 1981, p. 73).

Causes of Death

The most common causes of death are constantly changing as medical interventions improve. Degenerative diseases are currently the main causes of death in the United States (Seale, 2000). In 2000 the fifteen leading causes of death were, in order: heart disease, cancer, stroke, chronic lower respiratory diseases, accidents (unintentional injuries), diabetes, influenza and pneumonia, Alzheimer's disease, kidney disease, septicemia, suicide, chronic liver disease and cirrhosis, hypertension, homicide, and pneumonitis caused by solids and liquids (usually from aspirating material into the lungs) (Miniño et al., 2002). Older people die more often than younger people from chronic diseases, specifically, cancer and heart disease, regardless of gender, race, or ethnic background (Anderson, 2002).

The increase in deaths caused by chronic illness has prolonged the terminal stage of dying, and one consequence is that the dying process is less visible today than in the past. According to Bern-Klug, Gessert, and Forbes (2001), we have "traded in a dying process that was straightforward and recognizable for a dying process that is often unrecognized, invisible, and confounding" (p. 38). Dying people also experience more disabilities that prevent them from carrying out activities of daily living, such as bathing, dressing, and eating (Seale, 2000). Moreover, dying people and their families experience more anxiety, depression, and stress during these extended terminal phases, resulting in more psychosocial issues than people faced in the past.

These changes have influenced how older people, and the health professionals who care for them, manage death and dying. People demand more control over their death, including where and how they die, than they once did. They want to die with dignity, in peace, and without pain.

Metzger and Kaplan (2001, p. 7) made several recommendations in their review of end-of-life treatment today:

- Pain and other physical and psychological symptoms should be alleviated and comfort maximized by medical care that conforms to best-practice standards and is consistent with the person's values and preferences.
- The physical and emotional environment should be as pleasant and supportive as possible and include time spent with loved ones and other people of choice.
- Dying people and their families should be cared for in a manner that respects their inherent dignity.
- Dying people should be able to exercise personal autonomy (control) to the extent that they desire and is feasible.
- Dying people who wish to do so should be able to explore issues of meaning and spirituality with support from others.

These guidelines require a shift in how we think about health and death. Table 11.1 summarizes differences in the characteristics of traditional models and the new "expanded" models of health care.

Hospitals, nursing homes, and assisted living facilities will need increasing numbers of social workers with training and expertise in end-of-life issues. Health

TABLE 11.1 Characteristics of a Shift in the Conception of Health and Health Care

Old Model	*Expanded Model*
Definition: health as physical health and the absence of disease	**Definition:** health as wellness, including mental, social, and physical health
Goal: to find a cure for disease	**Goal:** to promote functional capacity and well-being
Context: acute episodic illness and treatment of disease	**Context:** includes chronic illness and treatment of the whole person as well as acute illness and treatment of disease
Value: defeat death	**Value:** prevent illness, injury, and untimely death; relieve suffering; and care for those who cannot be cured

Source: Metzger and Kaplan, 2001, p. 7.

professionals and patients' families will seek help from social workers about psychosocial issues and holistic care at the end of life. People will seek help with advance directives and end-of-life planning, coping with a life-threatening diagnosis, living with terminal illness, and experiencing meaningful death. Social workers will encounter terminally ill older people in various stages of dying and in different settings, including some people who have just received a life-threatening diagnosis and others who are undergoing treatment for their condition.

The death trajectory can be conceptualized as encompassing five phases: death as remote, diagnosis of a life-threatening illness, living with dying, the deathbed, and postdeath, or bereavement. See table 11.2 for an outline of these phases, which we summarize here and review in greater depth later in this chapter. (See chapter 12 for the discussion of bereavement.)

When death is remote, people think about it from a distance. This is the first stage of death awareness. It is still far enough off to be abstract. People change their views on death as they experience changes in hair color, vision, and hearing and as their parents grow older and die. Death becomes more real and imminent. Yet people continue to think vaguely of death until they are diagnosed with a life-threatening illness.

Since Congress enacted the Patient Self-Determination Act in 1991, health professionals are required to ask people about advance directives when they enter a hospital. *Advance directive* is a general term used to describe two types of documents, the living will and the medical power of attorney. The living will includes instructions about the use of life-sustaining treatments (such as supplemental feeding, dialysis, respiratory support, and cardiopulmonary resuscitation) when a patient is in a terminal state. The durable power of attorney for health care, also called a health care proxy, identifies one or more people who will make medi-

TABLE 11.2   The Death Trajectory

Death Trajectory	Death as remote	Diagnosis	Living with dying	Deathbed	Post-death
	END-OF-LIFE PLANNING	COMMUNICATING BAD NEWS	CLINICAL COUNSELING	SUPPORT	BEREAVEMENT COUNSELING
Micro issues	Patient Self-Determination Act and advance directives Living wills Health Care Proxies WIlls Funerals/memorials Burial options Legacies	Information and referral Decision making Teaching coping skills	Psychosocial counseling Pain management Mediation Interdisciplinary team work	The "good death" Death setting Family counseling Psychoeducation	Bereavement counseling
Macro issues	Implementation of requirements of Patient Self-Determination Act Physician-assisted suicide Euthanasia	Health inequities Access to health care	Empowerment Advocacy Palliative care	Awareness Death setting	Family leave policies

cal decisions on behalf of a patient who becomes mentally incompetent to make health treatment decisions (Last Acts, 2002).

Social workers often are the professionals who talk to patients about their plans and preferences at the end of life. Social workers can review available options about living wills, health care proxies, burial options, and legacies with these patients, who are often uninformed about advance directives.

The second stage of death is the diagnosis. Death becomes a reality when someone is diagnosed with a life-threatening illness. Social workers need to help patients understand their illness and make decisions about their treatment. Most patients want information about coping with the diagnosis and reducing the stress involved with their treatment. Preventative interventions can help elderly patients manage medical interventions without experiencing debilitating anxiety or depression. Many patients need social workers to help them with insurance policies, Medicare, and Medicaid benefits. Social workers need to advocate on behalf of clients who encounter obstacles in obtaining adequate health coverage. In some instances coalitions such as the Older Women's League or AARP are needed to challenge inequities in health care.

The third stage, living while dying, occurs when people know that they are dying and that their time is limited. Many issues revolve around symptom management at this time. Social workers must know how to assess patients' pains and discomforts and how to communicate with other health professionals who can provide palliative care. Interdisciplinary teams can deliver comprehensive end-of-life care and treat patients physically, emotionally, and spiritually.

The deathbed phase revolves around the actual death and the ways that people experience it. Social workers assume multiple roles at this stage. They educate others about death and its characteristics, inform families about managing symptoms and expressing care, identify the needs of dying people and their family members, and facilitate communication within families. Social workers must also work with others to raise social awareness about what constitutes a comfortable death, or a "good death." Health professionals as well as laypeople will benefit from knowing more about death and dying and learning how to create a meaningful environment for peaceful and spiritual death. We discuss these phases in depth in the pages that follow.

Phase 1: Death as Remote; End-of-Life Planning

End-of-life planning can range from writing a will to completing an advance directive to preparing a memorial service. According to Pearlman, Cole, Patrick, Starks, and Cain (1995), advance care planning, another term for end-of-life planning, "is intended to maximize beneficial medical treatment decisions in the event of mental incapacitation, promote shared understanding of relevant values and preferences between the patient and both her healthcare providers and family members, reduce burden on and conflict with family members at the time of future decision-making, and avoid errors of overtreatment and under treatment when patients can no longer indicate for themselves what they consider to be worthwhile treatment" (p. 359).

Advance care planning typically involves assessments of the patient's understanding of his medical history and current condition and his experiences with death. It also includes evaluations of his support systems, spirituality, decision-making style, family involvement, preference for death location, interest in hospice, inhibiting factors, finances, and personal, family, and community resources

(Ratner, Norlander, and McSteen, 2001). A small part of the planning process involves helping people to complete advance directives or living wills.

Ideally, advance care planning should be completed before a crisis or incapacitation occurs. According to Norlander and McSteen (2000), end-of-life planning ought to take place when the client

- is unlikely to survive for one or two more years
- had more than two hospitalizations following emergency room visits in the last twelve months or is older than sixty-five and has had an admission to an intensive care unit
- has had a change in functional status, with dependencies in two or more activities of daily living
- has illnesses or conditions that could be considered either life threatening or life limiting, such as cancer, heart disease/lung disease, diabetes, autoimmune disease such as lupus, osteoporosis (which leads to a 30% mortality rate for women older than eighty with a fractured hip), chronic renal failure/ dialysis, morbid obesity, depression, dementia, failure to thrive, and lifestyle choices such as smoking or chemical abuse

Advance Directives

The most basic end-of-life planning involves completing advance directives. Under the Patient Self-Determination Act (PSDA) health care facilities that receive reimbursements from Medicare or Medicaid must ask patients on admission if they have an advance directive and to inform them of their right to complete an advance directive. The PSDA was intended to provide competent adults with the opportunity to communicate their preferences for medical treatment before they become unable to articulate them. This increases their control over the care that they receive at the end of life and allows them to convey their wishes in writing or during conversations with physicians. See chapter 16 for more discussion about advance directives.

Problems with Advance Directives

Low completion rates are the most common problem with advance directives. Fewer than 25% of Americans have a written document stating their preferences for care at the end of life (Kahana, Dan, Kahana, and Kercher, 2004). Only about 50% of those with a terminal illness have an advance directive (Miles, Koepp, and Weber, 1996; Drought and Koenig, 2002).

Many people misunderstand and misinterpret these documents. In addition, family members often disagree with the instructions expressed in an advance directive. Some people eschew advance directives altogether, simply because they prefer not to think about death. People who do complete advance directives typically spend more time discussing end-of-life issues with their health care providers than people who do not, and they are more confident that their preferences are understood than those who do not have advance directives (A. T. Beck, Brown, Boles, and Barrett, 2002).

Cultural variations also influence people's reactions to advance directives. For example, Navajos often avoid discussion of death and serious illness for fear that such talk will create health problems (Werth, Blevins, and Toussaint, 2002). Many Hispanic and African American groups also are less inclined to complete advance directives than other groups are (Romero, Lindeman, Koehler, and Allen, 1997; Kahana et al., 2004). Elderly African Americans are more likely to prefer life-sustaining treatments but discuss advance care planning with their physicians less often, have or desire fewer living wills, and are generally less familiar with advance care planning than are members of other groups (S. Murphy, Palmer, Frank, Michel, and Blackhall, 1995; Bradley, 2002).

Another common problem with advance directives revolves around disagreements among family members. Few families discuss end-of-life care or a relative's wishes regarding life-sustaining interventions before a crisis occurs. Families are even less likely to have held these discussions if the relative has dementia (Uhlmann, Pearlman, and Cain, 1988; Drought and Koenig, 2002). Family members often avoid talking to health professionals about these issues because pressing current obligations prevent them from considering long-term issues. (See Lorenz et al., 2004, for more information about families and advance directives.)

Social workers can help these families by anticipating family members' confusion about progressive illness and by initiating talks about the future. Most families are relieved when health professionals bring up issues about death and dying. They feel more in control when they know what to expect and are able to anticipate different scenarios as the disease worsens.

Another problem, lack of compliance, results from many factors. Advance directives are sometimes inaccessible because they are located in a different state or are locked away in someone's office. Health care professionals are often unsure how to proceed if family members disagree with each other. Despite these limitations, social workers will increasingly become involved in assisting older people and their families to plan in advance for end-of-life care.

Planning Programs

Norlander and McSteen (2000) have devised a unique program in which social workers visit a terminally ill patient's home several times to discuss end-of-life preferences. The objective is to fulfill a person's wish to die at home. In another successful approach Gockel, Morrow-Howell, Thompson, Pousson, and Johnson, (1998) implemented an educational intervention in which social workers told patients about and explained advance directives at a walk-in clinic. Social workers can help clients plan for end-of-life care by informing them about the alternatives available, by helping them to complete the necessary forms, navigating bureaucracies, advocating for clients' preferences, and participating in groups that advocate for quality end-of-life care, such as Promoting Excellence in End-of-Life Care, a national program of the Robert Wood Johnson Foundation. For more information about Promoting Excellence, consult its website at www.promotingexcellence. org/index.html.

Funerals and Burial Options

Most families base their decision to bury or cremate a deceased loved one on tradition and religious preferences, and many people remain uninformed about burial options. Norms about final arrangements are sometimes unclear and vary across families, religions, socioeconomic status, and ethnic and cultural backgrounds. For example, many Chinese people expect to be buried with jewelry and prefer not to be cremated. Many Vietnamese people place spices, such as coffee and tea, in the casket, and Filipinos sometimes put needles and thread in the coffin. People from some Asian cultures include the deceased's personal belongings so that the decedent can avoid returning to search for these items (see Braun and Nichols, 1997, for more information on these cultural variations among Asian Americans).

Bern-Klug, Ekerdt, and Wilkinson (1999) outline several reasons that social workers should help families with final arrangements. Family members are often in crisis and overwhelmed with loss immediately after a loved one dies. These arrangements are sometimes expensive and are irrevocable; family members cannot change their minds later. Finally, because time is limited, people generally must decide on burial and funeral options within twenty-four hours of the death. According to Bern-Klug and colleagues (1999), social workers who have knowledge of public benefits and experience in consumer advocacy and discharge planning are ideally situated to help families with final arrangements.

Bern-Klug and colleagues (1999) have identified several areas in which social workers can help clients with final arrangements. These include the disposition of the body, the type of ceremony or memorial that will be held, and referrals to appropriate services. By talking with family members about the deceased person, social workers can help them to decide how best to remember their loved one in a ceremony or ritual that has meaning for them. Social workers' knowledge of community resources, home health care, and hospices, and their membership on interdisciplinary teams, place them in a unique position to inquire about clients' preferences and to communicate these to others.

Physician-Assisted Suicide

Physician-assisted suicide is sometimes confused with decisions about withholding (not starting) and withdrawing (stopping) treatment. Advance directives allow people to specify in advance, before they become incapacitated, their decision not to receive treatment. Treatment typically includes cardiopulmonary resuscitation (CPR), advanced cardiac life support, renal dialysis, nutritional support and hydration, mechanical ventilation, organ transplantation or other surgery, pacemakers, chemotherapy, and antibiotics (DeSpelder and Strickland, 2002). Withholding or withdrawing treatment differs from interventions that assist people in dying, that is, that actively help someone to die, which is illegal in the United States. Physician-assisted suicide actively and intentionally hastens a person's death. Physician-assisted suicide refers to providing terminally ill patients with the means to kill themselves, usually by prescribing a medication that the patient takes without the assistance of the physician. The physician may or may not be present when the patient dies. Physician-assisted suicide is illegal in the United States except in the state of Oregon (Ardelt, 2003b).

Oregon enacted the Death with Dignity Act in 1997, legalizing physician-assisted suicide for terminally ill people who request it. The legislation has provisions to ensure that patients who choose assisted suicide are terminally ill, have adequate decision-making capacity, are not depressed or acting impulsively, and have been offered alternatives.

Data on the outcome of the legislation are contradictory. Several researchers, for example, Ganzini and colleagues (2000), and Sullivan, Hedberg, and Fleming (2000), have found that desire for control was a more important reason for requesting physician-assisted suicide than depression, lack of social support, or fear of being a financial drain on family members.

Ethnic differences toward physician-assisted suicide are well documented. In a rigorous analysis Braun, Tanji, and Heck (2001) found that the strongest supporters (90%) of physician-assisted suicide are Japanese, and people of Chinese descent are the next most positive (77%). Approximately 75% of whites accept physician-assisted suicide. The strongest opponents are Filipinos, with only 33% supporting this option. Residents of Hawaii are almost evenly split, with about 51% showing a favorable response. Differences within groups are as strong as those between groups.

In a recent study of social workers' experiences with physician-assisted suicide in Oregon, P. J. Miller, Mesler, and Eggman (2002) report that social workers are anguished about situations involving physician-assisted suicide. The complex ethical and moral dilemmas that arise when people request this option overwhelm and confuse the social workers. Their training inadequately prepared Oregon social workers for end-of-life care, according to the findings of P. J. Miller and colleagues (2002). As the public debate on physician-assisted suicide grows and baby boomers age, social workers must prepare themselves for increasing numbers of requests for physician-assisted suicide.

Euthanasia

Euthanasia originally referred to a painless or peaceful death. Today most people use the term to refer to *passive* euthanasia, which is when health professionals withhold or withdraw treatment from people who are terminally ill or severely injured and allow the patient to die from the illness or injury. Many view passive euthanasia as an act of omission. Voluntary passive euthanasia is legal and generally accepted in the United States. In 1990 the U.S. Supreme Court granted permission for competent adults to refuse medical treatment, and Congress passed the Patient Self-Determination Act the next year (Ardelt, 2003b; Walker, 2003).

Active euthanasia is a deliberate act to end a person's life, and it can be involuntary, nonvoluntary, or voluntary (DeSpelder and Strickland, 2002). Involuntary euthanasia occurs without the patient's consent, and represents about 1% of cases in the Netherlands, where euthanasia has long been practiced. However, even in the Netherlands involuntary euthanasia is illegal; only voluntary euthanasia is accepted there. Nonvoluntary euthanasia happens when a relative or surrogate decision maker initiates the request to end a terminally ill patient's life. Voluntary euthanasia involves the intentional termination of a terminally ill person's life, usually by a physician at the patient's request. The Netherlands has guidelines that include a terminal diagnosis confirmed by a second opinion, the patient's desire to die, and unbearable suffering.

Social Work Ethics

Although medical doctors are directly involved with various medical treatments, social workers will continue to play a major role in assisting terminally ill patients with advance care planning, advance directives, and physician-assisted suicide, such as in Oregon. According to the Code of Ethics of the National Association of Social Workers, social workers with minimal or inadequate training should not work with clients in these areas. Instead, they should refer clients to social workers who are trained in these fields. The policy statement, approved by the NASW Delegate Assembly in 1993 and reconfirmed in 1999, articulates NASW's position concerning end-of-life decisions, and social workers practicing in the field of aging should review it. The statement is based on the principle of client self-determination but emphasizes that social workers should also enhance quality of life and help people identify the end-of-life options available to them. The statement also says that if social workers are unable to help with decisions about assisted suicide or other end-of-life choices, they have a professional obligation to refer patients and their families to competent professionals who are available to address these issues.

The Association of Oncology Social Work also offers a detailed position paper, "The Association of Oncology Social Work Position Paper on Active Euthanasia and Assisted Suicide," which is available at the association's website at www.aosw. org/mission/euthanasia.html and offers guidelines for social workers. Social workers face difficult ethical decisions when a terminally ill patient requests help to die. They must understand state and federal laws regulating physician-assisted suicide and consider the NASW Code of Ethics and policy statement regarding end-of-life decisions, discussed earlier. Miller, Hedlund, and Murphy (1998) offer a useful model for social workers that covers diagnosis, treatment, symptoms, and need for care, for assessing patients' requests for help with suicide. The model takes into account psychosocial functioning along with an individual's cultural context.

Phase 2: Diagnosis—Communicating Bad News

Physicians vary enormously in how they communicate with patients and, specifically, in how they inform patients about life-threatening conditions. Many medical schools are strengthening curricula on end-of-life care, and an increasing number are offering specialties in palliative medicine. Nurses have also launched several initiatives to increase end-of-life content in textbooks, curricula, and practice. The Project on Death in America's Social Work Leadership Development Awards seek to promote innovative research and training projects based on partnerships between social work schools and practice sites in order to advance ongoing development of social work practice, education, and training in the care of the dying.

Because almost all social workers learn basic communication skills like active and empathetic listening, they can help newly diagnosed older clients understand and cope with serious illnesses. At this stage social workers can assist by providing information and referral, assistance in decision making, and teaching coping skills.

Information and Referral

People are usually in shock and have difficulty assimilating medical information when they first learn that they have a life-threatening illness. Few people learn all they need or want to know during the meeting with their physician when their illness is first diagnosed. People also differ in their knowledge and understanding of medical terminology.

Social workers can help people understand their diagnosis and how it will affect their life. Bern-Klug and colleagues (2001) suggest that social workers act as "context interpreters" by providing individuals and families with the information that they must have in order to understand the natural course of an illness, the probable dying trajectory, and the medical decisions that they must make. Social workers with adequate medical knowledge can help dying people place their condition into a context they can manage. Social workers should interpret confusing or abstruse medical information for clients, or if they are unable to explain or are unsure of something, they should know how and where to refer clients for more information. Social workers can help clients cope with their feelings about their diagnosis, death, and treatment decisions.

Many newly diagnosed cancer patients benefit from talking to others who are struggling with similar health issues. Mutual support groups help cancer patients feel less alone and provide them with an outlet to more freely express their feelings. People in these groups often exchange information about experimental treatments and symptom management.

Oncology social workers who are trained to focus on the psychosocial effects of cancer at all stages complete psychosocial assessments of patients' and families' responses to a cancer diagnosis. This includes evaluating the extent of the client's knowledge of cancer and its treatment and identifying family members' strengths, coping skills, and supports; their ethnic, spiritual, and cultural concerns; and their awareness of community resources. These social workers develop treatment plans to enhance, maintain, and promote the client's optimal psychosocial functioning throughout cancer treatment, and these practitioners use various clinical interventions to address current issues as well as problems that will arise. Oncology social workers collaborate with other professionals in the planning and provision of services to cancer patients and their families. In addition, they advocate to protect patients' dignity, confidentiality, legal rights, and access to care (Association of Oncology Social Work, 2001). Thus they are trained to work with cancer patients on multiple levels.

Social workers must consider cultural differences in discussing a diagnosis because some families prefer to shield their loved ones from the knowledge that they are dying. Even talking about death is sometimes considered inappropriate (see Yeo and Hikoyeda, 2000). Blackhall, Murphy, Frank, Michel, and Azen (1995) found that while African Americans and European Americans believe that patients should be told that they have a terminal illness, Korean Americans and Mexican Americans are more inclined to keep this information from their relatives and to value family instead of individual decisions about treatments. Cultural influences will also affect how people treat a life-threatening illness.

Social workers can help families understand the vicissitudes of dying as well as the typical paths to death. Clinicians should also aim to reduce patients' uncertainties by reassuring them that others will accept them throughout the dying process, no matter what happens to them (Twycross, 1999). According to Bern-Klug and colleagues (2001, p. 44), "Most people who are dying—or at increased risk of dying—benefit from a 'big picture' of the end-of-life journey they are making, including discussions about the possible paths to dying and death." By providing this information, social workers can help families control some end-of-life events, such as the location and manner of death.

Decision Making

Although some diagnoses leave patients with few treatment decisions, other diagnoses, such as prostate or breast cancer, require patients to choose among various treatment options. These decisions generally involve cultural, religious, and psychosocial considerations, such as quality of life and attitudes about dying. Social workers can help people investigate their options and the effect of different choices on their life. By encouraging patients to discuss their priorities, social workers can help them figure out what is most important to them. Patients can more easily complete advance directives after they have explored their feelings and wishes about death and dying. Because family members sometimes differ from one another about treatment decisions, social workers should facilitate communication within families and ensure that everyone's voice is heard.

Inequities in treatment options sometimes emerge when a client's physicians or other health professionals treat them differently from younger or wealthier patients. In these instances social workers must advocate for their clients and challenge unjust, discriminatory policies. Organizations such as NASW that are comprised of many social workers are more influential than individuals. Health inequities on the basis of age, gender, and race continue to be a serious problem for many people when they explore their treatment options.

Teaching Coping Skills

Social workers with training in managing anxiety and with knowledge of effective coping skills can teach stress management techniques to newly diagnosed patients. Although people react to their diagnosis in various ways, social workers can reduce people's fears about dying and help them prepare for death. The most typical reactions include anxiety about physical discomfort and pain, uncertainty about dying, concerns about dignity, and fears about the unknown after death (DeSpelder and Strickland, 2002). Social workers can help people with a terminal illness find hope. At first, clients hope that the symptoms are insignificant or that even if the diagnosis is terminal, they have many good years left to live. Eventually, they hope for a pain-free death and a feeling that they have made some sort of meaningful contribution.

Although coping styles are influenced by personality characteristics and responses learned throughout life, as well as by age, religion, and marital status, people can learn to cope in ways that will improve their circumstances. In one study of women with breast cancer Glanz and Lerman (1992) found that coping differences explain at least half the variance in the women's emotional adjustment.

Social workers can empower clients by assessing their coping styles and working with them to evaluate the effectiveness of their stress reduction strategies. Social workers can inform clients about different coping techniques and their efficacy in various situations. For example, while problem-solving methods are often effective in reducing stress and when the situation is alterable, emotion-focused (especially meaning-based coping) methods are more helpful with intractable stressors.

Therapeutic Coping Model

Folkman and Greer (2000) propose a therapeutic program, based on a revised conceptual model of coping, to promote and maintain psychological well-being among those struggling with serious illnesses. Folkman and Greer recommend that clinicians first look beyond traditional psychiatric symptoms, which are usually negative reactions such as anxiety and depression, to help people with serious illness. Folkman and Greer emphasize positive experiences, even in unalterable situations, and discuss meaning-based coping that helps people "relinquish untenable goals and formulate new ones, make sense of what is happening, and appraise benefit where possible" (p. 13). The positive feelings that emerge from meaning-based coping can coexist with negative affect, not necessarily at exactly the same moment but fairly close in time.

People can also find benefits in their struggle with terminal illness by admiring their strength, reappraising their current activities, cognitively reframing their experiences, and improving their relationships. Another strategy involves setting new goals and identifying a purpose in life that the client has neglected or never previously considered. The focus is not on how to eliminate one's illness but rather on how to live and die in a more meaningful way, one that the client might have ignored before the diagnosis.

Folkman and Greer (2000) recommend three major therapeutic goals: creating conditions for challenge, encouraging behavior to achieve goals, and maintaining a positive attitude. Clinicians can help older people view their situation as challenging by encouraging them to think differently about their illness. For example, social workers can ask the client specific questions or make requests, such as "Tell me about a time recently when something happened that really mattered to you, something important"—and follow up with inquiries that elicit more detail. (See Folkman and Greer, 2000, for more information about this process.) When people view a stressful situation as a challenge instead of as a threat or loss, they unleash opportunities for mastery or gain that, in turn, invoke positive affect such as excitement, eagerness, or optimism. Social workers can help clients reframe their struggles and identify realistic goals, such as arranging a family gathering to give gifts or finishing their memoirs, depending on the client's illness, energy, and resources.

In addition to creating the conditions for challenge, Folkman and Greer (2000) recommend encouraging the client to achieve goals. This involves creating plans that may include others and may involve revising goals so that they are more realistic. Folkman and Greer stress the importance of working toward goals, which engages clients in pursuits that are meaningful to them.

Finally, Folkman and Greer (2000) maintain that clinicians should help clients maintain a positive attitude even if this coexists with feelings of loss or depression. Folkman and Greer explain that well-being in people with serious illnesses is different from the absence of negative feelings. Instead, it involves opportunities to achieve positive affect by engaging in rewarding activities and experiences.

PHASE 3: LIVING WITH DYING—CLINICAL COUNSELING

People vary in how long they live and struggle with a terminal illness, depending upon the type of illness and when it was diagnosed. The duration from diagnosis to death is sometimes so short that people remain unaware that they are dying. In other cases this period may last for more than ten years. In fact, many men with prostate cancer die from other causes before the cancer kills them. The differences between a rapid dying trajectory and a protracted one influence how clients prepare for death and how others will react. It shapes clients' interpersonal interactions as well as their priorities, such as whether they choose to start or finish particular tasks.

Tasks and Concerns of the Dying

Death is a normative event, not a pathological one, according to Doka (1993), and dying people still have things to work on, achieve, and contribute. Doka has identified several tasks that terminally ill people may focus on, depending upon whether they are in the acute, chronic, or terminal phase of dying. For example, during the acute phase people focus on understanding their disease and finding ways to cope with it. They must manage symptoms and side-effects during the chronic phase. The terminal phase involves preparing for death and saying good-bye. Kastenbaum (2000) cautions others about setting guidelines or tasks at the end of life, especially in a society that values work and productivity. He fears that by emphasizing tasks, experts will create stress for dying people to "die right." According to Kastenbaum, death provides a fundamental structure from which people conceptualize life and society, and dying people contribute to society despite their physical deterioration. Caregivers' lives revolve around dying people, and other healthy people need dying people to remind them of their mortality.

Dying people confront physical, psychological, social, and spiritual issues (Corr, 1992). While they must cope with physical declines in their body's functioning, symptoms (including pain) that arise from failing health, and increasingly limited functioning on a daily basis, people with terminal illness must also struggle with psychological concerns about control, security, and continued involvement in life. Social issues often revolve around how to maintain their attachments to their loved ones, what issues to let go of, and how to interact or not interact when others are present. Spiritual challenges include finding meaning in their circumstances, connecting to and maintaining harmony with others, and resolving their relationship with the universe. Many terminally ill people strive to understand their link to a higher being or ultimate reality (Twycross, 1999).

Members of the International Work Group on Death, Dying and Bereavement (1990) define *spirituality* as being "concerned with the transcendental, inspirational and existential way to live one's life as well as in a fundamental and profound sense, with the person as a human being" (p. 75). Social workers must assess dying people's spiritual needs along with their physical, psychological, and social needs, and clinicians must know when and how to offer spiritual assistance to dying people. Twycross (1999) explains that dying people usually say when they need spiritual help. For example, people often need spiritual assistance when they express hopelessness, meaninglessness, or powerlessness, which can sometimes lead to withdrawal and suicide, or when they exhibit loneliness, isolation, and vulnerability through such comments as "I can't endure this anymore." Other signs that clients could benefit from spiritual care include anger, resentment, or bitterness about former relationships; a sense of guilt or shame that that they are being punished for bad deeds; concern that they are unworthy of care or of the treatment being offered; unresolved feelings about death resulting in fear of sleep and the dark; or vivid dreams and nightmares, such as being trapped (Twycross, 1999).

Caregivers and health professionals can offer spiritual assistance in many ways. They include respecting a dying person's spiritual beliefs and preferences and developing resources to meet the client's spiritual needs; showing care and support by being present, compassionate, and hopeful; and allowing dying people to be themselves by communicating "unconditional acceptance" of them (P. O'Connor, 1993).

Dying people most often experience hope when they have relief from pain and symptoms, set realistic goals or minigoals, and have meaningful relationships that include humor and reminiscence (Twycross, 1999). When death is imminent, hope often revolves around a relationship with a higher being, relationships with others, and being rather than achieving. Some people simply hope not to be left alone to die and that they will have a peaceful death. According to O'Connor (1993), "our greatest task as caregivers is to protect our patients from this ultimate tragedy of depersonalization and to sustain them in a 'personalized' environment that recognizes individuals' needs and attempts to reduce individual fear" (p. 140).

Assessment

Cohen and Leis (2002) developed the McGill Quality of Life Questionnaire to evaluate the quality of life of terminally ill people. It covers (1) the patient's state, including her physical and cognitive functioning, psychological state, and physical condition; (2) the quality of palliative care; (3) the physical environment; (4) relationships; and (5) outlook. The Quality of Life in Life-Threatening Illness—Patient Version is a similar assessment tool (see Cohen and Leis, 2002, for more information). The Edmonton functional assessment, which is being tested for use with terminally ill patients, focuses more on physical and cognitive/affective functioning (Kaasa and Wessel, 2001). Moody, Beckie, Long, Edmonds, and Andrews (2000) use the McCanse Readiness for Death Instrument with elderly hospice patients to identify terminally ill patients who could benefit from interventions that facilitate their readiness to die. Byock and Merriman's Missoula-VITAS Quality of Life Index (1998) was designed to comprehensively assess the lives of dying people and their care at the end of life. The World Health Organization's Quality of Life Instrument (known as WHO QOL-100) and WHO QOL-BREF, a shorter, twenty-six-item version, are appropriate for cross-cultural situations. The WHO QOL spirituality, religiousness, and personal belief module is also useful when assessing quality of life at the end of life (Saxena, O'Connell, and Underwood, 2002). The most comprehensive resource for assessment measures of end-of-life care is located at the website of the Toolkit project at www.chcr.brown.edu/pcoc/toolkit. htm (Teno, Byock, and Field, 1999). Toolkit is a research initiative to develop assessment instruments to measure quality of care and quality of life of patients diagnosed with terminal illnesses.

Evaluating Depression

Van Loon (1999) offers a useful framework for examining depression among terminally ill people who want to die, and she recommends greater reliance on psychological rather than physical symptoms of depression when assessing dying people. She suggests that clinicians inquire directly about a client's depression and motives for suicide, and she believes that desire-to-die statements can be expressions of depression or suicidal ideation, a coping strategy, an acceptance of death, or a rational choice of suicide. Clinicians should ask the client whether his depression is unreasonable and whether and why he feels suicidal. This usually uncovers the dying person's feelings of pain, loneliness, and social isolation, which can be addressed through medication, increased social support, or cognitive interventions. In addition, this approach reveals the dying client's feelings about death, such as how accepting he is of his death and whether he views dying as a "rational choice," an important consideration among those seeking physician-assisted suicide.

Individual Care

An individualized care model that is based on a comprehensive assessment with the ABCDEF method (described in earlier chapters) ensures that dying people's unique needs are met within their social context. Kagawa-Singer (1998) and Hickman (2002) suggest that clinicians focus on the client's values, needs, and preferences when individualizing care. Hickman (2002) suggests that practitioners should embrace the client's definition of her family, recognize cultural biases inherent in the medical system, acknowledge the diversity of health care practices, incorporate different perspectives on autonomy, and establish a treatment approach that is sensitive to these issues.

Cancer self-help groups are also excellent resources that can offer hope, help people feel less alone, and provide people with opportunities for advocacy and empowerment (Gray, 2001). Although some people feel uncomfortable talking in groups, others benefit from knowing other terminally ill patients who are struggling with similar issues. People often learn different coping approaches in these groups. Social workers should carefully assess patients before referring them to support groups, however, because these groups are ineffective with reluctant participants.

Pain Management

Pain management is an important aspect of this terminal stage, and social workers should know how to evaluate dying people's pain and discomfort. Although most experts agree that 95% of all serious pain can be treated safely, many dying patients receive inadequate pain relief (Last Acts, 2002). In a survey conducted in 1999, researchers found that more than half of all Americans older than sixty-five suffer pain, but 40% of people who rate their chronic pain as moderate or severe fail to get pain relief (American Pain Society, 1999; see also Pro Health, 2002).

Experts argue that careful pain assessment and the use of medication at regular intervals around the clock, instead of "as needed," is essential for successfully managing a patient's pain (Haylock, 2002). Social workers should familiarize themselves with common pain assessment tools. (See Haylock, 2002, for an in-depth discussion of pain management and pain assessment.)

Bern-Klug and colleagues (2001) encourage social workers to develop skills in helping individuals and their families "articulate the intensity, duration, and quality (for example, aching, sharp, numbing, or cramping) of pain and request help from physicians" (p. 44). By treating a dying person's symptoms, such as nausea, shortness of breath, dizziness, and intense itchiness, family members or professionals working with them can substantially improve the dying person's final days.

Palliative care aims to relieve pain and other physical symptoms, but it also emphasizes emotional and spiritual support for patients and their families. According to van der Kloot Meijburg (2000, p. 113), "palliative care is a means of enhancing the well-being of the patient in the last stages of his or her life to help the patient make peace with his or her respective circumstances." Although more physicians (39%) are treating dying patients' pain than in the past, few doctors who provide palliative care are board certified in palliative medicine (Last Acts, 2002). In addition, palliative care should involve an interdisciplinary team of professionals, including social workers, to provide holistic treatment. Without a mix of disciplines the client is unlikely to receive integrated care that treats more than just physical symptoms.

Advocacy

Collective action or "coalition building" is the best way to change policies and methods that institutions, including hospitals and nursing homes, follow on end-of-life care (Hickman, 2002). Last Acts, the Association of Oncology Social Workers, and the Project on Death in America are examples of organizations that have focused effectively on improving end-of-life care. Gerontological social workers must work on multiple levels to successfully eradicate inequities in quality of life and quality of care among dying people in the United States. We especially need better policies to alleviate dying people's pain.

State policies on prescribing opioid analgesics are often outmoded and prevent people from receiving adequate pain relief. Such policies significantly affect the treatment of terminally ill people. The American Bar Association adopted a resolution in 2000 to encourage state, federal, and territorial governments to facilitate the treatment of pain. In addition, many insurance policies limit coverage for pain medications.

Organizations devoted to improving pain management are increasing. For example, the Pain and Policy Study Group at the University of Wisconsin—Madison is committed to identifying and addressing barriers to the availability of opioids in national policies and health care organizations. In addition, the Federation of State Medical Boards of the United States adopted guidelines in 1998 to improve pain treatment. Unfortunately, variations in state policies still result in too many people who die in pain. Unless more social workers and other health professionals advocate for changes in pain treatment, many dying people will be denied benign or peaceful deaths.

Phase 4: The Deathbed

Kastenbaum (2000) describes deathbed scenes as "symbolic constructions that draw upon both idiosyncratic personal experiences and culturally available themes, events, and meaning fragments" (p. 255). Deathbed scenes are opportunities for significant "rites of passage" and represent "the border, the edge, the precipice" (p. 255). When a dying relative reaches the end stage of a terminal illness, family members work at acknowledging and reconciling this final stage with their daily activities. Dying people may breathe harder, refuse nourishment, and exhibit incontinence. Family members oscillate between watching their loved one slip away and anticipating a crisis.

Symptoms of Actively Dying

People usually exhibit several symptoms when they are actively dying: their body systems slow down; their breathing patterns change and become irregular (for example, shallow breaths followed by deep breaths and periods of panting); their breathing becomes more difficult (dyspnea); their congestion increases (noisy and moist breathing; gurgling sounds); and their appetite and thirst decline. Additional symptoms include nausea and vomiting; incontinence; sweating; restlessness and agitation (for example, jerking, twitching, and pulling at bed linen or clothing); disorientation and confusion (for example, about time, place, and identity of people); decreased socialization; progressive detachment; changes in skin color as their circulation decreases (their limbs may become cool and perhaps bluish or mottled); increased sleeping; and decreases in consciousness.

Symptoms at the Time of Death

At the time of death the person's throat muscles relax and secretions in the throat may cause noisy breathing ("the death rattle"); breathing ceases; muscle contractions may occur, and the chest may heave as if to breathe; the heart may beat for a few minutes after breathing stops, and a brief seizure may occur; the person cannot be aroused; the eyelids may be partly open with the eyes in a fixed stare; the mouth may fall open as the jaw relaxes; and the body may release the contents of the bowel and bladder.

The Good or Appropriate Death

Various factors influence the deathbed scene, but the most significant is whether a death is unanticipated and acute rather than protracted and chronic. According to DeSpelder and Strickland (2002), a "good death" typically includes the following characteristics:

- Knowledge that death is coming and an understanding of what to expect
- The ability to retain reasonable control over what happens
- Dignity and privacy
- Adequate control of pain relief and other symptoms
- Choice about where death occurs (home or elsewhere)
- Access to information and expertise of whatever kind is needed
- Access to desired spiritual and emotional support
- Access to hospice or palliative care in any location (home, hospital, or elsewhere)
- Having a say about who is present and who shares the end
- The ability to issue advance directives that ensure the person's wishes are respected
- Adequate time to say good-bye
- The ability to leave when it is time to go and to not have life prolonged pointlessly

Weisman (1972) offers the concept of an "appropriate death" that includes minimal pain, independent functioning and mobility when possible, psychosocial needs that are well met, residual personal and social conflicts that are resolved to the extent possible, wishes that are seriously considered, and control that is freely relinquished to trusted others. Most important, others must respect the unique ways that people die while taking into account their personal wishes; their cultural, ethnic, and religious influences; and their reactions to pain and other symptoms associated with dying.

According to Byock (1997), dying offers people a chance for continued growth and the completion of several developmental tasks, including

- A sense of completion of worldly affairs: transfer of financial, legal, and formal social responsibilities (including completing a will and arranging a funeral or memorial service)
- A sense of completion in relationships with community: closure of multiple social relationships (employment, commerce, organizational, and congregational)
- A sense of meaning about life: life review (the telling of stories) and transmission of knowledge and wisdom
- Experiencing love of self: self-acknowledgment and self-forgiveness
- Experiencing love of others: acceptance of worthiness
- A sense of completion in relationships with family and friends: reconciliation, fullness of communication, and closure in each important relationship
- Acceptance of the finality of life and of existence as an individual
- A sense of new self (personhood) beyond personal loss
- A sense of meaning about life in general
- Surrender to the transcendent, to the unknown: letting go

Cultural Variations

Cultural factors influence people's preferences for a "good" or "appropriate death." For example, in an in-depth analysis of naturalized Cambodian Americans and Filipino Americans, G. Becker (2002) found that most people want to return to their homeland to die because they yearn for the social support that they feel is lacking in the United States. Social workers must carefully consider cultural factors at this stage and help families achieve a "good death" that is consistent with their cultural beliefs. Death rituals among many Cambodian Americans revolve around preparing the dying person for a rebirth. Among Filipino Americans, family and friends are expected to surround the dead person twenty-four hours a day with vigils, flowers, and lighted candles. They offer nightly prayers for the deceased for nine days, then again on the fortieth day. Other rituals continue for weeks, and a prayer or gathering is held annually to recognize the death anniversary. Cultural differences in the meaning of death and in the treatment of dying people substantially influence how people respond to advance directives, communicate their pain, request or refuse life-sustaining interventions, and grieve for loved ones. Cultural differences can also influence how health professionals respond to and treat patients' complaints about pain. In a study of black and white elderly nursing home residents, Engle, Fox-Hill, and Graney (1998) discovered that black patients are undertreated for pain more often than white patients.

Talamantes, Gomez, and Braun (2000) recommend that practitioners use a values history form to assess a client's preferences for end-of-life care. Ideally, this form should consider the client's attitudes about autonomy, hierarchy, time, trust, family, and orientation toward spirits.

Braun, Tanji, and Heck (2001) emphasize the importance of taking a good history that includes open-ended questions about people's education and experiences and that, most important, considers their level of religiosity, their propensity to plan ahead, support for discussing and documenting their wishes, the extent to which they feel that their death is a part of a larger plan or is outside their control, whether they believe discussing death will make it occur, and how much they would like to share or give away their decision-making power. In addition, Braun and colleagues underscore the importance of establishing relationships with dying patients before talking to them about end-of-life issues.

The Death Setting

Half of older Americans die in hospitals, although about 25% die at home (Last Acts, 2002). Place of death substantially influences how people die, and some settings are better equipped to manage people's pain and discomfort than others. The norms and ambience of certain locations also affect end-of-life care. Hospitals, nursing homes, and private homes, especially those that use hospice programs, treat dying people and their needs in different ways. These settings are changing as palliative care becomes increasingly available and accepted by physicians. Next we discuss the most salient characteristics of these settings.

Hospitals. Many people enter the hospital with the hope that their medical condition will improve or that something can be done, and family members are often unaware that their loved one is dying. People are usually pressured to submit to a battery of tests and invasive procedures after they enter a hospital. Patients with terminal illnesses are often neglected and die alone in the hospital. In a study of how much time health professionals and family members spend with seriously ill hospitalized patients with poor prognoses, Sulmasy and Rahn (2001) learned that patients spend most of their time alone (more than 18.5 hours per day). Even when patients say they want comfort care instead of aggressive intervention, they are often given invasive life-sustaining treatments when they enter a hospital (Somogyi-Zalud, Zhong, Hamel, and Lynn, 2002). Some hospitals have begun to offer palliative care, but few offer comprehensive programs. Approximately 42% report that they train staff how to manage chronic and acute pain, and only about 23% include hospices. Even fewer (13.8%) operate palliative care programs that are directed by specially trained physicians (Last Acts, 2002).

Nursing homes. Although more and more people enter nursing homes for short stays and then return to their community, about 25% of older people die in nursing homes. The proportion of deaths that occurs in nursing homes is projected to double by 2018 as hospital stays become even shorter (Brock and Foley, 1998; National Center for Health Statistics, 1996). Many residents suffer from inadequate relief from persistent pain because of the lack of palliative care in nursing homes (Happ et al., 2002). In a study of nursing home residents hospitalized in the last six weeks of life, Happ and colleagues (2002) found that most end-of-life care in nursing homes violates accepted standards of palliative care. Residents often die alone, and family members are poorly informed about residents' conditions. Formal hospice services are underused or are implemented with only one week of death. Kayser-Jones (2002) observed that pain among dying people residing in nursing homes is inadequately assessed, monitored, or managed, that depression and loneliness are ignored, and that families receive only limited information.

Dying people in nursing homes are often sequestered in special units where they are inconspicuous to other residents. Froggatt (2001) found that nursing homes often use transitional spaces where the staff can pay greater attention to dying people's needs, but this usually results in dying people's spending more time alone and less time interacting with others in public spaces. These residents become stigmatized and experience a "social death," that is, "the cessation of the individual as an active agent in other people's lives" (Froggatt, 2001, p. 320). Staff members and other residents often treat these dying people as if they have already died.

It is easier to ignore the realities associated with aging and dying when people who are dying or who have threatening illnesses are out of sight. Such practices often occur even though they violate almost every profession's recommendations for quality end-of-life care. In a project supported by the Retirement Research Foundation and the John A. Hartford Foundation Institute for Geriatric Nursing, Mezey and colleagues (2000) identified several guidelines for end-of-life care in nursing homes.

In addition to these guidelines, Mezey and colleagues (2000) recommend that the state and federal government exercise oversight responsibility for the quality of end-of-life care in nursing homes. They further recommend that health care professionals should gain competency in end-of-life care.

Social workers will play an increasingly important role in implementing high-quality end-of-life care in nursing homes. Bern-Klug is conducting one of the first in-depth studies of the psychosocial needs of nursing home residents and their families at the end of life. Her research, which is supported by the Project on Death in America, will identify the most important issues that social workers must address among clients who are dying in nursing homes.

Homes and hospices. Most older people prefer to die at home (Gallup International Institute, 1997; Pritchard, Fisher, and Lynn, 1998); however, most die in hospitals (Fried et al., 1999). Cantwell, Turoc, Brenneis, and Hanson (2000) found that the most significant factor influencing whether someone dies at home is that the patient and caregiver agree about it. If they disagree, the dying patient is less likely to die at home.

The availability of hospice care also affects the location of a death. Pritchard and colleagues (1998) found that when the only alternative is home care, physicians recommend that families use a hospital for their terminally ill relative. J. Gallo, Baker, and Bradley (2001) also observed that the availability of health resources (such as hospice), type of illness, and demographic characteristics (such as gender, race, marital status, and residence in a higher income area) are predictive of at-home deaths. When hospice care is available, many older people take advantage of the resources and opportunities that it provides, and hospice patients are more likely than nonhospice patients to die at home (Connor, 1998; Last Acts, 2002). See chapter 16 for a more in-depth discussion of hospice care.

Social workers will be increasingly involved in providing end-of-life care in the future. Multidisciplinary teams that include well-trained social workers with cultural competence are needed to deliver quality care at the end of life. Social workers must know how to work with dying older people at various stages of the dying trajectory. Unfortunately, most social workers say that they feel ill prepared to provide end-of-life care and want their coursework to pay more attention to death, dying, and bereavement (Christ and Sormanti, 1999).

Social workers will continue to redefine and establish their roles in end-of-life care as they work more with older people with terminal illness. Some social workers will focus on the personal level and offer counseling to dying people and their families. Others will work in the community to improve end-of-life care services. The best end-of-life care is holistic and incorporates a biopsychosocial cultural perspective on multiple levels. All social workers must challenge medical policies that discriminate against patients because of their age, gender, or socioeconomic status.

CASE 11.1

Mr. Appleby is a seventy-five-year-old African American who was diagnosed with lung cancer five years ago. Mr. Appleby's wife cares for him; he has become increasingly weak from chemotherapy treatments. He has been admitted to a local Veterans Affairs (VA) hospital several times for treatment of acute anemia, fluid buildup, and breathing problems. His physician has asked Mr. Appleby's social worker to evaluate him for hospice care.

The social worker uses the ABCDEF practice guide to holistically and comprehensively assess Mr. Appleby. He has become increasingly lethargic and moderately depressed as his cancer has spread. Mr. Appleby's support systems are strong and include members of his church, who regularly bring food and other supplies to assist the family.

The social worker evaluates Mr. Appleby's pain, which is considered a fifth vital sign by the U.S. Department of Veterans Affairs, by asking him to rate the severity of his pain on a scale, with zero representing no pain and 10 indicating severe pain. This initial screening concerns the social worker because Mr. Appleby reports that his pain is at a level of 4. She promptly schedules an appointment for him with his primary care physician and the hospital's hospice coordinator.

The social worker discusses hospice with the Applebys, although they are reluctant to accept it. They are pleased with the support that they have been receiving from their church, the community, and family members. After extensive discussion the social worker respects the Applebys' refusal of hospice services and arranges home health care services. In addition, because Mr. Appleby is eligible for VA services, the social worker locates a VA nurse who can make home visits. The social worker also conducts an in-depth and systematic assessment of Mr. Appleby's pain by examining its severity, location, quality, duration, cause, and course and whether it is acute or chronic, functional or pathological. The nurse and social worker use the OPQRST approach (onset, palliating and provoking factors, quality, radiation, severity, and temporal factors) (Twycross, 1999) to guide their initial assessment. The assessment includes such questions as when did your pain begin? Did it continue for several days or did it end within a few hours? They evaluate palliating factors by asking Mr. Appleby what alleviates his pain. And they explore provoking factors by asking him what exacerbates his pain. To evaluate the quality of his pain they ask him for descriptions, for example, "What, exactly, is your pain like?" To determine whether his pain radiates, they ask whether it spreads anywhere. They evaluate the severity of his pain by asking him to use a scale from zero to 10 (or faces with smiles and grimaces to represent pain) to rate it. They also ask him, "How much does the pain affect your life?" "Is this degree of pain tolerable or acceptable to you?" Finally, they assess the temporal factors by asking him, "When did your pain begin?" "When does it come or when is it most severe?" "Is it there all the time or does it come and go?" "Is it worse at any particular time of the day or night?" The social worker's assessment of Mr. Appleby's pain is facilitated by the relationship that they had established during the previous year.

The social worker works closely with the VA nurse and primary care physician to arrange adequate palliative care for Mr. Appleby. They follow the World Health Organization's three-step analgesic ladder to administer pain treatment (World Health Organization, 1990). In addition, they tell Mrs. Appleby that she may administer the medication around the clock instead of as needed to prevent "breakthrough pain."

Most important, the social worker talks extensively with the family about various pain management options and addresses the Applebys' concerns about addiction. The social worker also takes into account Mr. Appleby's psychological, social, and spiritual needs when devising the treatment plan.

The social worker actively listens to the Applebys' different concerns about pain management. Mr. Appleby believes in God and an afterlife, and he and his family value the love, care, and warmth that church members provide. The social worker concludes that Mr. Appleby's greatest needs at this time revolve around his physical care and pain management. Except for his mild depression, for which the physician prescribes antidepressants, Mr. Appleby and his family are coping well with his condition. Their strong social supports and religious involvement offer Mr. Appleby meaning and hope that he will not die alone. Although the Appleby family declines hospice care, Mrs. Appleby, their children, and church members believe that they can provide appropriate care for Mr. Appleby. The social worker feels that she can work successfully with the family and health care team to ensure that Mr. Appleby receives adequate pain treatment.

In this situation the social worker arranged proper care for Mr. Appleby by assessing his pain and arranging and coordinating services for him. Mr. Appleby's suffering would have worsened had the social worker failed to intervene. This example shows how social workers can actively improve end-of-life care for patients and advocate for their needs.

Discussion Questions

1. What roles can gerontological social workers play when helping clients cope with death and dying?
2. What are some cultural differences in how people conceptualize death, and how can social work implement culturally competent practice when counseling dying people?
3. How can hospitals improve care for dying people?
4. How can society enhance the quality of life for dying people and increase the number of people who experience a "good death"?

CHAPTER 12

Bereavement in Later Life

ALL MARRIED PEOPLE WILL EXPERIENCE WIDOWHOOD unless they divorce, separate, or die before their spouse. Loss of a spouse or partner is one of the most stressful experiences that anyone can undergo (Holmes and Rahe, 1967). Almost 7% of the population is widowed. Although the rise in divorce rates has resulted in fewer widowed people, 11.2 million widows and 2.7 million widowers were living in the United States in 2003. Among those older than sixty-five in 2003, 14% of the men were widowed, as were 44% of the women (U.S. Census Bureau, 2004b). Sixty percent of women older than seventy-five are widowed, as are 21% of men in this age group. Widowhood continues to be primarily a women's issue, although this is changing; as men live longer and marry women closer to them in age, the ratio of widows to widowers will decrease in this century.

Social workers encounter bereaved people in many settings, including hospitals, hospices, nursing homes, retirement communities, senior citizen centers, and adult day centers. Social workers must be prepared to assess loss, differentiate complicated from uncomplicated grief, and tailor counseling to the specific needs of the bereaved client. Social workers must also know the various components of grief and understand the ways that personal, social, and cultural factors influence how people respond to loss.

The primary intent of this chapter is to highlight the complicated nature of bereavement. We draw heavily from literature on older widows and widowers, which contains most of the existing empirical work on grieving. Although we discuss bereavement within the context of widowhood, the issues apply to any lifelong relationship or partnership. We consider many influences on bereavement, such as gender and ethnic differences, coping strategies, and circumstances of death. In the first section we discuss the ways that bereavement in late life differs from the losses that young people experience, define bereavement and grief, and discuss myths about bereavement. In the second section we review contemporary theories of bereavement, specifically, the stress paradigm, attachment theory, the dual process model of bereavement, and meaning-making models, and we show how they build on each other. In the third section, which is devoted to assessment, we identify factors that influence recovery. Later in the chapter we discuss interventions for uncomplicated and complicated grief, respectively. In the final section we apply concepts and techniques to a case example.

LATE LIFE BEREAVEMENT

On one hand, bereavement later in life is easier than when it occurs during young adulthood or middle age (Moss, Moss, and Hansson, 2001). Older adults cope better with death than younger people, presumably because older people have had more experience with loss. Older people also are better at regulating their emotions and generally evidence less affect intensity than younger adults (Lawton, Kleban, Rajagopal, and Dean, 1992). In addition, as people age they usually use more effective coping skills and have more warning before their spouse dies.

At the same time the loss of a spouse after many years of marriage affects many areas of the survivor's life, which places older people at risk for bereavement overload. Bereavement creates major changes in people's roles, identities, social supports, finances, and living facilities, and when health or financial stressors arise, bereavement becomes a chronic rather than an acute stressor (Sanders, 1980–81; O'Bryant and Hansson, 1995). Older bereaved people are especially vulnerable to depression and mortality, specifically, from cardiovascular disease (see Williams, 2002). Older bereaved men are twice as likely to die than are married men (C. Schaefer, Quesenberry, and Wi, 1995; R. Schulz and Beach, 1999). The ripple effects from the death of their spouse complicate bereavement for many elderly people.

DEFINING GRIEF AND BEREAVEMENT

Bereavement is an event that refers to the actual loss. It is typically followed by grief reactions, such as intense pining, yearning, and anger or protest reactions. Mourning represents the cultural manifestations of grieving. This is influenced by ethnic, religious, and class background. Rando (1993) defines *mourning* as a process that occurs when bereaved people reorient their relationship to the deceased, their own sense of self, and their external world. Grieving is what people do in response to bereavement. It is a bereaved person's reaction to the death of a loved one and typically occurs on multiple levels, physically, affectively, cognitively, and spiritually. Martin and Doka (2000) define *grief* as the psychic energy that results from the tension created by an individual's strong desire to (1) maintain her assumptive world as it was before the loss; (2) accommodate herself to the newly emerging reality resulting from her loss; and (3) incorporate this new reality in an emerging assumptive world (p. 14).

Grieving takes place on concrete and abstract levels. On a concrete level bereaved people reconstruct their routine, their social circle, and their physical environment. On an abstract level grieving individuals contemplate the uncertainties, imperfections, and mysteries of life. They struggle to make sense of life's mysteries after a loved one dies.

Components of Grief

Grief is a complex emotion that includes behavioral, cognitive, physiological, and emotional elements. Behavioral responses include crying, restlessness, and social withdrawal. Cognitive reactions are typically manifested in disbelief, preoccupation with the deceased, and problems with concentration. Physiological reactions are characterized by fatigue, loss of appetite, sleep disturbances, somatic disorders, and decreased immunity to diseases. The emotions that people feel are most often shock, anxiety, yearning, despair, depression, guilt, anger, and loneliness (Vinokur, 2002).

Grief differs from yearning, although it is a core ingredient of grief (Vinokur, 2002). Yearning is an obtrusive wish or need to recover the lost person. It is a preoccupation with the lost person and is accompanied by intense sadness upon the realization that the deceased is unattainable. The grieving person has a strong wish to reunite with the lost person, and crying, sadness, and intense pining ensue. Yearning is also characterized by searching behavior, which is often manifested in restlessness and aimless wandering. People become intensely vigilant. They remain alert for the return of the lost person and oscillate between hoping to reunite with the lost person and the realization that the deceased will never return. A deceased spouse's clothes or chair can be an intensely painful reminder, but bereaved people go back and forth, from deliberately looking at reminders to avoiding events or occasions that are too painful. Over time the pining, searching, intense pain, and sadness lessen. These reactions recur but are intermittent (Bowlby, 1980; Parkes, 1996). Despite cultural differences in emotional expressions of grief, most people cry in response to bereavement (Rosenblatt, 2001; W. Stroebe and Stroebe, 1987).

Grief also differs from emotional turbulence, which includes shock, anxiety, and intrusive thoughts, although emotional turbulence is another important component of grief. Emotional turbulence is affected by the suddenness of the loss and the extent to which people prepare for their spouse's death. When deaths occur unexpectedly or a partner is unable to communicate with his spouse before death, the survivor has more intrusive thoughts about the death. Prolonged death, on the other hand, often creates anxiety (Carr, House, Wortman, Nesse, and Kessler, 2001). The least anxious widowed people are those whose spouse dies in a nursing home.

Depression is another commonly experienced aspect of grief. Most widowed people undergo a major depression six months after their spouse's death; it usually shifts to a depressed mood after eighteen months. Many widowed people are more depressed, sad, and lonely than married people even four years later (Sonnega, 2002). Although grief and depression share many common attributes, they also differ in several important ways. Depressed people typically have lower self-esteem and feel more guilt than people who are bereaved but not depressed. Whereas many depressed people feel suicidal, worthless, and struggle with their functional capacities, people who are grieving maintain their self-worth and positive outlook. When bereaved people hold negative evaluations of themselves, others, the world, and the future and feel helpless and hopeless about everything, they are exhibiting more depression than grief.

Grief Stages

Most models of grief include three phases: an initial period of shock, disbelief, and denial that may last for weeks; an acceptance of the reality of the loss, which is an acute phase of mourning that may last for months and is characterized by intense feelings of sadness, despair, anxiety, loneliness, and anger; and a restitution, or acceptance, phase, when the intense feelings of grief subside, feelings stabilize, and bereaved people reinvest in new relationships and activities (Nolen-Hoeksema and Larson, 1999).

Experts have become increasingly skeptical about models of grief that refer to stages, for example, Simos (1979) and Parkes (1997). People's grief reactions vary according to the circumstances of the death, the cultural context, the survivor's attachment style, and the quality of the relationship with the decedent. People can experience different phases simultaneously or at different times or even take respites from intense grieving by visiting with friends, neighbors, and family members. People also differ in the intensity with which they grieve, and certain feelings are more intense than others at different times. While some bereaved individuals feel extreme panic or anger, others focus more on positive experiences that they had with the deceased; still others may feel relief after a spouse dies, especially if they have been engaged in extensive caregiving.

THE MYTHS OF BEREAVEMENT

Researchers studying bereavement continue to improve their research designs. They have diversified their samples, included more controls for potentially confounding variables, and added baseline measures and control groups, such as married people, for comparisons with bereaved respondents. As a result of these improved studies experts believe that many previous assumptions about bereavement are unsubstantiated. Wortman and Silver (1989) challenged many previous assumptions about grieving in a controversial publication that provoked a flurry of responses. They identified five myths about coping with loss.

The Myth of Intense Distress

The first myth is the expectation of intense distress following a major loss. Although most bereaved people suffer enormously following the death of a loved one, some individuals are only mildly distressed. In their review of the literature Wortman and Silver (2001) found that 30% to 40% of bereaved people reported symptoms of depression, more than half demonstrated more moderate depression, and a substantial minority displayed minimal distress. Some bereaved people even demonstrated positive emotions without later developing complicated grief reactions. Wortman and Silver (2001) concluded that grief reactions vary depending upon personality and the circumstances of the loss.

The Myth of Delayed Grief

The second myth is that failure to experience distress is pathological. Many experts (e.g., Worden, 2002; Simos, 1979) have cautioned that bereaved people who fail to experience grief following the loss of a spouse will inevitably undergo delayed grief reactions. Wortman and Silver (2001) found few studies that support this view. Instead, they observed that some bereaved people experience relief after loved ones die, most often in cases where the deaths were prolonged or extensive medical care was needed.

The Myth of Working Through Grief

The importance of working through the loss is the third myth that Wortman and Silver (1989, 2001) identified. Many experts argue that bereaved people must confront their feelings of loss or they will adjust poorly to their loss and encounter psychological problems later. Experts, such as Bowlby (1980), Lopata

(1975), and Parkes and Weiss (1983), have argued that bereaved people must "work through" their feelings and directly confront their despair and sadness by expressing their responses and reflecting on them. Simos states, "Each phase [of grieving] must be experienced to a peak of intensity before it can be resolved" (1979, p. 34), Similarly, Worden (2002, p. 30) explains, "It is necessary to acknowledge and work through this pain or it can manifest itself through physical symptoms or some form of aberrant behavior." Sanders (1999, p. 86) states: "Obsessive ruminations are a necessary part of working through the grief. There seems to be no shortcut."

M. Stroebe (1992–93) and M. Stroebe and W. Stroebe (1991) and others, for example, Bonanno and Kaltman (1999), conclude that grief work and preoccupation with negative emotions during the initial stages of bereavement are unnecessary for a positive bereavement outcome. Several studies (Bonanno and Keltner, 1997; Bonanno, 1999) have found that for some people, detachment from grief and feelings of distress after bereavement lead to a more positive recovery than a focus upon their feelings of loss. Based on evidence from cross-cultural studies, Stroebe observes that grieving is inappropriate in some settings (see M. Stroebe, 1992–93 for a more in-depth discussion of these cultural differences). She also criticized previous researchers for failing to differentiate grief work from rumination, which includes more obsessional and negative elements.

Fraley and Shaver (1999) claim that the critical issue is whether the absence of grief results from unresolved feelings of loss, specifically, whether the attachment that bereaved individuals had with a spouse was secure or insecure. Fraley and Shaver also explain that while suppression works for some people, it backfires when people's defenses are fragile or disorganized.

The Myth of the Necessity of Breaking Down Attachments

The fourth myth about bereavement involves the necessity of breaking down attachments, a perspective that started with Freud (1917/1957) and other psychoanalytic authors. These writers emphasized decathexis and the need for bereaved people to withdraw their psychic energy from the deceased and redirect it to new relationships.

Several studies show that many bereaved people *maintain* their attachments to their deceased loved one. Zisook and Shuchter (1993) found that more than half of bereaved spouses felt that their deceased partner was still with them thirteen months after death. Klass, Silverman, and Nickman (1996) revised their initial hypotheses after they found that many bereaved individuals derive comfort and solace from maintaining their connection to a lost loved one. Wortman and Silver (2001) caution, however, that continued attachment can create problems for survivors in some instances, particularly when the attachment is manifested in holding on to the deceased's belongings.

The Myth of Recovery

The final myth is the expectation of recovery, that bereaved people will inevitably return to their previous levels of functioning. Many bereaved people continue to experience psychological pain and grieve for many years after the loss of a loved one (see review in Wortman and Silver, 2001). Some bereaved people mourn as long as fifteen years after the loss and never return to their previous levels of functioning (Bonanno et al., 2002).

CONTEMPORARY MODELS OF BEREAVEMENT

Although experts are developing many new models of bereavement as new findings emerge, the stress paradigm, attachment model, dual process model of bereavement, and meaning-making models are the most widely accepted. Each model focuses on a different aspect of bereavement. Next we highlight their salient principles, but we encourage social workers to explore each model in greater depth.

The Stress Paradigm

People experience stress when the demands of a situation exceed their resources. Events and situations that give people time to prepare, identify, and organize their resources are usually less stressful than unexpected events (Pearlin, 1982; George, 1993; Thoits, 1983). Uncontrollable situations are especially stressful because people feel more helpless and hopeless when they are unable to change adverse circumstances. Chronic stressors, such as caring for an ill spouse over a long period of time, often cause depression and ill health and increase the likelihood of additional or multiple stressors.

People react differently to the loss of a spouse, depending on the circumstances of the death, including their degree of preparation, the presence of chronic stressors such as caregiving, and whether the loss led to new stressors. For example, widows who must learn how to manage household expenses for the first time have more problems adapting to their new lifestyle than women who always paid the bills and kept track of family finances. Similarly, widowers whose wives made all their social arrangements risk social isolation and loneliness after their spouse dies.

Folkman (2001) offers a revised model of coping that is applicable to bereavement. The model focuses on the adaptive tasks of coping that bereaved people must address. These include managing and accepting feelings of loss; reorganizing their identity, social relationships, and daily routines; discovering meaning in their loss and emotional pain; and reinvesting in new commitments and activities. Folkman argues that bereavement and coping generally include challenges and demands that affect negative *and* positive feelings. In her study of bereaved partners who cared for loved ones with AIDS, Folkman (2001) learned that positive emotions are just as important to survivors as negative emotions. For example, positive reappraisal, that is, reframing a situation to see it in a positive light, helps bereaved individuals adapt to difficult experiences because they focus more on the meaning of events. These individuals develop a greater acceptance of death, enhanced strength and self-worth, and more compassion for others. In a study comparing the importance of personality influences (extroversion and neuroticism) with coping styles (emotion focused and problem focused) and avoidant coping, Meuser and Marwit (1999–2000) found that long-standing personality indicators have less influence on bereavement outcome than how bereaved people cope. These findings underscore the value of taking into account the bereaved person's coping strategies, especially reappraisal, reframing, and finding meaning.

Folkman (2001) found that positive feelings emerge during active problem-solving coping, when caretakers engage in specific tasks such as managing pain medications, transporting someone to the doctor, or arranging the memorial. Active problem solving and positive reappraisal increase bereaved people's feelings of control and mastery, which in turn counteract their feelings of helplessness and despair. This lessens the negative affect and increases positive feelings during stressful times. Bonanno (2001) also found that positive emotions improve the bereavement outcome.

Attachment Theory

Bowlby (1980) studied the dynamics and processes involved in bonding, forming attachments, and separating; he found that people's responses to loss grow out of their earlier attachments with parental figures. Bowlby and others, for example, Parkes and Weiss (1983), observe that the responses of many adults who lose a romantic attachment resemble the reactions of infants who are separated from a significant caretaker. Bowlby describes an early "protest phase" of separation, characterized by anxiety, anger, and denial, after an initial numbing reaction or disbelief. If the separation continues, the person enters a phase of despair, marked by preoccupation with the lost person and feelings of intense yearning, a core reaction to loss and separation from a loved one. During the despair phase people are vigilant for the return of the lost person, and they despair when this does not occur. Over time, when the lost people are never recovered, bereaved people enter the phase of detachment (later called reorganization), in which the survivor reinvests in new activities and relationships (Bowlby, 1980; Fraley and Shaver, 1999). Parkes (2002) tried to investigate attachment style and bereavement outcomes empirically. In a preliminary study using a retrospective questionnaire, he found that people who report having secure attachments to their parents during childhood evidence less grief and distress than those who tended to cling and demonstrate separation distress with parental figures during childhood. Those who had learned to avoid attachments had difficulty expressing their feelings during bereavement. Finally, those who were rejected and depressed in childhood evidenced more disorganized/disoriented patterns of attachment, became depressed during bereavement, and were more inclined to use alcohol to escape their painful feelings. Further research is needed to better understand how attachment styles affect bereavement patterns.

The Dual Process Model of Coping with Bereavement

In an attempt to integrate traditional models with recent research, M. Stroebe and Schut (1995, 1999) and M. Stroebe, Schut, and Stroebe (1998) proposed the dual process model of coping with bereavement. This model is organized around three concepts: loss-oriented coping, restoration-oriented coping, and oscillation (see figure 12.1).

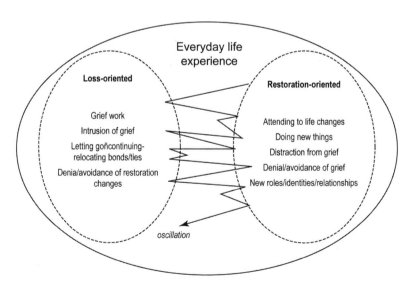

FIGURE 12.1 The Dual Process of Coping with Bereavement
Source: Stroebe and Schut. (1999). The Dual Process Model of Coping with Bereavement. *Death Studies,* vol. 23, pp. 197–224, Used by permission.

Loss-oriented coping occurs most often during the early stages of bereavement when people concentrate on, deal with, and process some aspect of the loss experience itself (M. Stroebe and Schut, 1999, p. 212). Loss-oriented coping resembles "grief work" and involves focusing on the deceased person, the circumstances of the loss, and negative feelings, such as yearning, despair, and painful longing. Restoration-oriented coping, on the other hand, comprises what the survivor needs to deal with (e.g., social loneliness) and how to deal with it (e.g., by avoiding solitariness) and not with the result of this process (e.g., restored well-being and social reintegration) (p. 214). Restoration-oriented coping includes attending to life changes, doing new things, distracting oneself from grief, and establishing new roles, identities, and relationships. Oscillation refers to the "alternation between loss- and restoration-oriented coping, the process of juxtaposition of confrontation and avoidance of different stressors associated with bereavement" (M. Stroebe and Schut, 1999, p. 215). This back-and-forth process between loss-oriented and restoration-oriented coping helps people adjust to their loss without grieving continually. According to M. Stroebe and Schut (1999), people preserve their physical and mental health by periodically taking time off from grieving to participate in activities, such as socializing with friends and family or taking part in church or community events. Loss-oriented and restoration-oriented coping coexist and are expressed intermittently, but people engage in more loss-oriented actions during the early stages of bereavement and more restoration-oriented activities later. In addition, people usually experience more negative affect in the beginning, but they eventually feel better when they socialize more and meet new people.

Richardson and Balaswamy (2001) tested the dual process model in an analysis of two hundred older widowers in their second year of bereavement. Richardson and Balaswamy compared elderly men who were widowed less than five hundred days with those who were widowed for more than five hundred days in order to examine the effect of loss and restoration factors at earlier and later stages of bereavement. Richardson and Balaswamy found that the early bereaved expressed more negative affect and less positive affect than the later widowers. In addition, both loss-oriented and restoration-oriented activities were important early *and* later in bereavement. Although the circumstances surrounding the loss (e.g., whether husbands had provided medical care to wives, and whether their wives died at home or in a hospital setting) influenced the men's negative feelings, restoration-oriented interactions (e.g., involvement with neighbors) also affected a widower's well-being during early stages of bereavement. Widowers who dated experienced higher levels of positive affect than those who were not dating. Both loss-oriented and restoration-oriented variables were important influences on well-being during the later stage of bereavement as well.

Some circumstances surrounding the loss will linger and affect well-being later. For example, if a spouse suffered while dying, the bereaved person recovers more slowly. A wife's suffering apparently has long-term effects that are unlike those of other loss variables, such as extent of medical care provided or location of death, which appear to resolve more quickly. Turvey and colleagues (1999) and Carr (2003) have also found more depression among bereaved people whose spouses experienced pain at the time of death. Many of these bereaved people also had more anxiety, yearning, and intrusive thoughts. When a loved one suffers, family members often feel guilty, distressed, and helpless (Doka, 1997).

Meaning Construction and Loss

Neimeyer (2001a) argues that a "new wave" of grief theory is emerging that recognizes the complexity and cultural diversity involved in bereavement and the varied patterns of grieving that individuals demonstrate. In addition, the new wave includes skepticism about the universality of phase or stage models and about a predictable emotional path leading to readjustment and separation from the deceased. These new conceptualizations of loss also acknowledge that successful grieving often involves continued symbolic bonds with deceased people instead of a complete emotional withdrawal.

According to Neimeyer (2001a, p. 4), "Viewed in its broadest terms, this suggests the gradual emergence of a new paradigm for grief theory, research, and practice, one founded on the postulate that *meaning reconstruction in response to a loss is the central process in grieving*." Similarly, Attig (2001) explains that when a spouse dies, the survivor must relearn her world on many levels, including emotionally, behaviorally, physically, and biologically, as well as socially, intellectually, and spiritually. The survivor accomplishes this by moving in two directions at once. On one hand, the bereaved person returns to a familiar world and tries to find that which can sustain her through bereavement; on the other hand, the survivor must establish new daily routines, new connections, new identities, and new meaning.

Calhoun and Tedeschi (2001) believe that clinicians can help bereaved people find meaning. By exploring clients' reflections and questions since the loss, social workers can help bereaved clients reconstruct their life and struggle to make sense of their world without their deceased loved one. Spiritual and religious issues are especially useful in this process. At the same time Calhoun and Tedeschi caution that bereaved people do not search for meaning until they are ready and motivated to explore these issues. Calhoun and Tedeschi underscore the importance of timing and allowing clients to introduce the search for meaning. If the social worker introduces it prematurely, the client will resist.

ASSESSING BEREAVED PEOPLE

The new wave of grief counseling also considers the diverse grief reactions that people experience when they lose a spouse. This approach suggests that social workers should avoid stereotyping bereaved people's reactions and should encourage clients to express their thoughts and feelings regardless of what "phase" they are in. This includes understanding that some people engage in grief work, but others "keep busy" without necessarily developing delayed grief responses.

The circumstances of a death are one of the most important areas that social workers must initially explore with the bereaved individual. By encouraging the client to talk about the circumstances of death, the social worker demonstrates that he can tolerate the client's emotional distress. Social workers also help bereaved people tell their story in their own words and from their own point of view. This establishes rapport without inadvertently imposing any preconceived notions about bereavement. Substantively, researchers have successfully identified several circumstances that affect grieving. As we discuss later, these circumstances include whether the death was unexpected and the extent of forewarning, whether medical care was necessary and, if so, for how long, whether the spouse suffered, the location of the spouse's death, and whether the surviving spouse was present at the moment of death.

Unexpected or Anticipated Death

Most experts have assumed that unexpected deaths result in more difficult bereavements than deaths that permit the survivor to anticipate grief (O'Bryant, 1990–91). Others, for example, Sanders (1982–83) and Richardson and Balaswamy (2001), have found that anticipated deaths, specifically, deaths that require extensive medical care, are more difficult for survivors. Carr, House, Wortman, and colleagues (2001) observe that the effects of bereavement vary according to the specific grief reaction, for example, intrusive thoughts, yearning, or depression, that they measured. In a longitudinal study of older widows and widowers, Carr and colleagues found that unexpected death increases the intensity of bereaved people's intrusive thoughts (unwelcome memories of the deceased or of events surrounding the death that affect sleeping and concentration) but have minimal affect on postloss feelings of shock, anger, depression, or overall grief. By eighteen months after the loss, most intrusive thoughts have faded. Traumatic reactions occur most often when the spouse dies a violent death, such as from an accident, suicide, or homicide (Zisook, Chentsova-Dutton, and Shuchter, 1998). L. C. Barry,

Kasl, and Prigerson (2002) report that bereaved people's *perceptions* of their preparedness for a death are most significant. Complicated grief reactions arise more often among those who feel unprepared for a loved one's death.

Provision of Care

Carr and colleagues (2001) found higher levels of anxiety among bereaved individuals when their spouses died after a prolonged illness. Sanders (1982–83) found that survivors of people who die after suffering long-term chronic illnesses show greater feelings of isolation and alienation than survivors whose spouses died after a short-term chronic illness. Richardson and Balaswamy (2001) similarly found that widowers who provided extensive medical care exhibit more negative affect during bereavement than widowers who were uninvolved in caretaking. These findings suggest that chronic stressors, which typically accompany protracted illnesses, negatively affect postbereavement outcome. Contrary to previous assumptions, older people, at least, may find adjustment to the loss of a spouse whose death was protracted to be more difficult in some ways than the adjustment to an unexpected death. This is especially true for those whose dying spouse required extensive care.

Pain and Suffering

Bereavement is more difficult when loved ones suffer before they die. Several studies, for example, Richardson and Balaswamy (2001), Turvey and colleagues (1999), and Carr (2003), have found that, in contrast to nonpainful deaths, deaths in which the deceased was in pain led to more negative grief reactions among survivors. These reactions also lingered during later stages of bereavement after other factors, such as the manner of death or whether the bereaved had provided medical care, were resolved.

Location of Death

The location of death, specifically, whether a spouse dies at home or in a nursing home, also affects bereavement. Richardson and Balaswamy (2001) and Pritchard and colleagues (1998), observed that when a spouse dies at home, the survivor feels less distress. At the same time, contrary to what one might expect, Carr and colleagues (2001) report that bereaved people adjust more quickly when their spouse died in a nursing home. Presumably, these bereaved people confronted multiple losses during their spouse's illness and experienced major changes when they placed their spouse in the nursing home.

Communication About Death

One reason that survivors often adjust better when their spouse dies at home is that a familiar and comfortable setting often promotes better communication between spouses. When dying people and their spouses talk about death and the dying process, survivors feel more in control of their bereavement and demonstrate a stronger sense of mastery (Carr et al., 2001).

Presence at Death

Bereaved people who are with their spouse at the moment of death experience less psychological distress than those who are not present when their spouse dies (see Bennett and Vidal-Hall, 2000). Carr (2003) found that bereaved people who were with their spouse at the moment of death experience fewer intrusive thoughts during the first six months of bereavement and less anger than those who were not present when their spouse died.

Relationship Before Death

Many researchers once assumed that conflictual or ambivalent marriages result in more complicated bereavement, but recent studies demonstrate that a stronger bond and more intense attachments between spouses lead to greater distress during bereavement. Carr and colleagues (2000) used a longitudinal analysis to examine how the quality of older people's marriages influence their psychological adjustment during bereavement. Carr's team found that close marriages result in greater psychological distress, and conflictual marriages result in lower levels of grief, especially yearning. The most critical predictor of bereavement distress is the extent to which the spouse felt dependent on his loved one. Wives who were highly dependent on their husbands for instrumental support, such as for home maintenance, financial management, meal preparation, and housework, were especially anxious during bereavement.

ABCDEF Assessment

The ABCDEF assessment framework helps social workers contextualize the bereaved person's situation by taking into account his (A) actions and behaviors; (B) biological state or health; (C) cognitive style, specifically, coping strategies and meaning-making attempts; (D) demographic or background characteristics; (E) environmental resources; and (F) feelings.

Actions and Behaviors (A)

Bereaved people engage in a wide variety of behaviors and must attend to many activities. Funerals, memorial services, and other death rituals must be arranged during the very early stages of bereavement. Social interactions with friends, co-workers, family members, and others who knew the deceased are also common at this time. Visiting the cemetery, managing budgetary and other financial matters, and organizing the personal belongings of the deceased occupy a bereaved person's time later. Social workers must assess these bereavement-related behaviors as well as nonbereavement activities, including involvement in work, organizations, and other recreational activities. The social worker must examine the amount, duration, and intensity of a bereaved person's involvement in loss *and* restoration-oriented activities.

Biological Influences (B)

Bereaved people's health and functional skills substantially influence their capacity to reach out to others and engage in community activities. When bereaved people's health problems prevent them from driving, they can easily become isolated from others during a time when they most need support. Social workers must carefully assess how well bereaved people are taking care of themselves and identify those who are at risk for stress-related illnesses. Bereavement adversely affects people's immune systems, and bereaved people have higher morbidity and mortality rates even when age, education, and gender are taken into account (C. Schaefer et al., 1995). Neuroendocrine, immune, and sleep disruptions frequently occur during bereavement (Hall and Irwin, 2001).

Cognitive Understanding (C)

Social workers must also assess bereaved people's worldview, especially their spiritual and religious beliefs. A prospective study of middle-aged bereaved people found that those with strong spiritual beliefs resolve the death of a loved one more quickly than people without spiritual beliefs (Walsh, King, Jones, Tookman, and Blizard, 2002). Social workers also should examine two cognitive constructs—rumination and meaning making—that are important predictors of recovery during bereavement.

Bereaved people who ruminate are at greater risk for depression and chronic grieving. Nolen-Hoeksema (2001) defines *rumination* as "engaging in thoughts and behaviors that maintain one's focus on one's negative emotions and on the possible causes and consequences of those emotions" (p. 546). Ruminators go over and over negative events and feelings and focus on why they feel so negatively. Although these individuals often report that they are trying to understand their negative feelings or find meaning in them, they rarely acquire insight. Instead, rumination usually increases their distress, especially their depression, anxiety, and anger, because it focuses on negative thoughts and negative memories, which in turn exacerbate their negative mood (Nolen-Hoeksema, 2001). Rumination prevents people from actively solving their problems and searching for constructive solutions. It can also inhibit people from engaging in routine activities that could offer them more gratification and a better sense of control. In addition, because other people grow tired of individuals who go over and over the same problems or thoughts, ruminators often feel criticized and rejected by others.

Meaning making is another important cognition that social workers should assess. Janoff-Bulman (1992) and Janoff-Bulman and Berg (1998) explain that three basic assumptions are challenged after a loved one dies: that the world is a benevolent place; that the world is meaningful, that is, makes sense; and that the self is worthy. Severe traumas associated with a loss often interfere with a bereaved person's capacity to rebuild her assumptive world. Social workers must help those who are threatened cognitively by a loss to make sense of their experiences. According to Fleming and Robinson (2001, p. 655), the goal in these instances "is a rebuilding process by which the survivor once again perceives the world and self in positive terms, but, at the same time, incorporates the trauma-loss within the new assumptive world."

Neimeyer (1998) has shown that people who engage in a "rebuilding process" after a loss recover more easily than those who continue to feel shattered. Social workers must explore how a bereaved client makes sense of a death. This includes examining the types of coping strategies that people use, specifically, the extent to which they use positive reappraisal, positive event interpretation, and other constructive cognitive processes, all of which facilitate meaning making.

Demographic Indicators

Background information offers clues about how gender and cultural background inevitably affect bereavement. Several studies, for example, Schut, Stroebe, van den Bout, and de Keijser (1997) now conclude that widows and widowers cope differently with the loss of a spouse. For example, widowers generally experience higher rates of depression than widows (Richardson and Balaswamy, 2001), but widows who were highly dependent on their spouses for emotional support and instrumental assistance are at greater risk for prolonged or chronic grieving (Carr et al., 2000). Financial resources become especially important for widows, who often abruptly lose income after their spouse dies. Umberson, Wortman, and Kessler (1992) found that the primary factor related to widowhood and depression among women was financial strain, but among men it was household management. Because the predictors for recovery during bereavement differ for older men and women, social workers must carefully assess high-risk areas, such as dependence for women and social isolation for men.

Ethnic background is another important demographic variable that social workers should assess because, like individual differences, cultural differences affect how people grieve. According to Rosenblatt (2001), grieving varies enormously across cultures with respect to how a death is understood, the possibility for future reunion with the dead, the meaning of various emotions following the death, the things people say to themselves and others following a death, and beliefs about death. Grieving also differs across places, times, and groups in terms of how, when, or even whether grief reactions are expressed, how much bereaved people focus on the loss, and how much the death interferes with daily routines and social interactions.

In some subcultures the open expression of grief is inappropriate; for example, the Balinese rarely cry in bereavement (Rosenblatt, 2001). Cultural factors affect the manner in which bodies are prepared, the timing and nature of burial or cremation, the bereavement period, and the reactions of others. Muslims usually bury the body within twenty-four hours, and only certain individuals are allowed to touch the dead body; Muslims also disapprove of cremation. In contrast, many Hindus believe that cremation is the best way for the soul to carry on. They view death as the end of the body but not the soul (Kamel, Mouton, and McKee, 2002). Buddhists believe in cremating the body after it has been washed and dressed in new clothes. In Japan death rituals are rooted in Buddhism; a major part of Buddhist rituals involves preparing the dead for their new status with the "generalized dead" of the family, the community, and the nation while preparing the survivors for their new lives. The decedent is moving toward enlightenment, while the survivor continues their bond. Forty-nine days is usually the period during which these transitions occur (Klass, 2001).

Doka (2002) recommends that clinicians engage bereaved clients in a dialogue about their cultural practices and ask them about their ethnic traditions. At the same time Doka warns against overgeneralizing and stereotyping people based on their ethnic background because individual differences within cultures are so pervasive. According to the "Last Acts Statement on Diversity and End-of-Life Care" (2001), providers need to know how to attend to diverse cultural practices in a way that is meaningful, does not promote patient or family stereotyping, and helps the providers understand and cope with their own biases. This includes respecting patients' or families' desire (or reluctance) to share information openly; understanding the different ways that individuals express pain, suffering, and distress; and understanding the unique spiritual or religious meaning and attitudes that patients and families may attach to illness, medical treatment, and death.

Environmental Factors (E)

Living arrangements and social support systems influence recovery during bereavement. Numerous studies (e.g., Cleiren, 1993; Dimond, Lund, and Caserta,

1987) demonstrate the importance of social resources for well-being during widowhood. In fact, a high level of social support is one of the single most consistent predictors of a positive recovery during bereavement (Gass, 1987). Utz, Carr, Nesse, and Wortman (2002) found that while being widowed led to increases in social support, it resulted in a decrease in involvement with formal supports. Utz and colleagues found that most of the increase in social contact was the social support offered to bereaved people, not social support that they sought.

Gender differences in social support among bereaved people suggest that widowers may be especially at risk for social isolation following bereavement. In addition, the factors that predict social interaction among widowers differ from those that influence sociability among widows. Social support also buffers the adverse effects of loss among bereaved men but not among bereaved women (Umberson et al., 1992).

Feelings (F)

People's feelings provide a barometer of recovery. They reveal where clients are in the bereavement process, in what areas they need help, how they cope, and their style or pattern of grieving. For example, angry bereaved people may need help channeling their feelings into constructive actions that increase their sense of control and help them resolve their angry feelings. In these cases social workers must assess how a bereaved person's anger affects his support systems and to what extent the anger has alienated potential supports. Chronic grievers may need help with their cognitive constructions, specifically, with meaning making or alternatives to ruminating. A careful assessment of the types of feelings that a bereaved client is experiencing helps social workers identify the high-risk client and develop interventions that are tailored to the client's unique circumstances.

Disordered or Atypical Mourning

Although many clinicians have identified complicated grief reactions, recent scholars question the validity of these disorders and recommend continued research on the validity of the notion of disordered mourning (see M. Stroebe, van Son, et al., 2000). M. Stroebe, van Son, and colleagues (2000) identify several problems with current conceptualizations of complicated or pathological grief. The most significant problem lies in the inconsistency in labeling. While some investigators refer to complicated grief reactions, others call them disordered, pathological, or traumatic. These labels mean the same thing in some instances but refer to different syndromes in others. Another problem involves the lack of consensus about the conceptualization of and criteria for complicated grief. M. Stroebe, van Son, and colleagues (2000) caution experts against concluding that complicated mourning results from personality differences; many circumstances also contribute to complicated reactions. Finally, because few studies have systematically assessed the cultural and social contexts underlying disordered mourning, M. Stroebe, van Son, and colleagues (2000) argue that more work is needed to ferret out these important influences.

Although consensus panels (see, for example, Prigerson et al., 1999) have resolved some issues, more studies are needed to validate current conclusions. The literature most frequently addresses three types of disordered mourning or complicated grief reactions—chronic grief, traumatic grief, and delayed or inhibited grief—and we discuss those here. However, ongoing efforts to study complicated grief reactions will inevitably change current thinking about these issues, and social workers should remain abreast of these developments as they occur.

Chronic Mourning

Chronic mourning, which was first conceptualized by Bowlby (1980), is one of the most common types of disordered mourning. According to Fraley and Shaver (1999), chronic mourning is "characterized by protracted grief and prolonged difficulty in normal functioning" (p. 739). Individuals who suffer from chronic mourning are overly preoccupied with thoughts of their missing partner. Adults who maintain anxious, insecure connections in their relationships are more inclined to evidence extreme distress after a relationship ends. They may cry, cling, and yearn for the lost person's return for extended periods of time. Parkes (1996) claims that these people have "grief-prone personalities" (p. 140). They often had low self-esteem and score high on neuroticism indexes (Shaver and Brennan, 1992).

Bonanno and colleagues (2002) distinguish chronic grievers from the chronically depressed. Unlike those who are chronically depressed, chronic grievers rarely demonstrate any preloss depression. In her analysis of different styles of grieving, Bonanno's team (2002) found that chronic grievers are more likely to positively evaluate their spouse and their marriage. They were also highly dependent on their spouse for emotional support and tended to score low on sense of control. The chronically depressed had more negative evaluations of their marriage and had the poorest interpersonal skills, the lowest perceived coping efficacy, and the lowest scores of any group on extraversion, conscientiousness, agreeableness, openness, and emotional stability.

Traumatic Grief

Another type of disordered mourning, which resembles chronic mourning, is traumatic grief (sometimes referred to as complicated grief). People suffering from traumatic grief struggle with their daily routine. They frequently have low self-esteem and are so focused on a loss that they avoid others or ignore them when socializing for several months after the loss (Prigerson and Jacobs, 2001b). They may remain stunned or dazed and intermittently experience acute separation distress.

Traumatic grief is comprised of two clusters of basic symptoms: separation distress and traumatic distress (Prigerson and Jacobs, 2001b). Separation distress is at the core of this disorder and is characterized by an intrusive, distressing preoccupation with the deceased person that includes yearning, longing, or searching. These bereaved people are hypervigilant to cues in the environment that remind them of the deceased, and their distress can continue for years or even for decades. The precipitating factor is a supportive, close, and security-involved relationship to the deceased that has a symbiotic quality to it. These individuals were highly dependent on the deceased for self-esteem, support, and social interaction, and few maintained interests or resources outside this relationship. The source of the distress is the absence of the lost person and the wish to be reunited with the deceased, not a specific horrific experience with the deceased. Because the distress is intense, these bereaved people are at high risk for suicide.

M. Stroebe, Schut, Stroebe, and colleagues (2002) conceptualized the attachment style of those diagnosed with traumatic grief as "insecure-fearful." The death leaves them so traumatized that they are unable to think or talk coherently. They experience abrupt, maladaptive oscillations between loss and restoration-oriented actions. Thoughts about the deceased spouse intrude and interfere with their concentration, leaving these bereaved people feeling out of control.

The second cluster of core symptoms underlying traumatic grief is traumatic distress that is specific to bereavement. These symptoms are manifested in avoiding reminders of the deceased; feeling purposelessness and futility about the future; a sense of numbness or detachment resulting from the loss; feeling shocked, stunned, or dazed by the loss; having difficulty acknowledging the death; feeling that life is empty and unfulfilling without the deceased; having a fragmented sense of trust, security, and control; and experiencing anger at the death (Prigerson and Jacobs, 2001b). Another symptom, which Prigerson and Jacobs added in a subsequent journal article (2001a), is a feeling that a part of oneself has died.

Prigerson and Jacobs (2001b) developed two assessment tools for traumatic grief. The first is called the Traumatic Grief Evaluation of Response to Loss, which is available from Prigerson and Jacobs, and the second is the Inventory of Traumatic Grief, or the Inventory of Complicated Grief—Revised (see Prigerson and Jacobs, 2001b).

Delayed or Inhibited Grief

Delayed grief refers to a situation in which normal grief reactions are demonstrated after an extensive delay. Worden (2002) suggests that delayed grief results from inadequate mourning at the time of the original loss; grieving is carried forward and expressed in a seemingly exaggerated way with a subsequent loss. A later loss, ostensibly less significant than the original one, triggers such a strong grief response that the bereaved person often recognizes her exaggerated reactions. Stigmatized deaths, such as suicides, sometimes cause bereaved people to unintentionally delay grieving. Delayed grieving also sometimes occurs, for example, when a bereaved person consciously suppresses his feelings for the sake of others or when he has other responsibilities to meet. Multiple losses that result in bereavement overload can also contribute to delayed grief reactions.

Few investigators have substantiated the existence of delayed grief. If it exists, very few people manifest this type of reaction. Using a longitudinal design of older people, Bonanno and colleagues (2002) observed that although about 23% of bereaved people evidence chronic grief or chronic depression, only 4% of respondents exhibited delayed grief, that is, their grief reactions were initially inhibited or minimal and later appeared (Bonanno et al., 2002). Most investigators, for example, Bonanno and Field (2001), Zisook and Shuchter (1986), and Bonanno (2001), have found even lower percentages of people who delay grieving.

Counseling Uncomplicated Grief

Grief counseling works best for those who seek help, who are in high distress, and, most important, who are at risk for complicated grief (Schut, Stroebe, van den Bout, and Terheggen, 2001). Counseling is largely ineffective with people who grieve normally or when it is provided as a result of outreach efforts. Grief counseling can have adverse effects if it is used preventatively with people who have not asked for help. When grief counseling is offered too hastily, before bereaved people's natural support systems have responded, friends and family members sometimes withdraw their support, especially if they sense that a bereaved person has alternatives (Schut et al., 2001).

Clients vary in what they find useful during counseling. Some clients simply appreciate knowing that help is available, whether they use it or not. Others are glad to learn that their feelings are normal and that the acute pain of grief will eventually subside. One widow might learn how to manage her bills, while another gains new interpersonal skills or coping strategies. Some bereaved people benefit from self-help groups; others need individual counseling.

The conclusions from reviews of the efficacy of bereavement counseling underscore the significance of assessment. By comprehensively evaluating a bereaved client's context, circumstances, and personality, social workers can more effectively individualize grief counseling. The tremendous variability in the types of grief that people experience requires an integrated, holistic approach to counseling.

Models of grief counseling are developing rapidly, although few have been validated empirically. Worden (2002) offers a brief but potentially useful model to facilitate uncomplicated grief that focuses on the tasks of mourning. This approach provides bereaved people with information about normal grief processes; offers and maximizes their social support; normalizes and validates people's feelings; and evaluates and teaches about coping. Rando (1993) has identified six functions, which she calls the "R processes," that resemble Worden's four tasks. In the next section we focus on selected contemporary models of bereavement, specifically, M. Stroebe and Schut's dual process model of bereavement (1999), as extended to counseling; and, finally, grief counseling from a meaning-making perspective. These should be used with caution until investigators evaluate their efficacy, especially with diverse populations. In the last section we apply these models to complicated grief reactions.

Stroebe and Schut's Dual Process Model

M. Stroebe and Schut (1999) incorporated principles from earlier grief models in the dual process model of bereavement: first, bereaved people must accept not only the reality of loss but also the reality of a changed world; second, they must experience the pain of grief *and* take time off from the pain of grief; third, they must adjust to life without the deceased *and* master the changed (subjective) environment; fourth, people must relocate the deceased emotionally, move on, *and* develop new roles, identities, and relationships (M. Stroebe, Schut, Stroebe, et al., 2002). M. Stroebe, Schut, Stroebe, and colleagues (2002) also recognize that a person's perceptions of a death and the loss, *along with* individual background variables, influence how that person will cope, such as whether she will use problem- or emotion-focused coping, during bereavement. See table 12.1 for a comparison of Stroebe's tasks with Bowlby's and Worden's.

Meaning-Making Approaches

Nadeau (2001) describes the use of a meaning-making perspective when counseling grieving families. She emphasizes listening to clients' stories because they illuminate the meanings that people attribute to their loss. In addition to finding meaning, many bereaved people grow and enhance their well-being, that is, they function better as a result of bereavement.

Davis (2001) concluded that two distinct processes comprise the meaning-making perspective. One process—finding meaning—involves making sense of the

TABLE 12.1 Comparison of Models

Phase Model (Bowlby, 1980)	Task Model (Worden, 1991)	Dual Process Model (M. Stroebe and Schut, 1999)
Shock	Accepts reality of loss	Accepts reality of loss and of changed world
Yearning/protest	Experiences pain of grief	Experiences pain of grief and takes time off from pain of grief
Despair	Adjusts to life without deceased	Adjusts to life without deceased and masters the changed (subjective) environment
Restitution	Relocates deceased emotionally and moves on	Relocates deceased emotionally, moves on, and develops new roles, identities, relationships

Source: Stroebe (2002). Used by permission.

loss and focuses on maintaining or rebuilding a threatened worldview. The other process—finding benefit—consists of maintaining or rebuilding a threatened sense of self. Finding benefit can be manifested in growth of character, change in life perspective, or strengthened relationships with others.

Finding Meaning

According to S. C. Thompson (1998), one strategy involves the client's changing his life schema (how he perceives and understands the world) or the cognitive representation (interpretation) of his life to coincide or be consistent with the loss. Bereaved people can reorder their priorities and change their goals to emphasize those that are more realistic or more easily achieved. People in mourning can also redirect their self-perceptions into more positive ones, such as perceiving themselves as resilient or as a survivor. Another approach involves reinterpreting an event or loss by using a positive focus or changing the perspective. Making social comparisons with others who are worse off is an effective strategy that helps bereaved people achieve perspective. Thompson (1998) recommends that clinicians help bereaved people reestablish more control in their life by helping them accept some outcomes and focus on areas that they can control, whether at a job or on a project or in relationships.

Various obstacles prevent bereaved people from finding meaning and achieving control. Some losses are easier to recover from and make sense of than others. Suicides and violent deaths are especially disturbing and difficult to grieve. People who think irrationally, avoid examining the circumstances, and adhere rigidly to certain beliefs struggle more to find meaning than those who openly reflect about their situation (Thompson, 1998). According to Harvey, Orbuch, Weber, Merbach, and Alt (1992), some people need as much as two hundred hours of counseling to resolve bereavement issues and achieve some closure for the loss. In addition, bereaved people must feel comfortable talking about and focusing on the death and remain open to alternative conceptualizations of events.

Janoff-Bulman and Berg (1998) explain that when a major loss occurs, such as when a spouse dies, people's assumptions about life, which they take for granted, are usually shattered, and a significant task of mourning involves finding meaning by rebuilding and reconstructing these assumptions.

Calhoun and Tedeschi (2001) caution clinicians that some clients avoid existential concerns and remain comfortable without exploring the meaning of events. In these instances the clinician should not pressure the client to "find meaning." According to Davis and Nolen-Hoeksema (2001), meaning making can exacerbate bereaved people's distress when they believe that what happened to them was senseless and random. These bereaved people will benefit less from finding meaning and more from focusing on the personal significance of the event, that is, figuring out how they may have grown or developed new strengths as a result of their experience. Davis and Nolen-Hoeksema found that searching for meaning is most beneficial to bereaved people during the first few months following the death, but later, as the death becomes more remote, this process is less therapeutic.

Finding Benefit or Personal Growth

Although clients should pave the way for discussions about finding benefit, social workers can facilitate the process in various ways. Gamino, Sewell, and Easterling (2000) found four factors that predict positive outcomes and personal growth: seeing some good result from the death; having a chance to say good-bye to the loved one; intrinsic spirituality; and spontaneous positive memories of the decedent. Gamino and colleagues suggest that clinicians can facilitate positive growth by helping mourners recast their stories of death and loss in positive ways that can still include sorrowful aspects. When a bereaved person missed an opportunity to communicate with his loved one before he died, the clinician can help the grieving person find symbolic ways to say good-bye, such as writing a letter or visiting the gravesite. Bereaved people who have a religious affiliation might find comfort by becoming more involved with their organization by finding additional spiritual resources. Finally, instead of avoiding reminders of the deceased, clinicians can help bereaved clients celebrate special memories, which often strengthens their connections to their loved one.

Personal growth can emerge from transformations that make the grieving person more independent of the deceased. For example, some older widows who for the first time learn to manage their bills, attend to home repairs, and fix their cars feel empowered when they master new skills. Many bereaved women from this cohort often feel self-sufficient for the first time in their lives. Social workers help these women by encouraging their independence. Personal growth occurs when an individual's social resources, coping skills, or personal resources are enhanced after bereavement (J. Schaefer and Moos, 2001).

Personal growth is manifested in different ways. While some people redefine their roles and relationships, others discover their inner strengths. Many bereaved people become more sensitive and compassionate toward others as a result of their bereavement experience. Some help others with their grief. People also feel more vulnerable and realize the finiteness of their life after someone close to them dies. They become more patient and more tolerant of others, and they appreciate each day more than they did before their loss.

Social workers who are sensitive to bereaved clients' needs and unique trajectories through bereavement will more effectively help clients find benefits from their bereavement experience. Most bereaved people comment that they achieved the most personal growth after the intense grieving period subsided, when they felt ready to reinvest in life and strong enough to try out new activities and relationships. Social workers who understand the roller-coaster emotions of bereavement will collaborate more effectively with their older bereaved clients and help them recover and move forward.

COUNSELING COMPLICATED GRIEF

Counseling Traumatic Grief

Although many experts agree that traumatic grief (or complicated grief) exists and that it should be included in the *DSM*, they have not yet agreed on how to treat this disorder. Pilot studies that test different treatments for traumatic grief are ongoing, but more sophisticated investigations will shed light on the interventions that work best in various situations. In one pilot study designed to evaluate treatment for bereaved people diagnosed with traumatic grief, Shear, Frank, Foa, and Cherry (2001) found success using a reenactment of the death, exposure to the activities and situations that the grieving person has been avoiding, and interpersonal therapy. The grief symptoms and associated anxiety and depression significantly improved in participants in this treatment.

Counseling Chronic Grief

A lack of consensus continues on how best to treat chronic grief, and clinical models to help bereaved people with attachment problems are still undeveloped. M.

Stroebe, Schut, Stroebe, and colleagues (2002) have begun to identify some areas that clinicians can address when working with bereaved people struggling with chronic grief.

Chronic grievers who evidence insecure-dependent attachments will most likely benefit from engaging in more restoration-oriented coping strategies that lead them away from dwelling on loss-related circumstances and help them to reinvest in life. In addition, because many chronic grievers were overly dependent on their spouses, these bereaved people need gentle nudging toward more independent functioning and a loosening of their bonds to the deceased.

Some chronic grievers also need to identify the factors behind their fears and strengthen cognitions that will enhance their feelings of mastery. Many bereaved people fear the intrusion of thoughts that make them feel out of control. In these situations the only effective treatment may be confrontation and exposure to their fears.

Counseling Bereaved People Who Are Depressed

Zisook and Shuchter (2001) have identified treatment guidelines for bereaved clients who are experiencing depression. Zisook and Shuchter worry that these individuals will go untreated because clinicians inappropriately delay treating them. Although the *DSM-IV* (1994) advises waiting for two months after the death of a loved one to begin treatment, Zisook and Shuchter warn against this because bereaved people who are depressed are at high risk for cardiovascular disease and immune dysfunction. Zisook and Shuchter believe that "to delay diagnosis could be to deprive the bereaved and depressed individual from much needed, potentially life-saving treatment" (2001, p. 783). They argue that health experts should treat a bereaved person's depression, even though it is a normal reaction to the death of a spouse, if it remains pervasive, persistent, and painful, interferes with the survivor's functioning or resolution of grief, and indicates a depressive syndrome.

Zisook and Shuchter (2001) also recommend treating bereaved people with minor or subsyndromal depression because of their high risk for severe illness. Bereaved individuals who experience high distress soon after bereavement are more likely to exhibit high distress later, and they are at risk for complicated grief reactions. Prophylactic treatments are recommended for any bereaved person with a history of depression.

Zisook and Shuchter (2001) outline several guidelines and recommendations for clinicians who are treating bereaved people who are both grieving *and* manifesting depression. These guidelines identify high-risk situations and procedures that are especially important to follow with these clients.

Ms. Murphy, seventy-five, lost her husband to prostate cancer one year ago, after fifty-five years of marriage. Her physician has referred her to a social worker for counseling because Ms. Murphy feels that she is unable to carry on with her life and has been sleeping and eating poorly. When the social worker sees Ms. Murphy, she encourages her to discuss her feelings. This helps develop rapport and sets Ms. Murphy at ease. The social worker encourages Ms. Murphy to talk about her husband's death and the circumstances, for example, the extent and duration of the medical care that he needed, how prepared she felt for his death, where her husband died, whether they were able to communicate about his dying, and whether she was present at the moment of his death. Ms. Murphy tearfully describes how bad she felt when she was unable to properly care for her husband. Ms. Murphy had cared for her husband extensively and had become increasingly exhausted. Although she had some help from a nurse and from her children, Ms. Murphy was the primary caretaker. As his cancer spread, Mr. Murphy became increasingly uncomfortable and was unable to move. He fell on several occasions, and she was unable to lift him without help. Despite these caregiving challenges, Mr. Murphy wanted to die at home. The Murphys contacted a home health care agency in the community that provided them with more assistance until Mr. Murphy died.

In addition to assessing the circumstances of the death, the social worker uses the ABCDEF practice guide to assess Ms. Murphy. Her behavior or actions (A) are limited. She engages mostly in loss-oriented activities, visiting her husband's grave several times a week, sleeping a lot, crying, and sometimes watching television. She has rarely visited her children, friends, or neighbors since her husband's death. Her biological functioning (B) or health is adequate. She has high blood pressure, which is under control with medication, and she feels weak, tired, and exhausted, but she is otherwise in good health. The cognitive assessment (C) reveals that Ms. Murphy frequently ruminates about her husband's death and always tends to dwell on negative thoughts. She regrets that she didn't urge him to see a doctor sooner. Some ruminations focus on her fears about life now and how she will manage without her husband. Her entire world had revolved around her husband and children, and she was proud of her caregiving. Ms. Murphy never worked outside the home. She describes herself as a nurturing wife and as someone who took good care of her family.

The demographic indicators (D) reveal that Ms. Murphy once enjoyed going to church but stopped going after she got married. She lives alone and her finances are secure. Although she has three children, they live out of state and visit only every few months. Her environmental resources (E) include neighbors and friends, but she restricted her social life while caring for her husband so that she could remain at his bedside. She spent little time with friends or on hobbies. Her feelings (F) include depression, anxiety, and yearning for her deceased husband. She still can't believe he is gone. Ms. Murphy describes her attachment style as one in which she often becomes "overly dependent" on others. Although she has frequently felt anxious in the past, she has never experienced serious depression.

The social worker concludes that Ms. Murphy is struggling with chronic and traumatic grief. Her excessive dependency on her husband over the years contributed to her difficulties now. She also evidences the salient symptoms of traumatic grief. She suffers from separation distress characterized by an intrusive, distressing preoccupation with her deceased husband, along with yearning, longing, and vigilance. The precipitating factor was his death after a long and dependent relationship. She exhibits traumatic distress by disbelieving that he is gone; she feels that her life is empty and unfulfilling without him; she has a fragmented sense of trust, security, and control; and she feels that a part of herself has also died.

The social worker recognizes the interrelationships of Ms. Murphy's limited activities (A), bleak cognitive outlook and excessive ruminations (C), and her feelings (F) of fear, depression, and anxiety. Her ruminations, which exacerbate her depression and anxieties, limit her involvement in restoration-oriented activities that could help Ms. Murphy move on with her life.

In collaboration with Ms. Murphy the social worker devises short-term and long-term treatment plans. The short-term goal is to alleviate Ms. Murphy's distress, specifically, her anxiety, fears, depression, and yearning. In addition to referring her for a medication evaluation, the social worker recommends that they work together, using desensitization and exposure techniques to gradually introduce Ms. Murphy to restoration-oriented activities, such as visiting with her children or going out with friends. She also teaches Ms. Murphy distraction and thought-stopping techniques to reduce her ruminations. The social worker strives to gather Ms. Murphy's social supports to help her shift toward more restoration-oriented coping. After Ms. Murphy's extreme distress subsides, the social worker also recommends guided imagery to help Ms. Murphy begin to reframe and revise the traumatic scenes, such as her husband's falling, that are still disturbing her. The demographic indicators (D) and cognitive assessment (C) reveal that her religion and her church might be a potential resource for her.

The long-term goals include helping Ms. Murphy confront her dependencies and insecure-fearful attachment styles that have prevented her from feeling competent and experiencing a sense of mastery about her abilities. The social worker refers Ms. Murphy to a support group of other widows who are also struggling with dependency issues.

Many widows from Ms. Murphy's generation sacrificed their own development to care for their families and naturally felt afraid and unsure of themselves when they were on their own. In supporting these women's efforts to grow more self-sufficient, social workers intervene on individual *and* social structural levels. This integrated approach has helped Ms. Murphy and others like her to reframe their struggles. Instead of seeing themselves as inadequate individuals, they are learning to see that they were victims of societal expectations that women care for family members and maintain the household. Many widows from this generation have rebuilt their lives and discovered strengths that they never knew they had. By using an integrated intervention approach, social workers help widows and widowers achieve their fullest potential.

Discussion Questions

1. Which myths of bereavement did you believe in, and where did you acquire these beliefs?
2. Identify a loss that you experienced in your life, and discuss which theory of bereavement, such as the stress paradigm, dual process model, attachment theory, and meaning-making model, best explains your grief reactions.
3. What did you find most helpful to you when you were grieving? What was least helpful?
4. How can society better support people during bereavement?

CHAPTER 13

Work and Retirement

R ETIREMENT IS MORE COMPLEX TODAY than in the past for various reasons. New options in part-time employment and partial retirement have emerged, and more retired women and retirees from diverse backgrounds comprise the retirement population. People also spend more years in retirement than in the past. In 1940 the average man spent nine years in retirement, about 15% of his lifespan, but by 1990 this had increased to at least fourteen years of retirement, which is more than 20% of his lifespan (U.S. Congress, 1992). In addition, many people retire early if they have the money and their company's support.

Although social workers have traditionally focused on older people's families, especially concerns about caregiving, elderly abuse, and intergenerational matters, social workers must also understand how work and retirement influence older people's lives. Gerontological social workers will encounter more and more older workers who are seeking guidance about retirement planning, retirement decisions, and postretirement adjustment.

In this chapter we discuss retirement trends and their implications for the meaning of retirement in this century. After summarizing various theories pertaining to retirement, we identify retirement issues that older people are likely to face in different retirement phases. We suggest interventions to address these issues and offer a case example to illustrate key points.

Retirement in the Twenty-first Century

People will experience multiple transitions, diverse lifestyles, and various work trajectories in the twenty-first century. Workers enter a "third age" when they leave long-term careers and jobs for those that fit better with their needs and skills and provide more intrinsic satisfaction. Many will begin second careers, an increasingly common phenomenon both before and during retirement. Others will switch to "bridge jobs," when they gradually shift from full-time to part-time or part-year work, sometimes with a different employer or in a different occupation. One study found that almost half of retirees (44%) work for pay at some point after retirement (Moen, Erickson, Agarwal, Fields, and Todd, 2000). Older workers will comprise more of the labor force than in the past (see figures 13.1 and 13.2). The number of older workers will continue to rise, and by 2015 about 20% of the labor force will be comprised of older workers, according to unpublished 2004 estimates from the U.S. Bureau of Labor Statistics. By 2025 more than thirty-three million older people are likely to be in the labor force (Burtless and Quinn, 2001). Many older adults will remain productive well into their nineties.

Older women, especially those aged 55 to 64, are responsible for most of this growth (see figure 13.3). Since 1950 more women in every age group are working, and the number of working women aged 55 to 64 has almost doubled. In 1950, 27% of the women in this age group worked, compared to 52% in 1999 (Purcell, 2000). From 1994 to 2000 employment increased not only among women in this age group but also among those aged 62 to 64.

Although the group of older workers aged 65 and older has grown more slowly than the group aged 55 to 64, the older group also has grown. In 1990, 16.3% of men and 8.6% of women older than 65 worked, whereas 18.6% of men and 10.6% of women in this age group were working in 2003 (U.S. Census Bureau, 2004b). This will continue until 2012, when older men will make up 20.8% of the labor force and older women will account for 12.2% of all workers (Census Bureau, 2004b).

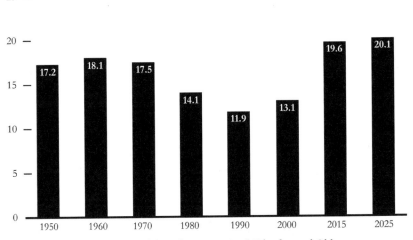

FIGURE 13.1 Percentage of the Labor Force Aged Fifty-five and Older, 1950–2025
Source: U.S. General Accounting Office, 2001.

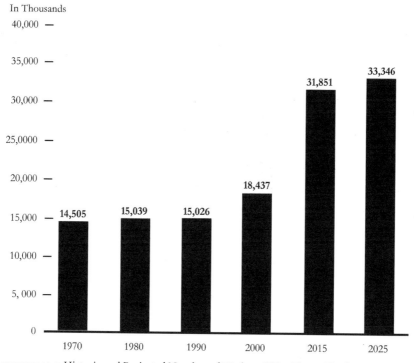

FIGURE 13.2 Historic and Projected Number of Workers Older Than Fifty-five, 1970–2025
Source: U.S. General Accounting Office, 2001.

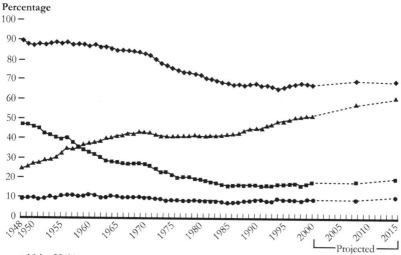

◆ Males 55-64
■ Males 65 and older
▲ Females 55-64
● Females 65 and older

FIGURE 13.3 Labor Force Participation Rates for Older Workers, by Gender, 1948–2015
Source: U.S. General Accounting Office, 2001.

These trends have several causes. First, more and more retirees will need to work to supplement their income. Declines in pension coverage and lack of savings among baby boomers will force many people to work longer than they expected. People will retire later, and increasing numbers of retirees will need to work to supplement their income, which may be lower than they expected. Also, a shrinking labor supply, as well as a shift from a manufacturing-based economy to a less physically demanding one that is based on producing and disseminating information, have increased the need for older workers. In addition, retirement policies now keep people working longer; legislation passed in 1983 increased from 65 to 67 the age at which people can receive full Social Security retirement benefits, and the 2000 amendment to the Social Security Act repealed the earnings test for those older than sixty-five. Finally, the phased retirement or flexible employment, which some employers are offering their older workers, will allow companies even greater flexibility in their retirement programs as they strive to retain older workers.

THE MEANING OF RETIREMENT

As the labor force ages and becomes more diverse, traditional definitions of retirement have become obsolete. People once defined retirement economically, that is, according to whether someone has stopped working and receives a public and/or private pension. But retirement is no longer a single event that occurs at a single point in time. More and more people are leaving careers for jobs that allow them to move gradually into part-time or part-year work.

Traditional concepts of retirement have especially failed to consider women's career trajectories. Compared to men, women take more time off from work for caregiving; they more often work at sites that provide "under the table" compensation (often as caregivers to the elderly in home settings); and their jobs typically pay less. Many women conceptualize retirement differently from men because of these gender differences in employment (Moen, 2001). Szinovacz and DeViney (1999) observed that reproductive history and marital status influence women's self-definitions of retirement. Price (2000) identified three themes—loss of social contacts, loss of professional challenges, and confronting stereotypes—that are associated with women's retirement. In her 1987 study Gibson found that 40% of retired older blacks continued searching for full- or part-time work or declared themselves disabled. She also identified unretired-retired people who were older than fifty-five and were not working but did not consider themselves retired. Zsembik and Singer (1990) reported different perceptions of retirement that exist among Mexican Americans, who often have intermittent work histories. In a study of Korean Americans M. Kim (1992) found three different conceptualizations of retirement—retirement as the termination of employment, retirement as leisure, and retirement as grandparenting. Various life circumstances, including disability status, spouse's employment, work history, and self-employment, affect people's definitions of retirement (Szinovacz and DeViney, 1999).

Theories of Adjustment to Retirement

The most common theories used to understand retirement include role theory, continuity theory, activity theory, and, more recently, life course theory and feminist gerontology. (See chapter 2 for a more in-depth discussion of theories.)

Role theory, which prevailed during the 1970s and early 1980s, emphasized the centrality of work and marital roles and viewed role exits, such as widowhood and retirement, as significant sources of distress and unhappiness. According to Blau (1973), roles exits cause problems because they require people to relinquish roles that they have already learned and to shift to new roles, such as retirement, which may be more ambiguous and disregarded.

Continuity theorists, who typically used longitudinal research designs, conceptualized retirement as an extension of earlier life stages as people try to maintain their previous levels of self-esteem, earlier lifestyle patterns, and long-standing values. Although some previous studies (e.g., George and Maddox, 1977) demonstrated stability in well-being during retirement, others found that continuity is possible only if retirees can maintain their preretirement lifestyle during retirement. Richardson and Kilty (1991) found that many retired women, specifically, women of low occupational status, are unprepared for the loss of income that occurs after retirement.

Activity theorists contended that people adjust best to retirement when they maintain high levels of activity and continue the same levels of involvement that they experienced in middle age (Havighurst, 1963). Retirees who lead active and socially involved lives and who participate in many groups and organizations presumably enjoy their later years more than those who mostly stay at home and avoid these activities. Although several studies (e.g., Albrecht, 1951) showed strong associations between high levels of activity and well-being, many well-adjusted retirees enjoy their solitude.

Critical gerontologists (e.g., Ovrebo and Minkler, 1993; Estes, 2001) adopted a broader view that considered the political and socioeconomic influences on retirement. These gerontologists analyzed discriminatory retirement policies and institutional ideologies that account for significant retirement gaps between men and women and between whites and minorities in pension coverage, Social Security benefits, and other retirement resources. Their view of retirement was more integrated and recognized structural *and* individual influences on retirement and the interplay between them.

Feminist gerontologists, for example, Browne (1998) and Richardson (1999b), criticize traditional models of retirement for their exclusion of women and people of diverse ethnic and cultural backgrounds, whose work histories do not always follow a linear path. These gerontologists focus on older women who are at risk for poverty because of a lifetime of poor wages, intermittent work histories, segregated work sites, lack of compensation for caregiving, and wage-based pensions. The feminist gerontologists also maintain that those who study or work with older women must understand the personal choices that women make about their jobs, marriages, and families and the systemic forces that affect these choices. By increasing the control and influence that women have over their personal and public lives, gerontologists will more successfully empower older women and emancipate them from oppressive environments.

Moen (1996) and J. Kim and Moen (1999, 2002) propose a life course perspective that examines retirement within the context of cohort and historical influences, structural factors, *and* situational exigencies. Moen (1996) demonstrates how these contextual influences change the roles that people experience throughout life and the manner in which they fulfill these roles. For example, gender differences in the meaning and importance of work affect women's work trajectories, which in turn substantially influence their retirement experiences. Structural factors, specifically, national and corporate policies, determine the choices and the amount of control that people have over their retirement decisions and lifestyles. More women live in poverty than men during retirement because retirement policies are generally wage based and discriminate against women who work without pay at home, caring for others. Situational exigencies that influence people's retirement experiences include their education, occupation, and marital status. The life course view of retirement focuses on the historical, social, and personal context of retirement and considers when, how, and why people retire.

Szinovacz (2003) underscores the relationships between early life course decisions and retirement experiences in her discussion of the life course model. She explains that, like most life transitions, retirement is influenced by early life experiences, such as years in the labor force, wages, retirement benefits, and the stability of a person's career. Women's childbearing patterns also affect retirement. Women who take time out to raise children are more likely to work later than mothers who continued to work. Those who delayed childbearing also remained in the labor force longer than those who had children when they were younger.

Szinovacz (2003) maintains that adjustment to retirement involves multiple domains in a person's life. Individual attributes, such as health, income, and occupation, and retirement policies affect people's adjustment to retirement. Individual and social structural factors influence how long people work, when they retire, and how well they adjust to retirement. People's experiences vary according to their background characteristics, work history, individual attributes, and social context. A multidisciplinary perspective that incorporates biopsychosocial influences is also needed to understand people's adjustment to retirement.

The Phases of Retirement

Most experts agree that retirement is a process rather than a discrete event and that the transition includes multiple stages. Atchley (1988), who was one of the first to describe the retirement process, identified eight phases in the transition from work to retirement. These include a preretirement stage, a honeymoon period that immediately follows retirement, a routine phase, rest and relaxation, disenchantment, and a final routine phase. Ekerdt, Bosse, and Levkoff (1985) also identified a honeymoon phase during the first six months of retirement but a reduction in life satisfaction thirteen to eighteen months after retirement. Richardson and Kilty (1988) observed that retirees' well-being declines six months after they retire, but one year later they feel better. Moen (2003) found gender differences in retirement satisfaction depending on the length of retirement and other influences, such as marital quality.

This chapter discusses retirement as being organized around three phases: preretirement, the retirement decision, and postretirement adjustment. Some issues are more relevant to some retirement phases than others. Table 13.1 depicts these issues and interventions to address them, which we discuss within the context of the three retirement phases.

The Preretirement Phase

Workers think more and more about leaving work during the preretirement stage, and they begin preparing for this transition as retirement approaches. Evans, Ekerdt, and Bosse (1985) found that the preretirement process often begins when people start to talk about retirement with their relatives, friends, and coworkers and initiate financial plans for retirement; this is usually at least fifteen years before they actually retire.

One of the most important preretirement activities is thinking about leisure and financial matters. Workers typically know little about their retirement benefits when they start working, but they become more interested in retirement finances when they enter the preretirement phase. They prepare financially by learning about public and private pensions, individualized retirement accounts, personal savings, and other retirement investments. However, few workers understand how

TABLE 13.1 Retirement Counseling (ABCDEF Model)

ABCDEF Model	Preretirement		The Decision to Retire		Retirement Adjustment	
	ASSESS:	INTERVENE:	ASSESS:	INTERVENE:	ASSESS:	INTERVENE:
A (Actions)	Planning	Preretirement counseling	Voluntary/involuntary	Cognitive therapy	Activities/Hobbies	Psychosocial counseling
	Years Worked	Retirement reform	Full/partial	Employment counseling	Work	Employment counseling
	Wages			Retirement reform		Retirement reform
B (Biological)	Health	Health counseling	Health	Health counseling	Health	Health counseling
C (Cognition)	Attitudes	Cognitive therapy	Mastery	Cognitive therapy	Mastery	Cognitive therapy
	Worldview/spirituality	Existential therapy	Ageism	Advocacy	Worldview/spirituality	Existential therapy
D (Demographics)	Income	Retirement reform	Income	Retirement reform	Income	Retirement reform
	Occupation/education	Social Security reform	Occupation/education	Employment counseling	Occupation/education	Employment counseling
	Gender/ethnicity	Employment counseling	Gender/ethnicity	Cultural sensitivity	Gender/ethnicity	Cultural sensitivity
	Marital status	Marital counseling	Marital status	Marital counseling	Marital status	Marital counseling
E (Environment)	Social supports	Psychosocial counseling	Social supports	Psychosocial counseling	Social supports	Psychosocial counseling
		Task-centered counseling		Task-centered counseling		Task-centered counseling
		Support groups		Support groups		Support groups
F (Feelings)	Emotional wellbeing	Psychosocial counseling	Anxiety	Exposure/action	Anxiety	Exposure/action
	Depression	Grief counseling	Depression	Concrete services	Depression	Concrete services
				Cognitive therapy		Cognitive therapy

retirement benefits are calculated. In Gustman and Steinmeier's 2001 study, only about half of the participants knew what their benefits would be. Even among those who said they understood the benefits that they would actually receive, only 27% were within 25% of the actual income. Women were less informed than men, and whites had more knowledge of their benefits than blacks or Hispanics. Low-income people and elderly people who expected to rely on Social Security understood their benefits the least, whereas affluent individuals were the most informed.

Few people engage in any retirement preparation beyond financial planning (Turner, Bailey, and Scott, 1994). In a study of three thousand public employees Richardson (1990) found that only about one-third of the men and about one-quarter of the women felt that they had prepared well for retirement. People avoid planning for retirement for many reasons, but most commonly it is because their income is inadequate to allow them to set aside money for retirement. People who are highly committed to their careers also plan less for retirement than alienated workers (Kilty and Behling, 1986; Richardson and Kilty, 1989). Some people avoid thinking about retirement because they have negative feelings about it. They often contemplate retirement during middle age, when physiological and psychological changes can lead workers to confront their mortality for the first time.

People who seek counseling during the preretirement phase are usually forty to sixty years old and are often confronting such midlife concerns as aging, loss, and death. Psychosocial interventions that incorporate supportive and existential counseling can help these clients. Retirees' feelings, especially about growing older, can affect their preparation for retirement. Older people who associate retirement with death or decline should be encouraged to explore their feelings about aging and to examine their fears. They may need to grieve the loss of time, youth, childbearing, and achievement. Many retirees are concerned about moving on to a new and unfamiliar stage and fear that they lack the knowledge and skills to cope with these later years. Some are anxious about becoming mentally and physically incapacitated and burdening their family members. Others worry about making new friends, not having fun, and adapting to less structure and a retiree identity.

Psychosocial counseling that emphasizes listening, life review, and supportive therapy can help people resolve these issues by encouraging them to identify, understand, and accept the varied feelings that come with aging. The goal is to facilitate clients' management of their feelings of loss, to help them experience and accept these feelings, and then to gradually encourage them to experiment with new and unfamiliar activities and events without the security that they obtained from their previous roles and obligations. Most people who confront and work through these midlife issues feel more integrated later, as they accept contradictory urges and establish new goals. Social workers can also lessen potential retirees' anxieties by providing them with information about what to expect during retirement and by encouraging them to try out retirement behaviors, such as engaging in a new hobby. These clients can benefit from help in developing new routines, new hobbies, new friends, and new sources of identity outside work. This fosters socialization and prepares workers for the next stage. As workers gain more knowledge about retirement and aging, they feel less anxious and fearful about these issues. Those who successfully resolve unsettling concerns from the past and redefine their goals for the future usually look forward to retirement.

Many companies offer preretirement counseling to their employees. The benefits of preretirement planning, especially informal planning, are unequivocal. Those who plan for retirement typically adjust better than those who do not, and those who plan informally benefit the most. They usually have a clearer idea of their needs, higher morale, more favorable attitudes toward retirement, and fewer longings for their former jobs than unprepared retirees (Taylor and Doverspike, 2003; L. Dorfman, 1989; J. Kim and Moen, 2001; Mutran, Reitzes, and Fernandez, 1997; Taylor-Carter, Cook, and Weinberg, 1997; Teaff and Johnson, 1983).

Preretirement counseling may be either limited or comprehensive. Limited programs emphasize finances and focus on pension information, business investments, and other retirement benefits, whereas comprehensive programs include recreation and hobbies, housing options, advance directives, health care, and successful aging. Trained group leaders usually facilitate discussions, and speakers may include people with expertise on a wide range of topics, including finances, legal considerations, health care, housing, money management, insurance, Social Security, and Medicare.

Many preretirement planning programs, which typically emphasize financial planning, would help more retirees if they addressed more social issues. Some retirees miss their coworkers and the social interactions that these relationships offer (Moen et al., 2000). Most preretirement planning programs also ignore the many structural barriers that affect how well people plan for their later years. For example, people need financial resources to prepare for retirement. Workers at low-paying jobs lack the funds to invest for retirement, and their employers rarely provide pension benefits. Social workers must advocate for retirement policies that are less discriminatory toward women and people from nontraditional backgrounds. Preretirement programs can address the needs of low-income retirees by including information on relevant social services and postretirement employment, specifically, programs to help older people find jobs.

The Retirement Decision

The increasing complexity of deciding when and how to retire requires more involvement by counselors to help people identify which options will benefit them most. Although many workers who can afford to retire early will continue to leave career jobs, more and more older people who are in good health will remain working for as long as possible. People who enjoy their work and have a good income are more likely to delay retirement as long as they remain healthy. Many women who remained in the labor force during their childbearing years are strongly invested in their careers and choose to delay retirement (Pienta, 1999). Other older women and elderly members of minority groups work beyond the typical retirement age because they need the income. Workers without pension coverage and those with spotty work histories, such as women who work only part time in order to care for family members, tend to work longer. Some people retire involuntarily because they become sick, need to care for an ill spouse or other family member, or are laid off and are unable to find work.

According to Atchley (1988), the decision to retire initially involves a comparison of the anticipated financial and social needs during retirement, expected financial resources, and current social satisfactions. Atchley believes that most people begin to contemplate retirement because they look forward to it and want more time for leisure and nonwork activities. He recognizes, however, that some workers must choose retirement before they are ready because of external pressures, including health problems, family responsibilities, coworkers' attitudes, employer's demands, and unemployment.

In an attempt to identify factors underlying people's retirement decisions, Kilty and Richardson (1988) conducted a factor analysis and found four factors. The first involves informal discussions of retirement plans with family and friends, reading literature about retirement, and engaging in leisure pursuits in preparation for the transition. The second cluster focused on formal retirement plans. The third factor clustered around the timing of retirement, specifically, whether to retire early, late, or on time. Voluntariness of retirement was the concern of the fourth factor. People's decisions about retirement involve many considerations. Ekerdt, Vinick, and Bosse (1989) found that although many workers change their minds several times about when and how to retire, they proceed smoothly and systematically once they decide. Income, attitude, health, and family obligations, including a spouse's retirement, usually affect the timing of retirement.

Financial resources, and especially the availability of pension coverage, are probably the most important factors influencing the retirement decision. Workers with pension benefits will typically make their retirement decision with an eye on the specific terms of their company's policies. Most pension programs are wage based, and the amount that they pay out depends on the number of years that the employee has worked for the company; for the current cohort of seniors and for boomers, vesting rights often took ten years to earn, although now the vesting period can be as short as three years. Few companies provide portable pensions that workers can carry over to a different employer. Many workers retire earlier than they planned because their employer offers a retirement buyout, a mechanism that has been popular since the 1980s.

Health also affects when people retire (George, Fillenbaum, and Palmore, 1984). Workers in poor health with adequate pensions retire early, especially if their jobs are physically demanding; unfortunately, many older workers who are not healthy delay their retirement because their pension is not adequate, and other financial resources, including health insurance, are limited. Those who believe that they are in poor health often leave work, whether they actually are unhealthy or not. They believe that if they live a more leisurely life, without the demands of the workplace, they can take better care of themselves. These individuals choose to retire before they become too sick to enjoy it. A spouse's ill health can also affect the timing of retirement; in some instances a sick spouse (especially a spouse who needs expensive assistance) may delay the healthy spouse's retirement, whereas in other situations a spouse's illness may hasten it (Szinovacz and DeViney, 2000). Clearly, health can influence the retirement decision in various ways.

Family concerns, including the quality of the individual's marriage, also affect the timing of retirement. Myers and Booth (1996), as well as Szinovacz and DeViney (2000), found that spouses who enjoy their marriage might view retirement as an opportunity for them to spend more time together in shared activities. The timing of a husband's retirement substantially influences the timing of a wife's decision to stop working, but a husband's retirement is rarely based upon when his wife stops working, according to Smith and Moen (1998). They concluded that a husband's retirement is viewed as a "family event," whereas a wife's often falls into the "tagalong category." Arber and Ginn (1995) observed that despite trends toward mutual decision making in marriages, men are more likely than women to pressure their spouse to retire. Family conflict can arise when marital equilibrium is disrupted or when one spouse threatens the gender role ideology within the marriage. Kulik and Barelli (1997) found that retired husbands whose wives are still working sometimes experience "status anxiety" and marital conflicts, including more marital arguments (Szinovacz and Schaffer, 2000).

Several researchers, for example, J. Kim and Moen (2002), have documented that women consider their family situations more often than men do when making decisions about retirement. The illness of an aging parent affects the retirement of many older women, who are often the primary caretakers (Richardson, 1993). Caregivers frequently retire or work less because of conflicts between work and family obligations (Brody, 2004). They often feel that they have few options, even when supportive services are available. Hatch and Thompson (1992) looked at the factors that lead women to retire and found that having an ill or disabled household member, such as a husband or parent, who requires assistance is the best predictor of retirement. Husbands sometimes retire when their wives need care because husbands are more uneasy than their wives about combining work and caregiving, according to Szinovacz and DeViney (2000). Some wives continue working even when their husbands are ill because their family needs the income.

Older people who retire involuntarily may need cognitive behavioral therapy. When people retire because of circumstances beyond their control, they are at a greater risk for depression and anxiety (Kilty and Richardson, 1989; Szinovacz, 2003). Peretti and Wilson (1978–79) found that involuntary retirees have higher suicide rates and express greater anomie and alienation than those who retire according to plan. Older people who maintain control over whether they work or retire experience higher levels of well-being than those who feel forced into decisions about working or retiring (Barnes-Farrell, 2003; J. Kim and Moen, 2002).

Cognitive behavioral therapy that focuses on the negative thoughts of discouragement and hopelessness that these older people often feel is especially efficacious in these situations. By helping these older people to reframe events and recognize structural influences, such as ageism, that affect how many employers view older workers, social workers can empower these older people. They will feel more in control of events when they acquire a better understanding of these factors. For example, retirees who are pressured to retire but later find a rewarding part-time job may feel better about retirement than involuntary retirees who cannot obtain employment. Retirees who feel more control over their decisions are less vulnerable to depression.

Involuntary retirees are high suicide risks, and social workers should always assess their suicide potential. Social workers who deem a retiree at high risk for suicide should intervene immediately to ensure that the person is safe and find a protective, therapeutic environment where prompt and proper treatment is available (see chapter 7 for more information on the suicide lethality index and counseling suicidal elderly people).

The goals of intervention during this phase are to help older people feel in control of their decision about leaving work (even if they must retire involuntarily) and to assist them in making the best possible decisions regarding when and how to retire. Individual interventions will help many workers with their retirement decision, but social workers who advocate for innovative retirement policies that expand the options for older people will help more people retire successfully. Too many older people believe that they must either work full time at their primary job or retire completely, when they would rather work fewer hours (Moen et al., 2000).

Support groups are sometimes helpful because they help to lessen the stigma of unemployment or forced retirement by showing these older people that they are not alone. These groups offer social interactions for people while they are unemployed—social isolation is a major issue contributing to depression. The groups also offer support during the job search, and members offer each other job-hunting tips.

Social workers must also engage in advocacy on behalf of older workers. Social workers can advocate for older workers by challenging ageist assumptions, for example, that older workers are less productive than younger workers. When employers pressure their employees to retire early, they damage these workers' self-esteem (Feldman, 2003). Social workers can also collaborate with older clients to support legislation that will protect older workers.

The proposed Phased Retirement Liberation Act would allow employers greater flexibility in their retirement programs as more and more organizations strive to retain older workers. Phased retirement options are already available in a few organizations. Studies, for example, Graig and Paganelli (2000), show that workers *and* employers benefit from gradual retirements, partial retirements, and part-time work. The elimination of mandatory retirement laws and the end of the earnings test for Social Security eligibility will also make it easier for older people to work in their later years. Nearly three-quarters (72%) of workers aged seventy and older work on a part-time basis (Summer, O'Neill, and Shirey, 2000).

Successful interventions take into account the personal choices that people make about their jobs, marriages, and families, within the context of social policies and other systemic influences.

Postretirement Adjustment

Most people adjust well to retirement and cope with the many inevitable changes that occur with age, but longer retirements mean that people will experience more varied problems. Some people—especially those with limited resources—struggle during retirement.

Retirement problems can emerge at any time, but most appear during the first year of retirement when people first confront the changes in their resources and disruptions in their lifestyle. Richardson and Kilty (1991) observed that both men and women have the greatest decline in well-being during the first six months after retirement, although their study also identified several patterns of adjustment. Some retirees maintain their life satisfaction and exhibit minimal changes during the first year, whereas others become happier after they retire. A minority demonstrate lower morale and unhappiness during the initial transition to retirement.

Researchers have identified several factors that affect people's satisfaction with retirement. These include social support, occupational status, retirement preparation, health, family relations (specifically marriage and caregiving), voluntary retirement, socioeconomic status, and postretirement employment.

Although numerous studies document the importance of social support and life satisfaction later in life, investigators examining retirement adjustment have overlooked the significance of support and satisfaction (Taylor and Doverspike, 2003). Older people who relied on coworkers for social contact are especially vulnerable to loneliness during retirement unless these older people have maintained their friendships with nonwork peers or easily develop new friends. Retirees who relocate are more prone to depression and loneliness if they leave old friends. While some older people easily find new friends, others feel lost around unfamiliar faces. Taylor and Doverspike (2003) suggest that practitioners assess retirees' social support and help them identify rewarding social experiences if they feel lonely after leaving their work friends.

Workers in high-status occupations adjust better to retirement than those in low-status jobs (Richardson and Kilty, 1991). The loss of the work role is apparently more detrimental to people in low-status occupations. Retirees who work at low-status jobs may have more difficulty maintaining status and respect after they stop working. On the other hand, many physicians and attorneys retain their professional influence after they retire. These retirees may miss the gratification that comes from feeling productive. In these instances gerontological social workers can help these retirees find either new work or gratifying hobbies that meet their need to feel productive.

As distinctions between work and leisure become increasingly blurred, older adults will take on more and more responsibility for decisions about retirement and whether to work later in life. Social workers will be called upon to help older people evaluate their resources, assess their stamina and well-being, and determine the continued role in their life of employment and productivity, paid and unpaid, as they age. Traditional views of retirement as a time of play and no work are no longer appropriate. People will continue to contribute, accomplish, and engage in meaningful work throughout their later years.

Social workers must also prepare to assist older people seeking postretirement employment. Older adults who remain productive adjust better than those who withdraw from activities. Moen and colleagues (2000) found that at least among men, the most satisfied retirees worked, whereas the most dissatisfied retirees were unemployed.

Marriage is usually a buffer against mental and physical illness during retirement, and several studies find higher retirement satisfaction among those who are married (Mutran et al., 1997; George and Maddox, 1977). Moen and colleagues (2000) observed declines in marital satisfaction during the early stages of retirement, but marital quality improved after two years. Kulik (2001) found that married men and women reported less enjoyment after they retire and that couples engage in more individual activities during retirement. Marriages are least satisfying when one spouse retires and the other continues working, and marital strain, spousal conflict, and lower marital satisfaction are more common when the wife continues working after her husband retires (Moen et al., 2001; Szinovacz and Schaffer, 2000). Marriage is especially important among newly retired women, according to J. Kim and Moen (1999), and it apparently mediates the effect of retirement for this group. Couples make adjustments immediately following retirement, although most adjust to the changes within two years (Moen et al., 2001). They are most vulnerable during the early stages when their roles and lifestyles change. Those who prepare for marital changes during preretirement may avoid the initial decline in marital enjoyment that sometimes occurs after retirement. Marital therapy for retirees who are struggling with these role changes and other aging issues might also help older couples during the retirement transition. Social workers can help retired couples better negotiate the increased time that they spend together at home and in recreation.

Socioeconomic status, which includes income and occupational status, is the most significant predictor of retirement satisfaction. People with adequate incomes travel more and participate in various leisure activities during retirement without worrying about the costs. Low-income retirees continually encounter financial adversities (Richardson and Kilty, 1991). The loss of financial resources is stressful and has enormous psychological costs. Impoverished older women experience inordinate emotional distress, low self-esteem, and excessive anxiety as they cope with paying bills and managing their expenses. They live more restricted lives, engage in more limited types of leisure, and worry more about money, health, and access to medical care.

J. Kim and P. Moen (1999) observed that the morale of newly retired men improves after they stop working, but newly retired women face an increase in depression and a decline in well-being. Although women's lifetime work histories have become more stable by their later years, researchers consistently find gender differences in older people's incomes. See chapter 15 for more information about poverty. Several factors, including lack of compensation for caregiving, poor wages, intermittent work histories, segregated work sites, and the wage-based nature of both public and private pension systems contribute to these higher rates of poverty among older women and minorities.

One of the most obvious reasons that women's poverty is so prevalent during retirement is that women's jobs pay less than men's. Inequalities during the life course result in lower earnings for women than men at every age, resulting in fewer wage-based retirement benefits. Women who receive Social Security benefits based on their own work records average substantially less per month than men. These gender inequities are unlikely to diminish because working women continue to earn significantly less than men.

White men more often work at jobs that have pensions, whereas the jobs of many women and minority group members often lack adequate health and retirement benefits (U.S. Census Bureau, 2000). In 2000, 46% of men and only 29% of women older than sixty-five received a pension benefit (Purcell, 2000). Richardson and Kilty (1997) found that retired women consistently report fewer total retirement resources than retired men, even after women's career patterns and number of years worked are taken into account.

Women's increased involvement in paid work will improve their pension status only if they work long enough to become vested in a pension plan. Women are more likely than men to work part time, as consultants, and in shared jobs that are not protected by a pension (U.S. Bureau of Labor Statistics, 2000). Federal laws permit employers to exclude from pension coverage employees who work fewer than twenty hours a week or fewer than a thousand hours a year. This lack of pension coverage among working women means that substantial numbers of women depend solely on Social Security during retirement.

Another reason that women have less retirement income than men is that they spend more time caring for others and fewer years in the labor force, and they are more likely than men to retire because of caregiving and family responsibilities (Calasanti and Slevin, 2001; Moen et al., 2000). Most caregivers raise children, support husbands, and care for ill family members without any compensation for their work. This is enormously costly for women. Older women will not achieve parity with older men unless retirement policies account for women's caregiving throughout the life course.

Many women pay more into Social Security than they receive in benefits. Dually entitled beneficiaries (people who qualify for benefits both as retired workers and as a present/former spouse) under Social Security suggest that a woman should benefit from working, but she does not if her spouse's benefits or earnings are greater than her own. In addition, divorced women qualify for benefits based on their ex-husband's record only if they were married for at least ten years and if she did not remarry. Widows encounter different problems. Because women typically outlive their husbands, they often deplete their husband's retirement income, except for Social Security. Although the federal Retirement Equity Act of 1984 directs employers to pay survivor's benefits directly to widows, problems continue. Many couples do not select the survivor benefit option. Even if they do, employers usually provide only about two-fifths of what the former spouse received when he was alive (Older Women's League, 1998). Although in the future fewer women will receive Social Security benefits as married and widowed beneficiaries, more women will be affected by divorce (Iams and Butrica, 1999). According to Butrica (2000), only 12% of women in the 1931–35 birth cohort will be divorced, compared to 20% of women in the 1956–60 birth cohort.

Retirement programs that are based on wages alone continue to exacerbate earlier inequities. Retirement parity will be achieved only when discriminatory work and hiring practices throughout the work years are eradicated, when women who work in female-dominated professions receive wages comparable to their male counterparts', and when women are adequately compensated for caregiving. Social workers must advocate for societal changes and retirement reforms that take into account the economic and psychological costs of caregiving if they hope to improve women's adjustment to retirement. These changes are consistent with an integrated practice model that recognizes interactions between the personal and political, public and private, and paid and unpaid work. Not until retirement inequities are addressed on multiple levels and through multiple strategies will retired women age as successfully as retired men.

CASE 13.1

Mr. Jenkins is sixty and worked at a bank for more than thirty years, until a larger company bought it, and he decided to retire because he had suffered a mild heart attack a few years earlier. Although he receives retirement benefits, Mr. Jenkins and his wife, who works as an elementary school teacher, still struggle to pay their mortgage and other expenses. Their two adult sons are on their own but have no money to spare.

Mr. Jenkins misses working and interacting with coworkers. He initially enjoyed his time off from work, but he became frustrated and bored after several weeks. His wife now expects him to pick up the house, wash clothes, do laundry, buy groceries, and cook dinner while she works. She becomes angry when he does not attend to these chores, and their relationship has deteriorated into constant arguments. One son eventually convinces his father to consult a social worker.

The social worker listens to Mr. Jenkins share his frustrations and disappointment about retiring sooner than he expected. She uses the ABCDEF practice guide to assess him and concludes that he is mildly depressed but not hopeless or suicidal. He is in good health except for his heart problems, which are under control. But he lost his social outlets when he left the bank. Mr. Jenkins misses the gratification and social interactions he experienced from work and feels unprepared for retirement. After evaluating his options with the social worker, Mr. Jenkins decides to seek a part-time job. The social worker refers Mr. Jenkins to a support group for seniors seeking work, but because he is primarily concerned about his marriage, the social worker suggests that Mr. and Ms. Jenkins come in to talk.

After setting ground rules about taking turns talking and not interrupting, the social worker asks the Jenkinses to share their perspectives about their marriage. Several themes emerge as they share their stories. The central issue involves role conflicts and their expectations for one another. Ms. Jenkins expects her husband to do more housework while he is home and she is working. Mr. Jenkins feels that this is demeaning and that his wife has lost respect for him now that he isn't "bringing home the bacon." His feelings of becoming "demasculinized" are affecting the couple's sexual relations. Although they both have noticed that their roles have changed, they are surprised to realize that their relationship has degenerated to this extent. After the Jenkinses share their feelings, the social worker conducts a more comprehensive evaluation of their relationship, including their individual and marital histories.

The social worker encourages the Jenkinses to talk more about the role changes. They agree that this is an area that they want to explore in greater depth. The social worker and the Jenkinses agree to spend more time examining these changes and the effects on their relationship.

Many couples experience changes in their marriage after one or both people retire or stop working (Szinovacz and Ekerdt, 1995; Moen, Kim, and Hofmeister, 2001). The equilibrium in the relationship can change without either person's realizing it, and the resulting instability creates marital conflict and confusion. Moen (2003) suggests that gerontologists can better understand family and other relationships in late life by conceptualizing them as "linked lives," another critical concept within the life course model. Moen explains that work and career development has become an increasingly joint process of marital partners that involves a "gendered process, embedded in existing and frequently outdated institutional arrangements predicated on a gendered division of labor" (2003, p. 239). Moen recommends that gerontologists look more closely at the ways that work and family lives intersect and consider the ways that institutions, historical changes, and ideological shifts influence work and family life. In this example Mr. Jenkins's job loss affected his marriage more than it affected him, and the social worker recognized the interpersonal interactions that contributed to his wife's stress by inviting her to participate. The linked lives concept is consistent with an integrated gerontological practice perspective that views older people in relation to their partners, children, friends, neighbors, communities, and institutions.

DISCUSSION QUESTIONS

1. What barriers do older workers face at their jobs and in the labor force?

2. How can gerontological social workers help older people with work and retirement?

3. What social policies do we need to protect and strengthen older workers? What controversial issues lurk behind these policies?

4. What current social policies focus on older women's poverty, and how might they be changed to better address these issues? What new ones do we need to decrease poverty in late life?

PART 4

Sociopolitical Issues

CHAPTER 14

Economic Policies and Aging

GERONTOLOGICAL SOCIAL WORKERS must work on multiple levels, using micro and macro interventions to help older people, who inevitably present complex and multifaceted problems during counseling. Unless social workers apply an integrated practice model, such as the ABCDEF practice framework discussed in previous chapters, their assistance to older people will be inadequate. The integrated practice model, introduced in Chapter 3, is grounded in a multidisciplinary perspective that emphasizes micro and macro interventions. In part 4 we address the salient sociopolitical influences that affect older persons (see parts 2 and 3 for reviews of psychological and social psychological gerontological issues, respectively). In this chapter we discuss general economic issues affecting older people and focus on late life poverty in chapter 15. We review Medicare, Medicaid, and other health care issues, including end-of-life care, in chapter 16 and conclude in chapter 17 with a discussion of the Older Americans Act and the many services that have emerged as a result of this legislation, as well as other initiatives that gerontology practitioners must understand.

In chapter 13 we discussed the phases of retirement and other factors that influence older adults' adjustment to retirement, and we continue to discuss retirement in this chapter. However, we now address the major national economic and retirement policies, which also influence how well people adjust to retirement, within the context of a "three-legged stool," representing Social Security, private pensions, and personal savings. Because of its importance we focus on Social Security but recognize that privatization is part of the discussion of retirement reform. The case example at the conclusion of this chapter illustrates how insecure many older people feel about their economic future and how vulnerable they are to inevitable life changes.

We begin this chapter with an overview of the economic status of the nation's older population, including economic inequities based on gender, race, ethnicity, and marital status.

Economic Status of the Nation's Elders

The economic status of elders in the United States is diverse. The ranks of senior citizens include the nation's most affluent and most disadvantaged. But most seniors have modest incomes. In 2001 almost a third (31.8%) had annual incomes of less than $10,000, and almost a third (31.2%) had incomes greater than $25,000. The median annual income for households headed by someone older than sixty-five was $33,938. About 1 in 10 seniors (10.1%) had an income below the federal poverty level, and another 6.5% had incomes near the poverty level (between poverty level and 125% of the poverty level). (Administration on Aging [AOA], 2003a). Figure 14.1 shows the distribution of the elderly by income in 2001.

The U.S. retirement system tends to reproduce the inequalities of the labor force. Those who have low wages during their working years will most likely have limited retirement income. As a result income in later life is a function of gender and race, just as it is among the nation's younger age groups. In 2001 the median personal income for men older than sixty-five was $19,688 and for women of the same age it was $11,313 (AOA, 2003a). Further, as table 14.1 shows, the median income of households headed by African Americans older than sixty-five was only 62% that of white households in the same age group. Similarly, the median income of households headed by older Hispanics represented 66% of the median

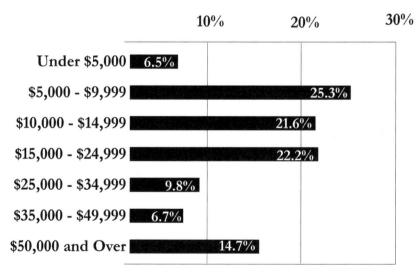

FIGURE 14.1 Distribution of Senior Citizens by Income, 2001
Note: Based on data from the Census Bureau and Social Security Administration.
Source: Administration on Aging, 2003a.

TABLE 14.1   Median Income of Households by Age and Race—1998

Ethnicity	Age of Household Head		
	55–64	65+	75+
White	$45,803	$22,442	$18,205
Black	$25,200	$13,936	$12,886
Hispanic	$28,765	$14,729	$12,886
Overall	$43,167	$21,442	$18,205
Percentage of White Median Income			
Black	55%	62%	71%
Hispanic	63%	66%	67%

Source: U.S. Census Bureau, 1999, table 1.

income for white households. Further examination of table 14.1 reveals that the difference between white households and minority households tends to be greater among the younger age group (55 to 64) than among the older groups. This probably illustrates the equalizing effect of Social Security. As this chapter explains, the program was designed to provide more income replacement for low-income workers than for more affluent workers.

An individual's economic status in late life depends on many factors, but sources of income, gender, ethnic background, and home ownership are especially important, as this chapter will show.

Sources of Income

Personal vulnerability is largely determined by the source of income. If an individual receives all or most of her income from wages, she is vulnerable to unemployment. A person who depends entirely on Social Security for income is vulnerable to political decisions that determine the fate of this program. An older adult who relies on income from assets is vulnerable to changes in interest rates and fluctuations in the value of those assets. As we review the sources of income for American elders, consider the implications of the figures in table 14.2 for their personal vulnerability.

As Americans move through their older years, the importance of each major source of income varies. For example, among those younger than 65 a majority receive income from earnings. This number steadily declines past the traditional retirement age: 44% of those aged 65 to 69 receive income from earnings, yet only 4% of those 85 and older do.

TABLE 14.2   Income Sources of Elderly Americans:
Percentages with Income from Each Source

Source	Percentage by Age						
	55–61	62–64	65–69	70–74	75–79	80–84	85+
Earnings	80	64	44	26	14	7	4
Retirement Benefits	26	62	89	93	94	96	95
Social Security	13	53	86	91	91	94	93
Benefits other than Social Security	16	30	41	44	43	41	33
Other public pensions	7	12	15	15	14	15	13
Railroad Retirement	0	0	1	1	1	1	1
Government employee pension	6	11	14	14	14	14	11
Military	1	2	2	2	2	1	2
Federal	1	3	5	5	5	6	4
State/local	4	7	8	8	7	7	6
Private pensions or annuities	10	20	28	31	31	28	22
Income from assets	61	60	60	59	60	62	55
Interest	57	57	57	57	57	59	62
Other income from assets	37	35	32	30	26	27	22
Dividends	33	31	27	26	22	22	17
Rent or royalties	11	10	11	9	8	8	7
Estates or trusts	0	0	0	0	0	0	0
Veterans' benefits	2	2	4	4	6	6	3
Unemployment compensation	4	3	1	1	0	0	0
Workers' compensation	2	2	1	1	0	0	0
Public assistance	5	6	5	5	4	3	6
SSI	5	5	5	5	4	3	6
Other public assistance	1	1	0	0	0	0	0
Personal contributions	2	1	1	1	1	1	0

Source: SSA, 2003, table 1.1.

Table 14.2 clearly illustrates the transfer from earnings to retirement benefits. Whereas only 26% of those aged 55 to 61 draw retirement benefits, a majority of those who are older do. This figure increases dramatically between the ages of 62 and 64 (62%) and 65 and 69 (89%). The vast majority (more than 90%) of those older than 70 receive income from retirement benefits. Further, the most important source of retirement benefits for Americans of retirement age (62 and older) is Social Security. Compared to this program, other public pensions play a fairly limited role in providing income for the elderly.

A majority of all older Americans receives income from assets. For this group, interest is the most important income source, followed by dividends. Each time the Federal Reserve lowers interest rates to stimulate economic growth, it takes money away from this large group of elders. Similarly, when publicly traded companies reduce or withhold their dividends, a large group is affected.

Race and Gender

The relative importance of the various sources of income varies by gender and marital status. For example, as we noted in Chapter 13, older women rely more heavily on Social Security than men do. For nearly two-thirds (74%) of unmarried women older than sixty-five, Social Security represents more than half their income. This is true of only 53% of married couples in the same age group (Social Security Administration [SSA], 2003, table 6.B2). Of course, older women live longer than their male counterparts, so they are more likely to be unmarried.

Whites are more likely than members of minority groups to have income from any of these sources. Whites also are more likely to have income from Social Security, public and private pensions, and assets. Whereas 91% of whites received income from Social Security in 2000, only 88% of African Americans and 77% of Hispanics did. The same year 43% of older whites had income from public and private pensions, compared to 33% of African Americans and 22% of Hispanics. Similarly, 63% of older whites had income from assets, compared to less than 30% of African Americans and Hispanics (Hungerford, Rassette, Iams, and Koenig, 2002).

Home Ownership

Although it does not produce income, a home is a significant asset for most of the nation's elderly. In this regard they have advantages that young adults do not. Whereas only 55% of Americans aged 30 to 34 owned their homes in the second quarter of 2003, a whopping 83% of those aged 65 to 69 enjoyed the benefits of home ownership. This number declined slightly with age, to 78% of those aged 75 and older (U.S. Census Bureau, 2003b). Of course, home ownership can be a double-edged sword. As elders "age in place," they may find themselves house rich but cash poor. Reverse mortgages, also called home equity conversions, were designed to address this problem by providing income for life in exchange for title to the residence. These programs require careful scrutiny, but they can significantly enhance the quality of life for elders in this situation.

The Government's Role in
Providing for Retirement Security

The political climate of the early years of the twenty-first century emphasizes individual, as opposed to collective, responsibility, not just for retirement income but for a wide range of human needs. As Atchley and Barusch (2003) note, a tendency to blame the vulnerable tends to surface during economic downturns. When they are faced with personal insecurity, Americans may feel unable or unwilling to shoulder the burden of those in need. The history of U.S. retirement policies does reveal a persistent tension between advocates of collective responsibility and those who emphasize private initiative for solving problems.

A quick glance at the players on each side suggests that personal interest cannot be ruled out as a motivating force. Social workers, for example, frequently advocate for interventions in the form of government programs to solve the financial problems of the needy. Cynics would point out that expansion of government programs has the secondary benefit of increasing employment opportunities within the social work profession. Similarly, financial and business interests tend to favor private initiative and oppose programs such as Social Security. Stockbrokers would be the first to benefit from "privatization" of the Social Security program, because it would put billions of dollars and millions of individual retirement accounts under their purview. Understanding the nuances of public policy debates requires looking beyond the rhetoric to personal interests that may explain the positions and behavior of lobbyists for all perspectives. As we review the history of government involvement in retirement security, the constant process of compromise and accommodation is apparent as nations attempt to reconcile the interests of key stakeholders.

Social Security in Western Europe

Industrial expansion in nineteenth-century Europe exposed people to new risks, even as it brought them together in rapidly growing urban centers.[1] European industrial workers faced three fears: poverty in old age, illness, and unemployment. Early income security programs were designed to address these fears.

As several historians have pointed out, the motivation to address workers' concerns was probably not entirely altruistic. Authoritarian regimes developed the first income security programs because they needed to increase workers' stake in

---

1. For a more detailed discussion of the development of social security, see Swaan (1988).

government and their loyalty to the nation-state (Flora, 1983; Flora and Heiden-heimer, 1981; Rimlinger, 1971).

The regime of Otto Von Bismarck in what was then known as Prussia (now Germany) is illustrative. Europe's first social insurance program was established under his regime in a series of laws passed in the 1880s. One popular myth holds that Bismarck established the program to force some of his aged political foes into retirement. But historians favor the emergence of socialism as a more compelling explanation (Swaan, 1988).

Karl Marx lived in Prussia from 1818 to 1883. In 1848 he and Friedrich Engels published the *Communist Manifesto*, which called for the worker revolution that they both saw as inevitable. Their ideas found fertile ground among the industrial laborers of Western Europe, and socialism quickly became a threat to established interests. Labor organizers opposed legislation to establish a social security program—small pensions, accident insurance, and national medical coverage—in Prussia because it would remove any incentive for workers to try to establish Marx's worker utopia. Labor leaders argued that workers should have allegiance to the international proletariat, rather than to a nation. The legislation passed despite their opposition; however, as Swaan (1988) notes, union leaders and Socialist Party officials were quickly "integrated into the state's fabric as executives of the national insurance system" (p. 188). Thus labor "agitators" were among the first to be co-opted by the new income security system, their loyalty to the state secured by their willingness to serve.

England followed Prussia in the development of social insurance for workers. Great Britain had a complex and well-established system for poor relief under the Elizabethan Poor Law (Trattner, 1989). Parish authorities, whose power and livelihood derived from the program, collected taxes. These officials and others responsible for aid to the indigent argued that poverty was the result of personal failings and that efforts to relieve it should focus on moral reform. In essence they argued that the fear of poverty was necessary to sustain motivation among indus-trial workers and was good for their moral fiber. But as industrialization advanced, these authorities were overwhelmed by the need, particularly of older workers. With the 1906 election of a Liberal government came an activist regime that, with the support of the new Labour Party, enacted social insurance legislation (includ-ing the Old Age Pensions Act of 1908).

Most nations in Western Europe established social insurance for workers before World War I (1914–18) began. Throughout the Continent these programs would serve three important nation-building functions. Programs of forced savings through paycheck deductions converted wages into accumulated capital, a large reserve that would be available for government initiatives and programs. The new systems also required government bureaucracies to collect and monitor workers' contributions and dispense benefits. This meant more government employees, offices, forms, and procedures—in essence, more government. Finally, social insurance helped secure workers' loyalty to the state. Through their contributions workers bought a stake in their government. Any effort to topple a regime would entail the loss of the workers' investment in the social insurance program.

France did not establish a social insurance system until 1930. The "petit bourgeoisie" was a well-established political and economic force, and historians attribute the nation's delay in establishing social security to its opposition (Swaan, 1988). For several decades these small property owners feared that government control of large sums of capital would disrupt their businesses. Essentially, they feared that they would be less able to borrow money. They argued that income security would reduce workers' incentive to accumulate personal savings. As we will show, both concerns have surfaced in recent arguments about restructuring the Social Security program of the United States. Eventually, historians argue, the support of moderate labor organizations and the erosion of the bourgeois power base permitted France to establish social insurance.

Social Security in the United States

Individualism survived in the United States longer than it did in Western Europe. Some have attributed this to the presence of the Western frontier, others to various flaws in the national character. At any rate, Americans consistently rejected attempts to establish social insurance for workers, arguing that they should assume personal responsibility for protecting themselves from the three fears. Americans attributed failure to accumulate savings to a moral failure—"improvidence."

Those who could afford it purchased private insurance against accidents and illness. These policies would offer some retirement income because retirement was generally the result of physical disability. In 1910 about half the workforce had such insurance (Achenbaum, 1986). Those who had not provided for their own retirement income were left to the mercies of their families or to the limited private charitable assistance that was available.

But even as early as 1829, the more privileged classes of workers had publicly funded pensions. The nation's first federal retirement program awarded pensions in the 1780s to veterans of the Revolutionary War. The Federal Employees Retirement Program was established in 1920. Initiatives at the state level created mini social security programs. By 1931 eighteen states had established compulsory old-age insurance programs for workers (Piven and Cloward, 1971), and by 1933 twenty-one states and the territories of Alaska and Hawaii operated relief programs for the dependent elderly (Achenbaum, 1986).

Some companies also provided private pensions. In 1875 the American Express Company established the nation's first private pension plan. Large employers like public utilities, railroads, and major manufacturing firms offered limited pension coverage to employees. Federal legislation in the 1920s triggered the expansion of private pensions. So the nation had a growing class of fortunate employees that enjoyed pension protection and was willing to blame those who didn't for their improvidence.

Proposals for national social insurance programs were unsuccessful in this context. During the Progressive Era (roughly, 1890–1930) advocates such as Abraham Epstein and I. M. Rubinow argued for these programs. Epstein founded the American Association for Old-Age Security in 1927 to advance his proposal for social insurance. But for the most part neither workers nor politicians supported these "radical" ideas. Indeed, many believed that the Supreme Court would find mandatory social insurance to be unconstitutional (Kingson and Berkowitz, 1993).

The Great Depression was not the first economic upheaval in the United States, but its duration and intensity were overwhelming. As Andrew Achenbaum explains:

> Between October 1929 and June 1932, the common-stock price index dropped from 260 to 90. The nation's real GNP [gross national product], which had risen 22 percent between 1923 and 1929, fell 30.4 percent over the next four years. Nearly 5,000 banks, with deposits exceeding $3.2 billion, became insolvent; 90,000 businesses failed. Aggregate wages and salaries in 1933 totaled only 57.5 percent of their 1929 value. The gross income realized by farmers was cut nearly in half; the farm-product index took a dive from 105 to 51 between 1928 and 1932. More than a thousand local governments defaulted on their bonds.... Insecurity pervaded the land. (1986, p. 16)

"Provident" Americans lost the savings that they had so carefully accumulated. Employed Americans lost their jobs. Incomes that had once seemed secure evaporated overnight. The notion of personal responsibility for economic calamity became laughable. Middle-class Americans realized that hard work and decent morals would not insulate them from economic calamity. Unemployment and poverty, once so easily attributed to personal failures, now seemed to call for a collective solution. Local and voluntary relief efforts were simply overwhelmed by need, as were state relief programs. The nation's Republican president, Herbert Hoover, urged Americans to "stay the course," suggesting that the market would naturally correct the situation.

But in times of great suffering Americans expect government to take action. Recognizing the need to move elders out of the labor force to make way for younger workers, many suggested the use of taxes to provide guaranteed income to the elderly. Francis Townsend, a retired doctor living in California, organized "Townsend Clubs" to support his proposal that all Americans older than sixty who were not in the labor force be given $200 per month on the condition that they spend the money within thirty days. Others, including the writer Upton Sinclair and Senator Huey P. Long, advanced similar ideas.

When 1932 arrived with no economic recovery in sight, New York governor Franklin D. Roosevelt was swept into the presidency with a clear mandate to take forceful action. Roosevelt immediately created the Committee on Economic Security (CES), under the direction of Edwin E. Witte. The CES was charged with drafting proposals for "New Deal" programs. Frances Perkins, a social worker, became the first woman to hold a cabinet post when FDR named her secretary of labor. Together, Witte and Perkins drafted the Social Security Act, "the most comprehensive social welfare bill that any president had ever asked Congress to consider" (Kingson and Berkowitz, 1993, p. 35).[2] One key policy goal was to encourage seniors to retire, freeing up jobs for younger workers. Therefore the program included a "retirement test": to receive full benefits a senior would have to demonstrate that he or she had no earnings. When Congress approved the measure in 1935, it was only a skeleton of what Social Security would become. Its old-age insurance provided benefits only to retired workers, not to their survivors or workers with disabilities. The original program covered only about half the labor force, excluding many farm and domestic workers, state and local employees, and the self-employed. Like the current program, it was financed by mandatory contributions from employees and employers. This aspect of the program survived two constitutional challenges.

The U.S. Supreme Court heard both Social Security challenges in 1937: *Charles C. Steward Machine Co.* v. *Davis*, and *Helvering et al.* v. *Davis*. In the first case the Charles C. Steward Machine Company of Alabama sued to recover its share of Social Security payroll taxes, claiming that they represented an illegal excise tax. The Court upheld the constitutionality of the tax, finding that the magnitude of the depression justified federal intervention. In the second case a shareholder with Edison Electric Illuminating Company of Boston argued that deduction of payroll taxes from wages would produce unrest among employees and "would be followed by demands of increases in wages and that corporation and shareholders would suffer irreparable loss" (*Helvering,* 1937). In rejecting this argument, the Court relied on the concept of general welfare:

2. A detailed history of Social Security is available at www.ssa.gov/history/chrono.html (October 29, 2004). For a brief international history of social insurance, see www.ssa.gov/history/briefhistory3.html (October 29, 2004).

Congress may spend money in aid of the general welfare.... The purge of nation-wide calamity that began in 1929 has taught us many lessons. Not the least is the solidarity of interests that may once have seemed to be divided. Unemployment spreads from state to state, the hinterland now settled that in pioneer days gave an avenue of escape [is gone].... The hope behind this statute is to save men and women from the rigors of the poorhouse as well as from the haunting fear that such a lot awaits them when journey's end is near. (*Helvering*, 301 U.S. at 640)

These constitutional challenges focused on the only compulsory element of the Social Security Act, old-age insurance. With the cases decided, the program was put into place. Retirement benefits were financed by employer and employee contributions of 1% each on a wage base of $3,000, with a maximum contribution of $30 per year. Benefits were paid out at age sixty-five and amounted to about $22 per month for single workers and $36 per month for couples. To allow a reserve to accumulate, no benefits were paid until 1940. The first benefit paid was $22 per month to Miss Ida Fuller, a retired secretary. Fuller lived to be more than one hundred years old. She paid less than $100 in Social Security taxes and collected about $21,000 in benefits (J. Schulz, 1995). Other women have fared less well.

Although we are focusing on the old-age insurance program in this chapter, we must note that the Social Security Act of 1935 included assistance to dependent children, public health services, unemployment compensation, and aid to the blind. It also established a grant-in-aid program for states to manage that provided assistance to indigent elders. This would later be replaced by Supplemental Security Income (SSI), which we discuss in chapter 15.

Old-Age and Survivor's Insurance for Workers

The 1935 law offered only rudimentary coverage for the nation's workers. With his reelection in 1936 FDR resolved to greatly expand this protection. The 1939 amendments to the Social Security Act expanded coverage, adding benefits for survivors and dependents of eligible workers.

These protections would continue to expand for four decades. In 1950 Congress added farmworkers and the self-employed to the program, bringing coverage to about 90% of the labor force. Later, Congress made provision for early retirement, allowing eligible workers to retire at sixty-two with 80% of the benefit that they would have received at sixty-five. In 1972 Congress established the cost of living adjustments (COLAs), which linked benefit increases to growth in the Consumer Price Index. In 1977 Congress put into place procedures for "indexing" earnings.

Indexing adjusts earnings for inflation in benefit computations, resulting in more generous treatment of earnings from the early years of a worker's career.

The 1980s marked the beginning of an era of retrenchment. By this time program expansions had eroded reserves, and the Old Age and Survivors Insurance (OASI) Trust Fund was in jeopardy. Anticipating the demands that would be presented by the baby boom cohort of Americans born between 1946 and 1968, President Ronald Reagan appointed a bipartisan commission, the National Commission on Social Security Reform, to recommend measures to restore the program's fiscal solvency. Based on the commission's recommendations, the following measures were implemented in 1983 amendments to the law:

1. *Revisions in the cost of living adjustment (COLA).* The COLA was subjected to a one-time delay, and a "stabilizer" was placed on future COLAs. When the trust fund falls below certain levels, the COLA is automatically indexed, not to the Consumer Price Index but to the average increase in wages (if it is lower). Because the income of the trust fund depends on wages, the COLA is insurance against erosion in times of high inflation and low employment. The stabilizer has not been implemented.

2. *Taxation of benefits.* In an extremely controversial measure retirees with incomes greater than $25,000 per year for individuals and $32,000 per year for couples found that as much as half of their benefits were subject to federal income tax.

3. *Increased retirement ages.* Gradual increases in the age for receipt of full retirement benefits began in 2003. By 2027 the retirement age for full benefits will be sixty-seven. Early retirement would result in 70% of full benefits, rather than 80%.

4. *Work incentives.* In a radical shift from the historic intent of the program, the commission recommended that seniors be encouraged to secure paid employment. Congress increased the amount that beneficiaries could earn through employment before their Social Security benefits were reduced. Employees older than seventy were no longer subject to benefit reductions from earned income.

The work of the national commission was pivotal in two respects: its recommendations enhanced the program's solvency, and the process of reform undertaken by the commission greatly reduced the influence of partisan politics and improved the quality of technical information used in debates about the program.

The 1983 amendments set the stage for later revisions that were primarily designed to improve the system's solvency and fund the retirement of the baby boom generation. In 2000, in a rare unanimous vote of both houses, Congress eliminated the retirement test entirely. Under the Senior Citizens' Freedom to Work Act of 2000, Social Security beneficiaries now are allowed to earn wages without any reduction in their benefits.

How OASI Operates

The Old Age and Survivors Insurance (OASI) program is the primary source of retirement income in the United States, providing benefits to more than forty million retired workers and their families in 2002 (Office of Management and Budget, 2001). Although it was intended as only one leg in the three-legged stool representing retirement income, many elders depend entirely on Social Security. In 2000, 21% of Americans aged seventy-five or older received all their income from Social Security. This was true of 18% of Americans aged sixty-five or older (SSA, 2003, table 6.A1).

OASI represents a carefully crafted compromise between two key policy objectives: giving a fair investment to seniors in general ("equity") and providing adequate benefits to low-income seniors ("adequacy"). Equity is achieved because benefits are based on contributions. Thus an individual's benefits are proportionate to the amount she has invested in the program. To achieve adequacy low-income wages are subject to more generous replacement, thus ensuring adequate income to low-wage workers.

To achieve equity an individual's benefits are computed on the basis of his contributions. Benefits are based on a person's "average indexed monthly earnings" (AIME). Not all earnings are subject to payroll tax. In 2003 income in excess of $87,000 per year was not taxed and therefore was not included in earnings computations. This figure is known as the "wage cap" and is adjusted annually for inflation. The system adjusts for inflation of a worker's earnings between the ages of twenty-one and sixty-two that were subject to the payroll tax. Then the five years with lowest earnings are dropped. The resulting total is averaged to produce the AIME. To be eligible to draw Social Security benefits, an individual must have worked in a job covered by the program and have earned at least $890 per quarter (this is adjusted annually) for forty quarters (i.e., ten years).

Adequacy guarantees seniors enough income for a modest lifestyle in later life. The "replacement rate" of OASI is designed to ensure adequacy. Benefit computations "replace" lower earnings more generously than they do high earnings. In 2003 the first $606 of a worker's AIME were replaced at a rate of 90%. Earnings from $606 to $3,653 were replaced at 32%. Finally, earnings between $3,653 and the wage cap of $7,250 were replaced at 15%. Under this formula a worker with low earnings will have a higher replacement rate than one with high earnings. This does not mean her Social Security check will be larger but that the difference between working income and Social Security income will be less than it would be for someone with high earnings.

Funding for OASI is authorized by the Federal Insurance Contribution Act (FICA) and comes from the payroll tax. Originally set at 1% of earnings to a cap of

$3,000, in 2003 this tax totaled 15.3% of wages up to $87,000. Half this amount is withheld from employees' wages, and the other half is paid quarterly by employers. Most of the tax (12.4%) is allocated to the Old Age, Survivors, and Disability Insurance fund (10.7% to OASI, 1.7% for disability insurance). The remaining 2.9% goes to finance Medicare.[3] High-income workers pay more tax, and low-income workers receive more generous replacement income. This aspect is sometimes described as the "redistributive" feature of Social Security. In contrast, the payroll tax is a regressive tax in that it collects a higher proportion of the income of low-wage workers than of very high-wage workers. This is true because wages greater than $87,000 are not subject to the tax.

Money collected through payroll taxes is credited to four trust funds: the OASI trust fund pays benefits to retirees, their dependents, and survivors; the DI (disability insurance) trust fund pays benefits to the disabled. The hospital insurance and supplemental medical insurance trust funds pay Medicare benefits. These funds are overseen by the six-member Social Security and Medicare boards of trustees. These include the secretaries of the treasury, labor, and health and human services; the commissioner of Social Security; and two members appointed by the president and confirmed by the Senate to represent the public. Some funds have income from sources other than the payroll tax, such as general revenues and beneficiary premiums.

The actuarial status of the OASI program has been the subject of much debate. At present revenue to the OASI trust fund exceeds expenditures. In 2002, for example, assets in the OASI trust fund grew by $146 billion—about $40 million per day. Each year the trustees issue a report that projects the future solvency of these programs. The report represents a best guess based on current economic indicators. The 2003 report suggested that OASI revenues will continue to exceed expenditures for sixteen years. This means that until 2018 the fund will continue to take in more than it spends (see table 14.3). At that time the fund would begin spending the interest earned on its assets. This is projected to continue until 2030, when the fund would begin spending assets. Current projections suggest that the assets of the OASI trust fund will be exhausted by 2044. At that time program revenue is expected to be sufficient to pay 73% of program costs. Relatively small adjustments made today—either by reducing benefits or increasing revenue—could prevent the eventual depletion of trust fund assets. The magnitude of these adjustments increases as time passes. But even if no change is made until the fund is depleted, society does have other alternatives for meeting its obligations to retirees and their

---

3. The wage cap applies only to the OASI contribution. There is no wage cap for Medicare contributions.

TABLE 14.3   Key Dates for Social Security Trust Funds*

Key Dates for the Trust Funds	Oasi	Di	Oasdi	Hi**
First year that outgo exceeds income, excluding interest	2018	2008	2018	2013
First year that outgo exceeds income, including interest	2030	2018	2028	2018
Year that trust fund assets are exhausted	2044	2028	2042	2026

*Based on the "intermediate assumption" or "best estimates" provided by the trustees.
**OASI = Old Age and Survivors Insurance; DI = Disability Insurance; OASDI = Old Age, Survivors, and Disability Insurance; HI = Hospital Insurance.
Source: Social Security and Medicare Boards of Trustees, 2004.

families. These might include, for example, short-term infusions of funds from general revenues.

Women and OASI

Although the Social Security law has been amended repeatedly, the program continues to reflect the dominant family form of 1935, when most women relied on a working man for their income. In fact, as we saw earlier, in its original version Social Security did not address the income needs of women who did not work. Indeed, until 1977 men seeking to receive survivor's benefits were required to demonstrate financial dependency.

As a dependent, a woman (or a man) is now entitled to 50% of the benefit that her (or his) spouse receives upon retirement. The survivor receives 100% of the deceased partner's benefit. So a couple receives 150% of the retiree's benefit (100% for the retiree and 50% for the nonworking spouse). Upon the worker's death the spouse receives benefits as the survivor, which represents a one-third reduction in household income. Widowed people may not claim benefits until they are sixty years old. If they do choose to draw benefits at that age, the benefit is reduced. Those who apply at sixty-two also receive reduced benefits.

Whereas provisions for wives and widows were established in 1939, divorcees did not receive coverage until 1965. At that time provision was made for women who had been married for at least twenty years. They received full dependent benefits, regardless of the marital status (or number of marriages) of their ex-husband. In 1977 that period was decreased to ten years. If she remarries, a divorced woman will have the choice of receiving the benefits to which she was entitled before her remarriage or switching to those to which she would be entitled under her new marriage. (Few people are aware of this provision, and anecdotal evidence suggests that some women live with their partners instead of marrying, rather than risk losing their Social Security benefits.)

Women are more likely than men to rely on Social Security as their sole source of income. For unmarried women—including widows—who are sixty-five or older, Social Security comprises 51% of their total income. In contrast, Social Security benefits make up only 37% of the retirement income of unmarried elderly men, and only 34% of elderly couples' income. Further, at the end of 2002 women's average monthly retirement benefit from Social Security was $774, compared to an average of $1,008 for men (Social Security Online, n.d.).

The Social Security system is vulnerable to criticism for its treatment of working women. Usually, because of departures from the workforce and lower lifetime wages, a working woman receives greater benefits as her husband's dependent than she would if her check were based on her employment history. Because she must choose one benefit or the other, she receives no benefit for the payroll taxes paid during her employment years. This violates the principle of equity, because working women receive no return for their investment in the program.

Another equity failure is related to the benefits received by low- to moderate-earning dual income couples. Typically, these couples receive lower benefits than couples in which one partner earns a high income and the other is not employed.

Proposed OASI Reforms

Social Security reforms usually produce "winners" (those who stand to get more money) and "losers" (those who would get less). The odds that Congress will approve any given reform can sometimes be estimated by comparing the political clout of its winners and losers. The reform proposals that we discuss in this section address two concerns that we introduced earlier. Privatization proposals are designed to address the fiscal status of the program. Earnings sharing and caregiver credits are designed to improve the program's treatment of women.

"Privatizing" Social Security

In 1979 José Piñera, then labor minister of Chile, oversaw the final stages of "privatizing" that nation's pension system. The short-term results were deemed satisfactory, and at the end of his term in Chile's government Piñera came to the United States to advance the case for privatizing the U.S. Social Security system (Dreyfus, 1996). He promoted the idea through the Cato Institute, a conservative think-tank that promotes government deregulation and the free market, and captured the attention of President Bill Clinton. Clinton included a privatization proposal in his 1999 State of the Union address and appointed a Social Security advisory council to develop privatization recommendations. After fairly acrimonious debate, the council presented three proposals, all of which involved investing some trust fund reserves in private capital markets. President George W. Bush embraced privatization enthusiastically and pursued it even through the stock market declines of 2000–2. The poor economy in subsequent years meant that privatization proposals were placed on the back burner. But with Republican victories in the 2004 election, privatization of Social Security resurfaced as one of President George W. Bush's top policy goals. The president proposed to allow workers to deposit a percentage of their Social Security payments in private accounts. Because this threatens the financial soundness of Society Security, some officials proposed replacing these funds through expanded government borrowing or benefit reductions.

Earnings Sharing

Proposals to establish "earnings sharing" would combine the earnings of a married couple and allocate half the combined total to the husband and half to the wife for the duration of the marriage. This change would benefit divorced people who were married for less than ten years by giving them credit for their ex-spouse's earnings. It would also eliminate the inequality experienced by dual career couples. To keep the proposal revenue neutral the gains experienced by these groups would be offset by losses to those who receive benefits as dependents and had no work history of their own. These proposals disadvantage the very people who are privileged today by a system that favors the 1935 family.

Caregiver Credits

With growing recognition of the important role of family caregivers, proposals to grant Social Security credits to caregivers are likely to resurface. Because caregiving disproportionately affects women, they are the most likely winners in any proposal to give Social Security credit for caregiving. Typically, these proposals would offer credit for as long as five years of no or minimal earnings while a worker is living with a young child or caring for a disabled family member. The credits attempt to compensate for the unpaid labor of caregiving. Yet they have been criticized as unfair to working caregivers, because credits give no benefit to those who do double duty—meeting family care responsibilities without leaving the workforce.

The importance of the Social Security program for America's elders cannot be overstated. It is a vital source of support for the most vulnerable and offers improved quality of life to the middle class. It offers protection from the economic hardships endemic to a capitalist economy and represents an important contract that benefits young and old. The program's vulnerability does not stem from systemic flaws but from systematic and deliberate efforts to undermine public confidence in its promise (Quadagno, 1989). As advocates, social workers can help generate public support for the program, and as practitioners they can ensure that individual seniors receive their due.

PRIVATE PENSIONS: SECOND LEG IN THE RETIREMENT STOOL

Most Americans think of pensions as private contracts between employers and employees. Yet the term *private* is a misnomer when applied to pensions. Few other personal assets have been as profoundly influenced by public policy.

Indeed, with the exception of some pioneering companies like American Express, employers did not establish pensions until public policies offered incentives for them to do so. The Revenue Act of 1921 exempted both employer contributions and pension fund income from federal income taxes. This favorable tax treatment triggered an expansion of pensions.

A similar expansion followed the wage-and-price controls imposed to control inflation during World War II. Given the labor shortage, companies were motivated to offer other incentives to job candidates. A generous pension was one such incentive. The number of workers covered by pensions increased from about four million in the late 1930s to ten million by 1950 (J. Schulz, 1995). The combination of two public policies—wage-and-price controls and tax laws—led to the establishment of millions of private pensions.

These early pensions presented several problems: (1) they tended to treat top executives much more favorably than regular employees; (2) workers often lost their benefits through mergers, closures, and bankruptcies; (3) in some spectacular scandals companies squandered and lost their pension reserves; (4) some workers were fired just months before they became eligible for a pension; and (5) workers' survivors (most of them widows) received no income from pensions.

Americans looked to government to address these problems. In 1974 Congress passed comprehensive legislation to regulate pensions. The Employee Retirement Income Security Act (ERISA) restricted the extent to which employers could use pensions only to reward "key employees"—that is, highly paid executives. It strengthened standards governing the financial management of pension funds, and it limited the number of years that an employer could require before a worker had the legal right to receive pension benefits—before the worker became "vested." Then, in 1984, ERISA was amended by the Retirement Equity Act to require that plans provide the option of a "joint and survivor annuity." Under this provision workers can elect to provide income for their survivors at the cost of a reduced annuity during the worker's lifetime.

Congress addressed the problem of mergers, closures, and bankruptcies by establishing the Pension Benefit Guarantee Corporation in 1974. The PBGC manages a mandatory insurance program for pension programs. Funded through mandatory employer contributions, the PBGC pays workers whose company has gone belly up a fraction of the benefits to which they would otherwise be entitled.

Although business representatives opposed each of these regulatory reforms, the laws have not slowed the growth of pensions. Twenty million workers were covered in 1960 and 35 million in 1979. By 1995 an estimated 42 million workers, roughly half the labor force, were covered (J. Schulz, 1995). Of course, those who have pension coverage tend to be workers in "good" jobs, with union representation, decent wages, and a modicum of employment security. Low-income workers, minorities, and women are disproportionately represented among workers without pension coverage.

The nature of pensions changed in the 1980s. Most pensions that were set up before the 1960s were "defined benefit" programs, that is, they promised a specific monthly income based on earnings and years of service. These plans offer workers a measure of security but impose financial pressures on their employers. Workers are insured by the PBGC, and they know what their pension income will be when they retire.[4] During the 1980s many employers began offering "defined contribution" programs under which a specified amount (usually a fixed percentage of earnings) is deposited into a tax-sheltered retirement account. The now-familiar "401K" is an example of a defined contribution plan. These plans are not insured by the PBGC, and the monthly retirement benefit is unpredictable because the value of the retirement account rises and falls with fluctuations in the financial markets.

The decline in defined benefit plans has been marked in recent years. The PBGC reported a 63% drop in the number of defined benefit plans between 1985 and 1998 (PBGC, 1998). In 1980 defined benefit plans were the main pension plans for 80% of workers who were covered by private pensions. By 1998 that share had fallen to less than 50%.

The spectacular failure of the Enron Corporation in 2002 illustrated the risks of defined contribution plans. Like many companies, Enron offered employees a 401K plan that was heavily invested in company stock. When the Enron stock lost its value, employees lost their retirement savings. As of this writing, Congress was developing proposals to reduce the insecurity that has been introduced by the expansion of defined contribution plans.

PERSONAL SAVINGS: TRULY THE THIRD LEG

The Federal Reserve reported in 2002 that Americans' already low rate of savings had declined (Brawnstein and Welch, 2002). Nonetheless, a majority of seniors

---

4. Unlike Social Security benefits, pension income does not include inflationary adjustments.

TABLE 14.4   Income Sources and Average Income by Source for
Americans Aged Sixty-five and Older, 2000

Income source	Percentage with income from this source	Mean income from this source*
Earnings	17.0	$25,376
Social Security	2.0	9,473
Supplemental Security Income	3.7	3,884
Public assistance	0.2	1,856
Veterans' benefits	3.5	8,018
Survivors' benefits	5.5	9,415
Disability benefits	0.7	8,283
Public and private pensions	35.9	11,709
Interest	58.1	3,945
Dividends	21.1	4,115
Rents, royalties, trusts	8.7	6,580

*For those who receive income from the source.
Source: U.S. Census Bureau, 2001a.

receive at least some interest income from personal savings (Federal Interagency Forum, 2004). In 2000 the mean interest income received was modest ($3,945). About 21% of older adults received dividend income, which averaged $4,115 for the year. Finally, a small minority (8.7%) enjoyed some income from rents, royalties, and trusts. This latter category yielded on average $6,580 in 2000 (see table 14.4). Clearly, personal saving is not a primary source of income for the nation's seniors. Ironically, both inflation and declining interest rates jeopardize income from savings. Inflation erodes the value of the savings, while declining interest rates reduce the ability of savings to generate income.

The savings-and-loan debacle of 1989–95 illustrated the willingness of government to intervene to protect Americans' savings. At a cost of untold trillions the federal government salvaged the recently deregulated savings-and-loan industry, preventing losses to thousands of savers. The nation's monetary policies also have an effect on personal savings, as the Federal Reserve Board manipulates interest rates in an attempt to stabilize the economy (Lewis and Widerquist, 2002). With interest rates at historic lows in the first five years of the twenty-first century, the majority of seniors who did have interest income undoubtedly experienced a pinch. Finally, proposals to eliminate capital gains tax will clearly benefit the few who enjoy income from dividends and rents, lowering the taxes that they will pay when they liquidate their assets.

CASE 14.1

At sixty-seven Mr. Peterson was ready to retire and enjoy his retirement. His company threw a party for him at a local hotel. The food was good and the wine plentiful. The evening was marked by jubilant speeches, gently chiding him for deserting the staff and teasing him about his golf game. But everyone agreed that Mr. Peterson had paid his dues. For twenty-three years he had worked his way through the ranks to a midlevel position in the auto parts company. Mr. Peterson's firm provided a defined-contribution pension plan. His accumulated reserves amounted to $750,000—"nearly a million," as he put it. This would provide a comfortable income for Mr. Peterson and his wife, Alma. They planned to purchase a winter home in Arizona and enjoy some cruises. Mr. Peterson might even improve his golf game. Social Security did not figure prominently in his calculations. He anticipated that he would receive about $1,800 per month from Social Security, a relatively small proportion of his projected retirement income. The Petersons had no savings to speak of.

Most of Mr. Peterson's retirement fund was invested in stocks. But he didn't spend his first year of retirement watching and worrying. The Petersons enjoyed a cruise around the world. Then came 2001, and before Mr. Peterson knew what was happening, his retirement reserves had dwindled to less than half their original value. In December 2001 Alma Peterson had a major stroke and needed extensive physical therapy. Mr. Peterson was initially appalled as the medical bills rolled in and later became resentful as the coverage limits of Medicare became painfully apparent. With no supplemental insurance the Petersons were forced to draw on their decimated retirement fund to pay for her care.

After their dreams of a second home and a life of leisure evaporated, the Petersons found that their retirement was marked by insecurity and worry. Another health crisis could wipe them out, and Mr. Peterson considered returning to work.

As Mr. Peterson became increasingly anxious about his finances and worried about how he could pay for his and his wife's retirement, he contacted his long-time employer and inquired about consulting opportunities. But after several fruitless conversations with his colleagues, Mr. Peterson sought help from a social worker, who was employed at a local community mental health center and who had a reputation for helping older adults.

The social worker comprehensively assessed Mr. Peterson using the ABCDEF practice guide discussed in earlier chapters. The social worker also met with Ms. Peterson to listen to her perspective on their situation. After completing the ABCDEF evaluation, the social worker concluded that the Petersons were concerned primarily about their health and economic changes. The couple's actions (A) were normal, and their behaviors indicated no functional limitations. Their health and biological functioning (B) were generally good, and Ms. Peterson benefited from her physical therapy sessions. Their cognitive functioning (C) was excellent, although they often coped by ruminating about events. Their demographic (D) and personal background information revealed that neither had received psychiatric treatment or experienced excessive anxiety in the past. Their environmental circumstances (E) showed that they socialized well and nurtured their friendships. They enjoyed many leisure activities that they had recently discontinued to save money. The assessment of their feelings (F) showed that Mr. Peterson blamed himself for the loss of their retirement income and felt like a failure.

The social worker concluded that the Petersons had many strengths, including excellent interpersonal skills that might benefit others. Because the social worker was assisting several retired men who also had lost substantial retirement assets in the stock market decline, she organized a support group for men, most of whom planned to return to work for economic reasons, and invited Mr. Peterson, who enthusiastically agreed to join. The social worker, who facilitated the group, organized several sessions around topics relevant to older workers, such as interviewing, finding job openings, and rewriting their resumes. The intent was to empower the retirees by raising their awareness that others were struggling with similar situations. By helping these older men to reframe their problems in sociopolitical terms, that is, as an unexpected downturn in the stock market that had affected many older people and not as a personal failure, the social worker hoped to lessen the men's anxieties. Moreover, the group members' support for one another helped them feel less alone with their problems and strengthened their social connections. The social worker understood how the nation's economic crisis affected the quality of life, well-being, and insecurities of these older people.

In many ways the Petersons are typical of their generation. They have little or no personal savings and relied heavily on accumulated pension reserves for retirement income. The pension provided by Mr. Peterson's employer was part of a growing trend toward defined-contribution pension plans and away from the guaranteed income provided by defined-benefit plans. As a result Mr. Peterson, like many other workers and retirees, bore the risk of market fluctuations. The stock market drop of 2000–2 reduced his retirement security. As a result the Petersons joined the majority of older Americans. More than half (59%) of the nation's seniors receive more than half their retirement income from Social Security (SSA, 2003). If Mr. Peterson reenters the labor force, he will become one of the few men older than sixty-five (17.5% in 2000) who rely on earnings for income later in life (U.S. Census Bureau, 2001a).

The Petersons relied on Medicare for health insurance and were surprised that it did not protect them from financial devastation in a catastrophic illness. As we will discuss in chapter 15, Medicare is less effective than ever at covering health care costs for seniors.

This chapter offered an introduction to the economic status of elders in the United States. This diverse group includes the nation's most affluent and its most disadvantaged, and the gap between them is widening.

In an analysis of retirement resources that used data from two waves of a Social Security beneficiary survey, Gregoire, Kilty, and Richardson (2002) corroborated the findings of other investigators, such as Rubin, White-Means, and Daniel (2000), that income inequities among those older than sixty-five are increasing. In addition, as in the labor market, economic disadvantage disproportionately affects women and minorities (see chapter 15).

The Social Security system is the single most important source of retirement income for the nation's elderly and was developed in response to the turmoil of the Great Depression. Before the 1980s Social Security in the United States expanded steadily. The 1983 amendments to the Social Security Act were pivotal in restoring the solvency of the system and improving the technical content of the discussion of the nation's most important retirement system. OASI represents a compromise between the values of equity (fair return on investment) and adequacy (sufficient income to sustain a person). The program has been criticized for its treatment of women. Reform proposals include privatization and earnings sharing.

Discussion Questions

1. Why do you think farmworkers and domestic employees were not included in the original Social Security Act?
2. Are the self-employed covered by Social Security? Please explain.
3. Web assignment: Go to www.ssa.gov/history/hfaq.html, select three questions, and review the responses provided. Write an essay describing your reaction to this information.
4. Consider the status of major airlines in the United States. Both United and Delta sought to reduce their pension obligations in efforts to stave off bankruptcy. Does the protection offered by the Pension Benefit Guarantee Corporation encourage business to renege on their pension commitments? Why or why not?

CHAPTER 15

Poverty and Aging

REDUCTION OF POVERTY AMONG ELDERLY Americans is one of the most significant policy achievements of the twentieth century. Yet millions of elders continue to live with income below the poverty threshold, and still more experience financial vulnerability. Some people argue that these elders were "improvident"—that their poverty is a sign of personal failure. But poverty in late life can be traced to societal failures—restricted educational and employment opportunities, gender bias in the workplace, discrimination against immigrants, and the lack of financial security for family caregivers. Poverty increases an individual's risk of mental and physical illness. As we discussed in chapter 6, depression among older women is sometimes attributed to their low income. Thus practitioners in mental health and health care settings are likely to observe firsthand the consequences of macroeconomic trends that leave many of the nation's elders in poverty. In fact, inequality is increasing, a trend that has implications for low-income elders.

Measuring Economic Hardship

The federal poverty threshold, also called the poverty level, is the nation's most well-known measure of economic hardship. It was developed in 1964 by Mollie Orshansky of the Social Security Administration to support Lyndon Johnson's War on Poverty. The poverty threshold was based on the "economy food plan," the least expensive of four food plans devised in 1961 by the U.S. Department of Agriculture. This plan estimated the cost of maintaining a minimally adequate diet during a temporary financial setback. To establish the poverty threshold Orshansky set the ratio of food expense to total income at one-third. So, for a given household size, the poverty threshold was three times the cost of eating according to the economy food plan.

Initially, poverty levels for female-headed households, rural households, and households headed by the elderly were lower than those for the rest of the population. In the case of female-headed and elder-headed households, this has been attributed to lower caloric requirements. Women and the elderly do not require as many calories as the general population. Rural households were expected to derive some of their food from home gardens. Over the years the thresholds for both rural and female-headed households were raised to equal the general poverty threshold. This did not happen for households headed by elders. Asked why this was the case, a poverty historian replied that no organized constituency advocates for the needs of low-income elders. (See G. M. Fisher, 1992, for background on the development of the federal poverty threshold.)

As a result the poverty level for the elderly is 8% to 10% lower than the rate for the population younger than sixty-five. In 2003 the poverty threshold for a sixty-four-year-old living alone was $9,573 per year, while the threshold for a sixty-five-year-old living alone was $8,825, a difference of 7.8%. Of course, elders generally do require fewer calories than young adults. Nonetheless, a large body of nutritional research since the 1960s has established that their nutrient requirements are comparable, and some senior citizens have greater nutritional requirements than the young.[1]

Although the poverty threshold is an administratively convenient number, even Orshansky acknowledged that the federal poverty threshold is flawed as a measure of economic deprivation (Orshansky, 1988). Binstock describes the thresholds as "little more than politically and administratively constructed frames of reference" (1986, p. 60). He suggests that valid measures of hardship in old age would incorporate household expenditure patterns as well as the ability to cope with hardship. Expenditure patterns of low-income households reveal the sacrifices involved in making do with insufficient income—impossible tradeoffs as people give up food or medications to pay the rent and avoid homelessness (Barusch, 1994; F. L. Cook and Kramek, 1986). Further, there is some evidence that older people may have greater difficulty coping with economic deprivation than young adults (Binstock, 1986).

Radner (1992) suggests that uncertainty is an important aspect of hardship. Inflation and medical expenses represent important threats to the economic security of the elderly (see chapter 14). Public assistance programs provide a vital safety net for some. But, as Holden and Smeeding (1990) point out, households whose

---

1. The Census Bureau distinguishes the nutritional needs of old and young for statistical purposes, but the U.S. Department of Health and Human Services makes no such distinction in determining eligibility for its programs.

income is between the poverty level and twice that amount are more vulnerable to some economic risks than those with lower incomes. Such economic risks include lack of insurance for acute health care, lack of assets from which to draw when faced with long-term care needs, Social Security benefits high enough to make the household ineligible for Medicaid, high housing costs, and chronic disabilities. Based on census data, Holden and Smeeding concluded that 35% of older people face at least two of these risks. Further, they suggest that "tweeners" (individuals with incomes between 100% and 150% of the poverty threshold) experience even greater economic vulnerability than the poor because they often do not qualify for public assistance.

A final consideration in the measurement of poverty is the use of a "point in time" approach. Poverty measures based on a single moment in time do not provide insight into the extent to which a population has *ever* experienced economic deprivation. As anyone whose parents (or grandparents) lived through the Depression knows, economic deprivation can have a lasting influence on a person's sense of security, habits, and even physical health. A person's risk of poverty over a lifetime is much higher than the risk in any given year. Holden, Burkhauser, and Myers (1986) found that the risk of poverty during a ten-year period was twice as high for elderly couples as their peak poverty rate in any single year. For widows the risk was almost 30% higher than the highest rate in a single year. With any risk, a longer time frame means that more people are exposed. So measures that look at a single year underestimate the number of people who experience poverty over an extended period. For example, suppose that in 1995, 50% of older adults were poor and that 50% of older adults were again found to be poor the next year. The risk of poverty in those specific years was 50%. But in 1996 some of those who had been poor the previous year were not, and some who were not poor in 1995 became poor. Suppose half the 1996 poor were "new." That would mean that the proportion of elderly who experienced poverty during the two-year period of 1995–96 would have been 75% (50% in 1995, and another 25% in 1996). Holden and colleagues also found that only about 20% of the elderly poor had an income that was always below the poverty threshold. Most move back and forth from marginal status (slightly above poverty) to poverty status.

Who *Is* Poor in Old Age?

The link between poverty in old age and people's experience with oppression at younger ages becomes obvious upon consideration of which populations are at highest risk for poverty in the United States. Poverty rates also reveal that advanced age, as well as marital status, increase an individual's risk of poverty (see table 15.1).

TABLE 15.1   Poverty Rates by Age, Race, and Gender, 2000

			Race		
Gender/Age	White	White, Non-Hispanic	Black	Hispanic	Total
MALE					
65–74	6.3%	5.3%	13.3%	20.1%	7.0%
75+	6.7	6.3	22.4	13.1	8.2
FEMALE					
65–74	8.7	8.0	23.5	18.0	10.5
75+	12.9	12.4	29.1	21.8	14.0
BOTH					
65–74	7.6	6.8	19.4	18.9	8.9
75+	10.4	10.0	26.4	18.5	11.7

Source: U.S. Census Bureau, 2001a.

Among both men and women the unmarried have higher rates of poverty than those who are married.

Older Americans who are members of ethnic minority groups experience higher rates of poverty than whites. In 2000 African American elders had the highest risk of poverty, with a rate of 22.4%. This compares to 18.8% for older Hispanics and 8.8% for elderly whites who are not Hispanic. Women are also at higher risk for poverty. In 2000 older women of all races had a poverty rate of 12.2%, compared to 7.5% for older men (U.S. Census Bureau, 2001a). Across gender and racial groups the very old have higher rates of poverty than the "young old." As table 15.1 shows, very old African American women have the highest rates of poverty. The income received by 29.1% of these women—nearly 1 in 3—is below the federal poverty threshold. Their risk of poverty is *more than five times* that of younger white, non-Hispanic men.

As Barusch (2002) notes, the groups with the highest risk of poverty—minorities, women, and the very old—represent the fastest-growing subgroups of the elderly population in the United States. Since 1930 the population of Americans older than sixty-five has quadrupled, increasing by 414%. The fastest-growing subgroup within the elderly population is the very old. Since 1930 the number of Americans aged seventy-five or older has seen a sevenfold increase, growing by 733%. Other fast-growing groups include older Americans of color, whose numbers have seen a sixfold increase, or 624%, since 1930, and older women, whose numbers have increased by 506% during the same period (Barusch, 2002).

What Are the Consequences of Poverty for the Elderly?

Generalizing about individual responses to poverty is difficult. For some, late life poverty is just more of the same. These individuals, who have experienced lifelong poverty, often find that old age brings access to resources and programs that were not available to them when they were younger. They are eligible for senior housing, for example, and such services as senior centers and meals under the Older Americans Act. Becoming eligible for Supplemental Security Income—granted to the disabled, aged, and blind—can mean relief from a lifetime of struggling for money. Others find themselves in poverty during their later years as the result of specific events, such as a divorce, death, or illness. People with middle-class backgrounds often have more resources to draw on in their social support systems, so they are more likely to receive assistance from family and friends. They also tend to continue to view themselves as middle class but temporarily disadvantaged. Put simply, poverty means doing without. But most people who live in poverty do not let it affect their self-image. Few people with poverty-level incomes identify themselves as "poor" (Barusch, 1994, 1997).

In general, the poor have more functional limitations, poorer health outcomes, more mental health problems, and higher mortality than their more financially secure peers (Grundy and Sloggett, 2003; Lobmayer and Wilkinson, 2000; Porell and Miltiades, 2002). This is probably the result of many factors. Low-income elders report higher levels of lifetime exposure to environmental health hazards (Berney et al., 2000). Low-income neighborhoods are associated with higher rates of crime. Of course, access to health care, especially preventative care, is restricted for the disadvantaged. Finally, as many have noted, the stress of being poor in an affluent nation can take its toll.

TRENDS

Declining Poverty

In 2002, 3.6 million Americans aged sixty-five and older (10.4% of the senior population) had income below the federal poverty threshold. Included in that figure are 745,000 elders (2.2% of the over-sixty-five population of the United States) whose income is less than half the poverty level. Not included are 2.2 million seniors (6.5%) whose income falls 100% and 125% of the poverty threshold (Proctor and Dalaker, 2003).

These figures represent a decline since 1959 in both the number and the percentage of older Americans in poverty (1959 is the first year for which poverty

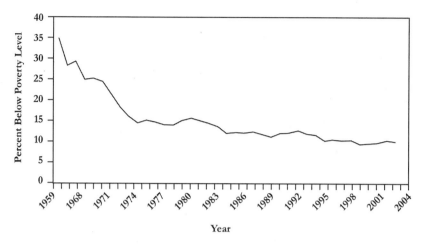

FIGURE 15.1 Historic Trends in Poverty Among American Elders, 1959–2001
Source: U.S. Census Bureau, 2002.

figures are available). According to the Census Bureau (2002), in 1959, 5.5 million older Americans had incomes that were below the poverty level, and they represented more than 1 in 3 (35.2%) of the nation's seniors, as figure 15.1 shows. Indeed, until the 1980s an older person in the United States had a significantly higher risk of poverty than a younger adult.

Rising Inequality

Although the number and proportion of older Americans living in poverty has diminished, the contrast between rich and poor has increased. Inequality in the United States is increasing. During the first two decades after World War II (1947 to 1968) inequality steadily declined (Weinberg, 1996). Americans of all economic classes saw their incomes rise. This ended during the 1970s, when a combination of economic stagnation and inflation began to erode wages. The 1970s and 1980s and, to a lesser extent, the 1990s were marked by a "pulling apart" of American income groups. The rich enjoyed greater income, whereas those with limited means experienced stagnant or declining incomes. For the general U.S. population inequality in household income increased from the early 1970s to the end of the 1990s (Gilbert and Kahl, 1992; Bernstein, McNichol, Mishel, and Zahradnik, 2000). This change was associated with a subtle shift in the nation's class structure, with more Americans finding themselves in high- or low-income groups and fewer in the middle-income category (Gilbert and Kahl, 1992).

A similar trend has been observed among the nation's elderly. Rubin, White-Means, and Daniel (2000) used census data to examine inequality among the elderly between 1967 and 1997. Their results suggest that the ten years between 1967 and 1977 were marked by a reduction in inequality among households headed by people who were sixty-five or older. This trend reversed itself, and between 1977 and 1997 inequality for this age group increased. This produced what these authors describe as "a declining ability of lower-income elderly persons to maintain their standard of living relative to the higher-income elderly" (Rubin et al., 2000, p. 29).

It is one thing to describe trends in inequality and quite another to explain them. Economists have identified several potential explanations. Some attribute rising inequality to economic trends, such as the loss of manufacturing jobs and the growth of high-tech jobs that require sophisticated skills and higher education; others note changes in social policy that have reduced the tax burden of the rich and diminished support for the poor. Still others suggest that immigration has increased the number of low-income Americans. Finally, observing that most studies use household rather than individual incomes to measure inequality, some note that increased numbers of single-parent and single-person households move significant numbers from middle-class to lower-class status (Ryscavage 1999).

Explanations of rising inequality among the elderly emphasize the competing roles of private pensions and Social Security. Private pensions duplicate the inequalities of the U.S. labor market. Those with good jobs during their working years have good pensions in old age, whereas those with less good jobs have little or no pension coverage. So private pensions maintain or increase inequality in later life. In contrast, the Social Security retirement system is designed to provide a better return to low-income workers. As we discussed in chapter 14, Social Security benefits provide greater earnings replacement at lower income levels. So in 2003 income of less than $606 per month was replaced at a 90% rate, whereas income of more than $7,250 per month was not replaced at all (see sidebar). Low-income workers receive proportionately more from Social Security than upper-income workers. Thus Social Security acts to decrease (but not eliminate) inequality in later years.

Is inequality itself a social problem? What difference does it make? Some argue that equality alone has no value. As Oliver Wendell Holmes said, "I have no respect for the passion of equality, which seems to me merely idealizing envy." Yet others suggest that extreme inequality jeopardizes the cohesiveness of society. A growing body of research has attempted to document the effects of inequality. International comparisons have suggested an association between inequality (usually measured as the proportion of a nation's gross national product that goes to

SOCIAL SECURITY REDUCES BUT DOES NOT ELIMINATE, ECONOMIC INEQUALITY

The Social Security system reduces inequality through its formula for replacing earnings, but it does not eliminate income differences between individuals. Consider the hypothetical cases of Mr. James and Ms. Morton. Mr. James spent his career as a midlevel manager at a major corporation, where Ms. Morton worked in the clerical pool. Neither married, so their benefits are based solely on their work histories. Ms. Morton's earnings averaged $23,000 per year, or $1,916 per month. As a corporate executive, Mr. James earned much more than she did. His salary averaged $80,000 per year, or $6,666 per month—more than three times Ms. Morton's earnings.

In 2003, when Ms. Morton and Mr. James both retired at sixty-five, the Social Security Administration used the following formula to compute their benefits:

90% replacement of earnings below $606 per month
35% replacement of earnings from $606 to $3,653
15% replacement of earnings from $3,653 to $7,250

Thus Mr. James's monthly Social Security check would be approximately $2,556 (90% of $606 = $545; 35% of $3,653 minus $606 = $1,066; and 15% of $6,666 minus $3,653 = $945). Ms. Morton would receive a monthly benefit of $1,004 (90% of 606 = $545 plus 35% of $1,916 minus $606 = $459).

Ms. Morton's monthly benefit of $1,004 is less than Mr. James's $2,556, but the difference between their Social Security benefits is not as great as the difference between the incomes they earned while working. Of course, benefit computations are more complex than this example. Nevertheless, this illustrates the way Social Security reduces, but does not eliminate, economic inequality.

the lowest 70% of the income distribution) and life expectancy at birth (O'Rand, 2001). Some international studies suggest that greater inequality is associated with higher mortality, particularly infant mortality (Lobmayer and Wilkinson, 2000). Similarly, studies within the United States have documented an association between inequality and such health measures as mortality and adverse birth outcomes. For a well-reasoned critique of these studies see Mellor and Milyo (2002).

Clearly, the interests of the rich diverge from those of the poor. It is difficult for those from affluent backgrounds to empathize with the disadvantaged. This is less so of members of the middle class, for whom poverty is only one job loss, divorce, or major illness away. So the erosion of the middle class can undermine public support for programs that provide relief for the needy. Thus rising inequality can make poverty more burdensome for those who experience it, even as their numbers are reduced.

PROGRAMS FOR LOW-INCOME ELDERS

Social Security as an Antipoverty Program

Social Security has been termed the nation's most effective antipoverty program. Its influence was demonstrated in an important study by the Center on Budget and Policy Priorities (Porter, Larin, and Primus, 1999). Researchers analyzed five years of census data (1993–97) to determine the number of elders in each state who would have been poor if they had not had Social Security benefits. The results showed that Social Security lowered the number of elders in poverty from 15.3 million to 3.8 million in 1997. Without Social Security nearly half (47.6%) of the U.S. elderly population would have been poor. The study also revealed that most (60%) of those lifted from poverty by Social Security were women. Because they live longer, the indexing of Social Security benefits to inflation is especially important to women. Further, women are more likely than men to rely exclusively on Social Security for their retirement income (see chapter 14).

Supplemental Security Income

The Supplemental Security Income (SSI) program was established in 1972 (and implemented in 1974) to provide a minimum guaranteed income to the elderly, the blind, and the disabled. SSI combined several state-administered, categorical programs (Aid to the Blind; Aid to the Disabled; and Old Age Assistance) into one. Eligibility is based on both categorical status (recipients must be either aged, blind, or disabled) and financial resources. The program is administered as a federal-state partnership. State agencies manage eligibility determination and may supplement SSI payments, and the Social Security Administration manages federal contributions and regulation of the program. Since its inception SSI has been remarkably unchanged, but it has seen enrollment growth since the mid-1980s (USGAO, 1995).

In 1990 the commissioner of Social Security appointed the SSI Modernization Panel to review the program and suggest modifications. Chaired by Dr. Arthur Flemming (a former Social Security commissioner), the panel undertook an exhaustive study of the program. Its report, released in 1992, identified major weaknesses in SSI and recommended a series of reforms. These included increasing benefits to 120% of the poverty threshold, adding staff to reduce delays in eligibility determination, eliminating the reduction in benefits for recipients who live with family members, and increasing the program's asset limits (Social Security Administration, 1992).

Although it largely ignored the recommendations of the SSI Modernization Panel, Congress revised SSI, along with other welfare programs, with the 1996 Personal Responsibility and Work Opportunity Reconciliation Act (PRWORA). Under this welfare reform legislation legal immigrants lost access to both SSI and food stamps unless they and/or their spouses had worked for ten years and had not received benefits. After the 1996 reforms took effect, an estimated 500,000 immigrants (more than half of whom were elderly) became ineligible for SSI. Another 940,000 immigrants (many of them elderly) lost their eligibility for food stamps (U.S. General Accounting Office, 1998).[2] The Balanced Budget Act of 1997 restored the SSI benefits for most of these immigrants, but this measure did not restore benefits for immigrants who arrived after August 1996.

Current Structure

SSI has a strict means test. Income must be less than the monthly benefit amount. In 2003 the federal share was $552 per month for individuals and $829 per month for couples. In-kind income, including food, clothing, or shelter (or "something" that can be exchanged for food, clothing, or shelter) is considered in determining eligibility. If an applicant lives with a family member who provides shelter and food, the applicant is eligible to receive only one-third of the federal SSI benefit. Individuals may not own assets worth more than $2,000; the assets ceiling for couples is $3,000. These asset limits have not been increased since 1984. Homes, adjoining land, household goods, and automobiles do not count as assets when calculating eligibility for SSI, but life insurance policies with a face value in excess of $1,500 per person do count (further information about SSI eligibility is available at the Social Security Administration's SSI home page, www.ssa.gov/notices/supplemental-security-income/).

Benefit levels vary from state to state. Although the federal monthly benefit is fixed, some states supplement this. The number of states providing a supplement has declined in recent decades. As of 2003, nine states (California, Hawaii, Nevada, Massachusetts, New Jersey, New York, Pennsylvania, Rhode Island, and Vermont) and the District of Columbia did so. With the federal benefit and state supplement, an elderly SSI recipient in California who lived alone would have received $757 per month, and a couple would have received $1,344 per month in 2003. If a person has income from working, the first $65 does not affect his or her SSI benefit level. Those who earn more than $65 will find their SSI benefit decreased by 50% of the earned income.

---

2. Although states were allowed to prohibit legal immigrants from participating in Medicaid, most have continued to provide Medicaid benefits to immigrants who were in the program before welfare reform as well as to new immigrants who have been in the United States for five years.

The SSI program, while "ideally suited to serve as a vehicle for reducing poverty among the elderly" (Zedlewski and Meyer, 1987, p. 14), fails to fulfill its promise for two reasons: nonparticipation and inadequate benefits. Only half the aged who are eligible for SSI benefits participate in the program (Zedlewski and Meyer, 1987). A 1979 study conducted by the Social Security Administration concluded that women were among those most likely to be nonparticipants (Menefee, Edwards, and Schieber, 1981). Concern about access problems led the U.S. Administration on Aging to fund an extensive outreach program from 1990 to 1997 to raise public awareness of the program and simplify the application process. The program helped identify processes that would simplify eligibility determination but had little effect on the operation of SSI. Another set of demonstration projects was funded in 2003 to focus on outreach to the homeless, according to J. Rosen (2004), director of Homelessness and Mental Health Volunteers of America.

Those who do participate in SSI find that the program's benefits are insufficient to raise recipients above the poverty level. For example, in 2003 an elderly individual living in a state that did not supplement SSI would have received $552 per month, for an annual income of $6,633. The federal poverty threshold for that person was $735 per month, $8,825 per year. M. Moon (1990) based her critique of SSI on this difference between benefit levels and the poverty threshold and further argues that the program is unfair to women. Benefits for couples are more generous than those for individuals. Individuals are most often women living alone, whereas couples invariably include men. In 2003 older individuals received an SSI benefit equal to 74% of the poverty threshold, but older couples received 82%.

Because SSI is means tested, a recipient's income cannot exceed the eligibility threshold. If an older person receives income from Social Security that is less than the SSI eligibility threshold, SSI payments will supplement that income to bring it up to the threshold. Because SSI eligibility standards have not changed over the years, while Social Security payments have increased annually, fewer people are "dually eligible."

Food Stamps

Congress established the food stamp program in 1964 when it enacted Public Law 88-525, the Food Stamp Act, which was superseded by the Food Stamp Act of 1977 and subsequent amendments. The program is operated by the U.S. Department of Agriculture and provides vouchers to eligible households for the purchase of food items. It was intended to reduce the effects of agricultural price supports on the needy and to enable the poor to have a nutritionally balanced diet. The costs of the program are borne primarily by the Agriculture Department, which covers 100% of benefit costs and 50% of administrative costs. Remaining administrative costs are borne by state and county governments, which are charged with administering the program.

Eligibility requirements are established at the federal level. Food stamp recipients must have incomes below the federal poverty threshold. Households may have as much as $2,000 in countable assets, such as a bank account. Homes and some vehicles are not countable assets. Households in which at least one person is older than sixty may have assets worth as much as $3,000 and retain their eligibility for food stamps (U.S. Department of Agriculture, 2004).

The food stamp program has been criticized for providing inadequate benefits. The minimum benefit is $10 per month, and advocates seek to raise that to $25 a month. The average monthly benefit for households headed by the elderly was $166 per month in 2000. For elders living alone the average was $44 (Food Research and Action Center, 2003).

In 1996 changes under the PRWORA reduced participation in the food stamp program. The Department of Agriculture reported that participation in January 1998 dropped to 20.3 million participants, a decline of 14% from the previous year. Approximately 6.73 million people have left the program since passage of the PRWORA. The act changed the food stamp program in several ways: it reduced the level of benefits, denied benefits to most legal immigrants, and created time limits for receipt of benefits by able-bodied adults without children.

In 2000 the Agriculture Department estimated that 1.48 million elderly (6% of all elderly households) in the United States did not have enough of the right kinds of foods to maintain their health (Nord and Andrews, 2002). Yet only a fraction (about 30 percent) of eligible seniors participate in the food stamp program. Nonparticipation has been attributed to the inadequacy of food stamp benefits, lack of information about the program, the difficulty of applying for benefits, and the stigma associated with public assistance.

Medicaid

In 1950 the first federal program of medical care for indigent Americans was established as a grant-in-aid program. Authorized by the Social Security Act Amendments of 1950, this program offered a federal match to states wishing to provide medical care to participants in other public assistance programs; however, not all states elected to participate.

In 1965 Medicaid was established under Title XIX of the Social Security Act. Like the original program of medical care for the indigent, Medicaid would operate as a federal-state partnership, with the federal match determined on the basis of poverty levels in the state. The Medicaid program was more generous than its predecessor. Nonetheless, it would be seventeen years before all states offered

Medicaid coverage. Arizona was the holdout, waiting until 1982 to participate in the program.

Unlike Medicare, Medicaid is means tested and serves clients of all ages. Although Medicare is overseen by the Social Security Administration, the direct administration of Medicaid is carried out by each state. The states vary in their eligibility requirements and in medical services covered, although some services are required by federal law. These include inpatient and outpatient hospital services; physician, midwife, and nurse-practitioner care; laboratory and X-ray services; nursing home and home health care; and rural health clinic services. States may provide additional services. These commonly include prescription drugs, clinic services, hearing aids, dental care, prosthetic devices, and long-term care for the mentally retarded.

Medicaid provides health care to millions of Americans. Eligibility requirements are both means tested and categorical. So, in addition to having limited income and assets, clients must belong to a covered group. These groups include children, pregnant women, the elderly, and people with disabilities. Eligibility requirements vary from state to state. Some states take advantage of the "medically needy option," to allow those who are in one of the groups covered by Medicaid to "spend down" and participate in the program. Under this option an individual with limited income and high medical expenses can become eligible for Medicaid after spending a given amount on medical expenses.

PRWORA denied Medicaid coverage (with the exception of emergency services) to some immigrants. In 2001 Medicaid enrolled an estimated 37.7 million Americans, of whom 4 million (10.6%) were elderly. Medical assistance payments that year totaled $216.1 billion, of which 26.5% was spent on elderly beneficiaries (U.S. Department of Health and Human Services, 2003b). Medicaid has been subjected to cost-containment measures that have reduced benefits, limited eligibility, and decreased the number of participating providers (for further details see chapter 16).

International Perspectives

Wide differences exist in the extent of both inequality and poverty, even among developed nations. Nearly all developed countries saw increased inequality during the 1980s, but the increases were greatest in the United States and Great Britain, and least in the nations of Scandinavia. Among the developed nations belonging to the Organization for Economic Cooperation and Development (OECD), the United States has high inequality, as well as high rates of poverty, among the elderly (Gottschalk and Smeeding, 1997). Indeed, when social assistance is taken into account, the United States has by far the highest rate of poverty among OECD nations (Smeeding, Rainwater, and Burtless, 2001).

The United States also fares poorly when compared to other nations on the proportion of elders in poverty. In a 1993 study of eight Western industrialized nations,[3] researchers found that "the United States has everywhere the highest elderly poverty rates of the countries studied" (Smeeding, Torrey, and Rainwater, 1993, p. 7).

Proposed Reforms

The declining poverty rates for elders shown in figure 15.1 make it tempting to conclude that the problem of poverty among the aged has been solved and that we need only allow the trend to continue. But demographic projections suggest that the answer may not be that simple. Because the fastest-growing groups in the U.S. elderly population (women, the very old, and minorities) are those most likely to experience poverty, we need structural changes in our retirement system or we may see a reversal in the nation's long trend of reduced poverty among the elderly.

One recurring theme in studies of poverty among the elderly is that in the United States single unmarried elders (most of them women) fare much worse than couples. Indeed, widows have been identified as a group left at high risk of poverty by the structure of the U.S. retirement system. Unmarried women make up almost 60% of the elderly poor, yet they represent only a third of the total elderly population (Hungerford, 2001). And, of course, the vast majority (80%) of unmarried women are widows. Some scholars who have examined this problem from a lifespan perspective have suggested that Social Security benefits be adjusted to increase income to survivors (most of them widows) and decrease the benefit for spouses. This would effectively transfer benefits from a time when a woman is at low risk for poverty (while she is living with a man) to a time of high poverty risk (when she is living alone) (Iams and Sandell, 1998; Social Security Advisory Council, 1997). Of course, as Hungerford (2001) observes, not all widows experience a drop in income with the loss of their husbands. But for the majority who do, reforms such as this might cushion the blow and reduce their risk of poverty in old age.

As the primary safety net for low-income elders, SSI is a natural target of reform efforts. The recommendations of the SSI Modernization Panel led to several

3. The countries were Canada, Australia, Sweden, France, Germany, the Netherlands, the United States, and the United Kingdom.

advocacy efforts, among them, proposals to raise benefits to the poverty threshold and suggestions that the asset limit for eligibility be increased. The Social Security Administration has initiated an SSI outreach program in an attempt to increase participation in the program.

From a more proactive position any reform that reduces the effects of discrimination and oppression will affect the distribution of poverty in old age. Today poverty is concentrated among the very old, women, and people of color—all populations that are subject to discrimination and devaluation. As educational and employment opportunities become more evenly distributed, we should find that the face of poverty in late life more closely mirrors that of the general aged population. While greater access to educational and employment opportunities may not reduce the overall risk of poverty, they may result in a more equitable distribution of that risk.

CASE 15.1

Sandra Hill was a spectacular preteen. She has dozens of photographs to prove it. She pranced through the halls of the school for "colored children" in the rural town of her birth, attracting nearly every eye in the place. But the school for "coloreds" stopped at the sixth grade. Black Americans who wanted more education had to go live with friends or relatives in the city, and she wasn't about to do that. At fourteen she met the love of her life—Jefferson Teemley. Seven years older, he had a good job at a gas station, he didn't drink or smoke, and he sang in the church choir.

Sandra Hill was married "before you could say 'boo!'" and five years later she and her husband were the proud parents of three children. They lived with her family through the Great Depression and had just moved into their own home when Jefferson went off to World War II and was killed. Ms. Teemley became a statistic: a black single mother with no visible means of support. She considered Aid to Dependent Children, but someone said the program didn't give assistance to black Americans. Luckily, she was able to find employment as a clerk in a nearby shipyard, and her parents took care of the children. At the end of World War II, when other women were urged to return home and be mothers, Ms. Teemley clung to her job until her employer told her he had to let her go. The men coming back from war needed those jobs. So Ms. Teemley became a maid in the home of white people who gave her their children's hand-me-down clothes and toys.

Of course, her employers did not pay Social Security tax, so Ms. Teemley never accumulated the credits necessary to receive benefits. Ms. Teemley was healthy and able to work until she reached sixty-three, when she suffered a

broken pelvis in an automobile accident that left her permanently and to-
tally disabled. Her profound disability made Ms. Teemley eligible for SSI,
which supports her today. At eighty-two she lives on $552 from SSI, $44 in
food stamps, and what she can scrape up from babysitting jobs.[4] She relies on
Medicaid to pay for her health care. Her home of fifty years is in a rundown
neighborhood, but she has friends nearby who look out for her. Her children
pay for her arthritis medicine when they can, which is not often. They are
struggling to meet the needs of growing families. Ms. Teemley would rather
do without than ask them for help.

Ms. Teemley's case manager recognizes that Ms. Teemley has led a charmed
life in many ways. She married the man of her dreams and has wonderful
children. She has lived to an age that she never expected to reach. Her parents
didn't live as long as she has, and many of her friends have passed on. Ms.
Teemley considers her long life as a blessing from God. This feeling is an important part of her self-image (Barusch, 1997). Based on her comprehensive
assessment of Ms. Teemley, the social worker is impressed with Ms. Teemley's
resilience. She nurtures her relationships, persists in finding work, and, despite her accident, expediently applied for SSI.

The social worker understands the many sociopolitical forces that, unfortunately, prevent Ms. Teemley from fully enjoying her later years. The many
years of economic disadvantage have accumulated and have led her into an
impoverished lifestyle, which many older single women inevitably confront.
Ms. Teemley illustrates what Tally and Kaplan (1956) first called "double
jeopardy." Her gender and race place her at an elevated risk of poverty. Like
nearly 1 in 3 (29%) African American women older than seventy-five, Ms.
Teemley lives on an income below the federal poverty threshold. Most elders
who are eligible for SSI do not participate in the program; some experts argue that this is the case because its benefits are so meager that it simply isn't
worth the time and energy required to establish eligibility. Families do what
they can to supplement meager federal benefits, and help with medications
is especially important, given their rising cost. If Ms. Teemley moved in with
her family, her SSI check would be reduced by a third. Technically, she is
required to report family assistance (and her babysitting money) as income.
If she did, her benefits would be reduced for every dollar she earned above
$65 per month.

4. Her SSI benefit represents the entire federal SSI contribution for seniors living in Georgia, which
does not provide a state supplement. The $44 in food stamps was the average benefit in 2003 for a
senior living alone.

The lower risk of poverty in old age represents a tremendous victory for U.S. social policy, brought about largely as a result of expanded Social Security coverage. Millions of seniors enjoy financial security that their predecessors could only imagine. Yet millions continue to live in poverty or near poverty during late life. For them poverty is not a call to arms. It just means doing without things that other people take for granted, like a safe neighborhood, adequate food, and life-saving medicine. Inequality has risen in the United States to an extent that is unprecedented, both in our nation's history and in comparison to other countries. Although the direct consequences of inequality are hard to document, it is safe to suggest that the growing ranks of billionaires have little in common with SSI recipients. Because the U.S. political system is increasingly controlled by the affluent, there is little reason to expect that anyone will pay serious attention to policies and programs that alleviate the harm done by poverty in later life. However, a safety net remains in place, and reform proposals are floated from time to time.

Discussion Questions

1. Social Security was established in 1935—why did it take until the 1980s for the poverty rate among the elderly to equal the rate for younger adults?

2. Why do you think that the poverty threshold for households headed by the elderly has never been adjusted, whereas that for farm households and women-headed households has?

3. What program changes would you recommend to increase enrollment of low-income elders in SSI?

4. What effect do you think the proposed privatization of Social Security could have on inequality among future generations of elders in the United States?

CHAPTER 16

Health Policies and Aging

B IOLOGICAL AND SOCIAL FACTORS interact in many ways, and access to health care often determines the outcome of these interactions. Unfortunately, health and economic inequities persist that adversely affect the lives of many older people. Chronic illnesses affect many older people today partly as a result of medical advances, such as vaccinations and antibiotics, that have made formerly acute and even fatal diseases manageable. As the population ages and people die more often from protracted, chronic illnesses than acute diseases, the need for end-of-life and long-term care will grow.

National health policies need to be reformed as the population changes. Medicare, which focuses more on acute than chronic illnesses, inadequately addresses the health and long-term care needs of most older adults, and Medicaid, the health insurance program for the poor, applies to only a segment of the population. Many older people also remain skeptical that their needs will be addressed by the recent extension of Medicare to cover prescription drugs—and of the cost to the nation of providing such coverage.

Social workers and other gerontology practitioners must understand how health policies do and do not address the health care needs of older people. In this chapter we focus on major public health policies, specifically, Medicare and Medicaid, but we also discuss relevant end-of-life care issues, including hospice, palliative care, and advance directives, that concern many older Americans. We illustrate the complexities inherent in our nation's health care system by presenting a case example about a family struggling to find proper medical care for their aging relative.

HEALTH STATUS OF THE ELDERLY

We tend to think of old age as a time of functional impairment and poor health. Normal biological aging is associated with physical changes that leave an individual more vulnerable to illness and accidents (see chapter 2). Yet only about a third of Americans aged sixty-five and older (34.5% of this group in 2001) have any kind of activity limitation because of chronic illness. When specific activities such as activities of daily living (ADLs) and instrumental activities of daily living (IADLs) are considered, the extent of limitations is even less. In 2001 only 6.4% of those aged sixty-five and older had an ADL limitation, whereas 12.6% had limitations with the more difficult IADLs

Activity limitations because of chronic diseases increase with age. In 1995 Trupin and Rice reported that 34% of Americans aged 65 to 74 have such limitations, compared to 45% of those 75 and older. The five most common chronic diseases among Americans aged 65 and older are arthritis, heart disease, cataracts, hearing impairment, and hypertension.

There is good evidence that Americans' "active life expectancy" is increasing. Between 1997 and 2001 the proportion of elders who experienced activity limitations declined. Table 16.1 shows this trend (see also Manton, Corder, and Stallard, 1993).

The health status of seniors varies. Although about a third of seniors have some kind of activity limitation because of a chronic condition, another third (38.7% in 2001) describe their health as "excellent" or "very good" (National Center for Health Statistics [NCHS], 2002). In any given year, about 1.5 million seniors live in nursing homes (NCHS, 2002). Yet each year more than 250,000 seniors participate in the Senior Olympics and National Senior Games, and thousands more compete in sports for adults of all ages.

INCREASING NEED FOR LONG-TERM CARE

Long-term care is generally defined in contrast to acute care. Where acute care is designed to cure short-term conditions, long-term care is designed to optimize functioning in the face of chronic illness. Today long-term care occurs in a vari-

TABLE 16.1 Trends in Activity Limitations Experienced
by Americans Aged Sixty-five and Older

	1997	*2001*
Any activity limitation due to chronic disease	38.7%	34.5%
IADL limitation	13.7%	12.6%
ADL limitation	6.7%	6.4%

Source: Centers for Disease Control, 2003, table 56, pp. 205–7.

ety of settings, including nursing homes, assisted living facilities, board-and-care homes, and private homes.

Simple demographics, along with developments in medical treatment, contribute to a dramatic increase in the need for long-term care. The oldest old (those 85 and older) have long been the nation's fastest-growing age group, and the proportion of any age group in need of long-term care increases with age. As Kunkel and Applebaum (1989) documented, roughly 4.2 of individuals aged 65 to 69 have a severe need for personal care. This compares to 23.7% of those aged 85 to 89 and more than half (52.2%) of those 95 and older. Even if the health status of future cohorts includes fewer activity limitations, improvements in medical care will allow growing numbers to reached advanced age—hence the indisputable prediction that the nation's health care system (like its family caregivers) will face increased demand for long-term care in coming decades.

Public Health Policies and the Elderly

In some respects the elderly are privileged by the U.S. health care system. They are the only age group in the country that has access to universal health insurance (through Medicare). And they are categorically eligible to receive Medicaid coverage in case of financial need. But the ageism that pervades other arenas of U.S. culture is also present in the nation's health care system. Medicare faces a fiscal crisis in coming years. Older adults who seek care may find increasingly limited choices of doctors as physicians opt out of Medicare. Further, seniors may not have access to life-saving treatment options that would be available to younger patients. Indeed, some critics have argued that seniors have a "duty to die" and get out of the way (Slater, 1984, p. 1).

The federal government was involved in health care before the establishment of Medicaid in 1964. The Hill-Burton Act of 1946 provided federal funding for hospital construction with the requirement that hospitals receiving these funds provide care to the indigent. Further, the 1950 amendments to the Social Security Act provided for limited federal participation in meeting the medical needs of public assistance recipients.

Through Medicaid "the poor were promised that they would soon have access to mainstream medical care and that health care was a basic right" (U.S. Congress, 1990, p. 7). Medicaid was set up as a federal-state partnership, primarily funded through federal dollars, with a matching requirement for the states. Administration was to be done by the states, with federal regulation and oversight. Medicaid programs do not provide health care directly. Instead, they reimburse providers for the cost of caring for low-income patients.

During Medicaid's first thirty years the population eligible for the program expanded. Initially, Medicaid was available only to recipients of public assistance. Later, Congress required the states to cover all pregnant women and infants living in households with income up to 185% of the poverty level, as well as low-income people with disabilities.

Partly as a result of this expanded beneficiary pool, the demands of the Medicaid program on state and federal budgets increased dramatically. Total expenditures more than doubled from 1988 to 1992. In 1992 Medicaid spent $88.6 billion to provide health care to 27 million low-income people. By 2001 the Congressional Budget Office (CBO, 2001) projected federal spending at $115 billion for that year. At the same time the matching funds for Medicaid consumed an ever-growing share of state budgets.

This growth in spending was not entirely because new groups were entering the beneficiary pool. As the Kaiser Commission on the Future of Medicaid (1993) argued, only one-third of the growth in cost stemmed from enrollment increases. Another third was attributed to medical price inflation and the remainder to state use of "Medicaid maximization strategies" designed to increase a state's haul of federal Medicaid dollars. For example, a state might transfer clients to Medicaid from state-funded programs for the medically indigent, effectively transferring a portion of the state's health care costs to the federal government.

Medicaid Cost Containment

Concern about rising Medicaid costs has fueled efforts at cost containment. Congress has made significant attempts since the mid-1980s to reduce costs—attempts that have accelerated in the economic downturn that began in 2001. Early efforts included adoption of a prospective payment system, reductions in payments to providers, eligibility restrictions, and managed care. More recently, states have reduced benefits and applied diverse measures to reduce Medicaid's prescription drug costs.

The Social Security Amendments of 1983 (P.L. 98-21) initiated the Hospital Prospective Payment System to reduce Medicaid expenses throughout the country. Instead of reimbursing hospitals for all reasonable costs, this system provides payment at a fixed rate based on the patient's diagnosis. Diagnosis related groups (DRGs) were established to determine the payment schedule. Under this system of prospective payment a hospital receives the same amount for every patient with a certain diagnosis, regardless of the services provided. While DRGs were designed to promote efficiency, their use has led to early hospital discharges. Patient advocates and service providers agree that the system has led hospitals to discharge patients "quicker and sicker," which places demands on families to provide care at home (Fischer and Eustis, 1989). In 1989 Congress extended the prospective payment system to physicians as well as hospitals.

Medicaid has also seen reductions in payments to providers. In 1990 Medicaid payments to physicians averaged 50% of their charges and 60% of the Medicare rate (Physician Payment Review Commission, 1991). The result of these cuts has been a drop in the number of physicians who are willing to serve Medicaid patients (Derlet and Kinser, 1994).

Transfer of Assets

Because Medicare's coverage of long-term care is extremely limited, Medicaid is becoming the de facto long-term care insurance for many of the nation's elders. Families anticipating nursing home placement have used a procedure commonly known as "transfer of assets" to make their relatives eligible for Medicaid coverage. Often they move a senior's estate into a "Medicaid qualifying trust," which was designed to hold the assets until the relative's death but keep them just inaccessible enough to make the grantor eligible for Medicaid.

Congress has enacted several reform measures to stymie this practice. The 1982 Tax Equity and Fiscal Responsibility Act allowed states to place liens on the property of Medicaid recipients unless the home was occupied by a spouse, a disabled or dependent child, or a sibling who had lived in the home for more than a year and had equity in it. Later, under the Medicare Catastrophic Care Act (MCCA) of 1988, institutionalized patients were deemed ineligible for Medicaid coverage if, within thirty months before applying for Medicaid, they disposed of assets for less than fair market value. This "look-back provision" did not apply to a house that was transferred to a spouse, a child younger than twenty-one, a disabled or blind adult child, an adult child who had lived in the house and cared for the patient for at least two years before the patient was institutionalized, or a sibling who had equity in the home and had lived in it for at least a year before the majority owner moved to a nursing home. If assets were transferred, Medicaid held up the applicant's eligibility for as long as thirty months or the amount of time it would have taken to "spend down" the assets in question. Exceptions were made for those who could prove that the assets were not transferred to secure Medicaid coverage.

Provisions that govern Medicaid eligibility today are substantially similar to those passed in 1988. The "look-back" period has been increased to thirty-six months. But if money was transferred into a trust, the period is sixty months. And the "penalty period"—the time during which Medicaid will not pay for care—now has no limit. Federal regulations do allow states to waive this penalty period if its imposition will cause "undue hardship."

Despite governmental efforts to restrict the use of Medicaid by the nonpoor, the practice of "elder law" continues, with many lawyers devoting their time to enabling members of the middle and upper classes to preserve their inheritance by putting their elderly relatives on Medicaid.

Medicare

Many of today's seniors remember a time when Americans did not have health insurance. Indeed, before World War II most people simply paid for their health care out of pocket. We knew a physician who enjoyed telling stories of the barter system used during the Depression, when his patients would bring live chickens and produce to exchange for his services. Of course, those who could not afford to pay for care were dependent on private charities for what care they did receive.

The United States saw a major expansion of employee benefits such as pensions and health insurance during the 1940s and 1950s. This was partially the result of laws that provided tax advantages to companies that established these benefits and partly the result of competition for labor. During this period growing numbers of American workers were covered by company-sponsored health insurance programs. But retired workers—the elderly—did not benefit from this expanded coverage. In 1963 only 56% of the nation's seniors had hospital insurance (U.S. Congress, 1990). For them Medicare would mark a revolutionary change in health care access.

Although Medicare was not established until 1964, discussion of national health insurance began as early as 1912, with a proposal by Theodore Roosevelt's Bull Moose Party. Indeed, during the 1930s, when the Social Security program was being developed, the possibility of establishing national health insurance was explored. Faced with vigorous opposition from medical professionals, President Franklin Delano Roosevelt concluded that national health insurance was too controversial and might scuttle the New Deal (Corning, 1969).

So it was not until 1964 that President Lyndon Johnson signed Title XVIII of the Social Security Act, establishing Medicare as a program of comprehensive health insurance for Americans who were eligible for Social Security retirement benefits. Medicare passed despite powerful resistance from the American Medical Association. The leadership of the AMA feared that Medicare was one step toward "socialized medicine," which many worried would allow government interference to mar the doctor-patient relationship.

The 1964 legislation established the basic structure of Medicare. The program has two parts: Part A and Part B. Known as "hospital insurance," Part A covers some hospital, skilled nursing home, and home health services, as well as hospice care. Part B is called "medical insurance." It partially pays for doctors, therapists, ambulance, and diagnostic services as well as prostheses, medical equipment, and some other medical services and supplies. Enrollment is handled through the Social Security Administration. Application for retirement benefits automatically triggers the Medicare application process. Part A (hospital) coverage is provided without charge. Unless the beneficiary instructs Social Security to do otherwise, she is automatically enrolled in Part B (outpatient) coverage, and the monthly premium is deducted from each Social Security check. Those who do not sign up for Part B when they enroll in Medicare may do so during a general enrollment period, held from January 1 through March 31 each year.

Financing for Medicare comes from three sources: a payroll tax, premiums paid by Medicare beneficiaries, and the general revenues of the United States. The Medicare payroll tax amounts to 2.9% of wages, with half paid by the employer and half by the worker. Unlike the payroll tax that finances Social Security retirement benefits, the Medicare tax is not subject to a wage cap but is applied to all wages. Part A (hospital insurance) and Part B (medical insurance) are financed differently. Part A is financed through the payroll tax, whereas Part B is funded through premiums and general revenues. Like Medicaid, Medicare is overseen at the federal level by the Centers for Medicare and Medicaid Services (formerly, the Health Care Financing Administration).

From its establishment to the 1980s Medicare saw steady expansion of benefits and improved quality control. The 1972 Social Security Amendments added coverage for people with disabilities and victims of end-stage renal disease. This legislation also established professional standards review organizations (PSROs) as a vehicle for quality control. Hospice coverage was added in the 1982 amendments to the Social Security Act, and PSROs were replaced with peer review organizations.

In 1988 Congress enacted the MCCA to establish increased benefits (including prescription drug coverage), financed through a surtax on enrollees whose incomes were high enough that they owed federal income tax. Those subject to the surtax complained bitterly, arguing that they were being asked to do something required of no other segment of the population: pay for the care of others in their age group. Most MCCA provisions were repealed in 1989 before they went into effect.

Since then the costs of Medicare have grown exponentially, fueling repeated efforts at cost containment. The Hospital Prospective Payment System, described earlier, was applied to Medicare as well as Medicaid, and DRGs became fixed parts of the landscape of health care for seniors. The system effectively reduced Medicare hospital expenditures and has since been applied to services provided by physicians and other health care providers (Physician Payment Review Commission, 1991).

Managed care was introduced to the Medicare program with the passage of the Balanced Budget Act of 1997. This measure initiated what some considered "the most significant changes in the Medicare program since the program's inception in 1965" (Longest, 2002, p. 386). Sometimes called the "Part C" of Medicare, the "Medicare + Choice" program was established to encourage Medicare recipients to enroll in managed care plans rather than the traditional Medicare program. Some of these plans promised to decrease seniors' out-of-pocket medical costs by providing prescription drug coverage and eliminating or reducing copayments and deductibles. These expanded benefits were supposed to be financed through the increased efficiency of managed care.

Under Medicare + Choice contracts managed care providers received a flat fee to serve a specific population. This gave managed care organizations (most of which were health maintenance organizations, or HMOs) an incentive to be efficient—to make sure that appropriate care is provided without unnecessary or duplicative services. Because they offer the prospect of better integration for chronic conditions, managed care organizations in theory had the potential to of-fer better care for seniors. Because they were not permitted to reject patients, these contracted managed care organizations might buffer seniors from the increasingly common experience of being turned down by physicians who no longer accept Medicare patients.

Medicare recipients responded favorably to this new program, and enrollment in the managed care plans rose steadily and rapidly, from one million in 1987 to more than six million in 1998. But increased enrollment in managed care did not translate into savings for the Medicare program. As researchers (Feder and Moon, 1998; Nichols, 1998) observed, the marketing departments of managed care orga-nizations were very successful at attracting relatively healthy Medicare clients and discouraging those with expensive health care needs.

But even with this "creaming" in effect, managed care organizations were un-able to collect enough to satisfy their business objectives. In the late 1990s Medi-care managed care organizations began to go under. At the end of 1998 about 440,000 elders in thirty states were dropped from Medicare health maintenance organizations. Many were forced to return to traditional Medicare with its hefty copayments and deductibles.

The Medicare + Choice program continues under the rubric of Medicare Ad-vantage, but its lessons are mixed. Indeed, as is becoming clear with the general U.S. population, the private health insurance market is probably unable to efficiently meet the health insurance needs of the elderly. As Feder and Moon point out:

On the one hand, Medicare's new process of choice can be regarded as fa-cilitating beneficiaries' ability to obtain a responsive health plan that, among other things, provides better coordination and perhaps more affordable care. On the other hand, choice in a competitive insurance market poses some significant risks. As a single insurance plan for most of the past thirty years, Medicare has avoided one of the most distressing features of competitive private health insurance markets: the segmentation of the healthy from the sick. When beneficiaries have a choice of plans, they will pay less if the plan they choose has more healthy than sick people. Similarly, insurers will profit more to the extent that their enrollees are healthy rather than sick. These incentives undermine the fundamental purpose of insurance—spreading the risk of illness—and concentrate the costs of illness on those most likely to experience it. Not only does this concentration serve as a disadvantage for the sick relative to the healthy, it may also serve as a disadvantage to the poor, relative to the better off. (1998, p. 8)

Medicare Prescription Coverage

The Medicare program has been criticized for years for failing to provide coverage for prescription medications. Since the development of Medicare, prescription medications have emerged as a dominant aspect of health care in the United States. Advocates of prescription coverage argue that today medications can prevent or delay the onset of conditions that would be extremely costly to treat. The nation's seniors and their physicians recognized the efficacy of the new generation of prescription medications, and as a result the elderly's out-of-pocket expenses for drugs became a significant proportion of their health care costs. Indeed, as some have noted, the proportion of income that seniors spent on out-of-pocket health care expenses reached and may have even exceeded the proportion that they paid before Medicare was developed. Clearly, demand for prescription coverage under Medicare was high, and in time various schemes were floated to provide and finance that coverage.

Meanwhile the cost of prescription medications in the United States was rising dramatically. Pharmaceutical companies argued that these price increases were necessary to support the lengthy and complex research and development process required to bring new drugs to market. Critics attributed the price increase at least in part to new advertising. In addition to adding to the drug companies' expenses, this advertising triggered increased demand (and hence increased prices) for medications. This is the direct result of a 1985 decision by the U.S. Food and Drug Administration to lift the ban on prescription drug advertising aimed at the general public. Canada still bans the practice, as do most European countries. In 2001 pharmaceutical manufacturers spent $19.1 billion on advertising (Kaiser Family Foundation, 2003).

Indeed, U.S. drug prices have increased at an especially high rate. As Families USA (2004) has reported, in 2003 the prices for the top thirty drugs used by seniors increased by 6.5%, or 4.3 times the rate of inflation. For the five-year period from 1995 to 2000, prices for the top fifty drugs rose 22% on average—roughly twice the general rate of inflation for the same period (Families USA, 2001).

Drug price increases have greater effects on seniors than on other groups. Although seniors represented just more than 13% of the population in 2002, they accounted for more than 34% of prescriptions and 42% of all drug spending (Families USA, 2001). The Congressional Budget Office estimated that outpatient prescription drug expenses for elders would average $2,439 per person in 2003 (CBO, 2002).

Unlike the United States, Canada regulates the prices charged for medications sold within its borders. Americans pay substantially more for medications than their northern neighbors. Canadian pharmacies have found a new market for their wares, offering an array of devices to allow Americans to purchase their drugs in Canada. These include online pharmacies and bus trips across the border. Congress enacted legislation to allow Americans to reimport prescription medications from Canada (because they were doing so anyway), but regulations were never issued because the Bush administration's Department of Health and Human Services refused to certify that any drug bought in Canada is safe and effective—a certification that is necessary before the agency can develop regulations to guide reimportation.

So, faced with increased prescription drug costs, seniors in the United States have pursued several alternatives: some purchase medications from Canadian pharmacies; some buy medications through programs such as that offered by AARP, which gives them a discount; some purchase insurance that includes prescription coverage; some pay out of pocket for the medications; and some just do without potentially life-saving drugs. Of course, many support the idea that Medicare should offer them prescription drug coverage.

The pharmaceutical industry has become a major source of funding for political campaigns. In 2000 U.S. Rep. Bernard Sanders, I-Vt., reported that campaign contributions by pharmaceutical companies increased by 57% between 1995 and 1999. Further, according to Public Citizen (2003), the national nonprofit public interest organization, pharmaceutical companies spent $91.4 million in 2002 on lobbying activities and employed 675 lobbyists. Of course, the U.S. pharmaceutical industry has been extremely profitable, with the top ten companies recording profits of $35.9 billion in 2002 (Public Citizen, 2003). In this context Congress undertook to develop a Medicare prescription drug benefit in 2003.

During the 2002 election cycle President George W. Bush announced that reforming Medicare would be a high priority for his administration. The Republican Party's leadership had begun drafting legislation to add prescription coverage, with an estimated price tag of $400 billion over ten years. Democrats criticized the legislation but offered little serious opposition. The Senate version of the bill— sponsored by Majority Leader Bill Frist, R-Tenn., and four cosponsors—passed with a narrow majority. At the same time a bill was working its way through the House, sponsored by Speaker Dennis Hastert, R-Ill., and twenty cosponsors. By July 2003 both houses had approved their bills, but negotiations to resolve the differences between House and Senate versions were lengthy and inconclusive. In November the AARP endorsed the legislation and began a $4 million advertising campaign on its behalf. With this pivotal endorsement the conference reached agreement, and the president signed the Medicare Prescription Drug, Improvement and Modernization Act on December 8, 2003.

As the law stands, Medicare beneficiaries may able to purchase a Medicare discount card that provides a reduction in the costs of medications. The law also established that prescription coverage under the voluntary program would begin on January 1, 2006, offered through private insurance companies with government subsidies. The benefit would include a $250 deductible, then would cover 25% of drug costs from $251 to $2,250 each year. Costs from $2,250 to $3,600 would not be covered, a gap that is known as the "doughnut hole." Medicare would cover 95% of annual drug costs in excess of $5,100. The program could establish a formulary, or list of approved drugs for specific conditions. Beneficiaries who bought drugs that were not on the formulary would find that these purchases would not count toward their deductible. Beneficiaries would, for the first time, receive differential treatment under Medicare based on their income. Traditionally, the program has treated all enrollees alike. Under the Medicare Modernization Act the premium for Part B will increase for upper-income beneficiaries. In addition, drug benefits for low-income seniors are structured to offer lower copayments and deductibles. These changes raise concern that means testing will turn Medicare, a universal insurance program, into a welfare program. Nonetheless, Medicare spending continues to be a significant public policy concern, and these changes may represent a cost-effective approach to helping those in need.

In addition to the prescription drug benefit, the law includes several lesser-known provisions. First, it would prohibit private insurance companies from writing new Medigap drug policies that would compete with the new Medicare program. Existing policies would be allowed to continue coverage. Second, many advocates argue that the law sets the stage for privatization of Medicare. It does this by requiring enrollees to purchase their drug benefit through private insurers and by supporting private managed care organizations through "comparative cost adjustment" demonstration programs. Finally, the law provides partial subsidies to companies that continue to offer prescription coverage to their retirees. Reactions to the legislation have been mixed, with some agreeing with Sen. Ted Kennedy, D-Mass., that it could destroy the forty-year-old Medicare program. Many fear that retirees who have coverage through their former employers will lose it, because the tax subsidy does not compensate firms for the entire cost of coverage. Others worry that the prohibition on competing drug coverage will restrict seniors' choices, as will the use of a Medicare formulary. Democrats worry that encouraging private insurance companies to compete with Medicare will undermine the program. Meanwhile, fiscal conservatives are wary of the $400 billion price tag that increases the nation's record debt. Democrats vowed to repeal the measure if they had prevailed in the 2004 elections. The AARP has been sharply criticized for its endorsement, with some noting that the organization derives nearly one-fourth of its income from sales of health insurance to its members. As a result, some argue, the AARP has a conflict of interest—on one hand charged with representing the interests of seniors and on the other drawing a profit from its insurance business. It is quite possible that this law will undergo revision before it takes effect in 2006. Indeed, in 2004 members of Congress submitted more than sixty bills to "fix" various aspects of the Medicare Modernization Act.

PUBLIC POLICY AND PRIVATE HEALTH COVERAGE

The U.S. health care system is a carefully balanced integration of private and public entities. The balance is susceptible to changing political and economic conditions, which determine the power and roles of government and private companies. Typically, private firms operate on a for-profit basis. Caregivers hired or reimbursed by these companies may experience tension between their obligation to help produce a profit and their mandate to provide care. Public policy regulates these companies in an attempt to protect consumers and ensure an acceptable level of care.

Traditionally, the state insurance commissioners have regulated the health insurance industry. The independence of state regulators is sometimes called into question when there is a revolving door between the state regulatory agency and executive jobs at insurance companies. In recent years the federal government has become more involved in regulating health insurance providers. Legislation such as the Health Insurance Portability and Accountability Act of 1996 and the Patients' Bill of Rights (should it ever pass) represent attempts by the federal government to ensure acceptable levels of patient care. Legislation such as the Medicare Prescription Drug, Improvement, and Modernization Act of 2003 provides government subsidies to encourage insurance companies to enter the Medicare market. Thus the U.S. government both regulates and supports private health insurance providers.

Private insurance companies offer coverage of two health risks of advanced age: the risk that arises from gaps in Medicare coverage and the risk of needing long-term care.

Medigap Insurance

In 2000 about 69% of people covered by Medicare had private insurance to supplement their Medicare benefits (Health Care Financing Administration, 2000). Most people with private coverage are middle- and upper-income elders. About half purchase individual policies, and half receive coverage as part of their retirement benefits. Nearly all these Medicare supplement policies are designed primarily to cover copayments and deductibles connected with the services that Medicare covers. They are of no help in paying for care that Medicare does not cover. Thus these policies typically do not include prescription drug and long-term care coverage.

Until 1989 the array of Medicare supplement policies (also known as "Medigap" policies) was confusing to most older adults. In 1989 Congress enacted legislation that standardized Medigap policies. Since 1992 insurers have been allowed to market only ten standard policies, ranging from the most basic coverage to policies that offer drug coverage. About 6% of Medigap policy holders have drug coverage (Chollet, 2001). According to an Internet search in 2003, these policies cost from $407 per year for the most basic coverage to a high of $5,005 per year for more comprehensive coverage.

Long-Term Care Insurance

Private insurance companies have been writing long-term care policies since 1982. Long-term care coverage is much less popular than health insurance but is growing in both availability and popularity. Government policy has contributed to that growth: the federal government and several states offer tax incentives to individuals who purchase long-term coverage. For example, some states exempt people with long-term care insurance from Medicaid spend-down provisions, making them immediately eligible for Medicaid coverage when their insurance benefits run out. The federal government offers limited tax deductions for the premiums for these policies.

In the early days of their development, long-term care policies were often problematic. Companies used deceptive sales tactics, and policies had small print that exempted major conditions like Alzheimer's from coverage. Partly as a result of government intervention, these sales practices have improved. And thanks in part to consumer education programs, fewer individuals are purchasing policies that do not meet their needs. Still, the development of long-term care insurance has been slowed by the perception that Medicaid coverage will be available to individuals who need long-term care. Nonetheless, as states restrict Medicaid coverage of nursing home care, and as providers refuse to accept Medicaid clients, the demand for private coverage of long-term care will increase.

END-OF-LIFE CARE

Although most Americans prefer to die at home, a majority die in hospitals. In 1998 the National Center for Health Statistics reported that 56% of deaths occur in acute care settings like hospitals and clinics. Another 19% occur at home, whereas 21% die in nursing homes (National Center for Health Statistics, 1998). Although it is still high, the percentage of deaths that occur in hospitals has decreased since 1980. Some attribute this to the establishment of Medicare's prospective payment system and use of DRGs (Sager, Easterling, Kindig, and Anderson, 1989). Yet others acknowledge that without community-based services, such as those provided under hospice, fewer people would be dying at home (Tolle, Rosenfeld, Tilden, and Park, 1999). In both cases public policy decisions were instrumental in the care of the dying.

The Hospice Movement

The last three decades of the twentieth century saw an evolution in the care of the dying, with the hospice movement front and center. The first well-known hospice, St. Christopher's, was established in London in 1967 under the direction of Dr. Cicely Saunders. The primary goal at St. Christopher's was to keep the dying patient free of pain and any memory or fear of pain. In addition, the staff offered comfort and companionship to the families. Families, including children, were free to visit at any time (except Mondays, when family members were given a day off and did not have to feel guilty about not visiting), and the staff encouraged families to help with the patient's care. Patients often went back and forth between the hospice and home. The median length of stay at St. Christopher's was two to three weeks. About half the patients returned home to die after a ten-day stay with the hospice staff (Saunders, 1976).

Interest in the hospice movement has grown steadily in the United States. In 1977 the country had about 50 hospices in various stages of development. By 2001 the National Hospice and Palliative Care Organization (2003) estimated that thirty-two hundred hospices were operating in the United States and its territories, serving approximately 775,000 patients and their families.

Hospices do not all follow the model of St. Christopher's. Davidson (1979) identified four basic models: hospital based, home care, free standing, and self-help. Hospital-based hospices operate under the auspices of a traditional acute care facility, and some struggle with the conflict between the pain management objectives of hospice and the treatment objectives of a hospital. Home care models offer staff and volunteer support to those caring for a dying person in their home. These hospices lack the facilities and physical structure of the hospital but generally enjoy greater autonomy. Free-standing hospice facilities usually offer both inpatient and home-based care. The inpatient care is provided in a more homelike environment than is usually found in a hospital or nursing home. Some hospices of this type operate in conjunction with nursing homes. The fourth hospice model is based on a self-help philosophy, with volunteers and lay counselors providing services at modest cost. These models have not yet been systematically evaluated.

Studies that have compared hospice patients with other terminally ill people have found hospice patients to be more mobile, to rate their pain as less severe, and to see their physicians and nurses as more accessible. Spouses of hospice patients were also less anxious and spent more time visiting than spouses of other terminally ill patients (Parkes, 1975). More recently, Mor and Masterson-Allen (1987) reported results of an extensive literature review on hospice outcomes. They found that symptom control and emotional support provided by hospices were comparable or superior to those offered in hospitals and that the cost of hospice care, especially if delivered in the home, was less.

The hospice movement got a boost with the 1982 passage of the Tax Equity and Fiscal Responsibility Act, or TEFRA (P.L. 97-248). This legislation added hospice to the benefits covered by Medicare. This extended hospice coverage to everyone who is eligible for Medicare Part A coverage and has a life expectancy of six months or less. Of course, the prospective payment system applies to hospice care, so hospice facilities receive a fixed daily rate regardless of what services they deliver. There was some concern that this could spawn a new generation of hospice facilities less committed to total patient care and more interested in maximizing revenues. Indeed, Levy (1989) suggests that the very institutionalization of hospice care through Medicare could be the downfall of the movement, which has been characterized by efforts outside the medical establishment.

Advance Directives

Today many elders use advance directives to express their preference regarding medical treatment in the event that they become incapacitated. The two approaches most commonly used are a living will (see figure 16.1) and a durable power of attorney. A living will is designed to provide specific requests about medical procedures that a person may or may not want if he becomes incapacitated. A durable power of attorney is used to designate a legal representative for the purpose of directing medical care if a person is unable to express her wishes. Unlike a "simple" power of attorney, the durable power of attorney remains in effect if its executor becomes incompetent or disabled.

All states now recognize the living will as providing legally enforceable instructions regarding medical care. Indeed, the Patient Self-Determination Act of 1990 (P.L. 101-508) requires health care institutions participating in Medicare and Medicaid to provide their patients with written information regarding living wills. These institutions must ask whether patients have an advance medical directive and document the reply in their medical records. Those interested in preparing a living will can find useful information through the U.S. Living Will Registry at www.uslivingwillregistry.com.

Cost Containment and End-of-Life Care

End-of-life care is expensive, so it has been a natural target for measures designed to control Medicare costs. Some cheerful irony lies in the observation that cost-containment measures may have had the secondary effect of improving end-of-life care. Yet financial pressures could undermine the successes of the hospice movement. DRGs were established to control health care costs under Medicare by setting a fixed fee schedule for patients with a given diagnosis, regardless of services delivered. The intent was to introduce an incentive to hospitals to minimize the use of procedures that were not medically necessary. And, as we have discussed, the system has reduced hospital costs under Medicare. Because patients are discharged from the hospital earlier, they receive more of their care at home and in subacute facilities. For many this means that they will die at home rather than in a hospital (Sager et al., 1989).

On the other hand, Medicare coverage for hospice care operates under a prospective payment system. Hospice providers receive a fixed amount for each day that they provide care to a dying patient, regardless of the services provided. There is some concern that the incentives introduced by this system will weaken the commitment to care that has marked the hospice movement to date.

Physician-Assisted Suicide

As we discussed in chapter 7, older people (particularly older white men) have the highest rate of suicide of any group in the United States. Indeed, for most subgroups of the U.S. population the risk of suicide increases with age. This is largely attributed to the increased risk of terminal illness among the nation's elders. While

I, _____, recognize that the best health care is based upon a partnership of trust and communication with my physician. My physician and I will make health care decisions together as long as I am of sound mind and able to make my wishes known. If there comes a time that I am unable to make medical decisions about myself because of illness or injury, I direct that the following treatment preferences be honored:

If, in the judgment of my physician, I am suffering with a terminal condition from which I am expected to die within six months, even with available life-sustaining treatment provided in accordance with prevailing standards of medical care:

___I request that all treatments other than those needed to keep me comfortable be discontinued or withheld and my physician allow me to die as gently as possible; OR

___I request that I be kept alive in this terminal condition using available life-sustaining treatment. (THIS SELECTION DOES NOT APPLY TO HOSPICE CARE.)

If, in the judgment of my physician, I am suffering with an irreversible condition so that I cannot care for myself or make decisions for myself and am expected to die without life-sustaining treatment provided in accordance with prevailing standards of care:

___I request that all treatments other than those needed to keep me comfortable be discontinued or withheld and my physician allow me to die as gently as possible OR

___I request that I be kept alive in this irreversible condition using available life-sustaining treatment (THIS SELECTION DOES NOT APPLY TO HOSPICE CARE.)

Additional requests: (After discussion with your physician, you may wish to consider listing particular treatments in this space that you do or do not want in specific circumstances, such as artificial nutrition and fluids, intravenous antibiotics, etc. Be sure to state whether you do or do not want a particular treatment.)

_____

After signing this directive, if my representative or I elect hospice care, I understand and agree that only those treatments needed to keep me comfortable would be provided and I would not be given available life-sustaining treatments.

Note: This form is not a complete legal document and is presented for illustrative purposes only.
Source: Alderman, n.d.

FIGURE 16.1 Living Will Form

teenage suicides generate hue and cry for prevention programs, most of us are complacent when we learn that a terminally ill older person chose to commit suicide. We are less complacent, however, at the prospect that an older adult who is in unbearable pain might seek a physician's assistance to die. This process, known as physician-assisted suicide, has been the focus of tremendous controversy.

Dr. Jack Kevorkian, a retired pathologist in Michigan, did more than anyone to bring physician-assisted suicide to public attention. Before his 1999 second-degree murder conviction for his involvement in the death of fifty-two-year-old Thomas Youk, Kevorkian acknowledged that he had assisted in the suicides of at least ninety-two people.

Several organizations are working to secure legal protection for physicians who help patients commit suicide.[1] Proponents offer several arguments. First, they suggest that when the suffering associated with terminal illness is unbearable and cannot be relieved, it strips the patient of dignity and deprive his life of meaning. Second, proponents note that physicians are already helping patients to commit suicide by allowing them access to overdoses of medication and that decriminalizing the actions of these physicians would open them to public scrutiny and ensure that decisions are made in a balanced way that protects the rights of the terminally ill. Finally, proponents note that a nation such as the United States, which places high value on individual dignity, should not deprive terminally ill people of assistance in ending their lives. (See Orentlicher, 1996, for a detailed review of the legal aspects of these arguments.)

Opponents of assisted suicide argue that it is the duty of medical practitioners to relieve the suffering of the terminally ill.[2] If physicians have an "easy out" in assisted suicide, they will not make the heroic efforts necessary to relieve pain. Second, opponents suggest that assisted suicide is one step down a "slippery slope" that could lead to euthanasia of undesirable or disabled people. Finally, opponents argue that a terminally ill patient who is in unremitting pain is not competent to make an informed decision regarding the value or meaning of her life.

In November 1994 Oregon voters made theirs the first state in the nation to legalize physician-assisted suicide, passing Measure 16 by a slim margin (51%–49%). The new law was immediately challenged, and a federal district judge issued a permanent injunction barring the measure from taking effect. In 1997 the U.S. Court of Appeals for the Ninth Circuit reversed this ruling. The same year the Supreme Court refused to review the case. In 2000 U.S. Attorney General John

1. Groups that support assisted suicide include Americans for Death with Dignity, Choice in Dying, Death with Dignity, and the Euthanasia Research and Guidance Organization.
2. Those opposed to assisted suicide include the Roman Catholic Church, Not Dead Yet, the International Anti-Euthanasia Task Force, and American Disabled for Attendant Programs Today.

Ashcroft announced his intention to revoke the licenses of physicians who assist in suicides. Oregon filed suit against this action in federal court. A judge ruled that the Death with Dignity Act would remain in effect until the case, *Oregon v. Ashcroft*, was decided.

Under the provisions of the act an adult resident of Oregon whose terminal illness has been confirmed by two physicians may make a written request for medication that can be used to commit suicide. The request must include the signatures of two witnesses who verify that it was made voluntarily. One witness must be a nonrelative who will not be affected by the patient's death. The law requires that the attending physician inform the patient of the probable effect of the medication, as well as treatment alternatives, including comfort care, hospice, and pain control. The measure requires that counseling be offered to patients who appear to be suffering from a psychiatric or psychological disorder. A consulting physician must review the patient's records and confirm in writing both the terminal diagnosis and the patient's ability to make an informed decision. The law also requires a waiting period of fifteen days between the patient's first request and the delivery of a written prescription. It also requires that specific documents be maintained by the physician and reports of all lethal prescriptions delivered to the health department. The Oregon Health Department issues annual reports on the Death with Dignity Act. In 1998 sixteen people used medication prescribed under the law to end their lives. In 2003 forty-two people did so (Oregon Department of Human Services, 2004).

CASE 16.1

When Winston Carpenter was forty-five, he learned that he had dangerously high cholesterol. This shouldn't have been much of a surprise, because both of his brothers suffer from the condition and are devoted consumers of the statin drugs designed to control it. Neither Winston nor his brothers considered the probable source of their condition. Indeed, they were surprised when their sixty-eight-year-old mother had her first heart attack. Never a fan of doctors, Martha Carpenter had no idea how clogged her veins were until she was gardening one day and suddenly felt like she'd been hit in the chest with a baseball bat. Mrs. C., as everyone called her, dialed "911" on her cell phone and was rushed to the emergency room; doctors performed bypass surgery later that day. Her sons flew to Cincinnati from both coasts to hover over her bed and cluck at her resistance to medical care.

Winston and his brothers had left by the time their mother received the first set of bills from the hospital. Medicare didn't *quite* cover all the costs of her care, and Mrs. C. was going to have a hard time paying her share from what had once seemed like a comfortable income. The doctors had prescribed a whole set of medications—some to control pain, some to thin her blood, some to lower her cholesterol. It was a dizzying and expensive array, and Mrs. C. decided to buy some, but not all, of the pills. She found that they lasted longer if she split the dose in half, and the effect seemed about the same. She got along fine for the next year, and her sons commented to friends that bypass surgery was becoming as common as appendectomies. Winston nagged her about exercising and keeping her cholesterol down, and his mother blithely lied to keep him off her back.

No one was prepared for the stroke five years later that ended Mrs. C.'s independence. Despite months in rehabilitation she never did regain her mobility, and her sons reluctantly concluded that she was not going to be able to return home. Winston flew to Cincinnati to handle arrangements. Going through his mother's mail, he confronted the reality of Medicare's limitations for the first time. His mother had no supplemental insurance, let alone long-term care insurance. Between the hospital and the rehab center Winston was looking at thousands of dollars in bills. On his mother's income it would take years to pay them all. And she still needed care. She had exhausted her Medicare coverage for rehab and was urged to transfer to a skilled nursing facility.

In a hastily arranged conference call Winston and his brothers discussed the possibility of selling the family home and cashing in the stocks and bonds that their father had left in trust. Before doing that they agreed that they needed professional help. A friend recommended an "elder law" specialist in town, and Winston went to see her. The lawyer explained that the family could preserve some of Mrs. C.'s assets by immediately transferring them to her sons. After a three-year waiting period she could be eligible for Medicaid coverage, which would pay for her nursing home stay. Winston and his brothers promised their mother that they would not sell the family home, and they agreed to pay for her care during the waiting period. It would represent a hardship for all of them but would preserve their inheritance.

Winston went shopping for a nursing home that would take his mother. She was a "private pay" patient, so most places he visited would take her. Many had rooms available and would be delighted to have her. But when Winston looked at the costs, he gagged. He couldn't imagine spending $5,000 per month for her care. Surely, he could do better. But the less expensive assisted living facilities would not accept residents with severe mobility restrictions, and the nursing homes that charged less were simply unacceptable. Winston decided to take his mother into his home. After all, he was single, and how much care could she need, anyway?

The rehab center discharged his mother into his care, and Winston rented the equipment that he would need to keep her comfortable: a hospital bed, a bedside commode, a walker, and some odds and ends. He even found a nice older woman to sit with his mother five days a week for $7.50 per hour. Surely, he had done the right thing. His mother enjoyed being in his home and actually seemed to improve for a while. But one day when he returned from work, Winston found the door unlocked and a note from the "elder sitter": "Have taken your mother to the General Hospital." She had had another stroke, and this time was near death. After another hurried conference call, Winston's brothers rushed to her side. She was clearly fading, and doctors gave her no more than a month to live.

After two days in intensive care, the hospital moved Mrs. C. out of intensive care and into a more general ward. Given her condition, her sons agreed to have a "do not resuscitate" (DNR) order placed in her chart. The next day, with all three of her sons in the room, Mrs. C. had a devastating seizure. Her body arched and her eyes bulged. Winston ran to the nurses' station and asked for help. Eventually, a nurse walked to the room. In an irritated tone she explained that Mrs. C. was "DNR," and the hospital staff could do nothing. Clearly, the hospital was not a good place for Mrs. C. to die. Winston decided to take her back to his home. The discharge specialist would make arrangements for hospice care.

Mrs. C. died five days later in Winston's home. She was seventy-four. Hospice workers managed her medications and catheter in those last days. A social worker and nurse visited daily, keeping tabs on both her condition and that of her primary caregiver, Winston. Winston was devastated by the loss but grateful that his mother had not suffered for a long time. He and his brothers were spared the pain and expense of a long nursing home stay, and some could use their inheritance to finance their children's college tuition.

Heart disease is the leading causes of death among people aged sixty-five and older in the United States, accounting for 33% of the deaths in this age group in 2000 (Anderson, 2002).[3] Advances in cardiac care have dramatically increased survival rates following a first heart attack. But they aren't inexpensive. Like Mrs. C., many Americans find the cost of life-saving health care beyond their means. Most, like her, do not carry long-term care insurance, and only 20.6% have private insurance to help to pay Medicare's deductibles and copayments (Centers for Disease Control, 2003, table 130).

---

3. The second leading cause of death among U.S. elders is cancer, which accounted for 22% of the deaths in this age group in 2000 (Anderson, 2002).

Indeed, the out-of-pocket expenses that seniors pay today are comparable to what they paid before the advent of Medicare. This is partly the result of reductions in coverage but primarily because of the rising cost of health care. And, as anyone who listens to the news these days knows, Medicare (still) pays minimally for prescription medications. Many elders adopt Mrs. C's strategies for reducing the cost of their drugs—ignoring some prescriptions and taking lower doses than their doctors order (a phenomenon that doctors call noncompliance).

Like Mrs. C., many find that their health expenses rise dramatically at the end of their lives. In her case tens of thousands of dollars were spent to give her another five years of life—most of which she enjoyed, though her final months were marked by pain and discomfort.

Mrs. C. was spared the need to rely on Medicaid for long-term care. But lacking a family member who is willing and able to provide care, many people spend their last months in a nursing home. Those who are provident make legal arrangements to transfer their assets, enabling them to use Medicaid to pay for their care. While this preserves the inheritance for their children, it certainly undermines the program's ability to meet its intended purpose—providing health care to the poor.

Mrs. C. was among a minority of Americans who was able to die at home. Although most Americans say that they would prefer to die at home, a majority of deaths still occurs in hospitals. The hospice movement has made great strides, both reducing the costs and improving the quality of care for the dying. With the advent of living wills growing numbers of seniors are able to prevent heroic, but ultimately futile, efforts to keep them alive by requesting DNR orders when they are terminally ill. Proponents of assisted suicide would go further, arguing that all Americans (not just residents of Oregon) should be able to request a physician's assistance to end their lives. Opponents have argued that this will result in lower quality of care for the dying, as health professionals give up on patients. Opponents note that patients with DNR orders receive less attention and care. This was certainly the case for Mrs. C.

Hope is central to the U.S. health care system and pivotal to American health policies. Old patients do not inspire hope. After all, "they're just going to die anyway." So a challenge for health care providers and health policy makers who serve the elderly is to recover their hope. Rather than hoping for an indefinitely prolonged existence, they might hope for a few good days—for the opportunity to say good-bye—for respite from chronic pain—or just for a delay in functional decline. When a patient or a population group is declared "beyond hope" or incapable of growth, the natural human reaction is abandonment. But as seniors have demonstrated time and again, hope springs eternal. The way Americans care for their elders, like the way they care for the dying, should reflect their hopes for this and future generations. Among its other gifts, the hospice movement is teaching Americans to approach end-of-life care with a hopeful perspective. May this perspective pervade the entire system designed to care for elders in their most vulnerable moments.

DISCUSSION QUESTIONS

1. How do you think the establishment of a single-payer health system would affect seniors in the United States? How would it affect insurance companies?

2. What is the appropriate role of government in the private health insurance market? Should it limit the ability of companies to draw a profit? Should it subsidize companies that are entering unpredictable markets? Should it protect consumers from unethical sales practices on the part of private firms?

3. If historic trends show improved functional status among the nation's elders, why do most experts agree that the demand for long-term care will increase? Are family members going to be called upon to meet that increased demand? What factors will facilitate and/or impede the family's ability to provide long-term care?

4. Select a piece of federal or state legislation that relates to private health care providers. What role of government does this law illustrate?

CHAPTER 17

Improving the Quality of Life: Social Services and Aging

GERONTOLOGICAL SOCIAL WORKERS most often help older adults by linking them to community services. The social worker linked Ms. D'Amico to a caregiver support group and respite services in case 3.1. In case 3.2 Mr. Paul needed transportation services. Social workers play a major role in the delivery of social services to the elderly, often serving as staff and administrators in public agencies. The profession's role here has proved important—improving, and even saving, the lives of many elders. Despite the importance of social services, they have consistently been underfunded. This leaves to social workers the difficult task of allocating scarce resources in the face of unmet needs. With this perspective in mind, in this chapter we focus on the role of the Older Americans' Act in meeting the service needs of the nation's elders, exploring the history, current structure, and tensions of its programs. We also briefly discuss private social service providers.

OLDER AMERICANS ACT

Congress passed the Older Americans Act in 1965, when the Vietnam War had not yet eclipsed the War on Poverty and widespread optimism generated a belief that all social problems could be solved—even the problems of age. In keeping with the times, the objectives of the law were lofty (see figure 17.1), and the services that it funded were universal—available to anyone aged sixty or older, regardless of income or assets.[1] The goals of the law present a compelling mandate for professionals who work with the elderly—one that would energize and organize efforts

---

1. The Social Services Block Grant is another source of limited funding for services to older Americans. Congress has provided significantly less money to the block grant program in recent years, so funding tends to be available only to those with very low incomes and multiple service needs (see www.acf.hhs. gov/programs/ocs/ssbg/ [January 27, 2005] for more information on the block grant program).

[I]n keeping with the traditional American concept of the inherent dignity of the individual … the older people of our Nation are entitled to, and it is the joint and several duty and responsibility of the governments of the United States, the several states and their political subdivisions, and of Indian tribes to assist our older people to secure equal opportunity to the full and free enjoyment of the following objectives:

(1) An adequate income in retirement in accordance with the American standard of living;

(2) The best possible physical and mental health which science can make available and without regard to economic status;

(3) Obtaining and maintaining suitable housing, independently selected, designed and located with reference to special needs and available at costs which older citizens can afford;

(4) Full restorative services for those who require institutional care, and a comprehensive array of community-based, long term care services adequate to appropriately sustain older people in their communities and in their homes, including support to family members and other persons providing voluntary care to older individuals needing long-term care services.

(5) Opportunity for employment with no discriminatory personnel practices because of age;

(6) Retirement in health, honor, dignity—after years of contribution to the economy;

(7) Participating in and contributing to meaningful activity within the widest range of civic, cultural, educational and training, and recreational opportunities;

(8) Efficient community services, including access to low-cost transportation, which provide a choice in supported living arrangements and social assistance in a coordinated manner and which are readily available when needed, with emphasis on maintaining a continuum of care for vulnerable older individuals;

(9) Immediate benefit from proven research knowledge, which can sustain and improve health and happiness;

(10) Freedom, independence, and the free exercise of individual initiative in planning and managing their own lives, full participation in the planning and operation of community-based services and programs provided for their benefit, and protection against abuse, neglect, and exploitation.

FIGURE 17.1   Older Americans Act of 1965: Declaration of Objectives

greatly in excess of the federal resources devoted to the cause. This is the fundamental paradox of the Older Americans Act—wonderful (if unachievable) goals and paltry resources.

Supporters of the measure argue that the federal appropriations have been, if not abundant, at least sufficient. They note that programs under the act were *designed* to involve national, state, and local governments and community providers. The federal money served as a catalyst, permitting the establishment of a network of planning and service agencies that would eventually blanket the entire country.

Critics emphasize the hopelessly ambitious goals of the law and the limited reach of its services. They suggest that the primary role of the law was symbolic—recognizing the needs and importance of senior citizens—and are pained by the failure of services to come within reach of the goals of the Older Americans Act.

History

The history of the Older Americans Act can be traced through shifting federal appropriation levels. R. B. Hudson (1994) identified three epochs in the funding of the act: the "near pittance period" (1966–71), the "extraordinary expansion period" (1972–81), and the "level funding" period (1982–90). We can add a fourth epoch to Hudson's typology, because the 1990s were a period of dramatic growth for programs under the Older Americans Act, which we discuss later in the chapter. Figure 17.2 illustrates historic trends in appropriations for the U.S. Administration on Aging, the agency created by the act.

During the "near pittance" period the agency's annual appropriation went from $545,000 to $33.6 million. In 1972 Congress brought the national senior nutrition program under the purview of the Administration on Aging, requiring additional appropriations and triggering what Hudson called the "extraordinary expansion"

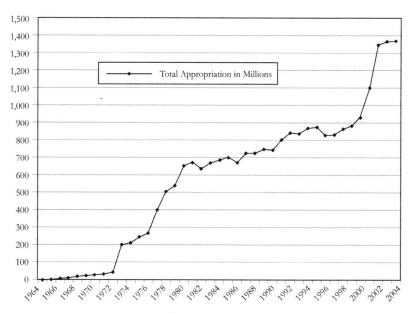

FIGURE 17.2 Appropriations for the Administration on Aging, 1964–2004
Source: Office of Budget and Finance, Administration on Aging.

period. By 1981 the agency's annual funding had grown more than twentyfold, to $675.9 million. This was astronomical growth, even in an era of high inflation. The Reagan era signaled an end to this growth, and in 1982 the appropriation for services to older Americans dropped for the first time in the agency's history. Eight years later, in 1990, the annual appropriation had increased by only 17%, to $747.7 million. Between 1990 and 2001 appropriations increased to $1.1 billion. The early Bush years saw continued growth in appropriations for senior services, because administration of the National Caregiver Support Program, with initial funding of $125 million, and of the Nutrition Services Incentive Program were handed to the Administration on Aging. The nutrition program rewards states that efficiently deliver nutritional services to the elderly. Because states could receive commodities in lieu of cash under this program, it was administered by the Department of Agriculture until 2004. The transfer brought an additional $150 million into the budget of the Administration on Aging. Funding for a fifth White House Conference on Aging also appeared in the 2004 budget for the agency.

Since its introduction, the Older Americans Act has been amended at least fourteen times. In 1972 Congress authorized grants for the development of congregate meal services. As Table 17.1 shows, congregate meals remain the largest single item in the Administration on Aging's budget.

TABLE 17.1   Appropriations Under the Older Americans Act

Activity	2001 Appropriation	2005 Budget Request
Congregate Meals	$378,356,000	$388,646,000
Home/Community-based Supportive Services (Senior Centers)	$325,027,000	$357,000,000
Home-delivered meals	$151,978,000	$180,985,000
National Family Caregiver Support	$124,981,000	$161,867,000
Nutrition Services Incentive Program	$150,000,000	$149,183,000
Grants to Indian Tribes	$23,457,000	$26,612,000
Preventive Health Services	$21,120,000	$21,919,000
Protection of Vulnerable Older Americans	$14,181,000	$18,559,000
Program Administration	$17,216,000	$18,482,000
Alzheimer's Disease Demonstration Grants	$8,962,000	$11,500,000
Aging Network Support Activities	$12,234,000	$13,373,000
White House Conference on Aging	NA	$4,558,000
Program Innovations	$25,430,000	$23,843,000
Total Discretionary Budget Authority	$1,252,942,000	$1,376,527,000

Source: Administration on Aging, 2004.

Congress amended the law again the next year to create a network of area agencies on aging, which were given major responsibility for planning, coordinating, and advocating for local programs that would benefit older people. These amendments also created special authorization for home-delivered meals and required states to set up nursing home ombudsman programs.

The 1978 amendments required that states "provide assurances that preference will be given to providing services to older individuals with the greatest economic or social need, with particular attention to low-income minority individuals." These amendments signaled a major shift in the focus of services under the law, from broad-based services that targeted the senior population as a whole to a more differentiated approach that directed services toward those with greatest need. This shift continued with the 1984 amendments, which clarified the definition of "low income" in relation to the federal poverty threshold. Finally, in both 1984 and 1987 Congress approved provisions that emphasized services to rural residents (R. B. Hudson, 1994).

Services for frail elders and their families were significantly expanded with the 2000 amendments to the Older Americans Act. These established the National Caregiver Support Program, designed to provide services to family members who are caring for frail elders. The program was initially funded with $125 million, allocated on the basis of the proportion of Americans older than seventy who live in each state. The law directs the states to provide information, assistance, counseling and training, respite, and supplemental services to family caregivers at all income levels, whether they are caring for older adults, grandchildren, or relatives with disabilities.

A comparison of the 1966 and 2003 appropriations under the Older Americans Act reveals the increasing complexity of programs that operate under it. The 1966 appropriations funded two categories: Title II, Grants for State and Community Programs on Aging, and Title IV, Training, Research and Discretionary Projects and Programs. Table 17.1 details the 2003 appropriations.

Current Structure

The Older Americans Act consists of seven titles:

Title I: Declaration of Objectives and Definitions
Title II: Establishment of the U.S. Administration on Aging
Title III: Provision of Grants to State and Community Programs on Aging
Title IV: Establishment of Training, Research, and Discretionary Projects
Title V: Establishment of Community Service Employment Program for Older
    Adults

Title VI: Provision of Grants for Native American Tribes
Title VII: Protection of the Rights of Vulnerable Elders

Today the network that serves senior citizens includes fifty-six state agencies on aging in the territories and states, along with 655 area agencies on aging. Generally, area agencies do not provide services directly. Instead, they contract with local agencies and organizations to deliver these services. Under the law states provide four basic types of social services: information and access services, community-based services, in-home services, and services designed to protect elders' rights. The availability of these services varies widely across the country. Typically, large cities offer a greater array of services, whereas those available in rural areas and small towns are more limited. In part these variations reflect the limited federal funding that has been provided for senior services. Area agencies have developed a diversified funding base, drawing from state and local government appropriations and raising money through grants from philanthropic organizations such as the United Way. Area agency services are probably more extensive in locations with the greatest capacity to supplement their federal funding.

Use of Services Under the Older Americans Act

The service network in the United States expanded greatly in the last decades of the twentieth century, largely because of the Older Americans Act. Yet only a few seniors use community-based services. In 1984 a special Supplement on Aging was added to the National Health Interview Survey conducted by the Census Bureau. This is the most recent, detailed look at service use by seniors throughout the country (National Center for Health Statistics, 1993).[2] The survey found that only 1 in 5 Americans older than sixty-five (21.5%) had used any community service in the previous year. The most widely used service was the senior center, which was accessed by 15.1% of respondents, followed by senior center meals (7.8%), special transportation services (4.3%), visiting nurses (2.9%), home-delivered meals (1.9%), home health aides(1.6%), and homemaker services (1.4%).

Four factors influence the use of services: predisposing factors, enabling factors, need factors, and barriers. Predisposing factors include personal and familial characteristics that make a person more (or less) likely to use formal services. Gender is one of these, as women are generally more likely than men to use a wide range of services. Enabling factors are characteristics of the environment that support

2. A second Supplement on Aging survey was conducted in 1994, but reports on use of community services are not yet available.

service use. The presence of a good transportation system, for example, might be an enabling factor. Need also determines service use. The 1984 survey found that those who lived alone were somewhat more likely than those who lived with others to use senior centers. That year, 20% of seniors who lived alone reported using centers, compared to 12% of those who lived with others. People who live alone are probably more likely to need the socialization offered by a senior center. At times, though, need may be less of a determinant of use than we might expect or hope. For example, sometimes an extremely frail person is unable to transport himself to a service location. Or a severely depressed person may lack the energy to call for help. Barriers to using these services can be either the absence of enabling factors (such as transportation) or characteristics of the service itself, include lengthy waiting lists, difficult eligibility determination, and insensitivity to minority cultures.

Information and Access Services

Information and access services educate older adults and help them get the help that they need. At a minimum these services usually include information and referral, outreach, and transportation. Some area agencies on aging also provide training on such topics as health insurance, caregiving, and retirement planning. Assessment and case management (sometimes known as "care management") may also be provided.

Information and referral services may be an older person's first contact with the social service system. Area agencies on aging deliver these programs in most areas. The U.S. Administration on Aging has established a website (www.eldercare.gov) and a toll-free number (1-800-677-1116) for use by anyone who wants to locate an area agency.

Outreach services seek out older people in need of services, who often become known to the program through relatives or neighbors. Outreach workers contact older people and refer them to appropriate agencies. Sometimes outreach workers make agency contacts on behalf of older people, helping them to apply for benefits like Medicaid, SSI, and food stamps.

Transportation services provided through area agencies are usually limited, offering rides to critical appointments such as medical exams or treatments. An older adult may receive a voucher to use a taxi or (in larger cities) the agency may dispatch specialized vans or buses.

Assessment and Case Management Services

Social workers frequently staff assessment and case management services. In this role they determine the resources, abilities, and needs of an older adult, then refer the person to the services he needs. The case manager may also monitor service delivery to ensure that what is provided meets the identified needs.

Case management is becoming recognized as an important professional subspecialty. In 1990 the Case Management Society of America (CMSA) was established to create standards for practice and provide training and support to case managers. CMSA has established a certification process and identified six essential activities of case management: assessment, coordination, planning, monitoring, implementation, and evaluation. (See www.cmsa.org for more information about this organization.)   .

Community-Based Services

Community-based services include a wide array of programs designed to enhance the older person's quality of life. Typically, these include employment services, senior centers, congregate meals, adult day services, and volunteer programs.

Employment services seek to connect older workers with jobs. Sometimes these services maintain a list of retired people who are available for short-term or part-time employment. These services may also sponsor "job clubs" where unemployed elders share information and social support in their job search. Assistance may also include skills assessment, job testing, and training.

Senior centers are located in most large communities and are usually operated by private nonprofit corporations. The typical senior center adopts a flexible program that offers congregate meals, recreational opportunities, health screenings, and a variety of educational programs. Membership tends to be drawn from a wide area rather than a single neighborhood. Those who participate in senior centers tend to be healthy and ambulatory. The National Institute for Senior Centers estimates that the United States has more than twelve thousand centers serving about ten million people (Beisgen and Kraitchman, 2003). The quality of facilities ranges from new, spacious buildings constructed for the purpose to shabby homes or storefronts converted for this use. Senior centers often serve as a focal point for the coordination of services to older people in a community.

Congregate meals programs bring older people to a central site for meals. In addition to nutritional support, these meals provide fellowship and an opportunity to learn about other programs. Many senior centers operate congregate meals programs. Congregate meals continue to be the largest single program in the Administration on Aging's budget, although some of the cost is defrayed through participant contributions.

Adult day services offer daytime programs for older people who are being cared for by their families but cannot be left alone. Services range from meals and custodial care to physical therapy, rehabilitation, and psychotherapy. Adult day services allow family caregivers to be employed while still assuming primary responsibility for the care of their loved ones.

Volunteer programs such as Foster Grandparents, the Retired Senior Volunteer Program (RSVP), and the Service Corps of Retired Executives (SCORE) offer opportunities for older adults to contribute to the community. The Foster Grandparent program is one of the oldest Administration on Aging services. Under this program elders provide important support to children in need. The RSVP program offers a variety of service opportunities to retired executives. SCORE enables retirees from careers in business to provide assistance and advice to owners of small businesses. Participation in these programs can improve morale, and perhaps even ward off depression, by enhancing the meaning and structure of the senior citizen's daily life (Freedman 1994; Morrow-Howell, Hinterlong, and Sherraden, 2001).

In-Home Services

Services delivered in the home typically focus on low-income seniors who are functionally impaired and isolated. In-home services include a wide range of programs designed to improve the quality of life and to prevent or delay the elder person's placement in an institution. These include Meals on Wheels, homemaker services, chore services, telephone reassurance, friendly visiting, energy assistance and weatherization, emergency response systems, home health services, personal care services, and respite care.

Meals on Wheels may be the best known of the in-home services. Volunteers or paid staff deliver meals to older people in their homes. Usually, the person who delivers the meals becomes an important social contact (sometimes the only contact) for an older person. The meals tend to be large, and many seniors find that they provide an entire day's nutrition.

Homemaker services provide household support to semi-independent older people living in their homes. In addition to the usual housekeeping chores such as cleaning, shopping, and laundry, some programs offer home maintenance and food preparation services. Homemaker services should be calibrated to a person's level of impairment. Highly impaired people may need a homemaker to come in daily, whereas others may need only occasional help with especially difficult tasks. Chore services include the less routine aspects of home maintenance, such as minor repairs, yard work, and cleaning the gutters.

Telephone reassurance services give isolated older people a point of contact and a sense of continuity. In an ideal phone reassurance program the people working the phones are trained in referral and know the older person through regular telephone visits. Regular calls assure older people that someone cares and will be checking on them. Volunteers often provide these services, which are especially helpful in rural areas. Another program, known as friendly visiting, is also frequently staffed by volunteers, who regularly stop in at an older person's home to socialize and check up on the client.

Energy assistance and weatherization are usually available on a limited basis to elders with low income. Money is provided to help pay their energy bills, and in some cases the program pays for the installation of energy-efficient modifications, such as attic insulation to cut energy usage.

Emergency response systems usually involve an electrical device that the senior can use to notify a central location in the event of an emergency.

A health professional often delivers home health services to the home and may help with such tasks as medication monitoring, physical therapy, skilled nursing care, and training caregivers.

Personal care services usually do not require a professional. A staff member of the agency on aging helps with personal care tasks such as bathing, dressing, eating, and walking.

Respite care provides temporary personal and nursing care to disabled elders. The purpose of the care is to provide relief to informal caregivers. Respite programs are designed to prevent caregiver burnout and allow impaired older people to remain in the community as long as possible.

Services to Protect Elders' Rights

Services designed to protect elders' rights tend to focus on assisting frail, vulnerable older people. These include nursing home ombudsman programs, elder abuse programs, and legal services.

Nursing home ombudsmen monitor care in nursing homes, investigate complaints from residents or family members, and serve as advocates for the rights of nursing home residents (Nelson, Huber, and Walter, 1995). Ombudspersons also create and maintain communication links between residents, nursing home administrators and staff, and nursing home regulators.

Elder abuse programs, often known as "adult protective services," are generally designed to prevent the abuse and neglect of older people—usually by family members. Although only about 3% of elders are believed to experience abuse or neglect, this small percentage represents nearly one million elders. See chapter 10 for the detailed discussion of elder abuse. Most programs use interdisciplinary teams, interagency cooperation, advocacy programs, victim support groups, and in-service training. All states require that those professionals who become aware of the abuse or neglect of an older or disabled person report this to state authorities.

Legal services can include a range of activities, from routine preparation of a will to guardianship or conservatorship, in which a professional takes responsibility for older people who can no longer be responsible for themselves.

Tensions in Older Americans Act Programs

Given the ambitious goals of the Older Americans Act, its programs have consistently been underfunded. Indeed, the 2003 appropriation for services under the law amounted to less than $30 for every potentially eligible American (those aged sixty or older). Clearly, it is impossible for services mandated by the law to meet the needs of *every* older American. The challenge for program administrators and managers is to allocate these funds in a way that optimizes their effect. Over the years this has translated into a focus on specific needy populations, such as elders with low income, elderly members of minority groups, elders living in rural settings, and the very frail.

This creates a new tension for the program. Vulnerable seniors are unlikely to vote, let alone advocate for increasing program budgets when they are under review. The popularity of these elder services has been linked to their capacity to reach mainstream, middle-class seniors—AARP members, who are able to make their voices heard in the political process. An old aphorism holds that services for the poor quickly become poor services. An ongoing challenge for the administrators and staffs of programs funded under the Older Americans Act will be ensuring that the constituents of their programs have the political clout to fight for them, even as these programs target the populations with the greatest need.

Another tension that affects elder services relates to the increasing demands for "cost effectiveness." Those who look at services from the perspective of cost effectiveness regard public social services as an "investment" that they believe should provide a reliable (and measurable) return. Thus home- and community-based services are often "marketed" as an opportunity to reduce nursing home placement. Because we all know how expensive nursing homes are, we tend to think that any less expensive service that prevents or delays placement will inevitably reduce government expenditures. As R. L. Kane and R. A. Kane (1980) point out, this assumption ignores the problem of "shifting targets." That is, some people who receive the service may not have gone into a nursing home even if they had not received the service. It is impossible to predict placement with complete accuracy. As a result even the most carefully targeted services will reach some people who would not have entered a nursing home. While these services may enhance the quality of life for elders and their families, it is hard to establish cost effectiveness based on such ephemeral benefits. Thus as the long-term care demonstration projects have shown, the expansion of community-based services may not result in cost savings.

Private Social Services

As the number of older Americans grows, so does the demand for social services. Middle-income and affluent elders can often purchase these services through the private market. Private firms offer a range of services. In large cities it is not unusual to find in-home services advertised in the newspaper and the Yellow Pages. A growing number of private firms offer assessment and case management to those able to pay their fees.

Of course, private organizations are subject to public policies. Medicare reimbursement policies deeply influence the size and vitality of the home health care industry. Similarly, employees of private firms are subject to laws and regulations governing the licensing of professionals. Some private firms depend on referrals from their local area aging agencies, and state ombudsmen can be called upon to investigate complaints against private providers.

The U.S. network of services for elders is complex, involving all levels of government and public and private service providers. Another layer of complexity is added, as the following example illustrates, when the effective care of senior citizens requires a partnership between formal service providers and family members.

CASE 17.1

Mattie Benevidez worked as a server for most of her life. Her husband, Alfredo, came to the United States from Mexico as a young man and eventually became a citizen. He worked his way up to being an assistant manager at Sears. They had three children who did well in school and were able to finish college. Being able to send his children to college was a great source of pride to Alfredo. At sixty-five he retired with Social Security and a small pension. The Benevidezes had five years together before he died of complications related to diabetes.

Ms. Benevidez thought that she was prepared for losing her husband. After all, he was seven years older than she. But she hadn't begun to imagine how much she would miss him. Loneliness became her constant enemy. Her two sons lived hundreds of miles away, and her daughter was busy with her small children. Ms. Benevidez got a dog, which helped a lot, and in time she learned to accept and even enjoy the quiet in her home.

Then one winter day Ms. Benevidez slipped on the ice and her life changed completely. She called Antonia, her daughter, who called the paramedics. They rushed Ms. Benevidez to the emergency room, and after hours of waiting and worrying the doctors told her that she had fractured her hip. A fairly short hospital stay was followed by weeks in a nursing home for rehabilitation. Ms. Benevidez was eager to return home to her dog, but the doctor said that she was too frail. She recommended that Ms. Benevidez move to an assisted living facility, but she could not afford to do so.

Finally, Antonia talked to a friend, who recommended that she call the local area agency on aging. After several tries, she found the number in the government pages of the phone book. The woman who answered the phone sounded very old, but she was able to make an appointment for Antonia to meet with a case manager. The case manager (a young woman with a master's in social work) explained that she would conduct an assessment, both of Ms. Benevidez's physical condition and of her resources, then would recommend services to help her. Antonia was delighted that the case manager was able to visit her mother the next day. Public social services provided through her local aging agency allowed Ms. Benevidez to return home, greatly improving the quality of life for both her and her family members. Ms. Benevidez has a low income, so she is eligible for such services as homemaker care that are ordinarily reserved for people with the greatest economic need. Of course, it is unclear whether these services actually saved the government money in her case. Initially, one would assume that by preventing her from entering a nursing home, the services more than paid for themselves. After all, nursing home care is much more expensive than these services. But would Ms. Benevidez *really* have entered a nursing home? Or would she have moved in with her daughter? It is quite likely, given the cultural background of this family, that Ms. Benevidez would have lived with her daughter instead of going into a nursing home. In this case her daughter would have sacrificed a great deal to meet her mother's needs. So, rather than preventing nursing home placement, the services that Ms. Benevidez received may have reduced the burden of caregiving for her daughter—allowing her to remain employed and care for her growing children. This more amorphous benefit is difficult to use in budget arguments. It is easy to put a price on a nursing home placement that was avoided but much harder to establish the dollar value of improved family life. For this reason it is sometimes easier to argue that social services save money by preventing nursing home placement than to address this more complex, if more accurate, reality.

Social service programs are deeply affected by changing perceptions of the elderly. Thanks in part to the success of Social Security, today's seniors are more affluent than the elderly were in 1966. As Binstock (1983) observes, when seniors are perceived as "greedy geezers," Americans become critical of programs that use age as the basis for eligibility, particularly if these programs fail to meet the needs of the most vulnerable. The challenge for the network of age-based programs will be to respond credibly to this criticism while maintaining the integrity and political viability of programs funded under the Older Americans Act.

Discussion Questions

1. How is your state using funding from the National Caregiver Support Program to help family caregivers? How does your state allocate this money? Do you think that the priorities reflected in this funding are consistent with the objectives of the Older Americans Act?

2. This chapter generally assumes that social services for the elderly are underfunded. Do you think that they are? Why or why not? How would you determine the need for public social services in a community?

3. Are social services for the elderly cost effective? Why or why not?

4. Do you think that elders who are members of ethnic minority groups should be considered especially in need of social services? Why or why not?

REFERENCES

To access websites whose URLs begin with the prefix *http://ferret*, the reader first must download a free program that permits access to TheDataWeb, a joint project of the U.S. Census Bureau and the Centers for Disease Control. TheDataWeb is a collection of on-line data libraries offering, among others, census data, health, and economic data. To learn more about TheDataWeb and to download the software, readers should consult www.thedataweb.org/.

Abels, P., & Abels, S. L. (2001). *Understanding narrative therapy.* New York: Springer.

Achenbaum, W. A. (1986). *Social Security: Visions and revisions.* Cambridge: Cambridge University Press.

Adams, G., & Beehr, T. (Eds.). (2003). *Retirement: Reasons, processes, and results.* New York: Springer.

Adams, W. L., & Cox, N. S. (1997). Epidemiology of problem drinking among elderly people. In Gurnack, *Older adults' misuse of alcohol, medicines, and other drugs* (pp. 1–23).

Adler, K., Patterson, T., & Grant, I. (2002). Physiological challenges associated with caregiving among men. In Kramer & Thompson, *Men as caregivers* (pp. 127–50).

Administration on Aging. (2002). *U.S. Administration on Aging strategic action plan FY 2003–2008.* Washington, DC: Department of Health and Human Services.

———. (2003a). *April: Income and poverty among the elderly.* www.aoa.gov/press/did_you_know/2003/april_pf.asp (February 1, 2005).

———. (2003b, August). *A statistical profile of Hispanic older Americans aged 65+.* www.aoa.gov/prof/Statistics/minority_aging/Facts-on-Hispanic-Elderly.pdf (November 11, 2004).

———. (2004). *Legislation and budget: Current budget information—FY 2005 budget request.* www.aoa.gov/about/legbudg/current_budg/legbudg_current_budg.asp (February 2, 2005).

Adorno, T. W. (1973). *Negative dialectics.* London: Routledge.

Albert, S. M., & Logsdon, R. G. (Eds.). (2002). *Assessing quality of life in Alzheimer's disease.* New York: Springer.

Albrecht, R. (1951). The social roles of older people. *Journal of Gerontology, 6,* 138–45.

Alderman, R. M. (n.d.). Directive to physicians and family or surrogate. *The People's Lawyer.* www.peopleslawyer.net/willform.html (November 4, 2004).

Aldwin, C. (1994). *Stress, coping, and development.* New York: Guilford.

Aldwin, C., & Gilmer, D. (2004). *Health, illness, and optimal aging: Biological and psychosocial perspectives.* Thousand Oaks, CA: Sage.

Alecxih, L., Zeruld, S., & Olearczyk, B. (n.d.). *Characteristics of caregivers based on the survey of income and program participation.* National Family Caregiver Support Program Issue Briefs. www.aoa.gov/prof/aoaprog/caregiver/careprof/progguidance/background/program_issues/AlecxihMonograph.pdf (November 3, 2004).

Alexander, F., & Duff, R. W. (1988, summer). Drinking in retirement communities. *Generations,* pp. 58–62.

Alexopoulos, G. S., Abrams, R. C., Young, R. C., & Shamoian, C. A. (1988). Cornell scale of depression and dementia. *Biological Psychiatry, 23,* 271–84.

Allen, D., & Landis, R. (1997). Substance abuse in elderly individuals. In P. D. Nussbaum (Ed.), *Handbook of neuropsychology and aging* (pp. 111–37). New York: Plenum.

Alvidrez, J., & Arean, P. (2002–2003). Physician willingness to refer older depressed patients for psychotherapy. *International Journal of Psychiatric Medicine, 32,* 21–35.

Alzheimer's Association. (2003, December). *Facts: Statistics about Alzheimer's disease.* www.alz.org/Resource Center/FactSheets/FSAlzheimerStats.pdf (January 31, 2004).

Alzheimer's Disease Education and Referral Center & National Institute on Aging. (1999). *Progress report on Alzheimer's disease.* (NIH publication no. 99-4664.) Silver Spring, MD: Authors.

American Pain Society. (1999, February 17). *Chronic pain in America: New survey of people with chronic pain reveals out-of-control symptoms impaired daily lives.* Press release. www.ampainso.org/whatsnew/release030499.htm (August 29, 2002).

Anderson, R. N. (2002). Deaths: Leading causes for 2000. *National Vital Statistics Reports, 50,* 1–10. www.cdc.gov/nchs/data/nvsr/nvsr50/nvsr50_16.pdf (November 2, 2003).

Anetzberger, G. (2000). Caregiving: Primary cause of elder abuse? *Generations, 24*(2), 46–52.

Anetzberger, G., Palmisano, B., Sanders, M., Bass, D., Dayton, C., Eckert, S., & Schimer, M. (2000). A model intervention for elder abuse and dementia. *Gerontologist, 40,* 492–97.

Applewhite, S. R. (1988). *Hispanic elderly in transition: Theory, research, policy, and practice.* New York: Greenwood.

Arber, S., & Ginn, J. (1995). Choice and constraint in the retirement of older married women. In S. Arber & J. Ginn (Eds.), *Connecting gender and ageing* (pp. 69–86). Philadelphia: Open University Press.

Ardelt, M. (2003a). Empirical assessment of a three-dimensional wisdom scale. *Research on Aging, 25*(3), 275–324.

———. (2003b). Physician-assisted death. In C. D. Bryant (Ed.)., *Handbook of death and dying* (vol. 1, pp. 424–34). Thousand Oaks, CA: Sage.

Argüelles, S., Klausner, E., Argüelles, T., & Coon, D. (2003). Family interventions to address the needs of the caregiving system. In Coon, Gallagher-Thompson, & Thompson, *Innovative interventions to reduce dementia caregiver distress* (pp. 99–118).

Association of Oncology Social Work. (2001). *Standards of practice in oncology social work*. www.arthritis.org/conditions/speakingofpain/factsheet.asp (August 29, 2002).

Atchley, R. (1988). *Social forces and aging* (5th ed.). Belmont, CA: Wadsworth.

———. (1989). A continuity theory of normal aging. *Gerontologist, 29,* 183–90.

———. (1993). Critical perspectives on retirement. In Cole, Achenbaum, Jakobi, & Kastenbaum, *Voices and visions of aging* (pp. 3–19).

Atchley, R., & Barusch, A. S. (2003). *Social forces and aging* (10th ed.). Belmont, CA: Wadsworth/Thomson Learning.

Atkinson, R. M. (1995). Treatment programs for aging alcoholics. In Beresford & Gomberg, *Alcohol and aging* (pp. 186–210).

———. (2000). Substance abuse. In C. E. Coffey & J. L. Cummings (Eds.), *Textbook of geriatric psychiatry* (2nd ed., pp. 367–400). Washington, DC: American Psychiatric Press

———. (2002). Alcohol use in later life: Scourge, solace, or safeguard of health. *American Journal of Geriatric Psychiatry, 10*(6), 649–59.

Atkinson, R. M., & Misra, S. (2002). Further strategies in the treatment of aging alcoholics. In Gurnack, Atkinson, & Osgood, *Treating alcohol and drug abuse in the elderly* (pp. 131–51).

Atkinson, R. M., Tolson, R. L., & Turner, J. A. (1990). Late versus early onset problem drinking in older men. *Alcoholism: Clinical and Experimental Research, 14*(4), 574–79.

Atkinson, R. M., Turner, J., & Tolson, R. (1998). Treatment of older adult problem drinkers: Lessons learned from "The class of '45." *Journal of Mental Health and Aging, 4,* 197–214.

Attig, T. (2001). Relearning the world: Making and finding meanings. In Neimeyer, *Meaning reconstruction and the experience of loss* (pp. 33–53).

Babor, T. F., de la Fuenta, J. R., Saunders, J., & Grant, M. (1992). *AUDIT: The Alcohol Use Disorders Identification Test: Guidelines for its use in primary health care*. Geneva: World Health Organization.

Baltes, M., & Carstensen, L. (1996). The process of successful ageing. *Ageing and society, 16,* 397–422.

———. (1999). Social-psychological theories and their applications to aging: From individual to collective. In Bengston & Schaie, *Handbook of theories of aging* (pp. 209–26).

Baltes, P. (1993). The aging mind: Potential and limits. *Gerontologist, 33*(5), 580–94.

Baltes, P., & Smith, J. (1999). Multilevel and systemic analyses of old age: Theoretical and empirical evidence for a fourth age. In Bengston and Schaie, *Handbook of theories of aging* (pp. 153–73).

———. (2003). New frontiers in the future of aging: From successful aging of the young old to the dilemmas of the fourth age. *Gerontology, 49,* 123–35.

Barker, J. (2004). Lesbian aging: An agenda for social research. In G. Herdt & B. de Vries (Eds.), *Gay and lesbian aging: Research and future directions* (pp. 29–72). New York: Springer.

Barlow, D. H. (1988). *Anxiety and its disorders*. New York: Guilford.

Barlow, D. H., & Craske, M. G. (2000). *Mastery of your anxiety and panic (MAP-3): Client workbook for anxiety and panic.* San Antonio, TX: Graywind/Psychological.

Barnes-Farrell, J. (2003). Beyond health and wealth: Attitudinal and other influences on retirement decision-making. In Adams & Beehr, *Retirement* (pp. 159–87).

Barrowclough, C., King, P., Colville, J., Russell, E., Burns, A., & Tarrier, N. (2001). A randomized trial of the effectiveness of cognitive-behavioral therapy and supportive counseling for anxiety symptoms in older adults. *Journal of Consulting and Clinical Psychology, 69*(5), 756–62.

Barry, K. L. (1999). *Brief interventions and brief therapies for substance abuse* (Treatment Improvement Protocol [TIP] Series No. 34). Rockville, MD: Substance Abuse and Mental Health Services Administration, U.S. Department of Health and Human Services.

Barry, K. L., Oslin, D., & Blow, F. C. (2001). *Prevention and management of alcohol problems in older adults.* New York: Springer.

Barry, L. C., Kasl, S. V., & Prigerson, H. G. (2002). Psychiatric disorders among bereaved persons: The role of perceived circumstances of death and preparedness for death. *American Journal of Geriatric Psychiatry, 10*(4), 447–57.

Bartels, S., Coakley, E., Oxman, T., Constantino, G., Oslin, D., Chen, H., Zubritsky, C., Cheal, K., Durai, U.N., Gallo, J., Llorente, M., & Sanchez, H. (2002). Suicidal and death ideation in older primary care patients with depression, anxiety, and at-risk-alcohol use. *American Journal of Geriatric Psychiatry, 10*(4), 417–27.

Bartels, S., Horn, S., Smout, R., Dums, A., Flaherty, E., Jones, J., Monane, M., Taler, G., & Voss, A. (2003). Agitation and depression in frail nursing home elderly patients with dementia. *American Journal of Geriatric Psychiatry, 11*(2), 231–38.

Barusch, A. S. (1994). Older women in poverty: Private lives and public policies. New York: Springer.

———. (1997). Self-concepts of low-income older women: Not old or poor, but fortunate and blessed. *International Journal of Aging and Human Development, 44*(4), 269–82.

———. (2002). *Foundations of social policy: Social justice, public programs, and the social work profession.* Belmont, CA: Wadsworth.

Bastida, E., & Gonzalez, G. (1995). Mental health status and needs of the Hispanic elderly: A cross-cultural analysis. In Padgett, *Handbook on ethnicity, aging, and mental health* (pp. 99–112).

Baum, C., Kennedy, D. L., Knapp, D. E., Juergens, J. P., & Faich, G. A. (1988). Prescription drug use in 1984 and changes over time. *Medical Care, 26*, 105–14.

Baumeister, R. F. (1990). Suicide as escape from self. *Psychological Review, 97*, 90–113.

Baumgarten, M., Becker, R., & Gauthier, S. (1990). Validity and reliability of the Dementia Behavior Disturbance Scale. *Journal of the American Geriatrics Society, 38*, 271–84.

Beach, D. L., & Kramer, B. J. (1999). Communicating with the Alzheimer's residents: Perceptions of care providers in a residential facility. *Journal of Gerontological Social Work, 32*(3), 5–26.

Beautrais, A. (2002). A case-control study of suicide and attempted suicide in older adults. *Suicide and Life-Threatening Behavior, 32*, 1–9.

Beck, A. T., Brown, J., Boles, M., & Barrett, P. (2002). Completion of advance directives by older health maintenance organization members: The role of attitudes and beliefs regarding life-sustaining treatment. *Journal of the American Geriatrics Society, 50,* 300–6.

Beck, A. T., Epstein, N., Brown, G., & Steer, R. (1988). An inventory for measuring clinical anxiety: Psychometric properties. *Journal of Consulting and Clinical Psychiatry, 56*(6), 893–97.

Beck, A. T., Kovacs, M., & Weissman, A. (1979). Assessment of suicidal intention: The scale for suicide ideation. *Journal of Consulting and Clinical Psychology, 47,* 343–52.

Beck, A. T., Rush, J., Shaw, B., & Emery, G. (1979). *Cognitive therapy of depression.* New York: Guilford.

Beck, A. T., Weissman, A., & Lester, D. (1974). The measurement of pessimism: The hopelessness scale. *Journal of Consulting and Clinical Psychology, 42,* 861–65.

Beck, C. (1995). *Affect changes as outcomes of behavioral interventions* (2R01 AG10321–04). Washington, DC: National Institute on Aging.

Beck, J. G., & Averill, P. (2004). Older adults. In R. G. Heimberg, C. L. Turk, & D. S. Mennin (Eds.), *Generalized anxiety disorder: Advances in research and practice* (pp. 409–33). New York: Guilford.

Beck, J. G., & Stanley, M. A. (1997). Anxiety disorders in the elderly: The emerging role of behavior therapy. *Behavior Therapy, 28,* 83–100.

Beck, J. G., Stanley, M. A., & Zebb, B. J. (1995). Psychometric properties of the Penn State Worry Questionnaire in older adults. *Journal of Clinical Geropsychology, 1,* 33–42.

———. (1999). Effectiveness of the Hamilton Anxiety Scale with older generalized anxiety disorder patients. *Journal of Clinical Geropsychology, 5,* 281–90.

Becker, G. (2002). Dying away from home: Quandaries of migration for elders in two ethnic groups. *Journal of Gerontology, 57B*(2), S79–95.

Bedard, M., Molloy, W., Squire, L., Dubois, S., Lever, J., & O'Donnell, M. (2001). The Zarit Burden Interview: A new short version and screening version. *Gerontologist, 41*(5), 652–57.

Beekman, A. T., de Beurs, E., van Balkom, A. J., Deeg, D. J., Van Dyck, R., & van Tilburg, W. (2000). Anxiety and depression in later life: Co-occurrence and communality of risk factors. *American Journal of Psychiatry, 157,* 89–95.

Beisgen, B. A., & Kraitchman, M. C. (2003). *Senior centers: Opportunities for successful aging.* New York: Springer.

Bengston, V. L. (1973). *The social psychology of aging.* Indianapolis: Bobbs-Merrill.

Bengston, V. L., & Schaie, K. W. (Eds.). (1999). *Handbook of theories of aging.* New York: Springer.

Bennett, K. M., & Vidal-Hall, S. (2000). Narratives of death: A qualitative study of widowhood in later life. *Ageing and Society, 20,* 413–28.

Beresford, T., & Gomberg, E. (Eds.). (1995). *Alcohol and aging.* New York: Oxford University Press.

Bergeron, L. R. (1999). Decision-making and adult protective services workers: Identifying critical factors. *Journal of Elder Abuse and Neglect, 10*(3/4), 87–113.

Bergeron, L. R., & Gray, B. (2003). Ethical dilemmas of reporting suspected elder abuse. *Social Work, 48*(1), 96–105.

Berg-Weger, M., Rubio, D. M., & Tebb, S. S. (2000a). The Caregiver Well-being Scale revisited. *Health and Social Work, 25,* 255–63.

———. (2000b). Living with and caring for older family members: Issues related to caregiver well-being. *Journal of Gerontological Social Work, 33*(2), 47–62.

Berkman, B., & Harootyan, L. (2003). *Social work and health care in an aging society: Education, policy, practice, and research.* New York: Springer.

Berkman, B. J., Maramaldi, P., Breon, E., & Howe, J. (2002). Social work gerontological assessment revisited. *Journal of Gerontological Social Work, 40*(1), 1–14.

Bern-Klug, M., Ekerdt D. J., & Wilkinson, D. S. (1999). What families know about funeral-related costs: Implications for social work practice. *Health and Social Work, 24*(2), 128–37.

Bern-Klug, M., Gessert, C., & Forbes, S. (2001). The need to revise assumptions about the end of life: Implications for social work practice. *Health and Social Work, 26*(1), 38–48.

Berney, L., Blane, D., Smith, D. G., Gunnell, D. J., Holland, P., & Montgomery, S. M. (2000). Socioeconomic measures in early old age as indicators of previous lifetime exposure to environmental health hazards. *Sociology of Health and Illness, 22*(4), 415–30.

Bernstein, J. E., McNichol, E., Mishel, L., & Zahradnik, R. (2000). *Pulling apart: A state-by-state analysis of income trends.* Washington, DC: Center on Budget and Policy Priorities, Economic Policy Institute. www.cbp.org/1–18–00srp-part1.pdf (January 6, 2005).

Berry, J. W., & Sam, D. L. (1997). Acculturation and adaptation. In J. W. Berry, M. H. Segall, & Cigdem Kagitçibasi (Eds.), *Handbook of cross-cultural psychology: Vol. 3. Social behavior and applications* (2nd ed., pp. 291–326). Boston: Allyn & Bacon.

Berry, J. W., Trimble, J. E., & Olmedo, E. L. (1986). Assessment of acculturation. In W. J. Lonner & J. W. Berry (Eds.), *Field methods in cross-cultural research* (pp. 291–324). Thousand Oaks, CA: Sage.

Best, S., & Kellner, D. (1991). *Postmodern theory: Critical interrogations.* New York: Guilford.

Binstock, R. (1983). The aged as scapegoat. *Gerontologist, 23,* 136–43.

———. (1986). Perspectives on measuring hardship: Concepts, dimensions, and implications. *Gerontologist, 26*(1), 60–62.

Birren, J. E. (Ed.). (1996). *Encyclopedia of gerontology.* San Diego: Academic Press.

Birren, J. E., & Bengston, V. (Eds.). (1988). *Emergent theories of aging.* New York: Springer.

Birren, J. E., & Schroots, J. (1996). History, concepts, and theory in the psychology of aging. In J. E. Birren & K. Warner Schaie (Eds.), *Handbook of the psychology of aging* (4th ed., pp. 3–23). San Diego: Academic Press.

Blackhall, L. J., Murphy, S. T., Frank, G., Michel, V., & Azen, S. (1995). Ethnicity and attitudes toward patient autonomy. *Journal of the American Medical Association, 274,* 820–25.

Blake, D., Weathers, F. W., Nagy, L. M., Kaloupek, D. G., Klauminzer, G., Charney, D. S., & Keane, T. M. (1990). A clinician rating scale for assessing current and life-time PTSD: The CAPS-1. *Behavior Therapist, 13*, 187–88.

Blau, Z. (1973). *Old age in a changing society.* New York: New Viewpoints.

Blazer, D. G. (1995). Depression. In G. L. Maddox (Ed.), *Encyclopedia of aging* (2nd ed., pp. 265–66). New York: Springer.

———. (2002). *Depression in late life* (3rd ed.). New York: Springer.

———. (2004). Alcohol and drug problems. In D. Blazer, D. C. Steffens, & E. W. Busse (Eds.), *Textbook of geriatric psychiatry* (3rd ed., pp. 351–67). Washington, DC: American Psychiatric Press.

Blazer, D. G., & Koenig, H. G. (1996). Suicide. In Birren, *Encyclopedia of gerontology* (pp. 529–38).

Blazer, D. G., George, L., & Hughes, D. (1991). The epidemiology of anxiety disorders: An age comparison. In Salzman & Lebowitz, *Anxiety in the elderly* (pp. 17–30).

Blazer, D. G., Hughes, D. C., & George, L. K. (1987). The epidemiology of depression in an elderly community population. *Gerontologist, 27*, 281–87.

Blow, F. (1998). *Substance abuse among older adults.* (DHHS publication no. [SMA] 98-3179). Rockville, MD: Substance Abuse and Mental Health Services Administration, U.S. Department of Health and Human Services.

Blow, F., & Barry, K. L. (2003). *Use and misuse of alcohol among older women.* Bethesda, MD: National Institute on Alcohol Abuse and Alcoholism.

Blow, F., Walton, M., & Chermack, S. (2000). Older adult treatment outcomes following elder-specific inpatient alcoholism treatment. *Journal of Substance Abuse Treatment, 19*, 67–75.

Blumenthal, H. T. (2003). The aging-disease dichotomy: True or false? *Journal of Gerontology: Medical Sciences, 58A*(2), 138–45.

Blumenthal, M. D. (1975). Measuring depressive symptomatology in the general population. *Archives of General Psychiatry, 32*, 971–78.

Bonanno, G. A. (1999). The concept of "working through" loss: A critical evaluation of the cultural, historical, and empirical evidence. In A. Maercker & M. Schuetz-Wohl, & Z. Solomon (Eds.), *Posttraumatic stress disorder: Vulnerability and resilience in the life-span (pp. 221–48).* Göttingen, Germany: Hogrefe & Huber.

Bonanno, G. A. (2001). Grief and emotion: A social-functional perspective. In Stroebe, Hansson, Stroebe, & Schut, *Handbook of bereavement research* (pp. 493–515).

Bonanno, G. A., & Field, N. P. (2001). Examining the delayed grief hypothesis across 5 years of bereavement. *American Behavioral Scientist, 44*, 798–16.

Bonanno, G. A., & Kaltman, S. (1999). Toward an integrative perspective on bereavement. *Psychological Bulletin, 125*(6), 760–76.

Bonanno, G. A., and Keltner, D. (1997). Facial expressions of emotion and the course of bereavement. *Journal of Abnormal Psychology, 106*, 126–37.

Bonanno, G. A., Lehman, D. R., Tweed, R. G., Haring, M., Wortman, C., Sonnega, J., Carr, D., & Nesse, R. M. (2002). Resilience to loss and chronic grief: A prospective study from preloss to 18-months postloss. *Journal of Personality and Social Psychology, 83*, 1150–64.

Borson, S., Brush, M., Gil, E., Scanlan, J., Vitaliano, P., Chen, J., Casman, J., Sta Maria, M. M., Barnhart, R., & Roques, J. (1999). The clock drawing test: Utility for dementia detection in multiethnic elders. *Journal of Gerontology: Medical Sciences, 54A*(11), M534–40.

Bowlby, C. (1993). *Therapeutic activities with persons disabled with Alzheimer's disease and related disorders.* Gaithersburg, MD: Aspen.

Bowlby, J. (1980). *Attachment and loss: Vol. 3. Loss—Sadness and depression.* New York: Basic Books.

Bowlby Sifton, C. B. (2000). Maximizing the functional abilities of persons with Alzheimer's disease and related dementias. In Lawton & Rubinstein, *Interventions in dementia care* (pp. 11–37).

Bradley, E. (2002). *The attitudes and beliefs of African Americans concerning end-of-life treatment: A developmental perspective.* Dissertation proposal, Ohio State University College of Social Work, Columbus.

Branch, L., Horowitz, A., & Carr, C. (1989). The implications for everyday life of incident self-reported visual decline among people over age 65 living in the community. *Gerontologist, 29*, 359–65.

Braun, K. L., & Browne, C. V. (1998). Perceptions of dementia, caregiving, and help-seeking among Asian and Pacific Islander Americans. *Health and Social Work, 23*, 262–74.

Braun, K. L., & Nichols, R. (1997). Death and dying in four Asian American cultures: A descriptive study. *Death Studies, 21*(4), 327–42.

Braun, K. L., Takamura, J. C., Forman, S. M., Sasaki, P. A., & Meininger, L. (1995). Developing and testing outreach materials on Alzheimer's disease for Asian and Pacific Island Americans. *Gerontologist, 35*, 122–26.

Braun, K. L., Tanji, V., & Heck, R. (2001). Support for physician-assisted suicide: Exploring the impact of ethnicity and attitudes toward planning for death. *Gerontologist, 41*, 51–60.

Brawnstein, S., & Welch, C. (2002). Financial literacy: An overview of practice, research, and policy. U.S. Federal Reserve, Division of Consumer and Community Affairs. www.federalreserve.gov/pubs/bulletin/2002/1102lead.pdf (January 27, 2005).

Brennan, P. L., & Moos, R. H. (1991). Functioning, life context, and help-seeking among late-onset problem drinkers: Comparisons with nonproblem and early-onset problem drinkers. *British Journal of Addictions, 86*, 1129–50.

Brennan, P. L., Moos, R. H., & Kim, J. Y. (1993). Gender differences in the individual characteristics and life contexts of late-middle-aged and older problem drinkers. *Addiction, 88*(6), 781–90.

Bridges-Parlet, S., Knopman, D., & Thompson, T. (1994). A descriptive study of physically aggressive behavior in dementia by direct observation. *Journal of the American Geriatrics Society, 42*, 192–97.

Brock, D. B., & Foley, D. J. (1998). Demography and epidemiology of dying in the U.S. with an emphasis on deaths of older persons. *Hospice Journal, 1–2*, 49–60.

Brod, M., Stewart, A., & Sands, L. (2000). Conceptualization of quality of life in dementia. In Albert & Logsdon, *Assessing quality of life in Alzheimer's disease* (pp. 3–16).

Brod, M., Stewart, A., Sands, L., & Walton, P. (1999). Conceptualization and measurement of quality of life in dementia: The Dementia–QOL Instrument. *Gerontologist, 39*(1), 25–36.

Brody, E. M. (2004). *Women in the middle: Their parent care years* (2nd ed.). New York: Springer.

Brower, K. (1998). Alcohol withdrawal and aging. In E. L. Gomberg, A. M. Hegedus, & R. A. Zucker (Eds.), *Alcohol problems and aging* (pp. 359–72). Bethesda, MD: U.S. Department of Health and Human Services.

Brown, D. (1996). Marital status and mental health. In Neighbors & Jackson, *Mental health in black America* (pp. 77–94).

Brown, K. S. (Ed.). (1999). *Assessing an older adult's readiness for medical rehabilitation.* New York: Wiley.

Brown, R. A., DiNardo, P. A., & Barlow, D. H. (1994). *Anxiety disorders schedule for DSM-IV.* Albany: Center for Stress and Anxiety, State University of New York.

Browne, C. (1998). *Women, feminism, and aging.* New York: Springer.

Bryson, K., & Casper, L. M. (1999). *Current populations reports: Special studies* (P23-198). Washington, DC: U.S. Census Bureau.

Bucholz, K., Sheline, Y., & Helzer, J. (1995). The epidemiology of alcohol use, problems, and dependence in elders: A review. In Beresford & Gomberg, *Alcohol and aging* (pp. 19–41).

Bullock, K., Crawford, S., & Tennstedt, S. (2003). Employment and caregiving: Exploration of African American caregivers. *Social Work, 48*(2), 150–62.

Burgess, E. (1954). Social relations, activities and personal adjustment. *American Journal of Sociology, 54,* 352–60.

Burkhardt, J. (2002). *Benefits of transportation services to health programs.* Rockville, MD: Community Transportation Association of America & WESTAT.

Burnette, D. (1999). Social relationships of Latino grandparent caregivers: A role theory perspective. *Gerontologist, 39*(1), 49–58.

———. (2000a). Grandparents as family caregivers: Advances in mental health practice, programming, and policy. *Journal of Mental Health and Aging, 6*(4), 263–67.

———. (2000b). Latino grandparents rearing grandchildren with special needs: Effects on depressive symptomatology. *Journal of Gerontological Social Work, 33*(3), 1–16.

Burnside, I. (1996). Reminiscence. In Birren, *Encyclopedia of gerontology* (pp. 399–406).

Burtless, G., & Quinn, J. (2001). Retirement trends and policies to encourage work among older Americans. In P. P. Burdetti, R. V. Burkhauser, J. M. Gregory, & H. A. Hunt (Eds.), *Ensuring health and income security for an aging workforce.* Washington, DC: National Academy of Social Insurance.

Buschsbaum, D., Buchanan, R., Lawton, M. J., & Schnoll, S. (1991). Alcohol consumption patterns in a primary care population. *Alcohol and Alcoholism, 26,* 215–20.

Butler, R. (1963). The life review. *Psychiatry, 26,* 65–76.

Butler, R., Lewis, M., & Sunderland, T. (1998). *Aging and mental health.* Boston: Allyn & Bacon.

Butrica, B. A. (2000). Divorced women at retirement: Projections of economic well-being in the near future—Statistical data included. *Social Security Bulletin, 63,* 3–12.

Byock, I. (1997). *Dying well: The prospect for growth at the end of life*. New York: Putnam's.

Byock, I., & Merriman, M. P. (1998). Measuring quality of life for patients with terminal illness: The Missouri-VITAS quality of life index. *Palliative Medicine, 12*(4), 231–44.

Cahill, S., South, K., & Spade, J. (2000). *Outing age: Public policy issues affecting gay, lesbian, bisexual, and transgender elders*. New York: Policy Institute of the National Gay and Lesbian Task Force Foundation.

Calasanti, T. (1996). Incorporating diversity: Meaning, levels of research, and implications for theory. *Gerontologist, 36*(2), 147–56.

Calasanti, T., & Slevin, K. (2001). *Gender inequalities and aging*. Walnut Creek, CA: AltaMira Press.

Calhoun, L., & Tedeschi, R. (2001). Posttraumatic growth: The positive lessons of loss. In Neimeyer, *Meaning reconstruction and the experience of loss* (pp. 157–72).

Campisi, J., Dimri, G., & Hara, E. (1996). Control of replicative senescence. In E. Schneider, & J. Rowe (Eds.), *Handbook of the biology of aging* (4th ed., pp. 121–49). New York: Academic Press.

Cantwell, P., Turoc, S., Brenneis, C., & Hanson, J. (2000). Predictors of home death in palliative care cancer patients. *Journal of Palliative Care, 16*, 23–30.

Carmin, C., Pollard, C. A., & Gillock, K. (1999). Assessment of anxiety disorders in the elderly. In P. Lichtenberg (Ed.), *Handbook of assessment in clinical gerontology* (pp. 59–90). New York: Wiley.

Carp, F. (2000). *Elder abuse in the family: An interdisciplinary model for research*. New York: Springer.

Carr, D. (2003). A good death for whom? Quality of spouse's death and psychological distress among older widowed persons. *Journal of Health and Social Behavior, 44*, 215–32.

Carr, D., House, J., Kessler, R., Nesse, R., Sonnega, J., & Wortman, C. (2000). Marital quality and psychological adjustment to widowhood among older adults: A longitudinal analysis. *Journal of Gerontology: Social Sciences, 55B*, S197–S207.

Carr, D., House, J., Wortman, C., Nesse, R., & Kessler, R. (2001). Psychological adjustment to sudden and anticipated spousal loss among older widowed persons. *Journal of Gerontology: Social Sciences, 56B*(4), S237–48.

Carstensen, L. (1993). Motivation for social contact across the life span: A theory of socioemotional selectivity. In J. E. Jacobs (Ed.), *Nebraska symposium on motivation, 1992: Developmental perspectives on motivation* (Vol. 40, pp. 209–54). Lincoln: University of Nebraska Press.

———. (1995). Evidence for a life-span theory of socioemotional selectivity. *Current Directions in Psychological Science, 4*, 151–56.

Carstensen, L. L., Edelstein, B. A., & Dornbrand, L. (Eds.). (1996). *The practical handbook of clinical gerontology*. Thousand Oaks, CA: Sage.

Carstensen, L. L., Gross, J., & Fung, H. (1997). The social context of emotion. *Annual Review of Gerontology and Geriatrics, 17*, 325–52.

Carstensen, L. L., Isaacowitz, D. M., & Charles, S. T. (1999). Taking time seriously: A theory of socioemotional selectivity. *American Psychologist, 54*(3), 165–81.

Carstensen, L. L., Rychtarik, R., & Prue, D. (1985). Behavioral treatment of the geriatric alcohol abuser: A long-term follow-up study. *Addictive behaviors, 10,* 307–11.

Casado, B., & Leung, P. (2001). Migratory grief and depression among elderly Chinese American immigrants. *Journal of Gerontological Social Work, 36,* 5–26.

Casper, L. M., & Bryson, K. (1998). *Co-resident grandparents and their grandchildren: Grandparent maintained families* (Population Division Working Paper Series 26). Washington, DC: U.S. Census Bureau.

Cassidy, J., & Shaver, P. R. (Eds.). (1999). *Handbook of attachment: Theory, research, and clinical applications.* New York: Guilford.

Center for Substance Abuse Treatment. (1994). *Practical approaches in the treatment of women who abuse alcohol and other drugs.* (Publication No. [SMA] 94-3006). Rockville, MD: U.S. Department of Health and Human Services.

Centers for Disease Control and Prevention. (2003). *Health, United States, 2003.* www.cdc.gov/nchs/hus.htm (November 1, 2003).

Chadiha, L., & Adams, P. (2003). Physical health and economic well-being of older African American women: Toward strategies of empowerment. In Berkman & Harootyan, *Social work and health care in an aging society* (pp. 149–76).

Chapin, R., & Cox, E. O. (2001). Changing the paradigm: Strengths-based and empowerment-oriented social work with frail elders. *Journal of Gerontological Social Work, 36*(1/2), 165–79.

Chappell, N. L., & Reid, R. C. (2002). Burden and well-being among caregivers: Examining the distinction. *Gerontologist, 42*(6), 772–80.

Charles C. Steward Machine Co. v. *Davis,* 301 U.S. 458 (1937). www.ssa.gov/history/supreme2.html (October 29, 2004).

Chastain, S. (1992). The accidental addict. *Modern Maturity, 35,* 39.

Chibnall, J., & Tait, R. (2001). Pain assessment in cognitively impaired and unimpaired older adults: A comparison of four scales. *Pain, 92,* 173–86.

Chiriboga, D. (1995). Social supports. In G. L. Maddox (Ed.), *Encyclopedia of aging* (2nd ed., pp. 890–93). New York: Springer.

Chodosh, J., Buckwalter, G., Blazer, D., & Seeman, T. (2004). How the question is asked makes a difference in the assessment of depressive symptoms in older persons. *American Journal of Geriatric Psychiatry, 12,* 75–83.

Choi, N., & Mayer, J. (2000). Elder abuse, neglect, and exploitation: Risk factors and prevention strategies. *Journal of Gerontological Social Work, 33*(2), 5–24.

Chollet, D. J. (2001). *Medigap coverage for prescription drugs.* Testimony before the U.S. Senate Committee on Finance, April 24, 2001.

Christ, G., & Sormanti, M. (1999). Advancing social work practice in end-of-life care. *Social Work in Health Care, 30*(2), 81–99.

Clark, D. (1997). Panic disorder and social phobia. In D. Clark & C. Fairburn (Eds.), *Science and practice of cognitive behaviour therapy* (pp. 121–53). New York: Oxford University Press.

Cleiren, M. (1993). *Bereavement and adaptation: A comparative study of the aftermath of death.* Washington, DC: Hemisphere.

Closser, M. H., & Blow, F. C. (1993). Special populations: Women, ethnic minorities, and the elderly. *Psychiatric Clinics of North America, 16*(1), 199–209.

Cohen, S. R., & Leis, A. (2002). What determines the quality of life of terminally ill cancer patients from their own perspective? *Journal of Palliative Care, 18*(1), 48–62.

Cohen-Mansfield, J. (2000). Approaches to management of disruptive behaviors. In Lawton & Rubinstein, *Interventions in dementia care* (pp. 39–63).

———. (2003). Agitation in the elderly: Definitional and theoretical conceptualizations. In D. Hay, D. Klein, L. Hay, G. Grossberg, & J. Kennedy (Eds.), *Agitation in patients with dementia: A practical guide to diagnosis and management* (pp. 1–21). Washington, DC: American Psychiatric Publishing.

Cohen-Mansfield, J., & Creedon, M. (2002). Nursing staff members' perceptions of pain indicators in persons with severe dementia. *Clinical Journal of Pain, 18*(64–73).

Cohen-Mansfield, J., & Werner, P. (1998a). The effects of an enhanced environment on nursing home residents who pace. *Gerontologists, 38*(2), 199–208.

———. (1998b). Predictors of aggressive behaviors: A longitudinal study in senior day care centers. *Journal of Gerontology: Psychological Sciences, 53B*(5), P300–10.

Cohen-Mansfield, J., Marx, M. S., & Rosenthal, A. S. (1989). A description of agitation in a nursing home. *Journal of Gerontology: Medical Sciences, 44,* M77–84.

Cohen-Mansfield, J., Werner, P., & Marx, M. S. (1990). Screaming in nursing home residents. *Journal of the American Geriatrics Society, 38,* 785–92.

Cole, T., Achenbaum, W. A., Jakobi, P., & Kastenbaum, R. (Eds.). (1993). *Voices and visions of aging: Toward a critical gerontology.* New York: Springer.

Collins, P. H. (2000). *Black feminist thought: Knowledge, consciousness, and the politics of empowerment.* New York: Routledge.

Comijs, H. C., Dijkstra, W., Bouter, L. M., & Smit, J. H. (1999). Hostility and coping capacity as risk factors of elder mistreatment. *Social Psychiatry and Psychiatric Epidemiology, 34,* 48–52.

Congress, E. P. (1999). *Social work values and ethics: Identifying and resolving professional dilemmas.* Belmont, CA: Wadsworth.

Congressional Budget Office. (2001). *An analysis of the president's budgetary proposals for FY 2001.* www.cbo.gov/showdoc.cfm?index = 1908amp;sequence = 3&from = 5 (January 6, 2005).

———. (2002). *Issues in designing a prescription drug benefit for Medicare. Chapter 1: Medicare beneficiaries drug spending and coverage.* www.cbo.gov/showdoc.cfm?index = 3960&sequence = 3 (January 6, 2005).

Conn, D. (2004). Other dementias and mental disorders due to general medical conditions. In J. Sadavoy, L. F. Jarvik, G. T. Grossberg, & B. S. Meyers (Eds.), *Comprehensive textbook of geriatric psychiatry* (3rd ed.) (pp. 545–77). New York: W. W. Norton.

Connor, S. R. (1998). *Hospice: Practice, pitfalls, and promise.* Washington, DC: Taylor & Francis.

Conwell, Y. (1992). Depression as a "cause" of late-life suicide. *Crisis, 13,* 55–56.

Conwell, Y., Duberstein, P. R., Connor, K., Eberly, S., Cox, C., & Caine, E. (2002). Access to firearms and risk for suicide in middle-aged and older adults. *American Journal of Geriatric Psychiatry, 10*(4), 407–16.

Conwell, Y., Duberstein, P. R., Cox, C., Herrmann, M. S., Forbes, N., & Carne, E. D. (1998). Age differences in behaviors leading to completed suicide. *American Journal of Geriatric Psychiatry, 6,* 122–26.

Cook, F. L., & Kramek, L. M. (1986). Measuring economic hardship among older Americans. *Gerontologist, 26*(1), 38–48.

Cook, S., Miyahara, S., Bacanu, S., Perez-Madrinan, G., Lopez, O., Kaufer, D., Nimgaonkar, V., Wisniewski, S., DeKosky, S., & Sweet, R. (2003). Psychotic symptoms in Alzheimer's disease. *American Journal of Geriatric Psychiatry, 11*(4), 406–13.

Cook-Daniels, L. (1997). Lesbian, gay male, bisexual and transgendered elders: Elder abuse and neglect issues. *Journal of Elder Abuse and Neglect, 9*(2), 35–49.

Coon, D., Gallagher-Thompson, D., & Thompson, L. (Eds.). (2003). *Innovative interventions to reduce dementia caregiver distress* (pp. 3–27). New York: Springer.

Coon, D., Ory, M., & Schulz, R. (2003). Family caregivers: Enduring and emergent themes. In Coon, Gallagher-Thompson, & Thompson, *Innovative interventions to reduce dementia caregiver distress* (pp. 3–27).

Corning, P. (1969). The second round—1927 to 1940, chap. 2. In *The Evolution of Medicare: From idea to law.* Social Security Administration: The history of Medicare. www. ssa.gov/history/corningchap2.html (January 6, 2005).

Corr, C. A. (1992). A task-based approach to coping with dying. *Omega: Journal of Death and Dying, 24,* 81–94.

Cottrell, L. (1933). Roles and marital adjustment. *Publications of the American Sociological Society, 27,* 107–12.

Cox, C. (2000a). Empowerment practice: Implications for interventions with African American and Latina custodial grandmothers. *Journal of Mental Health and Aging, 6*(4), 385–97.

———. (2000b). *To Grandmother's house we go and stay: Perspectives on custodial grandparents.* New York: Springer.

———. (2002). Empowering African American custodial grandparents. *Social Work, 47*(1), 45–54.

Cox, E. O. (1999). Never too old: Empowerment—The concept and practice in work with frail elderly. In W. Shera & L. Wells (Eds.), *Empowerment practice in social work: Developing richer conceptual foundations* (pp. 178–95). Toronto: Canadian Scholars' Press.

Cox, E. O., & Parsons, R. R. (1994). *Empowerment-oriented social work practice with the elderly.* Pacific Grove, CA: Brooks/Cole.

———. (1996). Empowerment-oriented social work practice: Impact on late life relationships of women. In K. Roberto (Ed.), *Relationships between women in later life* (pp. 129–43). New York: Harrington Park.

Craft, B., Johnson, D., & Ortega, S. (1998). Rural-urban women's experience of symptoms of depression related to economic hardship. *Journal of Women and Aging, 10,* 3–18.

Craig, Y. (1998). Intergenerational mediation: Its potential for contributing to the prevention of elder abuse. *Journal of Social Work Practice, 12*(2), 175–79.

Craske, M. (1996). Cognitive-behavioral approaches to panic and agoraphobia. In K. Dobson & K. Craig (Eds.), *Advances in cognitive-behavioral therapy* (pp. 145–73). Thousand Oaks, CA: Sage.

Cristofalo, V. (1996). Ten years later: What have we learned about human aging from studies of cell cultures? *Gerontologist, 36*(6), 737–41.

Crits-Christoph, P., Gibbons, M., & Crits-Christoph, K. (2004). Supportive-expressive psychodynamic therapy. In R. G. Heimberg, C. L. Turk, & D. S. Mennin (Eds.), *Generalized anxiety disorder: Advances in research and practice* (pp. 293–319). New York: Guilford.

Cumming, E., & Henry, W. (1961). *Growing old: The process of disengagement.* New York: Basic Books.

Cummings, J. L., Gega, M., Gray, K., Rosenberg-Thompson, S., & Carusi, D. A. (1994). The neuropsychiatric inventory: Comprehensive assessment of psychopathology in dementia. *Neurology, 44,* 2308–14.

Curran, J. S. M. (1995). Current provision and effectiveness of day care services for people with dementia. *Reviews in Clinical Gerontology, 5,* 313–20.

Damron-Rodriguez, J., & Corley, C. (2002). Social work education for interdisciplinary practice with older adults and their families. *Journal of Gerontological Social Work, 39*(1), 37–55.

Dannefer, D. (1988). What's in a name? An account of the neglect of variability in the study of aging. In Birren & Bengston, *Emergent theories of aging* (pp. 356–84).

———. (2003). Cumulative advantage/disadvantage and the life course: Cross-fertilizing and social science theory. *Journal of Gerontology: Social Sciences, 58B*(6), S327–37.

Dannefer, D., & Uhlenberg, P. (1999). Paths of the life course: A typology. In Bengston and Schaie, *Handbook of theories of aging* (pp. 306–26).

Davidson, G. W. (1979). Hospice care for the dying. In H. Wass (Ed.), *Dying: Facing the facts* (pp. 101–19). New York: McGraw-Hill.

Davies, C., & Williams, D. (2002). *The Grandparent Study 2002 Report.* Washington, DC: AARP.

Davis, C. (2001). The tormented and the transformed: Understanding response to loss and trauma. In Neimeyer, *Meaning reconstruction and the experience of loss* (pp. 137–55).

Davis, C. G., & Nolen-Hoeksema, S. (2001). Loss and meaning: How do people make sense of loss? *American Behavioral Scientist, 44,* 726–41.

Day, K., Carreon, D., & Stump, C. (2000). The therapeutic design of environments for people with dementia: A review of the empirical research. *Gerontologist, 40*(4), 397–416.

de Jong, P., Ormel, J., Slaets, J., Kempen, G., Ranchor, A., van Jaarsveld, C., Scaf-Klomp, W., & Sanderman, R. (2004). Depressive symptoms in elderly patients predict poor adjustment after somatic events. *American Journal of Geriatric Psychiatry, 12*(1), 57–64.

Derlet, R.W., & Kinser, D. (1994, September 29). Access of Medicaid recipients to outpatient care. *New England Journal of Medicine, 331*(13), 877–78.

DeSpelder, L. A., & Strickland, A. L. (2002). *The last dance: Encountering death and dying* (6th ed.). Boston: McGraw Hill Higher Education.

Devanand, D. P., Miller, L., Richards, M., Marder, K., Bell, K., Mayeux, & Stern, Y. (1992). The Columbia University Scale for Psychopathology in Alzheimer's Disease. *Archives of Neurology, 49,* 371–76.

Diagnostic and statistical manual of mental disorders. (1994). (4th ed.). Washington, DC: American Psychiatric Association.

Diagnostic and statistical manual of mental disorders. (2000). (4th ed., TR). Washington, DC: American Psychiatric Association.

Dick, L. P., & Gallagher-Thompson, D. (1996). Late life depression. In M. Hersen & V. Van Hasselt (Eds.), *Psychological treatment of older adults* (pp. 181–208). New York: Plenum.

DiClemente, C., Bellino, L., & Neavins, T. (1999). Motivation for change and alcoholism treatment. *Alcohol Research and Health, 23*(2), 86–92.

Dilworth-Anderson, P., Williams, I., & Gibson, B. (2002). Issues of race, ethnicity, and culture in caregiving research: A 20-year review (1980–2000). *Gerontologist, 42*(2), 237–72.

Dimond, M., Lund, D. A., & Caserta, M. S. (1987). The role of social support in the first two years of bereavement in an elderly sample. *Gerontologist, 27*, 599–604.

Doka, K. (1993). *Living with life-threatening illness: A guide for patients, their families, and caregivers.* Lexington, MA: Lexington Books.

———. (1997). When illness is prolonged: Implications for grief. In K. Doka (Ed.), *Living with grief when illness is prolonged* (pp. 5–15). Washington, DC: Hospice Foundation of America.

———. (2002, April 24). *Living with grief: Loss in later life.* Bereavement teleconference. Hospice Foundation of America, Washington, DC.

Dorfman, L. T. (1989). Retirement preparation and retirement satisfaction in the rural elderly. *Journal of Applied Gerontology, 8*, 432–50.

Dressel, P. M., Minkler, M., & Yen, I. (1999). Gender, race, class and aging: Advances and opportunities. In M. Minkler & C. L. Estes (Eds.), *Critical gerontology: Perspectives from political and moral economy* (pp. 275–94). Amityville, NY: Baywood.

Dreyfus, R. (1996). The biggest deal: Lobbying to take Social Security private. *American Prospect, 26*, 72–75.

Drought, T. S., & Koenig, B. (2002). "Choice" in end-of-life decision making: Researching fact or fiction? *Gerontologist, 42*, 114–28.

Duberstein, P., Conwell, Y., & Cox, C. (1998). Suicide in widowed persons: A psychological autopsy comparison of recently and remotely bereaved older subjects. *American Journal of Geriatric Psychiatry, 6*, 328–34.

Dupree, L., & Schonfeld, L. (1999). Management of alcohol abuse in older adults. In M. Duffy (Ed.), *Handbook of counseling and psychotherapy with older adults* (pp. 632–49). New York: Wiley.

Dupree, L. W., Broskowski, H., & Schonfeld, L. (1984). The gerontology project: A behavioral treatment program for elderly alcohol abusers. *Gerontologist, 24*, 510–16.

Dura, J. R., Stukenberg, K. W., & Kiecolt-Glaser, J. K. (1990). Chronic stress and depressive episodes in older adults. *Journal of Abnormal Psychology, 99*, 284–90.

Dyer, C., & Goins, A. (2000). The role of the interdisciplinary geriatric assessment in addressing self-neglect of the elderly. *Generations, 24*(2), 23–30.

Eaton, W., Kramer, M., Anthony, J. C., Dryman, A., Shapiro, S., & Locke, B. Z. (1989). The incidence of specific DIS/DSM-III mental disorders: Data from the NIMH epidemiologic catchment area program. *Acta Psychiatric Scandinavian, 79*, 109–25.

Egan, G. (1986). *The skilled helper: A model for systematic helping and interpersonal relating.* Pacific Grove, CA: Brooks/Cole.

Ekerdt, D., Bosse, R., & Levkoff, S. (1985). Am empirical test for phases of retirement: Findings from the Normative Aging Study. *Journal of Gerontology, 40,* 95–101.

Ekerdt, D., Vinick, B., & Bosse, R. (1989). Orderly endings: Do men know when they will retire? *Journal of Gerontology, 44,* 528–35.

Elder, G., Jr., & Johnson, M. K. (2003). The life course and aging: Challenges, lessons, and new directions. In R. A. Settersten Jr. (Ed.), *Invitation to the life course* (pp. 49–81). Amityville, NY: Baywood.

Emlet, C., Crabtree, J., Condon, V., & Treml, L. (1996). *In-home assessment of older adults: An interdisciplinary approach.* Gaithersburg, MD: Aspen.

Engle, V. F., Fox-Hill, E., & Graney, M. (1998). The experience of living-dying in a nursing home: Self-reports of black and white older adults. *Journal of the American Geriatrics Society, 46,* 1091–96.

Erikson, E. H. (1963). *Childhood and society* (2nd ed.). New York: W. W. Norton.

Estes, C. (1993). The aging enterprise revisited. *Gerontologist, 33,* 292–98.

————. (2001). *Social policy and aging: A critical perspective.* Thousand Oaks, CA: Sage.

Evans, L., Ekerdt, D., & Bosse, R. (1985). Proximity to retirement and anticipatory involvement: Findings from the Normative Aging Study. *Journal of Gerontology, 40,* 368–74.

Ewing, J. A. (1984). Detecting alcoholism: The CAGE Questionnaire. *Journal of the American Medical Association, 252,* 1905–7.

Falcon, L., & Tucker, K. (2000). Prevalence and correlates of depressive symptoms among Puerto Rican elders in Massachusetts. *Journal of Gerontology: Social Sciences, 55B*(2), S108–16.

Families USA. (2001). *Enough to make you sick: Prescription drug prices for the elderly.* www.familiesusa.org/site/DocServer?docID=4361 (January 6, 2005).

———— (2004). Sticker shock: Rising prescription drug prices for seniors. www.familiesusa.org/site/DocServer/Sticker_Shock.pdf?docID=3541 (January 17, 2005).

Family Circle & Kaiser Family Foundation. (2000). *National survey on health care and other elder care issues: Summary of findings and chart pack.* Menlo Park, CA: Kaiser Family Foundation.

Fast, B., & Chapin, R. (1997). The Strengths Model with older adults: Critical practice components. In D. Saleeby (Ed.), *The Strengths perspective in social work practice* (2nd ed., pp. 115–30). New York: Longman.

Feder, J., & Moon, M. (1998). Managed care for the elderly: A threat or a promise? *Generations, 22*(2), 6–10.

Federal Interagency Forum on Aging-Related Statistics. (2004, November). *Older Americans 2004: Key indicators of well-being.* Washington, DC: U.S. Government Printing Office.

Feil, N. (1992). *Validation.* Cleveland, OH: Edward Feil Productions.

————. (1993). *The validation breakthrough.* New York: Health Professions Press.

Feldman, D. (2003). Endgame: The design and implementation of early retirement incentive programs. In Adams & Beehr, *Retirement* (pp. 83–114).

Femiano, S., & Coonerty-Femiano, A. (2002). Principles and interventions for working therapeutically with caregiving men: Responding to challenges. In Kramer & Thompson, *Men as caregivers* (pp. 337–58).

Fernandez, M., Mutran, E., Reitzes, D., & Sudha, S. (1998). Ethnicity, gender, and depressive symptoms in older workers. *Gerontologist, 38,* 71–79.

Fields, F., & Casper, L. (2001). *America's families and living arrangements: Population characteristics.* Washington, DC: U.S. Census Bureau.

Fillenbaum, G. (1995). Multidimensional functional assessment. In G. L. Maddox (Ed.), *The encyclopedia of aging* (2nd ed., pp. 653–54). New York: Springer.

Finch, C., & Seeman, T. (1999). Stress theories of aging. In Bengtson and Schaie, *Handbook of theories of aging* (pp. 81–97).

Finkel, S. I., Lyons, J. S., & Anderson, R. L. (1993). A brief agitation rating scale (BARS) for nursing home elderly. *Journal of the American Geriatrics Society, 41,* 50–52.

Finlayson, R. E. (1995). Misuse of prescription drugs. *International Journal of the Addictions, 30* (13&14), 1871–1901.

———. (1998). Prescription drug dependence in the elderly: The clinical pathway to recovery. *Journal of Mental Health and Aging, 4,* 233–49.

Finlayson, R. E., & Davis, L. J., Jr. (1994). Prescription drug dependence in the elderly population: Demographic and clinical features of 100 inpatients. *Mayo Clinic Proceedings, 69,* 1137–45.

Finlayson, R. E., & Hofman, V. (2002). Prescription drug misuse: Treatment strategies. In Gurnack, Atkinson, & Osgood, *Treating alcohol and drug abuse in the elderly* (pp. 155–74).

Finney, J. W., Moos, R. H., & Brennan, P. L. (1991). The Drinking Problem Index: A measure to assess alcohol-related problems among older adults. *Journal of Substance Abuse, 3,* 395–404.

Fischer, L. R., & Eustis, N. N. (1989). Quicker and sicker: How changes in Medicare affect the elderly and their families. *Journal of Geriatric Psychiatry, 22*(2), 163–91.

Fisher, G. M. (1992, winter). The development and history of the poverty thresholds. *Social Security Bulletin, 55*(4), 3–14. For a summary see http://aspe.hhs.gov/poverty/papers/hptgssiv.htm (September 30, 2003)

Fisher, J.E., & Noll, J. P. (1996). Anxiety disorders. In Carstensen, Edelstein, & Dornbrand, *The practical handbook of clinical gerontology* (pp. 304–23).

Fiske, A., Gatz, M., & Pedersen, N. (2003). Depressive symptoms and aging: The effects of illness and non-health related events. *Journal of Gerontology: Psychological Sciences, 57B,* P320–28.

Fitzgerald, J. L., & Mulford, H. A. (1992). Elderly vs. younger problem drinker "treatment" and recovery experiences. *British Journal of Addiction, 87*(9), 1281–91.

Fleming, S., & Robinson, P. (2001). Grief and cognitive-behavioral therapy: The reconstruction of meaning. In Stroebe, Hansson, Stroebe, & Schut, *Handbook of bereavement research* (pp. 647–69).

Flint, A. J. (1994). Epidemiology and comorbidity of anxiety disorders in the elderly. *American Journal of Psychiatry, 151*(5), 640–49.

Flint, A. J., & Rifat, S. (1998). The treatment of psychotic depression in later life: A comparison of pharmacotherapy and ECT. *International Journal of Geriatric Psychiatry,* 23, 23–28.

Flora, P. (Ed). (1983). State, economy and society in Western Europe, 1815–1975: A data handbook. Vol. 1: The growth of mass democracies and welfare states. Frankfurt: Campus Verlag.

Flora, P., & Heidenheimer, A. J. (Eds). (1981). *The development of welfare states in Europe and America.* New Brunswick, NJ: Transaction.

Folkman, S. (2001). Revised coping theory and the process of bereavement. In Stroebe, Hansson, Stroebe, & Schut, *Handbook of bereavement research* (pp. 563–84).

Folkman, S., & Greer, S. (2000). Promoting psychological well-being in the face of serious illness. *Psycho-Oncology, 9,* 11–19.

Folkman, S., Chesney, M., McKusick, L., Ironson, G., Johnson, D. S., & Coates, T. J. (1991). Translating coping theory into an intervention. In J. Eckenrode (Ed.), *The social context of coping* (pp. 239–60). New York: Plenum.

Folstein, M. F., Folstein, S. E., & McHugh, P. R. (1975). "Mini-mental State": A practical method for grading the cognitive state of patients for the clinician. *Journal of Psychiatric Research, 12,* 189–98.

Food Research and Action Center (2003). *Food stamps and the elderly.* www.frac.org/ html/news/fsp/fsfactselderly.htm (October 2, 2003).

Forsell, Y., & Winblad, B. (1999). Incidence of major depression in a very elderly population. *International Journal of Geriatric Psychiatry, 14,* 368–72.

Fox, C. D., Berger, D., Fine, P. G., Gebhardt, G. F., Brabois, M., Kulich, R. J., Lande, S. D., McCarberg, B., & Portenoy, R. (2000, January 11). Pain assessment and treatment in the managed care environment: A position statement from the American Pain Society. *American Pain Society Managed Care Forum.* www.ampainsoc.org/managedcare/ position.htm (August 29, 2002).

Fozard, J., & Gordon-Salant, S. (2001). Changes in vision and hearing with aging. In J. E. Birren & K. Warner Schaie (Eds.), *Handbook of the psychology of aging* (5th ed., pp. 241–66). San Diego: Academic Press.

Fraley, R. C., & Shaver, P. R. (1999). Loss and bereavement: Attachment theory and recent controversies concerning "grief work" and the nature of detachment. In Cassidy & Shaver, *Handbook of Attachment* (pp. 735–59).

Franson, K., Chesley, D., & Kennedy, J. (2003). Beta-blockers, benzodiazepines, and other miscellaneous agents. In D. Hay, D. Klein, L. Hay, G. Grossberg, & J. Kennedy (Eds.), *Agitation in patients with dementia: A practical guide to diagnosis and management* (pp. 187–96). Washington, DC: American Psychiatric Publishing.

Fraser, N., & Nicholson, L. (1988). Social criticism without philosophy: An encounter between feminism and postmodernism. *Theory, Culture and Society, 5,* 373–94.

Fraser-Smith, N., Lesperance, T., & Talajic, M. (1995). Depression and 18-month prognosis after myocardial infection. *Circulation, 91,* 999–1005.

Freedman, M. (1994). Seniors in national and community service: A report prepared for the Commonwealth Fund's Americans Over 55 at Work Program. Philadelphia: Public/Private Ventures.

Freud, S. (1949). *An outline of psychoanalysis* (J. Strachey, Trans.). New York: W. W. Norton.

———. (1917/1957). *Mourning and melancholia.* In J. Strachey (Ed.), *The standard edition of the complete psychological works of Sigmund Freud* (Vol. 14, pp. 152–70). London: Hogarth.

Fried, T. R., van Doorn, C., O'Leary, J. R., Tinetti, M. E., & Drickamer, M. A. (1999). Older persons' preferences for site of terminal care. *Annals of Internal Medicine, 131,* 109–12.

Friedman, E., & Havighurst, R. (1954). *The meaning of work and retirement.* Chicago: University of Chicago Press.

Friedman, S. (Ed.). (1997). *Cultural issues in the treatment of anxiety.* New York: Guilford.

Froggatt, K. (2001). Life and death in English nursing homes: Sequestration or transition? *Ageing and Society, 21,* 319–32.

Fukukawa, Y., Nakashima, C., Tsuboi, S., Niino, N., Ando, F., Kosugi, S., & Shimokata, H. (2004). The impact of health problems on depression and activities in middle-aged and older adults: Age and social interactions as moderators. *Journal of Gerontology: Psychological and Social Sciences, 59B,* P19–26.

Fuller-Thomson, E., & Minkler, M. (2000). The mental and physical health of grandmothers who are raising their grandchildren. *Journal of Mental Health and Aging, 6*(4), 311–23.

———. (2003). Housing issues and realities facing grandparent caregivers who are renters. *Gerontologist, 43*(3), 92–98.

Fullmer, E. M., Shenk, D., & Eastland, L. (1999). Negating identity: A feminist analysis of the social invisibility of older lesbians. *Journal of Women and Aging, 11*(2–3), 131–48.

Fulmer, T. (2003). Try this: Elder abuse and neglect assessment. *Journal of Gerontological Nursing, 29*(1), 8–10.

Fulmer, T., Street, S., & Carr, K. (1984). Abuse of the elderly: Screening and detection. *Journal of Emergency Nursing, 10*(3), 131–40.

Futterman, A., Thompson, L., Gallagher-Thompson, D., & Ferris, R. (1995). Depression in later life: Epidemiology, assessment, etiology, and treatment. In E. E. Beckman & W. R. Leber (Eds.), *Handbook of depression* (2nd ed., pp. 494–525). New York: Guilford.

Gallagher, D. (1986). Assessment of depression by interview methods and psychiatric rating scales. In L. W. Poon (Ed.), *Handbook for clinical memory assessment of older adults* (pp. 205–25). Washington, DC: American Psychiatric Association.

Gallagher, D., & Thompson, L. (1983). Cognitive therapy for depression in the elderly: A promising model for treatment and research. In L. Breslau & J. Haug (Eds.), *Depression and aging: Causes, care and consequences* (pp. 168–92). New York: Springer.

Gallagher-Thompson, D. (2001). Caregivers of chronically ill elderly. In G. L. Maddox (Ed.), *Encyclopedia of aging* (3rd ed., vol. 1, pp. 160–62). New York: Springer.

Gallagher-Thompson, D., & Thompson, L. (1996). Applying cognitive-behavioral therapy to the psychological problems of later life. In Zarit & Knight, *A guide to psychotherapy and aging* (pp. 61–82).

Gallagher-Thompson, D., Hargrave, R., Hinton, L., Arean, P., Iwamasa, G., & Zeiss, L. M. (2003). Interventions for a multicultural society. In Coon, Gallagher-Thompson, & Thompson, *Innovative interventions to reduce dementia caregiver distress* (pp. 50–73).

Gallo, J., Rabins, P., & Illife, S. (1997). The "research magnificent" in later life: Psychiatric epidemiology and the primary care of older adults. *International Journal of Psychiatry in Medicine, 27,* 185–204.

Gallo, W., Baker, M., & Bradley, E. (2001). Factors associated with home versus institutional death among cancer patients in Connecticut. *Journal of the American Geriatrics Society, 49,* 771–77.

Gallup International Institute. (1997). *Spiritual beliefs and the dying process: A report on a national survey.* New York: Nathan Cummings Foundation.

Gamino, L., Sewell, K., & Easterling, L. (2000). Scott and White grief study—phase 2: Toward an adaptive model of grief. *Death Studies, 24,* 633–40.

Ganzini, L., Nelson, H., Schmidt, T., Kraemer, D., Delorit, M., & Lee, M. (2000). Physicians' experiences with the Oregon Death with Dignity Act. *New England Journal of Medicine, 342,* 557–63.

Garner, D. (1999). *Fundamentals of feminist gerontology.* New York: Haworth.

Gass, K. A. (1987). The health of conjugally bereaved older widows: The role of appraisal. *Research in Nursing and Health, 10,* 39–47.

Gatz, M., Kasl-Godley, J., & Karel, M. (1996). Aging and mental disorders. In J. E. Birren & K. Warner Schaie (Eds.), *Handbook of the psychology of aging* (4th ed., pp. 308–22). San Diego: Academic Press.

Gaugler, J. E., Jarrot, S., Zarit, S., Stephens, M., Townsend, A., & Greene, R. (2003). Adult day service use and reductions in caregiving hours: Effects on stress and psychological well-being for dementia caregivers. *International Journal of Geriatric Psychiatry, 18,* 55–62.

Gaugler, J. E., Kane, R. A., & Langlois, J. (2000). Assessment of family caregivers of older adults. In R. L. Kane & R. A. Kane (Eds.), *Assessing the well-being of older people: Measures, meaning, and practical applications* (pp. 320–59). New York: Oxford University Press.

Generations United. (2002). *Fact sheet: Grandparents and other relatives raising children: Their inclusion in the National Family Caregiver Support Program.* Washington, DC.

George, L. K. (1993). Sociological perspectives on life transitions. *Annual Review of Sociology, 19,* 353–73.

———. (2004). Social and economic factors related to psychiatric disorders in late life. In D. Blazer, D. C. Steffens, & E. Busse (Eds.), *Textbook of geriatric psychiatry* (3rd ed. pp. 139–61). Washington, DC: American Psychiatric Press.

George, L., & Maddox, G. (1977). Subjective adaptation of loss of the work role: A longitudinal study. *Journal of Gerontology, 39,* 364–71.

George, L., Fillenbaum, G., & Palmore, E. (1984). Sex differences in antecedents and consequences of retirement. *Journal of Gerontology, 39,* 364–71.

Germain, C., & Bloom, M. (1999). *Human behavior in the social environment: An ecological view.* (2nd ed.). New York: Columbia University Press.

Germain, C., & Gitterman, A. (1996). *The life model of social work practice* (2nd ed.). New York: Columbia University Press.

Germane, P., Shapiro, S., & Skinner, E. (1985). Mental health of the elderly. *Journal of the American Geriatrics Society, 33,* 264–52.

Geron, S. (1997). Introduction: Taking the measure of assessment. *Generations, 21*(1), 5–9.

Geron, S., & Little, F. (2003). Standardized geriatric assessment in social work practice with older adults. In Berkman & Harootyan, *Social work and health care in an aging society* (pp. 269–96).

Gerson, S., Belin, T. R., Kaufman, M. S., Mintz, J., & Jarvik, L. (1999). Pharmacological and psychological treatments for depressed older patients: A meta-analysis and overview of recent findings. *Harvard Review of Psychiatry, 7,* 1–28.

Gibson, R. (1987). Reconceptualizing retirement for black Americans. *Gerontologist, 27,* 691–98.

Gil, J., Bernard, D., Martinez, D., & Beach, D. (2004). Polycomb CBX7 has a unifying role in cellular lifespan. *Nature Cell Biology, 6*(1), 67–72.

Gilbert, D., & Kahl, J. A. (1992). *The American class structure: A new synthesis* (4th ed.). Belmont, CA: Wadsworth.

Gilligan, C. (1982). *In a different voice.* Cambridge, MA: Harvard University Press.

Gilliland, B., & James, R. (1988). *Crisis intervention strategies.* Pacific Grove, CA: Brooks/Cole.

Gitlin, L., & Gwyther, L. (2003). In-home interventions: Helping caregivers where they live. In Coon, Gallagher-Thompson, & Thompson, *Innovative interventions to reduce dementia caregiver distress* (pp. 139–60).

Glanz, K., & Lerman, C. (1992). Psychological impact of breast cancer: A critical review. *Annals of Behavioral Medicine, 14,* 204–12.

Glaser, R., & Kiecolt-Glaser, J. K. (1997). Chronic stress modulates the virus-specific immune response to latent herpes simplex virus Type I. *Annals of Behavioral Medicine, 19,* 78–82.

Glied, S., & Kofman, S. (1995). *Women and mental health: Issues for health reform.* New York: Commonwealth Fund, Commission on Women's Health.

Glynn, R., Bouchard, G., LoCastro, J., & Laird, N. (1985). Aging and generational effects on drinking behaviors in men: Results from the Normative Aging Study. *American Journal of Public Health, 75,* 1413–19.

Gockel, J., Morrow-Howell, N., Thompson, E., Pousson, M., & Johnson, M. (1998). Advance directives: A social work initiative to increase participation. *Research on Social Work Practice, 8,* 520–28.

Gold, D. (1996). Introduction: Cross-fertilization of the life course and other theoretical paradigms. *Gerontologist, 36*(2), 224–25.

Gomberg, E. S. L. (1990). Drugs, alcohol, and aging. *Research Advances in Alcohol and Drug Problems, 10,* 171–213.

———. (1995). Older women and alcohol use and abuse. In F. J. Turner (Ed.), *Mental health and the elderly* (pp. 355–74). New York: Free Press.

Gomberg, E. S. L., & Zucker, R. A. (1998). Substance use and abuse in old age. In I. H. Nordhus, G. R. VandenBos, S. Berg, & P. Fromholt (Eds.), *Clinical Geropsychology* (pp. 189–209). Washington, DC: American Psychological Association.

Gomberg, E. S. L., Hegedus, A., & Zucker, R. (Eds.). (1990). *Alcohol problems and aging.* Bethesda, MD: U.S. Department of Health and Human Services.

Gonzalez, H., Haan, M., & Hinton, L. (2001). Acculturation and the prevalence of depression in older Mexican Americans: Baseline results from the Sacramento Area Latino Study on Aging. *American Journal of Geriatric Psychiatry, 49,* 948–53.

Goodman, C., & Silverstein, M. (2002). Grandmothers raising grandchildren: Family structure and well-being in culturally diverse families. *Gerontologist, 42*(5), 676–89.

Gottfries, C. G. (1998). Is there a difference between elderly and younger patients with regard to the symptomatology and aetiology of depression? *International Clinical Psychopharmacology, 13,* S13–18.

Gottlieb, B. H., Thompson, L., & Bourgeois, M. (2003). Monitoring and evaluating interventions. In Coon, Gallagher-Thompson, & Thompson, *Innovative interventions to reduce dementia caregiver distress* (pp. 28–49).

Gottschalk, P., & Smeeding, T. (1997). Cross-national comparisons of earnings and income inequality. *Journal of Economic Literature,* June, 633–87.

Graig, L., & Paganelli, V. (2000). Phased retirement: Reshaping the end of work. *Compensation and benefits management, 16,* 1–10.

Grant, B. F., Harford, T. C., Dawson, D. A., Chou, P. S., Dufour, M., & Pickering, R. P. (1994). Prevalence of DSM-IV alcohol abuse and dependence: United States, 1992. *Alcohol Health and Research World, 18,* 243–49.

Gratton, B., & Haber, C. (1996). Three phases in the history of American grandparents: Authority, burden, compassion. *Generations, 20*(1), 7–12.

Gray, R. (2001). Cancer self-help groups are here to stay: Issues and challenges for health professionals. *Journal of Palliative Care, 17*(1), 53–59.

Green, R., Cupples, L., Kurz, A., Auerbach, S., Go, R., Sadovnick, D., Duara, R., Kukull, W., Chui, H., Edeki, T., Griffith, P., Friedland, R., Bachman, D., & Farrer, L. (2003). Depression as a risk factor for Alzheimer's disease: The MIRAGE Study. *Archives of Neurology, 60*(5), 753–59.

Greenblatt, D., & Shader, R. (1991). Benzodiazepines in the elderly: Pharmacokinetics and drug sensitivity. In Salzman & Lebowitz, *Anxiety in the elderly* (pp. 131–73).

Greene, R. (2000). *Social work with the aged and their families* (2nd ed.). New York: Aldine de Gruyter.

Greene, R., & Galambos, C. (2002). Social work's pursuit of a common professional framework: Have we reached a milestone? *Journal of Gerontological Social Work, 39*(1), 7–23.

Gregoire, T., Kilty, K. M., & Richardson, V. E. (2002). Gender and racial inequities in retirement resources. *Journal of Women and Aging, 14*(3–4), 25–39.

Grieger, I., & Ponterotto, J. (1995). A framework for assessment in multicultural counseling. In J. Ponterotto, J. M. Casas, L. Suzuki, & C. Alexander (Eds.), *Handbook of multicultural counseling* (pp. 357–74). Thousand Oaks, CA: Sage.

Grossberg, G., & Desai, A. (2003). Management of Alzheimer's disease. *Journal of Gerontology: Medical Sciences, 58A*(4), 331–53.

Grundy, E., & Sloggett, A. (2003). Health inequalities in the older population: The role of personal capital, social resources and socioeconomic circumstances. *Social Science and Medicine, 56,* 935–47.

Gubrium, J. F., & Buckholdt, D. (1977). *Toward maturity.* San Francisco: Jossey-Bass.

Gubrium, J. F., & Holstein, J. (1999). Constructionist perspectives on aging. In Bengtson & Schaie, *Handbook of theories of aging* (pp. 287–305).

Gupta, R., & Yick, A. (2001). Validation of CES-D Scale for older Chinese immigrants. *Journal of Mental Health and Aging, 7*(2), 257–72.

Gurland, B., Golden, R., Teresi, J., & Challop, J. (1984). The SHORT-CARE: An instrument for the assessment of depression, dementia, and disability. *Journal of Gerontology, 39,* 166–69.

Gurland, B., Kuriansky, J., Sharpe, L., Simon, R., Stiller, P., & Birkett, P. (1977–78). The Comprehensive Assessment and Referral Evaluation (CARE)—Rationale, development and reliability. *International Journal of Aging and Human Development, 8*(1), 9–42.

Gurnack, A. (Ed.). (1997). *Older adults' misuse of alcohol, medicines, and other drugs.* New York: Springer.

Gurnack, A., Atkinson, R., & Osgood, N. (Eds.). (2002). *Treating alcohol and drug abuse in the elderly.* New York: Springer.

Gustman, A. L., & Steinmeier, T. L. (2001). *Imperfect knowledge, retirement and saving* (National Bureau of Economic Research Working Paper Series). Cambridge, MA.

Gutmann, D. (1964). An exploration of ego configuration in middle and later life. In B. Neugarten (Ed.), *Personality in middle and later life.* New York: Atherton.

Habermas, J. (1976). *Communications and the evolution of society.* Boston: Beacon.

Hall, M., & Irwin, M. (2001). Physiological indices of functioning in bereavement. In Stroebe, Hansson, Stroebe, & Schut, *Handbook of bereavement research* (pp. 473–92).

Hannappel, M., Carslyn, R. J., & Allen, G. (1993). Does social support alleviate the depression of caregivers of dementia patients? *Journal of Gerontological Social Work, 20,* 35–51.

Happ, B., Capezuti, E., Strumpf, N., Wagner, L. Cunningham, S., Evans, L., & Maislin, G. (2002). Advance care planning and end-of-life care for hospitalized nursing home residents. *Journal of the American Geriatrics Society, 50,* 829–35.

Harbison, J. (1999). Models of intervention for "elder abuse and neglect": A Canadian perspective on ageism, participation, and empowerment. *Journal of Elder Abuse and Neglect, 10*(3–4), 1–17.

Harel, Z., & Biegel, D. E. (1995). Aging, ethnicity, and mental health services: Social work perspectives on need and use. In Padgett, *Handbook on ethnicity, aging, and mental health* (pp. 217–41).

Harper, D. J., Manasse, P. R., James, O., & Newton, J. T. (1993). Intervening to reduce distress in caregivers of impaired elderly people: A preliminary evaluation. *International Journal of Geriatric Psychiatry, 8,* 139–45.

Harris, P. B. (2002). The voices of husbands and sons caring for a family member with dementia. In Kramer & Thompson, *Men as caregivers* (pp. 213–33).

Harvey, J. (Ed.). (1998). *Perspectives on loss: A sourcebook.* Philadelphia: Brunner/Mazel.

Harvey, J., Orbuch, R. L., Weber, A. L., Merbach, N., & Alt, R. (1992). House of pain and hope: Accounts of loss. *Death Studies, 16,* 99–124.

Harwood, D., Barker, W., Ownby, R., Mullan, M., & Duaru, R. (1999). Factors associated with depressive symptoms in non-demented community-dwelling elderly. *International Journal of Geriatric Psychiatry, 14,* 331–37.

Hatch, L. R., & Thompson, A. (1992). Family responsibilities and women's retirement. In M. Szinovacz, D. Ekerdt, & B. Vinick (Eds.), *Families and retirement* (pp. 99–113). Newbury Park, CA: Sage.

Havighurst, R. J. (1957). The social competence of middle-aged people. *Genetic Psychology Monogram, 56,* 297–375.

———. (1963). Successful aging. In R. Williams, C. Tibbits, & W. Donahue (Eds.), *Processes of aging* (vol. 1, pp. 299–20). New York: Atherton.

Hay, D., Klein, D., Hay, L., Grossberg, G., & Kennedy, J. S. (2003). *Agitation in patients with dementia: A practical guide to diagnosis and management.* Washington, DC: American Psychiatric Publishing.

Hayflick, L. (1995). Biological aging theories. In G. L. Maddox (Ed.), *The encyclopedia of aging* (2nd ed., pp. 113–18). New York: Springer.

Haylock, P. (2002). Managing cancer pain: Where we've come from, where we are, and what is left to do. *Illness, Crisis and Loss,* 10(1), 62–79.

Hays, J. C., Landerman, L. R., George, L. K., Flint, E. P., Koenig, H. G., Land, K. C., & Blazer, D.G. (1998). Social correlates of the dimensions of depression in the elderly. *Journal of Gerontology: Psychological Sciences, 53B,* P31–39.

Hayslip, B., Emick, M., Henderson, C., & Elias, K. (2002). Temporal variations in the experience of custodial grandparenting: A short-term longitudinal study. *Journal of Applied Gerontology,* 21(2), 139–56.

Health Care Financing Administration. (2000). *Medicare 2000: Thirty-five years of improving Americans' health and security.* Washington, DC: U.S. Government Printing Office. http://cms.hhs.gov/researchers/pubs/default.asp (January 6, 2005).

Heard, K., & Watson, T. S. (1999). Reducing wandering by persons with dementia using differential reinforcement. *Journal of Applied Behavior Analysis, 32,* 381–84.

Hebert, R., Levesque, L., Lavoie, J., Ducharme, F., Gendron, C., Preville, M., Voyer, L., & Dubois, M. (2003). Efficacy of a psychoeducative group program for caregivers of demented persons living at home: A randomized controlled trial. *Journal of Gerontology: Social Sciences, 58B*(1), S58–67.

Heisel, M., Flett, G., & Besser, A. (2002). Cognitive functioning and geriatric suicide ideation: Testing a mediational model. *American Journal of Geriatric Psychiatry, 10*(4), 428–36.

Held, D. (1980). *Introduction to critical theory.* Berkeley: University of California Press.

Helvering et al. v. Davis, 301 U.S. 619 (1937). www.ssa.gov/history/supreme1.html (October 28, 2004).

Helzer, J. E., Carey, K. E., & Miller, R. H. (1984). Predictors and correlates in older versus younger alcoholics. In G. Maddox, L. N. Robins, & N. Rosenberg (Eds.), *Nature and extent of alcohol problems among the elderly: Proceedings of a workshop* (Research monograph no. 14, pp. 83–99). Rockville, MD: National Institute on Alcohol Abuse and Alcoholism.

Hendricks, J. (1996). The search for new solutions. *Gerontologist, 36*(2), 141–44.

Herzog, A. R., & Markus, H. R. (1999). The self-concept in life span and aging research. In Bengston and Schaie, *Handbook of theories of aging* (pp. 227–52).

Hickman, S. (2002). Improving communication near the end of life. *American Behavioral Scientist, 46*(2), 252–67.

Hinrichsen, G. A. (1999). *Interpersonal psychotherapy for late-life depression.* In M. Duffy (Ed.), *Handbook of counseling and psychotherapy with older adults* (pp. 470–486). New York: John Wiley and Sons, Inc.

Hobbs, F. B., & Stoops, N. (2002). *Demographic trends in the 20th century, Census 2000 Special Reports* (Series CENSR-4). Washington, D.C.: U.S. Census Bureau.

Hoffmann, N. G., & Harrison, P. A. (1995). *SUDDS-IV manual.* St. Paul, MN: New Standards.

Hogervorst, E., Barnetson, L., Jobst, K. A., Nagy, Z., Combrinck, M., & Smith, A. D. (2000). Diagnosing dementia: Interrater reliability assessment and accuracy of the NINCDS/ADRDA Criteria versus CERAD Histopathological criteria for Alzheimer's disease. *Dementia and Geriatric Cognitive Disorders, 11,* 107–13.

Holden, K. C., & Smeeding, T. M. (1990). The poor, the rich, and the insecure elderly caught in between. *Milbank Quarterly, 16,* 227–39.

Holden, K. C., Burkhauser, R. V., & Myers, D. A. (1986). Income transitions at older stages of life: The dynamics of poverty. *Gerontologist, 26,* 292–97.

Hollinger, R. (1994). *Postmodernism and the social sciences: A thematic approach.* Thousand Oaks, CA: Sage.

Holmes, T. H., & Rahe, R. H. (1967). The social readjustment rating scale. *Journal of Psychosomatic Research, 11,* 213–18.

Hooyman, N., & Gonyea, J. (1995). *Feminist perspectives on family care.* Thousand Oaks, CA: Sage.

———. (1999). A feminist model of family care: Practice and policy directions. In D. Garner (Ed.), *Fundamentals of feminist gerontology* (pp. 149–69). Binghamton, NY: Haworth.

Hooyman, N., Browne, C., Ray, R., & Richardson, V. (2002). Feminist gerontology and the life course: Policy, research and teaching issues. *Gerontology and Geriatrics Education, 22*(4), 3–26.

Hopko, D. R., Stanley, M. A., Reas, D. L., Wetherell, J. L., Beck, J. G., Novy, D. M., & Averill, P. M. (2003). Assessing worry in older adults: Confirmatory factor analysis of the Penn State Worry Questionnaire and psychometric properties of an abbreviated model. *Psychological Assessment, 15,* 173–83.

Horkheimer, M., & Adorno, T. (1972). *Dialectic of enlightenment.* New York: Seabury.

Hudson, M., Beasley, C., Benedict, R., Carlson, J., Craig, B., & Mason, S. (1999). Elder abuse: Some African American views. *Journal of Interpersonal Violence, 14*(9), 915–39.

Hudson, R. B. (1994). The Older Americans Act and the defederalization of community-based care. In P. Kim (Ed.), *Services to the aging and aged: Public policies and programs*, pp. 45–75. New York: Garland.

Hughes, C. P., Berg, L., Danziger, W. L., Coben, L. A., & Martin, R. L. (1982). A clinical scale for the staging of dementia. *British Journal of Psychiatry, 140,* 566–72.

Hungerford, T. L. (2001). The economic consequences of widowhood on elderly women in the United States and Germany. *Gerontologist, 41*(1), 103–10.

Hungerford, T., Rassette, M., Iams, H., & Koenig, M. (2002). *Trends in the economic status of the elderly: 1976–2000.* Social Security Administration. www.ssa.gov/policy/docs/ssb/v64n3/v64n3p12.html (July 30, 2003).

Hwalek, M. A., & Sengstock, M. C. (1986). Assessing the probability of abuse of the elderly: Toward development of a clinical screening instrument. *Journal of Applied Gerontology, 5,* 153–73.

Iams, H. M., & Butrica, B. (1999, April 30). *Projected trends from the MINT model.* Paper presented to the 1999 Technical Advisory Panel to the Social Security Trustees, Washington, DC.

Iams, H. M., & Sandell, S. H. (1998). Cost-neutral policies to increase Social Security benefits for widows: A simulation for 1992. *Social Security Bulletin, 61*(1), 14–43.

Ibrahim, F. A., & Owen, S. V. (1994). Factor analytic structure of the Scale to Assess World View. *Current Psychology: Development, Learning, Personality, Social, 13,* 201–9.

Ibrahim, F. A., Roysircar-Sodowsky, G., & Ohnishi, H. (2001). Worldview: Recent developments and needed directions. In J. Ponterotto, J. M. Casas, L. Suzuki, & C. Alexander (Eds.), *Handbook of multicultural counseling* (2nd ed., pp. 425–56). Thousand Oaks, CA: Sage.

International Work Group on Death, Dying, and Bereavement. (1990). Assumptions and principles of spiritual care. *Death Studies, 14,* 75–81.

Inzitari, D., Rossi, M., Lamassa, M., Mugnai, S., Carlucci, G., Bianchi, C., & Amaducci, L. (1999). Validity of different linguistic versions of the Alzheimer's Disease Assessment Scale in an international multicenter Alzheimer's disease trial. *Dementia and Geriatric Cognitive Disorders, 10*(4), 269–77.

Iwamasa, G., Hilliard, K., & Kost, C. (1998). Geriatric depression scale and Japanese American older adults. *Clinical Gerontologist, 19,* 13–24.

Jackson, J. S., Williams, D. R., & Gomberg, E. (1998). Aging and alcohol use and abuse among African Americans: A life-course perspective. In Gomberg, Hegedus, & Zucker, *Alcohol problems and aging* (pp. 63–87).

James, R., & Gilliland, B. (2001). *Crisis intervention strategies.* Belmont, CA: Wadsworth/Thomson Learning.

Jamison, S. (1997). *Assisted Suicide: A decision-making guide for health professionals.* San Francisco: Jossey-Bass.

Janoff-Bulman, R. (1992). *Shattered assumptions: Toward a new psychology of trauma.* New York: Free Press.

Janoff-Bulman, R., & Berg, M. (1998). Disillusionment and the creation of value: From traumatic losses to existential gains. In Harvey, *Perspectives on loss* (pp. 35–47).

Joseph, C. (1997). Misuse of alcohol and drugs in the nursing home. In Gurnack, *Older adults' misuse of alcohol, medicines, and other drugs* (pp. 228–54).

Jung, C. (1933). *Modern man in search of a soul.* New York: Harcourt Brace.

———. (1960). *Collected works: Vol. 8. The stages of life.* New York: Pantheon.

———. (1969). *Collected works: Vol. 9.* Princeton, NJ: Princeton University Press.

Kaasa, T., & Wessel, J. (2001). The Edmonton functional assessment tool: Further development and validation for use in palliative care. *Journal of Palliative Care, 17*(5), 5–11.

Kagawa-Singer, M. (1998). The cultural context of death rituals and mourning practices. *Oncology Nursing Forum, 25,* 1752–56.

Kahana, B., Dan, A., Kahana, E., & Kercher, K. (2004). The personal and social context of planning for end-of-life care. *Journal of the American Geriatrics Society, 52,* 1163–67.

Kahn, R. L., Goldfarb, A. I., Pollack, M., & Peck, A. (1960). Brief objective measures for the determination of mental status in the aged. *American Journal of Psychiatry, 117,* 326–28.

Kail, B. L., & DeLaRosa, M. (1998). Challenges to treating the elderly Latino substance abuser: A not so hidden research agenda. In M. Delgado (Ed)., *Latino elders and the twenty-first century: Issues and challenges for culturally competent research and practice* (pp. 123–41). New York: Haworth.

Kaiser Commission on the Future of Medicaid. (1993). *The Medicaid cost explosion: Causes and consequences.* Baltimore: Kaiser Family Foundation.

Kaiser Family Foundation. (2003, June). *Impact of direct-to-consumer advertising on prescription drug spending.* www.kff.org/rxdrugs/loader.cfm?url=/commonspot/security/getfile.cfm&PageID=14378 (January 17, 2005).

Kamel, H., Mouton, C., & McKee, D. (2002). Culture and loss. In K. Doka (Ed.), *Living with grief: Loss in later life* (pp. 282–94). Washington, DC: Hospice Foundation of America.

Kane, R. A., & Kane, R. L. (1981). *Assessing the elderly: A practical guide to measurement.* Lexington, MA: D. C. Heath.

Kane, R. L. (2000). Mandated assessments. In R. L. Kane & R. A. Kane (Eds.), *Assessing older persons* (pp. 458–82). New York: Oxford University Press.

Kane, R. L., & Kane, R. A. (1980). Alternatives to institutional care of the elderly: Beyond the dichotomy. *Gerontologist, 20,* 249–59.

Kang, T., & Kang, G. E. (1995). Mental health status and needs of the Asian American elderly. In Padgett, *Handbook on ethnicity, aging, and mental health* (pp. 113–31).

Kashner, T. M., Rodell, D., Ogden, S., Guggenheim, F., & Karson, C. (1992). Outcomes and costs of two VA inpatient treatment programs for older alcoholic patients. *Hospital and community psychiatry, 43,* 985–89.

Kastenbaum, R. (1992). *The psychology of death.* New York: Springer.

———. (1994). Anxiety in old age. In B. Wolman & G. Stricker (Eds.), *Anxiety and related disorders* (pp. 209–25). New York: Wiley.

———. (2000). *The psychology of death* (3rd ed.). New York: Springer.

Katon, W., Lin, E., Russo, J., & Unutzer, J. (2003). Increased medical costs of a population-based sample of depressed elderly patients. *Archives of General Psychiatry, 60,* 897–900.

Katz, I. (1998). Diagnosis and treatment of depression in patients with Alzheimer's disease and other dementias. *Journal of Clinical Psychiatry, 59,* 38–44.

Katz, I. R., & Parmelee, P. A. Overview (1997). In Rubinstein & Lawton. *Depression in long-term and residential care* (pp. 1–25).

Katzman, R. (2000, July 9). *Epidemiology of Alzheimer's disease.* Paper presented at the World Alzheimer Congress 2000, Washington, DC.

Kayser-Jones, J. (2002). The experience of dying: An ethnographic nursing home study. *Gerontologist, 42*[special issue III], 11–19.

Kilty, K. M., & Behling, J. (1986). Retirement financial planning among professional workers. *Gerontologist, 25,* 525–30.

Kilty, K. M., & Richardson, V. E. (1988, November). *Factors in the retirement decision process.* Paper presented at the Annual Meeting of the American Gerontological Society, San Francisco.

———. (1989). Differences in depression between voluntary and involuntary retirees. Unpublished manuscript.

Kim, J., & Moen, P. (1999). *Work/retirement transitions and psychological well-being in late midlife* (BLCC Working Paper 99-10). Ithaca, NY: Cornell University.

———. (2001). Moving into retirement: Preparation and transitions in late midlife. In Lachman, *Handbook of midlife development* (pp. 487–527).

———. (2002). Retirement transitions, gender, and psychological well-being: A life-course, ecological model. *Journal of Gerontology: Psychological Sciences, 57B*(3), P212–22.

Kim, M. (1992). *Retirement attitudes, preparations, conceptualizations, and behavioral intentions among first-generation Korean Americans in midlife.* Unpublished doctoral dissertation, Ohio State University, Columbus.

Kincaid, M. M., Harvey, P. D., Parella, M., White, L., Putman, K. M., Powchik, P., Davidson, M., & Mohs, R. C. (1995). Validity and utility of the ADAS-L for measurement of cognitive and functional impairment in geriatric schizophrenic inpatients. *Journal of Neuropsychiatry and Clinical Neurosciences, 7,* 76–81.

King, C., Van Hasselt, V. B., & Segal, D. L. (1994). Diagnosis and assessment of substance abuse in older adults: Current strategies and issues. *Addictive Behaviors, 19,* 41–55.

Kingson, E. R., & Berkowitz, E. D. (1993). *Social Security and Medicare: A policy primer.* Westport, CT: Greenwood.

Kirkwood, T. (2002). Why does aging occur? In V. Cristofalo & R. Adelman (Eds.), *Annual Review of geriatrics and gerontology: Modern topics on the biology of aging* (pp. 41–55). New York: Springer.

Klass, D. (2001). Continuing bonds in the resolution of grief in Japan and North America. *American Behavioral Scientist, 44*(5), 742–63.

Klass, D., Silverman, P. R., & Nickman, S. L. (1996). *Continuing bonds: New understandings of grief.* Washington, DC: Taylor & Francis.

Klein, D., Steinberg, M., Galik, E., Steele, C., Sheppard, J., Warren, A., Rosenblatt, A., & Lyketsos, C. (1999). Wandering behaviour in community-residing persons with dementia. *International Journal of Geriatric Psychiatry, 14,* 272–79.

Klein, S. (Ed.). (1996). *A national agenda for geriatric education: White papers.* Rockville, MD: Health Resources and Services Administration.

Klein, W., & Jess, C. (2002). One last pleasure? Alcohol use among elderly people in nursing homes. *Health and Social Work, 27*(3), 193–97.

Klerman, G. L., Weissman, M. M., Rounsaville, B. J., & Chevron, E. S. (1984). *Interpersonal psychotherapy of depression.* New York: Basic Books.

Kline, D. W., & Scialfa, C. T. (1996). Visual and auditory aging. In J. E. Birren & K. Warner Schaie (Eds.), *Handbook of the psychology of aging* (4th ed., pp. 181–203). San Diego: Academic Press.

Knight, B., Teri, L., Wohlford, P., & Santos, J. (Ed.). (1995). *Mental health services for older adults.* Washington, DC: American Psychological Association.

Koenig, H. (1997). Mood Disorders. In P. D. Nussbaum (Ed.), *Handbook of neuropsychology and aging* (pp. 63–79). New York: Plenum.

Koenig, H. G., & Blazer, D. G. (1996). Depression. In Birren, *Encyclopedia of gerontology* (pp. 415–28).

Kohn, R., Westlake, R., Rasmussen, S., Marsland, R., & Norman, W. (1997). Clinical features of obsessive-compulsive disorder in elderly patients. *American Journal of Geriatric Psychiatry, 5*(3), 211–15.

Kohout, F., Berkman, L., Evans, D., & Cornoni-Huntley, J. (1993). Two shorter forms of the CES-D Depression Symptoms Index. *Journal of Aging and Health, 5,* 179–93.

Kolomer, S., McCallion, P., & Janicki, M. (2002). African-American grandmother carers of children with disabilities: Predictors of depressive symptoms. *Journal of Gerontological Social Work, 37*(3/4), 45–63.

Kosberg, J. (1988). Preventing elder abuse: Identification of high-risk factors prior to placement decisions. *Gerontologist, 28,* 43–50.

———. (1988). The abuse of elderly men. *Journal of Elder Abuse and Neglect, 9*(3), 69–87.

Kraaij, V., Arensman, E., & Spinhoven, P. (2002). Negative life events and depression in elderly persons: A meta-analysis. *Journal of Gerontology: Psychological and Social Sciences, 57B,* P87–94.

Kramer, A., & Willis, S. (2002). Enhancing cognitive vitality of older adults. *Current Directions in Psychological Science, 11*(5), 173–77.

Kramer, B. (2002). Men caregivers: An overview. In Kramer & Thompson, *Men as caregivers* (pp. 3–19).

Kramer, B., & Thompson, E., Jr. (Eds.). (2002). *Men as caregivers.* New York: Springer.

Krause, N. (2001). Social support. In R. Binstock & L. George (Eds.), *Handbook of aging and the social sciences* (pp. 272–94). San Diego: Academic Press.

Kubler-Ross, E. (1997). *The wheel of life: A memoir of living and dying.* New York: Scribner's.

Kulik, L. (2001). The impact of men's and women's retirement on marital relations: A comparative analysis. *Journal of Women and Aging, 13*(2), 21–37.

Kulik, L., & Barelli, H. Z. (1997). Continuity and discontinuity in attitudes toward marital power relations: Pre-retired vs. retired husbands. *Ageing and Society, 17,* 571–595.

Kumar, V., & Eisdorfer, C. (1998). *Advances in the diagnosis and treatment of Alzheimer's disease*. New York: Springer.

Kunkel, S. R., & Applebaum, R. A. (1989). *Estimating the prevalence of long-term disability for an aging society*. Oxford, OH: Scripps Gerontology Center.

Kuypers, J. A., & Bengtson, V. L. (1973). Social breakdown and competence: A model of normal aging. *Human Development, 16*, 181–201.

Lachman, M. (Ed.). (2001). *Handbook of midlife development*. New York: Wiley.

Lachs, M., & Pillemer, K. (1995). Abuse and neglect of elderly persons. *New England Journal of Medicine, 332*(7), 437–43.

Lachs, M., Williams, C., O'Brien, S., & Pillemer, K. (2002). Adult protective service use and nursing home placement. *Gerontologist, 42*(6), 734–39.

Laidlaw, K., Thompson, L., Dick-Siskin, L., & Gallagher-Thompson, D. (2003). *Cognitive behaviour therapy with older people*. West Sussex, U.K.: Wiley.

Landrine, H., & Klonoff, E. (1996). *African American acculturation*. Thousand Oaks, CA: Sage.

Landry-Meyer, L. (1999). Research into action: Recommended intervention strategies for grandparent caregivers. *Family Relations, 48*(4), 381–89.

Lang, F. R., & Carstensen, L. (1994). Close emotional relationships in late life: Further support for proactive aging in the social domain. *Psychology and Aging, 9*, 315–24.

———. (2002). Time counts: Future time perspective, goals, and social relationships. *Psychology and Aging, 17*(1), 125–39.

Lang, F. R., Staudinger, U., & Carstensen, L. (1998). Socioemotional selectivity in late life: How personality does (and does not) make a difference. *Journals of Gerontology: Psychological Science, 53B*, P21–30.

Last Acts Diversity Committee. (2001). *Last Acts statement on diversity and end-of-life care*. www.lastacts.org/statsite/5526la_tsk_publ.html (July 31, 2002). This site is now defunct.

Last Acts. (2002). *Means to a better end: A report on dying in America today*. www.rwjf. org/news/special/meansReport.pdf (December 21, 2004).

Lavretsky, H., Mistry, R., Bastani, R., Gould, R., Gokham, I., Huang, D., Maxwell, A., McDermott, C., Rosansky, J., Jarvick, L., & the UPBEAT Collaborative Group. (2003). Symptoms of depression and anxiety predict mortality in elderly veterans enrolled in the UPBEAT program. *International Journal of Geriatric Psychiatry, 18*, 183–84.

Lawton, M. P. (1979). *Clinical geropsychology: Problems and prospects, Master lectures on the psychology of aging*. Washington, DC: American Psychological Association.

———. (1991). A multidimensional view of quality of life in frail elders: The concept and measurement of quality of life in the frail elderly. In J. E. Birren, J. Lubben, J. C. Rowe, & D. E. Deutchman (Eds.), *The concept and measurement of quality of life* (pp. 3–27). San Diego: Academic Press.

Lawton, M. P., & Rubinstein, R. L. (Eds.). (2000). *Interventions in dementia care*. New York: Springer.

Lawton, M. P., Kleban, M. H., Moss, M., Rovine, M., & Glicksman, A. (1989). Measuring caregiving appraisal. *Journal of Gerontology, 44*(3), P61–71.

Lawton, M. P., Kleban, M. H., Rajagopal, D., & Dean, J. (1992). Dimensions of affective experience in three age groups. *Psychology and Aging, 7,* 171–84.

Lawton, M. P., Van Haitsma, K., & Klapper, J. (1996). Observed affect in nursing home residents with Alzheimer's disease. *Journal of Gerontology: Psychological Sciences, 51B,* P3–14.

Lawton, M. P., Van Haitsma, K., & Perkinson, M. (2000). Emotion in people with dementia: A way of comprehending their preferences and aversions. In Lawton & Rubinstein, *Interventions in dementia care* (pp. 95–119).

Lazarus, R. S., & Folkman, S. (1984). *Stress, appraisal, and coping.* New York: Springer.

Lee, G., Willetts, M., & Seccombe, K. (1998). Widowhood and depression: Gender differences. *Research on Aging, 20,* 611–30.

Lee, J. (1994). *The empowerment approach to social work practice.* New York: Columbia University Press.

Lee, J. (2001). *The empowerment approach to social work practice.* New York: Columbia University Press.

Leenaars, A. A., Maltsberger, J. T., & Neimeyer, R. A. (Eds.). (1994). *Treatment of suicidal people.* Washington, DC: Taylor & Francis.

Leitsch, S., Zarit, S., Towsend, A., & Greene, R. (2001). Medical and social adult day service programs. *Research on Aging, 23*(4), 473–98.

Lemke, S., & Moos, R. (2002). Prognosis of older patients in mixed-age alcoholism treatment programs. *Journal of Substance Abuse Treatment, 22,* 33–43.

———. (2003). Treatment and outcomes of older patients with alcohol use disorders in community residential programs. *Journal of Studies on Alcohol, 64*(2), 219–26.

Leventhal, H., Rabin, C., Leventhal, E., & Burns, E. (2001). Health risk behaviors and aging. In J. E. Birren, & K. Warner Schaie (Eds.), *Handbook of the psychology of aging* (5th ed., pp. 186–214). San Diego: Academic Press.

Levesque, L., Gendron, C., Vezina, J., Herbert, R., Ducharme, F., Lavoie, J. P., Gedron, M., Voyer, L., & Preville, M. (2002). The process of group intervention for caregivers of demented persons living at home: Conceptual framework, components and characteristics. *Aging and Mental Health, 6*(3), 239–47.

Levy, J. A. (1989). The hospice in the context of an aging society. *Journal of Aging Studies, 3*(4), 385–99.

Lewis, M. A., & Widerquist, K. (2002). *Economics for social workers: The application of economic theory to social policy and the human services.* New York: Columbia University Press.

Liberto, J., & Oslin, D. (1997). Early versus late onset of alcoholism in the elderly. In Gurnack, *Older adults' misuse of alcohol, medicines, and other drugs* (pp. 94–112).

Liberto, J., Oslin, D., & Ruskin, P. (1996). Alcoholism in the older population. In Carstensen, Edelstein, & Dornbrand, *The practical handbook of clinical gerontology* (pp. 324–48).

Light, J., Grigsby, J., & Bligh, M. (1996). Aging and heterogeneity: Genetics, social structure, and personality. *Gerontologist, 36*(2), 165–73.

Linn, M. (1978). Attrition of older alcoholics from treatment. *Addictive Diseases: An International Journal, 3,* 437–47.

Llorente, M. D., Eisdorfer, C., Loewenstein, D., & Zarate, Y. (1996). Suicide among Hispanic elderly: Cuban Americans in Dade County, Florida, 1990–1993. *Journal of Mental Health and Aging, 2,* 79–87.

Lobmayer, P., & Wilkinson, R. (2000). Income, inequality, and mortality in 14 developed countries. *Sociology of Health and Illness, 22*(4), 401–14.

Logsdon, R., Gibbons, L., McCurry, S., & Teri, L. (2000). Quality of life in Alzheimer's disease: Patient and caregiver reports. In S. Albert & R. Logsdon (Eds.), *Assessing quality of life in Alzheimer's disease* (pp. 17–30). New York: Springer.

Logsdon, R. G., Teri, L., McCurry, S., Gibbons, L., Kukull, W. A., & Larson, E. B. (1998). Wandering: A significant problem among community-residing individuals with Alzheimer's disease. *Journal of Gerontology: Psychological Sciences, 53B*(5), P294–99.

Longest, B. B. (2002). *Health policymaking in the United States.* (3rd ed.) Chicago: Health Administration Press.

Lopata, H. (1975). Grief work and identity reconstruction. *Journal of Geriatric Psychiatry, 8,* 41–55.

Lorenz, K., Lynn, J., Morton, S. C., Dy, S., Mularski, R., Shugarman, L., Sun, V., Wilkinson, A., Maglione, M., & Shekelle, P. G. (2004). *End-of-life care and outcomes. Evidence report/technology assessment No. 110.* Prepared by the Southern California Evidence-based Practice Center. (AHRQ publication no. 05-E004-2). Rockville, MD: Agency for Healthcare Research and Quality.

Lubben, J., & Gironda, M. (2003). Centrality of social ties to the health and well-being of older adults. In Berkman & Harootyan, *Social work and health care in an aging society* (pp. 319–50).

Luborsky, M. (1997). Attuning assessment to the client: Recent advances in theory and methodology. *Generations, 21*(1), 10–15.

Lugaila, T. (1998). *Marital status and living arrangements: March 1997* (Series P20-56). Washington, DC: U.S. Census Bureau.

Lyotard, J. F. (1984). *The postmodern condition.* Minneapolis: University of Minnesota Press.

Mabry, J. B., Bengston, V., and Rosenthal, C. (2001). Family. In G. L. Maddox (Ed.), *The encyclopedia of aging* (3rd ed., pp. 379–82). New York: Springer.

McCarthy, T. (1982). *The critical theory of Jurgen Habermas.* Cambridge, MA: MIT Press.

McFarland, P., & Sanders, S. (2003). A pilot study about the needs of older gays and lesbians: What social workers need to know. *Journal of Gerontological Social Work, 40*(3), 67–80.

McKhann, G., Drachman, D., Folstein, M., Katman, R., Price, D., & Stadlan, E. (1984). Clinical diagnosis of Alzheimer's disease: Report of the NINCDS-ADRDA Work Group under the auspices of Department of Health and Human Services Task Force on Alzheimer's Disease. *Neurology, 34,* 939–44.

McKinnon, Jesse. (2003, April). The black population in the United States: March 2002. *Current Population Reports* (P20-541). www.census.gov/prod/2003pubs/p20-541.pdf (November 11, 2004).

Madden, D. (2001). Speed and timing of behavioral processes. In J. E. Birren & K. Warner Schaie (Eds.), *Handbook of the psychology of aging* (5th ed., pp. 288–312). San Diego: Academic Press.

Malec, J. F., Richardson, J. W., Sinaki, M., & O'Brien, M. W. (1990). Types of affective response to stroke. *Archives of Physical Medicine and Rehabilitation, 71,* 278–84.

Manson, S. (1995). Mental health status and needs of the American Indian and Alaska Native Elderly. In Padgett, *Handbook on ethnicity, aging, and mental health* (pp. 132–41).

Manton, K. G., Corder, L. S., & Stallard, E. (1993). Estimates of change in chronic disability and institutional incidence and prevalence rates in the U.S. elderly population from 1982, 1984, and 1989 National Long Term Care Survey. *Journal of Gerontology: Social Sciences, 48*(4), S153–66.

Maramaldi, P., & Guevara, M. (2003). Cultural considerations in health care and quality of life. In Berkman & Harootyan, *Social work and health care in an aging society* (pp. 297–318).

Margolis, S., & Rabins, P. V. (1997). *The Johns Hopkins White Papers: Depression and Anxiety.* New York: Medletter.

Margolis, S., & Swartz, K. (1999). *The Johns Hopkins White Papers: Depression and anxiety.* New York: Medletter.

Martin, G. (2003). *The biology of aging:* The state of the art: Book review. *Gerontologist, 43*(2), 272–74.

Martin, T. L., & Doka, K. J. (2000). *Men don't cry . . . women do: Transcending gender stereotypes of grief.* Philadelphia: Brunner/Mazel.

Masoro, E. (2002). A conceptual assessment of age-associated physiological change in mammals. In V. Cristofalo & R. Adelman (Eds.), *Annual review of gerontology and geriatrics: Vol. 21. Modern topics in the biology of aging* (pp. 57–71). New York: Springer.

Mast, B., MacNeill, S., & Lichtenberg, P. (2004). Longitudinal support for the relationship between vascular risk factors and late-life depressive symptoms. *American Journal of Geriatric Psychiatry, 12*(1), 93–101.

Matsubayashi, K., Wada, T., Okumiya, K., Fujisawa, M., Taoka, H., Kimura, S., & Doi, Y. (1994). Comparative study of quality of life in the elderly between in Kahoku and in Yaku. *Nippon Ronen Igakkai Zasshi* [Japanese Journal of Geriatrics], *31*(10), 790–99.

Mazure, C., Maciejewski, P., Jacobs, S., & Bruce, M. (2002). Stressful life events interacting with cognitive/personality styles to predict late-onset major depression. *American Journal of Geriatric Psychiatry, 10*(3), 297–304.

Mega, M., Cummings, J., Fiorello, T., & Gornbein, J. (1996). The spectrum of behavioral changes in Alzheimer's disease. *Neurology, 46,* 130–35.

Mehta, K., Simonsick, E., Penninx, B., Schulz, R., Rubin, S., Satterfield, S., & Yaffe, K. (2003). Prevalence and correlates of anxiety symptoms in well-functioning older adults: Findings from the health aging and body composition study. *Journal of the American Geriatrics Society, 51,* 499–504.

Mellor, J. M., & Ivry, J. (Eds.). (2002). *Advancing gerontological social work education.* New York: Haworth.

Mellor, J. M., & Lindeman, D. (1998). The role of the social worker in interdisciplinary geriatric teams. *Journal of Gerontological Social Work, 30*(3–4), 3–7.

Mellor, J. M., & Milyo, J. (2002). Income inequality and health status in the United States: Evidence from the Current Population Survey. *Journal of Human Resources, 37*(3), 510–39.

Menefee, J. A., Edwards, B., & Schieber, S. J. (1981). Analysis of nonparticipation in the SSI program. *Social Security Bulletin, 44*, 3–21.

Metzger, M., & Kaplan, K. O. (2001). *Transforming death in America: A state of the nation report.* Washington, DC: Last Acts.

Meuser, T., & Marwit, S. (1999–2000). An integrative model of personality, coping and appraisal for the prediction of grief involvement in adults. *Omega: Journal of Death and Dying, 40*(2), 375–93.

Meyer, T. J., Miller, M. L., Metzger, R. L., & Borkovec, T. D. (1990). Development and validation of the Penn State Worry Questionnaire. *Behavioural Research and Therapy, 28*, 487–95.

Meyers, B., & Young, R. (2004). Psychopharmacology. In J. Sadavoy, L. F. Jarvik, G. Grossberg, and B. S. Meyers (Eds.), *Comprehensive textbook of geriatric psychiatry* (3rd ed.). (pp. 903–91). New York: W. W. Norton.

Mezey, M., Dubler, N., Bottrell, M., Mitty, E., Ramsey, G., Post, L., & Hill, T. (2000). *Guidelines for end-of-life care in nursing homes: Principles and recommendations.* New York: New York University Division of Nursing & Montefiore Medical Center Division of Bioethics.

Miles, S. H., Koepp, R., & Weber, E. P. (1996). Advance end-of-life planning: A research review. *Archives of Internal Medicine, 156*, 1062–68.

Miller, M., & Silberman, R. (1996). Using interpersonal psychotherapy with depressed elders. In Zarit & Knight, *A guide to psychotherapy and aging* (pp. 83–99).

Miller, P. J., Hedlund, S. C., & Murphy, K. A. (1998). Social work assessment at end of life: Practice guidelines for suicide and the terminally ill. *Social Work in Health Care, 26*, 23–36.

Miller, P. J., Mesler, M. A., & Eggman, S. (2002). Take some time to look inside their hearts: Hospice social workers contemplate physician-assisted suicide. *Social Work in Health Care, 35*(3), 53–65.

Miller, W. R., Benefield, R. G., & Tonigan, J. S. (1993). Enhancing motivation for change in problem drinkers: A controlled comparison of two therapist styles. *Journal of Consulting and Clinical Psychology, 61*(3), 455–61.

Miniño, A. M., Arias, E., Kochanek, M., Murphy, S., & Smith, B. (2002). *Deaths: Preliminary data for 2000.* Hyattsville, MD: National Center for Health Statistics.

Minkler, M., & Estes, C. (Eds.). (1991). *Critical perspectives on aging: The political and moral economy of growing old.* Amityville, NY: Baywood.

Minkler, M., & Roe, K. M. (1996). Grandparents as surrogate parents. *Generations, 20*(1), 34–38.

Minkler, M., Roe, K. M., & Price, M. (1992). The physical and emotional health of grandmothers raising grandchildren in the crack cocaine epidemic. *Gerontologist, 32*, 752–61.

Mittelman, M., Zeiss, A., Davies, H., & Guy, D. (2003). Specific stressors of spousal caregivers: Difficult behaviors, loss of sexual intimacy, and incontinence. In Coon, Gallagher-Thompson, & Thompson, *Innovative interventions to reduce dementia caregiver distress* (pp. 77–98).

Moen, P. (1996). A life course perspective on retirement, gender, and well-being. *Journal of Occupational Health Psychology, 1*(2), 131–44.

———. (2001). Moving into retirement: Preparation and transitions in late midlife. In Lachman, *Handbook of midlife development* (pp. 487–27).

———. (2003). Linked lives: Dual careers, gender, and the contingent life course. In W. Heinz & V. Marshall (Eds.), *Social dynamics of the life course* (pp. 237–58). New York: Aldine de Gruyter.

Moen, P., Erickson, W., Agarwal, M., Fields, V., & Todd, L. (2000). *The Cornell retirement and well-being study: Final report.* Ithaca, NY: Cornell University.

Moen, P., Kim, J., & Hofmeister, H. (2001). Couples' work/retirement transitions, gender, and marital quality. *Social Psychology Quarterly, 64,* 55–71.

Montano, C. B. (1999). Primary care issues related to the treatment of depression in elderly patients. *Journal of Clinical Psychiatry, 60,* 45–51.

Monteiro, I. M., Boksay, I., Auer, S. R., & Torossian, C. (1998). Reliability of routine clinical instruments for the assessment of Alzheimer's disease administered by telephone. *Journal of Geriatric Psychiatry and Neurology, 11*(1), 18–24.

Montgomery, A., Barber, C., & McKee, P. (2002). A phenomenological study of wisdom. *International Journal of Aging and Human Development, 54*(2), 139–57.

Moody, H. (1988). Toward a critical gerontology: The contribution of the humanities to theories of aging. In Birren & Bengston, *Emergent theories of aging* (pp. 19–40).

———. (1993). Overview: What is critical gerontology and why is it important? In Cole, Achenbaum, Jakobi, & Kastenbaum, *Voices and visions of aging* (pp. xv–xli).

Moody, L., Beckie, T., Long, C., Edmonds, A., & Andrews, S. (2000). Assessing readiness for death in hospice elders and older adults. *Hospice Journal, 15*(2), 49–65.

Moon, A. (2000). Perceptions of elder abuse among various cultural groups: Similarities and differences. *Generations, 24*(2), 75–80.

Moon, M. (1990). Public policies: Are they gender-neutral? *Generations, 14,* 59–63.

Moore, A. A., Beck, J., Babor, T., Hays, R., & Reuben, D. (2002). Beyond alcoholism: Identifying older, at-risk drinkers in primary care. *Journal of Studies on Alcohol, 63*(3), 316–21.

Moore, A. A., Morton, S. C., & Beck, J. C. (1999). A new paradigm for alcohol use in older persons. *Medical Care, 37*(2), 165–79.

Moore, A. A., Seeman, T., Morgenstern, H., Beck, J., & Reuben, D. (2002). Are there differences between older persons who screen positive on the CAGE questionnaire and the Short Michigan Alcoholism Screening Test—Geriatric Version? *Journal of the American Geriatrics Society, 50,* 858–62.

Mor, V. (2002). *Working Group 1: Patterns of care, Exploring the role of cancer centers for integrating aging and cancer research: Workshop report* (pp. 31–34). Bethesda, MD: National Institute on Aging and National Cancer Institute.

Mor, V., & Masterson-Allen, S. (1987). *Hospice care systems: Structure, process, costs, and outcome.* New York: Springer.

Mor, V., & Morris, J., et al., (1995). Minimum data set. In G. L. Maddox (Ed.), *The encyclopedia of aging* (2nd. ed., pp. 639–42). New York: Springer.

Morris, J. C., & Fulling, K. (1988). Early Alzheimer's disease: Diagnostic considerations. *Archives in Neurology, 45,* 345–49.

Morrow, R. (1994). *Critical theory and methodology.* Thousand Oaks, CA: Sage.

Morrow-Howell, N., Becker, S., & Judy, L. (1998). Evaluating an intervention for the elderly at increased risk of suicide. *Research on Social Work Practice, 8,* 28–46.

Morrow-Howell, N., Hinterlong, J., & Sherraden, M. (Eds.). (2001). *Productive aging: Concepts and challenges.* Baltimore: Johns Hopkins University Press.

Moskowitz, S. (1998). Private enforcement of criminal mandatory reporting laws. *Journal of Elder Abuse and Neglect, 9*(3), 1–22.

Moss, M. S., Moss, S. Z., & Hansson, R. O. (2001). Bereavement and old age. In Stroebe, Hansson, Stroebe, & Schut, *Handbook of bereavement research* (pp. 241–60).

Mueller, T., Kohn, R., Leventhal, N., Leon, A., Solomon, D., Coryell, W., Endicott, J., Alexopoulos, G., & Keller, M. (2004). The course of depression in elderly patients. *Journal of the American Geriatrics Society, 12*(1), 22–29.

Mui, A. (1998). Living alone and depression among older Chinese immigrants. *Journal of Gerontological Social Work, 30,* 147–66.

Mungas, D., Weiler, P., Franzi, C., & Henry, R. (1989). Assessment of disruptive behavior associated with dementia: The Disruptive Behavior Rating Scales. *Journal of Geriatrics, Psychiatry, and Neurology, 2,* 196–202.

Murphy, C., & Alexopoulos, G. (2004). Longitudinal association of initiation/perserveration and severity of geriatric depression. *Journal of the American Geriatrics Society, 12*(1), 50–55.

Murphy, S., Palmer, S., Frank, G., Michel, V., & Blackhall, L. (1995). Ethnicity and advance directives. *Journal of Law, Medicine, & Ethics, 24,* 108–17.

Murray, C. J., & Lopez, A. D. (1996). *The global burden of disease.* Boston: World Health Organization and Harvard University Press.

Mutran, E. J., Reitzes, D. C., & Fernandez, M. E. (1997). Factors that influence attitudes toward retirement. *Research on Aging, 19,* 251–73.

Myers, J. K., Goldman, E., Hingson, R., Scotch, N., & Mangione, T. (1984). Evidence for cohort or generational differences in the drinking behavior of older adults. *International Journal of Aging and Human Development, 14,* 31–44.

Myers, S., & Booth, A. (1996). Men's retirement and marital quality. *Journal of Family Issues, 17,* 336–58.

Nadeau, J. (2001). Family construction of meaning. In Neimeyer, *Meaning reconstruction and the experience of loss* (pp. 95–111).

Nagpaul, K. (2001). Application of elder abuse screening tools and referral protocol: Techniques and clinical considerations. *Journal of Elder Abuse and Neglect, 13*(2), 59–78.

Nahmiash, D., & Reis, M. (2000). Most successful interventions strategies for abused older adults. *Journal of Elder Abuse and Neglect, 12*(3–4), 53–70.

National Academy on an Aging Society. (1999). *Challenges for the 21st Century: Chronic and Disabling Conditions* (Issue brief 1).Washington, DC: Author.

———. (2000). *Caregiving: Helping the elderly with activity limitations.* (Issue brief no. 7). Washington, DC: Author.

National Alliance for Caregiving. (1997). *Family caregiving in the U.S.: Findings from a national survey: Final report.* Bethesda, MD: Author.

National Alliance for the Mentally Ill. (1997). *Nearly 40 percent of older suicide victims see doctor during week before killing themselves.* www.nami.org/Content/ContentGroups/ Press_Room1/19971/July_1997/Nearly_40_Percent_Of_Older_Suicide_Victims_See_ Doctor_During_Week_Before_Killing_Themselves.htm (July 30, 1997).

National Association of Social Workers. (1997). *Code of ethics.* Washington, DC: Author.

National Association of Social Workers Delegate Assembly. (1993). *NASW policy statement: Client self-determination in end-of-life decisions.* Washington, DC: National Association of Social Workers.

National Center for Health Statistics. (1993). Aging in the 80s: Age 65 years and over— Use of community services: Preliminary data from the Supplement on Aging to the National Health Interview Survey: United States, January—June, 1985. *Advance Data from Vital and Health Statistics* (pp. 121–30). (DHHS publication no. [PHS] 94-162). www.cdc.gov/nchs/data/series/sr_16/sr16_013.pdf (March 13, 2004).

———. (1996). *Vital statistics of the United States, 1992: Vol. 2. Mortality,* Part A. Washington, DC: U.S. Public Health Service.

———. (1998). *National Mortality Followback Survey.* www.cdc.gov/nchs/about/major/ nmfs/nmfs.htm (January 15, 2003).

———. (2002). *Early release of selected estimates from the National Health Interview Survey.* www.cdc.gov/nchs/about/major/nhis/released200202.htm (December 30, 2003).

———. (2003a). *Health, United States, 2003.* Hyattsville, MD: U.S. Department of Health and Human Services.

———. (2003b). *Summary health statistics for the U.S. population: National Health Interview Survey, 2001.* (DHHS publication no. [PHS] 2003-1545). Hyattsville, MD: U.S. Department of Health and Human Services.

National Center on Addiction and Substance Abuse at Columbia University. (1998). *Under the rug: Substance abuse and the mature woman.* (1998). New York: Author.

National Center on Elder Abuse. (2003a). *A fact sheet on caregiver stress and elder abuse.* www.elderabusecenter.org/pdf/family/fact_sheet.pdf (June 30, 2003).

———. (2003b, May 20). National Summit on Elder Abuse 2001: A call for action. *National action agenda on elder abuse.* www.elderabusecenter.org/default. cfm?p=actionagenda.cfm (June 30, 2003).

———. (2003c, June 24). *Frequently Asked Questions.* www.elderabusecenter.org/default.cfm?p=faqs.cfm (June 30, 2003).

National Center on Elder Abuse, American Public Human Services Association, & WESTAT. (1998, September). *The national elder abuse incidence study: Final report.* Washington, DC: U.S. Department of Health and Human Services. www.aoa.gov/eldfam/ Elder_Rights/Elder_Abuse/AbuseReport_Full.pdf (October 11, 2004).

National Hospice and Palliative Care Organization. (2003). *Hospice Facts and figures.* www.nhpco.org/files/public/Hospice_Facts_110104.pdf (December 21, 2004).

National Institute on Aging. (1999, March 9). NIA launches national study to treat mild cognitive impairment. *NIA News: Alzheimer's Disease Research Update.* www.alzheimers.org/nianews/nianews19.html (July 27, 2000).

————. (2004, October). *2003 Progress report on Alzheimer's disease.* (NIH publication no. 04-5570). Washington, DC: National Institutes of Health, U.S. Department of Health and Human Services.

National Institute on Aging & National Cancer Institute. (2002). *Exploring the role of cancer centers for integrating aging and cancer research: Workshop report.* Bethesda, MD: Author.

National Institute on Alcohol Abuse and Alcoholism. (1995). *The physicians' guide to helping patients with alcohol problems.* (NIH publication no. 95-3769). Rockville, MD: National Institute on Alcohol Abuse and Alcoholism.

Neighbors, H. W., & Jackson, J. (Eds.). (1996). *Mental health in black America.* Thousand Oaks, CA: Sage.

Neimeyer, R. (1998). *Lessons of loss: A guide to coping.* New York: McGraw Hill.

————. (2001a). Meaning reconstruction and loss. In Neimeyer, *Meaning reconstruction and the experience of loss* (pp. 1–9).

————. (Ed.). (2001b). *Meaning reconstruction and the experience of loss.* Washington, DC: American Psychological Association.

Nelson, H. W., Huber, R., & Walter, K. L. (1995). The relationship between volunteer long-term care ombudsmen and regulatory nursing home actions. *Gerontologist, 35*(4), 509–14.

Nerenberg, L. (2000). Developing a service response to elder abuse. *Generations, 24*(2), 86–92.

Neugarten, B. (1973). Personality change in late life: A developmental perspective. In C. Eisdorfer & M. P. Lawton (Eds.), *The psychology of adult development and aging* (pp. 331–35). Washington, DC: American Psychological Association.

Nichols, L. M. (1998). Building a marketplace for elderly consumers. *Generations, 22*(2), 31–36.

Niederehe, G. (1996). Psychosocial treatments with depressed older adults: A research update. *American Journal of Geriatric Psychiatry, 4,* S66–78.

Noelker, L. S., and Whitlach, C. J. (2001). *Informal caregiving.* In G. L. Maddox (ed.), *The encyclopedia of aging* (pp. 541–544). New York: Springer Publishing Company.

Nolen-Hoeksema, S. (2000). The role of rumination in depressive disorders and mixed anxiety/depressive symptoms. *Journal of Abnormal Psychology, 109,* 504–11.

————. (2001). Ruminative coping and adjustment to bereavement. In Stroebe, Hansson, Stroebe, & Schut, *Handbook of bereavement research* (pp. 545–62).

Nolen-Hoeksema, S., & Larson, J. (1999). *Coping with loss.* Mahwah, NJ: Erlbaum.

Noonan, A. E., & Tennstedt, S. (1997). Meaning in caregiving and its contribution to caregiver well-being. *Gerontologist, 37,* 785–95.

Nord, M., & Andrews, M. (2002). *Reducing food insecurity by half in the United States: Assessing progress towards a national objective.* (Food Assistance and Nutrition Research Report No. 26-2). U.S. Department of Agriculture. Economic Research Service. www.ers.usda.gov/publications/FoodReview/Sep2002/frvol25i2d.pdf (September 30, 2003).

Norlander, L., & McSteen, K. (2000). The kitchen table discussion: A creative way to discuss end-of-life issues. *Home Healthcare Nurse, 18*(8), 532–39.

Nursing Home Reform Act. 42 U.S.C. § 1395i-3 (a)-(h)(Medicare); § 13966r (a)-(h)(Medicaid) (1987).

O'Bryant, S. (1990–1991). Forewarning of husband's death: Does it make a difference? *Omega: Journal of Death and Dying, 22,* 227–39.

O'Bryant, S., & Hansson, R. O. (1995). Widowhood. In R. Blieszner & V. H. Bedford (Eds.), *Handbook of aging and the family* (pp. 440–58). Westport, CT: Greenwood.

O'Connor, M. K., Knapp, R., Husain, M., Rummans, T., Petrides, G., Smith, G., Mueller, M., Snyder, K., Bernstein, H., Rush, A., Fink, M., & Kellner, C. (2001). The influence of age on the response of major depression to electroconvulsive therapy: A C.O.R.E. Report. *American Journal of Geriatric Psychiatry, 9*(4), 382–90.

O'Connor, P. (1993). A clinical paradigm for exploring spiritual concerns. In K. Doka & J. Morgan (Eds.), *Death and spirituality* (pp. 133–41). Amityville, NY: Baywood.

Office of Management and Budget. (2001). Table 15-1. Federal resources in support of Social Security. www.whitehouse.gov/omb/budget/fy2002/bud15.html (December 14, 2004).

Ohayon, M., & Schatzberg, A. (2003). Using chronic pain to predict depressive morbidity in the general population. *Archives of General Psychiatry, 60*(1), 39–47.

Older Women's League. (1998). *Women, work, and pensions: Improving the odds for a secure retirement.* Washington, DC: Author.

————. (2001). *Faces of caregiving: OWL Mother's Day report.* Washington, DC: Author.

Olsen, R., Hutchings, B. L., & Ehrenkrantz, E. (1999). The physical design of the home as a caregiving support: An environment for persons with dementia. *Journal of Case Management, 8*(2), 125–31.

Olshansky, S. J., Hayflick, L., & Carnes, B. (2002). Position statement on human aging. *Journal of Gerontology: Biological Sciences, 57A*(8), B292–97.

Ondus, K., Hujer, M., Mann, A., & Mion, L. (1999). Substance abuse and the hospitalized elderly. *Orthopedic Nursing, 18*(4), 27–36.

O'Rand, A. (1996). The precious and the precocious: Understanding cumulative disadvantage and cumulative advantage over the life course. *Gerontologist, 36*(2), 230–38.

————. (2001). Stratification and the life course. In R. Binstock & L. George (Eds.), *The Handbook of aging and the social sciences* (pp. 197–213). San Diego: Academic Press.

Oregon Department of Human Services. (2004). *Sixth annual report on Oregon's Death with Dignity Act [DWDA].* Table 1: Demographic characteristics of 171 DWDA patients who died after ingesting a lethal dose of medication, by year, Oregon, 1998–2003. www.ohd.hr.state.or.us/chs/pas/ar-tbl-1.cfm (December 20, 2004).

Orentlicher, D. (1996, August 29). The legalization of physician-assisted suicide. *New England Journal of Medicine, 335*(9), 663–67.

Ormel, J., VonKorff, M., Oldehinkel, A. J., Simon, G., Tiemens, B. G., & Ustun, T. B. (1999). Onset of disability in depressed and non-depressed primary care patients. *Psychological Medicine, 29,* 847–53.

Ormel, J., VonKorff, M., Ustun, T. B., Pini, S., Korten, A., & Oldehinkel, R. (1994). Common mental disorders and disability across cultures: Results from the WHO collaborative study on psychological problems in general health care. *Journal of the American Medical Association, 272,* 1741–48.

O'Rourke, N., & Tuokko, H. A. (2003). Psychometric properties of an abridged version of the Zarit Burden Interview within a representative Canadian caregiver sample. *Gerontologist, 43,* 121–27.

Orshansky, M. (1988, October). Commentary: The poverty measure. *Social Security Bulletin, 51*(10), 22–24.

Ory, M. (2000). Afterword: Dementia caregiving at the end of the twentieth century. In Lawton & Rubinstein, *Interventions in dementia care* (pp. 173–79).

Oslin, D., & Holden, R. (2002). Recognition and assessment of alcohol and drug dependence in the elderly. In Gurnack, Atkinson, & Osgood, *Treating alcohol and drug abuse in the elderly* (pp. 11–31).

Ovrebo, B., & Minkler, M. (1993). The lives of older women: Perspectives from political economy and the humanities. In Cole, Achenbaum, Jakobi, & Kastenbaum, *Voices and visions of aging* (pp. 289–308).

Padgett, D. (Ed.). (1995). *Handbook on ethnicity, aging, and mental health.* Westport, CT: Greenwood.

Page, J. B., Rio, L., Sweeney, J., & McKay, C. (1985). Alcohol and adaptation to exile in Miami's Cuban population. In L. A. Bennett & G. M. Ames (Eds.), *The American experience with alcohol: Contrasting cultural perspectives* (pp. 315–32). New York: Plenum.

Palmore, E. (1995). Long-lived human populations. In G. L. Maddox (Ed.), *The encyclopedia of aging* (2nd ed., pp. 584–85). New York: Springer.

Paniagua, F. (1998). *Assessing and treating culturally diverse clients: A practical guide* (2nd ed.). Thousand Oaks, CA: Sage.

Parkes, C. M. (1975). Determinants of outcome following bereavement. *Omega: Journal of Death and Dying, 6,* 303–23.

———. (1996). *Bereavement: Studies of grief in adult life.* (3rd ed.). Philadelphia: Taylor and Francis.

———. (1997). Bereavement events and mental health in the elderly. *Reviews in Clinical Gerontology, 7,* 47–53.

———. (2002). Grief: Lessons from the past, visions for the future. *Death Studies, 26,* 367–85.

Parkes, C. M., & Weiss, R. (1983). *Recovery from bereavement.* New York: Basic Books.

Paveza, G. J., Cohen, D., Eisdorfer, C., Freels, S., Sernia, T., Ashford, J., Gorelick, P., Hirschman, R., Luchins, D., & Levy, P. (1992). Severe family violence and Alzheimer's disease: Prevalence and risk factors. *Gerontologist, 47,* 493–97.

Pearlin, L. I. (1982). The social contexts of stress. In L. Goldberger & S. Breznita (Eds.), *Handbook of stress* (pp. 367–79). New York: Free Press.

Pearlin, L., Mullan, J., Semple, S., & Skaff, M. (1990). Caregiving and the stress process: An overview of concepts and their measures. *Gerontologist, 30*(5), 583–94.

Pearlman, R. A., Cole, W. A., Patrick, D. L., Starks, H. E., & Cain, K. C. (1995). Advance care planning: Eliciting patient preferences for life-sustaining treatment. *Patient Education and Counseling, 26*, 353–61.

Pedersen, P., Draguns, J., Lonner, W., & Trimble, J. (Eds.). (2002). *Counseling across cultures* (5th ed.). Thousand Oaks, CA: Sage.

Penninx, W. J., Leveille, S., Ferrucci, L., Van Eijk, J., & Guralnik, J. (1999). Exploring the effect of depression on physical disability: Longitudinal evidence from the established populations for epidemiologic studies of the elderly. *American Journal of Public Health, 89*, 1346–52.

Pension Benefit Guarantee Corporation. (1998). *Pension insurance data book, 1998*. www. pbgc.gov/publications/databook/databk98.pdf (January 6, 2005).

Peretti, P., & Wilson, C. (1978–79). Contemplated suicide among voluntary and involuntary retirees. *Omega: Journal of Death and Dying , 9*, 193–201.

Peters, J., Kratzsch, T., Ruth, M., Berger, G., Schramm, U., & Frolich, L. (2000, July 12). *Combination of Mini-Mental State Exam and Clock Drawing Test leads to an enhanced sensitivity in screening for dementia*. Paper presented at the World Alzheimer Congress, Washington, DC.

Petersen, R. (2000, July 9). *Mild cognitive impairment: Transition from aging to Alzheimer's disease*. Paper presented at the World Alzheimer Congress 2000, Washington, DC.

Petersen, R. C., Smith, G. E., Waring, S. C., Ivnik, R. J., Tangalos, E. G., & Kokmen, E. (1999). Mild cognitive impairment: Clinical characterization and outcome. *Archives of Neurology, 56*(3), 303–8.

Pfeiffer, E. (1975). A short portable mental status questionnaire for the assessment of organic brain deficits in elderly patients. *Journal of the American Geriatrics Society, 23*, 433–41.

Physician Payment Review Commission. (1991, April). *Annual report to Congress, 1991*. Washington, DC: Author.

Physician Payment Review Commission. (1995). *Annual Report to Congress, 1995*. Washington, DC: Author.

Pienta, A. M. (1999). Early childbearing patterns and women's labor force behavior in later life. *Journal of Women and Aging, 11*, 69–83.

Pincus, A. (1970). Reminiscence in aging and its implications for social work practice. *Social Work, 15*, 47–53.

Pincus, H. A., Tanielian, T. L., Marcus, S. C., Olfson, M., Zarin, D. A., Thompson, J., & Zito, J. M. (1998). Prescribing trends in psychotropic medications: Primary care, psychiatry and other medical specialties. *Journal of the American Medical Association, 279*, 526–31.

Pinquart, M., & Sorensen, S. (2003). Associations of stressors and uplifts of caregiving with caregiver burden and depressive mood: A meta-analysis. *Journal of Gerontology Series B: Psychological Sciences and Social Sciences, 58*(2), P112–28.

Piven, F. F., & Cloward, R. A. (1971). *Regulating the poor: The functions of public welfare*. New York: Pantheon.

Porell, F. W., & Miltiades, H. B. (2002). Regional differences in functional status among the aged. *Social Science and Medicine, 54*(8), 1181–98.

Porter, K. H., Larin, K., & Primus, W. (1999). *Social Security and poverty among the elderly: A national and state perspective.* Washington DC: Center on Budget and Policy Priorities. www.cbpp.org/4-8-99socsec.htm (January 25, 2001).

President's Commission for the Study of Ethical Problems in Medicine and Biomedical and Behavioral Research. (1981). *Defining death: A report on the medical, legal and ethical issues in the determination of death* Washington, DC: Government Printing Office.

Price, C. (2000). Women and retirement: Relinquishing professional identity. *Journal of Aging Studies, 14*(1), 81–101.

Prigerson, H., & Jacobs, S. (2001a). Caring for bereaved patients: "All the doctors just suddenly go." *Journal of the American Medical Association, 286*(11), 1369–76.

———. (2001b). Traumatic grief as a distinct disorder: A rationale, consensus criteria, and a preliminary empirical test. In Stroebe, Hansson, Stroebe, & Schut, *Handbook of bereavement research* (pp. 613–37).

Prigerson, H., Shear, M. K., Jacobs, S. C., Reynolds, C. F., Maciejewski, P. K., Pilkonis, P. A., Wortman, C., Williams, J. B. W., Widiger, T. A., Rosenheck, R. A., Davidson, J ., Frank, E., Kupfer, D. J., & Zisook, S. (1999). Consensus criteria for traumatic grief: A preliminary empirical test. *British Journal of Psychiatry, 174,* 67–73.

Pritchard, R., Fisher, E., & Lynn, J. (1998). Influence of patient preferences and local health system characteristics on place of death. *Journal of the American Geriatrics Society, 46,* 1242–50.

Proctor, B. D., & Dalaker, J. (2003). *Poverty in the United States: 2002, Current Population Reports* (P60-222). Washington, DC: U.S. Census Bureau.

ProHealth (2002). Survey shows four of ten Americans suffer daily pain. ProHealth's ArthritisSupport.com. www.arthritissupport.com/library/showarticle.cfm/ID/479/e/1/T/Arthritis/ (February 24, 2005)

Pruchno, R. A., & McKenney, D. (2000). Living with grandchildren: The effects of custodial and coresident households on the mental health of grandmothers. *Journal of Mental Health and Aging, 6*(4), 269–89.

———. (2002). Psychological well-being of black and white grandmothers raising grandchildren: Examination of a two-factor model. *Journal of Gerontology: Psychological Sciences, 57B*(5), P444–52.

Public Citizen. (2003). *The other drug war: 2003.* Public Citizen Congress Watch, 2003. www.citizen.org/documents/Other_Drug_War2003.pdf (January 6, 2005).

Purcell, P. (2000, October). Older workers: Employment and retirement trends. *Monthly Labor Review,* pp. 19–30.

Quadagno, J. (1989). Generational equity and the politics of the welfare state. *Politics and Society, 17,* 360–76.

Quadagno, J., & Reid, J. (1999). The political economy perspective in aging. In Bengston & Schaie, *Handbook of theories of aging* (pp. 344–58).

Quinn, M. J., & Tomita, S. (1997). *Elder abuse and neglect* (2nd ed.). New York: Springer.

Rabins, P. V. (1992). Prevention of mental disorder in the elderly: Current perspectives and future prospects. *Journal of the American Geriatrics Society, 40,* 727–33.

Rabins, P. V., & Margolis, S. (2004). *Memory.* Baltimore: Johns Hopkins Medical Institutions.

Radford, S. A., & Bucks, R. S. (2000, July 9). *Emotion processing in Alzheimer's disease.* Paper presented at the World Alzheimer Congress 2000, Washington, DC.

Radner, D. B. (1992). *An assessment of the economic status of the elderly.* (ORS working paper no. 55). Washington, DC: Office of Research and Statistics, Social Security Administration.

Ramirez, R. R., & de la Cruz, P. G. (2003, June). The Hispanic population in the United States: March 2002. *Current Population Reports* (P20-545). www.census.gov/prod/2003pubs/p20-545.pdf (October 12, 2004).

Rando, R. (1993). *Treatment of complicated mourning.* Champaign, IL: Research Press.

Raschko, R. (1997). The Spokane Elder Care Program: Community outreach methods and results. In L. L. Heston (Ed.), *Progress in Alzheimer's disease and similar conditions* (pp. 233–43). Washington, DC: American Psychiatric Press.

Ratner, E., Norlander, L., & McSteen, K. (2001). Death at home following a targeted advance-care planning process at home: The kitchen table discussion. *Journal of the American Geriatrics Society, 49,* 778–81.

Ray, W., Taylor, J., Lichtenstein, M., & Meador, K. (1992). The nursing home behavior problem scale. *Journal of Gerontology, 47,* M9–16.

Reamer, F. G. (1998). *Ethical standards in social work: A review of the NASW Code of Ethics.* Washington, DC: NASW Press.

Reay, A., & Browne, K. D. (2002). The effectiveness of psychological interventions with individuals who physically abuse or neglect their elderly dependents. *Journal of Interpersonal Violence, 17*(4), 416–31.

Reeves, T., & Bennett, C. (2003, May). The Asian and Pacific Islander population in the United States: March 2002. *Current Population Reports.* (P20-540). www.census.gov/prod/2003pubs/p20-540.pdf (October 12, 2004).

Reid, M. C., & Anderson, P. A. (1997). Geriatric substance use disorders. *Medical Clinics of North America, 8*(4), 999–1016.

Regier, D. A., Boyd, J. H., Burke, J. K., Rae, D. S., Myers, J. K., Kramer, M., Robins, L. N., George, L. K., Karno, M. & Locke, B. Z. (1998). One-month prevalence of mental disorder in the US: Based on five epidemiological catchment area sites. *Archives of General Psychiatry, 45,* 977–986

Reis, M. (1999). Innovative interventions when seniors are abused. In J. Pritchard (Ed.), *Elder abuse work: Best practice in Britain and Canada* (pp. 378–407). London: Jessica Kingsley.

Reis, M., & Nahmiash, D. (1995). Validation of the caregiver abuse screen (CASE). *Canadian Journal on Aging, 14,* 45–60.

———. (1998). Validation of the indicators of abuse (IOA) screen. *Gerontologist, 38,* 471–80.

Reisberg, B., Borenstein, J., Salob, S. P., Ferris, S. H., Franssen, E., & Georgotas, A. (1987). Behavioral symptoms in Alzheimer's disease: Phenomenology and treatment. *Journal of Clinical Psychiatry, 48* (Suppl. 5), 9–15.

Reisberg, B., Ferris, S., de Leon, M. J., & Crook, T. (1982). The global deterioration scale for assessment of primary degenerative dementia. *American Journal of Psychiatry, 139,* 1136–39.

Reisberg, B., Ferris, S. H., de Leon, M. J., Schneck, M. K., Buttinger, C., & Borenstein, J. (1984). Functional staging of dementia of the Alzheimer type. *Annals of the New York Academy of Science, 435,* 481–82.

Reker, G. (1997). Personal meaning, optimism, and choice: Existential predictions of depression in community and institutional elderly. *Gerontologist, 37,* 709–16.

Reker, G., & Wong, P. (1988). Aging as an individual process: Toward a theory of personal meaning. In Birren & Bengston, *Emergent theories of aging* (pp. 214–46).

Reynolds, B. (1934). *Between client and community: A study in responsibility in social casework.* New York: Oriole.

Reynolds, C., Miller, M., Pasternak, R., Frank, E., Perel, J., Cornes, C., Houck, P., Mazumdar, S., Dew, M., & Kupfer, D. (1999). Treatment of bereavement-related major depressive episodes in later life: A controlled study of acute and continuation treatment with nortriptyline and interpersonal psychotherapy. *American Journal of Psychiatry, 156,* 202–7.

Richardson, V. E. (1990). Gender differences in retirement planning among educators: Implications for practice with older women. *Journal of Women and Aging, 2,* 27–40.

———. (1992). Service use among urban African American elderly people. *Social Work, 37*(1), 1–96.

———. (1993). *Retirement counseling: A handbook for gerontology practitioners.* New York: Springer.

———. (1999a). How circumstances of widowhood and retirement affect adjustment among older men. *Journal of Mental Health and Aging, 5,* 1–10.

———. (1999b). Women and retirement. In D. Garner (Ed.) *Fundamentals of feminist gerontology.* (pp. 49–66). New York: Haworth.

Richardson, V. E., & Balaswamy, S. (2001). Coping with bereavement among elderly widowers. *Omega: Journal of Death and Dying, 43*(2), 129–44.

Richardson, V. E., & Kilty, K. M. (1988, November). *The effects of gender and time on adjustment to retirement.* Paper presented at the annual meeting of the Gerontological Society of America, San Francisco.

———. (1989). Retirement planning among black professionals. *Gerontologist, 29,* 32–37.

———. (1991). Adjustment to retirement: Continuity vs. discontinuity. *International Journal of Aging and Human Development, 33,* 151–69

———. (1995). Gender differences in mental health before and after retirement. *Journal of Women and Aging, 7,* 19–35.

———. (1997). A critical analysis of expected and actual finances among retired women and men. *Journal of Poverty: Innovations on Social, Political and Economic Inequalities, 1*(1), 19–47.

Ridley, C., & Udipi, S. (2002). Putting cultural empathy into practice. In Pedersen, Draguns, Lonner, & Trimble, *Counseling across cultures* (pp. 317–33).

Riley, M. W. (1971). Social gerontology and the age stratification of society. *Gerontologist, 11,* 79–87.

————. (1996). Discussion: What does it all mean? *Gerontologist, 36*(2), 256–58.

Riley, M. W., Foner, A., & Riley, J. W. (1999). The aging and society paradigm. In Bengston & Schaie, *Handbook of theories of aging* (pp. 327–43).

Rimlinger, G. V. (1971). *Welfare policy and industrialization in Europe, America, and Russia.* New York: Wiley.

Rockwell, E., Jackson, E., Vilke, G., & Jeste, D. (1994). A study of delusion in a large cohort of Alzheimer's disease patients. *American Journal of Geriatric Psychiatry, 2,* 157–64.

Rogers, A. (1999). Factors associated with depression and low life satisfaction in the low-income, frail elderly. *Journal of Gerontological Social Work, 31,* 167–94.

Romero, L., Lindeman, R., Koehler, K., & Allen, A. (1997). Influence of ethnicity on advance directives and end-of-life decisions. *Journal of the American Medical Association, 277*(4), 298–99.

Ron, P. (2002). Depression and suicide among community elderly. *Journal of Gerontological Social Work, 38*(3), 53–71.

Ronen, T., & Dowd, T. (1998). A constructive model for working with depressed elders. *Journal of Gerontological Social Work, 30,* 83–99.

Roose, S. P., & Dalack, G. W. (1992). Treating the depressed patient with cardiovascular problems. *Journal of Clinical Psychiatry, 53,* 25–31.

Rose, A. M. (1965). The subculture of the aging: A framework for research in social gerontology. In A. M. Rose & W. A. Peterson (Eds.), *Older people and their social world* (pp. 3–6). Philadelphia: F. A. Davis.

Rosen, J. (2004). Personal communication with author. December 17, 2004. Rosen is director of Homelessness and Mental Health Volunteers of America.

Rosen, W. G., Mohs, R. C., & Davis, K. L. (1984). A new rating scale for Alzheimer's disease. *American Journal of Psychiatry, 141,* 1356–64.

Rosenblatt, P. (2001). A social constructionist perspective on cultural differences in grief. In Stroebe, Hansson, Stroebe, & Schut, *Handbook of bereavement research* (pp. 285–300).

Rosow, I. (1974). *Socialization to old age.* Berkeley: University of California Press.

Ross, M., Fisher, R., & MacLean, M. (2000). End-of-life care for seniors: The development of a national guide. *Journal of Palliative Care, 16*(4), 47–55.

Rovner, B. W. (1993). Depression and increased risk of mortality in the nursing home patient. *American Journal of Medicine, 94,* 19S–22S.

Rowles, G., & Reinharz, S. (1988). Qualitative gerontology. In G. Rowles & S. Reinharz (Eds.), *Qualitative gerontology* (pp. 3–33). New York: Springer.

Rubin, R. M., White-Means, S. L., & Daniel, L. M. (2000, November) Income distribution of older Americans. *Monthly Labor Review,* 19–30.

Rubinstein, R., & de Medeiros, K. (2004). Ecology and the aging self. In H. Wahl, R. J. Scheidt, & P. G. Windley (Eds.), *Annual review of gerontology and geriatrics: Aging in context: Socio-physical environments* (Vol. 21, pp. 59–84). New York: Springer.

Rubinstein, R., & Lawton, M. P. (Eds.). (1997). *Depression in long-term care and residential care.* New York: Springer.

Ruckdeschel, K., Thompson, R., Datto, C., Streim, J., & Katz, I. (2004). Using the Minimum Data Set 2.0 mood disturbance items as a self-report screening instrument for depression in nursing home residents. *American Journal of Geriatric Psychiatry, 12*(1), 43–49.

Ryscavage, P. (1999). *Income Inequality in America: An analysis of trends.* New York: M. E. Sharpe.

Sager, M. A., Easterling, D. V., Kindig, D. A., & Anderson, O. W. (1989). Changes in the location of death after passage of Medicare's prospective payment system: A national study. *New England Journal of Medicine, 320,* 433–39.

Salthouse, T., & Ferrer-Caja, E. (2003). What needs to be explained to account for age-related effects on multiple cognitive variables. *Psychology and Aging, 18*(1), 91–110.

Salthouse, T., Berish, D., & Miles, J. (2002). The role of cognitive stimulation on the relations between age and cognitive functioning. *Psychology and Aging, 17*(4), 548–57.

Saltz, C. (Ed.). (1997). *Social work response to the White House Conference on Aging: From issues to actions.* New York: Haworth.

Saltz, C., & Rosen, A. (1997). Social work response to the 1995 White House Conference on Aging. In Saltz, *Social work response to the White House Conference on Aging* (pp. 1–8).

Saluter, A. F. (1996). Marital status and living arrangements: March 1994. *Current Population Reports* (Series P20–484, p. A-7). Washington, DC: U.S. Government Printing Office.

Salzman, C., & Lebowitz, B. D. (Eds.). (1991). *Anxiety in the elderly: Treatment and research.* New York: Springer.

Sandburg, A. (1998). Changes in psychoactive drug prescribing over four years in 30 nursing facilities. *Consultant Pharmacist, 13*(1), 1–7.

Sanders, C. M. (1980–81). Comparison of younger and older spouses in bereavement outcome. *Omega: Journal of Death and Dying, 11,* 217–32.

———. (1982–83). Effects of sudden vs. chronic illness on bereavement outcome. *Omega: Journal of Death and Dying, 13,* 227–41.

———. (1999). *Grief: The mourning after.* New York: Wiley.

Sands, R. (1986). The encounter of meaninglessness in crisis intervention. *International Forum for Logotherapy, 9,* 102–8.

Sands, R., & Goldberg-Glen, R. (2000). Factors associated with stress among grandparents raising their grandchildren. *Family Relations, 49*(1), 97–195.

Sands, R., & Richardson, V. (1986). Clinical practice with women in their middle years. *Social Work, 31*(1), 36–43.

Sarton, M. (1987). *At seventy: The journal of May Sarton.* New York: W. W. Norton.

Satre, D., Mertens, J., Arean, P., & Weisner, C. (2003). Contrasting outcomes of older versus middle-aged and younger adult chemical dependency patients in a managed care program. *Journal of Studies on Alcohol, 64*(4), 520–31.

Saunders, C. (1976). St. Christopher's Hospice. In E. S. Schneidman (Ed.), *Death: Current Perspectives,* pp. 516–23. Palo Alto, CA: Mayfield.

Saxena, S., O'Connell, K., & Underwood, L. (2002). A commentary: Cross-cultural quality-of-life assessment at the end of life. *Gerontologist, 42*[special issue III], 81–85.

Schaefer, C., Quesenberry, C. P., & Wi, S. (1995). Mortality following conjugal bereavement and the effects of a shared environment. *American Journal of Epidemiology, 141,* 1142–52.

Schaefer, J., & Moos, R. (2001). Bereavement experiences and personal growth. In Stroebe, Hansson, Stroebe, & Schut, *Handbook of bereavement research* (pp. 145–67).

Schaie, K. W. (1995). Abilities. In G. L. Maddox (Ed.), *The encyclopedia of aging* (2nd ed., pp. 2). New York: Springer.

———. (1996). *Intellectual development in adulthood.* New York: Cambridge University Press.

Schaie, K. W., & Willis, S. L. (1986). Can intellectual decline in the elderly be reversed? *Developmental Psychology, 22,* 223–32.

Schiamberg, L., & Gans, D. (2000). Elder abuse by adult children: An applied ecological framework for understanding contextual risk factors and the intergenerational character of quality of life. *International Journal of Aging and Human Development, 50*(4), 329–59.

Schiffman, S. (1995a). Smell. In G. L. Maddox (Ed.), *The encyclopedia of aging* (2nd ed., pp. 867–68). New York: Springer.

———. (1995b). Taste. In G. Maddox (Ed.), *The encyclopedia of aging* (2nd ed., pp. 920–22). New York: Springer.

Schofield, M., & Mishra, G. (2003). Validity of self-report screening scale for elder abuse: Women's Health Australia Study. *Gerontologist, 43*(1), 110–20.

Schonfeld, L., & Dupree, L. W. (1995). Treatment approaches for older problem drinkers. *International Journal of the Addictions, 30*(13 & 14), 1819–42.

Schonfeld, L., Dupree, L., & Dickson-Fuhrmann, E. (2000). Cognitive-behavioral treatment of older veterans with substance abuse problems. *Journal of Geriatric Psychiatry and Neurology, 13*(3), 124–29.

———. (2002). Age-specific cognitive-behavioral and self-management treatment approaches. In Gurnack, Atkinson, & Osgood, *Treating alcohol and drug abuse in the elderly* (pp. 109–30).

Schulz, J. H. (1995). *The economics of aging* (6th ed.). Westport CT: Auburn House.

Schulz, R., & Beach, S. R. (1999). Caregiving as a risk factor for mortality: The Caregiver Health Effects Study. *Journal of the American Medical Association, 282,* 2215–19.

Schulz, R., O'Brien, A. T., Bookwala, J., & Fleissner, K. (1995). Psychiatric and physical morbidity effects of dementia caregiving: Prevalence, correlates, and causes. *Gerontologist, 35,* 771–91.

Schut, H. A., Stroebe, M. S., van den Bout, J., & de Keijser, J. (1997). Intervention for the bereaved: Gender differences in the efficacy of two counseling programmes. *British Journal of Clinical Psychology, 36,* 63–72.

Schut, H. A., Stroebe, M. S., van den Bout, J., & Terheggen, M. (2001). The efficacy of bereavement interventions: Determining who benefits. In Stroebe, Hansson, Stroebe, & Schut, *Handbook of bereavement research* (pp. 705–37).

Seale, C. (2000). Changing patterns of death and dying. *Social Science and Medicine, 51,* 917–30.

Segal, D. L., Hersen, M., Van Hasselt, V. B., Kabacoff, R. L., & Roth, L. (1993). Reliability of diagnosis in older psychiatric patients using the Structured Clinical Interview for *DSM-III-R. Journal of Psychopathology and Behavioral Assessment, 15,* 347–56.

Selai, C. E., Trimble, M., Rossor, M. N., & Harvey, R. J. (2000). The Quality of Life Assessment Schedule (QOLAS)—A new method for assessing quality of life (QOL) in dementia. In Albert & Logsdon, *Assessing quality of life in Alzheimer's disease* (pp. 31–48).

Settersten, R. A., Jr. (2003). Propositions and controversies in life-course scholarship. In R. A. Settersten Jr. (Ed.), *Invitation to the life course* (pp. 15–45). Amityville, NY: Baywood.

Shaver, P. R., & Brennan, K. A. (1992). Attachment styles and the "big five" personality traits: Their connections with each other and with romantic relationship outcomes. *Personality and Social Psychology Bulletin, 18,* 536–45.

Shear, M. K., Frank, E., Foa, E., & Cherry, C. (2001). Traumatic grief treatment: A pilot study. *American Journal of Psychiatry, 158(9),* 1506–8.

Sheehy, G. (1976). *Passages: Predictable crises of adult life.* New York: E. P. Dutton.

Sheikh, J. (1991). Anxiety rating scales for the elderly. In Salzman & Lebowitz, *Anxiety in the elderly* (pp. 251–65).

Sherrell, K., Buckwalter, K. C., & Morhardt, D. (2001). Negotiating family relationships: Dementia care as a midlife developmental task. *Families in Society, 82(4),* 383–92.

Shibusawa, T., & Mui, A. (2001). Stress, coping, and depression among Japanese American elders. *Journal of Gerontological Social Work, 36,* 63–81.

Shneidman, E. (1985). *Definition of suicide.* New York: Wiley.

Shue, V., Beck, C., & Lawton, M. P. (1996). Measuring affect in frail and cognitively impaired elders. *Journal of Mental Health and Aging, 2(3),* 259–71.

Shugarman, L. R., Fries, B. E., Wolf, R. S., & Morris, J. N. (2003). Identifying older people at risk for abuse during routine screening practices. *Journal of the American Geriatrics Society, 51(1),* 24–31.

Silverstein, M., & Marenco, A. (2001). How Americans enact the grandparent role across the family life course. *Journal of Family Issues, 22(4),* 493–522.

Simard, J. (2000). The memory enhancement program: A new approach to increasing the quality of life for people with mild memory loss. In Albert & Logsdon, *Assessing quality of life in Alzheimer's disease* (pp. 153–62).

Simon, B. (1994). *The empowerment tradition in American social work: A history.* New York: Columbia University Press.

Simoni-Wastila, L. (1998). Gender and psychotropic drug use. *Medical Care, 36(1),* 88–94.

Simos, B. G. (1979). *A time to grieve: Loss as a universal human experience.* New York: Family Service Association of America.

Sinha, D., Zemlan, F. P., Nelson, S., Bienenfeld, D., Thienhaus, O., Ramaswamy, G., & Hamilton, S. (1992). A new scale for assessing behavioral agitation in dementia. *Psychiatry Research, 41,* 73–88.

Sinoff, G., Ore, L., Zlotogorosky, D., & Tamir, A. (1999). Short anxiety screening test: A brief instrument for detecting anxiety in the elderly. *International Journal of Geriatric Psychiatry, 14,* 1062–71.

Slater, W. (1984). Latest Lamm remark angers the elderly. *Arizona Daily Star,* March 29, 1.

Smeeding, T. M., Rainwater, L., & Burtless, G. (2001). U.S. poverty in a cross-national context. In S. H. Danziger & R. H. Haveman (Eds.), *Understanding poverty.* Cambridge, MA: Harvard University Press. 162–189.

Smeeding, T. M., Torrey, B. B., & Rainwater, L. (1993). *Going to extremes: An international perspective on the economic status of the U.S. aged.* (Cross-national Studies in Aging Program project paper no. 13). All-University Gerontology Center, Maxwell School of Citizenship and Public Affairs, Syracuse University.

Smith, D. (2003, April). The older population in the United States: March 2002. *Current Population Reports* (P20-546). www.census.gov/prod/2003pubs/p20-546.pdf (November 11, 2004).

Smith, D., & Moen, P. (1998, August). Spousal influence on retirement: His, her, and their perceptions. *Journal of Marriage and the Family, 60,* 734–44.

Smith, J., & Freund, A. (2002). The dynamics of possible selves in old age. *Journal of Gerontology Series B: Psychological Sciences, 57* (6), P492–500.

Social Security Administration. (1992, September 4). *Supplemental Security Income modernization project: Final report;* Notice. Washington, DC: Government Printing Office.

———. (2003). *Income of the population 55 or older.* www.ssa.gov/policy/docs/statcomps/income_pop55/2000/incpop00.pdf (January 6, 2005).

Social Security Advisory Council. (1997). *Report of the 1994–1996 Advisory Council on Social Security.* www.ssa.gov/history/reports/adcouncil/report/toc.htm (January 6, 2005).

Social Security and Medicare Boards of Trustees. (2004). *Status of the Social Security and Medicare programs: A summary of the 2004 annual reports.* www.ssa.gov/OACT/TRSUM/trsummary.html (October 29, 2004).

Social Security Online. (n.d.). *How Social Security helps women today.* www.ssa.gov/organizations/educationalwomenfactsheet.htm (October 29, 2004).

Solomon, B. (1976). *Black empowerment: Social work in minority communities.* New York: Columbia University Press.

Solomon, J. C., & Marx, J. (2000). The physical, mental, and social health of custodial grandparents. In B. Hayslip & R. Goldberg-Glen (Eds.), *Grandparents raising grandchildren: Theoretical, empirical, and clinical perspectives* (pp. 183–206). New York: Springer.

Solomon, P. R., Hirschoff, A., Kelly, B., Brush, M., DeVeaux, R. D., & Pendlebury, W. W. (1998). A 7-minute neurocognitive screening battery highly sensitive to Alzheimer's disease. *Archives of Neurology, 55,* 349–55.

Somogyi-Zalud, E., Zhong, Z., Hamel, M. B., & Lynn, J. (2002). The use of life-sustaining treatments in hospitalized persons aged 80 and older. *Journal of the American Geriatrics Society, 50,* 930–34.

Sonnega, J. (2002). *Survey evidence of clinical wisdom: Special occasions and grief in the elderly widowed.* Ann Arbor: University of Michigan.

Sorensen, S., Pinquart, M., & Duberstein, P. (2002). How effective are interventions with caregivers? An updated meta-analysis. *Gerontologist, 42*(3), 356–72.

Spar, J. (1988). Principles of diagnosis and treatment in geriatric psychiatry. In L. Lazarus (Ed.), *Essentials of geriatric psychiatry: A guide for health professionals.* (pp. 102–12). New York: Springer.

Spector, A., Davies, S., Woods, B., & Orrell, M. (2000). Reality orientation for dementia: A systematic review of the evidence of effectiveness from randomized controlled trials. *Gerontologist, 40*(2), 206–12.

Spitzer, R. L., Williams, J. B. W., Givvon, F., & First, M. B. (1992). The structured clinical interview for *DSM-III-R* (SCID). *Archives of General Psychiatry, 49,* 624–29.

Spraggins, Renee E. (2003). *Women and men in the United States: March 2002: Population characteristics.* U.S. Census Bureau. www.census.gov/prod/2003pubs/p20-544. pdf (November 3, 2004).

Stanley, M. A., Beck, J. G., & Glassco, J. (1996). Treatment of generalized anxiety in older adults: A preliminary comparison of cognitive-behavioral and supportive approaches. *Behavior Therapy, 27,* 565–81.

Stanton, A., Danoff-Burg, S., Cameron, C., & Ellis, A. (1994). Coping through emotional approach: Problems of conceptualization and confounding. *Journal of Personality and Social Psychology, 66,* 350–62.

Staudinger, U. M. (1999). Older and wiser? Integrating results on the relationship between age and wisdom-related performance. *International Journal of Behavioral Development, 23,* 641–64.

Staudinger, U. M., & Bluck, S. (2001). A view on midlife development from life-span theory. In Lachman, *Handbook of midlife development* (pp. 3–39).

Steffens, D., Jays, J., & Krishman, K. (1999). Disability in geriatric depression. *American Journal of Geriatric Psychiatry, 7,* 34–40.

Stephens, M., & Franks, M. (1999). Intergenerational relationships in later-life families: Adult daughters and sons as caregivers to aging parents. In J. Cavanaugh & S. K. Whitbourne (Eds.), *Gerontology: An interdisciplinary perspective* (pp. 329–54). New York: Oxford University Press.

Sternberg, R. J., & Lubart, T. I. (2001). Wisdom and creativity. In J. E. Birren & K. Warner Schaie (Eds.), *Handbook of the psychology of aging* (5th ed., pp. 500–22). San Diego: Academic Press.

Stevens, D., Merikangas, K., & Merikangas, J. (1995). Comorbidity of depression and other medical conditions. In E. E. Beckman & W. R. Leber (Eds.), *Handbook of depression* (2nd ed., pp. 147–99). New York: Guilford.

Stewart, A., & Ware, J. (1992). *Measuring functioning and well being: The medical outcomes study approach.* Durham, NC: Duke University Press.

Stokes, S. C., Thompson, L., Murphy, S., & Gallagher-Thompson, D. (2001). Screening for depression in immigrant Chinese-American elderly: Results of a pilot study. *Journal of Gerontological Social Work, 36,* 27–41.

Strean, J. (1979). Role theory. In F. J. Turner (Ed.), *Social work treatment: Interlocking theoretical approaches* (pp. 385–407). New York: Free Press.

Street, D., & Quadagno, J. (1993). The state, the elderly, and the intergenerational contract: Toward a new political economy of aging. In K. Schaie & A. Achenbaum (Eds.), *Social impact on aging* (pp. 130–50). New York: Springer.

Streib, G., & Schneider, C. (1971). *Retirement in American society.* Ithaca, NY: Cornell University Press.

Stroebe, M. (1992–93). Coping with bereavement: A review of the grief work hypothesis. *Omega: Journal of Death and Dying, 26,* 19–42.

Stroebe, M., & Schut, H. (1995). *The dual process model of coping with loss.* Oxford: International Work Group on Death, Dying and Bereavement, St. Catherine's College.

————. (1999). The dual process model of coping with bereavement: Rationale and description. *Death Studies, 23*, 197–224.

Stroebe, M., & Stroebe, W. (1991). Does "grief work" work? *Journal of Consulting and Clinical Psychology, 59*, 479–82.

Stroebe, M., Hansson, R. O., Stroebe, W., & Schut, H. (Eds.). (2001). *Handbook of bereavement research: Consequence, Coping, and Care.* Washington, DC: American Psychological Association.

Stroebe, M., Schut, H., & Stroebe, W. (1998). Trauma and grief: A comparative analysis. In Harvey, *Perspectives on loss* (pp. 81–96).

Stroebe, M., Schut, H., Stroebe, W., van den Bout, J., Zech, E., Gergen, M., & Gergen, K. (2002). *Coping with attachment in bereavement: Toward better outcome prediction.* Ann Arbor, MI: CLOC Workshop, Institute for Social Research.

Stroebe, M., van Son, M., Stroebe, W., Kleber, R., Schut, H., & van den Bout, J. (2000). On the classification and diagnosis of pathological grief. *Clinical Psychology Review, 20*(1), 57–75.

Stroebe, W., & Stroebe, M. S. (1987). *Bereavement and health.* Cambridge: Cambridge University Press.

Strom, R., & Strom, S. (1993, March). *Problems encountered by grandparent support groups.* Paper presented at Generations United, Washington, DC.

————. (2000). Goals for grandparents and support groups. In B. Hayslip & R. Goldberg-Glen (Eds.), *Grandparents raising grandchildren: Theoretical, empirical, and clinical perspectives* (pp. 289–303). New York: Springer.

Sue, D., & Sue, D. (2003). *Counseling the culturally diverse: Theory and practice.* New York: Wiley.

Sullivan, A., Hedberg, K., & Fleming, D. (2000). Legalized physician-assisted suicide in Oregon—The second year. *New England Journal of Medicine, 342*, 598–604.

Sullivan, E., & Fleming, M. (1997). *A guide to substance abuse services for primary care clinicians: Treatment Improvement Protocol (TIP)* (Series 24). Rockville, MD: U.S. Department of Health and Human Services.

Sulmasy, D., & Rahn, M. (2001). I was sick and you came to visit me: Time spent at the bedsides of seriously ill patients with poor prognoses. *American Journal of Medicine, 111*, 385–89.

Sulsky, S., Jacques, P., Otradovec, C., Hartz, S., & Russell, R. (1990). Descriptors of alcohol consumption among noninstitutionalized nonalcoholic elderly. *Journal of the American College of Nutrition, 9*, 326–31.

Sultzer, D., Mahler, M., Mandelkern, M., Cummings, J., Van Gorp, W., Hinkin, C., & Berisford, M. (1995). The relationship between psychiatric symptoms and regional cortical metabolism in Alzheimer's disease. *Journal of Neuropsychiatry and Clinical Neurosciences, 7*, 476–84.

Summer, L., O'Neill, G., & Shirey, L. (2000). *How financially secure are young retirees and older workers?* (Vol. 2). Washington, DC: National Academy on an Aging Society.

Swaan, A. de. (1988). *In care of the state: Health care, education, and welfare in Europe and the USA in the modern era.* New York: Oxford University Press.

Swartz, K., & Margolis, S. (2004). *The John Hopkins White Papers: Depression and anxiety.* Baltimore: Johns Hopkins Medical Institutions.

Szanto, K., Reynolds, C. F. III, Frank, E., Stack, J., Fasiczka, A. L., Miller, M., Mulsant, B., Mazumdar, S., & Kupfer, D. (1996). Suicide in elderly patients: Is active vs. passive suicidal ideation a clinically valid distinction? *American Journal of Geriatric Psychiatry,* 4, 197–207.

Szinovacz, M. (2003). Contexts and pathways: Retirement as institution, process, and experience. In Adams and Beehr, *Retirement* (pp. 6–52).

Szinovacz, M., & DeViney, S. (1999). The retiree identity: Gender and race differences. *Journals of Gerontology,* 54B, S207–18.

———. (2000). Marital characteristics and retirement decisions. *Research on Aging,* 22(5), 470–98.

Szinovacz, M., & Ekerdt, D. (1995). Families and retirement. In R. Blieszner & V. H. Bedford (Eds.), *Handbook of aging and the family* (pp. 377–400). Westport, CT: Greenwood.

Szinovacz, M., & Schaffer, A. (2000). Effects of retirement on marital conflict tactics. *Journal of Family Issues,* 21, 367–89.

Talamantes, M., Gomez, C., & Braun, K. (2000). Advance directives and end-of-life care: The Hispanic perspective. In K. Braun, J. Pietsch, & P. Blanchette (Eds.), *Cultural issues in end-of-life decision making* (pp. 83–100). Thousand Oaks, CA: Sage.

Tally, T., & Kaplan, J. (1956). The Negro aged. *Gerontological Society Newsletter,* December 6, 3.

Tariot, P. N., Mack, J. L., Patterson, M. B., Edland, S. D., Weiner, M. F., Fillenbaum, G., Blazina, L., Teri, L., Rubin, E., Mortimer, J. A., Stern, Y., & the CERAD Behavioral Pathology Committee. (1995). The Behavior Rating Scale for Dementia of the Consortium to Establish a Registry for Alzheimer's Disease. *American Journal of Psychiatry,* 152, 1349–57.

Taulbee, L. R., & Folsom, J. C. (1966). Reality orientation for geriatric patients. *Hospital and Community Psychiatry, 17,* 133–35.

Taylor, M., & Doverspike, D. (2003). Retirement planning and preparation. In Adams and Beehr, *Retirement* (pp. 53–82).

Taylor-Carter, M. A., Cook, K., & Weinberg, C. (1997). Planning and expectations of the retirement experience. *Educational Gerontology, 23,* 273–88.

Teaff, J., & Johnson, D. (1983). Pre-retirement education: A proposed bill for tuition tax credit. *Educational Gerontologist, 9,* 31–36.

Tebb, S. S. (1995). An aid to empowerment: A caregiver well-being scale. *Health and Social Work, 20,* 87–92.

Tebb, S. S., & Jivanjee, P. (2000). Caregiver isolation: An ecological model. *Journal of Gerontological Social Work, 34,* 51–72.

Tennstedt, S., Cafferata, G. L., & Sullivan, L. (1992). Depression among caregivers of impaired elders. *Journal of Aging and Health, 4,* 58–76.

Teno, J. M., Byock, I., & Field, M. J. (1999). Research agenda for developing measures to examine quality of care and quality of life of patients diagnosed with life-limiting illness. *Journal of Pain and Symptom Management, 17*(2), 75–82.

Teresi, J., & Evans, D. (1996). Cognitive measures for chronic care populations. *Journal of Mental Health and Aging, 2,* 151–174.

Teresi, J., Abrams, R., Holmes, D., Ramirez, M., Shapiro, C., & Eimicke, J. (2002). Influence of cognitive impairment, illness, gender, and African-American status on psychiatric ratings and staff recognition of depression. *American Journal of Geriatric Psychiatry, 10,* 506–14.

Teri, L., & Gallagher-Thompson, D. (1991). Cognitive-behavioral interventions for treatment of depression in Alzheimer's patients. *Gerontologist, 31,* 413–16.

Teri, L., & Logsdon, R. (1991). Identifying pleasant activities for individuals with Alzheimer's disease: The Pleasant Events Schedule—AD. *Gerontologist, 31,* 124–27.

Teri, L., Logsdon, R. G., Uomoto, J., & McCurry, S. M. (1997). Behavioral treatment of depression in dementia patients: A controlled clinical trial. *Journal of Gerontology: Psychological Sciences, 52B*(4), P159–66.

Teri, L., Truax, P., Logsdon, R., Uomoto, J., Zarit, S., & Vitaliano, P. (1992). Assessment of behavioral problems in dementia: The revised memory and behavior problems checklist. *Psychology of Aging, 7,* 622–31.

Thoits, P. A. (1983). Dimensions of life events that influence psychological distress: An evaluation and synthesis of the literature. In H. B. Kaplan (Ed.), *Psychosocial stress: Trends in theory and research* (pp. 157–91). New York: Academic Press.

Thomas, E., & Biddle, B. (1966). Basic concepts for classifying the phenomena of role. In B. Biddle & E. Thomas (Eds.), *Role theory: Concepts and research* (pp. 23–45). New York: Wiley.

Thompson, E. (2002). What's unique about men's caregiving? In Kramer & Thompson, *Men as caregivers* (pp. 20–43).

Thompson, L., Gallagher, D., & Breckenridge, J. (1987). Comparative effectiveness of psychotherapies for depressed elders. *Journal of Consulting and Clinical Psychology, 55,* 385–90.

Thompson, L., & Gallagher-Thompson, D. (1997). Psychotherapeutic interventions with older adults in outpatient and extended care settings. In Rubinstein & Lawton, *Depression in long-term care and residential care* (pp. 169–84).

Thompson, S. C. (1998). Blockades to finding meaning and control. In Harvey, *Perspectives on loss: A source book* (pp. 21–34).

Tolle, S. W., Rosenfeld, A. G., Tilden, V. P., & Park, Y. (1999). Oregon's low in hospital death rates: What determines where people die and satisfaction with decisions on place of death? *Annals of Internal Medicine, 130,* 681–85.

Tornstam, L. (1992). The quo vadis of gerontology: On the scientific paradigm of gerontology. *Gerontologist, 32,* 318–26.

———. (1994). Aging and the religious dimension. In L. E. Thomas & S. A. Eisenhandler (Eds.), *Aging and the religious dimension.* Westport, CT: Auburn House.

Toseland, R. (1995). *Group work with the elderly and family caregivers.* New York: Springer.

Toseland, R., & Smith, T. (2003). *Supporting caregivers through education and training.* Washington, DC: National Family Caregiver Support Program, U.S. Administration on Aging.

Trattner, W. I. (1989). *From poor law to welfare state: A history of social welfare in America.* New York: Free Press.

Trupin, L., & Rice, D. (1995, June). Health status, medical care use, and number of disabling conditions in the United States. *Disability Statistics Abstract* (9). National Institute on Disability and Rehabilitation Research.

Trzepacz, P. T., McCue, M., Klein, I., & Levey, G. S. (1988). A psychiatric and neuropsychological study of patients with untreated Graves' disease. *General Hospital Psychiatry, 10*(1), 49–55.

Turnbull, J. E., & Mui, A. C. (1995). Mental health status and needs of black and white elderly: Differences in depression. In Padgett, *Handbook on ethnicity, aging, and mental health* (pp. 73–98).

Turner, M. J., Bailey, W. C., & Scott, J. P. (1994). Factors influencing attitude toward retirement and retirement planning among midlife university employees. *Journal of Applied Gerontology, 13,* 143–56.

Turvey, C., Carney, C., Arndt, S., Wallace, R., & Herzog, R. (1999). Conjugal loss and syndromal depression in a sample of elders aged 70 years or older. *American Journal of Psychiatry, 156,* 1596–1601.

Turvey, C., Conwell, Y., Jones, M., Phillips, C., Simonsick, E., Pearson, J., & Wallace, R. (2002). Risk factors for late-life suicide: A prospective, community-based study. *American Journal of Geriatric Psychiatry, 10*(4), 398–406.

Twycross, R. (1999). *Introducing palliative care* (3rd ed.). Oxon, Oxford: Radcliffe Medical Press.

Uhlenberg, P. (1996). Mortality decline in the twentieth century and supply of kin over the life course. *Gerontologist, 36,* 681–85.

Uhlmann, R. E., Pearlman, R. A., & Cain, K. C. (1988). Physicians' and spouses' predictions of elderly patients' resuscitation preferences. *Journal of Gerontology, 43,* M115–21.

Umberson, D., Wortman, C., & Kessler, R. (1992). Widowhood and depression: Explaining long-term gender differences in vulnerability. *Journal of Health and Social Behavior, 33,* 10–24.

U.S. Bureau of Labor Statistics. (2000). *Employment and earnings, 47*(8), 1–115.

U.S. Census Bureau. (1999). Money income in the United States. *Current Population Reports: Consumer Income* (P60-206). www.census.gov/prod/99pubs/p60-206.pdf (August 4, 2003).

———. (2000). *Statistical abstract of the United States: 2000.* Washington, DC: U.S. Government Printing Office.

———. (2001a). Table 1: Age, sex, household relationship, race and Hispanic Origin— Poverty status of people by selected characteristics in 2000. *Current population survey: Annual demographic survey, March supplement.* To access this table on line, Google its title. The first entry should be *Detailed Poverty (P60 Package) TOC.* Look to the right of its green URL for the word *cached,* and click on it. As of February 2, 2005, following that procedure led directly to the table.

———. (2001b). *Statistical abstract of the United States: 2001.* Washington, DC.

———. (2002). *Historical poverty tables: Table 3. Poverty status of people, by age, race, and Hispanic origin: 1959 to 2001.* www.census.gov/hhes/poverty/histpov/hstpov3.html (September 30, 2003).

―――. (2003a, May). Index of population. *Current Population Survey, March 2002* (Special Populations Branch, Population Division). www.census.gov/population/ socdemo/age (December 21, 2003).

―――. (2003b). *Housing vacancy survey: Second quarter, 2003.* www.census.gov/hhes/ www/housing/hvs/q203tab7.html (July 30, 2003).

―――. (2003c). *The older population in the United States: March 2002* (P20-546). Washington, D.C.: Author.

―――. (2004a). Grandchildren living in the home of grandparents: 1970 to present. Historical time series table CH-7. Fertility and Family Statistics Branch. *Annual social and economic supplement: 2003 Current Population Survey, Current Population Reports* (Series P20-553). www.census.gov/population/socdemo/hh-fam/tabCH-7.pdf (November 10, 2004).

―――. (2004b). *Statistical abstract of the United States: 2004–2005.* Washington, DC: Author.

U.S. Congress. House Select Committee on Aging. (1990). *Medicare and Medicaid's Twenty-fifth anniversary: Much promised, accomplished, and left unfinished.* (Committee publication no. 101-762). Washington, DC: U.S. Government Printing Office.

―――. House Select Committee on Aging. Subcommittee on Health and Long-term Care.. (1992). *Alcohol abuse and misuse among the elderly* (HR 102-852). Washington, DC: U.S. Government Printing Office.

U.S. Department of Agriculture. (2004). Food stamp program: Fact sheet on resources, income, and benefits. www.fns.usda.gov/fsp/applicant_recipients/fs_Res_Ben_Elig. htm (January 12, 2005).

U.S. Department of Health and Human Services. (1999). *Mental health: A report of the Surgeon General.* Rockville, MD: Author.

―――. (2003a). *2001–2002 Alzheimer's disease progress report.* NIH publication no. 03-5333. Washington, DC: National Institutes of Health.

―――. (2003b). *2003 CMS Statistics.* Centers for Medicare and Medicaid Services. http://cms.hhs.gov/researchers/pubs/03cmsstats.pdf (October 3, 2003).

U.S. Department of Transportation. (2004, February 11). FTA [Federal Transit Administration] fiscal year 2004 apportionments, allocations and program information. *Federal Register, 69*(28): Notices.

U.S. General Accounting Office. (1995, July 24). *Prescription drugs and the elderly: Many still receive potentially harmful drugs despite recent improvements* (Letter Report, GAO/ HEHS-95-152). Washington, DC: Author.

―――. (1998). *Welfare reform: Many states continue some federal or state benefits for immigrants* Report to the ranking minority member, U.S. Senate Subcommittee on Children and Families, Committee on Labor and Human Resources. www.gao.gov/ archive/1998/he98132.pdf (December 14, 2004).

―――. (2001). *Older workers: Demographic trends pose challenges for employers and workers.* GAO-02-85. Washington, DC: Author.

Utz, R., Carr, D. S., Nesse, R., & Wortman, C. (2002). The effect of widowhood on older adults' social participation: An evaluation of activity, disengagement, and continuity theories. *Gerontologist, 42*(4), 522–33.

van der Kloot Meijburg, H. (2000). The lessons we learn: Palliative care in the Netherlands. *Illness, Crisis and Loss, 8*(2), 109–19.

Van Grootheest, D. S., Beekman, M. I., Broese van Groenou, M. I., & Deeg, D. J. H. (1999). Sex differences in depression after widowhood. Do men suffer more? *Social Psychiatry Psychiatric Epidemiology, 34,* 391–98.

Van Loon, R. A. (1999). Desire to die in terminally ill people: A framework for assessment and intervention. *Health and social work, 24*(4), 260–68.

Van Reekum, R., Simard, M., Clarke, D. Binns, M., & Conn, D. (1999). Late-life depression as a possible predictor of dementia. *American Journal of Geriatric Psychiatry, 7,* 151–59.

Vinokur, A. (2002). *The structure and predictors of grief reactions: A prospective study of older widowed adults.* Ann Arbor: University of Michigan.

Vinton, L. (1999). Working with abused older women from a feminist perspective. *Journal of Women and Aging, 11*(2–3), 85–100.

Volicer, L., & Hurley, A. (2003). Management of behavioral symptoms in progressive degenerative dementias. *Journal of Gerontology: Medical Sciences, 58A*(9), 837–45.

Volicer, L., Hurley, A. C., Lathi, D. C., & Kowall, N. W. (1994). Measurement of severity in advanced Alzheimer disease. *Journal of Gerontology: Medical Sciences, 49,* M223–26.

von Strauss, E., Viitanen, M., DeRonchi, D., Winblad, B., & Fratiglioni, L. (1999). Aging and the occurrence of dementia: Findings from a population-based cohort with a large sample of nonagenarians. *Archives of Neurology, 56*(5), 587–92.

Waern, M., Rubenowitz, E., & Runeson, B. (2001). *Physical illness and suicide in late life* (abstract). Paper presented at the 10th Congress of the International Psychogeriatric Association, Nice, France.

Wagner, A. W., Teri, L., & Orr-Rainey, N. (1995). Behavior problems among dementia residents in special care units: Changes over time. *Journal of American Geriatrics Society, 43,* 784–87.

Walker, G. (2003). Medical euthanasia. In C. D. Bryant (Ed)., *Handbook of death and dying* (vol. 1, pp. 405–23). Thousand Oaks, CA: Sage.

Wallace, G. (2001). Grandparent caregivers: Emerging issues in elder law and social work practice. *Journal of Gerontological Social Work, 34*(3), 127–36.

Wallace, J. (1992). Reconsidering the life review: The social construction of talk about the past. *Gerontologist, 32*(1), 120–25.

Walsh, F. (1999). Families in later life: Challenges and opportunities. In B. Carter & M. McGoldrick (Eds.), *The expanded family life cycle: Individual, family, and social perspectives* (pp. 307–24). Boston: Allyn & Bacon.

Walsh, K., King, M., Jones, L., Tookman, A., & Blizard, R. (2002, June). Spiritual beliefs may affect outcome of bereavement: Prospective study. *British Medical Journal, 324,* 1–5.

Wan, T., & Odell, B. (1983). Major role losses and social participation of older males. *Research on Aging, 5,* 173–96.

Ware, J., & Sherbourne, C. (1992). The MOS 36-Item Short-Form Health Survey (SF-36): Conceptual framework and item selection. *Medical Care, 30,* 473–83.

Warren, W., Blackwell, A., & Morris, M. (1989). Age differences in perceiving the direction of self-motion from optical flow. *Journal of Gerontology: Psychological Sciences,* 44, P147–53.

Wasylkewycz, M. (2002). Elder abuse in the family: An interdisciplinary model for research [Book review]. *Journal of Marriage and the Family,* 64(1), 274–76.

Waxman, H., Carner, T., & Klein, M. (1984). Underutilization of mental health professionals by community elderly. *Gerontologist,* 24, 23–30.

Webster, J. D. (2003). An exploratory analysis of a self-assessed wisdom scale. *Journal of Adult Development,* 10(1), 13–22.

Weinberg, D. H. (1996). *A brief look at postwar U.S. income inequality.* Current Population Reports. (Publication no. P60-191). Washington, DC: U.S. Census Bureau.

Weisman, A. (1972). *On dying and denying: A psychiatric study of terminality.* New York: Behavioral Publications.

Weissman, J. J., Leaf, P. J., Tischler, G. L., Blazer, D. G., Karno, M., Bruce, M. L., & Florio, L. P. (1988). Affective disorders in the United States. *Psychological Medicine,* 18, 141–53.

Weissman, M., Marowitz, J., & Klerman, G. (2000). *Comprehensive guide to interpersonal psychotherapy.* New York: Basic Books.

Wells, A. (1995). Meta-cognition and worry: A cognitive model of generalized anxiety disorder. *Behavioral and Cognitive Psychotherapy,* 23, 301–20.

——— (2004). A cognitive model of GAD: Metacognitions and pathological worry. In R. C. Heimberg, C. L. Turk, & D. S. Mennin (Eds.), *Generalized anxiety disorder: Advances in research and practice* (pp. 164–86). New York: Guilford.

Wells, A., & Butler, G. (1997). Generalized anxiety disorder. In D. Clark & C. Fairburn (Eds.), *Science and practice of cognitive behaviour therapy* (pp. 155–78). New York: Oxford University Press.

Wells, K. B., Rogers, W., Burnam, M., & Camp, P. (1993). Course of depression in patients with hypertension, myocardial infarction, or insulin-dependent diabetes. *American Journal of Psychiatry,* 150, 632–38.

Welte, J. W. (1998). Stress and elderly drinking. In Gomberg, Hegedus, & Zucker, *Alcohol problems and aging* (pp. 229–46).

Wendt, P., Peterson, D., & Douglass, E. (1993). *Core principles and outcomes of gerontology, geriatrics and aging studies instruction.* Washington, DC: Association for Gerontology in Higher Education.

Werth, J., L., Jr., Blevins, D., & Toussaint, K. (2002). The influence of cultural diversity on end-of-life care and decisions. *American Behavioral Scientist,* 46(2), 204–19.

Wetherell, J., Gatz, M., & Craske, M. (2003). Treatment of generalized anxiety disorder in older adults. *Journal of Consulting and Clinical Psychology,* 71(1), 31–40.

White House Conference on Aging, 1995. (1996). *The road to an aging policy (final report).* Washington, DC: White House Conference on Aging.

White, K., & Barlow, D. (2002). Panic disorder and agoraphobia. In D. Barlow (Ed.), *Anxiety and its disorders: The nature and treatment of anxiety and panic* (pp. 328–79). New York: Guilford.

Whitlatch, C. J., Zarit, S. H., & von Eye, A. (1991). Efficacy of interventions with caregivers: A reanalysis. *Gerontologist, 31,* 9–14.

Whitley, D., Kelley, S., & Sipe, T. (2001). Grandmothers raising grandchildren: Are they at increased risk of health problems? *Journal of Mental Health and Aging, 6*(4), 105–14.

Whooley, M. A., & Browner, W. S. (1998). Association between depressive symptoms and mortality in older women. *Archives of Internal Medicine, 158,* 2129–35.

Wight, R. (2002). AIDS caregiving stress among HIV-Infected men. In Kramer & Thompson, *Men as caregivers* (pp. 190–209).

Williams, J. R. (2002). Effects of grief on a survivor's health. In K. Doka (Ed.), *Living with grief: Loss in later life* (pp. 191–206). Washington, DC: Hospice Foundation of America.

Willis, S. L., & Schaie, K. W. (1994). Cognitive training in the normal elderly. In F. Forette, Y. Christen, & F. Boller (Eds.), *Cerebral plasticity and cognitive stimulation* (pp. 91–113). Paris: National Gerontology Foundation.

———. (1999). Intellectual functioning in midlife. In S. L. Willis & J. D. Reid (Eds.), *Life in the middle* (pp. 225–64). San Diego: Academic Press.

Wilsnack, S., Vogeltanz, N., Diers, L., & Wilsnack, R. (1995). Drinking and problem drinking in older women. In Beresford & Gomberg, *Alcohol and aging* (pp. 263–92).

Wisocki, P. A. (1994). The experience of worry among the elderly. In G. C. L. Davey & F. Tallis (Eds.), *Worrying: Perspectives on theory, assessment and treatment.* (pp. 247–61). New York: Wiley.

Wisocki, P. A., Handen, B. B., & Morse, C. (1986). The worry scale as a measure of anxiety among home bound and community active elderly. *Behavior Therapist, 9,* 91–95.

Wolf, R. (1996). Understanding elder abuse and neglect. *Aging, 367,* 4–8.

———. (2001). Support groups for older victims of domestic violence. *Journal of Women and Aging, 13*(2), 71–83.

Wolfe, R., Morrow, J., & Fredrickson, B. L. (1996). Mood disorders in older adults. In Carstensen, Edelstein, & Dornbrand, *The practical handbook of clinical gerontology* (pp. 274–303).

Wong, S., Heiby, E., Kameoka, V., Dubanoski, J. (1999). Perceived control, self-reinforcement, and depression among Asian American and Caucasian American elders. *Journal of Applied Gerontology, 18,* 4–62.

Woodruff-Pak, D., & Papka, M. (1999). Theories of neuropsychology and aging. In Bengston & Schaie, *Handbook of theories of aging* (pp. 113–32).

Woods, B. (1999). The person in dementia care. *Generations, 23*(3), 35–39.

Worden, W. (2002). *Grief counseling and grief therapy* (3rd ed.). New York: Springer.

World Health Organization. (1990). *Cancer pain relief and palliative care* (Technical Report Series 804). Geneva: Author.

Wortman, C. B., & Silver, R. C. (1989). The myths of coping with loss. *Journal of consulting and clinical psychology, 57,* 349–57.

———. (2001). The myths of coping with loss revisited. In Stroebe, Hansson, Stroebe, & Schut, *Handbook of bereavement research* (pp. 405–29).

Yaffe, K., Blackwell, T., Gore, R., Sands, L., Reus, V., & Browner, W. S. (1999). Depressive symptoms and cognitive decline in nondemented elderly women: A prospective study. *Archives of General Psychiatry, 56*(5), 425–30.

Yee, D. (1997). Can long-term-care assessments be culturally responsive? *Generations,* *21*(1), 25–29.

Yeo, G., & Hikoyeda, N. (2000). Cultural issues in end-of-life decision making among Asians and Pacific Islanders in the United States. In K. Braun, J. Pietsch, & P. Blanchette (Eds.), *Cultural issues in end-of-life decision making* (pp. 101–26). Thousand Oaks, CA: Sage.

Zarit, S. H. (1997). Brief measures of depression and cognitive function. *Generations,* *21*(1), 41–43.

———. (2001). *Respite services for caregivers.* (NFCSP: Selected Issue Briefs). Department of Health and Human Services, Administration on Aging. www.aoa.gov/prof/aoaprog/caregiver/careprof/progguidance/background/program_issues/ZaritMonograph.pdf (January 18, 2005).

Zarit, S. H., & Knight, B. (Eds.). (1996). *A guide to psychotherapy and aging.* Washington, DC: American Psychological Association.

Zarit, S. H., & Whitlatch, C. J. (1992). Institutional placement: Phases of transition. *Gerontologist, 32,* 665–72.

Zarit, S. H., & Zarit, J. (1983). Cognitive impairment. In P. M. Lewinsohn & L. Teri (Eds.), *Clinical geropsychology* (pp. 38–81). Elmsford, NY: Pergamon.

Zarit, S., Reever, K. E., & Bach-Peterson, J. (1980). Relatives of the impaired elderly: Correlates of feelings of burden. *Gerontologist, 20*(6), 649–55.

Zarit, S., Stephens, M., Townsend, A., & Greene, R. (1998). Stress reduction for family caregivers: Effects of adult day care use. *Journal of Gerontology: Psychological and Social Sciences, 53B*(5), S267–71.

Zedlewski, S. R., & Meyer, J. A. (1987). *Toward ending poverty among the elderly and disabled: Policy and financing options.* Washington, DC: Urban Institute.

Zeidner, M., & Endler, N. S. (1996). *Handbook of coping: Theory, research, applications.* New York: Wiley.

Zeiss, A., & Steffen, A. (1996). Behavioral and cognitive-behavioral treatments: An overview of social learning. In Zarit & Knight, *A guide to psychotherapy and aging* (pp. 35–60).

Zimprich, D., & Martin, M. (2002). Can longitudinal changes in processing speed explain longitudinal age changes in fluid intelligence? *Psychology and Aging, 17,* 690–95.

Zisook, S., & Shuchter, S. R. (1986). The first four years of widowhood. *Psychiatric Annals, 16,* 288–94.

———. (1993). Major depression associated with widowhood. *American Journal of Geriatric Psychiatry, 1,* 316–26.

———. (2001). Treatment of the depressions of bereavement. *American Behavioral Scientist, 44*(5), 782–97.

Zisook, S., Chentsova-Dutton, Y., & Shuchter, S. R. (1998). Post-traumatic stress disorder following bereavement. *Annals of Clinical Psychiatry, 10,* 157–63.

Zsembik, B., & Singer, A. (1990). The problem of defining retirement among minorities: The Mexican-Americans. *Gerontologist, 30,* 749–57.

Zucker, R. (1998). Developmental aspects of aging, alcohol involvement, and their interrelationship. In Gomberg, Hegedus, & Zucker, *Alcohol problems and aging* (pp. 3–23).

Zung, W. W. K. (1971). A rating instrument for anxiety disorders. *Psychosomatics, 12,* 371–79.

Zusmand, J. (1966). Some explanations of the changing appearance of psychotic patients: Antecedents of the social breakdown syndrome concept. *Milbank Memorial Fund Quarterly, 64,* 63–84.

SUBJECT INDEX

NAME INDEX